Paradox 10/25/97

by refren
to cha ♡ **W9-DEC-178**   e
by val doesn't allow values,

Form Editor toolbar

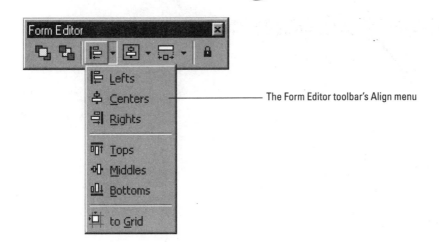

The Form Editor toolbar's Align menu

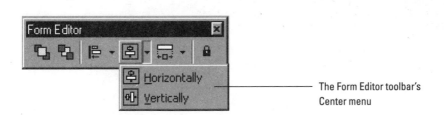

The Form Editor toolbar's Center menu

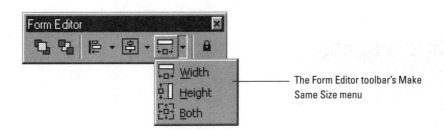

The Form Editor toolbar's Make Same Size menu

Mastering Visual Basic 5

Mastering™ Visual Basic® 5

Evangelos Petroutsos

SYBEX

San Francisco · Paris · Düsseldorf · Soest

Associate Publisher: Gary Masters
Acquisitions Manager: Kristine Plachy
Acquisitions & Developmental Editor: Peter Kuhns
Editor: Pat Coleman
Project Editor: Brenda Frink
Technical Editor: Scott Player
Graphic Illustrator: Patrick Dintino
Electronic Publishing Specialist: Deborah A. Bevilacqua
Production Coordinator: Grey B. Magauran
Proofreaders: Jennifer Metzger and Theresa Gonzalez
Indexer: Ted Laux
Cover Designer: Design Site
Cover Illustrator: Mike Miller

Screen reproductions produced with Collage Complete.

Collage Complete is a trademark of Inner Media Inc.

SYBEX is a registered trademark of SYBEX Inc.
Mastering is a trademark of SYBEX Inc.

TRADEMARKS: SYBEX has attempted throughout this book to distinguish proprietary trademarks from descriptive terms by following the capitalization style used by the manufacturer.

Netscape Communications, the Netscape Communications logo, Netscape, and Netscape Navigator are trademarks of Netscape Communications Corporation.

The author and publisher have made their best efforts to prepare this book, and the content is based upon final release software whenever possible. Portions of the manuscript may be based upon pre-release versions supplied by software manufacturer(s). The author and the publisher make no representation or warranties of any kind with regard to the completeness or accuracy of the contents herein and accept no liability of any kind including but not limited to performance, merchantability, fitness for any particular purpose, or any losses or damages of any kind caused or alleged to be caused directly or indirectly from this book.

Photographs and illustrations used in this book have been downloaded from publicly accessible file archives and are used in this book for news reportage purposes only to demonstrate the variety of graphics resources available via electronic access. Text and images available over the Internet may be subject to copyright and other rights owned by third parties. Online availability of text and images does not imply that they may be reused without the permission of rights holders, although the Copyright Act does permit certain unauthorized reuse as fair use under 17 U.S.C. Section 107.

Copyright ©1997 SYBEX Inc., 1151 Marina Village Parkway, Alameda, CA 94501. World rights reserved. No part of this publication may be stored in a retrieval system, transmitted, or reproduced in any way, including but not limited to photocopy, photograph, magnetic or other record, without the prior agreement and written permission of the publisher.

Library of Congress Card Number: 97-65358
ISBN: 0-7821-1984-0

Manufactured in the United States of America

10 9 8 7 6 5 4 3 2

Software License Agreement: Terms and Conditions

The media and/or any online materials accompanying this book that are available now or in the future contain programs and/or text files (the "Software") to be used in connection with the book. SYBEX hereby grants to you a license to use the Software, subject to the terms that follow. Your purchase, acceptance, or use of the Software will constitute your acceptance of such terms.

The Software compilation is the property of SYBEX unless otherwise indicated and is protected by copyright to SYBEX or other copyright owner(s) as indicated in the media files (the "Owner(s)"). You are hereby granted a single-user license to use the Software for your personal, noncommercial use only. You may not reproduce, sell, distribute, publish, circulate, or commercially exploit the Software, or any portion thereof, without the written consent of SYBEX and the specific copyright owner(s) of any component software included on this media.

In the event that the Software or components include specific license requirements or end-user agreements, statements of condition, disclaimers, limitations or warranties ("End-User License"), those End-User Licenses supersede the terms and conditions herein as to that particular Software component. Your purchase, acceptance, or use of the Software will constitute your acceptance of such End-User Licenses.

By purchase, use or acceptance of the Software you further agree to comply with all export laws and regulations of the United States as such laws and regulations may exist from time to time.

Software Support

Components of the supplemental Software and any offers associated with them may be supported by the specific Owner(s) of that material but they are not supported by SYBEX. Information regarding any available support may be obtained from the Owner(s) using the information provided in the appropriate read.me files or listed elsewhere on the media.

Should the manufacturer(s) or other Owner(s) cease to offer support or decline to honor any offer, SYBEX bears no responsibility. This notice concerning support for the Software is provided for your information only. SYBEX is not the agent or principal of the Owner(s), and SYBEX is in no way responsible for providing any support for the Software, nor is it liable or responsible for any support provided, or not provided, by the Owner(s).

Warranty

SYBEX warrants the enclosed media to be free of physical defects for a period of ninety (90) days after purchase. The Software is not available from SYBEX in any other form or media than that enclosed herein or posted to *www.sybex.com*. If you discover a defect in the media during this warranty period, you may obtain a replacement of identical format at no charge by sending the defective media, postage prepaid, with proof of purchase to:

SYBEX Inc.
Customer Service Department
1151 Marina Village Parkway
Alameda, CA 94501
(510) 523-8233
Fax: (510) 523-2373
e-mail: info@sybex.com
WEB: HTTP://WWW.SYBEX.COM

After the 90-day period, you can obtain replacement media of identical format by sending us the defective disk, proof of purchase, and a check or money order for $10, payable to SYBEX.

Disclaimer

SYBEX makes no warranty or representation, either expressed or implied, with respect to the Software or its contents, quality, performance, merchantability, or fitness for a particular purpose. In no event will SYBEX, its distributors, or dealers be liable to you or any other party for direct, indirect, special, incidental, consequential, or other damages arising out of the use of or inability to use the Software or its contents even if advised of the possibility of such damage. In the event that the Software includes an online update feature, SYBEX further disclaims any obligation to provide this feature for any specific duration other than the initial posting.

The exclusion of implied warranties is not permitted by some states. Therefore, the above exclusion may not apply to you. This warranty provides you with specific legal rights; there may be other rights that you may have that vary from state to state. The pricing of the book with the Software by SYBEX reflects the allocation of risk and limitations on liability contained in this agreement of Terms and Conditions.

Shareware Distribution

This Software may contain various programs that are distributed as shareware. Copyright laws apply to both shareware and ordinary commercial software, and the copyright Owner(s) retains all rights. If you try a shareware program and continue using it, you are expected to register it. Individual programs differ on details of trial periods, registration, and payment. Please observe the requirements stated in appropriate files.

Copy Protection

The Software in whole or in part may or may not be copy-protected or encrypted. However, in all cases, reselling or redistributing these files without authorization is expressly forbidden except as specifically provided for by the Owner(s) therein.

To my family

ACKNOWLEDGEMENTS

Many people contributed to this book, and I would like to thank all of them. I guess I should start with the programmers at Microsoft, for their commitment to Visual Basic. Visual Basic has evolved from a small, flexible programming tool to an awesome development tool. This constant improvement and the gradual introduction of new and increasingly advanced tools is simply amazing.

Special thanks to Father Serafim Casgoine for his fine job on Chapter 13, *Object Programming with Visual Basic,* and for his help during the last, almost hectic phases of the book. I hope we'll meet again in another project.

The next thanks goes to the talented people at Sybex. To all of them, and to each one individually. To Peter Kuhns, for his involvement from conception to production. He worked on this project as developmental editor and advisor and offered his help generously when needed in every aspect of the book. To technical editor Scott Player, for scrutinizing every paragraph and every line of code. To editor Pat Coleman, for taking this book personally and improving it in numerous ways. Her attention to detail was my security blanket. To project editor Brenda Frink, for graciously handling so many tasks at once, many of which I'll never know about. To production coordinator Grey Magauran, electronic publishing specialist Debi Bevilacqua, indexer Ted Laux, graphic illustrator Patrick Dintino, and so many more persons I haven't met but who were involved in the production of this book and added their expertise and talent.

Many thanks to InstallShield for putting together the browser for this CD on a very short notice. You should check out their software on the CD that comes with this book.

This book would not have been possible without the Internet. I wrote much of it while in Greece. The technical editor was in Utah, the editor was in Texas, and, of course, the Sybex people are in California. We all had to be in constant touch, and our cyberspace neighborhood trivialized large bodies of water and several time zones. And, so, finally I want to thank all the people who keep the Internet up and running, day and night—the people who maintain the servers, the routers, and the software and handle all the details of connecting users.

CONTENTS AT A GLANCE

TABLE OF CONTENTS

Chapter 11: Database Programming with Visual Basic 569

Chapter 14: Building ActiveX Controls   769

PART IV   From the Desktop to the Web   843

Chapter 15: Visual Basic and the Web   845

Chapter 16: The Scripting Model   903

INTRODUCTION

Several years ago, when Visual Basic was a "small" language, a Mastering book would cover every aspect of it. Since the first version, however, Visual Basic has evolved into a major development environment that covers every aspect of programming, from educational applications to database programming, and from financial applications to developing Internet components. Writing a book that even introduced all these topics would be out of the question. Especially a Mastering book.

The topics covered in this book were chosen to provide a solid understanding of the principles and techniques involved in developing applications with Visual Basic. Programming isn't about new keywords and new functions. I chose the topics I felt every programmer should master in order to master the language. One of the biggest chapters in this book discusses the graphics methods of Visual Basic. There's nothing new in this area, but graphics are such an important part of the language that the related techniques had to be explained in detail. Most chapters in this book are really version-independent. They will be just as useful to people who are still using version 4 of the language.

Another motivation for choosing the topics of the book was my desire to present useful, practical examples. Some of you may not find all topics equally interesting. My hope is that everyone will find something interesting and something of value, whether it is an application such as DirMap, a clear explanation of a topic, or the introduction to Internet programming techniques with Visual Basic.

Some chapters do deal with the new face of Visual Basic. If I could isolate a single feature of the language that could be considered the most important new feature, it would have to be the development of ActiveX controls. For the first time, Visual Basic can be used to develop ActiveX controls, and this feature opens enormous possibilities and new markets for VB developers. This aspect of Visual Basic is covered in Chapter 14, where I've tried to show the similarities between developing VB applications and ActiveX controls and demonstrate through the examples how you can apply your VB knowledge to developing custom ActiveX controls.

You will notice that the last part of the book is about the Web. This information was included because of its broad appeal. The Desktop and the Web are merging, and VB programmers should be able to apply their knowledge to the Web. Most of the last part of the book is about VBScript, which is a subset of Visual Basic. VBScript is the language used in developing Web applications—another lucrative market for VB developers. The chapters in the last part of the book are short compared with the others, not because I got tired toward the end of the book, but because my intention was to discuss the topics that are new to VB developers and avoid rehashing information that most VB programmers would find trivial.

Who Should Read This Book?

You don't need a solid knowledge of Visual Basic to read this book, but you do need a basic understanding of programming. You need to know the meaning of variables and functions and how an If Then structure works. The first two chapters are introductory, but they are not meant for the absolute beginner. Instead, they were included to introduce Visual Basic to users with programming experience in a different environment. Occasional users of previous versions of Visual Basic will also find interesting information in these chapters. If you have no programming experience, you should probably start with another, simpler book.

Chapter 3, *Visual Basic, the Language,* is mostly reference information about data types and procedures. It's information that every programmer needs from time to time. While reading the rest of the book or exploring the code of an application, you might need to look up how to use optional parameters or how to implement a collection. Consult Chapter 3. With Chapter 4, we get into real VB programming.

This book is addressed to the average programmer who wants to get the most out of Visual Basic. It covers the topics I feel are of use to most Visual Basic programmers. Visual Basic is an extremely rich programming environment, and I had to choose between a superficial coverage of many topics or an in-depth coverage of fewer topics. To make room for more topics, I have avoided including a lot of reference material and lengthy listings. For example, you won't find complete project listings or Form descriptions. I assume you can draw a few controls on a Form and don't really need long descriptions of the properties of the controls. I'm also assuming that you don't want to read the trivial segments of each application. Instead, the listings contain the "meaty" part of the applications; the procedures that explain the topic at hand. If you want to see the complete listing, it's all on the CD.

Many books offer their readers long, numbered sequences of steps to accomplish something. Following instructions simplifies certain tasks, but programming isn't about following instructions. It's about being creative; it's about being able to apply the same technique in several practical situations. And the way to exploit creatively the power of a language such as Visual Basic is to understand its principles and its programming model and develop a sense of how to apply the language to daily programming situations.

Each time I show you how to design an application, I provide a detailed, step-by-step procedure that will help you accomplish the task. But this book goes beyond that. I explain why things must be done in a certain way, and I present alternatives and try to connect new topics to those explained earlier in the book. In several chapters, I expand on applications developed in earlier chapters. Connecting new knowledge to something you have mastered already provides a positive feedback and a deeper understanding of the language.

The Structure of the Book

This book wasn't meant to be read from cover to cover, and I know that most people don't read computer books this way. Each chapter is independent of the others, although they make references to previous chapters. Each topic is covered in depth; however, I make no assumptions about the reader's knowledge of the topic. As a result, you may find the introductory sections of a chapter too simple. The topics discussed become progressively more advanced, and you will certainly find some new information in every chapter. Even if you are familiar with the aspect of the language discussed in each chapter, take a look at the examples. Some of them are what I would call "advanced." One of my goals was to simplify as many advanced topics as I could and demonstrate them with practical examples.

This book tries to teach through examples. Isolated topics are demonstrated with short examples, and at the end of many chapters you will build a large, practical application (a real-world application) that "puts together" the topics and techniques. Some of the more advanced applications may not be so easy to understand, and this is exactly where you shouldn't give up. Simpler applications would have made my (and your) life easier, but the book wouldn't deserve the title Mastering, and your knowledge of Visual Basic wouldn't be as complete.

Mastering Visual Basic 5 is organized in four parts.

Part I discusses the fundamentals of Visual Basic. In contains two introductory chapters, a reference chapter that discusses the absolute essentials (variables, procedures, and so on), and then moves to the building blocks of the language: Forms and ActiveX controls. The last chapter of the first part discusses graphics methods.

Part II is a collection of advanced and nontrivial topics. I discuss a few of the more advanced ActiveX controls, how to add multimedia elements to your applications, and how to write MDI applications. In this part of the book, you will find a chapter that introduces a powerful programming technique, recursive programming. The last chapter in the second part of the book is an introduction to database programming with Visual Basic.

Part III discusses ways to extend Visual Basic. You will find an introduction to the Windows API, and you will learn how to build ActiveX components, such as OLE servers and custom ActiveX controls.

Part IV deals with the newest in Visual Basic. It discusses various techniques for applying your knowledge of Visual Basic to the Web. In this part of the book, you will learn how to write applications for the Web and how to use custom ActiveX controls on Web pages. A good portion of this chapter deals with VBScript, a variation of Visual Basic you can use to program (or activate, as it's called) your Web pages.

How to Reach the Author

Despite our best efforts, the first edition of a book this size is bound to contain errors. Although printed media isn't as easy to update as a Web site, I will spare no effort to fix every problem you report (or I discover). If you have any problems with text or the applications in this book or if you have any general questions about Visual Basic, you can contact me directly at:

`76470.724@compuserve.com`

Although I can't promise a response to every question, I will fix any problems in the examples and provide updated versions. I would also like to hear any comments you may have on the book, about the topics you liked or not and how useful you found the examples. Your comments will be taken into consideration in future editions.

PART 1

Visual Programming: The Fundamentals of Visual Basic

Getting Started with Visual Basic

- Using the Integrated Development Environment (IDE)

- Developing your first VB project

- Designing the user interface

- Programming an application

- Developing event-driven programs in a visual environment

- Customizing your environment

This chapter introduces Visual Basic's Integrated Development Environment (IDE) and the basic principles of developing applications with visual tools and event programming. We will go through the steps of creating a few simple applications, and I'll explain the components of the visual development environment. In this chapter, I'll take you on a tour of the environment and discuss the basics of developing user interfaces. We'll then add a few lines of code. In the second chapter, we'll build more advanced, practical applications that demonstrate other features of the language.

> **NOTE** If you don't need the introductory material of this chapter, you can skip it entirely. You should, however, take a look at the new features of the Visual Basic IDE and its customization options. The corresponding sections are marked with a NEW icon.

One Language, Three Editions

I assume that you have installed Visual Basic 5. This means you have already decided which edition of Visual Basic you are going to use. Visual Basic comes in three flavors:

- The Visual Basic Learning Edition
- The Visual Basic Professional Edition
- The Visual Basic Enterprise Edition

The Visual Basic Learning Edition is the introductory edition that lets you easily create Windows applications. It comes with all the tools you need to build mainstream Windows applications, and most of the examples and applications in this book will work with the Learning edition.

The Visual Basic Professional Edition is for computer professionals and includes advanced features such as tools to develop ActiveX and Internet controls. The topics covered in Part IV, *From the Desktop to the Web,* require the Professional edition.

The Visual Basic Enterprise Edition is the most advanced edition and is aimed at programmers who build distributed applications in a team environment. It includes all the features of the Professional edition, plus tools such as Visual SourceSafe (a version control system) and the Automation and Component Manager, which are not covered in this book.

Depending on which edition of Visual Basic you installed, you may see fewer or more options in the menus and toolbars of the Visual Basic IDE. The options discussed in most of this book are present in all three editions. If some of the menu options in the figures are not present on your system, you are probably using the Learning edition.

The Integrated Development Environment

Visual Basic is not just a language. It's an Integrated Development Environment in which you can develop, run, test, and debug your applications. Start Visual Basic, and you'll see the window shown in Figure 1.1. Here you are prompted to select the type of project you want to create.

With Visual Basic, you can create the following types of applications.

Standard EXE   A Standard EXE project is a typical application. Most of the applications in this book are Standard EXE projects. These are the types of applications you developed with previous versions of Visual Basic.

ActiveX EXE, ActiveX DLL   These types of projects are available with the Professional edition. ActiveX components are OLE automation servers and are described in Chapter 13, *Object Programming with Visual Basic*. The two types of projects are identical in functionality, but are packaged differently (as executable files or Dynamic Link Libraries).

ActiveX Control   This type of project is also a feature of the Professional edition. Use it to develop your own ActiveX controls, which are described in Chapter 14, *Building ActiveX Controls*.

FIGURE 1.1

The types of projects
you can create with
Visual Basic

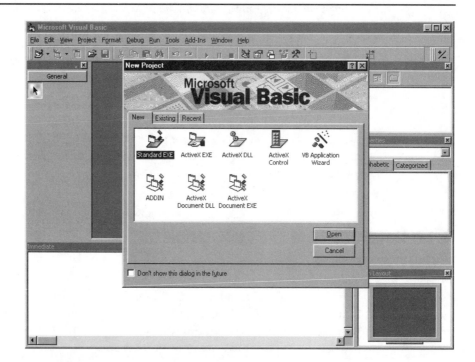

 ActiveX Document EXE, ActiveX Document DLL ActiveX documents
are in essence Visual Basic applications that can run in the environment of a container that supports hyperlinking. In simpler terms, this environment is a Web
browser, such as Internet Explorer.

 VB Application Wizard The Wizard takes you through the steps of setting
up the skeleton of a new application. I believe that you shouldn't use this Wizard
unless you can develop a project on your own. Modifying the skeleton code created by the Wizard is just as difficult, if not more, than developing your own
application from scratch. You should, however, experiment with this tool to see
the types of applications it can prototype for you.

 ADDIN You can create your own add-ins for the Visual Basic IDE. To do so,
select this type of project. This topic is rather advanced, and we won't look at it
in this book.

The window in Figure 1.1, earlier in this chapter, has three tabs:

- New

- Existing

- Recent

In the New tab, you can select the type of a new project, as explained already. Switch to the Existing tab to select an existing project and open it. To open a project you were working on recently, switch to the Recent tab, which contains the list of the most recently opened projects. In your daily projects, you'll be coming back to the project you were working on during the last few days, and this is where you can find them easily.

Select the Standard EXE icon in the New Project window, and then click on OK to open the window shown in Figure 1.2.

FIGURE 1.2

A new Visual Basic project

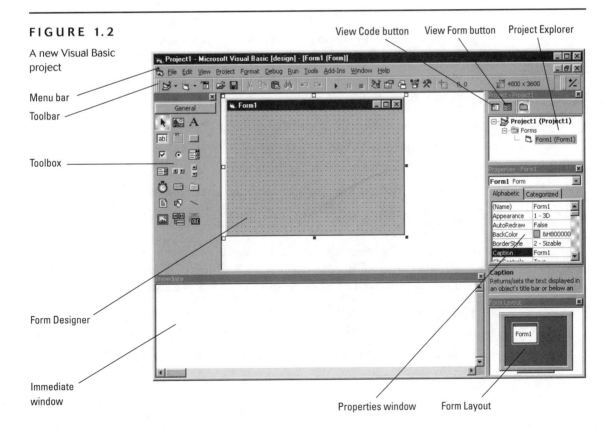

What you see on your screen now is the Visual Basic IDE, which is made up of a number of components. The main window, in the middle of the screen, contains a Form, named Form1. The Form is the application's window, and in it you place the elements of your application's user interface (checkboxes, command buttons, and so on). It is also the window that the user sees when running the application.

The Menu Bar

The menu bar contains the commands you need to work with Visual Basic. The basic menus are:

- **File**   Contains the commands for opening and saving projects and creating executable files and a list of recent projects.

- **Edit**   Contains editing commands (Undo, Copy, Paste, and so on) plus a number of commands for formatting and editing your code (Find, Replace).

- **View**   Contains commands for showing or hiding components of the IDE.

- **Project**   Contains commands that add components to the current project, references to Windows objects, and new tools to the Toolbox.

- **Format**   Contains commands for aligning the controls on the Form. A much-needed tool in previous versions of Visual Basic.

- **Debug**   Contains the usual debugging commands.

- **Run**   Contains the commands that start, break, and end execution of the current application.

- **Tools**   Contains tools you need in building ActiveX components and ActiveX controls; contains the command to start the Menu Editor and the Options command, which lets you customize the environment.

- **Add-Ins**   Contains add-ins that you can add and remove as needed. By default, only the Visual Data Manager Add-In is installed in this menu. Use the Add-In Manager command to add and remove add-ins.

- **Window**   Contains the commands to arrange windows on the screen; the standard Window menu of a Windows application.

- **Help**   Contains information to help you as you work.

The Toolbars

The toolbars give you quick access to commonly used menu commands. Besides the main toolbar, which is displayed by default below the menu bar, the Visual Basic IDE provides additional toolbars for specific purposes, such as editing, form design, and debugging. To view the additional toolbars, choose View ➤ Toolbars.

- The Standard toolbar is just below the menu bar and is displayed by default.

- The Edit toolbar contains the commands of the Edit menu.

- The Debug toolbar contains the commands of the Debug menu.

 • The Form Editor toolbar contains the commands of the Format menu.

To open and close toolbars, choose View ➤ Toolbars to display a submenu containing the names of the toolbars. These names are toggles and turn the corresponding toolbars on and off. Choose the Customize command to customize the appearance and contents of menus.

The Project Explorer

The window titled Project is the Project Explorer, which displays the components of the project. Simple projects, such as the ones we develop in this chapter, are made up of a single Form. In later chapters, you'll see projects that have multiple Forms and other types of components, such as modules and ActiveX controls.

The project components are organized in folders, and the Project window is called Project Explorer because it has the look of the Windows Explorer. As you will see in later chapters, Visual Basic 5 can manage projects, and groups of projects.

The Toolbox

The Toolbox contains the icons of the controls you can place on a Form to create the application's user interface. By default, the Toolbox contains the pointer icon and the icons of 20 ActiveX controls (explained in the section "The Elements of the User Interface"). To place a control (such as a command button) on a Form, you first select it with the mouse and then move the mouse over the Form. When the mouse is over the Form, it turns into a cross, and you can draw the control on the Form, just as you would draw a rectangle using a drawing application. The size of the rectangle determines the size of the control.

In addition to the default Toolbox (with the title General), you can create custom layouts by selecting Add Tab from the context menu, which appears when you right-click on the Toolbox. Instead of crowding the Toolbox with all the ActiveX controls you need for a project, you can create several tabs with icons on the Toolbox and organize the controls according to function.

To add a new tab to the Toolbox, follow these steps:

1. Right-click on the Toolbox to open the pop-up menu.

2. Choose Add Tab, and enter the name of the new tab. Visual Basic displays a new button (such as the General button) in the Toolbox.

3. Click on the new tab button to open the tab, and then right-click on it to display a pop-up menu.

4. Select Components, and Visual Basic displays a list of all ActiveX controls installed on your system.

5. To add to the current tab, check the checkbox in front of the names of the controls, as shown in Figure 1.3.

FIGURE 1.3

The Components window contains all the ActiveX controls present on your system, and you can select the ones you want to use in your projects.

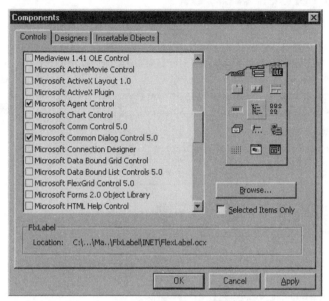

Where Do ActiveX Controls Come From?

Many places, indeed. Some ActiveX controls come with Windows, but are not installed by default. The Microsoft Common Dialog Control 5.0 (checked in Figure 1.3) comes with Windows 95, and if you place this control on your Forms, you can open the standard common dialog boxes, such as the Font and Color dialog boxes, from within your code. You can find many ActiveX controls at Microsoft's Web site (visit http:// www.microsoft.com/activex).

The Microsoft Agent Control was developed by Microsoft for use on Web pages and Desktop applications. If you are surfing the World Wide Web, you will run into many pages that use custom ActiveX controls, which will be automatically downloaded and installed on your system. Chapter 14, *Building ActiveX Controls,* shows you how to develop your own ActiveX controls, and, in addition, you will find a few custom ActiveX controls on the CD that comes with this book.

The Properties Window

The Properties Window contains the property settings for the selected control. *Properties* are attributes of an object, such as its size, caption, color, and so on. You can adjust the appearance of the controls on the Form with point-and-click operations. For example, you can set the string that appears on a command button by locating the Caption property in the Properties window and typing a new value, such as "Click me!" To change the color of a Form, locate the BackColor property in the Properties window, and click on the arrow button next to the current value of the color. Visual Basic displays a color selection box, as shown in Figure 1.4.

FIGURE 1.4

You can set most properties by pointing and clicking in the Properties window.

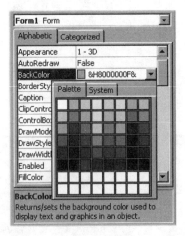

The Form Designer

The Form Designer is the main window in the middle of the screen, and in it you design and edit the application's user interface. The same window displays a text editor, with which you can enter and edit the application's code. The Form Designer displays two windows for each Form:

- The Form itself (the elements of the user interface)

- A Code window (the code behind the elements of the Form)

To switch between the two views, click on the little icons (View Code and View Form) at the top of the Project Explorer (see Figure 1.2, earlier in this chapter). Select the Form you want to view in the Project Explorer, and then click on one of the two View buttons to see the Form or its code.

The Form Layout

You use the Form Layout window, which is in the lower right corner, to determine the initial positions of the Forms in your application. You can move Forms around and place them on top of each other. This window is useful in applications that use multiple Forms, because you can specify how each Form is positioned with respect to the main Form. Figure 1.5 shows the placement of three Forms on the Desktop and their initial relative positions. The insert in the lower right corner shows how the placement of the Forms was specified in the Form Layout window.

FIGURE 1.5

Use the Form Layout window to specify the initial positions of your application's Forms.

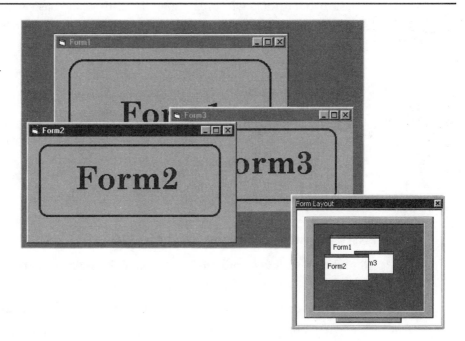

The Immediate Window

The Immediate window at the bottom is a debugging aid. While an application is running, you can stop it and use the Immediate window to examine or change the values of the application's variables and to execute Visual Basic commands in Immediate mode. The Immediate window is one of the reasons for the popularity of Visual Basic and for the popularity of the BASIC programming language in general. It lets you step into the application's code while it executes, change the values of the variables, even insert statements in the code, and then continue the execution of an application.

In the following sections, we will develop a few simple projects that demonstrate basic concepts of application development with visual tools and event-driven programming. It's introductory material, intended for people who are familiar with visual development or who program with other languages. We'll look at how to set up an application, how to design its user interface, and how to add code. Toward the end of the chapter, I will summarize the principles of event-driven programming and show you how to customize the IDE. This topic is last so that readers who are not familiar with Visual Basic will acquire some experience with the environment before attempting customization techniques.

Your First VB Project

When you select the Standard EXE type of project in the New Project window, Visual Basic creates a new project, which is named Project1. Project1 is the top item in the Project Explorer window. The Forms folder under the project name contains the names of all Forms that make up the project. As you will see in the next chapter, a project can have more than one Form.

Renaming and Saving the Project

You should start your projects by renaming their components and saving them, preferably in a new folder. To do so, follow these steps:

1. In the Project Explorer window, click on the project's name (Project1).

2. In the Properties window, select the value of the Name property (projects have a single property, the Name property) and enter the name MVB5_1 (for Mastering Visual Basic 5).

3. In the Project Explorer window, select the name of the Form. The Properties window now displays the Form's properties.

4. Locate the Name property, select it, and change it to Example1.

Your Project Explorer window should now look like the one in Figure 1.6.

FIGURE 1.6

The Project Explorer window after renaming the project's components

Now you are ready to save the project. To save a project, you must first save the Form(s) and then the project (more on this in Chapter 2, *Visual Basic Projects*, in which we'll look at the structure of a project and how it's saved on disk). When saving projects, try to use meaningful filenames so that you'll be able to locate them later. For the projects of this book, I had to use 8-character names, a limitation imposed by the CD production process.

Follow these steps to save the project:

1. Choose File (the File menu is shown in the left of Figure 1.7) ➢ Save Example1 As. (Visual Basic suggests the default name for the Form, so you must select the Save As command, not the Save command.)

FIGURE 1.7

The File menu and the Save File As window

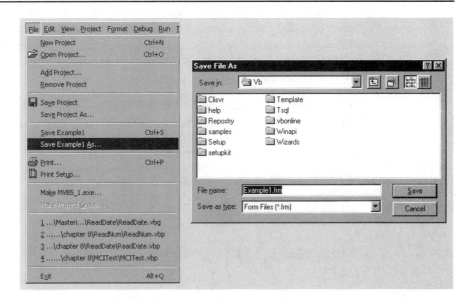

2. In the Save File As window (shown in the right half of Figure 1.7), click on the New Folder button to create a new folder, and save the project there. It is suggested that each project and its files be stored in a separate folder, but it is possible to store multiple projects in the same folder.

3. Name the new folder, and click on Save.

4. Choose File ➤ Save Project As. In the Save Project As window , enter a name for the project file and click on Save.

> **NOTE**
> The Form's name has nothing to do with the name of the file in which the Form is stored, and the Project's name has nothing to do with the name of the file in which the project is stored. It is customary, however, to use the same name for the Form or project and the file in which it is stored (or at least similar names).

The Elements of the User Interface

The user interface is what appears in the application's window when it runs. It consists of various elements with which the user can interact and control the application. The first element of the user interface is the Form. This is the window displayed at run time, and it acts as a container for all the elements of the interface. The elements in the user interface are common to all Windows applications, and they are all shown as icons in the Toolbox.

The icons in the Toolbox of the Visual Basic IDE and their names are shown in Figure 1.8. Let's run down quickly through the controls shown in the Toolbox.

FIGURE 1.8

The icons on the Toolbox represent the elements you can use to build user interfaces.

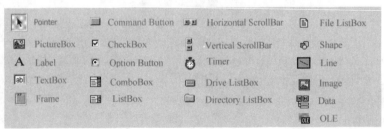

The TextBox Control   This control displays text that the user can edit. The TextBox control is a mini text editor, and its most important property is the Text property, which can set the text on the control or read the text that the user enters.

The Label Control   This control displays text on a Form that the user can't edit. Labels commonly identify other controls and can be transparent, so the text appears to be placed directly on the Form. You set the label's text with the Caption property.

The CheckBox Control   The checkbox presents one or more choices that the user can select. The CheckBox control's main property is Value, and it is 0 if the checkbox is cleared, and 1 if the checkbox is checked.

The Option Button Control   Option buttons, or radio buttons, appear in groups, and the user can chose only one of them. The Option button's main property is Checked, and it is True if the control is checked, and False otherwise.

The ListBox Control   This control contains a list of options from which the user can chose one or more. Unlike a group of checkboxes or option buttons, the ListBox control can contain many lines, and the user can scroll the list to locate an item. The selected item in a ListBox control is given by the Text property. Another important property of the ListBox control is the Sorted property, which determines whether the items in the list will be sorted or not.

The ComboBox Control   The ComboBox control is similar to the ListBox control, but it contains a text edit field. The user can either choose an item from the list or enter a new string in the edit field. The item selected from the list (or entered in the edit field) is given by the control's Text property.

The PictureBox Control   The PictureBox control is used to display images, and the images are set with the Picture property.

The Image Control   The Image control is similar to the PictureBox control in that it can display images, but it supports only a few features of the PictureBox control and requires fewer resources.

The Shape Control   The Shape control is used to draw graphical elements, such as boxes and circles, on the surface of a Form.

The Line Control   Similar to the Shape control, the Line control is used to draw lines on a Form.

 The Frame Control   This control is used to draw boxes on the Form and to group other elements.

File System Controls   You use these controls to add file-handling capabilities to your application. They are normally used together to provide an interface for accessing and exploring drives, folders, and files. The File System controls are:

 • **DriveListBox**   Displays the drives on the system in a drop-down list from which the user can select.

 • **DirListBox**   Displays a list of all folders in the current drive and lets the user move up or down in the hierarchy of the folders.

 • **FileListBox**   Displays a list of all files in the current folder.

 The Timer Control   You can use the Timer control to perform tasks at regular intervals. The main property of the Timer control is Interval, which determines how often the Timer notifies your application.

 The OLE Container Control   The OLE Container control is a window you can place on your Form to host documents from other applications, such as Microsoft Word and Microsoft Excel. Through this control, you can access the functionality of other applications, as long as they support OLE.

 The Data Control   This control provides point-and-click access to data stored in databases. It has many properties and methods, which are discussed in Chapter 11, *Database Programming with Visual Basic*.

Designing the User Interface

Designing the application's user interface consists of drawing the elements on the Form. In our first application, the user can select one of the three major credit cards (the form of payment) and one or more of the three items listed on the right of the Form shown in Figure 1.9.

FIGURE 1.9

Designing a user interface with Visual Basic controls

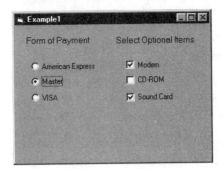

To design the Form shown in Figure 1.9, follow these steps:

1. In the Project Explorer, double-click on the name of the Form to open it in design mode, and in the Properties window, find the Caption property. This is the value that appears in the Form's caption bar, and its default value is Form1. Change it to Example1. The new name appears on the Form's caption bar even as you type its value in the Properties window.

2. Place a Label control near the top left corner of the Form.

3. With the Label control selected, switch to the Properties window and set the Label control's Caption property to Form of Payment. Notice that the Label control doesn't have a border by default.

4. Locate the Font property in the Properties window, and click on the button with the ellipsis next to the current font to open the Font dialog box.

5. Select an easy-to-read font. The example in Figure 1.9 uses 10 point MS Sans Serif.

6. Place another Label control next to the first one, and set its Caption property to Select Optional Items.

7. Switch back to the Properties window, and set the Font property of the new Label control to the same setting as the first one.

8. Now you can place the Option Button controls on the Form. Select the Option Button icon in the Toolbox, and draw a control on the Form. Make it large enough to hold the American Express caption.

9. While the first Option Button is still selected on the Form, move to the Properties window, and set its Caption property to American Express. Don't bother aligning the control or setting its Font or other properties yet.

10. Repeat steps 8 and 9 for the other two option buttons. Their captions should be Master and VISA.

11. Now place three CheckBox controls, and set their captions to Modem, CD-ROM, and Sound Card.

The elements of the interface are now on the Form, and you have two groups of controls that can be manipulated in common. For example, you can change the setting of the Font property for a number of controls at once. Follow these steps:

1. Select the three Option Buttons with the mouse, and then locate the Font property in the Properties window.

2. Click on the ellipsis button to open the Font dialog box.

3. Select a font, and it will apply to all selected controls.

To select multiple controls on the Form, hold down Shift (or Control) and click on them. If the controls you want to select are clustered together, you can select them by drawing a box around them with the mouse. The selected controls are indicated with handles.

Aligning the Controls

Now you must align the controls on the Form. This isn't a trivial step. Your application's user interface is its visible part, and what people think about your application depends a great deal on how the application looks. You are not expected to design the most spectacular user interface (not that it wouldn't help), but at the very least your controls must be perfectly aligned. If not, the Form will look crooked, out of whack. The Visual Basic IDE provides numerous commands for aligning controls, which are all on the Format menu and are explained next.

The Format Menu

The commands on the Format menu align and resize the selected controls on the Form. Here's a quick rundown of them, arranged according to their corresponding submenu.

Align   The commands on this menu align the edges or middles of the selected controls:

- **Lefts, Centers, Rights**   Aligns the left, center, and right sides of the selected controls; meaningful only if controls are stacked in a column.

- **Tops, Middles, Bottoms**   Aligns the top, middle, and bottom sides of the controls; meaningful only if controls are placed next to each other.

- **To Grid**   Aligns the controls to the nearest grid point.

Make Same Size   The commands on this menu make all selected controls the same size:

- **Height, Width, Both**   Makes the horizontal, vertical, or both dimensions of the controls equal.

Size to Grid   This command changes the size and/or position of the selected control(s) so that each corner aligns with the nearest grid point.

Horizontal Spacing   The commands on this menu control the horizontal spacing between selected controls:

- **Make Equal**   Makes all horizontal (vertical) distances between successive controls the same size.

- **Increase**   Increases the horizontal (vertical) distance between adjacent controls by one grid block.

- **Decrease**   Decreases the horizontal (vertical) distance between adjacent controls by one grid block.

- **Remove**   Removes any horizontal (vertical) space between adjacent controls.

Vertical Spacing   This menu controls the vertical spacing between selected controls and has the same commands as the Horizontal Spacing submenu, only these commands apply to the vertical arrangement of the controls.

Center in Form   This submenu contains two commands:

- **Horizontally**   Centers the selected control(s) in the width of the Form.

- **Vertically**   Centers the selected control(s) in the height of the Form.

Order   The Order submenu contains two commands that change the relative order of the selected control(s) by moving them in front or behind other controls. They work just like the commands of the same name in a drawing application, and you use them to manipulate the depth of each control. The *depth* is equivalent to a layer on which one or more controls reside. Objects on layers closer to the viewer hide the objects on layers behind them and are hidden by objects on layers in front of them.

- **Bring to Front**   Brings the selected control in front of other overlapping controls.

- **Send to Back**   Sends the selected control behind other overlapping controls.

Using the Format Menu

You can arrange your controls on the Form in many ways, and after you acquire some experience with the VB IDE, you'll be using these commands effectively.

To align the controls on the Example1 Form, follow these steps:

1. Select all three Option Button controls with the mouse. (To select multiple controls, hold down Shift or Control and click on each one.) Alternatively, you can draw a rectangle on the Form that encloses the desired controls.

2. Choose Format ➢ Align ➢ Lefts to align the left edges of the three controls.

3. With the three controls selected, choose Format ➢ Vertical Spacing ➢ Make Equal to make the distances between successive controls equal.

4. While the three controls remain selected, move them around with the mouse to the desired position. Click on any of the selected controls and drag it around. All the selected controls will move as a group.

Optionally, while the three controls remain selected, choose Format ➢ Lock Controls. This ensures that you won't ruin the alignment of the controls. Once a control is locked, you can't move it with the mouse or change its alignment. If your Form contains many carefully aligned controls, you should lock them; it doesn't take much to ruin the alignment. A simple action such as selecting a control to use as a reference to align other controls could move the control by a few pixels.

Running the Application

Now you can run and test the application. If you haven't had any experience with Visual Basic (or other visual development tools), you may be wondering, What application? We didn't type even a single line of code. Well, why do you think it's called Visual Basic and not Microsoft Basic or Windows Basic or anything else? Visual Basic uses visual tools to build a large section of the application. The user interface can be built almost entirely with point-and click-operations.

To run the application, choose Run ➢ Start or press F5. The application contains no code, but check out how much functionality is built into it. When you click on an Option Button, it is checked, and the previously checked option button is cleared. The checkboxes behave differently. Each time you click on a checkbox, it changes its state: If it is selected, it is cleared; if it is cleared, it becomes selected.

To stop the application, choose Run ➢ End. As you can see, the Visual Basic IDE is more than a program editor. It's an integrated environment in which you can design and run your applications.

Using the Immediate Window

Start the application again by pressing F5, and then interrupt it by pressing Ctrl+Break or by choosing Run ➢ Break. The application has been interrupted, but not terminated. At the bottom of the screen, you will see a window named Immediate, as shown in Figure 1.10. When you issue Visual Basic commands in this window, they execute immediately. Let's see how this works.

FIGURE 1.10

Commands entered in the Immediate window execute immediately.

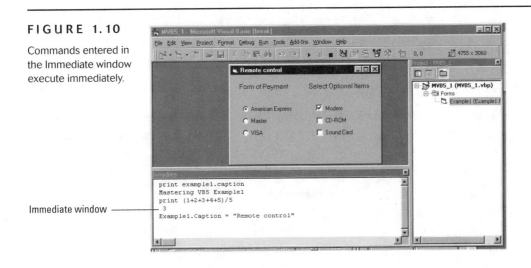

Immediate window

The States of Visual Basic

Visual Basic applications can be viewed in three distinct states:

- Design
- Execution
- Break

In *design state*, you can edit the user interface or add code to the application. All the windows of the IDE and its commands are available to you.

In *execution state,* the application is running. Only a few menu commands are available, and none of the windows of the IDE are available. You can neither edit the user interface nor add code to an application while it's running.

In the *break state,* the application's execution has been interrupted temporarily and can resume when you press F5 or choose Run ➢ Continue. The Immediate window is activated, and you can edit the code and issue commands in it. However, you can't edit the user interface.

Let's explore the role of the Immediate window while the application is in break state. Place the pointer in the Immediate window and type the following:

```
Print Example1.Caption
```

As you recall, Example1 is the name of the Form, and Caption is the name of the property that sets or reads the Form's caption. The previous statement displays the form's caption in the line below as soon as you press Enter.

The following statement displays the value 3:

```
Print (1+2+3+4+5)/ 5
```

This is a regular Visual Basic statement consisting of numeric values and arithmetic operators. It can appear anywhere in a Visual Basic application. You can issue all types of Visual Basic statements in the Immediate window, such as cos(3/100) or Rnd(), which returns a random number between 0 and 1.

The last statement shown in Figure 1.10:

```
Example1.Caption = "Remote Control"
```

does something quite interesting. It sets the value of the Form's Caption property. To display the application's window, press Alt+Tab. You will see that its caption has changed, as shown in Figure 1.10.

You use the Immediate window when you are designing and debugging applications, and with it you perform three common operations:

- Execute Visual Basic statements to perform simple tasks such as calculations

- Examine the values of the controls on the Form

- Set the values of the controls on the Form

These are extremely useful operations during an application's design and debugging phase. You don't have to write code to perform simple tasks. Merely type a statement in the Immediate window, and it executes as if it belonged to the current application.

You can issue even more complicated statements in the Immediate window, as long as they are all typed on the same line. To print six random numbers in the range 1 to 49, for instance, you can either issue six separate Print statements or write a small For...Next loop that prints the numbers. In an application's code, you would use the following structure:

```
For lucky = 1 To 6
    Print 1 + Int(Rnd()*48)
Next lucky
```

To issue the same statements in the Immediate window, you must type them in a single line. To enter more than one statement in a line (whether in the Immediate window or in your code), use the colon as separator:

```
For lucky = 1 To 6: Print 1 + Int(Rnd()*48): Next lucky
```

Enter this line in the Immediate window and press Enter to display the next six lucky numbers, as shown in Figure 1.11.

FIGURE 1.11

Executing multiple commands in the Immediate window

```
Immediate
For lucky = 1 To 6: Print 1 + Int(Rnd()*48): Next lucky
1
37
40
35
3
20
```

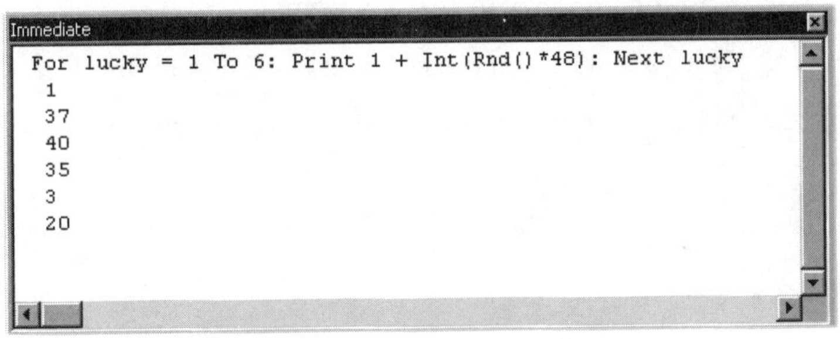

Programming an Application

Our next application is called MSVB_2, and you will find it in the Example2 folder in this chapter's folder on the CD. Start a new project, name the project MSVB_2 and name its Form Example2, and then save it in its own folder. The application's main window is shown in Figure 1.12.

FIGURE 1.12

The Example2 Form demonstrates a few properties of the TextBox control.

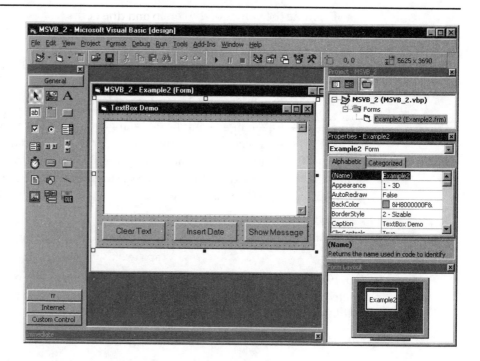

Now, follow these steps:

1. When you are back in the Visual Basic IDE, select the Form and change its Caption property to TextBox Demo.

2. Place a text box on the Form, as shown in Figure 1.12.

3. Select the text box, and in the Properties window, set its MultiLine property to True.

By default, the TextBox control accepts a single line of text, and the default setting of its MultiLine property is False. By setting it to True, you are specifying that the text box can accept multiple lines of text.

Since the text box can hold multiple lines of text, it is possible for the user to enter text that exceeds the height of the control. To make sure that every piece of the text in the control is visible, you must set its ScrollBars property to Vertical. When you do so, a vertical scroll bar appears on the right side of the control so that the user can scroll its contents up and down.

4. Locate the ScrollBars property in the Properties window, and expand the list of possible values by selecting the setting 2-Vertical. (The other possible values are 0-None, 1-Horizontal, and 3-Both.)

5. Place three command buttons, and set their Captions to Clear Text, Insert Date, and Show Message. We will program these buttons later to react when they are clicked.

6. From the Format menu, select the appropriate commands to make the size of all three command buttons the same, align their tops, and align them with the text box.

The application's interface is complete. Now run the application and check out the TextBox control. This control can add the basic functionality of a text editor to your applications. Notice how it wraps text as you type, and try out the editing keys. You can select text with the mouse and delete it, copy it to the Clipboard by pressing Ctrl+C, and paste it back by pressing Ctrl+V. You can even switch to another application, such as Notepad, copy some text with the other application's Copy command, and then paste it in the text box by pressing Ctrl+V.

Programming the Command Buttons

Now we must add some code behind the Form's buttons to perform the actions indicated by their captions. Obviously, the Clear Text button must clear the control by deleting any text on it. The Insert Date button displays the date in the control, and the Show Message button displays a message on the control. Follow these steps:

1. If the application is running, stop it by choosing Run ➤ End.

2. When the Form appears on the screen, double-click on the first command button. Visual Basic opens the Code window, shown in Figure 1.13.

FIGURE 1.13

The Code window for the Example2 application

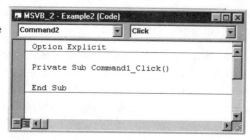

Preparing to Code

Before you start coding, choose Tools ➤ Options to open the Options dialog box:

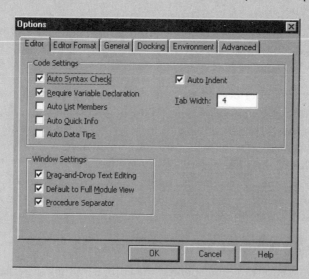

Select the Editor tab, and then clear the following checkboxes:

- Auto List Members
- Auto Quick Info
- Auto Data Tips

This action simplifies the process of entering code. I will explain later the meaning of these options and how they interfere with typing commands.

Visual Basic has inserted the following lines in the Code window and placed the pointer between them:

```
Private Sub Command1_Click()

End Sub
```

Command1 is the name of the control, and Click is the name of an event. This event is triggered every time the user clicks on the first command button. When this happens, Visual Basic looks for a subroutine named Command1_Click, and if it's found, it executes. In other words, if you want actions to execute every time the Command1 control is clicked, you must insert them in the Command1_Click subroutine.

The command to clear the TextBox control is as follows:

```
Text1.Text = ""
```

Text1 is the name of the control (it's the default name Visual Basic assigned to it when it was created), and Text is the name of the property that sets (or reads) the text on the control. Setting the Text property to an empty string in effect clears the text box. The Code window should now look like the one shown in Figure 1.14. Command1_Click() is an *event handler*, a procedure that specifies how the Command1 control must handle the Click event.

FIGURE 1.14

The Code window of the Example2 application with the code of the Clear Text button

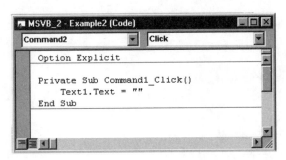

Now double-click on the second command button to display its subroutine for the Click event. To display the current date in the text box, the subroutine must contain the following line:

```
Private Sub Command2_Click()
    Text1.Text = Date()
End Sub
```

The Date() function returns the current date. Assigning its value to the Text property replaces the current contents of the control with the date.

The Click event handler for the third button is:

```
Private Sub Command3_Click()
    Text1.Text = "Welcome to Visual Basic 5.0"
End Sub
```

This subroutine displays the string "Welcome to Visual Basic 5.0" in the text box.

Run the application and test the operation of the command buttons. They perform simple operations, but their code is even simpler. Each time you click on the Insert Date or Show Message buttons, the current contents of the text box are cleared. Ideally, we should be able to insert the date and message in the text, not replace it.

SelText   To insert a string in the text box, you use the SelText property, which represents the selected text in the control. If you assign a value to the SelText property, the selected text (not the entire text) is replaced with the new value. Even if no text is selected, the new string is inserted at the location of the pointer in the text. The revised event handlers for the buttons Command1 and Command2 are shown next, along with the rest of the code. Implement these changes, and then run the application to see how the commands behave now. You have some practical and useful features in your editor, which is based on an ActiveX control.

Code 1.1: The Example2 Application

```
Option Explicit

Private Sub Command1_Click()
    Text1.Text = ""
End Sub

Private Sub Command2_Click()
    Text1.SelText = Date()
End Sub

Private Sub Command3_Click()
    Text1.SelText = "Welcome to Visual Basic 5.0"
End Sub
```

Grouping Controls

Our next application is called MSVB5-3, and its interface is shown in Figure 1.15. This example is another typical design with a peculiar requirement and demonstrates how to group controls.

FIGURE 1.15

The Example3 Form

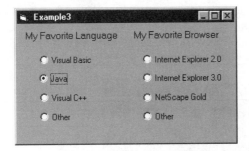

The design of this Form is straightforward. Place eight option buttons grouped in two blocks on the Form, set their captions as shown in Figure 1.15, and left-align each group's controls by choosing Format ➤ Align ➤ Left. The titles are placed on Label controls.

Run the application, and check out how the option buttons work. Each time you click on a control, the other controls are cleared. But this isn't how this application should behave, right? We want to be able to check one option button in each column. By default, Visual Basic checks one option button only, no matter how many you have placed on the Form. It can't group them without additional clues.

To create groups of controls, you place them on another control, which is called a *container*. The most common choice for the container control is the Frame control. Option buttons placed on different frames form separate groups, and Visual Basic maintains one checked option button in each group. Let's modify the application to create two groups of option buttons, as shown in Figure 1.16. Follow these steps:

1. Select the option buttons in the first group.

2. Choose Edit ➤ Cut. The option buttons are removed from the Form and stored in the Clipboard. We will use the Paste command to place them back on the Form later.

3. Draw a frame large enough to hold the option buttons you copied.

4. While the frame is selected, choose Edit ➤ Paste. The controls you removed from the Form earlier are pasted on the Frame control. They are not only grouped together, they are a permanent fixture of the Frame control. You can't move them outside the frame.

5. Repeat steps 1 through 4 with the other 4 option buttons. Select and copy them, place a second frame on the Form, and then paste the controls on it. Align the buttons as needed.

FIGURE 1.16

The option buttons of the Form shown in Figure 1.15, after they were grouped with the help of two frames

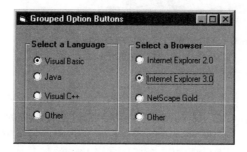

As you can see, the two labels are no longer needed because the two frames have their own captions. Let's delete the two labels and place the titles on the Frame controls. Follow these steps:

1. Select the first frame on the Form, and then locate its Caption property in the Properties window and set it to Select a Language.

2. Repeat step 1 for the second frame.

3. To turn on the bold attribute for both frames, select them, double-click on their Font property in the Properties window, and in the Font dialog box, click on Bold.

4. To delete the labels that are no longer needed, select each one and press Delete, or select them both with the mouse and then press Delete. You can also select both labels and then choose Edit ➤ Delete.

Run the application now, and check out how the Option buttons behave. Each group has its own checked button, and you can select both a language and a browser. You could have used the PictureBox control instead of the Frame control.

Prefer the Frame, however, because it visually isolates the members of each group. You can also use a PictureBox control without a visible border so that the option buttons appear as if they are directly on the Form. They will behave as grouped buttons, just as they do when they are placed on a frame.

You now have an idea how Visual Basic works, and you have an understanding of the basic principles of application development with Visual Basic. The two main themes in developing applications with Visual Basic are:

- Visual design

- Event-driven programming

To design the user interface of the application, you don't need more than a basic understanding of the controls (and you know what each control does from your experience with other Windows applications) and basic drawing capabilities. If you have used drawing applications, you can design a user interface with Visual Basic.

Programming the application isn't as simple, but there's a methodology you can't escape. A Visual Basic application isn't a monolithic program such as applications you may have developed with other languages. When you program in Visual Basic, you must first decide how the application interacts with the user. In other words, you must decide how each control reacts to user actions, such as the click of a mouse, keystrokes, and so on, and you must program these reactions. This is called *event-driven programming*, because the application does not determine the flow; instead, the events caused by the user determine the flow of the application. You program the application to react to various external conditions (events), and the user's actions determine the application's flow.

Let's put together the knowledge acquired so far and summarize the basic principles of application development.

Visual Development and Event-Driven Programming

Forms and controls are the basic elements in the user interface of any Windows application. In Visual Basic, these elements are called objects, because they are manipulated like objects. Objects have properties and methods, and they react to external events, as does any physical object. Your car, for example, is a physical object, and one of its properties is color. Normally, properties are set when an object is created. If you don't like the color of the car as you ordered it, you can still change it. Most control properties are set when the object is created (placed on the Form), but you can change a property later by assigning a new value to it. You can change a property at design time (through the Properties window) or at run time (through your code).

Visual Basic assigns default properties to every new control you place on a Form. The default Name property, for example, is the name of the control, followed by a number (Command1, Command2, and so on). The background color of most controls is either gray or white. You can examine the property values of a newly created control in the Properties window.

> **TIP**
>
> Take advantage of the following IDE feature: Controls inherit some properties from the Form. It's customary for all (or nearly all) controls on a Form to have the same Font property. If you place all the controls on the Form, you must change the Font property later. An alternative is to set the Form's Font property to the desired value so that all the controls placed on it will inherit the Form's font.

A few properties are available only at design time, and some others are available only at run time. You can't specify an item in a ListBox control at design time, because the control is empty. It is populated with Visual Basic statements when the program starts. (It is also possible to prepopulate the control at design time by assigning values to the List property, but the actual handling of the control's items takes place at run time.) The Text property of the ListBox control, therefore, has no meaning at design time. At run time, it is the control's most important property.

The MultiLine property of the TextBox control, on the other hand, determines whether the text box holds multiple lines of text. You can set this property only at design time, and it can't be changed at run time.

Some properties are only available at run time and are read-only. The number of items in a ListBox control is available at run time and is read-only. You can only find out the number of items in the control. To change their count, you must either add or remove items.

A Few Common Properties

The following properties apply to most objects.

Name   This property sets the name of the control, through which you can access the control's properties and methods.

Appearance   This property can be 0 for a flat look or 1 for a 3-D look. The examples in this book use the 3-D look for most controls.

BackColor   This property sets the background color on which text is displayed or graphics are drawn.

ForeColor   This property sets the foreground color (pen color or text color).

Font   This property sets the face, attribute, and size of the font used for the text on the control (text in a TextBox control, the caption of a label or command button, and so on).

Caption   This property sets the text that is displayed on many controls that don't accept input, for example, the text on a Label control, the caption of a Command Button control, and the strings displayed next to the CheckBox and OptionButton controls.

Text   This property sets the text that is displayed on the controls that accept user input, for example, the TextBox control. Some other controls that can accept text, such as the RichTextBox control, don't appear by default in the Toolbox.

Width, Height   These properties set the control's dimensions. Usually, the dimensions of a control are determined with the visual tools we have explored already. But you can read the control's dimensions or set them from within your code with these properties. The default units are twips, and there are 1440 twips in an inch (see Chapter 6, *Drawing and Painting with Visual Basic*, for a discussion of the twips units).

Left, Top   These properties set the coordinates of the control's upper left corner, expressed in the units of the container (usually a Form). The placement of a control on the Form can be specified with the Form Layout window, but you can change it from within your code with these two properties. The default units are twips, and there are 1440 twips in an inch (see Chapter 6, *Drawing and Painting with Visual Basic,* for a discussion of the twips units).

Enabled   By default, this property's value is True, which means that the control can get the focus. Set it to False to disable the control. A disabled control appears gray and can't accept user input.

Visible   Set this property to False to make a control invisible. Sometimes, you use invisible controls to store information that is used internally by the application and should not be seen or manipulated by the user.

A Few Common Methods

Objects have methods too, which are the actions they can carry out. You can think of methods as the actions of an object. For example, the methods of your VCR are the Play, Fast Forward, Rewind, Pause, and Record buttons. After you press one of these buttons, your VCR can perform without any further assistance from you. The Form object, for example, knows how to clear itself, and you can invoke the Cls method to clear a Form. A Form also knows how to hide itself, an action that you can invoke from within your code with the Hide method.

WARNING   Don't confuse methods with a control's built-in functionality. The TextBox control, for example, knows how to handle keystrokes and convert them into lines of text and display them. You need not call a special method to perform these actions.

Clear   Some methods are simple verbs that tell the object the action to carry out. The Clear method tells the control to discard its contents. If the object is a ListBox, the Clear method removes all its item from the control. The Clear method can also be applied to the Clipboard object, to clear its contents.

AddItem, RemoveItem   These methods are used to manipulate the items in a ListBox or ComboBox control. The application doesn't have to know how the items are stored in the control. It issues the AddItem method, and the control takes care of appending or inserting the new item in the list. And this exactly why methods are used. They are the actions each control can perform without any assistance from the programmer. In effect, methods hide the implementation details of the controls' features, and the programmer can exploit these features by calling a method, which is similar to setting a property value.

For example, to add the item "Canada" in the ListBox control named Countries (which presumably maintains a list of countries), use the following statement:

```
Countries.AddItem "Canada"
```

The ListBox control appends the string Canada at the end of the list. If the list is sorted (its Sorted property was set to True at design time), the new item is inserted in the proper order in the list. The AddItem method does a good deal of work behind the scenes, but as a programmer, you needn't worry about the details. All you need to know is the name of the method.

As you can see, to apply a method to a control, you specify the name of the control, followed by a period and then the name of the method. The syntax is nearly identical to the syntax of properties. The difference is that a method isn't assigned a value. Typically, a method accepts one or more parameters that tell it exactly how to perform an action.

Some methods, such as the Clear method, are quite simple. You merely specify the name of the control it applies to and the method's name. Some others require additional information. The AddItem method, for instance, which adds a new item to a ListBox control, must know the item to add. When you call this method, you must also supply the value of the item to be added to the list, as you saw in the previous example.

The PictureBox control provides a method for drawing lines. For the PictureBox control to draw a line, it must know the end coordinates of the line (line drawing and other drawing methods are explained in Chapter 6, *Drawing and Painting with Visual Basic*).

A Few Common Events

Events determine the control's reactions to external conditions. Events are recognized by the various controls, but are handled by your application. A command button will recognize that it was clicked upon, but it won't react to the event unless you provide some code. In other words, you must tell Visual Basic what to do when the user clicks on the specific command button, as we did in the second example in this chapter. Once you specify a subroutine for the control's Click event, this subroutine executes each time the control is clicked. The subroutine that determines how a control reacts to an event is called an *event handler*.

To write an event handler for a control, follow these steps:

1. Switch to the Code window, or double-click on the control for which you want to write the event handler.

2. In the top of the Code window, which is shown in Figure 1.17, you will see two drop down lists. The first contains the names of all the controls on the Form. Select the control for which you want to write an event handler. The second list contains all the events the selected control can recognize. Select the event for which you want to write an event handler.

FIGURE 1.17

To write an event handler, select the control's name from the list on the left and the event's name from the list on the right.

The combination of the control's name and the event's name is unique and is the name of the event handler. Each time an event takes place, Visual Basic looks for the subroutine made up of the name of the control on which the event took place and the name of the event. If such a handler exists, it's executed. If not, your application won't react to the event. (Typically, applications react to a small number of events.)

The two most common groups of events are mouse (events caused with the mouse) and keyboard (events caused with the keyboard).

Mouse Events

The events triggered by mouse actions are the most common events in programming with Visual Basic. Most of the elements of the user interface can be manipulated with the mouse, and programming mouse events is your number one job as a VB programmer. However, many users prefer the keyboard, even for operations that are simpler to carry out with the mouse, so you must not favor mouse operations to the exclusion of their keyboard equivalents.

Click, DblClick   The Click event takes place when the user clicks the left mouse button; the DblClick event takes place when the user double-clicks the left mouse button.

MouseDown, MouseUp   The MouseDown event takes place when the mouse button is pressed, and the MouseUp event takes place as it is released.

MouseMove   This event takes place continuously as the mouse is moved over a control. The order in which mouse events take place is as follows:

1. As the mouse is moved around, the MouseMove event is triggered continuously.

2. When the user presses a mouse button, the MouseDown event is triggered.

3. If the user continues to move the mouse around while holding down the button, the program keeps receiving MouseMove events.

4. When the user releases the mouse button, the MouseUp event is triggered.

5. If the left mouse button was held down, the Click event is triggered immediately after the MouseUp event.

When the mouse button is double-clicked, the following events take place:

1. Mouse Down

2. MouseUp

3. Click

4. Double-Click

5. MouseUp

It's a bit involved, but there will never be a reason to program all mouse events or the same control (unless you want to find out the order in which the events are received).

The mouse events you'll be using most often are the Click and DblClick events. If you want finer control of the mouse actions, you will have to program the MouseDown and MouseUp events. For example, if you want to know the coordinates of the point where the mouse was clicked, you will use the MouseDown and MouseUp events. The definitions of the Click and DblClick events are as follows:

```
Sub Click()

End Sub
```

and

```
Sub DblClick()

End Sub
```

Contrast these definitions with the definition of the MouseUp event:

```
Private Sub Text1_MouseUp(Button As Integer, Shift As Integer,
➥X As Single, Y As Single)

End Sub
```

The *Button* argument reports which mouse button caused the event. The *Shift* argument reports the status of the Shift, Control, and Alt keys; and the *X* and *Y* arguments are the coordinates of the point where the mouse button was released. Table 1.1 shows the values of the *Button* argument, and Table 1.2 shows the values of the *Shift* argument.

TABLE 1.1   The Values of the Button Argument

CONSTANT	VALUE	DESCRIPTION
vbLeftButton	1	Left button is pressed
vbRightButton	2	Right button is pressed
vbMiddleButton	4	Middle button is pressed

TABLE 1.2   The Values of the Shift Argument

CONSTANT	VALUE	DESCRIPTION
vbShiftMask	1	SHIFT key is pressed
vbCtrlMask	2	CTRL key is pressed
vbAltMask	4	ALT key is pressed

To find out which button caused the MouseDown or MouseUp event, use the following If structure:

```
If Button = vbLeftButton Then
    {process left button}
End If
```

You can write a mouse handler to simulate the double-click with the click of the middle mouse button (this will work with three-button mice only, but won't affect the operation of a two-button mouse). Insert the following lines in the MouseUp event handler:

```
Private Sub Form_MouseUp(Button As Integer, Shift As Integer,
➥X As Single, Y As Single)
    If Button = vbMiddleButton Then Call Form_DblClick
End Sub
```

This event handler monitors the MouseUp event for the middle button, and when it detects the event, it invokes the From_DblClick event handler. Notice that although you can't cause the DblClick event from within your code, you can call the event's handler.

Similarly, you can detect the state of the Shift key while the mouse button was pressed. Suppose you want to perform one action when the Command1 control is clicked and a different action when the same control is clicked with the Control key pressed. To do so, test the Shift argument with an If structure such as the following:

```
If Shift = vbCtrlMask Then
    {Mouse was pressed while Control key down}
End If
```

Keyboard Events

Keyboard events are generated by keystrokes. Usually, you must program the keyboard events for the controls that can accept text. In addition, you must provide code for the keyboard events of controls that can be manipulated with both the mouse and the keyboard, because many users prefer to work with the keyboard most of the time.

KeyDown, KeyUp   The KeyDown event is triggered when a key is pressed, and the KeyUp event is triggered when a key is released.

KeyPress   In practice, your code doesn't care about the KeyDown and KeyUp events. Most programs use the KeyPress event to find out which key was pressed. The KeyPress event is used frequently to write keyboard handlers for text boxes, because this event takes place before the character pressed is displayed in the text box. The definition of the KeyPress event is:

```
Private Sub Text1_KeyPress(KeyAscii As Integer)

End Sub
```

The *KeyAscii* argument is the ASCII character of the key pressed. You can use this event to even reject the character typed. Setting the *KeyAscii* argument to zero in effect chokes the keystroke, and the control never sees it. The character that corresponds to this ASCII code is:

```
Chr$(KeyAscii)
```

The ASCII codes of the numeric digits start at 48 (for the digit 0) and end at 57 (for the digit 9). The following event handler allows the user to enter only numeric digits in the Text1 text box:

```
Private Sub Text1_KeyPress(KeyAscii As Integer)
    If KeyAscii < 48 Or KeyAscii > 57 Then KeyAscii = 0
End Sub
```

Change   The Change event is triggered by various controls when their contents change. The Change event is generated for the TextBox control each time a new character is typed or deleted. It is generated for the CheckBox control every time the user changes its status by clicking on it.

Most Windows applications prompt you to save your data when it has been changed since the last Save operation. You can easily add this feature to your applications by setting a variable from within the Change event. When the user saves the contents of a text box, reset this variable to indicate that the user can quit the application without saving the control's contents. If the user types even a single character after saving the file, the variable is set from within the Change event to indicate that the text has been changed and that the application should prompt the user before exiting.

Focus

A fundamental concept in developing user interfaces that comply with the Windows standards is the focus. *Focus* is the ability of a control to receive user input via the keyboard. When an object has the focus, it can receive input from a user. Suppose you have a Form with two TextBox controls on it. At any time, only one of them can accept input (in other words, can recognize the keys pressed). The control that can accept input is said to have the focus. To enter text in the other text box, you must move the focus to it either with the mouse (by clicking on the second TextBox control) or via the keyboard (by pressing the Tab key).

GotFocus and LostFocus   There are two related events, GotFocus and LostFocus. When the focus is moved from one control to the other, the first control (the one that had the focus) receives the LostFocus event, and after that the second control (the one to which the focus was moved) receives the GotFocus event.

You can use the GotFocus event to initialize a control for editing, and you can use the LostFocus event to validate the data entered by the user. For example, you can copy the contents of a text box when it receives the focus so that you can restore its original contents later. After the user enters some data and moves to another control, you can examine the text box's contents from within your code and either accept them or restore them by assigning the temporary variable to the control's Text property.

You can also move the focus to another control by using the SetFocus method within your code. Figure 1.18 shows a data-entry Form with three TextBox controls. Each text box can store a single line of text (MultiLine property=False). The Enter key has no meaning on these controls, because there is no second line to move to. You can detect this keystroke from within the KeyUp event and move the focus to the next control.

FIGURE 1.18

The Focus application demonstrates how to move the focus from one control to the other from within your code.

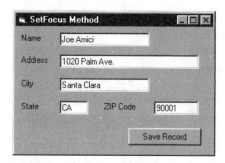

TIP Why use the Enter key to move the focus to another control? Because most data-entry operators would much rather work with the keyboard than the mouse. If you are typing data, the last thing you want is to have to reach for the mouse to select the next field. The Tab key will do the same, but the Enter key is easier to reach and can speed up typing.

VB5 at Work: The Focus Application

The Focus application, which you will find in the Focus folder on the CD, has five single-line text boxes in which the user can enter data. Every time the user presses Enter, the focus moves to the next control. To capture the Enter key, you use the KeyUp event, which reports the code of the key pressed.

Code 1.2: Capturing the Enter Key

```
Private Sub Text1_KeyUp(KeyCode As Integer, Shift As Integer)

    If KeyCode = 13 Then Text2.SetFocus

End Sub
```

The other text boxes have similar event handlers for the KeyUp event. When the user presses Enter while the last text box has the focus, the focus moves to the Save Record command button, as follows:

```
Private Sub Text5_KeyUp(KeyCode As Integer, Shift As Integer)

    If KeyCode = 13 Then SaveBttn.SetFocus

End Sub
```

This button doesn't save the data anywhere. It simply displays a message, clears the text boxes, and then moves the focus to the first text box.

Code 1.3: The Save Button

```
Private Sub SaveBttn_Click()

    MsgBox "Record Saved. Click OK to enter another"
    Text1.Text = ""
    Text2.Text = ""
    Text3.Text = ""
    Text4.Text = ""
```

```
        Text5.Text = ""
        Text1.SetFocus

End Sub
```

Tab Order

All Windows applications allow the user to move the focus from one control to the other with the Tab key. For this to happen, you must decide how the focus is moved from one control to the other. In other words, you must decide which control gets the focus each time the user presses Tab. This is known as Tab order. Each control has its own Tab order, which is by default the order in which the controls were created.

TIP   The Tab key doesn't produce spaces, even when used with a TextBox control. It always moves the focus to the next control in the Tab order.

Because controls are rarely placed on a Form in the same order they will be used, you need to be able to change the Tab order. You do so with the TabIndex property, which determines the control's position in the Tab order. The first control that is drawn has a TabIndex value of 0, the second has a TabIndex of 1, and so on. The focus is moved from each control to the one with the next TabIndex value. To change the order in which the focus moves from one control to another, you change the TabIndex property of the control. When the Tab order for a given control is changed, Visual Basic automatically renumbers the Tab order of the remaining controls on the Form to reflect insertions and deletions.

If you don't want the user to move to a specific control, you can remove it from the Tab order by setting its TabStop property to False. The TabStop property determines whether the control can get the focus, but does not determine its Tab order. Regardless of the setting of the TabStop property, you can always move the focus to any control with the mouse.

There is one control, the Option button, whose Tab order is handled specially. The members of an option button group have a single Tab stop. Since only one option button in the group can be checked at a time, it doesn't make sense to move the focus from one to the other. A user who wants to change the status of an option button through the keyboard can use the arrow buttons to check an option button—an action that clears the previously selected button.

Customizing the Environment

After familiarizing yourself with the IDE, you will probably want to customize it according to your taste and requirements. To access the customization tools, choose Tools ➤ Options to open the Options dialog, as shown in Figure 1.19. Let's now look at the various ways you can customize the IDE by using the settings in this dialog box.

The Editor Tab

You use the settings in this tab to customize the behavior of the code and project windows. Visual Basic lets you customize these two windows according to your personal preferences and your experience.

FIGURE 1.19

The Editor tab of the Options dialog box

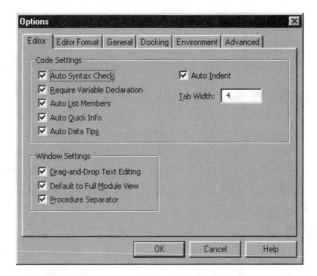

Code Settings

The Code settings let you specify the behavior of the text editor of the Code window. Use the settings on this tab to specify how much help you want Visual Basic to provide as you enter your code. The Code Settings section of the Editor tab has the following options.

Auto Syntax Check   Check this checkbox if you want Visual Basic to verify the syntax of every line of code as you enter it. If you make a syntax error, Visual Basic issues a warning, and the line turns red when you press Enter.

Require Variable Declaration   Check this checkbox if you want to require explicit variable declarations. If you check this option, the statement Option Explicit is added automatically on each Form and module.

Auto List Members   Check this checkbox to display a pop-up list with the members of a control. As soon as you type a control's name followed by a period (which means you are about to type a property or a method name), Visual Basic displays all the members (properties, methods, and events) of the control. Figure 1.20 shows the Auto List Members box with the members of the Text1 control (which is a TextBox control).

FIGURE 1.20

Auto Listing the members of the TextBox control

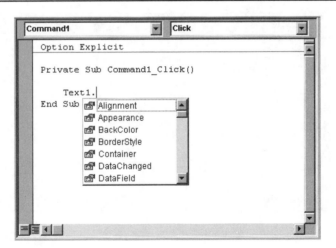

Auto Quick Info   Check this box to display information about functions and their parameters. For example, if you want to call the MsgBox() function in your Code and the Auto Quick Info feature is enabled, Visual Basic displays the syntax of the function for you. As you enter the arguments of the function, the current argument is highlighted in the little yellow box, as shown in Figure 1.21.

FIGURE 1.21

Auto Quick Information
for the MsgBox()
function

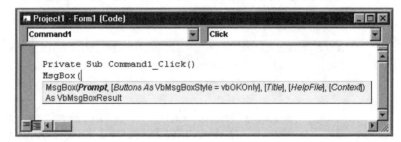

Auto Data Tips   Check this box to display the value of the variable over which your cursor is placed. Auto Data Tips are available in Break state only. If you break the execution of an application and switch to the Code window, you can place the pointer over a variable to see its value. Figure 1.22 shows this feature in action for the MSVB5-2 application. The Stop statement was inserted to interrupt the execution of the application.

FIGURE 1.22

The Auto Data Tips
feature displays the
values of the variables
while the program is in
Break state.

```
PieChart - Form1 (Code)

Command1                          Click

Private Sub Command1_Click()
Dim PieData(10) As Integer

    Form1.Cls
    For i = 0 To 9
        PieData(i) = 20 + Rnd() * 100
        Total = Total + PieData(i)
    Next                PieData(i) = 91

    Form1.DrawWidth = 2
    For i = 0 To 9
        arc1 = arc2
```

Auto Indent   Check this box if you want to be able to tab the first line of code; all subsequent lines start at that tab location.

Tab Width   Enter a number in this text box to set the tab width; the default value is 4 spaces. Valid values are in the range 1 to 32.

Window Settings

Use the Window settings to specify a few basic characteristics of the Code editor.

Drag-and-Drop Text Editing   Check this box to allow drag-and-drop operations from the Code window to the Immediate or Watch windows.

Default to Full Module View   Check this box to view a scrollable list of procedures when you edit code in a Code window. If this box is not checked, you can view only one procedure at a time.

Procedure Separator   Check this box to display the separator bars that appear between procedures in the Code window.

The Editor Format Tab

You use this tab (see Figure 1.23) to set the attributes for the type of text selected in the Code Colors list. Select the type of text from this list, and then specify how you want it to appear in the Code window.

FIGURE 1.23

The Editor Format tab of the Options dialog box

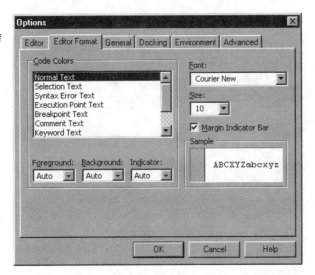

The General Tab

In this tab, you specify the settings of the grid, error-trapping, and Compile options for the current project, as shown in Figure 1.24.

Form Grid Settings

The Settings in this section let you specify the characteristics of the grid on which the controls are placed. These characteristics include the density of the grid points, whether the grid will be visible, and so on.

Show Grid   Check this box to specify that the grid on a Form is visible.

Grid Units   Displays the units used for measuring distances on the grid units, which are points.

Width, Height   In these text boxes, enter the numbers that determine the width and height of the grid cells.

Align Controls to Grid   Check this box if you want Visual Basic to automatically resize and reposition controls so that their outer edges are on grid lines.

FIGURE 1.24

The General Tab of the Options dialog box

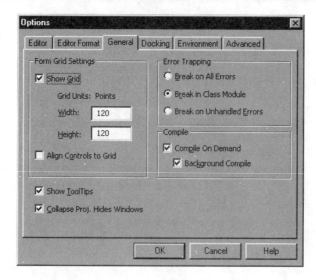

Show ToolTips   Check this box to display ToolTips for the toolbar and Toolbox items.

Collapse Proj. Hides Windows   Check this box to hide the window when a project is collapsed in the Project Explorer.

Error Trapping

The options in this section of the General tab let you specify under what conditions an error in an application will generate a run-time error and be interrupted.

Break on All Errors   Check this box if you want Visual Basic to enter Break state on any error, even if the error is handled by an error handler.

Break in Class Module   Check this box if you want any error in a class module without an error handler to cause the project to enter Break state.

Break on Unhandled Errors   When you check this box, any error causes the project to enter Break state if there is no active error handler.

Compile

The Compile options let you specify how and when Visual Basic will compile an application before it starts executing it.

Compile on Demand   Check this box if you want to compile code as needed, which allows the application to start sooner. If this checkbox is not cleared, Visual Basic compiles the entire project and then starts executing it. If you choose the Start with Full Compile command on the Run menu, Visual Basic ignores the Compile on Demand setting and performs a full compile.

Background Compile   When an application starts executing without a full compile, Visual Basic can use the idle time during run time to finish the project's compilation in the background if this checkbox is checked.

The Docking Tab

In this tab (see Figure 1.25) you specify which windows will be dockable. A *dockable window* is attached (or "anchored") to other windows that are dockable or to

FIGURE 1.25

The Docking tab of the
Options menu

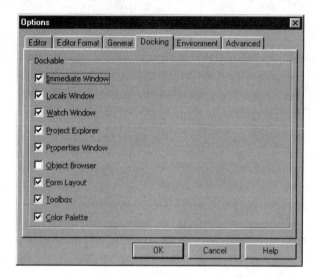

the main window. When you move a dockable window, it "snaps" to the new
location. You can move a nondockable window anywhere on the screen.

Check the box in front of the names of the windows that you want to behave as
dockable and clear the rest.

The Environment Tab

In this tab you specify various attributes of your Visual Basic development environment. Changes made in this tab (see Figure 1.26) are saved in the Registry and
loaded every time you restart Visual Basic.

When Visual Basic Starts

The following options let you specify what happens when you start Visual Basic
(whether it prompts you for a project name or starts a default executable program).

Prompt for Project   Check this button if you want Visual Basic to display
the New Project window when it starts.

FIGURE 1.26

The Environment tab of
the Options menu

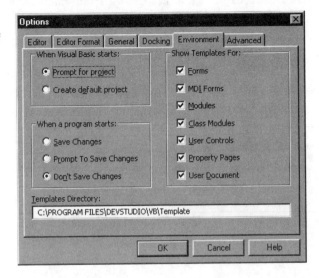

Create Default Project   Check this option if you want a default executable
(EXE) project to open each time you start Visual Basic.

The following options let you specify what happens when you start an application (when you press F5 or choose Start ➤ Run).

Save Changes   Check this option if you want to automatically save changes
to a project (without prompting) every time you run it. If this option is selected,
you won't lose changes when your application crashes Visual Basic. However,
if you are making extensive changes to your application, you may want to go
back to the previous version, and with this option selected, it will be too late.

Prompt to Save Changes   Check this option if you want Visual Basic to
always prompt you to save changes to your project when you run it.

Don't Save Changes   Check this option if you want Visual Basic not to save
the project automatically and not to prompt you to save it when you run it.

Show Templates For   Check the boxes in this section to specify which templates are displayed in the Project menu when you add an item to a project.

Templates Directory   Enter here the full path name of the folder where template files are stored.

The Advanced Tab

In this tab (see Figure 1.27), you set the options that are described next.

FIGURE 1.27

The Advanced tab of the Options dialog box

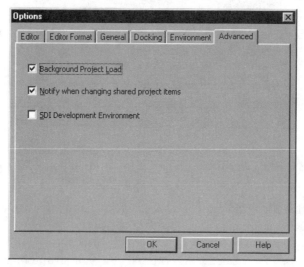

Background Project Load   Check this checkbox to specify that projects are loaded in the background. When projects are loaded in the background, control returns to the developer more quickly.

Notify When Changing Shared Project Items   Check this checkbox if you want Visual Basic to notify you when you change a shared project item such as a Form or module and try to save it.

SDI Development Environment   Check this checkbox if you want to work in as SDI (Single Document Interface) environment. In this book, we use the MDI (Multiple Document Interface) environment.

CHAPTER
TWO

2

Visual Basic Projects

- Developing a loan application

- Programming a math application

- Creating an application that uses multiple Forms

- Distributing executable files

The previous chapter introduced Visual Basic's development editor, basic controls, and the principles of event-driven programming. In this chapter, we expand on that introduction to the language by building some real-life applications. Among other topics, we'll look at how to write applications that have multiple windows, how to validate user input, and how to write error-trapping routines. We'll also look at several techniques you'll need as you work through the applications we develop in the rest of the book.

This chapter's goal is to explain the methodology for building applications. The code of the applications is rather simple, but it demonstrates user interface design and the basics of validating data and trapping errors.

> **NOTE** If you are a beginner, you may be thinking, "All I want now is to write a simple application that works—I'll worry about data validation later." It's never too early to start thinking about validating your code's data and error trapping.

As you will see, making sure that your application doesn't crash requires more code than the actual operations it performs! If this isn't quite what you expected, welcome to the club.

VB5 at Work: A Loan Calculator

We are now going to develop a practical application that calculates loan parameters. As you will soon see, it's easy to implement and demonstrates the steps for designing an application. Let's do away with the difficult part right off the bat. Visual Basic provides built-in functions for performing many types of financial calculations, and you only need a single line of code to calculate the monthly payment given the loan amount, its duration, and the interest rate. Designing the user interface, however, takes much more effort.

Regardless of the language you use to develop an application, you must go through the following process:

1. Decide what the application will do and how it will interact with the user.

2. Design the application's user interface.

3. Write the actual code.

How the Loan Application Works

The user should be able to specify the amount of the loan, the interest rate, and the duration of the loan in months. You must, therefore, provide three text boxes in which the user can enter these values, as shown in Figure 2.1. Another parameter affecting the monthly payment is whether payments are made at the beginning or at the end of each month, so you also want to provide a way for the user to specify whether the payments will be early (first day of the month) or late (last day of the month). The most appropriate type of control for entering Yes/No or True/False type of information is the Checkbox control.

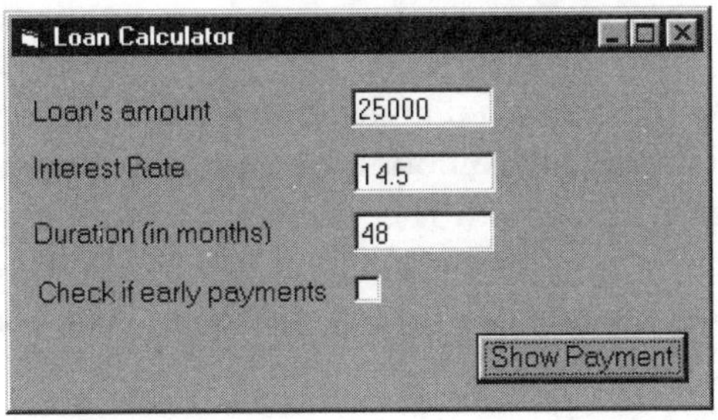

FIGURE 2.1

The Loan application is a simple financial calculator.

After the user specifies this information, clicking on a command button calculates the monthly payment and displays it in a message box. All the action takes place in the code for the Command Button's Click subroutine. The function for calculating monthly payments is called Pmt, and it must be called as follows:

```
MontlyPayment = Pmt(InterestRate, Periods, Amount, FutureValue, Due)
```

The interest rate (variable *InterestRate*) is specified as a monthly rate. If the interest rate is 16.5 percent, this value should be 0.165 / 12. The duration of the loan (*Periods*) is specified in number of months, and *Amount* is the loan's amount. The future value of a loan is zero (it would be a positive value for an investment), and the last parameter, *Due*, specifies when payments are due. If it's 0, payments are due at the beginning of the month; if it's 1, payments are due at the end of the month.

The present value of the loan is the amount of the loan with a negative sign. The present value of the loan is negative because you don't have the money now. You are borrowing it; it's money you owe to the bank. The future value of the loan is zero. The future value represents what the loan will be worth when it's paid off. This is what the bank owes you or what you owe the bank at the end of the specified period.

Pmt() is a built-in function that uses the five values in the parentheses to calculate the monthly payment. The values are called *arguments*. The Pmt() function and the other financial functions of Visual Basic are described in Appendix A.

The arguments are the values that the function requires to carry out the calculations. You need not know how the payment is calculated. The Pmt() function does the calculations and returns the result. To calculate the monthly payment on a loan of $25,000 with an interest rate of 14.5 percent payable over 48 months and due the last day of the payment period (which in our case is a month), you call the Pmt() function as follows:

```
Debug.Print Pmt(0.145 / 12, 48, -25000, 0, 0)
```

The value 689.45 will be displayed in the Immediate Execution window. Notice the negative sign in front of the amount. If you specify a positive amount, the result will be a negative payment. The payment and the loan's amount have different signs because they represent different cash flows. The last two arguments of the Pmt() function are optional. If you omit them, Visual Basic assumes they are zero. You could also call the Pmt function like this:

```
Debug.Print Pmt(0.145 / 12, 24, -25000)
```

NOTE You will see in Chapter 3, *Visual Basic, The Language,* that it is possible to write functions with optional arguments, but for now we will supply all values.

Calculating the amount of the monthly payment given the loan's parameters is quite trivial. Even if you have no idea how the payment is calculated, Visual Basic does it for you. What you need to know (or understand) are the parameters of a loan and how to pass them to the Pmt() function. You must also know how the interest rate is specified, to avoid invalid values.

Building the User Interface

Now, let's build the user interface. Start a new project, rename its Form to LoanCalc, and save the project as Loan.

Your first task is to decide the font and size of the text you'll use for most controls on the Form. Although we are not going to display anything on the Form directly, all the controls we place on it will have by default the same font as the Form (which is called the container of the controls). You can change the font later during the design, but it's a good idea to start with the right font. At any rate, don't try to align the controls if you are planning to change their fonts. This will, most likely, throw off your alignment efforts.

> **TIP**
>
> Try not to mix fonts on a Form. A Form or a printed page, for that matter, that includes type in several fonts appears to have been created haphazardly and is difficult to read.

The Loan application you will find on the CD uses 10 point MS Sans Serif. To change it, select the Form with the mouse, double-click on the name of the Font property in the Properties window to open the Font dialog box, and select the desired font and attributes.

To design the Form shown in Figure 2.1, earlier in this chapter, follow these steps:

1. Place three labels on the Form and assign the following captions to them:

    - **Label1**   Loan's amount
    - **Label2**   Interest Rate
    - **Label3**   Duration (in months)

    The labels should be large enough to fit their captions. You need not change the default names of the three Label controls on the Form because their captions are all we need. We aren't going to program them.

2. Place a TextBox control next to each label. Name the first text box (the one next to the first label) Amount and set its Text property to 25000, name the second text box IRate and set its value to 14.5, and name the third text box Duration and set its Text to 48. These initial values correspond to a loan of $25,000 with an interest rate of 14.5 percent and a payoff period of 48 months.

3. Next, place a CheckBox control on the Form. By default, the control's caption is Check1, and it appears to the right of the checkbox. Because we want the titles to be to the left of the corresponding controls, we will change this default appearance.

4. Select the checkbox with the mouse (if it's not already selected), and in the Properties window, locate the Alignment property. It's value is 0 - Left Justify. If you expand the drop-down list by clicking on the arrow button, you will see that this property has another setting, 1 - Right Justify. Select the alternate value from the list.

5. With the checkbox selected, locate the Name property in the Properties window, and set it to PayEarly.

6. Change the caption by entering the string "Check if early payments" in its Caption property field.

7. Place a Command Button control on the lower right corner of the Form. Name it ShowPayment, and set its caption to "Show Payment".

Aligning the Controls

Your next step is to align the controls. First, be sure that the captions on the labels are visible. Our labels contain lengthy captions, and if you didn't make them long enough, the captions may wrap to a second line and become invisible, like the one shown in Figure 2.2.

TIP

Be sure to make your labels long enough to hold their captions, especially if you are using a nonstandard font. A user's computer may substitute another font for a nonstandard font.

To align the controls on the Form, Visual Basic provides a number of commands, all of which are on the Format menu. Let's align the controls that are already on the Loan Form. Follow these steps:

1. Select the three labels and the checkbox, and left-align them by choosing Format ➤ Align ➤ Lefts.

2. Select the three text boxes, and left-align them by choosing Format ➤ Align ➤ Lefts. Do not include the checkbox in this selection.

FIGURE 2.2

The third label's caption is too long to be displayed in a single line.

3. With all three text boxes selected, use the mouse to align them over the box of the CheckBox control.

Your Form should now look like the one in Figure 2.1. Take a good look at it, and see if any controls are misaligned. In the interface design process, you tend to overlook small problems such as a slightly misaligned control. The user of the application, however, instantly spots such mistakes. It doesn't make any difference how nicely the rest of the controls are arranged on the Form; if one of them isn't, it attracts the user's eye.

Programming the Loan Application

Run the application now, and see how it behaves. Enter a few values in the text boxes, change the state of the checkbox, and test the functionality already built into the application. Clicking on the command button won't have any effect because we have not yet added any code. If you are happy with the user interface, stop the application, open the Form, and double-click on the command button. Visual Basic opens the Code window and displays the following three lines of the ShowPayment_Click event:

```
Option Explicit
```

```
Private Sub ShowPayment_Click()

End Sub
```

Place the pointer between the lines `Private...` and `End Sub` and enter the following lines:

```
Dim Payment As Single

Payment = Pmt(0.01 * IRate.Text / 12, Duration.Text, -Amount.Text,
➡0, PayEarly.Value)
MsgBox Format$(Payment, "#.00")
```

The Code window should now look like the one shown in Figure 2.3. Notice the underscore character at the end of the first part of the long line. The underscore lets you break long lines so that they will fit nicely in the Code window.

FIGURE 2.3

The Show Payment button's Click event subroutine

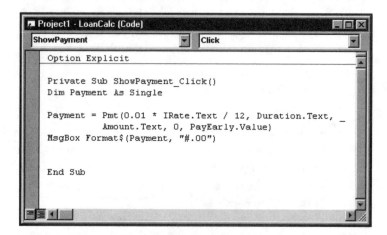

The first line declares a variable. It lets the application know that *Payment* is a placeholder for storing a floating point number. It then calls the Pmt() function, passing as arguments the values of the controls:

- The first argument is the interest rate. The value entered by the user is multiplied by 0.01 so that the value 14.5 (which corresponds to 14%) is passed to the Pmt() function as 0.145. Although we humans prefer to specify interest rates as integers (8%) or floating point numbers larger than 1 (8.24%), the Pmt() function expects to read a number less than 1. The value 1 corresponds to 100%. Therefore, the value 0.1 corresponds to 10%. This value is also divided by 12 to yield the monthly interest rate.

- The second argument is the duration of the loan in months (the value entered in the Duration text box), and the third argument is the loan's amount (the value entered in the Amount text box). The fourth argument (the loan's future value) is 0 by definition.

- The last argument must be the value 0 or 1, which specifies when payments are made. If they are made early in the month, this value should be 0. If they are made at the end of the month, it should be 1. As you know, the CheckBox control's Value property has a value 0 (if cleared) or 1 (if checked). You can therefore pass the quantity PayEarly.Value directly to the Pmt() function.

The second line displays the result in a message box, with the MsgBox function. Because the Pmt() function returns a precise number, such as 372.2235687646345, you must round and format it nicely before displaying it. Since the bank can't charge you anything less than a penny, you don't need extreme accuracy. Two fractional digits is sufficient. That's what the Format$() function does. It accepts a number and a string and formats the number according to the string (it's called the *formatting string*).

To format a number with two fractional digits, you set the formatting string to "#.00". This tells Visual Basic to round the number to two fractional digits and throw away the rest. The integer part of the number isn't affected. Moreover, if the result is something like 349.4, Visual Basic should format it as 349.40.

TIP

You almost always use the Format$() function when you want to display the results of numeric calculations, because most of the time you don't need Visual Basic's extreme accuracy. A few fractional digits are all you need. In addition to numbers, the Format$() function can format dates and time. It is explained in Appendix A.

Run the application now, and when the Form opens, click on the Show Payment button. The result for the loan described by the initial values of the controls on the Form is 689.45. This is the amount you'll be paying every month over the next 4 years to pay off a loan of $25,000 at 14.5%. Enter other values, and see how a loan's duration and interest rate affect the monthly payment.

Validating the Data

If you enter a nonnumeric value in one of the fields, the program crashes and displays an error message. For example, if you enter "twenty" in the Duration text box, the program displays the error message shown in Figure 2.4. A simple typing error crashed the program. This isn't the way Windows applications work. Your applications must be able to handle most user errors, provide helpful messages, and in general guide the user in running the application efficiently.

FIGURE 2.4

The Type mismatch error message means that you supplied a string where a numeric value was expected or vice versa.

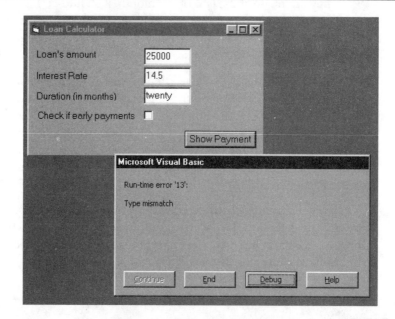

Click on the End button, and Visual Basic takes you back to the application's Code window. We must obviously do something about user errors. Applications must be foolproof and not crash with every mistake the user makes. One way to take care of typing errors is to examine each control's contents, and if they do not contain valid numeric values, display our own descriptive message and give the user another chance. Here's the revised ShowPayment_Click() subroutine that examines the value of each text box before attempting to use it in the calculations.

Code 2.1: The Revised ShowPayment_Click() Subroutine

```
Private Sub ShowPayment_Click()
Dim Payment As Single
```

```
Dim LoanIRate As Single
Dim LoanDuration As Integer
Dim LoanAmount As Integer

    If IsNumeric(Amount.Text) Then
        LoanAmount = Amount.Text
    Else
        MsgBox "Please enter a valid amount"
        Exit Sub
    End If
    If IsNumeric(IRate.Text) Then
        LoanIRate = 0.01 * IRate.Text / 12
    Else
        MsgBox "Invalid interest rate, please re-enter"
        Exit Sub
    End If
    If IsNumeric(Duration.Text) Then
        LoanDuration = Duration.Text
    Else
        MsgBox "Please specify the loan's duration as a number of
        ➥months"
        Exit Sub
    End If

    Payment = Pmt(LoanIRate, LoanDuration, LoanAmount, 0,
    ➥PayEarly.Value)
    MsgBox Format$(Payment, "#.00")

End Sub
```

First, we declare three variables, in which the loan's parameters will be stored: *LoanAmount, LoanIRate,* and *LoanDuration.* These values will be passed to the Pmt() function as arguments. Each text box's value is examined with an If structure. If the corresponding text box holds a valid number, its value is assigned to the numeric variable. If not, the program displays a warning and exits the subroutine without attempting to calculate the monthly payment. IsNumeric() is another built-in function that accepts a variable and returns True if the variable is numeric, False otherwise.

The IsNumeric() function accepts as an argument a value (of any type) and returns True if the value is a valid number. If the Amount text box holds a numeric value, such as 21000 or 21.50, the function IsNumeric(Amount.Text) returns True, and the following statement is executed. The following statement assigns the value entered in the Amount text box to the *LoanAmount* variable. If not, the Else clause of the statement is executed, which displays a warning in a message box and then exits the subroutine. The Exit Sub statement tells Visual Basic to stop executing the subroutine immediately, as if the End Sub line were encountered.

You can run the revised application and test it by entering invalid values in the fields. Notice that you can't specify an invalid value for the last argument. The CheckBox control won't let you enter a value; you can only check or clear it. Both options are valid. The LoanCalc application you will find on the CD contains this last version, with the error-trapping code.

The actual calculation of the monthly payment takes a single line of Visual Basic code. Displaying it requires another line of code. Adding the code to validate the data entered by the user, however, is an entire program. And that's the way things are.

Writing Well-Behaved Applications

A well-behaved application must contain data-validation code. If this application crashes because of a typing mistake, nothing really bad will happen. The user will try again or give up your application and look for a more professional one. If the user has been entering data for hours, the situation is much worse. It's your responsibility as a programmer to make sure that only valid data are used by the application and that the application keeps working, no matter how the user misuses it.

NOTE The applications in this book don't contain much data-validation code. They demonstrate specific techniques, and the data-validation code would obscure the "useful" code that applies to the topic at hand. You can use parts of the examples in your own applications, but you should provide your own data-validation code (and error-catching code, as you will see in the following section).

Now run the application one last time and enter an enormous amount. Try to find out what it takes to pay off our national debt with a reasonable interest rate in, say, 72 months. The program will crash again (as if you didn't know). This time the program will go down with a different error message. Visual Basic will complain about an "overflow."

TIP   What's an overflow? A numeric value so large that the program can't handle it.

An overflow error can't be caught with data-validation code. There's always a chance your calculations will produce overflows or other types of math errors. Data validation isn't going to help here. We need something called error trapping. *Error trapping* tells Visual Basic to trap errors and, instead of stopping the program, inform your code that an error has occurred and give your code a chance to handle it. We'll see how to prevent these types of errors in the next example.

VB5 at Work: A Math Calculator

Our next application is more advanced, but not as advanced as it looks. It's a math calculator with a visual interface and demonstrates how Visual Basic can simplify programming. If you haven't tried it, you may think that writing an application such as this one is way too complicated, but it isn't. The Math application is shown in Figure 2.5, and you will find it in this chapter's folder on the CD. The Math application emulates the operation of a hand-held calculator and implements the basic arithmetic operations. It has the structure of a working math calculator, and you can easily expand it by adding more features.

FIGURE 2.5

The Math application's window

Building the User Interface

Let's start by building the user interface. Start a new project, name its main Form MathCalc, and save the project as Math. Now, follow these steps:

1. Select a font that you like for the Form. All the command buttons you'll place on the Form will inherit this font. The MathCalc application on the CD uses 10 point MS Dialog font.

2. Add the Label control, which will become the calculator's display. Set its BorderStyle property to 1-Fixed Single so that it will have a 3-D look, as shown in Figure 2.5.

3. Draw the first command button on the Form, change its caption to "0", name it Digits, and set its Index to 0. We will create an array of buttons.

4. Place the button in its final position on the Form.

Creating an array of controls may sound strange, but here's why you do it. We could create 11 buttons and give them different names, for example, Digit1, Digit2, and so on. But then we would have to provide a separate subroutine for their Click event. One subroutine per command button. By creating an array of command buttons, we can provide a single subroutine for the Click event of all buttons. You will see later how this naming scheme simplifies our code.

5. Right-click on the button, and from the shortcut menu, select Copy. The command button is copied to the Clipboard, and now you can paste it on the Form (which is much faster than designing an identical button).

6. Right-click somewhere on the Form, and from the shortcut menu, select Paste to create a copy of the button you copied earlier. Visual Basic displays a dialog box with the following message:

```
You already have a control named 'Digits'. Do you want to
➥create a control array?
```

You want to create an array of command buttons, so click on Yes.

7. Repeat steps 5 and 6 nine more times, once for each numeric digit and the button with the period. Each time a new command button is pasted on the Form, Visual Basic gives it the name Digits and sets its Index property to a value that is larger than the previous one by 1. Each button's Index property will be the same as its caption, as long as you set the captions sequentially. If you place the command buttons for the digits in any other order, the application won't work. As you have guessed, we'll be using the Index property

to handle the buttons from within our code, and it's crucial that their captions are the same as their indices.

8. When the buttons of the numeric digits are all on the Form, place two more buttons, one for the C (Clear) operation and one for the period button. Name them ClearBttn and DotBttn, and set their captions accordingly. Use a larger font size for the period button to make its caption easier to read.

9. When all the buttons of the first group are on the Form and in their approximate positions, align them with the commands on the Format menu.

    a. First, align the buttons on a row and make their horizontal spacing equal. Then do the same with the buttons on a column, and this time make sure their vertical distances are equal.

    b. Now you can align the buttons on each row and each column separately. Use one of the buttons you aligned in the last step as the guide for the rest of them. The buttons can be aligned in many ways, so don't worry if somewhere in the process you ruin the alignment. There's always an Undo command in the Edit menu.

10. Now, place the command buttons for the operations. Table 2.1 lists their captions and names.

TABLE 2.1 Captions and Names for the Command Buttons

Caption	Name
+	Plus
—	Minus
*	Times
/	Div
+/—	PlusMinus
1/X	Over
=	Equals

11. Use the commands on the Format menu to align these buttons as shown in Figure 2.6.

FIGURE 2.6

Group the digit buttons in rows and columns to align them. Use the control with the blue handles as a reference for aligning the other controls.

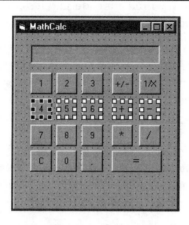

FIGURE 2.6

Group the digit buttons in rows and columns to align them. Use the control with the blue handles as a reference for aligning the other controls.

Programming the Math Application

Now you are ready to add some code to the application. Double-click on one of the numeric command buttons on the Form, and you will see the following in the Code window:

```
Private Sub Digits_Click(Index As Integer)

End Sub
```

This is the Click event's handler for all command buttons that represent digits. All buttons have the same name, and they are differentiated by their index. When the user clicks on one of them, Visual Basic generates the Digits_Click event and uses the *Index* argument to report the index of the button that was clicked.

What happens on your hand-held calculator when you press a numeric button? The corresponding digit is appended to the display. To emulate this behavior, insert the following line in the Click event handler:

```
Display.Caption = Display.Caption + Digits(Index).Caption
```

This line appends the digit clicked to the calculator's display. For example, if you have already entered the value 345, clicking on the digit 0 displays the value 3450 on the Label control that acts as the calculator's display.

TIP

A single line of code in a single Click event took care of all the numeric buttons. That's what an array of controls does for you. If you have multiple controls with identical behavior, create an array of controls. All the members of the array have the same handler (subroutine) for each event, and you need not repeat the code over and over.

The code behind the digit buttons needs a few more lines. If you run the application now, you'll see what happens after an operation is performed and the result is displayed. If you click on another digit, it is appended to the existing number. But this isn't the way your hand-held calculator works. The first time a digit button is pressed after a result is displayed, the display must clear and then print the new digit.

Code 2.2: The Digits_Click Event

```
Private Sub Digits_Click(Index As Integer)

    If ClearDisplay Then
        Display.Caption = ""
        ClearDisplay = False
    End If
    Display.Caption = Display.Caption + Digits(Index).Caption

End Sub
```

The *ClearDisplay* variable is declared as Boolean, and it can take a True or False value. Suppose the user has performed an operation, and the result is on the calculator's display. The user now starts typing another number. Without the If clause, the program continues to append digits to the number already on the display. This is not how the calculator works. When a new number is entered, the display must clear. And our program uses the *ClearDisplay* variable to know when to clear the display.

The Equals button sets the *ClearDisplay* variable to True to indicate that the display contains the result of an operation. The Digits_Click() subroutine examines its value each time a new digit button is pressed. If it's True, it clears the display and then prints the new digit on it. It also sets it to False so that when the next digit is pressed, the program won't clear the display again.

What if the user makes a mistake and wants to undo an entry? The typical hand-held calculator has no backspace key. The Clear key erases the current number on the display. Let's implement this feature. Double-click on the C button and enter the following code in its Click event:

```
Display.Caption = ""
```

And now we can look at the Period button. A calculator, no matter how simple, should be able to handle fractional numbers. The Period button works just like the digit buttons, with one exception. A digit can appear any number of times in a numeric value, but the period can appear only once. You must make sure that the user can't enter numbers such as 23.456.55. Once a period is entered, this button must not insert another one.

Code 2.3: The Period Button

```
Private Sub DotBttn_Click()
    If InStr(Display.Caption, ".") Then
        Exit Sub
    Else
        Display.Caption = Display.Caption + "."
    End If
End Sub
```

The InStr(Display.Caption, ".") function returns the number of periods in the number displayed. If this number is positive, the number already has one period, and another cannot be entered. In this case, the program exits the Subroutine. If the InStr() function returns 0, the period is appended to the number entered so far, as is a regular digit.

The InStr() function accepts two arguments, which are two strings, and returns the location of the second string in the first one. The following function returns 12 because the string "Visual" appears in the 12th character position in the longer string:

```
InStr("Welcome to Visual Basic", "Visual")
```

The following function, however, returns 0 because the string "Java" doesn't appear anywhere in the first string.

```
InStr("Welcome to Visual Basic", "Java")
```

The following expression:

```
InStr(Display.Caption, ".")
```

returns a positive number if the value already on the display contains a period. If that's the case, the program exits the subroutine without taking any action. If the value returned by the InStr() function is a positive number, the value entered is an integer, and the period is displayed.

Check out the operation of the application. We have already created a functional user interface that emulates a hand-held calculator with data-entry capabilities. It doesn't perform any operations yet, but we have already created a functional user interface with only a small number of statements.

The Math Operations

Now we can move to the interesting part of the application. Let's consider how a calculator works. When the user clicks on a plus button, the value on the display is stored in a variable. The program must make a note to itself that the current operation is an addition and then clear the display so that the user can enter another value. The user enters another value and then clicks on the Equals button to see the result. At this point, our program must do the following:

1. Read the value on the display.

2. Add that value to the first operand (which is stored in a variable).

3. Display the results.

Let's start by defining three variables:

- *Operand1*, the first number in the operation

- *Operator*, the desired operation

- *Operand2*, the second number in the operation

The Equals button must perform the following operation:

```
Operand1 Operator Operand2
```

Suppose the number on the display when the user clicks on the Plus button is 3342. The user then enters the value 23 and clicks on the Equals button. The program must carry out the addition:

```
3342 + 23
```

Had the user clicked on the division button, the operation would be:

```
3342 / 23
```

In both cases, the result is displayed (and it may become the first operand for the next operation).

The variables in the previous examples are local in the subroutines where they were declared. Other subroutines had no access to them; other subroutines couldn't read or set their values. Sometimes, however, variables must be accessed from many places in a program. The *Operand1*, *Operand2*, and *Operator* variables in this application must be accessed from within more than one subroutine, so they must be declared outside any subroutine. The same is true for the *ClearDisplay* variable. Let's see how the program uses the *Operator* variable.

When the user clicks on the Plus button, the program must store the value "+" in the *Operator* variable. This takes place from within the Plus button's Click event. But later on, the Equals button must have access to the value of the *Operator* variable in order to carry out the operation (in other words, it must know what type of operation the user specified). Because these variables must be manipulated from within more than a single subroutine, they must be declared outside any subroutine (see Figure 2.7).

FIGURE 2.7

The first few lines in the Math application's Code window. The variables declared outside any procedure are visible from any subroutine on this Form.

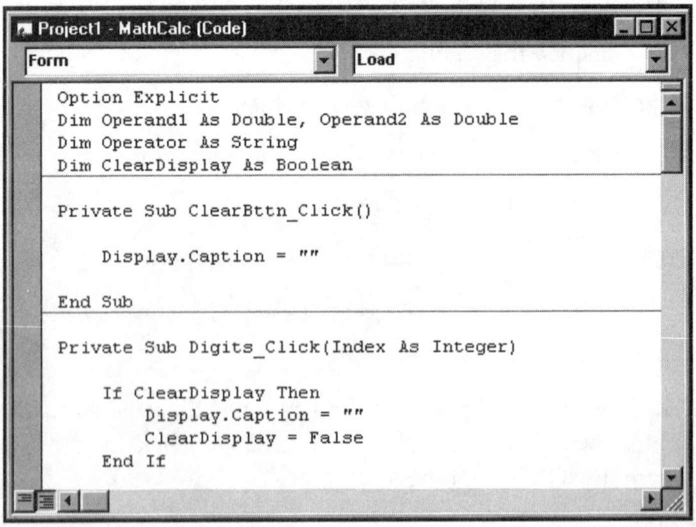

```vb
Option Explicit
Dim Operand1 As Double, Operand2 As Double
Dim Operator As String
Dim ClearDisplay As Boolean

Private Sub ClearBttn_Click()

    Display.Caption = ""

End Sub

Private Sub Digits_Click(Index As Integer)

    If ClearDisplay Then
        Display.Caption = ""
        ClearDisplay = False
    End If
```

Place the pointer at the top of the code window, right after the Option Explicit statement, and enter the following declarations:

```
Dim Operand1 As Double, Operand2 As Double
Dim Operator As String
Dim ClearDisplay As Boolean
```

The keyword Double is new to you. It tells Visual Basic to create a numeric variable with the greatest possible precision for storing the values of the operators. (Numeric variables and their types are discussed in detail in the next chapter.) The Boolean type takes two values, True and False. You have already seen how the *ClearDisplay* variable is used.

The variables *Operand1*, *Operand2,* and *Operator* are called Form-wide, because they are visible from any subroutine in the Form. If our application had another Form, these variables wouldn't be visible from the other Form(s). In other words, any subroutine on the Form on which the variables were declared can read or set the values of the variables, but no subroutine outside that Form can do so.

With the variable declarations out of the way, we can now implement the operator buttons. Double-click on the Plus button, and in the Click event's handler, enter the following lines:

```
Private Sub Plus_Click()

    Operand1 = Val(Display.Caption)
    Operator = "+"
    Display.Caption = ""

End Sub
```

The variable *Operand1* is assigned the value currently on the display. The Val() function returns the numeric value of its argument. As you recall, a Label's caption property is a string. For example, you can assign the value "My Label" to a Label's Caption property. The actual value stored in the Caption property is not a number. It is a string such as "428", which is different from the numeric value 428. That's why we use the Val() function to convert the value of the Label's caption to a numeric value.

The other three operator buttons do the same. The only difference is the symbol of the operator.

Code 2.4: The Click Event Handlers for the Operator Buttons

```
Private Sub Minus_Click()

    Operand1 = Val(Display.Caption)
    Operator = "-"
    Display.Caption = ""

End Sub

Private Sub Times_Click()

    Operand1 = Val(Display.Caption)
    Operator = "*"
    Display.Caption = ""

End

Private Sub Div_Click()

    Operand1 = Val(Display.Caption)
    Operator = "/"
    Display.Caption = ""

End Sub
```

So far, we have implemented the following functionality in our application: When an operator button is clicked, the program stores the value on the display in the *Operand1* variable and stores the operator in the *Operator* variable. It then clears the display so that the user can enter the second operand. After the second operand is entered, the user can click on the Equals button to calculate the result.

Code 2.5: The Equals Button

```
Private Sub Equals_Click()
Dim result As Double

    Operand2 = Val(Display.Caption)
    If Operator = "+" Then result = Operand1 + Operand2
    If Operator = "-" Then result = Operand1 - Operand2
    If Operator = "*" Then result = Operand1 * Operand2
    If Operator = "/" And Operand2 <> "0"
Then result = Operand1 / Operand2
    Display.Caption = result

End Sub
```

The *result* variable is declared as Double so that the result of the operation will be stored with maximum precision. The code extracts the value displayed in the Label control and stores it in the variable *Operand2*. It then performs the operation with a string of If statements:

- If the Operator is "+", the result is the sum of the two operands.

- If the Operator is "-", the result is the difference of the first operand minus the second.

- If the Operator is "*", the result is the product of the two operands.

- If the Operator is "/", the result is the quotient of the first operand divided by the second operand, provided that the divisor is not zero.

NOTE The division takes into consideration the value of the second operand, because if it's zero, the division can't be carried out. The last If statement carries out the division only if the divisor is not zero. If *Operand2* happens to be zero, nothing happens.

Now run the application and check it out. It works just like a hand-held calculator, and you can't crash it by specifying invalid data. We didn't have to use any data-validation code in this example because the user doesn't get a chance to type invalid data. The data-entry mechanism is foolproof. The user can enter only numeric values because there are only numeric digits on the calculator. The only possible error is to divide by zero, and that is handled in the Equals button.

Adding More Features

Now that we have implemented the basic functionality of a hand-held calculator, we can add features to our application. Let's add two more useful buttons:

- The +/- button, which inverts the sign of the number on the display

- The 1/X button, which inverts the number on the display

Open the Code window for each of the command buttons and enter the following code in the corresponding Click event handlers.

For the +/- button, enter the following:

```
Private Sub PlusMinus_Click()

    Display.Caption = -Val(Display.Caption)

End Sub
```

For the 1/X button, enter the following:

```
Private Sub Over_Click()

    If Val(Display.Caption) <> 0 Then Display.Caption = 1 /
    ➥Val(Display.Caption)

End Sub
```

As with the division button, we don't attempt to invert a zero value. The operation 1/0 is undefined and causes a run-time error.

One more feature you can add to the calculator is to limit the number of digits on the display. But don't do anything about it yet. Let's see if we can crash this application.

You can easily expand the Math application by adding function buttons to it. For example, you can add buttons to calculate common functions, such as cos, sin, log and so on. The Cos button calculates the cosine of the number on the display. The code behind this button's Click event is a one-liner:

```
Display.Caption = Cos(Display.Caption)
```

It doesn't require a second operand or keeping track of the operation. You can implement all math functions with a single line of code. Of course, you should add some error trapping, and in some cases, you can use data-validation techniques. The Sqr() function, which calculates the square root of a number, expects a positive argument. If the number on the display is negative, you can issue a warning:

```
If Display.Caption < 0 Then
    MsgBox "Can't calculate the square root of a negative number"
Else
    Display.Caption = Sqr(Display.Caption)
End If
```

The Log function can calculate the logarithms of positive numbers only. Other functions, however, can easily cause overflows. For example, the Exp() function can easily produce very large numbers.

Error Trapping

Crashing this application won't be as easy as crashing the Loan application. But it's not impossible either. Start multiplying very large numbers (start again with the national debt), and continue multiplying with large numbers. It will take a while, but eventually you will bring the program to a halt with an overflow error message. The result will eventually become larger than the largest number Visual Basic can represent and will generate the overflow message, as shown in Figure 2.8.

FIGURE 2.8

This error message is generated if you use the Math application to manipulate very large numbers.

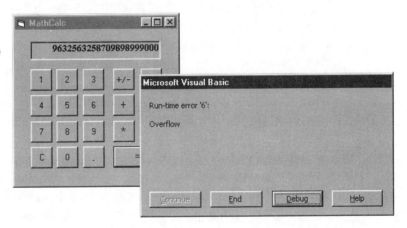

The error's number is 6, and its description is "Overflow" (one of the worst, because it can't be remedied easily). Many errors are caused by conditions that can be remedied from within your code. If a file wasn't found, for instance, you can prompt the user for another filename. If a field's value is empty, you can ask the user to enter a different value or to use a generic value. But the overflow is always the result of a series of math operations you can't undo.

How do you prevent this? Data validation isn't going to help. You just can't predict the result of an operation without actually performing the operation. And if the operation causes an overflow, you can't prevent it.

The solution is to *trap* the error. The overflow will occur no matter what, but you can trap it, and instead of letting the error message show up and embarrass you, you can handle it from within your code. To handle errors from within your code, you insert a so-called error trap, with the following statement:

```
On Error Goto ErrorLabel
```

The *ErrorLabel* entry is a label in your code. This statement asks Visual Basic to jump to the statement following the label ErrorLabel. (This has nothing to do with the Label control; it's a mark in the code that identifies a specific line and it can be any string.)

The structure of a subroutine with an error trap is as follows:

```
Sub MySubroutine()
On Error Goto ErrorHandler
    {statements}
    Exit Sub

ErrorHandler:
    MsgBox "Couldn't complete the operation. Aborting"
End Sub
```

The first statement isn't executable. It doesn't cause any action in your code. It simply tells Visual Basic that if an error occurs, it must execute the lines following the label *ErrorHandler*. *ErrorHandler* is not a statement or a keyword. It's a string that identifies the beginning of the error-handling code. Notice the colon at the end of the label. This is how Visual Basic knows that ErrorHandler is a label and not a procedure name.

If no error occurs during execution, the subroutine's statements are executed as if the error-trapping statements weren't there. After the subroutine's statements are executed and the Exit Sub statement is reached, the subroutine exits as usual. If an error occurs during the execution of the statements, however, the program jumps to the statement following the ErrorHandler label. The lines following the ErrorHandler label form an *error handler*. You handle the error in the error handler. The error handler shown in the example is generic; it displays a message and exits the subroutine.

Writing a Simple Error Handler

The error handler for our application must tell the user what kind of error occurred and then stop the operation. Let's examine its implementation. The overflow error will occur only when the Equals button is pressed, so this is the subroutine you must modify. Open the Code window, and in the button's Click event, add the underlined lines in Code 2.6.

Code 2.6: The Revised Equals Button

```
Private Sub Equals_Click()
Dim result As Double

On Error GoTo ErrorHandler

    Operand2 = Val(Display.Caption)
    If Operator = "+" Then result = Operand1 + Operand2
    If Operator = "-" Then result = Operand1 - Operand2
    If Operator = "*" Then result = Operand1 * Operand2
    If Operator = "/" And Operand2 <> "0"
Then result = Operand1 / Operand2
    Display.Caption = result
    ClearDisplay = True

    Exit Sub

ErrorHandler:
    MsgBox "The operation resulted in the following error"
& vbCrLf & Err.Description
    Display.Caption = "ERROR"
    ClearDisplay = True
End Sub
```

Most of the time, the error handler remains inactive and does not interfere with the operation of the program. If an error occurs, which most likely will be an overflow error, the program's control is transferred to the error handler. It doesn't make any difference which line in the code produces the error; the error handler is activated.

The error handler displays a message box with the description of the error, displays the string ERROR, and sets the *ClearDisplay* variable to True so that when another digit button is clicked, a new number will appear on the display. The vbCrLf constant inserts a line break between the literal string and the error's description.

NOTE

Err is the name of an object that represents the error. The two most important properties of the Err object are Number and Description. In the case of the overflow error, the error's number is 6, and its description is the string "Overflow." Notice that this code doesn't detect the type of error that occurred. It handles all errors in the same manner (by displaying the error message and the string ERROR on the calculator's display).

An Application with Multiple Forms

Few applications are built on a single Form. Most applications use two, three, even more Forms, which correspond to separate sections of the application. In this section, we are going to build an application that uses three Forms and lets the user switch among them at will. You'll see how to write an application that opens multiple windows on the Desktop. In Chapter 4, *Working with Forms*, we will explore the topic of multiple Forms in depth.

VB5 at Work: The Calculators Application

In the last section we designed two related applications; let's combine them into one. We will create a new project, call it Calculators, and add the two Forms we already designed. We will then design a third Form that will become our switching point. The new Form will let us load each of the two calculators, as shown in Figure 2.9.

To implement the new, multiwindow application, follow these steps:

1. Start a new Standard EXE project.

2. Choose Project ➤ Add Form to open the Add Form dialog box (see Figure 2.10). Click on the Existing tab, and locate the Form LoanCalc on your disk (or on the CD). The LoanCalc Form is added to the current project, and its name appears in the Forms folder under the project's name.

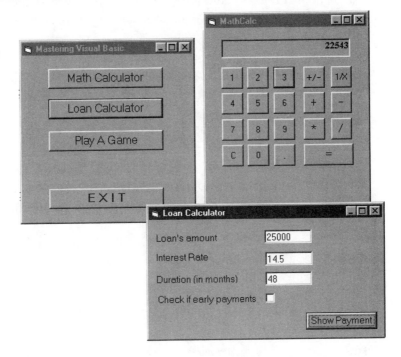

FIGURE 2.9

The window of the
Calculators application
loads and displays
the Math and Loan
calculators.

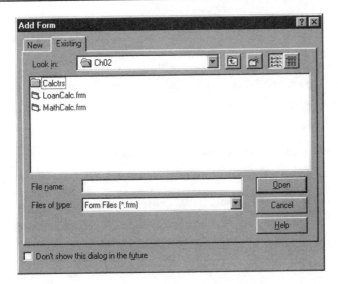

FIGURE 2.10

When you ask Visual
Basic to add a Form to
a project, you have the
option to create a
new Form or add an
existing one.

3. Choose Project ➤ Add Form, and locate the Form MathCalc in the Existing tab of the Add Form dialog box to add the Form of the MathCalc application to the project.

You now have a project with three Forms (the first one being an empty Form). If you run the application, you will see the following error message:

```
Must have Startup Form or Sub Main()
```

4. Open the Form1 Form in design mode, select it with the mouse, and in the Properties window, set its Name property to Calculators and its Caption to Mastering VB5.

5. Now add four command buttons on the Form, as shown in Figure 2.8, earlier in this chapter. The names and captions of these buttons are shown in Table 2.2.

TABLE 2.2   The Names and Captions of the Command Buttons

CAPTION	NAME
Math Calculator	ShowMath
Loan Calculator	ShowLoan
Play a Game	ShowGame
Exit	ExitButton

The code behind the first two buttons should show the MathCalc and LoanCalc Forms. To show a Form from within another, you must use the Show method, which has the following syntax:

```
Form.Show
```

The *Form* entry is the name of the Form you want to show.

6. Now, enter the following code in the Math Calculator button's Click event:

```
Private Sub ShowMath_Click()
    MathCalc.Show
End Sub
```

and the code behind the Loan Calculator is:

```
Private Sub ShowLoan_Click()
    LoanCalc.Show
End Sub
```

The Show method (as well as the Hide method, which hides an open window) is described in detail in Chapter 4, *Designing with Forms.* Invoking a Form from within another is a simple task.

The code behind the Play a Game button should also call the Show method of another Form, but it doesn't. I regret not developing a game for your enjoyment, but I did do something cute. When you click on this button, it jumps to another place on the Form.

Code 2.7: The Play a Game Button

```
Private Sub ShowGame_Click()
    ShowGame.Left = Rnd() * (Calculators.Width -
➥ShowGame.Width)
    ShowGame.Top = Rnd() * (Calculators.Height -
➥ShowGame.Height)
End Sub
```

This subroutine manipulates the Left and Top properties of the command button to move the button to a different position.

The last button, Exit, ends the application with the End statement:

```
Private Sub ExitButton_Click()
    End
End Sub
```

This is all it takes to create a multiwindow application based on some existing Forms. No changes in the existing Forms are required.

Now you can save the project. Choose File ➢ Save Project As, and in the Save dialog box, create a new folder and save the project in it.

On the CD, you will find the Calculators project in the Calcltrs folder. You may notice that only the project file and the application's main Form are stored in this folder. The Math and Loan Forms are still in their original folders. The structure of a Visual Basic project and how its components are stored on disk are discussed in the next section.

The StartUp Object

Now press F5 or choose Start ➤ Run to run the application. Instead of running the application, Visual Basic displays the following error message:

```
Must have a startup form or Sub Main()
```

Click on OK to open the Project Properties dialog box, as shown in Figure 2.11. Visual Basic wants to know which Form to display when it starts. By default, Visual Basic displays the Form named Form1 or starts by executing a subroutine called Main. Our project has neither, so Visual Basic needs more information in order to start the application.

FIGURE 2.11

Open the Project Properties dialog box to specify the Startup object.

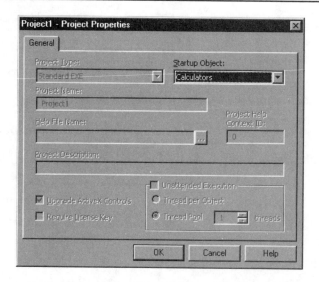

Obviously, the Startup object must call the Calculators Form, as shown in Figure 2.11. This is the only Form that can call the other two. Expand the Startup Object drop-down list, and select Calculators. Click on OK to start the application.

NOTE   You can also open the Project Properties dialog box by choosing Project ➤ Project Properties. If you do so, the dialog box will have more tabs than those shown in Figure 2.11. I'll explain this later when we look at how to package an application as an EXE file.

Now, run the application and see how it works. Click on the first two buttons in the main window to display the Loan and Math Forms. Switch from one window to the other, and click on the main Form's buttons while the two windows are open. Visual Basic doesn't open the corresponding window again, but moves the focus to it (brings it on top of any other window on the Desktop).

To close a window, click on the Close button (the little X button at the upper right corner of the window). You can close and open the Math and Loan windows as many times as you wish. If you close the application's main window, though, you will have to restart the application. This action is equivalent to clicking on the Exit button of the main Form.

A Project's Files

Each Visual Basic project is made up of a number of files that are all listed in the Project Explorer window, as shown in Figure 2.12. This figure shows the components of the Calculators project. Notice that the files are grouped in folders, according to their types. As mentioned in Chapter 1, *Getting Started with Visual Basic*, there can be more types of files. Not only can you have more types of files in the same project, you can have multiple projects, or a project group (discussed in Chapter 14, *Building ActiveX Controls*). In this section, we are going to look at the structures of the files making up a typical project: the Form and project files.

FIGURE 2.12

The components of the Calculators project

The project file is a list of all the files and objects associated with the project, as well as information about the environment (if you have changed some of the default settings). The contents of the project file are updated every time the project is saved. It's a text file that you can open and view with a text editor.

> **WARNING** Modifying the project file directly is not recommended, and you don't have good reason to do so.

You can, however, create project files from within a special application, which is usually called a code generator. A *code generator* is an application that creates the code of an application based on user-supplied data. The various Wizards, for instance, are code-generators; they generate code for the programmer. This code is usually the skeleton of an application that you must modify according to your requirements.

The Project File

If you open the Calc.vbp project file with a text editor, you will find the following references in it:

```
Form=..\MathCalc.frm
Form=Calc.frm
Form=..\LoanCalc.frm
Startup="Sub Main"
```

It contains a list of the Forms making up the project and the Startup Form (which is the Form displayed when the application starts). The project is stored in the Calcltrs folder, and the Forms MathCalc and LoanCalc are stored in the parent folder. The references to these files from within the Calc project file are relative. Thus, if you move the entire parent folder with its subfolder to a new location on your disk, the project file will still be able to locate the project's components.

The Form File

The Form files (FRM) are also text files and contain the descriptions of the controls on the Form and the corresponding code. Here is the contents of the Calc.frm file:

```
VERSION 5.00
Begin VB.Form Calculators
```

```
Caption              =    "Mastering Visual Basic"
ClientHeight         =    3480
ClientLeft           =    60
ClientTop            =    345
ClientWidth          =    3690
LinkTopic            =    "Form1"
ScaleHeight          =    3480
ScaleWidth           =    3690
StartUpPosition      =    3   'Windows Default
Begin VB.CommandButton ExitButton
   Caption              =    "E X I T"
   BeginProperty Font
      Name              =    "MS Sans Serif"
      Size              =    12
      Charset           =    0
      Weight            =    700
      Underline         =    0    'False
      Italic            =    0    'False
      Strikethrough     =    0    'False
   EndProperty
   Height               =    420
   Left                 =    570
   TabIndex             =    3
   Top                  =    2805
   Width                =    2490
End
Begin VB.CommandButton ShowGame
   Caption              =    "Play A Game"
   BeginProperty Font
      Name              =    "MS Sans Serif"
      Size              =    12
      Charset           =    0
      Weight            =    400
      Underline         =    0    'False
      Italic            =    0    'False
      Strikethrough     =    0    'False
   EndProperty
   Height               =    420
   Left                 =    570
   TabIndex             =    2
   Top                  =    1590
   Width                =    2490
End
```

```
Begin VB.CommandButton ShowLoan
    Caption             =     "Loan Calculator"
    BeginProperty Font
        Name            =     "MS Sans Serif"
        Size            =     12
        Charset         =     0
        Weight          =     400
        Underline       =     0     'False
        Italic          =     0     'False
        Strikethrough   =     0     'False
    EndProperty
    Height              =     420
    Left                =     570
    TabIndex            =     1
    Top                 =     915
    Width               =     2490
End
Begin VB.CommandButton ShowMath
    Caption             =     "Math Calculator"
    BeginProperty Font
        Name            =     "MS Sans Serif"
        Size            =     12
        Charset         =     0
        Weight          =     400
        Underline       =     0     'False
        Italic          =     0     'False
        Strikethrough   =     0     'False
    EndProperty
    Height              =     420
    Left                =     570
    TabIndex            =     0
    Top                 =     270
    Width               =     2490
End
End
Attribute VB_Name = "Calculators"
Attribute VB_GlobalNameSpace = False
Attribute VB_Creatable = False
Attribute VB_PredeclaredId = True
Attribute VB_Exposed = False
```

```
Private Sub ExitButton_Click()

    End

End Sub

Private Sub ShowGame_Click()

    ShowGame.Left = Rnd() * (Form1.Width - ShowGame.Width)
    ShowGame.Top = Rnd() * (Form1.Height - ShowGame.Height)

End Sub

Private Sub ShowLoan_Click()

    LoanCalc.Show

End Sub

Private Sub ShowMath_Click()

    MathCalc.Show

End Sub
```

The first definition is that of the Form, which begins with the following line:

```
Begin VB.Form Calculators
```

VB.Form is a Form object, and Calculators is its name. Following this line is a list of Form properties. The properties whose names begins with "Client" determine the position and size of the Form on the Desktop. The ScaleWidth and ScaleHeight properties determine the coordinate system of the Form. The positions of the controls on the Form are expressed in these units (coordinate systems are discussed in detail in Chapter 6, *Drawing and Painting with Visual Basic*).

After the properties of the Form, and before the End keyword that closes the definition of the Form (the one that begins as Begin VB.Form), are the definitions of the controls. The following line:

```
Begin VB.CommandButton ExitButton
```

marks the beginning of the first Command Button control on the Form, which is the Exit button. This definition ends with the End keyword. In between these two keywords are all the properties of the Exit command button. Notice that the Font property has a number of members and that they are all enclosed in a pair of BeginProperty/EndProperty keywords.

Following the definition of the controls is the Form's code. Code 2.8 shows the structure of an FRM file. It contains the headers of the controls only; the lines that correspond to the properties of the controls and the actual statements in the sub-routines are omitted to make the structure of the file easier to see. Ellipses denote the places where properties and code lines would otherwise appear.

Code 2.8: The Object Headers of the Calculators Form

```
VERSION 5.00
Begin VB.Form Calculators
   . . .
   Begin VB.CommandButton ExitButton
      BeginProperty Font
      . . .
      EndProperty
   . . .
   End
   Begin VB.CommandButton ShowGame
      BeginProperty Font
      . . .
      EndProperty
   . . .
   End
   Begin VB.CommandButton ShowLoan
      BeginProperty Font
      . . .
      EndProperty
   . . .
   End
   Begin VB.CommandButton ShowMath
      BeginProperty Font
      . . .
      EndProperty
   . . .
   End
End
Attribute VB_Name = "Calculators"
Attribute VB_GlobalNameSpace = False
Attribute VB_Creatable = False
Attribute VB_PredeclaredId = True
Attribute VB_Exposed = False
```

```
Private Sub ExitButton_Click()

End Sub

Private Sub ShowGame_Click()

End Sub

Private Sub ShowLoan_Click()

End Sub

Private Sub ShowMath_Click()

End Sub
```

As you can see, writing an application that automatically generates VB code is straightforward. You have to start with a similar project, see what information Visual Basic stores in the project and Form files, and use these files as guides.

Moving and Copying Projects

Sooner or later you'll have to move or copy a project to another folder. If you chose File ➤ Save Project As and save the project with the same (or a different) name in another folder, only the VBP file is stored in the new folder. The project's components remain in their original folders. This may not be what you expected, but that's how Visual Basic works. A project's components need not reside in the same folder, so Visual Basic isn't copying all the files along with the project file.

TIP Using components of existing projects is not only possible, it is desirable. You should never write code that duplicates existing code.

You shouldn't maintain multiple copies of the same file either. Suppose you create a custom Form for specifying colors. After this Form is tested and is working, you can use it from within multiple projects. This Form shouldn't be replicated in each project's folder. If you decide to add a feature to it later (and you will, no matter what), you will have to update multiple files. If you save this Form in a special folder, though, you can add it to any number of projects. If you update the Form, all the projects that use it will see the new Form.

TIP

You could save the file in your vb\common\forms folder, for example, and add it to each project that needs its functionality.

This is why Visual Basic doesn't enforce the one-folder-per-project rule. Create a folder for each project, and store all the files that are unique to the project in it, but add existing components to a new project from their original folders.

To save a project in a different folder, you must first copy all the files of the project to a new folder and only then save the project file in the same folder. If you first save the project to a new folder or under a different filename, your project won't see the new files. Instead, it will refer to the original files.

As mentioned, the VBP file contains references to the project's components. Of course, if you change the name or path of even a single component in your project, Visual Basic will prompt you to save the project file before you close it. An awareness of this detail can save you a good deal of frustration.

WARNING

There's nothing more frustrating than having identically named files in several folders and not knowing which ones are the latest versions. Even worse, you may end up updating one set of files and expect to see the changes in another set. This is an accident waiting to happen, and if you decide to move a project to another folder, always delete the files in the old folder.

You can also move projects to a different folder from within the Windows Explorer. Visual Basic uses relative path names in the VBP file, so if you move all the files to a new folder, the relative references are valid. However, you shouldn't count on this. It is possible that the VBP file will end up seeing files other than those you think it does, or it might not find the referenced files at all. It is best to use File menu commands when moving projects around.

Distributing an Executable File

So far, you have been executing applications within Visual Basic's environment. However, you can't expect the users of your application to have Visual Basic installed on their systems. If you develop an interesting application, you won't feel like giving away the code of the application (the source code, as it is called). Applications are distributed as executable files, along with their support files.

The users of the application can't see your source code, and your application can't be modified or made to look like someone else's application (that doesn't mean it can't be copied, of course).

NOTE   An *executable* file is a binary file that contains instructions only the machine can understand and execute. The commands stored in the executable file are known as *machine language*.

Applications designed for the Windows environment can't fit in a single file. It just wouldn't make sense. Along with the executable files, your application requires a number of so-called support files. If you are using any custom controls, the files in which they reside (they have the extension OCX) must be distributed with the application.

In general, Windows applications require a large number of support files, and these files may already exist on many of the machines on which your application will be installed. That's why it doesn't make sense to distribute huge files. Each user should install the main application and the support files that are not already installed on his or her computer.

Using the Application Setup Wizard

Distributing applications would be a complicated process if it weren't for the Application Setup Wizard. The Application Setup Wizard takes care of packaging your application for distribution.

The Wizard creates a new application, whose sole purpose is to install your application. It also breaks the installation program into pieces so that you can distribute your application on diskettes. The Application Setup Wizard comes with Visual Basic, and it's straightforward to use.

TIP   There are also other tools you can use for creating setup applications. One of them is called InstallShield, and you will find it on this book's CD.

Creating an Executable File

Before preparing the setup application, you must create an executable file for your application. This file will be represented as an icon on your Desktop, and you can run the application without starting Visual Basic and loading the project. Simply double-click on the application's icon on the Desktop (or a folder) to start the application.

To make an executable file for your project, follow these steps:

1. Choose File ➤ Make *project*.exe (*project* is the name of the project).

2. Enter the name and the location of the file, and Visual Basic creates the executable file.

You can set options for the executable files through the Project Properties dialog box. Follow these steps:

1. Choose Project ➤ Project Properties to open the Project Properties dialog box, as shown in Figure 2.13.

2. Select the Compile tab.

FIGURE 2.13

In the Compile tab of the Project Properties dialog box, you specify compilation options.

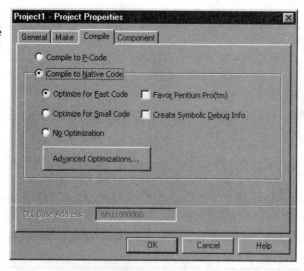

Now you are ready to specify options. Visual Basic can produce two types of executable files:

- P-code
- Native code

Compile to P-Code   When you select this option, Visual Basic compiles a project using p-code, which is pseudo-code that the CPU can't execute directly. BASIC has always been an interpreted language. Programs written in an interpreted language are not translated into machine language before they are executed. Instead, each line of code is translated into machine language as needed and then executed.

Interpreted programs are not as fast as compiled programs (which are translated into optimized machine language before execution). A p-code program is somewhere between the two. It's highly efficient code, but it can't be executed as is. A translation step is required. P-code, however, is closer to machine language than it is to Visual Basic, and the process of translating p-code to executable code is efficient.

NOTE   The main benefit of p-code is that it's compact and not much slower than pure executable code.

Compile to Native Code   When you select this option, Visual Basic compiles a project using native code, which is the machine language that the CPU understands and executes. The generated executable is faster than the equivalent p-code executable by as much as 20 times. This is a benchmark (a best-case scenario), and you shouldn't expect such dramatic improvements with your average applications. Use this option for applications that perform involved math operations.

When you compile to native code, you have the following options:

- **Optimize for Fast Code** maximizes the speed of the executable file by instructing the compiler to favor speed over size. To optimize the code, the compiler can reduce many constructs to functionally similar sequences of machine code.

- **Optimize for Small Code** minimizes the size of the executable file by instructing the compiler to favor size over speed.

- **No Optimization** compiles without optimizations.

- **Favor Pentium Pro** optimizes code to favor the Pentium Pro processor. Use this option for programs meant only for the Pentium Pro. Code generated with this option runs on other Intel processors, but it does not perform as well as if compiled with other options.

- **Create Symbolic Debug Info** generates symbolic debug information in the executable. An executable file created using this option can be debugged with Visual C++ or with debuggers that use the CodeView style of debug information. Setting this option generates a PDB file with the symbol information for your executable. This option is most likely to be used by Visual C++ programmers who also use Visual Basic.

Selecting Advanced Optimization Options

When you select Advanced Optimizations, Visual Basic opens the Advanced Optimizations dialog box, shown in Figure 2.14. You use these options to turn off certain checks that normally take place and ensure that your application works properly. To increase the speed of the executable file, you can turn off some or all of these checks by selecting the appropriate checkbox.

> **WARNING** Enabling these optimizations may prevent the correct execution of your program. You must understand what each option does and be sure the application doesn't require any of the options you turn off.

FIGURE 2.14

The Advanced Optimizations dialog box

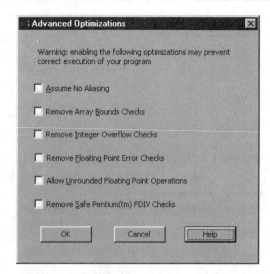

Assume No Aliasing   Check this checkbox to tell the compiler that your program does not use aliasing. *Aliasing* is a technique that lets your code refer to a variable (memory location) by more than one name. This technique is not used in this book, and you can safely select this option.

Remove Array Bounds Checks   By default, Visual Basic checks an array's bounds every time your code accesses the array to determine if the index is within the range of the array. If the index is not within array bounds, a run-time error is generated (which can be trapped from within the code). Select this option to turn off the array bounds checking and speed up applications that use arrays. However, the code that ensures that the array's bounds are not exceeded may cost more in execution time. If an array bound is exceeded, the results will be unexpected.

Remove Integer Overflow Checks   By default, Visual Basic checks every calculation for integer-style data types—byte, integer, and long—to ensure that the value is within the range of the data type. If the magnitude of the value being put into the data type is incorrect, a run-time error is generated. Select this option to turn off error checking and speed up integer calculations. If data type capacities are overflowed, you will get incorrect results.

Remove Floating Point Error Checks   By default, Visual Basic checks every calculation of a floating-point data type—Single and Double—to be sure that the value is within range for that data type and that there are no divide-by-zero or invalid operations. If the magnitude of the value being put into the data type is incorrect, an error occurs. Select this option to turn off error checking and speed up floating-point calculations. If data type capacities are overflowed, no error occurs, and you may get incorrect results.

Allow Unrounded Floating Point Operations   When this option is selected, the compiler uses floating point registers more efficiently, avoids storing and loading large volumes of data to and from memory, and compares floating points more efficiently.

Remove Safe Pentium FDIV Checks   Selecting this option removes the safety checking so that the code for floating-point division is faster, but may produce slightly incorrect results on Pentium processors with the FDIV bug.

Visual Basic, the Language

- Variables

- Constants

- Arrays

- Collections

- Procedures

- Subroutines

- Functions

- Arguments

- Statements

This chapter discusses the fundamentals of any programming language:

- Variables

- Procedures

A *variable* stores data, and a *procedure* is code that manipulates variables. To do any serious programming with Visual Basic, you must be familiar with these concepts. To write efficient applications, you need a basic understanding of some fundamental topics, such as the types, scope, and lifetime of variables and the procedures and argument-passing mechanisms.

As you have seen in the first two chapters, most of the code in a Visual Basic application deals with manipulating control properties. This chapter explores more formally how variables store data and how programs process variables. If you are familiar with Visual Basic, you might want to simply scan the following pages and make sure you are familiar with the concepts. You might also want to review some of the more advanced topics such as how to use variants and how to write functions with optional arguments.

If you are new to Visual Basic, you may find that some material in this chapter is over your head. This chapter covers basic concepts, definitions, and, in general, tedious but necessary material. Think of this chapter as a prerequisite for the more advanced techniques covered in the rest of the book. You can use it as a reference for topics discussed in subsequent chapters.

Variables

In Visual Basic, as in any other programming language, variables store values during a program's execution. For example, you're writing a program that frequently prompts the user for data, and you decide to add a personal touch to the interface. Every time the program needs data, it will display the user's name. Instead of writing an application for Joe Doe, another for Mary Jones, and so on, you can declare a variable that will store the user's name. When the program starts, it asks the user to enter his or her name. It then stores this name in a variable and during the course of the program uses it to display the user's name.

Variables are placeholders in which you can leave values and recall them at will. A variable has a name and a value. The variable *UserName*, for example, can have the value "Joe," and the variable *Discount* can have the value 0.35. *UserName* and *Discount* are variable names, and "Joe" and 0.35 are their values. When a variable's value is text (or string, as it's called), it must be enclosed in double quotes. In your code, you can refer to the value of a variable by the variable's name. For example, the following statement calculates the discount for the amount of $24,500:

```
MsgBox "You will save " & 24500 * Discount
```

The message that this expression displays depends on the value of the *Discount* variable. If you decide to offer a better discount, all you have to do is change the value of the *Discount* variable. You change the value of the *Discount* variable in a single place in your code, and the entire program is updated. If you didn't use the *Discount* variable, you would have to make many changes in your code. In other words, if you coded the previous line as follows:

```
MsgBox "You save " & 24500 * 0.35
```

you would have to look for every line in your code that calculates discounts and change the discount from 0.35 to another value.

Declaring Variables

In most programming languages, variables must be declared. In other words, you must tell the compiler which variables you are going to use in advance. Historically, the reason for doing this is to help the compiler. If the compiler knows the variables and their types, it can produce optimized code. When you tell the compiler that the variable *Discount* will hold a number, the compiler sets aside so many bytes for the *Discount* variable and is ready to use it.

Every time a compiled application runs into a new variable, it has to create it. Doing so doesn't take a lot of statements, but it does produce a delay that could have been avoided. If the compiler knows all the variables that are going to be used in the application ahead of time, it can produce the most compact and most efficient code.

One of the most popular yet intensely criticized features of BASIC was that it didn't force the programmer to declare all variables. As you will see, there are more compelling reasons than speed and efficiency for declaring variables.

Explicit Declarations

To declare a variable, use the Dim statement followed by the variable's name and type, as follows:

```
Dim meters As Integer
Dim greetings As String
```

TIP
We'll look at the various data types in detail shortly. In the meantime, you should know that a variable declared as an Integer can store only integer numbers.

The first variable, *meters,* will store integers, such as 3 or 1002, and the second variable, *greetings,* will store text, such as "Thank you for using Fabulous software". You can declare multiple variables of the same type in the same line, as follows:

```
Dim meters, inches, centimeters As Integer
```

When Visual Basic finds a Dim statement, it creates one or more new variables, as specified in the statement. That is, it creates a placeholder by reserving some space in memory and assigning a name to it. Each time this name is used in subsequent commands, Visual Basic uses this area in memory to read or set its value. For instance, when you use the following statement:

```
meters = 23
```

Visual Basic places the value 23 in the placeholder reserved for the variable *meters.* When the program asks for the value of this variable, Visual Basic reads it from the same area of memory. The following statement:

```
Print meters
```

causes Visual Basic to retrieve the value 23 from the area of memory named *meters.* It is also possible for a single statement to both read and set the value of a variable. The following statement increases the value of the *meters* variable:

```
meters = meters + 1
```

Visual Basic reads the value (say 23), adds 1 to it, and then stores the new value (24) in the same memory location.

Variable Naming Conventions

When declaring variables, you should be aware of a few naming conventions. A variable's name:

- Must begin with a letter.
- Can't contain an embedded period or any of the type-declaration characters.

- Must not exceed 255 characters.
- Must be unique within its scope (we'll look at the variable's scope shortly).

One good reason for declaring variables is so that Visual Basic knows the type of information the variable must store and can validate the variable's value. Attempting to assign a value of the wrong type to a declared variable generates a "Type Mismatch" run-time error.

For example, if you attempt to assign the value "Welcome" to the *meters* variable, Visual Basic won't execute the statement because this assignment violates the variable declaration. The *meters* variable was declared as Integer, and you are attempting to store a string in it. There are some interesting exceptions to this rule, and we'll look at them shortly. For example, it is possible to assign the value "103" to the variables *meters* (it's a string, but it represents a numeric value) and to assign the value 103 to the *greetings* variable (it is converted to the string "103" and then assigned to the string variable).

You can also declare variables without specifying their type. Visual Basic creates a generic variable that can hold any type. The following statement:

```
Dim temp, var, generic
```

creates three variables of the variant type. A variant can store all types of values and is an extremely flexible data type, but it requires more overhead than variables declared with a specific type.

Implicit Declarations

You can also choose not to declare variables. When Visual Basic meets an undeclared variable name, it creates a new variable on the spot and uses it. The new variable's type is Variant, the generic data type that can accommodate all other data types. Using a new variable in your code is equivalent to declaring it without type. Visual Basic adjusts its type according to the value you assign to it. Declare two variables, *var1* and *var2*, with the following statement:

```
Dim var1, var2
```

and then assign a text value to one and a numeric value to the other:

```
var1 = "Thank you for using Fabulous Software"
var2 = 49.99
```

The *var1* variable is a string variable, and *var2* is a numeric one. You can verify this with the TypeName() function, which returns a variable's type. The following statements print the types shown below:

```
Debug.Print "Variable var1 is " & TypeName(var1)
     Variable var1 is String
Debug.Print "Variable var2 is " & TypeName(var2)
     Variable var2 is Double
```

NOTE   The TypeName() function is explained in Appendix A.

Later in the same program you can reverse the assignments:

```
var1 = 49.99
var2 = "Thank you for using Fabulous software"
```

If you execute the previous Print statements again, you'll see that the types of the variables have changed. The *var1* variable is now a Double, and *Var2* is a string.

Finally, you can omit declaration statements, yet create typed variables with the variable declaration characters. To create a variable while the program executes, but still specify a data type, add a suffix that is one of the data declaration characters in Table 3.1.

TABLE 3.1   Data Type Definition Characters

SYMBOL	DATA TYPE	EXAMPLE
$	String	A$, messageText$
%	Integer	counter%, var%
&	Long	population&, colorValue&
!	Single	distance!
#	Double	exactDistance#

You can also declare variables using the Def*xxx* statements. For example, you can declare that all variables beginning with *a* and *b* are integers, with the DefInt statement:

```
DefInt a-b
```

You can use the following statements to declare ranges of variables based on their first character:

DefBool	DefByte	DefInt
DefLng	DefCur	DefSng
DefDbl	DefDate	DefStr
DefOb	DefVar	

Variable types that are declared with data type definition characters and the Def*xxx* statements are leftovers from older versions of BASIC and are, for the most part, obsolete.

Types of Variables

Visual Basic recognizes the following types of variables:

- Numeric
- String
- Variant
- Date
- Object

The two major variable types are numeric and string. *Numeric* variables store numbers, and *string* variables store text. *Variant* variables can store any type of data. On the surface, using variants may seem like a good idea (Why bother to specify the type if one type suits all?), but variants have their disadvantages.

We begin our discussion of variable types with numeric variables. Text is stored in string variables , but numbers can be stored in many formats, depending on the size of the number and its precision. That's why there are many types of numeric variables.

Date variables store dates, and Object variables store objects of all types.

Numeric Variables

You'd expect that programming languages would use a single data type for numbers. After all, a number is number. But this couldn't be farther from the truth. All programming languages provide a variety of numeric data types, including the following:

- Integers

- Floating-point numbers with limited precision

- Floating-point numbers with extreme precision

As you will see, there are many types of variables for storing numbers, and the reason is efficiency. For example, if you are manipulating the pixels of an image, you are calculating with integers. You don't need more precision than integer numbers can provide, and using integers speeds up the calculations considerably. In scientific calculations, you need all the precision you can get (and then some more); in that case, you should use the double-precision data type.

Different types of numbers are represented internally in different formats. All numeric values are truncated to a certain extent. The result of the operation 1/3 is 0.333333… (an infinite number of digits "3"). You could fill 16Mb of RAM with the digit "3," and the result would still be truncated. Here's a simple but illuminating example. In a new Form's Load event, declare two variables as follows:

```
Dim a As Single, b As Double
```

Single and *Double* are the two basic data types for storing *floating-point numbers* (numbers that have a fractional part), and the Double type can represent these numbers more accurately than the Single type. Enter the following statements:

```
a = 1 / 3
Debug.Print a
```

Now, Run the application and watch the result in the Immediate window:

```
0.3333333
```

There are seven digits to the right of the decimal point. Now execute the following statements in the Immediate window:

```
a = a * 100000
Debug.Print a
 33333.34
```

Not as accurate as you might have expected initially. The result isn't even rounded properly. If you divide a by 100000, the result is:

```
0.3333334
```

which is different from the number we started with (0.3333333). This is an important point in numeric calculations, and its called *error propagation*. In long sequences of numeric calculations, errors propagate. Even if you can tolerate the error introduced by the Single data type in a single operation, the cumulative error may be significant.

Let's perform the same operations with double-precision numbers. Add a second variable declaration in the Form:

```
Dim b As Double
```

and then add these lines to the Form's Load event handler:

```
b = 1 / 3
Debug.Print b
b = b * 100000
Debug.Print b
```

This time the following numbers:

```
0.333333333333333
33333.3333333333
```

are displayed in the Immediate window.

The choice of data types for your variables can make a difference in the results of the calculations. The proper variable types are determined by the nature of the values they represent. The choice of data types is frequently a tradeoff between precision and speed of execution (less precise data types are manipulated faster). Visual Basic supports the numeric data types in Table 3.2.

TABLE 3.2 The Visual Basic Numeric Data Types

DATA TYPE	WHAT IT DOES
Integer	Stores integer values in the range -32,768 to 32,767.
Long	Stores long integers in the range -2,147,483,648 to 2,147,483,647.

TABLE 3.2   The Visual Basic Numeric Data Types (continued)

DATA TYPE	WHAT IT DOES
Single	Stores single-precision floating-point numbers. It can represent negative numbers in the range -3.402823E38 to -1.401298E-45 and positive numbers in the range 1.401298E-45 to 3.402823E38. Notice that the Single data type can't represent exactly the 0 value.
Double	Stores double-precision floating-point numbers. It can represent negative numbers in the range -1.79769313486232E308 to -4.94065645841247E324 and positive numbers in the range 4.94065645841247E-324 to 1.79769313486232E308.
Currency	Stores fixed-point numbers with four fractional digits. The Currency data type can represent numbers in the range -922,337,203,685,477.5808 to 922,337,203,685,477.5807.

Integers are stored internally in two bytes, and Visual Basic handles integers efficiently, but you can represent only so many numbers with two bytes. Integers that exceed the specified range must be stored as Long integers. Long integers are stored in four bytes, and they cover a much larger range of values. If you know that a specific variable (such as a loop counter, for instance) will hold a small integer, declare it as an Integer. If the value of the integer may exceed the range of values that can be represented with two bytes, use a Long integer. Integer operations are faster and consume less memory than other data types.

If your variable can contain a fractional part, declare it as a Single, a Double, or a Currency variable. The Single data type is stored in four bytes, and the Double data type is stored in eight bytes. The main difference between the two types is not the range of values, but the accuracy with which values are represented. If you divide 5 by 3 as a Single data type, the result is:

```
1.666667
```

If you divide 5 by 3 as a Double data type, the result is:

```
1.66666666666667
```

The Double data type provides more accuracy, which is needed in math calculations. If you don't need more than a couple of fractional digits, use the Single data type. If you are concerned about accuracy, use the Double data type. Also use the Double data type if you are going to perform a series of math operations and the result of one operation will be used as an operand for the next. A little accuracy lost at every operation may substantially alter the final result.

The Currency data type can store fixed-point numbers and is suitable for financial calculations that don't need more accuracy than two fractional digits. This type supports four digits to the right of the decimal separator and fifteen digits to the left. This accuracy is adequate for financial calculations, but not for scientific calculations.

Accuracy of Numeric Types   The smaller the integer part of a floating-point number, the more fractional digits it can hold. For example, the result of the operation 5 divided by 3 expressed as a Double data type is:

```
1.66666666666667
```

The result of the operation 500000 divided by 3 expressed as a Double data type doesn't have as many fractional digits, however. Visual Basic reports the number as follows:

```
166666.666666667
```

The number had to be truncated at the ninth digit after the decimal point because Visual Basic has 8 bytes in which to fit the number. Some bytes of the larger number are allocated to the integer part, so there are fewer bytes left for representing the fractional part.

Some Tricks

If your calculations require the maximum precision possible, here are a couple of simple but effective tricks.

- *Bias the numbers.* If you are doing calculations in the range 100,010 to 100,100, subtract 100,000 from the initial numbers to reduce the values in the range 10 to 100. When you are done, add the bias 100,000 to the result.

- *Manipulate your expressions.* Examine your expressions and try to remove any redundancy. An expression such as *(a * b) / a* need not be calculated. The result is b, no matter what. If the previous expression is evaluated, it can't yield a more accurate result, and it's likely that it will yield a less accurate result. This is a simple example, but long expressions may contain redundancy that's not as obvious.

To declare variables of any of the previous types, use the Dim statement, followed by the name of the variable, the As keyword, and the variable's type. The following are all valid declarations of numeric variables:

```
Dim count As Integer
Dim DaysInCentury As Long
Dim Length As Single
Dim Area As Double
```

You can also combine multiple declaration on the same line. If the variables are of the same type, separate them with commas:

```
Dim Area As Double, Volume As Double
```

You can also specify multiple variables with different types in the same statement:

```
Dim Area As Double, Count As Integer
```

In the following statement:

```
Dim A, B, C As Integer
```

none of the A, B, and C variables will be declared as integers.

You can use other keywords in declaring variables, such as Private, Public, and Static. We will look at these keywords in later sections of this chapter. In the meantime, bear in mind that all variables declared with the Dim statement exist in the module in which they were declared. If the variable *Count* is declared in a function, it exists only in this function. You cannot access it from outside the function. Actually, you can have a *Count* variable in multiple functions. Each variable is stored locally. Such variables have different values and don't interfere with one another.

The Byte Data Type   None of the numeric types is stored in a single byte. In some situations, however, data is stored as bytes, and you must be able to access individual bytes. The Byte type holds basically an integer in the range 0 to 255. Bytes are frequently used to access binary files, image and sound files, and so on. Some API calls also use Byte arguments. To declare a variable as a Byte, use the following statement:

```
Dim n As Byte
```

The variable *n* can be used in numeric calculations too, but you must be careful not to assign the result to another Byte variable if its value may exceed the range of the Byte type. If the variables *A* and *B* are initialized as follows:

```
Dim A As Byte, B As Byte
```

```
A = 233
B = 50
```

the following statement:

```
MsgBox A + B
```

will display the correct result, even though it exceeds the value range of the Byte type. Attempting to assign this value to a Byte variable, though, with a statement such as the following:

```
B = A + B
```

generates an overflow run-time error. The result (288) can't be stored in a single byte. Visual Basic generates the correct answer and stores it internally as an Integer; that's why it can display the answer with the MsgBox function. But the assignment operation fails, because the result can't fit in a single byte.

NOTE The operators that will not cause overflows are the Boolean operators AND, OR, NOT, and XOR. These are not logical operators that return True or False. They combine the matching bits in the two operands and return another byte. If you combine the numbers 199 and 200 with the AND operator, the result is 192. The two values in binary format are 11000111 and 11001000. If you perform a bitwise AND operation on these two values, the result is 11000000, which is the decimal value 192.

String Variables

The String data type stores only text, and string variables are declared with the following statement:

```
Dim someText As String
```

You can assign any text to the variable *someText*. You can store nearly 2 gigabytes of text in a String variable. The following assignments are all valid:

```
someText = "Now is the time for all good men to come to the aid of
➥their country"
someText = ""
someText = "There are approximately 15,000 words in this chapter"
someText = "15,000"
```

The second assignment creates an empty string, and the last one creates a string that just happens to contain numeric digits, which are also characters. The difference between the variables

```
someNumber = 15000
```

and

```
someText = "15,000"
```

is that they hold different values. The *someText* variable holds the digits "1", "5", ",", "0", "0", and "0", and *someNumber* holds a numeric value. You can, however, use the variable *someText* in numeric operations, and you can use the variable *someNumber* in string operations. Visual Basic performs the necessary conversions for you. After all, when you attempt to divide "15,000" by another number, your intentions are obvious, and your application need not crash with a run-time error (as it would with other versions of BASIC).

Declare and initialize two string variables *A* and *B* as follows:

```
Dim A As String, B As String
A = "123"
B = "10"
```

Dividing *A* by *B* is a valid operation, even though the two variables are defined as strings. The following statement:

```
Debug.Print A / B
```

prints 12.3 in the Immediate window. This means that Visual Basic figured out that you wanted to use the two variables as numbers, converted them to integers, performed the division, and converted the result to the proper data type for you.

You can even use the two variables as both string and numeric values in the same expression. The following statement:

```
Debug.Print A & " divided by " & B & " is " & A / B
```

won't confuse Visual Basic. It will actually display this message:

```
123 divided by 10 is 12.3
```

Fixed-Length Strings   As you can see, string variables have variable lengths. They grow and shrink as needed to accommodate the values assigned to them. You can also specify fixed-length strings with a statement such as the following:

```
Dim someText As String * 1000
```

This variable is long enough to hold 1,000 characters. If you assign a string with fewer than 1,000 characters to it, the variable is padded with spaces. If you assign a string that exceeds the maximum declared length, it will be truncated.

Fixed-length strings are used in several situations. For example, you can declare a fixed-length string variable to accept user input when its maximum length is known. If a string variable's size will change drastically during the course of an application, you might want to declare it as fixed-length to prevent Visual Basic from having to resize it constantly.

Boolean Variables

The Boolean data type stores True/False values. Although a single bit would be adequate, for efficiency reasons Visual Basic allocates two bytes to this data type. Boolean variables are in essence integers that take the value -1 (for True) and 0 (for False). Boolean variables are declared as:

```
Dim failure As Boolean
```

and they are initialized to False.

Boolean variables are used in testing conditions, such as the following:

```
If failure Then MsgBox "Couldn't complete the operation"
```

They are also combined with the logical operators AND, OR, NOT, and XOR. The NOT operator toggles the value of a Boolean variable. The following statement:

```
running = Not running
```

is a toggle. If the variable *running* is True, it's reset to False, and vice versa. This statement is a shorter way of coding the following:

```
If running = True Then
   running = False
Else
   running = True
End If
```

Date Variables

Date and time values are stored internally as in a special way, but you need not really know the format. A variable declared as Date:

```
Dim expiration As Date
```

can store both date and time values. The following are all valid assignments:

```
expiration = "01/01/1997"
expiration = "02/23/1995"
expiration = "13:03:05 AM"
expiration = "02/23/1995 13:03:05 AM"
expiration = #02/23/1996 13:03:05 AM#
```

In the last statement, I didn't mistype pound signs instead of quotes. The pound sign tells Visual Basic to store a date and/or time value to the *expiration* variable, just as the quotes tell Visual Basic that the value is a string.

The Date data type is extremely flexible; Visual Basic knows how to handle date and time values without performing complicated conversions. You manipulate dates and times with the Date and Time functions, explained in Appendix A. You can, however, directly subtract two Date variables to find out their difference in days. Let's initialize two Date variables:

```
Dim day1 As Date, day2 As Date
day1 = Date()
day2 = "01/01/2000"
```

The *day1* variable will be the current date. The difference between the two dates:

```
MsgBox day2 - day1
```

is the number of days from the current date to the end of the millenium. On January 5, 1997, the difference was 1091 days. You can easily find the number of years, months, and days between the two dates with the help of the Year(), Month(), and Day() functions (also explained in Appendix A):

```
Years = Years(day2 - day1) - 1900
Months = Month(day2 - day1)
Days = Day(day2 - day1)
```

You can also add days to a Date variable. Integer values correspond to days. To add an hour, add 1/24 of a day; to add a minute add 1/(24*60) of a day. If *day1* is:

```
day1 = #11/3/96 1:03:05 PM#
```

the following Print statements will display the results shown:

```
Print day1 + 1
      11/4/96 1:03:05 PM
Print day1 + 1 / 24
      11/3/96 2:03:05 PM
```

```
Print day1 + 1 / (24 * 60)
     11/3/96 1:04:05 PM
```

When other numeric data types are converted to the Date data type, values to the left of the decimal represent date information, and values to the right of the decimal represent time. Midnight is 0, and midday is 0.5. Negative whole numbers represent dates before December 30, 1899. The date and time 6 hours from now is:

```
now + 0.25
```

If the current time is less then 6 hours from midnight, the date will change too:

```
Debug.Print now
1/9/97 11:40:54 AM
Debug.Print now+0.5
1/9/97 11:40:54 PM
Debug.Print now+0.75
1/10/97 5:40:07 PM
```

Object Variables

An Object variable is a reference to one of Visual Basic's many objects, and you can use an Object variable to access the actual object. You will see examples of Object variables in Chapter 9, *The Multiple Document Interface* (in which you will create new Forms as objects), and in Chapter 13, *Object Programming with Visual Basic* (in which you will learn how to access objects of other applications, such as Word documents, from within your Visual Basic applications).

Here is a simple example of an Object variable. A Form has two command buttons on it, Command1 and Command2. You can declare two Object variables, as:

```
Dim a As CommandButton, b As CommandButton
```

Each of these two Object variables can be set to one of the two command buttons with the following statements:

```
Set a = Command1
Set b = Command2
```

From now on, you can manipulate the two command buttons' properties through the variables *a* and *b*. To change the Caption property of the first command button, use a statement such as the following:

```
a.Caption = "Hi!"
```

To turn on the bold attribute of the second command button (so that its caption appears in bold), use the following statement:

```
b.FontBold = True
```

You will find more examples of Object variables in later chapters. You will also learn how to create your own objects, with their own properties and methods.

Variant Variables

This is the most flexible data type, and it can accommodate all other types. A variable declared as Variant (or a variable that hasn't been declared at all) is handled by Visual Basic according to the variable's current contents. If you assign an integer value to a Variant, Visual Basic treats it as integer. If you assign a string to a Variant, Visual Basic treats it as a string. Not only that, but Variants can hold different types in the course of the same program. Visual Basic performs the necessary conversions for you.

To declare a Variant, use the Dim statement without specifying a type as follows:

```
Dim myVar
```

You can also specify the Variant type to make the code cleaner:

```
Dim myVar As Variant
```

or don't declare the type at all. Every time your code references a new variable, Visual Basic creates a Variant for it. If the variable *validKey* hasn't been declared, when Visual Basic runs into the following line:

```
validKey = "002-6abbgd"
```

it creates a new Variant and assigns the value "002-6abbgd" to it.

You can use Variants both in numeric and in string calculations. Suppose the variable *modemSpeed* has been declared as Variant with the following statement:

```
Dim modemSpeed
```

and later in your code you assign the following value to it:

```
modemSpeed = "28.8"
```

The *modemSpeed* variable is a string variable that you can use in statements such as the following:

```
MsgBox "We suggest a " & modemSpeed & " modem"
```

This statement displays the following message:

```
"We suggest a 28.8 modem"
```

You can also treat the *modemSpeed* variable as a numeric value with the following statement:

```
MsgBox "A " & modemSpeed & " modem can transfer " & modemSpeed *
➥1000 / 8 & " bytes per second"
```

This statement displays the following message:

```
"A 28.8 modem can transfer 3600 bytes per second"
```

The first instance of the *modemSpeed* variable in the above statement is treated as a string, because this is the variant's type according to the assignment statement (we assigned a string to it). The second instance, however, is treated as a number (a single-precision number). Visual Basic converted it to a numeric value because it is used in a numeric calculation.

Another example of this behavior of Variants is the following:

```
A = "10"
B = "11"
Debug.Print A + B
Debug.Print A & B
```

Both Print statements print the string "1011". You are asking Visual Basic to add two strings, and this is how Visual Basic interprets your intentions. When applied to strings, the + and & operators are identical. If you change the definition of the second variable to the following:

```
B = 11
```

the first Print statement prints 21 (a numeric value), and the second Print statement prints the string "1011" as before.

Visual Basic knows how to handle variables in a way that "makes sense." The result may not be what you had in mind, but it certainly is dictated by common sense. If you really wanted to concatenate the strings "10" and "11", you should have used the & operator, which tells Visual Basic exactly what to do. Quite impressive, but for many programmers this is a strange behavior that can lead to subtle errors, and they avoid it. It's up to you to decide whether to use Variants and how far you will go with them. Sure, you can perform tricks with Variants, but you shouldn't overuse them to the point that others can't read your code.

WARNING   The plus operator is used in both numeric and string operations. In numeric operations, it adds two values. In string operations, it concatenates two values. This is the single operator that can introduce ambiguity when used with Variants. Visual Basic attempts to add the two values by converting them into numbers. If the conversion is successful, the + operator adds the two values; if not, a Type Mismatch run-time error is generated. When adding or concatenating Variants, use the operators + and & to help Visual Basic carry out the proper operation.

You can also store dates and times in the Variant type. To assign date or time values to Variants, surround the values with the pound sign, as follows:

```
date1=#03/06/1999#
```

All operations that you can perform with dates (discussed in the section "Date Variables") you can also perform with Variants.

Converting Variable Types

In some situations you will need to convert variables from one type into another. Table 3.3 shows the Visual Basic functions that perform data type conversions.

TABLE 3.3   The Data Type Conversion Functions of Visual Basic

FUNCTION	DESCRIPTION
Cbool	Converts its argument to Boolean
Cbyte	Converts its argument to Byte
CCur	Converts its argument to Currency
CDate	Converts its argument to Date
CDbl	Converts its argument to Double
CInt	Converts its argument to Integer
CLng	Converts its argument to Long

TABLE 3.3   The Data Type Conversion Functions of Visual Basic (continued)

FUNCTION	DESCRIPTION
CSng	Converts its argument to Single
CStr	Converts its argument to String
CVar	Converts its argument to Variant
CVErr	Converts its argument to Error

To convert the variable initialized as:

```
Dim A As Integer
```

to a Double, use the following function:

```
B = CDbl(A)
```

Suppose you have declared two integers, as follows:

```
Dim A As Integer, B As Integer
A = 23
B = 7
```

The result of the operation A / B is a single value. The following statement:

```
Debug.Print A / B
```

displays the value 3.285714. To get the same result with the greatest possible accuracy, use the CDbl() function:

```
Debug.Print CDbl(A / B)
```

which displays the value 3.28571438789368. It's the same value expressed as a Double and therefore more accurate.

User-Defined Data Types

In the previous sections, we assumed that applications create variables to store single values. As a matter of fact, most programs store sets of data of different types. For example, a program for balancing your checkbook must store several pieces of information for each check: the check's number, its amount, the date, and so on. All these pieces of information are necessary to process the checks, and ideally they should be stored together.

A structure for storing multiple values (of the same or different type) is called a *record*. Each check in the checkbook-balancing application is stored in a separate record, as shown in Figure 3.1. When you recall a given check, you need all the information stored in the record.

FIGURE 3.1

Pictorial representation of a record

Record Structure

CheckNumber	CheckDate	CheckAmount	CheckPaidTo

Array of Records

275	04/12/97	104.25	Gas Co.
276	04/12/97	48.76	Books
277	04/14/97	200.00	VISA
278	04/21/97	430.00	Rent

To define a record in Visual Basic, use the Type statement. It has the following syntax:

```
Type varType
    variable1 As varType
    variable2 As varType
    ...
    variablen As varType
End Type
```

After this declaration, you have in essence created a new data type that you can use in your application. You can declare variables of this type and manipulate them as you manipulate all other variables (with a little extra typing). The declaration for the record structure shown in Figure 3.1 is:

```
Type CheckRecord
    CheckNumber As Integer
    CheckDate As Date
    CheckAmount As Single
    CheckPaidTo As String*50
End Type
```

The CheckRecord structure can be used in the same way as regular variables. To define variables of this type, use a statement such as this one:

```
Dim check1 As CheckRecord, check2 As CheckRecord
```

To assign value to these variables, you must separately assign a value to each one of its components (they are called *fields*), which can be accessed by combining the name of the variable and the name of a field separated by a period, as follows:

```
check1.CheckNumber = 174
```

You can think of the record as an object and its fields as properties. Here are the assignment statements for a check:

```
check2.CheckNumber = 175
check2.CheckDate = #08/14/1996#
check2.CheckAmount = 240.00
check2.CheckPaidTo = "Books etc"
```

You can also create arrays of records with a statement such as the following (arrays are discussed later in this chapter):

```
Dim Checks(100) As CheckRecord
```

Each element in this array is a CheckRecord record and holds all the fields of a given check. To access the fields of the third element of the array, use the following notation:

```
Checks(2).CheckNumber = 175
Checks(2).CheckDate = #08/14/1996#
Checks(2).CheckAmount = 240.00
Checks(2).CheckPaidTo = "Books etc"
```

Records are used frequently to read from and write to random access files. This is a topic we aren't going to explore in this book.

Special Values

Variables have the values your program assigns to them. Before any value is assigned to them, numeric variables are zero, and string variables are zero length (""). There are, however, two special values: Empty and Null.

The Empty Value

If a Variant variable has been declared but has not yet been assigned a value, its value is Empty. The Empty value is different from a zero-length string. You can find out if a variable has been initialized with the IsEmpty() function:

```
If IsEmpty(var) Then MsgBox "Variable has not been initialized"
```

As soon as you assign a value to the variable, it is no longer Empty, and the IsEmpty() function returns False. You can also set a variable to Empty with the following statement:

```
var = Empty
```

The Empty value is used with numeric, string, and date variables. You can use the Empty value to reset variables before calling a procedure or if the objects they refer to have ceased to exist.

The Null Value

Null is commonly used in database applications to indicate that a field doesn't contain data or that an Object variable hasn't been assigned a value. The Null value is different from the Empty value. A variable of the types we have examined so far is never Null, unless you assign the value Null to it with the following statement:

```
var = Null
```

Uninitialized variables that refer to objects (databases, custom objects, collections, and so on) are Null, not Empty, as in the following:

```
If Not IsNull(varField) Then
  {process variable varField}
End If
```

If your code calls a function to create a new object, it must always check the value of the new *Object* variable with the IsNull() statement to verify that the object has been created.

Examining the Type of a Variable

Besides setting the types of the various variables and converting between types, you can examine the type of a variable with the VarType and TypeName functions. Both functions accept as argument the name of a variable, and they return a number (the VarType() function) or a string (the TypeName() function) indicating the type of the variable. The VarType() function returns one of the numbers shown in Table 3.4, depending on the type of its argument.

TABLE 3.4   The Numbers That the VarType() Returns

CONSTANT	VALUE	DESCRIPTION
vbEmpty	0	Empty (uninitialized)
vbNull	1	Null (no valid data)
vbInteger	2	Integer
vbLong	3	Long integer
vbSingle	4	Single-precision floating-point number
vbDouble	5	Double-precision floating-point number
vbCurrency	6	Currency value
vbDate	7	Date value
vbString	8	String
vbObject	9	Object
vbError	10	Error value
vbBoolean	11	Boolean value
vbVariant	12	Variant (used only with arrays of variants)
vbDataObject	13	A data access object
vbDecimal	14	Decimal value
vbByte	17	Byte value
vbArray	8192	Array

Is It a Number or a String?

Another set of Visual Basic functions return variables' data types, but not the exact type:

- **IsNumeric()**   Returns True if its argument is a number (Integer, Long, Currency, Single, or Double). Use this function to determine whether a variable holds a numeric value before passing it to a procedure that expects a numeric value or process it as a number.

- **IsDate()**   Returns True if its argument is a valid date (or time).

- **IsArray()**   Returns True if its argument is an array.

- **IsNull(), IsEmpty()**   Detect whether a variable has been initialized or is a Null value.

- **IsMissing()**   Returns True if a certain optional procedure argument is missing (you'll see how the IsMissing() function is used later in this chapter).

All these functions are described in Appendix A.

Forcing Variable Declarations

Visual Basic doesn't enforce variable declaration, which is a good thing for the average programmer. You are certainly familiar with the term *quick and dirty* as applied to programming. When you want to slap together a quick program, the last thing you need is someone telling you to decide which variables you are going to use and declare them before using them. When writing large applications, though, you will probably find that variable declaration is a good thing. It will help you write clean code and will simplify debugging. Variable declaration eliminates the source of the most common and peskier bugs. But most programmers accustomed to the free format of Visual Basic also carry their habits of quick-and-dirty coding to large projects.

If you have gotten spoiled, you can ask Visual Basic to enforce variable declaration for you. To do so, place the following statement in the declarations section of a Form or module:

```
Option Explicit
```

This statement tells the compiler to check each variable before using it and issue an error message if you attempt to use a variable without declaring it. If you omit the Option Explicit statement, Visual Basic creates variables as needed.

Let's consider an application for currency exchange. You could use the following statement to convert German marks to U.S. dollars:

```
USDollars = amount * 1.562
```

or you could assign the value 1.562 to the variable *DM2USD* and then use this variable in your code:

```
DM2USD = 1.562
USDollars = amount * DM2USD
```

The first time your code refers to the *DM2USD* variable name, Visual Basic creates a new variable and then uses it as if it were declared.

TIP

Another reason for declaring the variables in advance is to simplify debugging, especially in large applications. Suppose the variable *DM2USD* appears in many places in your application. If in one of these places you type *DM2UDS* instead of *DM2USD* and the program doesn't enforce variable declaration, the compiler creates a new variable, assigns it the value zero, and then uses it. Any amount converted with the *DM2UDS* variable will be zero! If the application enforces variable declaration, the compiler complain (the *DM2UDS* variable hasn't been declared), and you will catch the error. Many programmers, though, feel restricted by having to declare variables. Others live by that rule. Depending on your experiences with Visual Basic, you will decide for yourself.

For a small application, you don't have to declare variables. It's too much typing. But for large applications that may take weeks or months to develop, you should consider variable declaration. The Option statement must be included in every module in which you want to enforce variable declaration. If you decide to declare all variables in your projects, you can ask Visual Basic to insert the Option Explicit statement automatically in every module by checking the Require Variable Declaration checkbox in the Options dialog box (choose Tools ➤ Options), as shown in Figure 3.2.

WARNING

If you check the Require Variable Declaration checkbox while you are working on a project, Visual Basic automatically inserts the Option Explicit statement in any new modules, but not in existing modules. To enforce variable declaration in all modules, you must add the Option Explicit statement to any existing modules in your project manual.

FIGURE 3.2

The Options dialog box controls whether all variables in your projects must be declared explicitly.

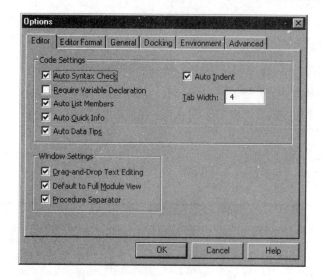

A Variable's Scope

In addition to its type, a variable also has a scope. The *scope* of a variable is the section of the application that can see and manipulate it. If a variable is declared within a procedure, only the code in the specific procedure has access to that variable. This variable doesn't exist for the rest of the application. This variable's scope is limited to a procedure, and it's called *local*.

Suppose you are coding the Click event of a command button to calculate the sum of all even numbers in the range 0 to 100. One possibility is the following:

```
Private Sub Command1_Click()
  Dim i As Integer
  Dim Sum As Integer
  For i = 0 to 100 Step 2
    Sum = Sum + i
  Next
  MsgBox "The sum is " & Sum
End Sub
```

The variables *i* and *Sum* are local to the Command1_Click() procedure. If you attempt to set the value of the *Sum* variable from within another procedure, Visual Basic creates another *Sum* variable and uses it. But this won't affect the variable *Sum* in the Command1_Click() subroutine.

Sometimes, however, you need to use a variable with a broader scope, such as one whose value is available to all procedures within the same Form or module. These variables are called *Form-wide* (or module-wide) and can be accessed from within all procedures in the component. In principle, you could declare all variables in the Form's declaration section, but this will lead to problems. Every procedure in the Form will have access to the variable, and you must be careful not to change the value of a variable without good reason.

Finally, in some situations the entire application must access a certain variable. In this case, the variable must be declared as *Public*. Public variables have a global scope (they are visible from any part of the application). To declare a Public variable, use the Public statement in place of the Dim statement. Moreover, Public variables may not appear inside procedures. They must be declared as Form variables or in a module.

The Lifetime of a Variable

In addition to type and scope, variables have a *lifetime*, the period during which they retain their value. Variables declared as Public exist for the lifetime of the application. Local variables, declared within procedures with the Dim or Private statement, live for as long as the procedure in which they were declared. When the procedure finishes, the local variables cease to exist, and the allocated memory is returned to the system. The same procedure can be called again, of course. In this case, the local variables are recreated and initialized again.

Variables declared in a Form, outside any procedure, take effect when the Form is loaded and cease to exist when the Form is unloaded. If the Form is loaded again, its variables are initialized, as if it's being loaded for the first time.

You can, however, force a local variable to preserve its value between procedure calls, with the Static keyword. Suppose the user of your application can enter numeric values at any time. One of the tasks performed by the application is to track the average of the numeric values. Instead of adding all the values each time the user adds a new value and dividing by the count, you can keep a running total with the function RunningAvg(), which is shown next:

```
Function RunningAvg(newValue)
  CurrentTotal = CurrentTotal + newValue
  TotalItems = TotalItems + 1
  RunningAvg = CurrentTotal / TotalItems
End Function
```

You must declare the variables *CurrentTotal* and *TotalItems* outside the function so that their values are preserved between calls. Alternatively, you can declare them in the function with the Static keyword:

```
Function RunningAvg(newValue As Double) As Double
Static CurrentTotal As Double
Static TotalItems As Integer

  CurrentTotal = CurrentTotal + newValue
  TotalItems = TotalItems + 1
  RunningAvg = CurrentTotal / TotalItems

End Function
```

The advantage of using Static variables is that they help you minimize the number of total variables in the application. All you need is the running average, and the RunningAvg() function does exactly that, without making its variables visible to the rest of the application. And, therefore, you don't risk changing their values from within other procedures.

TIP

You can declare all the variables in a procedure as static by prefixing the procedure definition with the keyword Static. The previous function could have been declared as `Static Function RunningAvg(newValue As Double) As Double`, and the local variables could be declared with the Dim statement as usual. The keyword Static may appear in front of every subroutine or function, including event handlers.

Constants

Some variables don't change value during the execution of a program. These are *constants* that appear many times in your code. If your program does math calculations, for instance, the value of pi (3.14159…) may appear many times in your code. These values are best represented by constants. Instead of typing the value 3.14159 over and over again, you can define a constant, name it *pi*, and use the name of the constant in your code. The following statement :

```
Area = 2 * pi * Radius
```

is much easier to understand than the equivalent:

```
Area = 2 * 3.14159 * Radius
```

You could declare *pi* could be declared as a variable, but constants are preferred for two reasons:

- *Constants can't change value.* This is a safety feature. Once a constant has been declared, you can't change its value in subsequent statements, and you can be sure that the value specified in the constant's declaration will take effect in the rest of the program.

- *Constants are processed faster than variables.* When the program is running, the values of constants don't have to be looked up. The compiler substitutes constant names with their values, and the program executes faster.

The manner in which you declare constants is similar to the manner in which you declare variables, except that in addition to supplying the constant's name you must also supply a value, as follows:

```
Const constantname [As type] = value
```

The As type part of the declaration is optional. If you omit it, the constant's type is determined by the value you assign to it. Constants also have a scope and can be Public or Private. The constant *pi*, for instance, is usually declared in a module as Public so that every procedure can access it:

```
Public Const pi As Double = 3.14159265358979
```

The *constantname* variable is a valid constant name that follows the same rules as variable names. The constant's value is a literal value or a simple expression composed of numeric or string constants and operators. You can't use functions in declaring variables. One way to define the value of *pi* is as follows:

```
pi = 4 * Atn(1)
```

However, you can't use this assignment in the constant declaration. You must supply the actual value. Constants can be strings too, such as:

```
Const ExpDate = #31/12/1997#
```

or:

```
Const ValidKey = "A567dfe"
```

Visual Basic uses constants extensively to define the various arguments of its methods and the settings of the various control properties. The value of a CheckBox control, for instance, can be 0 (unchecked), 1 (checked), or 2 (grayed). Instead of using statements such as the following:

```
Check1.Value = 0
Check2.Value = 2
```

use the built-in constants vbUnchecked and vbGrayed:

```
Check1.Value = vbUnchecked
Check2.Value = vbGrayed
```

The constants vbUnchecked and vbGrayed are built-in to the language, and you need not declare them. Their symbolic names make the code much easier to read and maintain. Visual Basic's constants are prefixed with *vb,* indicating that they are Visual Basic constants. Avoid this prefix when declaring your own constants. Other components of the language use different prefixes. For example, the Database Access Objects use constants with the *db* prefix.

Constant declarations may include other constants. In math calculations, the value *pi* is as common as the value 2 * *pi*. You can declare these two values as constant:

```
Public Const pi As Double = 3.14159265358979
Public Const pi2 As Double = 2 * pi
```

You can also create circular constant definitions, such as the following:

```
Const constant1 = constant2 * 2
Const constant2 = constant1 / 2
```

This circular definition doesn't lead anywhere (none of the constants has a value) and you must avoid them.

It's very unlikely that these two declarations will appear in the same module, but you may forget how you defined *constant1* in one of the modules and attempt to define *constant2* in terms of *constant1* in another module. If this happens, Visual Basic generates a run-time error. If you declare all your constants in a single module, they are easier to maintain and change.

TIP

When defining constant in terms of other constants, especially if they live in different modules, be sure you avoid circular definitions. Try to place all your constant declarations in the same module. If you have modules you use with several applications, try to include the module's name in the name of the constants to avoid conflicts and duplicate definitions.

Arrays

A standard structure for storing data in any programming language is an array. Whereas individual variables can hold single entities, such as a number, a date, or a string, arrays can hold sets of related data. An array has a name, as does a variable, and the values stored in it can be accessed by an index.

Suppose you use the variable *Salary* to store a salary:

```
Salary = 34000
```

What if you wanted to store 16 salaries, one for each employee? You could declare 16 variables, Salary1, Salary2, up to Salary16, or you could declare an array with 16 elements. An array contains a series of values that are distinguished by means of an index. Unlike simple variables, arrays must be declared with the Dim statement:

```
Dim Salary(15)
```

Salary is the name of an array that holds 16 values, the salaries of the 16 employees. Salary(0) is the first person's salary, Salary(1) the second person's salary, and so on. All you have to do is remember which person corresponds to each salary. You wouldn't even have to remember the names if you used another array that contained the names of the employees. Declare another array of 16 elements as follows:

```
Dim Names(15)
```

and then assign values to the elements of both arrays:

```
Names(0) = "Joe Doe"
Salary(0) = 34000
Names(1) = "Dave York"
Salary(1) = 62000
...
Names(15) = "Peter Smack"
Salary(15) = 10300
```

This structure is more compact and more convenient than having to hardcode the names of employees and their salaries in variables. To declare an array, use the Dim statement (or the Private statement), followed by the name of the array and the maximum number of elements it can hold in parentheses. Optionally, you can specify the type of the array's elements with the As keyword:

```
Dim Names(15) As String
Dim Salary(15) As Long
```

All elements in an array have the same data type. Of course, when the data type is Variant, the individual elements can contain different kinds of data (objects, strings, numbers, and so on). By default, the first element of an array has index 0. The number that appears in parentheses in the Dim statement is the array's upper limit (or upper bound) and is one less than the array's total capacity. The two arrays contain 16 elements each.

The array's first element need not be zero. You can specify the lower limit (or lower bound) explicitly in the Dim statement:

```
Dim Names(1 To 16) As String
Dim Salary(1 to 16) As Long
```

The lower bound can have any other value, provided it is smaller than the upper bound. The following declarations are valid:

```
Dim Array1(10 To 20) As Double
Dim Array2(100 to 900) As Long
```

although most arrays start at zero or 1.

> **TIP**
>
> If you feel uncomfortable with zero-based arrays, you can declare your arrays with one more element than required. Declare an array with 20 elements as Dim MyArray(20) and ignore the first element. Even better, you can include the statement Option Base 1 in your Form or module to force array indexing to start at 1. The Option Base 1 statement is similar to the Option Explicit statement and affects all the arrays in the current Form or module.

Multidimensional Arrays

One-dimensional arrays, such as those presented so far, are good for storing long sequences of one-dimensional data (such as names, temperatures, and so on). In some situations you will want to store sequences of multidimensional data. How would you store a list of cities and their average temperatures in an array? Or names and scores, years and profits, or data with more than two dimensions, such as products, prices, and units in stock? You could use two one-dimensional arrays or one two-dimensional array. Figure 3.3 shows two one-dimensional arrays, one of them with city names, the other with temperatures. The name of the third city is City(2), and its temperature is Temperature(2).

FIGURE 3.3

A two-dimensional array
and the two equivalent
one-dimensional arrays

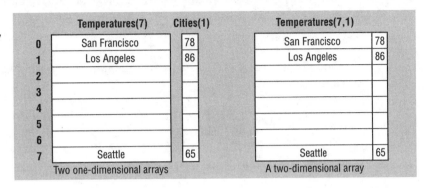

You can store the same data more conveniently in a two-dimensional array. A two-dimensional array has two indices. The first identifies the row (the order of the city in the array), and the second identifies the column (city or temperature). To access the name and temperature of the third city in the two-dimensional array, use the following indices:

```
Temperatures(2, 0)    is the third city name
Temperatures(2, 1)    is the third city's average temperature
```

The benefit of using multidimensional arrays is that they are conceptually easier to manage. The previous example doesn't demonstrate it very clearly, but here's another example. Suppose you are writing a game, and you want to track the positions of certain pieces on a board. Each square on the board is identified by two numbers, its horizontal and vertical coordinates. The obvious structure for tracking the board's squares is a two-dimensional array, in which the first index corresponds to the row number and the second index corresponds to the column number. The array could be declared as follows:

```
Dim Board(10, 10) As Integer
```

When a piece is moved from the square on the first row and first column to the square on the third row and fifth column, you assign the value 0 to the element that corresponds to the initial position:

```
Board(1, 1) = 0
```

And you assign 1 to the square to which it was moved, to indicate the new state of the board:

```
Board(3, 5) = 1
```

To find out if a piece is on the upper left square, you would use the following statement:

```
If Board(1, 1) = 1 Then
   {piece found}
Else
   {empty square}
End If
```

Notice that this array is not zero based. It just makes sense to waste the first element to code the application in a more familiar way. Board games don't have zero numbered rows or columns.

This notation can be extended to more than two dimensions. The following statement:

```
Dim Matrix(9, 9, 9)
```

creates an array with 1000 elements (10 x 10 x 10). You can think of a three-dimensional array as a cube made up of overlaid two-dimensional arrays, such as the one shown in Figure 3.4.

FIGURE 3.4

Pictorial representations of one-, two-, and three-dimensional arrays

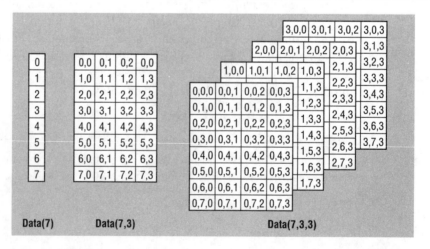

Dynamic Arrays

Sometimes you may not know how large to make an array. Instead of making it large enough to hold the maximum number of data (which means that most of the array may be empty), you can declare a dynamic array. The size of a dynamic array can vary during the course of the program. Or, you might need an array until the user has entered a bunch of data and the application has processed it and displayed the results. Why keep all the data in memory when they are no longer needed? With a dynamic array, you can discard the data and return the resources they occupied to the system.

To create a dynamic array, declare it as usual with the Dim statement (or Public or Private), but don't specify its dimensions:

```
Dim DynArray()
```

Later in the program, when you know how many elements you want to store in the array, use the ReDim statement to redimension the array, this time with its actual size:

```
ReDim DynArray(UserCount)
```

UserCount is probably a user-entered value.

The ReDim statement can appear only in a procedure. Unlike the Dim statement, ReDim is executable—it forces the application to carry out an action at run time. Dim statements are not executable, and they can appear outside procedures.

An array can be redimensioned to multiple dimensions. Declare it with the Dim statement outside any procedure as follows:

```
Dim Matrix() As Double
```

and then use the ReDim statement in a procedure to declare a three-dimensional array:

```
ReDim Matrix(9, 9, 9)
```

The ReDim statement can't change the type of the array. Moreover, subsequent ReDim statements can change the bounds of the array Matrix, but not the number of its dimensions. For example, you can't use the statement ReDim Matrix(99, 99) later in your code. Once an array has been redimensioned the first time, its number of dimensions can't change. The Matrix array will remain three-dimensional.

NOTE The ReDim statement can by issued only from within a procedure, and it can't appear in the declarations section of a Form or a module. In addition, the array to be redimensioned must be visible from within the procedure that calls the ReDim statement.

The Preserve Keyword   Each time you execute the ReDim statement, all the values currently stored in the array are lost. Visual Basic resets the values of the elements, as if they were just declared. (It resets Variants to Empty values, Numeric data types to zero, and Strings to empty strings.)

In most situations, when you resize an array, you no longer care about the data in it. You can, however, change the size of the array without losing its data. The ReDim statement recognizes the Preserve keyword, which forces it to resize the array without discarding the existing data. For example, you can enlarge an array by one element without losing the values of the existing elements using the UBound function as follows:

```
ReDim Preserve DynamicArray(UBound(DynArray) + 1)
```

If the array DynamicArray() holds 12 elements, this statement adds one element to the array (the element DynamicArray(12)). The values of the elements with indices 0 through 11 do not change.

Arrays of Arrays

One of the possibilities introduced to the language with the Variant data type is that of creating complex structures, such as arrays of arrays. If an array is declared as Variant, you can assign other types to its elements, and you can assign arrays. Suppose you have declared and populated two arrays, one with integers and another with strings. You can then declare a Variant array with two elements and populate it with the two arrays as follows:

```
Dim IntArray(10) As Integer
Dim StrArray(99) As String
Dim BigArray(2) As Variant

{populate array IntArray}
{Populate array StrArray}
```

```
BigArray(0) = IntArray()
BigArray(1) = StrArray()
```

Notice the empty parentheses after the array names. This notation signifies the entire array and is used in passing arrays to DLLs, as you will see in Chapter 12, *The Windows API*. The empty parentheses are equivalent to *IntArray(0)* and *StrArray(0)*. Had you supplied an index, part of the array would be assigned to the corresponding element of *BigArray*. The following statement:

```
BigArray(0) = IntArray(2)
```

assigns to the first element of the BigArray element the last 8 elements (2 through 9) of the array *IntArray*.

BigArray was declared as a one-dimensional array, but because each of its elements is an array, you must use two indices to access it. To access the third element of *IntArray* in *BigArray*, use the indices (0, 2). Likewise, the tenth element of the *StrArray* in *BigArray* is *BigArray(1, 9)*.

Collections

Arrays are convenient for storing related data, but accessing individual elements can be a problem. To print the temperature in Atlanta, for instance, you have to know the index that corresponds to Atlanta. If you don't, you have to scan each element in the array until you find Atlanta. Ideally, arrays should be accessed by their contents. For example, you should be able to look up the temperature in Atlanta with a statement such as the following:

```
Temperature("Atlanta")
```

In the past, programmers had to resort to creative programming techniques to manipulate array data. Visual Basic provides an alternative: collections. As does an array, a collection stores related items. Collections are objects and, as such, have properties and methods. The advantage of a collection over an array is that the collection lets you access its items via a key. If the city name is the key in the Temperatures() array, you can recall the temperature in Atlanta instantly by providing the key:

```
MsgBox "The temperature in Atlanta is " &
Temperatures.Item("Atlanta")
```

The *Item* argument is a method of the Collection object that returns a collection item based on its key or index. If you know the index of Atlanta's entry in the Collection, you can use a statement such as the following:

```
MsgBox "The temperature in Atlanta is " & Temperatures.Item(6)
```

Of course, if you are going to access a Collection's item with its index, there's no advantage in using collections over arrays.

To use a collection, you must first declare a *Collection* variable, as follows:

```
Dim Temperatures As New Collection
```

The keyword New tells Visual Basic to create a new collection and name it Temperatures.

The Collection object provides three methods and one property:

- **Add Method**   Adds items to the collection.
- **Item Method**   Returns an item by index or by key.
- **Remove Method**   Deletes an item from the collection by index or by key.
- **Count Property**   Returns the number of items in the collection.

Let's look at each of these members in detail.

Add (item, key, before, after)   To add a new element to a collection, assign its value to the *item* argument and its key to the *key* argument. To place the new item in a specific location in the array, specify one of the arguments *before* or *after* (but not both). To insert the new item before a specific element whose key (or index) you will specify, use the *before* argument. To place the new item after an item, specify this item's key or index with the *after* argument.

For example, to add the temperature for the city of San Francisco to the Temperatures collection, use the following statement:

```
Temperatures.Add 78, "San Francisco"
```

The number 78 is the value to be stored (temperature), and the string "San Francisco" is the new item's key. To insert this temperature immediately after the temperature of Santa Barbara, use the following statement:

```
Temperatures.Add 78, "San Francisco", , "Santa Barbara"
```

The extra comma denotes the lack of the *before* argument. The Add method supports named arguments, so the previous statement could also be written as follows:

```
Temperatures.Add 78, "San Francisco", after:= "Santa Barbara"
```

Collections aren't sorted; neither do they have a method to automatically sort their items. To maintain an ordered collection of objects, use the *before* and *after* arguments. In most practical situations, however, you don't care about sorting a collection's items. You sort arrays to simplify access of their elements; you don't have to do anything special to access the elements of collections.

Remove (index)   The Remove method removes an item from a collection. The *index* argument can be either the position of the item you want to delete or the item's key. To remove the city of Atlanta from your collection of temperatures, use the following statement:

```
Temperatures.Remove "Atlanta"
```

Or, if you know the city's order in the collection, specify the index in place of the key:

```
Temperatures.Remove 3
```

Item(index)   The Item method returns the value of an item in the collection. As with the Remove method, the index can be either the item's position in the collection or its key. To recall the temperature in Atlanta, use one of the following statements:

```
T1 = Temperatures.Item("Atlanta")
T1 = Temperatures.Item(3)
```

The Item method is the default method for a Collection object, so you can omit it when you access an item in a collection. The previous example could also be written as follows:

```
T1 = Temperatures("Atlanta")
```

TIP   Collection objects maintain their indices automatically as elements are added and deleted. The index of a given element, therefore, changes during the course of a program, and you shouldn't save an item's index value and expect to use it to retrieve the same element later in your program. Use keys for this purpose.

Count   The Count property returns the number of items in the collection. To find out how many cities have been entered so far in the Temperatures collection, use the following statement:

```
Temperatures.Count
```

You can also use the Count property to scan all the elements of the collection, with a For … Next loop such as the following:

```
For city = 1 To Temperatures.Count
      {process elements}
Next city
```

Actually, there is a better way to scan the elements of a Collection, which is explained next.

Processing a Collection's Items

To scan all the items in a Collection, Visual Basic provides the For Each … Next structure. Its syntax is as follows:

```
For Each item in Collection
  {process item}
Next
```

The *item* variable is the loop counter, but you don't have to initialize it or declare its type. The For Each statement scans all the items in the collection automatically. At each iteration, the *item* variable assumes the item's value.

Using Collections

Let's implement a Collection for storing the city names and temperatures. Start a new project and add the following declaration in the Form:

```
Dim Temperatures As New Collection
```

This statement creates a new Collection and names it Temperatures. Then enter the following code in the Form's Load event:

```
Private Sub Form_Load()

  Temperatures.Add 76, "Atlanta"
  Temperatures.Add 85, "Los Angeles"
  Temperatures.Add 97, "Las Vegas"
  Temperatures.Add 66, "Seattle"

End Sub
```

Of course, you can add as many lines as you wish, read the data from a disk file, or prompt the user to enter city names and temperatures at run time. New items can be added to the collection at any time.

Next, create a command button, set its Caption property to Show City Temperature, and enter the following code in its Click subroutine:

```
Private Sub Command1_Click()
On Error GoTo NoItem
  city = InputBox("What City?")
  temp = Temperatures.Item(city)
  MsgBox temp
  Exit Sub

NoItem:
  MsgBox "This city was not found in our catalog"

End Sub
```

This subroutine prompts users to enter the name of the city whose temperature they want to learn. The program then recalls the value of the collection's item, whose key is the city name supplied by the user. If the supplied key doesn't exist, a run-time error is generated, which is why we use the On Error statement. If the user enters a nonexisting city name, a run-time error is generated; Visual Basic intercepts it and executes the statements following the label NoItem.

Finally, add another command button to the Form, set its caption to Show Average Temperature, and enter the following code behind its Click event:

```
Private Sub Command2_Click()
  For Each city In Temperatures
    total = total + city
    Debug.Print city
  Next
  avgTemperature = total / Temperatures.Count
  MsgBox avgTemperature
End Sub
```

The Print statement displays each element in the Immediate window. The *city* entry is the name of the loop variable, and its value is not the city name. It's the item's value, which is the temperature in the current city. The counter of the For Each loop in the previous example could be named iCity, temp, or foo.

NOTE The key values in a Collection object are not stored as array elements in the Collection. They are only used for accessing the items of the Collection, just as array indices are used for accessing an array's elements.

Procedures

In the first couple of chapters, you learned to develop applications by placing code in event handlers. An *event handler* is a short segment of code that is executed each time an external (or internal to your application) condition triggers the event. When the user clicks on a control, the control's Click event handler executes. This handler is nothing more than a subroutine, which performs all the actions you want to perform when the control is clicked. It is separate from the rest of the code and doesn't have to know what would happen if another control is clicked or if the same control is double-clicked. An event handler is a self contained piece of code that's executed when needed.

A large application is broken into small segments called *procedures*. The two types of procedures are *subroutines* and *functions*—the building blocks of your applications. Your code is not a monolithic listing. It's made up of procedures, and you work on one procedure at a time. The one thing you've certainly learned about programming in Visual Basic so far is that the application is made up of small, self-contained segments.

For example, when you write code for a control's Click event, you concentrate on the event at hand, namely how the program should react to the Click event. What happens when the control is double-clicked is something you will worry about later, in the DoubleClick subroutine. This "divide and conquer" approach isn't unique to programming events. It permeates the Visual Basic language and is used to write even the longest applications, by breaking them into small, well-defined tasks. Each task is performed by a separate procedure that is written and tested separately from the others.

Procedures are useful for implementing repeated tasks, such as frequently used calculations. Suppose you are writing an application that, at some point, must convert inches to centimeters or calculate the smaller of two numbers. You can always do the calculations inline and repeat them in your code wherever they are needed, or you can write a procedure that performs the calculations and call this procedure. The benefit of the second approach is that code is cleaner and easier to understand and maintain. If you discover a more efficient way to implement the task, you need change it in only one place. If the same code is repeated in several places throughout the application, you will have to change every instance.

The Abs() Function   This function returns the absolute value of its argument. If the argument is positive, it returns it as is; if it's negative, it inverts its sign. The Abs() function could have been implemented as follows:

```
Function Abs(X As Double) As Double
   If X>=0 Then
      Abs = X
   Else
      Abs = -X
   End If
End Function
```

This is a trivial procedure, yet it's built into Visual Basic because it's used frequently in math and science calculations. Developers can call a single function rather than supplying their own Abs() functions. Visual Basic and all other programming languages provide a number of built-in functions—those needed most frequently by most developers. But each developer has special needs; you can't expect to find all the procedures you may ever need in a programming language. Sooner or later, you will have to supply your own.

Subroutines

A subroutine is a block of statements that carry out a well-defined task. The block of statements is placed with a pair of Sub/End Sub statements and can be invoked by name. The following subroutine displays the current date in a Message Box and can be called by its name, ShowDate:

```
Sub ShowDate()
  MsgBox Date()
End Sub
```

A subroutine normally performs a more complicated task than this one, but it's nevertheless a block of code isolated from the rest of the application. All the event procedures in Visual Basic, for example, are coded as subroutines. The actions that must be performed each time a command button is clicked are coded in the button's Click procedure. This subroutine is called each time the button is clicked.

The statements in a subroutine are executed, and when the End Sub statement is reached, control returns to the calling program. It is possible to exit a Subroutine prematurely with the Exit statement. For example, some condition may stop the subroutine from successfully completing its task.

Functions

A function is similar to a subroutine, but a function returns a result. Subroutines perform a task and don't report anything to the calling program; functions commonly carry out calculations and report the result. The statements making up a function are placed in a pair of Function/End Function statements. Moreover, because a function reports a result, it must have a type, as in the following:

```
Function NextDay() As Date
    NextDay = Date() + 1
End Function
```

The NextDay() function returns tomorrow's date by adding 1 day to the current date. Because it must report the result to the calling program, the NextDay() function has a type, as do variables, and the result is assigned to its name (something you can't do with subroutines).

Arguments

Both types of procedures are not as isolated from the rest of the application as the examples imply. Most procedures accept arguments from the calling program. An *argument* is a value you pass to the procedure and on which the procedure usually acts. This is how both subroutines and functions communicate with the rest of the application.

The examples you've seen so far were trivial. The subroutines that handle the various events provide none, one, or more arguments. The Click subroutine, for instance, doesn't have arguments because all you need is the name of the subroutine. The user has clicked on a control, and you must write the code to handle this event. You don't need any additional information.

The KeyPress subroutine provides an integer argument, which is the ASCII code of the character pressed. The definition of the KeyPress subroutine is as follows:

```
Private Sub Command1_KeyPress(KeyAscii As Integer)

End Sub
```

You specify arguments in the procedure declaration, but without the Dim statement. *KeyAscii* is an argument that conveys information about the key pressed. The code in the KeyPress subroutine will most likely process the keystroke, and it needs this information.

Functions accept arguments too and in many cases more than one. The function Min(), for instance, accepts two numbers and returns the smaller one:

```
Function Min(a As Variant, b As Variant) As Variant
  Min = IIf(a < b, a, b)
End Function
```

IIf is a built-in function that evaluates the first argument. If IIf is True, it returns the second argument. If IIf is False, it returns the third argument. Because the arguments of the Min() function were declared as Variants, the function works with all types of data, not just numeric data types.

When you call a procedure, you must supply values for all the arguments specified in the procedure's definition and in the same order. Moreover, the values of the arguments must match their declared type. If a procedure expects an Integer value, you shouldn't supply a Double value. Here's an example of a subroutine declaration:

```
Sub PrintLotto(num1, num2, num3, num4, num5, num6 As Integer)
```

This subroutine prints six highly desirable numbers, and when you call it, you must supply six integer values. The subroutine's code may declare additional variables, but these six variables are required. You can't even call this subroutine without them.

Calling Subroutines

To call a procedure, you use the Call statement and supply its name and arguments in parentheses, as follows:

```
Call PrintLotto(Num1, Num2, Num3, Num4, Num5, Num6)
```

You can omit the Call statement and call the subroutine by name. The arguments are supplied without the parentheses, as follows:

```
PrintLotto Num1, Num2, Num3, Num4, Num5, Num6
```

The number of arguments you supply to the subroutine and their types must match those in the procedure declaration.

Calling Functions

Functions are called by name, and a list of arguments follows this name in parentheses, as follows:

```
Degrees = Fahrenheit(Temperature)
```

In this example, the Fahrenheit() function converts the Temperature argument (which presumably is the temperature in degrees Celsius) to degrees Fahrenheit, and the result is assigned to the *Degrees* variable. Functions can be called from within expressions as the following shows:

```
MsgBox "40 degrees Celsius are " & Fahrenheit(40) & " degrees
Fahrenheit"
```

Suppose the function CountWords() counts the number of words and the function CountChars() counts the number of characters in a string. The average length of a word can be calculated as follows:

```
LongString = Text1.Text
AvgLen = CountChars(LongString) / CountWords(LongString)
```

The first statement gets the text of a TextBox control and assigns it to a variable, which is then used as an argument to the two functions. When the second statement executes, Visual Basic first calls the functions CountChars() and Count-Words() with the specified arguments and then divides the results they return.

You can call Functions in the same way that you call Subroutines, with the Call statement, but the result won't be stored anywhere. For example, the function Convert() may convert the text in a text box to uppercase and return the number of characters it converted. Normally, you call this function as follows:

```
nChars = Convert()
```

If you don't care about the return value, you can call the Convert() function with the Call statement:

```
Call Convert()
```

Argument-Passing Mechanisms

One of the most important procedural issues is the mechanism used to pass arguments. In the examples so far, I used the default mechanism—passing arguments by reference. The other mechanism is passing by value. Although most programmers use the default mechanism, it's important to know the difference between the two mechanisms and when to use each one.

Passing Arguments by Reference Passing arguments by reference gives the procedure access to the actual variable. The calling procedure passes the address of the variable in memory so that the procedure can change its value permanently. In earlier versions of BASIC, including Visual Basic, this was the only argument-passing mechanism.

Start a new Visual Basic project and enter the following function definition in the Form's Code window:

```
Function Add(num1 As Integer, num2 As Integer) As Integer

  Add = num1 + num2
  num1 = 0
  num2 = 0

End Function
```

This simple function adds two numbers and then sets them to zero. Next, place a command button on the Form and enter the following code in the button's Click event:

```
Dim A As Integer, B As Integer
A = 10
B = 2

Sum = Add(A, B)
Debug.Print A
Debug.Print B
Debug.Print Sum
```

This code displays the following results in the Immediate Execution window:

```
0
0
12
```

The changes made to the function's arguments take effect even after the function has ended. The values of the variables *A* and *B* have changed permanently.

Now change the definition of the function by inserting the keyword ByVal before the names of the arguments as follows:

```
Function Add(ByVal num1 As Integer, ByVal num2 As Integer) As
Integer
```

With this change, Visual Basic passes copies of the arguments to the function. The rest of the program remains the same. Run the application, click on the command button, and the following values display in the Immediate Execution window:

```
10
2
12
```

The function has changed the values of the arguments, but these changes remain in effect only in the function. The variables *A* and *B* in the Command1_Click() subroutine haven't been affected.

When passing an argument by reference, the argument type must match the declared type. In other words, you can't pass an Integer value if the procedure expects a Double value, even if they have the same value. For example, if the function Degrees() converts temperature values from Celsius to Fahrenheit, the definition of the function is as follows:

```
Function Degrees(Celsius as Single) As Single

  Degrees = (9 / 5) * Celsius + 32

End Function
```

This function is usually called as:

```
CTemp = 37
MsgBox Degrees(CTemp)
```

If CTemp has been declared an Integer, Visual Basic generates a run-time error and displays the following message:

```
ByRef argument type mismatch
```

This error message tells you that the argument you are passing to the function does not match the function declaration. The function expects a Single value and is passed an Integer.

You can get around this problem in two ways. The first is to convert the Integer value to a Single value and then pass it to the function:

```
MsgBox Degrees(CSng(CTemp))
```

You can also change the variable's declaration to a Single variable.

The second method is to let Visual Basic make the conversion, by enclosing the argument in parentheses:

```
MsgBox Degrees((CTemp))
```

Visual Basic converts the value to the type that matches the function's declaration.

Automatic Argument Type Matching

This technique is more flexible than the example indicates. Suppose you are prompting the user for the Celsius degrees with the InputBox() function. The InputBox() function returns a string that you must convert to a numeric value before passing it to the Degrees() function. You can skip the conversion by enclosing the string argument in parentheses:

```
CTemp = InputBox("Enter temperature in degrees Celsius")
MsgBox Degrees((CTemp))
```

Visual Basic performs the necessary conversion, and the Degrees() function accepts a numeric argument. You can also combine the two statements into one:

```
MsgBox Degrees((InputBox("Enter temperature in degrees
Celsius")))
```

In general, you pass arguments by reference only if the procedure has reason to change its value. If the values of the arguments are required later in the program, you run the risk of changing their values in the procedure. For example, if the Degrees() function changes the value of the CTemp argument, the variable won't have the same value before and after the call of the Degrees() function.

Passing Arguments by Value   When you pass an argument by value, the procedure sees only a copy of the argument. Even if it changes it, the changes are not permanent. The benefit of passing arguments by value is that the argument values are isolated from the procedure and only the program in which they are declared can change their values.

Passing arguments by value requires a bit of extra typing, since this isn't the default argument-passing mechanism. For example, to declare that the Degrees() function's arguments are passed by value, use the ByVal keyword in the argument's declaration as follows:

```
Function Degrees(ByVal Celsius as Single) As Single

    Degrees = (9 / 5) * Celsius + 32

End Function
```

To see what the ByVal keyword does, add a line that changes the value of the argument in the function:

```
Function Degrees(ByVal Celsius as Single) As Single

    Degrees = (9 / 5) * Celsius + 32
    Celsius = 0

End Function
```

Now call the function as follows:

```
CTemp = InputBox("Enter temperature in degrees Celsius")
MsgBox CTemp & " degrees Celsius are " & Degrees((CTemp)) & "
degrees Fahrenheit"
```

If the value entered in the Input Box is 32, the following message is displayed:

```
32 degrees Celsius are 89.6 degrees Fahrenheit
```

Remove the ByVal keyword from the function's definition and call the function as follows:

```
Celsius = 32.0
FTemp = Degrees(Celsius)
MsgBox Celsius & " degrees Celsius are " & FTemp & " degrees
Fahrenheit"
```

This time the program displays the following message:

```
0 degrees Celsius are 89.6 degrees Fahrenheit.
```

When the *Celsius* argument was passed to the Degrees() function, its value was 32. But the function changed its value, and upon return it was 0. Because the argument was passed by reference, any changes made by the procedure affected the variable permanently.

NOTE When you pass arguments to a procedure by reference, you are actually passing the variable itself. Any changes made to the argument by the procedure will be permanent. When you pass arguments by value, the procedure gets a copy of the variable, which is discarded when the procedure ends. Any changes made to the argument by the procedure won't affect the variable of the calling program.

Using Optional Arguments

Normally, when you want to call a procedure that expects three arguments, you must pass three arguments to the procedure, and you must pass them in the proper order. Suppose you wrote a function to evaluate math expressions, such as 3*cos(3.14159) + log(10). The function Evaluate() should expect a single argument, the expression to be evaluated, and return a Double value:

```
Function Evaluate(expression As String) As Double
```

The *expression* variable is the math formula to be evaluated.

What if you want to evaluate functions with an independent variable X, such as 3*cos(X) + log(10)? You would have to specify not only the expression, but also the value of X. A function that evaluates all types of expressions should be able to accept either one or two arguments.

TIP The alternative of passing a dummy second argument when one is not needed will also work, but it will make your code more difficult to understand.

Visual Basic lets you specify optional arguments with the Optional keyword preceding each optional argument. The definition of the Evaluate() function should be:

```
Function Evaluate(expression As String, Optional XValue As Double)
As Double
```

Once the first optional argument is specified, all following arguments in the definition must also be optional and declared with the Optional keyword. The Evaluate() function can now be called either with one or with two arguments:

```
Debug.Print Evaluate(397 / 3 - 102)
```

or

```
Debug.Print Evaluate(397 / sin(3) - 102)
```

Now, how does the procedure know which arguments it received and which it didn't? To find out whether an argument was supplied, use the IsMissing() function in the procedure. If an optional argument is not provided, the argument is actually assigned as a Variant with the value of Empty. The example below shows how to test for missing optional arguments using the IsMissing() function. The function Evaluate() should contain a statement such as the following:

```
If IsMissing(XValue) Then
    {process expression without an x value}
Else
    {process expression for the specified x value}
End If
```

Here's an example of a generic function that supports optional arguments. It doesn't actually evaluate math expressions, but it demonstrates how to use the IsMissing() function to check for missing arguments. First, declare the function as follows:

```
Function Evaluate(expression As String, Optional XValue As Double)
As Double
If IsMissing(XValue) Then
    MsgBox "Evaluating " & expression
Else
    MsgBox "Evaluating " & expression & " for X = " & XValue
End If
End Function
```

Next, call this function as follows:

```
Evaluate("3*x+5", 10)
```

and

```
Evaluate("3*10+5")
```

In each case, the Evaluate() function displays a different message. The first call to the function displays the following message:

```
Evaluating 3*x+5 for X = 10
```

The second call displays only this expression:

```
Evaluating 3*x+5
```

Providing a Default for an Optional Argument   You can also specify a default value for an optional argument. If the Evaluate() function must have a value for the *XValue* argument, you can define the function as follows:

```
Function Evaluate(expression As String, Optional XValue=0) As
Double
```

If the function is called without a value for the *XValue* argument, the Evaluate() function uses the value 0 for the missing argument.

For example, Visual Basic's financial functions (described in Appendix A) accept optional argument and specify default values for any missing arguments. The last argument of most VB financial functions is an integer that specifies whether loan payments are made at the beginning or at the end of the period. If you don't supply this value, these functions assume that payments are due at the end of the period.

The benefit of supplying default values for missing arguments is that your code doesn't have to check for missing arguments and then take a course of action depending on whether an argument's value was supplied. Using the default value, your program can proceed as if all arguments were supplied.

Passing an Unknown Number of Arguments

Generally, all the arguments that a procedure expects are listed in the procedure's definition, and the program that calls the procedure must supply values for all arguments. On occasions, however, you may not know how many arguments will be passed to the procedure. Procedures that calculate averages or, in general, process a number of values, can accept a few to several arguments whose count is not known at design time. In the past, programmers had to pass arrays with the data to similar procedures. Visual Basic 5 introduces the ParamArray keyword, which allows you to pass a variable number of arguments to a procedure.

Let's look at an example. Suppose you want to populate a ListBox control with elements. The method for adding an item to the ListBox control is AddItem and is called as follows:

```
List1.AddItem "new item"
```

This statement adds the string "new item" to the List1 ListBox control.

If you frequently add multiple items to a ListBox control from within your code, you can write either repeated statements or a subroutine that performs this task. The following subroutine adds a number of arguments to the List1 control:

```
Sub AddNamesToList(ParamArray NamesArray())

  For Each x In NamesArray
    List1.AddItem x
  Next x

End Sub
```

This subroutine's argument is an array, prefixed with the keyword ParamArray. This array holds all the parameters passed to the subroutine. To add a number of items to the list, call the AddNamesToList() subroutine as follows:

```
AddNamesToList "Robert", "Manny", "Richard", "Charles", "Madona"
```

or

```
AddNamesToList "Mercury", "Earth", "Mars", "Jupiter"
```

If you want to know the number of arguments actually passed to the procedure, use the UBound() function on the parameter array. The number of arguments passed to the AddNamesToList() subroutine is as follows:

```
UBound(NamesArray())
```

Here is another method for scanning all the elements of the parameter array:

```
For i = 0 to UBound(NamesArray())
  List1.AddItem NamesArray(i)
Next i
```

Named Arguments

You've learned how to write procedures with optional arguments and how to pass a variable number of arguments to the procedure. The main limitation of the argument-passing mechanism, though, is the order of the arguments. If the first argument is a string and the second argument is a date, you can't change their order. By default, Visual Basic matches the values passed to a procedure to the declared arguments by their order. That's why the arguments you've seen so far are called *positional arguments*.

This limitation is lifted by Visual Basic's capability to specify *named arguments*. With named arguments, you can supply arguments in any order, because they are recognized by name and not by their order in the list of the procedure's arguments. Suppose you've written a function that expects three arguments—a name, an address, and an e-mail address:

```
Function Contact(Name As String, Address As String, EMail As String)
```

When calling this function, you must supply three strings that correspond to the arguments *Name*, *Address*, and *EMail* in that order. However, there's a safer way to call this function: supply the arguments in any order by their names. Instead of calling the Contact function as follows:

```
Contact("Peter Evans", "2020 Palm Ave. Santa Barbara, CA 90000",
    "PeterEvans@SciNet.com")
```

you can call it this way:

```
Contact(Address:="2020 Palm Ave, Santa Barbara, CA 90000",
    EMail:="PeterEvans@SciNet.com", Name:="Peter Evans")
```

The equals sign assigns values to the names of the arguments. Because the arguments are passed by name, you can supply them in any order.

To test this technique, enter the following function declaration in a Form's code:

```
Function Contact(Name As String, Address As String, EMail As String)

    Debug.Print Name
    Debug.Print Address
    Debug.Print EMail

    Contact = "OK"

End Function
```

Then, call the Contact() function from within a button's Click event with the following statement:

```
Debug.Print Contact(Address:="2020 Palm Ave, Santa Barbara, CA
    90000", Name:="Peter Evans", EMail:="PeterEvans@SciNet.com")
```

You'll see the following in the Immediate Execution window:

```
Peter Evans
2020 Palm Ave, Santa Barbara, CA 90000
PeterEvans@SciNet.com
OK
```

The function knows which value corresponds to which argument and can process them the same way that it processes positional arguments. Notice that the function's definition doesn't change whether it's used with positional or named arguments. The difference is in how you call the function and how you declare it.

Named arguments make code safer and easier to read, but because they require a lot of typing, most programmers don't use them. Besides, programmers are so used to positional arguments that the notion of naming arguments is like having to declare variables when variants will do. Named arguments are good for situations in which you have optional arguments that require many consecutive commas, which may complicate the code.

Control Flow Statements

What makes programming languages flexible and capable of handling every situation and every programming challenge with a relatively small set of commands is the capability to examine external conditions and act accordingly. Programs are not monolithic sets of commands that carry out the same calculations every time they are executed. Instead, they adjust their behavior depending on the data supplied, on external conditions, such as a mouse click or the existence of a peripheral, or even on abnormal conditions generated by the program itself. For example, a program that calculates averages may work time and again until the user forgets to supply any data. In this case, the program attempts to divide by zero, and your program must detect this condition and act accordingly.

An application needs a built-in capability to test conditions and take a course of action depending on the outcome of the test. Visual Basic provides three control flow, or decision, structures:

- If...Then
- If...Then...Else
- Select Case

If ... Then ... End If

The If structure tests the condition specified and, if it's True, executes the statement(s) that follow. The If structure can have a single-line or a multiple-line syntax. To execute one statement conditionally, use the single-line syntax as follows:

```
If condition Then statement
```

Visual Basic evaluates the *condition* and, if it's True, executes the statement that follows. If the condition is not True, it continues with the statement following the If structure.

You can execute multiple statements by separating them with a colon:

```
If condition Then statement: statement: statement
```

Here's an example of a single-line If statement:

```
If Month(date) = 1 Then Year = Year + 1
```

You can break this statement into multiple lines, as shown here::

```
If Month(date) = 1 Then
  Year = Year + 1
End If
```

Some programmers prefer the multiple-line syntax of the If ... Then statement, even if it contains a single statement, because the code is easier to read.

If...Then...Else...End If

A variation of the If...Then statement is the If ... Then ... Else statement, which executes one block of statements if the condition is True and another if the condition is False. The syntax of the If ... Then ... Else statement is as follows:

```
If condition Then
        statementblock-1
Else
        statementblock-2
End If
```

Visual Basic evaluates the *condition*. If it's True, it executes the first block of statements and then jumps to the statement following the End If statement. If the condition is False, Visual Basic ignores the first block of statements and executes the block following the Else keyword.

Another variation of the If ... Then ... Else statement uses several conditions, with the Elseif keyword:

```
If condition1 Then
        statementblock-1
Elseif condition2 Then
        statementblock-2
Elseif condition3 Then
        statementblock-3
Else
   statementblock-4
End If
```

You can have any number of Elseif clauses. The conditions are evaluated from the top, and if one of them is True, the corresponding block of statements is executed. The Else clause will be executed if none of the previous expressions was True. Here's an example of an If statement with Elseif clauses:

```
If score < 50 Then
   Result = "Failed"
Elseif score < 75 Then
   Result = "Pass"
Elseif score < 90 Then
   Result = "Very Good"
Else
   Result = "Excellent"
End If
```

This statement is easier to read, but not as efficient in terms of execution time because Visual Basic evaluates all conditions, even if the first one is True.

Multiple If...Then Structures versus Elseif

Notice that once a True condition is found, Visual Basic executes the associated statements and skips the remaining clauses. It continues executing the program with the statement immediately after End If. That's why you should prefer the following complicated structure to the equivalent series of simple If statements:

```
If score < 50 Then
   Result = "Failed"
End If
```

```
If score < 75 And score >= 50 Then
  Result = "Pass"
End If
If score < 90 And score > =75 Then
  Result = "Very Good"
End If
If score >= 90 Then
  Result = "Excellent"
End If
```

Because the multiple ElseIf structure can create efficient but difficult-to-read code, there's an alternative: the Select Case statement.

Select Case

The Select Case structure compares the same expression to a different value. The advantage of the Select Case statement over multiple If...Then...Else statements is that it makes the code easier to read and maintain.

The Select Case structure tests a single expression, which is evaluated once at the top of the structure. The result of the test is then compared with several values, and if it matches one of them, the corresponding block of statements is executed. Here's the syntax of the Select Case statement:

```
Select Case expression
      Case value1
            statementblock-1
      Case value2
            statementblock-2
            .
            .
            .
      Case Else
            statementblock
End Select
```

And here's a practical example based on the Select Case statement:

```
Select Case WeekDay(Date)
Case 1
  DayName = "Monday"
```

```
  Message = "Have a nice week"
Case 6
  DayName = "Saturday"
  Message = "Have a nice weekend"
Case 7
  DayName = "Sunday"
  Message = "Did you have a nice weekend?"
Case Else
  Message = "Welcome back!"
End Select
```

The *expression* variable, which is evaluated at the beginning of the statement, is the number of the weekday, as reported by the WeekDay() function (a value in the range 1 to 7). The value of the *expression* is then compared with the values that follow each Case keyword. If they match, the block of the following statements up to the next Case keyword is executed, and the program skips to the statement following the End Select statement. The block of the Case Else statement is optional and is executed if none of the previous Case values match the expression.

Some Case statements can be followed by multiple values, which are separated by commas. Here's a revised version of the previous example:

```
Select Case WeekDay(Date)
Case 1, 2, 3, 4, 5
  Message = "Welcome back!"
  DayType = "Workday"
Case 6, 7
  Message = "Have a nice weekend"
  DayType = "Holiday"
End Select
```

The five workdays and the two weekend days are handled by two Case statements with multiple values. This structure doesn't contain a Case Else statement because all values are examined in the Case statements. The WeekDay() function can't return another value.

TIP   If more than one Case value matches the expression, only the statement block associated with the first matching Case executes.

Here are the equivalent If … Then … Else statements that would implement the previous example:

```
today = WeekDay(Date)
' MORE COMPACT NOTATION: If today > 0 And today < 6
If today = 1 or today = 2 or today = 3 or today = 4 or today = 5
Then
  Message = "Welcome back!"
  DayType = "Workday"
Else
  Message = "Have a nice weekend"
  DayType = "Holiday"
End If
```

To say the least, this coding is verbose. If you attempt to implement a more elaborate Select Case statement with If … Then … Else statements, the code becomes even more difficult to read. Here is the first example, implemented with If … Then … Else statements:

```
today = WeekDay(date)
If today = 1 Then
  DayName = "Monday"
  Message = "Have a nice week"
Elseif today = 6 Then
    DayName = "Saturday"
    Message = "Have a nice weekend"
Elseif today = 7 Then
    DayName = "Sunday"
    Message = "Did you have a nice weekend?"
End If
```

Of course, the Select Case statement can't substitute for any If … Then structure. The Select Case structure evaluates the expression before entering the Case statements. In contrast, the If...Then...Else structure can evaluate a different expression for each ElseIf statement.

Loop Statements

Loop statements allow you to execute one or more lines of code repetitively. Many tasks consist of trivial operations that must be repeated over and over again, and looping structures are an important part of any programming language. Visual Basic supports the following loop statements:

- Do...Loop
- For...Next
- While ... Wend

Do...Loop

The Do loop executes a block of statements for as long as a condition is True. There are two variations of the Do...Loop statement, but both use the same basic model. Visual Basic evaluates an expression, and if it's True, the statements are executed. If the expression is not True, the program continues, and the statement following the loop is executed.

The loop is executed either *while* the condition is True or *until* the condition becomes True. The two variations of the Do loop use the keywords While and Until to specify how long the statements are executed. To execute a block of statements while a condition is True, use the following syntax:

```
Do While condition
      statement-block
Loop
```

To execute a block of statements until the condition becomes True, use the following syntax:

```
Do Until condition
  statement-block
Loop
```

When Visual Basic executes the previous loops, it first evaluates *condition*. If *condition* is False, the Do While or Do Until loop is skipped (the statements aren't even executed once). When the Loop statement is reached, Visual Basic evaluates the expression again and repeats the statement-block of the Do While loop if the expression is True or repeats the statements of the Do Until loop if the expression is False.

The Do loop can execute any number of times as long as *condition* is True (or nonzero if the condition evaluates to a number). Moreover, the number of iterations need not be known before the loops starts. If *condition* is initially False, the statements may never execute.

Here's a typical example of using Do loops. Suppose the string MyText holds a piece of text (perhaps the Text property of a TextBox control), and you want to count the words in the text. We will assume that there are no multiple spaces in the text and that the space character separates successive words. To locate an instance of a character in a string, use the InStr() function, which accepts three arguments:

- The starting location of the search

- The text to be searched

- The character being searched

The following loop repeats for as long as there are spaces in the text. Each time the InStr() function finds another space in the text, it returns the location (a positive number) of the space. When there are no more spaces in the text, the InStr() function returns zero, which signals the end of the loop.

```
position = 1
Do While position > 0
  position = InStr(position + 1, MyText, " ")
  words = words + 1
Loop
Debug.Print words
```

The Do loop is executed while the InStr() function returns a positive number, which happens for as long as there are more words in the text. The variable *position* holds the location of each successive space character in the text. The search for the next space starts at the location of the current space plus 1 (so that the program won't keep finding the same space). For each space found, the program increments the value of the *words* variable, which holds the total number of words when the loop ends.

You may notice a problem with the previous code segment. It assumes that the text contains at least one word and starts by setting the *position* variable to 1. If the *MyText* variable contains an empty string, the program reports that it contains one word. To fix this problem, you must specify the condition as follows:

```
Do While InStr(position + 1, MyText, " ")
  position = InStr(position + 1, MyText, " ")
  words = words + 1
Loop
Debug.Print words
```

This code segment counts the number of words correctly, even if the *MyText* variable contains an empty string. If the *MyText* string variable doesn't contain any spaces, the function InStr(position + 1, MyText, " ") returns 0, which corresponds to False, and the Do loop isn't executed.

You can code the same routine with the Until keyword. In this case, you must continue to search for spaces until *position* becomes zero. Here's the same code with a different loop (the InStr() function returns 0 if the string it searches for doesn't exist in the longer string):

```
position = 1
Do Until position = 0
   position = InStr(position + 1, MyText, " ")
   words = words + 1
Loop
Debug.Print words
```

Another variation of the Do loop executes the statements first and evaluates the *condition* after each execution. This Do loop has the following syntax:

```
Do
       statements
Loop While condition
```

or

```
Do
       statements
Loop While condition
```

The statements in this type of loop execute at least once, since the condition is examined at the end of the loop. Could we have implemented the previous example with one of the last two types of loops? The fact that we had to do something special about zero-length strings suggests that this problem shouldn't be coded with a loop that tests the condition at the end. Since the loops' body will be executed once, the *words* variable is never going to be zero.

As you can see, you can code loops in a number of ways with the Do … Loop statement, and which you use depends on the problem at hand and your programming style.

For...Next

The For ... Next loop is one of the oldest loop structures in programming languages. Unlike the Do loop, the For ... Next loop requires that you know how many times the statements in the loop will be executed. The For ... Next loop uses a variable (it's called the loop's *counter*) that increases or decreases in value during each repetition of the loop. The For ... Next loop has the following syntax:

```
For counter = start To end [Step increment]
      statements
Next [counter]
```

(The keywords in square brackets are optional.) The arguments *counter, start, end,* and *increment* are all numeric. The loop is executed as many times as required for the *counter* to reach (or exceed) the *end* value.

In executing a For loop, Visual Basic does the following:

1. Sets *counter* equal to start.

2. Tests to see if *counter* is greater than *end.* If so, it exits the loop. If *increment* is negative, Visual Basic tests to see if *counter* is less than *end,* in which case it exits the loop.

3. Executes the statements in the block.

4. Increments *counter* by the amount specified with the *increment* argument. If the *increment* argument isn't specified, *counter* is incremented by 1.

5. Repeats the statements.

The following For ... Next loop scans all the elements of the numeric array *data()* and calculates their average:

```
For i = 0 To UBound(data)
  total = total + data(i)
Next i
Debug.Print total / UBound(a)
```

The single most important thing to keep in mind when working with For ... Next loops is that the loop's *counter* is set at the beginning of the loop. Changing the value of the *end* variable in the loop's body won't have any effect. The following loop:

```
endValue = 10
For i = 0 To endValue
  endValue = 100
  {more statements}
Next i
```

will be executed 10 times, not 100 times.

You can, however, adjust the value of the *counter* from within the loop. The following is an endless (or infinite) loop:

```
For i = 0 To 10
  Debug.Print i
  i = i - 1
Next i
```

This loop never ends because the loops *counter* in effect is never increased. (If you try this, press Control+Break to interrupt the endless loop.)

WARNING Manipulating the *counter* of a For ... Next loop is strongly discouraged. This practice will most likely lead to bugs such as infinite loops, overflows, and so on. If the number of repetitions of a loop isn't known in advance, use a the Do ... Loop or a While ... Wend structure (discussed in the following section).

The *increment* argument can be either positive or negative. If *increment* is positive, *start* must be less than or equal to *end*. If *increment* is negative, *start* must be greater than or equal to *end*. If this isn't the case, the loop's body will not be executed, not even once.

Finally, the *counter* variable need not be listed after the Next statement, but it makes the code easier to read, especially when For ... Next loops are nested within each other (nested loops are discussed in the section "Nested Control Structures" later in the chapter).

While ... Wend

The While ... Wend loop executes a block of statements while a condition is True. The While ... Wend loop has the following syntax:

```
While condition
  statement-block
Wend
```

If *condition* is True, all statements are executed, and when the Wend statement is reached, control is returned to the While statement, which evaluates *condition* again. If *condition* is still True, the process is repeated. If *condition* is False, the program resumes with the statement following the Wend statement.

The following While ... Wend loop prompts the user for numeric data. The user can type a negative value to indicate that all values are entered:

```
number = 0
While number => 0
  total = total + number
  number = InputBox("Please enter another value")
Wend
```

You assign the value 0 to the *number* variable before the loop starts, because this value can't affect the total. Another technique is to precede the While statement with an InputBox function to get the first number from the user.

Nested Control Structures

You can place control structures inside other control structures (such as an If...Then block within a For...Next loop). A control structure placed inside another control structure is said to be *nested*.

Control structures in Visual Basic can be nested to as many levels as you want. It's common practice to indent the bodies of nested decision structures and loop structures to make the program easier to read. Here is the structure of a nested For ... Next loop that scans all the elements of a two-dimensional array:

```
For irow = 0 To Ubound(Array2(0))
  For icol = 0 To Ubound(Array2(1))
    { process element Array2(irow, icol)) }
    Next icol
Next irow
```

The outer loop (with the irow counter) scans each row of the array, and the inner loop scans each column. The outer loop scans each element in the first row of the array, the elements of the second row, and so on until the entire array has been scanned. The loop's body can process the element Array2(irow, icol).

TIP

As mentioned, the presence of the counter names *icol* and *irow* are not really required after the Next statement. Actually, if you supply them in the wrong order, Visual Basic generates an error message. In practice, few programmers specify counter values after a Next statement because Visual Basic matches each Next statement to the corresponding For statement. If the loop's body is lengthy, you can improve the program's readability by specifying the corresponding counter name after each Next statement.

You can also nest control flow structures. The following structure tests a user-supplied value to determine if it's positive and, if so, determines whether the value exceeds a certain limit:

```
Income = InputBox("Enter your income")
If Income > 0 Then
  If Income > 20000 Then
    MsgBox "You will pay taxes this year"
  Else
    MsgBox "You won't pay any taxes this year"
  End If
Else
  MsgBox "Bummer"
End If
```

The *Income* variable is first compared with zero. If it's negative, the Else clause of the If...Then statement is executed. If it's positive, it's compared with the value 20,000, and depending on the outcome, a different message is displayed.

The Exit Statement

The Exit statement allows you to exit prematurely from a block of statements in a control structure, from a loop, or even from a procedure. Suppose you have a For ... Next loop that calculates the square root of a series of numbers. Because the square root of negative numbers can't be calculated (the Sqr() function generates a run-time error), you might want to halt the operation if the array contains an invalid value. To exit the loop prematurely, use the Exit For statement as follows:

```
For i = 0 To UBound(nArray())
  If nArray(i) < 0 Then Exit For
  nArray(i) = Sqr(nArray(i))
Next
```

If a negative element is found in this loop, the program exits the loop and continues with the statement following the Next statement. There are similar Exit statements for the Do loop (Exit Do), as well as for functions and subroutines (Exit Function and Exit Subroutine). If the previous loop was part of a function, you might want to assign an error code to the function and exit not only the loop, but the function itself:

```
For i = 0 To UBound(nArray())
  If nArray(i) < 0 Then
    MsgBox "Negative value found, terminating calculations"
    Exit Function
  End If
  nArray(i) = Sqr(nArray(i))
Next
```

If this code is part of a subroutine procedure, you use the Exit Subroutine statement. The Exit statements for loops are Exit For and Exit Do. There is no way (or compelling reason) to exit prematurely an If or Case statement. There is also an Exit Property statement, which we will look at in Chapter 14, *Building ActiveX Controls.*

Working with Forms

- Manipulating Forms

- Loading, showing, and hiding Forms

- Designing menus

- Developing shortcut and access keys

- Using drag-and-drop operations

- Dragging list items

In Visual Basic, the Form is the container for all the controls that make up the user interface. When a Visual Basic application is executing, each window on the Desktop is a Form. In previous chapters, we used Forms as containers, on which we placed the elements of the user interface. Now, we'll look at Forms, and at a few related topics, such as menus (Forms are the only objects that can have menus attached) and drag-and-drop operations. The Form is the top level object in a Visual Basic application, and every application starts with the Form.

Forms have a built-in functionality that is always available, without any programming effort on your part. You can move a Form around, resize it, and even cover it with other Forms. You do so with the mouse, with the keyboard, or through the Control menu. Forms have many trivial properties that I won't discuss here. Instead, let's jump directly to the properties that are unique to Forms and then look at how to manipulate Forms from within an application's code.

The Appearance of Forms

The main characteristic of a Form (see Figure 4.1)is the title bar, on which the form's caption is displayed. On the left end of the title bar is the Control Menu icon. Clicking on this icon opens the Control menu. On the right side of the title bar are three buttons—Minimize, Maximize, and Close. Clicking on these buttons minimizes, maximizes, and closes the Form. When a Form is maximized, the Maximize button is replaced by the Normal button, which restores the Form to its size and position before it was maximized.

FIGURE 4.1

The elements of
the Form

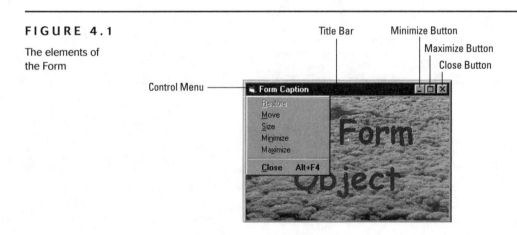

Title Bar   Minimize Button

Maximize Button

Close Button

Control Menu

The Control menu contains the following commands:

- **Restore** Restores a maximized Form to its size before it was maximized. Available only if the Form is maximized.

- **Move** Lets the user move the Form around with the mouse.

- **Size** Lets the user resize the control with the mouse.

- **Minimize** Minimizes the Form.

- **Maximize** Maximizes the Form.

- **Close** Closes the current Form

You can customize the appearance of the Form with the following Form properties.

MinButton, MaxButton These two properties are True by default. Set them to False to hide the corresponding buttons on the title bar.

ControlMenu This property is also True by default. Set it to False to hide the icon and disable the Control menu. Although the Control menu is rarely used, Windows applications don't disable it.

When the ControlMenu property is False, the three buttons on the title bar are also disabled. If you set the Caption property to an empty string, the title bar disappears altogether.

BorderStyle The BorderStyle property determines not only the style of the form's border, as its name implies, but also the appearance of the Form. The BorderStyle property can take one of the values shown in Table 4.1.

TABLE 4.1 The Values of the BorderStyle Property

VALUE	CONSTANT	DESCRIPTION
0-None	vbBSNone	The Form has no visible border or title bar and looks quite odd. It can't be moved around or resized, and this setting should be avoided.
1-Fixed Single	VbFixedSingle	The Form has a visible border, but can't be resized.

TABLE 4.1   The Values of the BorderStyle Property (continued)

VALUE	CONSTANT	DESCRIPTION
2-Sizable	VbSizable	This is the default value. The Form has a visible border and a title bar and can be repositioned on the Desktop and resized.
3-Fixed Dialog	VbFixedDialog	Fixed dialog box.
4-Fixed ToolWindow	vbFixedToolWindow	The Form has the look of a toolbar. It has a Close button only and can't be resized.
5-Sizable ToolWindow	VbSizableToolWindow	Same as the Fixed ToolWindow, but can be resized.

A typical application has more than a single Form. When an application starts, the main Form is loaded. You can control which Form is initially loaded by setting the Startup Object in the Project Properties window, shown in Figure 4.2. To open this dialog box, chose Project ➤ Project Properties.

FIGURE 4.2

In the Project Properties dialog box, you select the Form that is displayed when the application starts.

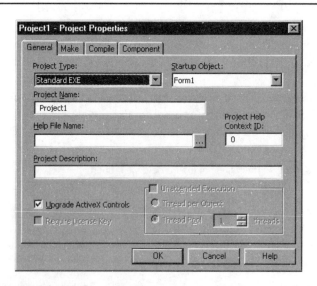

By default, Visual Basic suggests the name of the first Form it created when the project started, which is Form1. If you change the name of the Form, Visual Basic won't use the new name. Instead, when you try to start the application, Visual Basic displays an error message, indicating that you must specify the startup object, and then it displays the Project Properties window.

You can also start an application with a subroutine, without loading a Form. This subroutine must be called Main. If you specify the Main subroutine as the Startup Object in the Project Properties window of Figure 4.2, you must load and display the application's Forms from within the Main subroutine.

Loading, Showing, and Hiding Forms

Before we look at the methods and statements for displaying Forms, we must take a look at the possible states of a Form. A Form can be in one of the following states:

- **Not loaded**   The Form lives on a disk file and doesn't take up any resources.

- **Loaded but not shown**   The Form is loaded into memory, takes up the required resources, and is ready to be displayed.

- **Loaded and shown**   The Form is shown, and the user can interact with it.

Show   To show a Form, you use the Show method. If the Form is loaded but invisible, the Show method brings the specified Form to the top. If the Form isn't loaded, the Show method loads it and then displays it. The Show method has the following syntax:

```
formName.Show mode
```

The *formName* variable is the Form's name, and the optional argument *mode* determines whether the Form will be modal or modeless. It can have one of the following values:

- 0 Modeless (default)

- 1 Modal

A modal Form takes total control of the application and won't let the applications proceed unless the Form is closed. A modal Form, therefore, must have a Close button or some means for the user to close it so that he or she can return to the Form from which the modal Form was loaded. The InputBox() function displays a modal window. Unless the user clicks on the OK or Cancel button, the program can't continue. When an Input Box is displayed, you can't even switch back to the program's main window.

WARNING In effect, modal Forms disable all other parts of the application, but not any other applications that are running at the moment. When a modal Form is displayed, you can't switch to other Forms in the same application, but you can switch to other applications.

Modeless Forms are the norm. They interact with the user, and they allow the user to switch to any other Form of the application. All modeless Forms are equivalent in that the user can chose any Form and interact with it. If you don't specify the optional *mode* argument, the Show method displays the Form as modeless.

The Show method will also load the Form if necessary. Then why load and then show a Form if the Show method takes care of both steps? There are two reasons for loading Forms separately:

- Some Forms need not be displayed; you must only load them. These Forms may contain procedures needed by other applications or have a special function, such as doing something in the background. For example, a Form with a Timer control that tracks time or other events need not have a visible user interface.

- You can speed up the display of a Form by loading it ahead of time. Loading a Form takes time, especially if the Form contains large bitmaps or many controls. The delay associated with loading a Form can be avoided if the Form is loaded on startup. The loading time won't be reduced by loading a Form at startup, but after the application is loaded and running, there won't be any substantial delays. The Forms will be in memory, and the Show method can display them instantly.

Loading and Unloading Forms

To load and unload Forms, use the Load and Unload statements. The Load statement has the following syntax:

```
Load formName
```

And the Unload statement has this syntax:

```
Unload formName
```

The *formName* variable is the name of the Form to be loaded or unloaded. Unlike the Show method, which takes care of both loading and displaying the Form, the

Load statement doesn't show the Form. You have to call the Form's Show method to display it on the Desktop.

Once a Form is loaded, it takes over the required resources, so you should always unload a Form that's no longer needed. When a Form is unloaded, the resources it occupies are returned to the system and can be used by other Forms and/or applications. Because loading a Form isn't instant, especially if the Form contains bitmaps or other resources that entail loading large files, don't unload a Form frequently in the course of an application. If your application contains many Forms, balance the benefit of having them all in memory versus loading certain Forms as needed. Opening a database and setting up the related structures (we'll look at them in Chapter 11, *Database Programming with Visual Basic*), for instance, doesn't take place instantly, and your application shouldn't load and unload Forms that access databases. It's best to keep the Form loaded in memory and display it when the user needs it.

VB5 at Work: The FormLoad Application

By default, Visual Basic loads and displays the first Form of the project. If the loading process takes more than a second, the user simply has to wait. The Form-Load application demonstrates a technique for handling slow-loading Forms. You can't shorten the load time, but you can improve the subjective delay, the delay perceived by the user. The LoadForm application loads two Forms, and this takes a while. The delay is artificial, but it simulates a real-world condition.

The FormLoad application has three Forms, as shown in Figure 4.3. The first one, shown on top of the others, is a simple, quick-loading Form with a couple of messages. You could place your company logo or other useful (or, at least, less-boring) information on the first Form. Initially, the messages on the main Form indicate that the application is loading and ask the user to wait. This Form loads the two slow-loading Forms in the background. As each Form is loaded, the main Form's caption changes to indicate which Form is currently loading. After both Forms are loaded, the two command buttons at the bottom of the Form are enabled, and the messages on the Form change to those shown in Figure 4.3.

The absolutely essential code for loading the two Forms is as follows:

```
Load Form2
Load Form3
```

FIGURE 4.3

The FormLoad application loads two Forms in the background, reducing the perceived delay.

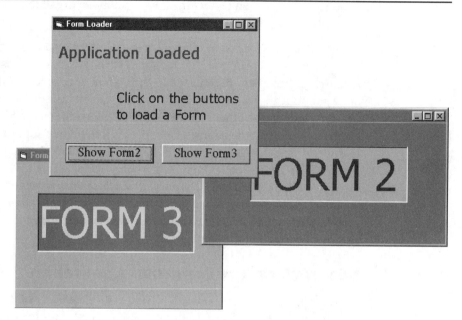

If you use these two lines to load the other Forms of the application, the first Form won't display properly before the loading process starts. Windows loads the Form in memory and then waits for an opportunity to draw it on the screen. Windows gets this opportunity when other applications aren't running. The first Form is loaded, and then the code on the Form starts executing. And while the code is running, nothing happens on the display. To give Windows a chance to load the first Form, display it, and then load the other two Forms, insert the following code in the first Form's Load event:

```
Private Sub Form_Load()

    Form1.Show
    Form1.Refresh
    Form1.Caption = "Loading Form2..."
    Load Form2
    Form1.Caption = "Loading Form3..."
    Load Form3

    Form1.Caption = "Form Loader"
    Command1.Visible = True
    Command2.Visible = True
```

```
Label1.Caption = "Application Loaded"
Label2.Caption = "Click on the buttons to load a Form"
```

End Sub

If you omit the Form1.Show method, the main Form won't be displayed before the other two Forms are loaded. The Refresh method tells Visual Basic to update the display before executing the following commands. By default, Visual Basic refreshes the display only when it gets a chance, and this is when it's not executing any code. If you load a Form from within your code, you must call the Refresh method to redraw the screen.

The program then sets the main Form's caption to a message indicating that Form2 is being loaded and loads Form2. After Form2 is loaded, it does the same for Form3. It displays a similar message in its caption and loads the Form. After both Forms are loaded, it resets its caption and makes the two buttons at the bottom visible so that the user can display the Forms Form2 and Form3. The code behind the Show Form2 button is:

```
Form2.Show
```

And the code behind the Show Form3 button is:

```
Form3.Show
```

Run the application and see how it works. To contrast this approach with the default behavior of Visual Basic, comment out the lines that load the two Forms. If you do so, the Forms are loaded when the user clicks on the corresponding button. They will be loaded just as slow as before, but there's a big difference. This delay is perceived by the user. When you click on a button, you want something to happen. But with a slow-loading Form, nothing happens for a few seconds. When an application is starting, though, you will put up with some delay, in other words, the perceived delay. The Forms will take just as long to load in either case, but loading them when the user isn't actually working is less obtrusive and therefore more tolerable. A Form that takes more than a second to load at run time takes points from your application. It makes it look amateurish, not well designed, and certainly not as user friendly as it should be.

Here's how I simulated the delay. The Load events of the Form2 and Form3 Forms contain the following code:

```
Private Sub Form_Load()
    Dim LTime
    LTime = Timer()
    While Timer() - LTime < 5
```

```
    Wend
End Sub
```

The Timer() function returns the number of seconds elapsed since midnight and is used to delay the loading for 5 seconds. The total delay is 10 seconds, 5 for each Form. This code works well unless you start the application a few seconds before midnight. The Timer() function is reset at midnight.

The DoEvents Statement   As mentioned, Windows doesn't deal with the display if it's busy executing code. In other words, the update of the display has a low priority in the Windows "to-do" list. The code that implements the artificial delay in the loading of a Form is a tight loop. While it's executing, it takes over the application. You can switch to another application if you wish (Windows 95 is a multitasking environment), but the FormLoad application appears to be frozen. For example, you can't resize the application's main Form or move it around. Many users like to reposition Forms on the desktop or resize them when the application starts. The FormLoad application is frozen because the code that's executing doesn't give Windows a chance to handle the display.

To give Windows a chance to do something about the display, you must call the DoEvents statement. The DoEvents statement tells your application to give Windows a chance to take care of its own chores. It doesn't relinquish control to the operating system; it simply gives it a little time to take care of any pending tasks, and the control is returned immediately to the application. To experiment with the DoEvents statement, modify the While loop as shown here:

```
Private Sub Form_Load()
    Dim LTime
    LTime = Timer()
    While Timer() - LTime < 5
        DoEvents
    Wend
End Sub
```

Now run the application and see how it reacts when you attempt to reposition or resize the main Form while the two Forms are being loaded. The application is no longer frozen. It reacts to external events as it should.

The DoEvents statement can introduce significant delays. If you have a loop that might execute a million times, you can't return control to the operating system with each iteration. Each time a new process takes control of the CPU, some overhead is required. It doesn't take long, but if you add up these delays, the DoEvents statement may harm your application rather than help it. Using the

DoEvents statement effectively takes some experience and experimentation. We will come back to this topic in Chapter 6, *Drawing and Painting with Visual Basic*, and we will look at a few techniques for balancing the requirements of quick code execution and proper application behavior.

Controlling One Form from within Another

You've learned how to load a Form from within another. In many situations, this is all the interaction you need between Forms. Each Form is designed to operate independently of the others, and they can communicate via global variables. In other situations, however, you may need to control one Form from within another. Controlling the Form means accessing its controls and setting or reading their values from within another form's code.

Look at the two Forms in Figure 4.4, for instance. These are Forms of the TextPad application, which we are going to develop in Chapter 5, *Basic ActiveX Controls*. TextPad is a text editor and is a single-Form application, with the exception of the Search and Replace command. All other operations on the text are performed with the commands of the menu you see on the main Form. When the user wants to search for and/or replace a string, the program displays another Form, on which the user specifies the text to find, the type of search, and so on. When the user clicks on one of the Form's buttons, the corresponding code must access the text on the other Form and search for a word or replace a string with another. You'll see how this works in Chapter 5. In this chapter, we will develop a simple example to demonstrate how you can access another Form's controls.

FIGURE 4.4

The Search & Replace Form acts on the contents of a control on another Form.

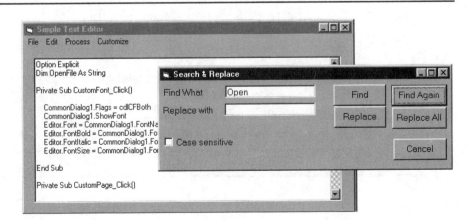

Accessing a Form's controls from within another is straightforward. Simply prefix the control's name with the name of the Form. For example, to access the Text property of the Text1 control on the Form, you use the following expression:

```
Text1.Text
```

To access the same property from within another Form, you use this expression:

```
Form1.Text1.Text
```

Form1 is the name of the Form to which the Text1 control belongs. You can actually have a Text1 control on two Forms, Form1 and Form2. The expression `Text1.Text` is the Text property of the Text1 control on either control. If the following statement:

```
Text1.Text = "some text"
```

is executed from within Form1, it assigns the string "some text" to the Text1 control on the Form1 Form. If the same statement is executed from within Form2, it assigns the same string to the Text1 control on the Form2 Form. To access the control on the other Form, you prefix the expression with the name of the Form.

TIP

You can actually manipulate the properties of the controls on a Form that is not loaded. Visual Basic loads the Form and changes its property, but does not display the Form. When the Form is later displayed, you will see that the property has changed value.

Accessing Forms from within Their Controls

You can also control the Form from within the various controls, using the Parent property. The active control on a Form (the control that has the focus) is returned by the ActiveControl property. The expression `ActiveControl` returns a handle (a reference) to the active control. If the active control is the Command1 command button, the expression `ActiveControl` is a synonym for Command1.

One of the properties of the ActiveControl object is the Parent property, which returns a handle to the object on which the active control is placed. Since most controls are placed on Forms, the expression `ActiveControl .Parent` is a reference to the current Form. To access the Form's Caption property, for instance, use a statement such as the following:

```
ActiveControl.Parent.Caption = "I belong to this Form"
```

With similar expressions, you can access all the members of the Form (properties and methods) and even pass them as arguments to procedures.

Suppose you have a subroutine that can perform certain actions on Forms. In our example, the action is simple: It paints the Form red. Instead of writing a subroutine for each Form, you can pass to this subroutine a handle to the Form it must act upon. Here is the definition of the subroutine:

```
Sub DoSomethingWithForm(Frm As Object)
    MsgBox "I will paint the " & Frm.Name & " Form"
    Frm.BackColor = vbRed
End Sub
```

This subroutine accepts as an argument an object, which is presumably the Form whose background it must change. The subroutine can be called from within any control's code with a statement such as the following:

```
Private Sub Command1_Click()
    DoSomethingWithForm ActiveControl.Parent
End Sub
```

The expression `ActiveControl.Parent` is a reference to the object that contains the active control. If the command button is placed on another control, and not on the Form, this example may not work.

To use this technique in your applications, you must first examine the type of object passed to the DoSomethingWithForm() subroutine and make sure that it has a BackColor property. You can do so with the TypeOf keyword, which is explained in the section "Drag-and-Drop Operations," later in this chapter.

VB5 at Work: The Forms Application

The Forms application demonstrates the Load and Unload statements and the Show and Hide methods as well as how to access the properties and methods of one Form from within another. The application's main Form, shown in Figure 4.5, is called Form Handling. This Form contains two groups of identical controls, under the headings Form2 and Form3. (Only Form2 is shown in Figure 4.5. Form3 is identical to Form2; it just contains a different graphic.) These two Forms are loaded, shown, and hidden from within the main Form. You can also specify whether the Forms will be shown as modal or modeless.

FIGURE 4.5

The Forms application demonstrates how to manipulate Forms from within other Forms.

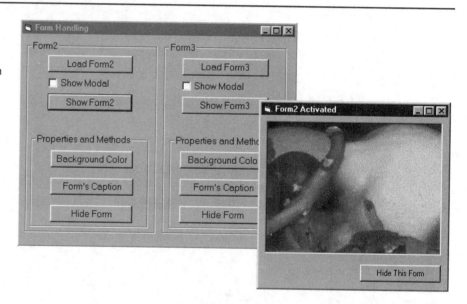

After the Forms Form2 and Form3 are loaded, you can use the buttons in the lower half of the main Form to set their BackColor and Caption properties and to call their Hide method. Let's look at the code behind the various buttons of the Forms application's main Form.

Code 4.1: The Load Form2 Button

```
Private Sub LoadForm2_Click()

    If LoadForm2.Caption = "Load Form2" Then
        Load Form2
```

```
        LoadForm2.Caption = "Unload Form2"
    Else
        Unload Form2
        LoadForm2.Caption = "Load Form2"
    End If

End Sub
```

The Load Form2 button is a toggle. If the Form is already loaded, it unloads it and sets its own caption accordingly. The Show Form2 button calls the Show method to show the Form2 Form (whether or not it's been loaded). The code behind the Show Form2 button takes into consideration the state of the Show Modal checkbox. If it's checked, it shows the Form as modal.

Code 4.2: The Show Form2 Button

```
Private Sub ShowForm2_Click()

    Form2.Show Form2Modal.Value

End Sub
```

The checkbox's Value property is 0 or 1, which happens to be the same as the valid values of the Show method's Mode argument.

The Background Color button sets the background color of the Form2 Form to a random color.

Code 4.3: The Background Color Button

```
Private Sub Form2Color_Click()

    Form2.BackColor = QBColor(Rnd() * 15)

End Sub
```

And the Form's Caption button sets the caption of the Form with the following statement.

Code 4.4: The Caption Button

```
Private Sub Form2Caption_Click()

    Form2.Caption = "Caption changed!"

End Sub
```

Finally, the Hide Form button hides the Form by calling its Hide method.

Code 4.5: The Hide Form Button

```
Private Sub HideForm2_Click()

    Form2.Hide

End Sub
```

The code behind the buttons of the second group on the Forms application is quite similar, only it refers to the Form3 Form instead of Form2.

The Activate and Deactivate Events   When more than one Form is displayed, the user can switch from one to the other with the mouse or by pressing Alt+Tab. Each time a Form is activated, the Activate event takes place. The Forms application uses the Activate event to set the Form's caption to a message indicating that this is the current Form:

```
Private Sub Form_Activate()

    Form2.Caption = "Form2 Activated"

End Sub
```

Likewise, when a Form is activated, the previously active Form receives the Deactivate event, which the application uses to change the Form's caption:

```
Private Sub Form_Deactivate()

    Form2.Caption = "Form2 Inactive"

End Sub
```

NOTE   It is possible to manipulate the properties and call the methods of the controls on a Form from within another Form, but the events are reported to the controls themselves. In other words, you can't capture the events of one form's controls from within another Form.

Designing Menus

Menus are one of the most important and most characteristic elements of the Windows user interface. Even in the old days of character-based displays, menus were used to display methodically organized choices and guide the user through an application. Despite the visually rich interfaces of Windows applications and the many alternatives, menus are still the most popular means of organizing a large number of options. Many applications duplicate some or all of their menus in the form of icons on a toolbar, but the menu is a standard fixture of a Form. You can turn the toolbars on and off, but not the menus.

Menus can be attached only to Forms, and you design them with the Menu Editor. To see how the Menu Editor works, start a new Standard EXE project, and when Form1 appears in the design window, choose Tools ➢ Menu Editor to open the Menu Editor, as shown in Figure 4.6. Alternatively, you can click on the Menu Editor button on the toolbar. The Menu Editor's window (shown in Figure 4.6) will appear.

FIGURE 4.6

The Menu Editor's window displaying a simple menu structure

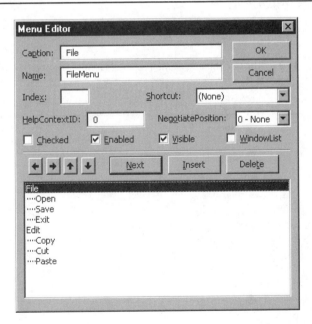

In this window you can specify the structure of your menu by adding one command at a time. Each menu command has two mandatory properties:

- **Caption**   The string that appears on the application's menu bar.

- **Name**   The name of the menu command. This property doesn't appear on the screen, but your code uses it to program the menu command.

The Caption and Name properties of a menu item are analogous to the properties that have the same name as the Command Button or Label control. Caption is what the user sees on the Form, and Name is the means of accessing the control from within the code. As far as your code is concerned, each menu command is a separate object, just like a Command Button or a Label control.

To add commands to the Form's menu bar, enter a caption and a name for each command. As soon as you start typing the command's caption, it also appears in a new line in the list at the bottom of the Menu Editor window. Let's create the menu structure shown in Figure 4.6. This menu contains two commands, File and Edit. When the user clicks on either one, the submenus are displayed.

Table 4.2 shows the Caption and Name properties for each command.

TABLE 4.2   The Caption and Name Properties for the File and Edit Commands

CAPTION	NAME
File	FileMenu
Open	FileOpen
Save	FileSave
Exit	FileExit
Edit	EditMenu
Copy	EditCopy
Cut	EditCut
Paste	EditPaste

The commands that belong to each menu form the corresponding submenu and are indented from the left. To design the menu follow these steps:

1. Open a new Form in the Design pane, and choose Tools ➤ Menu Editor to open the Menu Editor window.

2. In the Caption box, type the caption of the first command (File).

3. In the Name box, enter the command's name (FileMenu).

4. Press Enter or click on Next to enter the next command. Repeat steps 1 through 3 for all the commands listed.

If you run the application now, all the commands you've entered are displayed along the Form's menu bar. If the window isn't wide enough to fit the entire menu, some of the menu's commands are wrapped to a second line.

To create the menu hierarchy (make the commands appear under the File and Edit headings), you must indent them. Select the Open command in the list and click on the button that has the right-pointing arrow. Do the same for the Save, Copy, Cut, and Paste commands. Your Menu Editor window should look like the one in Figure 4.6, earlier in this chapter.

If you run the application now, the menu has the proper appearance. Each subordinate command appears under the first-level menu command to which it belongs. To view the subordinate commands, click on the corresponding top-level command. For example, to select the Paste command, first open the Edit menu.

You can nest menu commands to more than two levels by selecting a command and pressing the button with the right-pointing arrow more than once. When a menu command leads to a submenu, an arrow appears to its right, indicating that, if selected, it will lead to a submenu.

TIP

To create a separator bar in a menu, create a command as usual and set its Caption to a hyphen (-). A horizontal line is displayed in the place of the command. Separator bars divide menu items into logical groups, and even though they have the structure of regular menu commands, they don't react to the mouse click.

The remaining properties on the Menu Editor window are optional and are described next.

The Index Property   You can create an array of menu commands. All the commands have the same name and a unique index that distinguishes them. When appending a list of recently opened filenames in the File menu, it's customary to create an array of menu commands (one for each filename); all have the same name but a different index.

The Checked Property   Some menu commands act like toggles, and they are usually checked to indicate that they are on or unchecked to indicate that they are off. To display a checkmark next to a menu command initially, select the command from the list by clicking on its name, and then check the Checked box in the Menu Editor window. You can also access this property from within your code, to change the checked status of a menu command at run time, by manipulating its Checked property.

The Enabled Property   Some menu commands aren't always available. The Paste command, for example, has no meaning if the Clipboard is empty. To indicate that a command can't be used at the time, you set its Enabled property to False. The command then appears grayed in the menu, and although it can be selected with the mouse, it can't be activated. You can set the initial status of a command by checking or clearing the Enabled box in the Menu Editor window. You can also toggle the status of a menu command from within your code by manipulating its Enabled property.

The Visible Property   Set a command's Visible property to False to remove it temporarily from the menu. The Visible property isn't used frequently in menu design. In general, you should prefer to disable a command to indicate that it can't be used (some other action is required to enable it). Making a command invisible frustrates users, who may try to locate the command in another menu.

Window List   This option is used with MDI (Multiple Document Interface) applications to maintain a list of all open windows. The Window List option is explained in Chapter 9, *The Multiple Document Interface*.

TIP

The place to set menu control properties is the Menu Editor window. Each menu command, however, is another object on the Form to which it belongs, as are command buttons. It is therefore possible to set a menu object's properties through the Properties window. You can't, however, select a command on the menu bar and then look up its properties in the Properties window. You must expand the list of objects above the properties, select the menu object you are interested in by name, and then view (or change) the menu object's properties.

Programming Menu Commands

Menu commands are similar to controls. They have certain properties that you can manipulate from within your code, and they recognize a single event, the Click event. If you select a menu command at design time, Visual Basic opens the code for the Click event in the Code window. The name of the event handler for the Click event is composed of the command's name followed by an underscore character and the event's name, as with all other controls.

You can also manipulate the menu command's properties from within your code. These properties are the ones you can set at design time, through the Menu Editor window. Menu commands don't have methods you can call.

Most menu object properties are toggles. To change the Checked property of the FontBold command, for instance, use the following statement:

```
FontBold = Not FontBold
```

If the command is checked, the checkmark will be removed. If the command is unchecked, the checkmark will be inserted in front of its name.

You can also change the command's caption at run time, although this practice isn't common. The Caption property is manipulated only when you create dynamic menus by adding and removing commands at run time, as you will see in the section "Adding Commands at Run Time."

Using Access and Shortcut Keys

Menus are a convenient way of displaying a large number of choices to the user. They allow you to organize commands in groups according to their function, and they are available at will. Opening menus and selecting commands with the mouse, however, can be an inconvenience. When using a word processor, for example, you don't want to have to take your hands off the keyboard and reach for the mouse. To simplify menu access, Visual Basic supports *access keys* and *shortcut keys*.

Access Keys

Access keys allow the user to open a menu by pressing the Alt key and a letter key. To open the Edit menu in all Windows applications, for example, you can press Alt+E. E is the Edit menu's access key. Once the menu is open, the user can select a command with the arrow keys or by pressing another key, which is the command's shortcut key. For example, with the Edit menu open, you can press P to invoke the Paste command or C to copy the selected text.

Access keys are designated by the designer of the application, and they are marked with an underline character. The underline under the character E in the Edit menu denotes that E is the menu's access key and that the keystroke Alt+E opens the Edit command. To assign an access key to a menu command, insert the ampersand symbol (&) in front of the character you want to use as an access key in the menu's caption.

NOTE   If you don't designate access keys, Visual Basic uses the first character in each top-level menu as its access key. The user won't see the underline character under the first character, but will be able to open the menu by pressing the first character of its caption while holding down the Alt key. If two or more menu captions begin with the same letter, the first menu will open.

Because the & symbol has a special meaning in menu design, you can't use it as is. To actually display the & symbol in a caption, prefix it with another & symbol. For example, the caption &Drag produces a command with the caption Drag, and the first character is underlined because it's the access key. The Caption Drag && Drop will create another command, whose caption will be Drag & Drop. Finally, the string &Drag && Drop will create another command with the caption Drag & Drop, with the first character underlined.

Shortcut Keys

Shortcut keys are similar to access keys, but instead of opening a menu, they run a command when pressed. Assign shortcut keys to frequently used menu commands so that users can reach them with a single keystroke. Shortcut keys are combinations of the Control key and a function or a character key.

To assign a shortcut key to a menu command, drop down the Shortcut list in the Menu Editor and select a keystroke. You don't have to insert any special characters in the command's Caption, nor do you have to enter the keystroke next to the caption. It will be displayed next to the command automatically. Figure 4.7 shows some of the possible shortcut keys you can assign to your menus.

FIGURE 4.7

Unlike access keys, shortcut keys can't be assigned at will. You must select them from the Shortcut list.

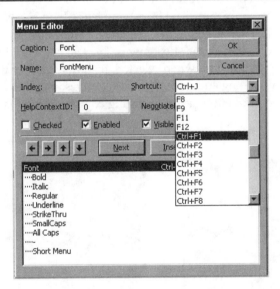

<table>
<tr><td colspan="2">Menu Editor</td><td>☒</td></tr>
<tr><td>Ca<u>p</u>tion:</td><td>Font</td><td>OK</td></tr>
<tr><td>Na<u>m</u>e:</td><td>FontMenu</td><td>Cancel</td></tr>
</table>

Inde<u>x</u>:   <u>S</u>hortcut: Ctrl+J

HelpContextID: 0   Ne<u>g</u>otiate

☐ <u>C</u>hecked   ☑ <u>E</u>nabled   ☑ <u>V</u>isible

← → ↑ ↓   <u>N</u>ext   Ins

F8
F9
F11
F12
Ctrl+F1
Ctrl+F2
Ctrl+F3
Ctrl+F4
Ctrl+F5
Ctrl+F6
Ctrl+F7
Ctrl+F8

Font   Ctrl
····Bold
····Italic
····Regular
····Underline
····StrikeThru
····SmallCaps
····All Caps
·····
····Short Menu

TIP

When assigning access and shortcut keys, take into consideration some well-established Windows standards. Users expect Alt+F to open the File menu. Don't use Alt+F for the Format menu. Likewise, when the Edit menu is open, pressing C selects the Copy command and pressing t selects the Cut command. Don't use the C key as a shortcut for the Cut command.

Manipulating Menus at Run Time

Dynamic menus change at run time and display more or fewer commands, depending on the current status of the program. This section explores two techniques for implementing dynamic menus:

- Creating short and long versions of the same menu
- Adding and removing menu commands at run time

Creating Short and Long Menus

A common technique in menu design is to create long and short versions of a menu. If a menu contains many commands, and most of the time only a few of them are needed, you can create one menu with all the commands and another with the most common ones. The first menu is the long one, and the second is the short one. The last command in the long menu should be Short Menu, and, when selected, it should display the short menu. The last command in the short menu should be Long Menu, and, when selected, it should display the long menu. Figure 4.8 shows a long and a short version of the same menu. The short version omits the not so frequently used formatting commands and is easier to handle.

FIGURE 4.8

The two versions of the Font menu of the LongMenu application

To implement the LongMenu command, start a new project and create a menu that has the structure shown in Table 4.3.

TABLE 4.3 The Structure of the LongMenu Command

COMMAND NAME	CAPTION
FontMenu	Font
mFontBold	Bold
mFontItalic	Italic
mFontRegular	Regular
mFontUline	Underline
mFontStrike	StrikeThru
mFontSmallCaps	SmallCaps
mFontAllCaps	All Caps
separator	"-" (an underscore without the quotes)
MenuSize	Short Menu

The code that shows/hides the long menu is in the MenuSize command's Click event:

Code 4.6: The MenuSize Menu Item's Click Event

```
Private Sub MenuSize_Click()

    If MenuSize.Caption = "Short Menu" Then
        MenuSize.Caption = "Long Menu"
    Else
        MenuSize.Caption = "Short Menu"
    End If
    mFontUline.Visible = Not mFontUline.Visible
    mFontStrike.Visible = Not mFontStrike.Visible
    mFontSmallCaps.Visible = Not mFontSmallCaps.Visible
    mFontAllCaps.Visible = Not mFontAllCaps.Visible

End Sub
```

This subroutine doesn't do much. It simply toggle the Visible property of certain menu commands to False and changes the command's caption to "Short Menu" or "Long Menu," depending on the menu's current status.

Adding and Removing Commands at Run Time

We'll conclude our discussion of menu design with a technique for building dynamic menus, which grow and shrink at run time. Many applications maintain a list of the most recently opened files in their File menu. When you first start the application, this list is empty, and as you open and close files, it starts to grow.

To create a dynamic menu, you first create a control array of menu commands. In the Menu Editor window, add a menu option and set its Index property to 0. You can then add commands with the same name and consecutive Index values. You don't have to add more options at design time. One command with its Index property set to 0 is adequate to create the menu control array. You can use this array's name and an index value to add new options at run time.

> **TIP**
>
> The elements of a menu control array must be contiguous in the menu control list box and must be at the same level of indention.

Figure 4.9 shows the RTMenu application, which demonstrates how to add to and remove items from a menu at run time.

FIGURE 4.9

The RTMenu application

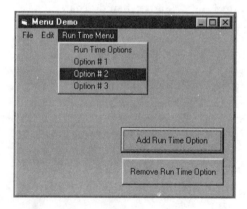

Initially, the form's menu contains the following items:

File

    Open

    Save

    Exit

Edit

    Copy

    Cut

    Paste

Run Time Menu

Commands grouped in submenus are indented from the left. The last command's Name is RunTimeOptions, and its Index is 0. Once a command option is specified as a control array, you can easily add members to the RunTimeOptions() array with the Load method.

The two buttons at the bottom of the Form add to and remove commands from the Run Time Menu. Each new command is appended at the end of the menu, and the commands are removed from the bottom of the menu (the most recently added commands).

Code 4.7: The RTMenu Application

```
Option Explicit
Dim RTmenu

Private Sub AddCommand_Click()

    RTmenu = RTmenu + 1
    If RTmenu = 1 Then RunTimeOptions(0).Caption = "Run Time
Options"
    Load RunTimeOptions(RTmenu)
    RunTimeOptions(RTmenu).Caption = "Option # " & RTmenu

End Sub

Private Sub RemoveCommand_Click()

    If RTmenu = 0 Then
```

```
        MsgBox "Menu is empty"
        Exit Sub
    End If
    Unload RunTimeOptions(RTmenu)
    RTmenu = RTmenu - 1

End Sub
```

New menu commands are appended to the existing menu with the Load method. The argument of the Load method is the name of a menu command with a new Index value. The variable *RTMenu* keeps track of the number of commands under the Run Time Menu menu object. Each time a new command is added to this menu, *RTMenu* is incremented by 1. The Remove Run Time Option button uses the Unload method to remove commands from the same menu. The argument to the Unload method is the index of the command to be removed. This sample application removes commands from the bottom of the menu, but you could remove any command by specifying its order in the menu.

> **NOTE**
> The Load and Unload methods are not new to you. We used them in the first section of the chapter to load and unload Forms. In addition to these two methods, you can also call the Hide method, to hide menu commands. Calling the Hide method is equivalent to setting the corresponding command's Visible property to False.

Creating Pop-Up Menus

Nearly every Windows application provides a context menu (or shortcut menu, as it's sometimes called) that the user can invoke by right-clicking on a Form or a control. The pop-up menu (or floating menu) is a regular menu, but it's not anchored on the Form. It can be displayed anywhere on the Form.

Pop-up menus are invoked with the PopupMenu method. First, you create a menu as usual. Suppose you have designed the basic File and Edit menus for an application, and they are displayed on the Form as usual. To make the application a bit easier to use, you can also display the Edit menu as a pop-up menu. If the Edit menu's name is EditMenu, you can insert the following line in a control's MouseUp event:

```
Private Sub Form_MouseUp(Button As Integer, Shift As Integer, X As
➥Single, Y As Single)
```

```
    If Button = 2 Then PopupMenu EditMenu
End Sub
```

(We use the MouseUp event because it reports which button was pressed.)

If the right mouse button is pressed, the code calls the Form's PopupMenu method to display the Edit menu. The PopupMenu method is usually called from within TextBox and PictureBox controls, because these controls can carry out editing operations.

> **TIP**
>
> If you don't want the pop-up menu to appear in the application's menu bar, you must still create the menu as usual with the Menu Editor and then set its Visible property to False. Each time the menu is invoked with the PopupMenu method, Visual Basic ignores the setting of the Visible method.

The PopupMenu method has the following syntax:

```
PopupMenu menuname, flags,x, y, boldcommand
```

Only the first argument is required, and it is the menu's name, as shown in the Menu Editor window. The other arguments are optional. The *x* and *y* arguments are the coordinates of a point on the Form (or control) where the menu will be displayed. The *flags* argument defines the location and behavior of a pop-up menu and can have one of the values shown in Table 4.4.

TABLE 4.4   The Values for the *flags* Argument

CONSTANTS	DESCRIPTION
Location	
vbPopupMenuLeftAlign	(default) The specified x location defines the left edge of the pop-up menu.
VbPopupMenuCenterAlign	The pop-up menu is centered around the specified x location.
VbPopupMenuRightAlign	The specified x location defines the right edge of the pop-up menu.

TABLE 4.4   The Values for the *flags* Argument (continued)

CONSTANTS	DESCRIPTION
Behavior	
vbPopupMenuLeftButton	(default) The pop-up menu triggers the Click event when the user clicks on a menu item with the left mouse button only.
vbPopupMenuRightButton	The pop-up menu triggers the Click event when the user clicks on a menu item with either the right or the left mouse button.

To specify a value from each group, combine them with the OR operator. The following code displays a pop-up menu with its top border centered on the Form, which triggers Click events for menu items that are clicked with either mouse button.

```
x = ScaleWidth / 2
y = ScaleHeight / 2
Form1.PopupMenu EditMenu, vbPopupMenuCenterAlign Or _
        vbPopupMenuRightButton, X, Y
```

The last argument, BoldCommand, specifies the name of a menu command that should appear in bold. Only one command in the menu can be bold, and bold is commonly used to denote the default (or suggested) option.

Drag-and-Drop Operations

A unique characteristic of the Windows user interface is the ability to grab a control and drop it on another. This feature is called *drag-and-drop* and is used extensively in the Windows Desktop metaphor. Nearly every item on the Windows Desktop can be dragged and dropped on various other items, such as the Recycle Bin, the printers, folders, and so on.

The same principles can be used in applications. Figure 4.10 is a typical example. The Form in Figure 4.10 contains the three file controls that let the user select and view any folder on the disk. The two lists (Move to Temp and Move to Tape) are destinations for various files. You could provide buttons to move files from the FileListBox control to either list, but the most convenient way to move files to the two ListBox controls on the Form is to drag-and-drop them.

FIGURE 4.10

The ListDrop application demonstrates the kind of functionality you can add to your user interface with drag-and-drop operations.

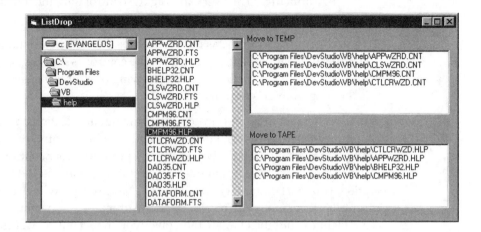

Open the ListDrop project and test-drive the application. To specify the files to be copied to the Temp folder or the tape drive (these features aren't implemented in the code, but you can easily add the code to actually move or copy the selected files), drag them from the FileListBox control to the corresponding List. To undo an action, you can drag a filename from one of the two lists back to the file list. When a filename is moved from the file list to one of the two ListBox controls, the file isn't removed from the file control (you would have to delete the file to remove it from the FileListBox control). When you move a selected filename from the Move to Temp or Move to Tape lists back to the FileListBox control, however, the name of the file is removed from the corresponding list.

Load and run the ListDrop application and check out its ease of operation and its functionality. Compare it with any other user interface design based on more traditional controls, such as command buttons, and you will see that drag-and-drop features can significantly enhance your application's interface. User interfaces based on drag-and-drop operations aren't common, but when an application can benefit from this type of interface, you should implement it. As you will see, doing so is quite easy and is based on a small number of properties, methods, and events.

The DragMode Property   Nearly all controls have a DragMode property, which determines whether a control can be dragged or not with the mouse. The DragMode property can have one of the following settings:

- **0-Manual**   Drag operations must be initiated from within the code.

- **1-Automatic**   The user can drag the control with the mouse.

When you set a control's DragMode property to Automatic, Visual Basic displays the control's outline as the user moves the control around and notifies the controls that happen to be underneath the control as it's dragged. Visual Basic doesn't perform any actions, such as copying one control's text onto another. This is the programmer's responsibility.

To implement drag-and-drop features in your applications, you must first decide which controls can be dragged and on which control they can be dropped. The control being dragged is the source control. All other controls on the Form are the destinations of the drag-and-drop operation. To initiate a drag-and-drop operation, you must either set a control's DragMode property to Automatic or call the control's Drag method. The DragMode=Automatic setting and the Drag method are identical, but the Drag method gives you more control over the operation. For example, you may not initiate a drag operation if the source control is empty.

The DragDrop and DragOver Methods   A drag operation ends with a drop operation, that is, when the user releases the mouse button. By default, controls don't react to the drop operation. To make a control react when another control is dropped on it, you must supply some code in its DragDrop event, whose definition is as follows:

```
Sub control_DragDrop(Source As Control, X As Single, Y As Single)
```

The *control* item can be any control on the Form. *Source* is an object that represents the control that was dropped. It's not a control's name or other property; it's an object variable. You can use it to access the various properties of the control that was dropped. *X* and *Y* are the coordinates of the mouse at the moment the source control was dropped on the destination control.

In addition to reacting to the dropping of a source control, the destination control can react to the movement of a control being dragged over it. This condition is detected with the DragOver event, which is generated as long as the source control is dragged over the destination control. The definition of the DragOver event is as follows:

```
Private Sub control_DragOver(Source As Control, X As Single, Y As
➡Single, State As Integer)
```

Source is the control being dragged, *X* and *Y* are the current coordinates of the mouse, and the *State* argument corresponds to the transition state of the control being dragged. It can have one of the following values:

- 0   The source control entered the target's area.
- 1   The source control left the target's area.
- 2   The source control moves over the target's area.

VB5 at Work: The DrpEvnts Application

To see these events in actions, let's design the application shown in Figure 4.11. The application is called DrpEvnts, and you will find it in this chapter's folder on the CD.

FIGURE 4.11

The DrpEvnts application

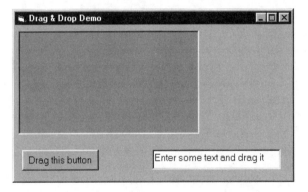

The application monitors the dragging of the command button and reacts as follows.

- When the button is first dragged over the picture box, the picture box is painted red.
- When the button leaves the picture box, the picture box is painted green.
- If the user drops the button while it's over the picture box, the picture box is painted blue.

To design the application, follow these steps:

1. Start a new project and place a picture box and a command button on the Form.

2. Set the PictureBox control's Background property to a green color, and set the command button's DragMode property to 1-Automatic.

3. Enter the following code in the PictureBox control's DragOver event handler:

```
Private Sub Picture1_DragOver(Source As Control, X As Single, Y
➡As Single, State As Integer)

    If State = 0 Then Picture1.BackColor = vbRed
    If State = 2 Then Form1.Caption = "Source Control moves
    ➡over the PictureBox"
    If State = 1 Then
        Picture1.BackColor = vbGreen
        Form1.Caption = "Drag & Drop Demo"
    End If

End Sub
```

And enter the following code in the control's DragDrop event:

```
Private Sub Picture1_DragDrop(Source As Control, X As Single, Y
➡As Single)

    Picture1.BackColor = vbBlue

End Sub
```

Run the application and see how it monitors the movement of the mouse. The *State* argument of the DragOver event takes the value 0 only when the button is dragged over the PictureBox control for the first time. After that, the DragOver event is triggered as the button is moved over the picture box, but the *State* argument is 2. Finally, as the button is moved outside the area of the PictureBox control, the DragOver event is triggered one last time, and this time its *State* argument is 1.

Notice that the code of this application is concentrated in the two drag-related events of the Picture Box control and that you didn't have to supply any code for the Command Button's events. Simply setting its DragMode property to Automatic was enough to add the dragging capability to the control. Moreover, the code doesn't use the Source argument of the two events. The Picture Box control would react exactly the same, no matter which control you dragged over or dropped on it.

The TypeOf Keyword   The DragDrop and DragOver events' *Source* argument represents an object so that the destination control can figure out which control was dropped on it. To access the name of the control that was dropped, use the following expression:

```
Source.Name
```

Suppose you want to read the Text property of TextBox controls and the Caption property of Label controls when they are dropped on the destination control. Use the following expressions to return these two properties:

```
Source.Text
Source.Caption
```

But you have to know whether the dropped control was a TextBox control or a Label control. If not, your code may attempt to access the Label's Text property or the TextBox's Caption property and crash with a run-time error.

To find out the type of object dropped, use the TypeOf keyword. It has the following syntax:

```
TypeOf objectname Is objecttype.
```

The *objectname* item is an object, and *objecttype* is an object type. To find out whether the source control is a TextBox control, use an If structure such as the following:

```
If TypeOf Source Is Textbox Then
    MsgBox Source.Text
End If
```

You can use the TypeOf keyword anywhere in any Visual Basic application, but it's commonly used in drag-and-drop operations. We'll use this keyword later in our applications to differentiate the various types of controls being dropped.

Mouse Conflicts

Let's experiment a little with dragging operations. We'll add a line of code to the Command Button's Click event to make the button react to the mouse click by displaying a message in the Immediate window with the following statement:

```
Debug.Print "I was clicked"
```

Run the application and click on the Drag and Drop button with the mouse. No message will appear in the Immediate window. When Visual Basic starts a drag-and-drop operation, it doesn't generate the usual mouse events (Click or Mouse-Down). If you reset the button's DragMode property to 0 (Manual), Visual Basic will start responding to the mouse events on the button, but it won't drag it.

> **NOTE**
>
> When a control's DragMode property is set to True, it stops reacting to the usual mouse events. All you can do is drag the control around, but you can't count on its usual mouse events.

To make matters even worse, add a TextBox control on the Form, set its property to Automatic, and then run the application again. You can enter text in the control, move the control around, but the editing operations of the mouse are gone. If you attempt to select some text with the mouse, a drag operation starts. The editing features of the mouse are taken over by the dragging operations.

Our experiments indicate that automatic dragging must be designed carefully. You can't simply set a control's DragMode to Automatic and expect it to work as before. If the control is a Label, you don't have to worry about editing it. Setting its DragMode property to Automatic isn't going to cause any serious problems, except that you won't be able to use the common mouse events. If you don't need the Click event handler of the Label control in your application, you can set the control's DragMode to Automatic and implement drag-and-drop features. If you set a command button's DragMode to Automatic, you can't count on the control's Click event. The solution to these conflicts is to implement drag-and-drop features manually. You'll see how this is done, but first let's look at a couple of applications.

VB5 at Work: The DragDrop Application

The DragDrop application, shown in Figure 4.12, consists of a single Form that contains a Label, a TextBox, and a PictureBox control. The Label and TextBox controls' DragMode property is set to 1-Automatic, so you can drag them on any other control. Run the application, enter some text in the text box (without using the mouse's editing features, just the keyboard), and then drop the text box on the label.

FIGURE 4.12

The DragDrop
application

If you enter the full path name of an image file in the text box and then drop the control on the Label control, the filename is copied to the Label control. If you drop it on the picture box, the image is displayed there. These are two common uses of drag-and-drop operations.

Code 4.8: The DragDrop Event Handler Code for the TextBox Control

```
Private Sub Text1_DragDrop(Source As Control, X As Single, Y As
Single)
    If TypeOf Source Is Label Then
        Text1.Text = Label1.Caption
    End If
End Sub
```

In this event handler, we make sure that the control being dropped is the Label control, and we assign the TextBox control's Text to the Label control's Caption. You may think that we didn't have to test for the object being dropped, since the Label is the only object that can be dropped on the TextBox control. That's not quite true. You can actually drop an object on itself.

The DragDrop event handler for the Label control is similar.

Code 4.9: The DragDrop Event Handler Code for the Label Control

```
Private Sub Label1_DragDrop(Source As Control, X As Single, Y As
➥Single)
If TypeOf Source Is TextBox Then
    Label1.Caption = Source.Text
End If
End Sub
```

The Label control reacts to the drop of the TextBox control by copying the text to the Label's Caption property. The PictureBox control reacts differently to the drop of either control: It assumes that the contents of the label or the text box control is the filename of an image, which it attempts to display.

Code 4.10: The DragDrop Event Handler Code for the PictureBox Control

```
Private Sub Picture1_DragDrop(Source As Control, X As Single, Y As
➥Single)
Dim imgName
If TypeOf Source Is TextBox Then
    imgName = Source.Text
Else
    imgName = Source.Caption
End If
On Error GoTo NOIMAGE
Picture1.Picture = LoadPicture(imgName)
Exit Sub

NOIMAGE:
    MsgBox "This is not a valid file name"

End Sub
```

First, it extracts the label's caption or the text box's text (depending on the source control), and then it assigns this string to its Picture property. The error handler is there to prevent run-time errors, should the control contain an invalid filename.

NOTE
The drop event can trigger any action on the destination control. It is common to use drag-and-drop operations to allow the user to move information among text boxes or list boxes, but as this example demonstrates, you can process the data dropped on the destination control in any way you see fit.

VB5 at Work: The FormDrop Application

Our next application demonstrates drag-and-drop operations among multiple Forms. The FormDrop application consists of three Forms. The main Form contains two columns of labels, which contain state and city names. The other two Forms each contain a ListBox control, and they are initially empty. The user can drag any of the labels on the main Form and drop them on one of the two lists, which reside on different Forms.

Design the Forms as shown in Figure 4.13. Place any type of data you want in the Label controls.

FIGURE 4.13

The DropForm application lets you drag-and-drop controls among different Forms.

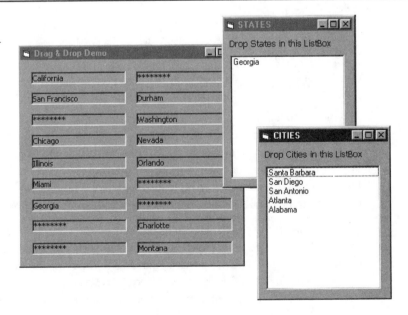

When the main Form is loaded, it must display the other two Forms. Enter the following code in its Load event handler:

```
Private Sub Form_Load()
    DropForm2.Show
    DropForm2.Move DropForm1.Left + DropForm1.Width + 500,
    ➡DropForm1.Top
    DropForm3.Show
    DropForm3.Move DropForm1.Left + DropForm1.Width + 500,
    ➡DropForm1.Top + DropForm2.Height

End Sub
```

The Move method is used to place the smaller Forms to the right of the main Form.

The interesting code is in the DragDrop event handlers of the two ListBox controls.

Code 4.11: The DragDrop Event Handler Code of the ListBox Control on the States Form

```
Private Sub List1_DragDrop(Source As Control, X As Single, Y As
➡Single)
    If Source.Caption = "********" Then
        Beep
        Exit Sub
    End If
    List1.AddItem Source.Caption & "  (" & Source.Parent.Name & ")"
    ➡Source.Caption = "********"
End Sub
```

When a label is dropped on this control, its Caption is set to asterisks to indicate that it can't be dropped again. Since only Label controls can be dropped on the two ListBox controls, there is no need to test for the type of object being dropped. We use the `Source.Caption` expression directly to access the label's caption. The DragDrop event handler for the ListBox control on the Cities Form is identical. Only the name of the ListBox control changes (List2 instead of List1).

Notice that besides the caption of the control that was dropped on the list box, we add the name of the Form from which the label came in parentheses. The expression `Source.Parent` gives you access to the Form to which the source control belongs. Through this expression, you can access the properties of the Form from which the source control came. The expression `Source.Parent.Name` returns the name of the Form on which the labels with the city and state names are placed.

The drag operation's destination control doesn't care where the source control came from. The argument Source has all the information it needs to access the source control's properties, regardless of whether it resides on the same or another Form.

Manual Drag

Now we are going to look at how you can drag editable controls (such as the text box) without sacrificing the control's editing features. To initiate a drag operation manually, call the Drag method. Calling the Drag method for a control is equivalent to setting its DragMode property to 1-Automatic for as long as the control is being dragged. After the control is dropped somewhere on the Form, the DragMode property is reset. The DragMode property doesn't change, but the control behaves temporarily as if its DragMode property were set to 1-Automatic.

When do you call the Drag method of a control? First, you must decide how the application will differentiate between regular editing operations with the mouse and dragging operations. One safe approach is to use the Control or Alt key with the mouse to drag the control. All the functions of the mouse are available as usual. If the mouse button is pressed while the Control key is down, though, the code initiates a drag operation by calling the control's Drag method.

VB5 at Work: The TextDrop Application

Let's see how this is done. Figure 4.14 shows a Form with two TextBox controls and a Label control. The project is called TextDrop and can be found on the CD.

FIGURE 4.14

The TextDrop application demonstrates the differences between automatic and manual dragging.

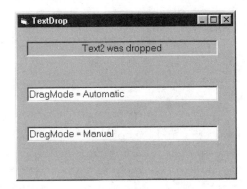

The two text boxes have their DragMode property set to Automatic and Manual, as indicated by the displayed messages. Both text boxes can be dropped on the Label control. Let's start by looking at the code behind the Label control's Drag-Drop event.

Code 4.12: The Label Control's DragDrop Event

```
Private Sub Label1_DragDrop(Source As Control, X As Single, Y As
➥Single)

    Label1.Caption = Source.Name & " was dropped"

End Sub
```

This subroutine displays a message with the name of the control that was dropped on the label. There is no need to test for the type of the control, since all controls have a Name property.

The first control can be dropped automatically. This means that you can edit the contents of the first text box using only the keyboard. To select a range of text on the control, you hold down the Shift key and press the arrow keys. If you drag the mouse on the first text box, it will start moving. Drop it on the Label control, and watch the label's caption change to reflect the name of the control that was dropped.

The second text box can be edited as usual. To drag it, you click on the control while holding down the Control key and then start dragging it. The Drag method of the control is called from within the MouseDown event and if the Control button is pressed.

Code 4.13: The Second TextBox Control's MouseDown Event

```
Private Sub Text2_MouseDown(Button As Integer, Shift As Integer, X
➥As Single, Y As Single)

    If Shift = 2 Then
        Text2.Drag
    End If

End Sub
```

Run the TextDrop application and see how it behaves. The Drag method is quite simple and will become your tool for adding drag-and-drop features to editable controls. You should also use the Drag method with noneditable controls, such as labels or command buttons, that should also react to the common mouse events.

Dragging List Items

Another problem with drag-and-drop operations is that while you're dragging a large control, Visual Basic moves the control's outline around. If the source control is a ListBox control, there's no need to drag the entire control; drag only the selected element. The trick is to drag a smaller control, such as a Label control, whose dimensions are the same as the item's dimensions. In the last section, we are going to look at this technique and demonstrate some practical examples of drag-and-drop operations.

VB5 at Work: The ListDrop Application

The application shown in Figure 4.15 is called ListDrop, and you will find it in the ListDrop folder on the CD. The operation of this application was explained in the section "Drag and Drop Operations," earlier in this chapter.

FIGURE 4.15

The ListDrop application demonstrates how to simulate drag-and-drop operations with isolated List items.

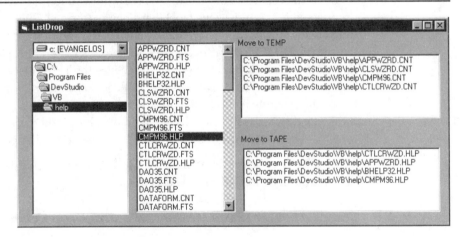

The Form contains all the controls you see on it plus an invisible Label control. When the user clicks the mouse over a ListBox control, the invisible Label control (called DragLabel) is resized to the width of the corresponding ListBox control and to the height of a line in the list, and it is repositioned over the selected item in the list. Its Drag method is called to initiate a drag operation.

Code 4.14: The FileListBox Control's MouseDown Event Handler

```
Private Sub FileList_MouseDown(Button As Integer, Shift As Integer,
➡X As Single, Y As Single)
```

```
    Dim DY
    DY = TextHeight("A")     ' Height of an item
    DragLabel.Move FileList.Left, FileList.Top + Y - DY / 2, _
    ➥FileList.Width, DY
    DragLabel.Drag ' Drag label instead of item

End Sub
```

The DragLabel control can be dropped on any other control on the Form. When it's dropped on the TEMPList control, the following lines are executed:

```
Private Sub TEMPList_DragDrop(Source As Control, X As Single, Y As
Single)

    If ListDrop.ActiveControl.Name = "FileList" Then
    ➥TEMPList.AddItem Dir1.Path & "\" & FileList.filename

End Sub
```

The ListBox control can't use the Source argument to find out which control was dropped on it. It's always the label that's being dropped. The control in which the drag operation was initiated remains active to the end of the drag-and-drop operation, so the TEMPList control can access the ActiveControl property of the Form to figure out where the item is coming from. Since the TEMPList and TAPEList controls can only accept data from the FileList control, in their DragDrop event handler they must examine the ActiveControl's Name property. If it's FileList (the name of the FileListBox control), the selected item must be added to the corresponding list's contents. The code of the TAPEList_DragDrop event handler is identical.

When the user selects an item in the TEMPList and TAPEList controls to remove, the code in Code 4.15 is executed:

Code 4.15: The TEMPList Control's DragDrop Event Handler

```
Private Sub TEMPList_MouseDown(Button As Integer, Shift As Integer,
➥X As Single, Y As Single)
Dim DY
    DY = TextHeight("A")     ' Height of item
    DragLabel.Move TEMPList.Left, TEMPList.Top + Y - DY / 2,
    ➥TEMPList.Width, DY
    DragLabel.Drag ' Drag label instead of item
End Sub
```

Again, a drag operation is initiated. The item is removed from the corresponding list if it's dropped on the FileList control.

Code 4.16: The FileList Control's DragDrop Event Handler

```
Private Sub FileList_DragDrop(Source As Control, X As Single, Y As
➡Single)

If ListDrop.ActiveControl.Name = "TEMPList" Then
    TEMPList.RemoveItem TEMPList.ListIndex
ElseIf ListDrop.ActiveControl.Name = "TAPEList" Then
    TAPEList.RemoveItem TAPEList.ListIndex
End If

End Sub
```

There are a few more lines of code here because the program must figure out the control that initiated the drag-and-drop operation and remove the selected item from the corresponding list. Again, the code uses the form's ActiveControl property to figure out where the item came from.

NOTE You may have noticed the following odd behavior: The DragLabel control need not become visible before the Drag method is called. Its outline will be dragged as if it were visible. Normally, you wouldn't be able to drag an invisible control, but the Drag method doesn't seem to care about the control's Visible property.

If you open the ListDrop application on the CD, you will see that the controls that don't react to the dropping of the control have the following code in their DragOver event:

```
Private Sub Drive1_DragOver(Source As Control, X As Single, Y As
➡Single, State As Integer)

    If State = 0 Then Source.MousePointer = 12
    If State = 1 Then Source.MousePointer = 0

End Sub
```

The controls that can't be used as destinations for the drag-and-drop operation react to the DragOver event by setting the pointer to a stop icon, to indicate that they are not valid receptors for the current operation. It is customary to include these two lines of code to all the controls that won't react to the DragDrop event.

CHAPTER
FIVE

5

Basic ActiveX Controls

- The TextBox control

- The ListBox control

- The ComboBox control

- The ScrollBar control

- The Slider control

- The Common Dialogs control

- The File controls

In the previous chapters, we explored the environment of Visual Basic and the principles of event-driven programming, which is the core of Visual Basic's programming model. In the process, we examined briefly a few basic controls, through the examples. Visual Basic provides many more controls, and all of them have a multitude of properties. Most of the properties have obvious names, and you can set them either from the Properties window or from within your code.

This chapter explores several of the basic ActiveX controls in depth. These are the controls you'll be using most often in your applications, because they are the basic building blocks of the Windows user interface.

Rather than look at controls' background and foreground color, font, and other trivial properties, however, we'll look at the properties unique to each control and at how these properties are used in building a user interface.

> **NOTE** This chapter is not going to discuss every property and every method of every control. That would take another book, and its value would be questionable. Most properties are quite simple to use and easy to understand.

The TextBox Control

The text box is the primary mechanism for displaying and entering text and is one of the most common elements of the Windows user interface. The TextBox control is a small text editor that provides all the basic text-editing facilities—inserting and selecting text, scrolling the text if it doesn't fit in the control's area, even exchanging text with other applications through the Clipboard.

An extremely versatile data-entry tool, the text box can be used for entering a single line of text, such as a number or a password, or for entering a text file, such as an INI or a BAT file. Figure 5.1 shows a few typical examples created with the TextBox control.

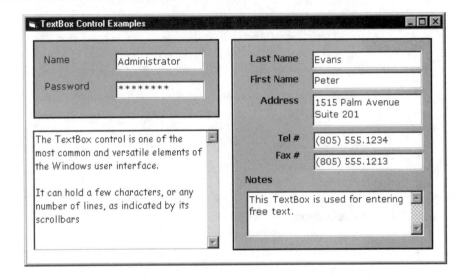

FIGURE 5.1

Typical uses of the
TextBox control

All the text boxes in Figure 5.1 contain text, some a single line, some several lines. The scroll bars you see in some text boxes are part of the control. These scroll bars are attached to the control automatically whenever the control's contents exceed the visible area of the control.

With the exception of graphics applications, the TextBox control is the bread and butter of any Windows application. By examining its properties and designing a text editor based on the TextBox control, you will see that most of the application's functionality is already built-in to the control.

Basic Properties

Let's start with the properties that determine the appearance and limits of the TextBox control, which can be set through the Properties window, and then look at the commands that allow you to manipulate the control's contents.

MultiLine   This property determines whether the TextBox control will hold a single line or multiple lines of text. By default, the control holds a single line of text. To change this behavior, set the MultiLine property to True.

ScrollBars   This property controls the attachment of scroll bars to the TextBox control if the text exceeds the control's dimensions. Single-line text boxes can have a horizontal scroll bar so that the user can view any part of a long line of text. Multi-line text boxes can have a horizontal or a vertical scroll bar or both. Scroll bars will appear only if needed, and you won't see them at design time.

If you attach a horizontal scroll bar to the TextBox control, the text won't wrap automatically as the user types. To start a new line, the user must press Enter. This arrangement is useful in implementing editors for programs in which lines must break explicitly. If the horizontal scroll bar is missing, the control inserts soft line breaks when the text reaches the end of a line, and the text is wrapped automatically.

MaxLength   This property determines the number of characters the TextBox control will accept. Its default value is zero, which means the text may be of any length, up to the control's capacity limit (discussed in a moment). To restrict the number of characters the user can type, set the value of this property accordingly.

TIP   The MaxLength property of the TextBox control is often set to a specific number in data-entry applications. This prevents users from entering more characters than can be stored in a database field .

A TextBox control with its MaxLength property set to 0, its MultiLine property set to True, and its ScrollBars property set to 2 (vertical) is on its own a functional text editor. Place a text box with these settings on a Form, run the application, and check out the following:

- Enter text and manipulate it with the usual editing keys, such as Delete, Insert, Home, and End.

- Select multiple characters with the mouse or with the arrows while holding down the Shift key.

- Move segments of text around with Copy (Ctrl+C) and Paste (Ctrl+V) operations.

- Exchange data with other applications through the Clipboard.

And all this without a single line of code! Shortly you'll see what you can do with the TextBox control if you add some code to your application, but first let's look at a few more properties of TextBox control.

The TextBox Maximum: 64Kb

The amount of text you can place in a TextBox control is limited to approximately 64Kb (a single-line text box can hold only 255 characters). This is adequate for moderately sized text files, but you may run into files that won't fit in a text box. (In this case you must resort to a RichTextBox control, which is covered in Chapter 7, *Advanced ActiveX Controls.*

This is exactly what happens when you attempt to open a large file with Notepad, which is based on the TextBox control. Notepad prompts you to open the file with WordPad, which is based on the RichTextBox control; it doesn't have a size limitation.

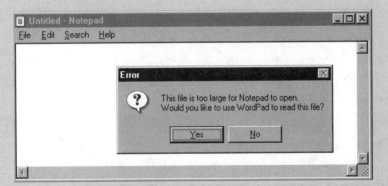

If you are using an application based on the TextBox control and enter the maximum number of characters, you won't be allowed to type any more characters. There will be no warnings; the control handles this situation silently by ignoring the characters typed. You can, however, perform certain editing operations, such as deleting characters to make room for additional text or sending data to the Clipboard, as long as the total number of characters in the text box doesn't increase.

Manipulating the Control's Text

Most of the properties for manipulating text in a TextBox control are available at run time only. Here's a breakdown of each property.

Text   The most important property of the TextBox control is the Text property, which holds the control's text. This property is also available at design time so that you can assign some initial text to the control. At run time, use this property to extract the text entered by the user or to replace the existing text by assigning a new value to the Text property. The Text property is a string and can be used as an argument with the usual string manipulation functions of Visual Basic. The following function:

```
Len(Text1.Text)
```

returns the number of characters in the text box. The following Instr$ function:

```
Instr$(Text1.Text, "Visual")
```

returns the location of the first occurrence of the string "Visual" in the text.

To store the control's contents in a file, use a statement such as the following:

```
Write #fnum, Text.Text
```

Similarly, you can read the contents of a text file into a TextBox control with a statement such as the following:

```
Text1.Text=Input$(LOF(fnum), fnum)
```

The *fnum* entry is the file number, which was presumably opened for input with an Open statement.

> **WARNING**   Before you use the Text property, you must make sure that the size of a file the user will open doesn't exceed the 64Kb limit of the control. If it does, you must reject the operation and prompt the user accordingly. Use the LOF() function, which returns the length of an open file, before attempting to assign the file's contents to the Text property of the control.

PasswordChar   Available at design time, the PasswordChar property turns the characters typed into any character you specify. If you don't want to display the actual characters typed by the user (when entering a password, for instance), use this property to define the character to appear in place of each character the user types.

The default value of this property is an empty string, which tells the control to display the characters as entered. If you set this value to an asterisk ("*"), for example, the user sees an asterisk in the place of every character typed. This property does not affect the control's Text property, which contains the actual characters. If a text box's Password property is set to any character, the user can't even copy or cut the text. Any text that's pasted on the control will appear as a sequence of asterisks or as whatever character has been specified with the PasswordChar property.

Text Selection

The TextBox control provides three properties for manipulating the text selected by the user: SelText, SelStart, and SelLength. For example, the user can select a range of text with a click-and-drag operation, and the selected text appears in reverse color, just as with any text-editing application.

SelText The SelText property returns the selected text. If you want to manipulate the currently selected text from within your code, use the SelText property. For example, you can replace the current selection by assigning a new value to the SelText property. To convert the selected text to uppercase, use the UCase$() function, which does exactly that:

```
Text1.SelText =UCase$(Text1.SelText)
```

To delete the current selection, assign an empty string to the SelText property.

The other two properties, SelStart and SelLength, return (or set) the location and length of the selected text in the control.

SelStart and SelLength The SelStart property returns or sets the position of the first character of the selected text, somewhat like placing the cursor at a specific location in the text and selecting text by dragging the mouse. The SelLength property returns or sets the length of the selected text. The most common use of these two properties is to extract the user's selection or to select a piece of text from within the application. One example is to extract the location of a string in the text.

The Form shown in Figure 5.2 contains a text box and two labels. Each time the user selects some text with the mouse, the following lines are executed from within the control's MouseUp event, and they display the selected text's starting location and length in the two labels:

```
Label1.Caption = "SelStart = " & Text1.SelStart
Label2.Caption = "SelLength = " & Text1.SelLength
```

This example reads the values of the SelStart and SelLength properties. If you assign values to them, you can select text from within your application.

FIGURE 5.2

The SelStart and Sel-Length properties let you select text from within your application.

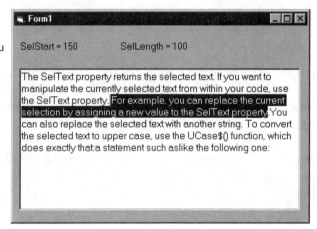

Suppose the user is seeking the word *Visual* in the control's text. The Instr$() function will locate the string, but it will not select it. The found string may even be outside the visible area of the control. You can add a few more lines of code to select the word in the text and highlight it so that the user will spot it instantly:

```
seekString = "Visual"
textStart = Instr$(Text1.Text, seekString)
  If textStart > 0 Then
        Text1.SelStart = textStart
        Text1.SelLength = Len(seekString)
End If
```

These lines locate the string "Visual" (or any user-supplied string stored in the *seekString* variable) in the text and select it by setting the SelStart and SelLength properties. Moreover, if the string is outside the visible area of the control, the text scrolls up or down so that the selected text becomes visible.

As far as the appearance of the selected text goes, it doesn't make any difference whether it was selected by the user or by the application; it appears in reverse color, as is common with all text editors.

The few lines of code shown here form the core of a text editor's Search command. Replacing the current selection with another string is as simple as assigning a new value to the SelText property, which provides you with an easy implementation of a Search and Replace operation. Designing a Form to include the control on which the Search and Replace strings will be entered and the command buttons will take more effort than implementing the search and replace logic!

TIP

The SelStart and SelLength properties always have a value, even if no text has been selected. In this case, SelLength is 0, and SelStart is the current location of the pointer in the text. If you want to insert some text at the pointer's location, simply assign it to the SelText property.

The selected text remains highlighted even when the focus is moved to another control or Form. This is a nice feature, but you can change the appearance of the selected text, if you want, with the HideSelection property. Its default value is False, which is why the text remains highlighted even when the text box loses the focus. If you set the HideSelection property to True, the selected text is highlighted only as long as the TextBox control has the focus.

VB5 at Work: The TextPad Application

The TextPad application, shown in Figure 5.3, demonstrates most of the TextBox properties and methods described so far. TextPad is a basic text editor that you can incorporate in your programs and customize for special applications. The Text-Pad's Form is covered by a TextBox control. Every time the user changes the size of the Form, the application adjusts the size of the TextBox control accordingly.

FIGURE 5.3

The TextPad application is a text editor that demonstrates the most useful properties and methods of the TextBox control.

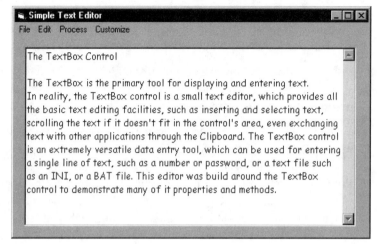

The menu bar of the Form contains all the commands you'd expect to find in text-editing applications:

- **File**

    - **New**   Clears the text

    - **Open**   Loads a new text file from disk

    - **Save**   Saves the text to its file on disk

    - **Save As**   Saves the text with a new filename on disk

    - **Exit**   Terminates the application

- **Edit**

    - **Copy**   Copies selected text to the Clipboard

    - **Cut**   Cuts selected text

    - **Paste**   Pastes the Clipboard's contents to the text

    - **Select All**   Selects all the text in the control

    - **Find**   Displays a dialog box with Find & Replace options

- **Process**

    - **Upper Case**   Converts selected text to uppercase

    - **Lower Case**   Converts selected text to lowercase

    - **Number Lines**   Numbers the text lines

- **Customize**

  - **Font**   Sets the text's font, size, and attributes

  - **Page Color**   Sets the control's background color

  - **Text Color**   Sets the color of the text

Design this menu as explained in Chapter 4, *Working with Forms*. File menu options are implemented with the Common Dialogs control, which is discussed shortly. As you will see, you don't have to design the File Open and File Save dialog boxes. All you have to do is place another control on the Form and set a few properties; Windows takes it from there. The application will display the standard File Open and File Save dialog boxes, in which the user can select or specify a filename; the program then reports this filename to the application.

The options on the Edit menu move selected text to and from the Clipboard. For the TextPad application, all you need to know about the Clipboard are the SetText method, which places a string on the Clipboard, and the GetText method, which retrieves text from the Clipboard and copies it to a string variable (see Figure 5.4).

FIGURE 5.4

The Copy, Cut, and Paste operations aren't limited to the TextPad application. Use them to exchange text with any other application.

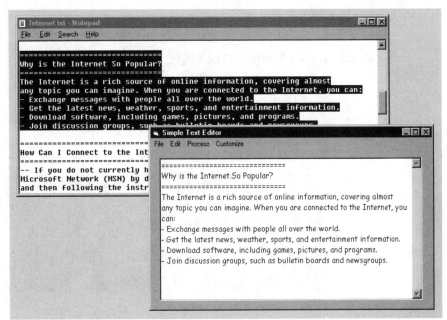

The Copy command, for example, is implemented with a single line of code (Editor is the name of the TextBox control):

```
Private Sub EditCopy_Click()

    Clipboard.SetText Editor.SelText

End Sub
```

The Cut command does the same, but it also clears the selected text:

```
Private Sub EditCut_Click()

    Clipboard.SetText Editor.SelText
    Editor.SelText = ""

End Sub
```

The Paste command assigns the contents of the Clipboard to the current selection:

```
Private Sub EditPaste_Click()

    Editor.SelText = Clipboard.GetText

End Sub
```

If no text is currently selected, the Clipboard's text is pasted at the pointer's current location.

Search and Replace Operations

The last option in the Edit menu —and the most interesting—displays a Search & Replace dialog box (shown in Figure 5.5). This dialog box works like the Find and Replace dialog box of Word and many other Windows applications.

FIGURE 5.5

The TextPad's Search & Replace dialog box

The buttons in the Search & Replace dialog box are relatively self-explanatory:

- **Find** locates the first instance of the specified string in the text. In other words, Find starts searching from the beginning of the text, not from the current location of the pointer. If a match is found, the Find Again, Replace, and Replace All buttons are enabled.

- **Find Again** locates the next instance of the word in the text.

- **Replace** replaces the current instance of the found string with the replacement string and then locates the next instance of the same string.

- **Replace All** replaces all instances of the string specified in the Find String box with the string in the Replace With box.

Whether the search is case-sensitive depends on the status of the Case Sensitive CheckBox control. The Find command checks the status of this checkbox and sets the *compare* variable accordingly. This variable is then used with the InStr() function to specify the type of search.

The actual search is performed with the InStr() function, which searches the text in the TextBox control for the specified string. If the string is found, the program highlights it by selecting it and then stores its position in the *position* variable. The *position* variable is declared as a Form-wide variable so that it can be used later by the Find Again button to specify the starting location of the new search.

Code 5.1: The Find Button

```
Private Sub FindButton_Click()
Dim compare As Integer

position = 0
If Check1.Value = 1 Then
  compare = vbBinaryCompare
Else
  compare = vbTextCompare
End If
position = InStr(Position + 1, Form1.Editor.Text, Text1.Text, compare)
If position > 0 Then
  ReplaceButton.Enabled = True
  ReplaceAllButton.Enabled = True
  Form1.Editor.SelStart = Position - 1
```

```
      Form1.Editor.SelLength = Len(Text1.Text)
      Form1.SetFocus
   Else
      MsgBox "String not found"
      ReplaceButton.Enabled = False
      ReplaceAllButton.Enabled = False
   End If
End Sub
```

The Find button examines the value of the Check1 CheckBox control, which specifies whether the search will be case-sensitive and sets the value of the *compare* variable accordingly. The *compare* variable is passed to the InStr() function and tells it how to search for the desired string. If the InStr() function locates the string, the program selects it by setting the text box's SelStart and SelLength properties. If not, it displays a message and disables the Replace and Replace All buttons on the Form.

The code of the Find Again button is the same, but it doesn't reset the *position* variable to zero. This way, the InStr() function locates the next instance of the same string.

The Replace button replaces the current selection with the replacement string and then locates the next instance of the find string. The Replace All button, does the same thing as the Replace button, but it continues to replace the found string until no more instances can be located in the text.

The code behind the Find Again, Replace, and Replace All buttons is quite similar to the code of the Find button and really doesn't need repeating. If you open the TextPad sample application, you can see the differences.

When you have the application open, consider modifying the code so that the Find button starts searching for the string from the current pointer's location. To do this, pass the pointer's location as the first argument to the InStr() function:

```
position = InStr(Form1.Editor.SelStart, Form1.Editor.Text,
➡Text1.Text, compare)
```

You might also want to limit the search operation in the selected text only. You must pass the location of the first selected character to the InStr() function as before, and in addition you must make sure that the located string falls within the selected range, which is from Form1.Editor.SelStart to Form1.Editor.SelStart + Form1.Editor.SelLength:

```
If Position > Form1.Editor.SelStart + Form1.Editor.SelLength Then
   MsgBox "String not found"
```

```
Else
   Form1.Editor.SelStart = Position - 1
   Form1.Editor.SelLength = Len(Text1.Text)
End If
```

Capturing Keystrokes

The TextBox control has no unique methods or events, but it's quite common in programming this control to capture and process the user's keystrokes. The KeyPress event occurs every time a key is pressed, and reports the character that was pressed. You can use this event to capture certain keys and modify the program's behavior, depending on the character typed.

Suppose you want to use the TextPad application (discussed earlier) to prepare messages for transmission over a telex line. As you may know, a telex can't transmit lowercase characters or special symbols. The editor must convert the text to uppercase and replace the special symbols with their equivalent strings: DLR for $, AT for @, O/O for %, BPT for #, and AND for &. You can modify the default behavior of the TextBox control from within the KeyPress event so that it converts these characters as the user types.

The TLXPad, which you will find in this chapter's folder on the CD, is identical to the TextPad application but customized for preparing telex messages. (Not that the telex is growing in popularity, but there are situations in which some custom preprocessing of the data is required. By capturing keystrokes, you can process the data as they are entered, in real time. For example, you could make sure that numeric values fall within a given range, make sure that hexadecimal digits don't contain invalid characters, and so on.) The only difference is the modified application's KeyPress event.

Code 5.2: TLXPad Application

```
Private Sub Editor_KeyPress(KeyAscii As Integer)
Dim TLXSymbols As String
Dim ch As String * 1

   TLXSymbols = "@#$%&"
   ch = Chr$(KeyAscii)
   If InStr(TLXSymbols, ch) Then
      KeyAscii = 0
   Else
      KeyAscii = Asc(UCase$(Chr$(KeyAscii)))
      Exit Sub
   End If
```

```
Select Case ch
  Case "@": Editor.SelText = "AT"
  Case "#": Editor.SelText = "BPT"
  Case "$": Editor.SelText = "DLR"
  Case "%": Editor.SelText = "O/O"
  Case "&": Editor.SelText = "AND"
End Select

End Sub
```

This event handler replaces the special symbols with a string, and it also converts alphanumeric characters to uppercase. The line that converts the alphanumeric characters to uppercase needs some explanation. The KeyAscii argument of the KeyPress event reports the ASCII value of the key presses, not the actual character:

```
KeyAscii = Asc(UCase$(Chr$(KeyAscii)))
```

Before deploying the UCase$() function to convert the character to uppercase, you must convert the ASCII value to a character. This is what the function Chr$() in the preceding long statement does. To understand it, read it from right to left: First it extracts the actual character typed from its ASCII value, then it converts the character to uppercase, and finally it converts the character back to an ASCII value, which is returned to the application. The KeyPress event handler is executed before the keystroke is passed to the TextBox control, and that's why you can modify the keystrokes from within the control's KeyPress event.

Another common feature in text-editing applications is the assignment of special operations to the function keys. The Notepad application, for example, uses the F5 function key to insert the date at the cursor's location. You can do the same with the TextPad application, but you can't use the KeyPress event—the KeyAscii argument does not report function keys. The events that can capture the function keys are the KeyDown event, which is generated when a key is pressed, and the KeyUp event, which is generated when a key is released. Also, unlike the KeyPress event, the KeyDown and KeyUp events do not report the ASCII value of the character, but instead report its *keycode* (a special number that distinguishes each key on the keyboard, also known as the *scancode*).

The keycode is unique for each key, not each character. Lower- and uppercase characters have different ASCII values, but the same keycode, because they are on the same key. The number 4 and the $ symbol have the same keycode because the same key on the keyboard generates both characters. When the key's keycode is reported, the KeyDown and KeyUp events also report the state of the Shift, Control, and Alt keys.

To be able to use the KeyDown and KeyUp events, you must know the keycode of the key you want to capture. The keycode for the function key F1 is 112, the keycode for F2 is 113, and so on. To capture a special key, such as the F1 function key, and assign a special string to it, program the key's KeyUp event. The following event handler uses the F5 and F6 function keys to insert the current date and time in the document. It also uses the F7 and F8 keys to insert two predefined strings in the document.

Code 5.3: KeyUp Event Examples

```
'Should be globally defined constants
Const DateInputKey = 116
Const TimeInputKey = 117
Const SpecialInput1Key = 118
Const SpecialInput2Key = 119
{more code}

  Select Case KeyCode
    Case DateInputKey:      Editor.SelText = Date
    Case TimeInputKey:      Editor.SelText = Time
    Case SpecialInput1Key:  Editor.SelText = "MicroWeb Designs, Inc"
    Case SpecialInput2Key:  Editor.SelText = "Another long,
    ➡common string you can insert with a single keystroke"
  End Select

End Sub
```

Notice the definitions of the constants that make the code easier to read and that simplify its maintenance.

With a little additional effort, you can provide users with a dialog box that lets them assign their own strings to function keys. You will probably have to take into consideration the status of the Shift argument, which reports the status of the Shift, Control, and Alt keys, according to Table 5.1. Windows is already using many of the function keys, and you shouldn't reassign them. For example, the F1 key is the standard Windows context-sensitive Help key, and users will be confused if they press F1 and see the date appear in their documents.

TABLE 5.1 The Values of the Shift Argument of the KeyDown and KeyUp Events

CONSTANT	VALUE	DESCRIPTION
vbShiftMask	1	Shift key is down
vbCtrlMask	2	Ctrl key is down
vbAltMask	4	Alt key is down

To find out whether one or more of the Shift keys were down the moment another key was pressed, use the AND operator with the Shift argument. The following If structure detects the Shift key:

```
If Shift AND vbShiftMask Then
      {Shift key was down}
End If
```

To detect combinations of the Shift keys, use statements such as this one:

```
If (Shift AND vbShiftMask) AND (Shift AND vbAltMask) Then
      {Shift and Alt keys were down}
End If
```

The ListBox and ComboBox Controls

The ListBox and ComboBox controls present lists of choices from which the user can select one or more. The ListBox control occupies a user-specified amount of space on the Form and is populated with a list of items; the user can select one or more with the mouse. The items must be inserted in the ListBox control through the program. Users cannot enter data in a list; they can only select items, which will be manipulated by the application when they click on a button or take some other action.

The ComboBox control also contains multiple items but occupies less space on the screen. The ComboBox control is an expandable ListBox control: The user can expand it to make a selection and retract it after the selection is made. The real advantage to the ComboBox control, however, is that the user can enter new information in the ComboBox, rather than being forced to select only the items listed.

The ComboBox control may seem more useful, but its use isn't as common as ListBox controls. This section first examines the properties and methods of the ListBox control. Later, you'll see how the same properties and methods can be used with the ComboBox control.

Basic Properties

The ListBox control, as well as the ComboBox control, provide a few properties that can be set at design time. Because they determine the basic functionality of the control and can't be changed at run time, we'll start with these fundamental properties.

MultiSelect   This property determines how the user can select the list's items and must be set at design time (at run time, you can only read this property's value). The MultiSelect property's values determine whether the user can select multiple items and which method will be used for multiple selection. MultiSelect values are shown in Table 5.2.

TABLE 5.2   The MultiSelect Property Values

SETTING	DESCRIPTION
0	Multiple selection not allowed (the default).
1	Simple multiple selection. A mouse click (or pressing the spacebar) selects or deselects an item in the list. To move the focus to another item, use the arrow keys.
2	Extended multiple selection. Press Shift and click the mouse (or press one of the arrow keys) to span the selection. This will highlight all the items between the previously selected item and the current selection. Press Ctrl and click the mouse to select or deselect an item in the list.

Sorted   Items can be inserted by the application into a ListBox or ComboBox control, but inserting them at the proper place and maintaining some sort of organization would be quite a task for the programmer. If you want the items to be always sorted, set the control's Sorted property to True. This property must be set at design time and is read-only at run time.

The ListBox control is basically a text control and won't sort numeric data properly. To use the ListBox control to sort numbers, you must first format them with leading zeros. For example, the number 10 will appear in front of the number 5, because the string "10" is smaller than the string "5". If the numbers are formatted as "010" and "005", they will be sorted correctly.

The items in a sorted ListBox control are in ascending and case-sensitive order. Moreover, there is no mechanism for changing this default setting. The items "aa", "aA", "AA", "Aa", "ba", and "BA" will be sorted as follows:

"AA"

"Aa"

"aA"

"aa"

"BA"

"ba"

Uppercase characters appear before the equivalent lowercase characters, but both upper- and lowercase characters appear together. All words beginning with B appear after the words beginning with A and before the words beginning with C. Within the group of words beginning with B, those beginning with B appear before those beginning with b.

Style   This property can be set only at design time. This property determines the appearance of the control. Its value can be 0 (Standard) or 1 (Checkbox). The two lists shown in Figure 5.6 illustrate the Standard and Checkbox appearance of the ListBox control. Notice that the list on the left is unsorted and that the list on the right is sorted.

FIGURE 5.6

The two ListBox controls on this Form show the two distinct looks of the control.

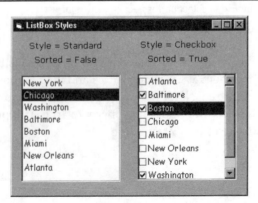

The ListBox Control's Methods

To manipulate a ListBox control from within your application, you should be able to:

- Add items to the list
- Remove items from the list
- Access individual items in the list

Add Item   The first two operations are performed with the AddItem and RemoveItem methods. The AddItem method's syntax is as follows:

```
List1.AddItem item, index
```

The *item* parameter is the string to be added to the list, and *index* is its order. The first item's order in the list is zero. The *index* argument is optional; if you omit it, the string is appended at the bottom of the list. If the control's Sorted property is set to True, the item is inserted in its proper place in the list, regardless of the value of the *index* argument.

Remove Item   To remove an item from the list, you must first find its position (*index*) in the list, which you must then supply to the RemoveItem method. The syntax of the method is as follows:

```
List1.RemoveItem index
```

The *index* parameter is the order of the item to be removed, and this time it's not optional. The following statement:

```
List1.RemoveItem 0
```

removes the item at the top of the list.

Clear   The Clear method removes all the items from the control. Its syntax is simple:

```
List1.Clear
```

Manipulating the List's Items

To access individual items, you can use several properties that are unique to the List-Box (and ComboBox) control. Removing an item from a list requires that you know its order in the list, but the Remove method's argument is rarely used. Usually, you rely on the user to select the items to be removed; otherwise, the items will be selected from within your code, based on their values. The ListBox control provides several properties that let you manipulate the items from within your code.

ListCount   This is the number of items in the List.

List0   This is an array that holds the list's items. The element List(0) holds the first element of the list, List(1) holds the second item, and so on up to List(ListCount-1), which holds the last item. The List() array is used frequently in scanning all the List items. The following loop, for instance, scans all the items of the List1 control, looking for and removing blank strings:

```
For itm = List1.ListCount - 1 to 0 Step -1
  If List1.List(itm) = "" Then
      List1.RemoveItem itm
  End If
Next
```

Notice that the loop scans the elements of the List() array backward. Can you see why? If the list were scanned forward, each time an item was removed, the list's length would decrement by 1, and the loop would be executed more times than there are items in the List, causing a run-time error. Scanning the items backward prevents this.

List Index   This is the index of the selected item in the List. If multiple items are selected, ListIndex is the index of the most recently selected item. If the application needs to remove items from a list, you must use this property to remove the selected item. The following statement:

```
List1.RemoveItem List1.ListIndex
```

removes the selected item from the List1 control, but only if an item is selected. If no item is selected at the time the RemoveItem method is invoked, the ListIndex property has a negative value; any attempt to remove an item with a negative index results in a run-time error. To avoid this error, check the value of the ListIndex property first:

```
If List1.ListIndex >= 0 Then
      List1.RemoveItem List1.ListIndex
End If
```

After removal of the item, the indices of the following items are adjusted accordingly.

Selected   This property is an array, similar to the List property, with elements that have a True or a False value, depending on the status of the corresponding list element (the value is True if the element is selected; otherwise, it is False).

Because there is no property equivalent to the ListIndex property for multiple selected items, the only way to find out which elements have been selected—and before you can process them—is to examine all the elements of the Selected array (you'll see shortly an example of this technique).

SelCount   This property reports the number of selected items in a ListBox control with its MultiSelect property set to 1 (Simple) or 2 (Extended). It is commonly used in conjunction with the Selected array in processing the selected items in the control. If a ListBox control allows multiple elements to be selected, you might want to use the checkbox style for your list's items. Set the Style property to 1 so that the list's items will be displayed as checkboxes, like the ones shown in Figure 5.5, earlier in this chapter.

NewIndex   This property returns the index of the item most recently added to a ListBox control. This property is used commonly with the ItemData property discussed in the section "Indexing with the List Control."

VB5 at Work: The ListDemo Application

The ListDemo application (shown in Figure 5.7) demonstrates the basic operations of the ListBox control. The two ListBox controls operate slightly differently. The first one has the default configuration: Only one item can be selected at a time, and new items are appended after the existing item. The second ListBox control has its Sorted property set to True and its MultiSelect property set to 2 (Extended). This means that the elements of this control are always sorted, and the user can select multiple cells with the Shift and Control keys.

The Add New Element buttons use the InputBox() function to prompt the user for input, and then they add the user-supplied string to the ListBox control. The code is identical for both buttons.

Code 5.4: The Add New Element Buttons

```
Private Sub Command5_Click()
Dim listItem As String

  listItem = InputBox("Enter item to add to the list")
  If Trim(listItem) <> "" Then
    List1.AddItem listItem
  End If

End Sub
```

FIGURE 5.7

The ListDemo application demonstrates most of the operations you will perform with ListBox controls.

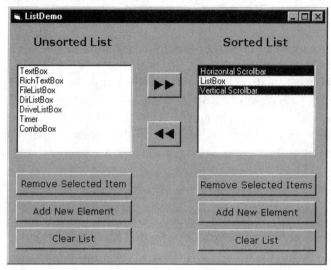

Notice that the subroutine examines the data entered by the user to avoid adding blank strings to the list. The code for the Clear List button is also straight-forward; it simply calls the Clear method to remove all entries from the corresponding list.

The code for the Remove Selected Item button is different from that for the Remove Selected Items button. The reason: The first can have only one selected item; the second can have multiple selected items. To delete an item, you must have at least one item selected (explained earlier).

Code 5.5: Remove Selected Item Button

```
Private Sub Command3_Click()

  If List1.ListIndex > 0 Then
    List1.RemoveItem List1.ListIndex
  End If

End Sub
```

The code for the Remove Selected Items button must scan all the items of the list and remove the selected one(s).

Code 5.6: The Remove Selected Items Button

```
Private Sub Command4_Click()
Dim i As Integer
```

```
  If List2.SelCount = 1 Then
    List2.RemoveItem List2.ListIndex
  ElseIf List2.ListCount > 1 Then
    For i = List2.ListCount - 1 To 0 Step -1
      If List2.Selected(i) Then
        List2.RemoveItem i
      End If
    Next i
  End If

End Sub
```

The code examines the control's SelCount property, which specifies the number of selected items. If ListCount equals one, it moves the item. If the number of selected items is more than one, the program scans the entire list and removes the items that have their Selected property set to True. Notice also that the list is scanned backward, as explained in the discussion of the RemoveItem method.

The Arrows

The two Command Buttons between the two ListBox controls transfer selected items from one list to another. The first arrow button can transfer a single element only, after it ensures that the list contains a selected item. First, it adds the item to the second list, and then it removes the item from the original list.

Code 5.7: The Top Arrow Button

```
Private Sub Command1_Click()

  If List1.ListIndex >= 0 Then
    List2.AddItem List1.Text
    List1.RemoveItem List1.ListIndex
  End If

End Sub
```

The second arrow button transfers items in the opposite direction. Its code is similar to that of the Remove Selected Items button. The arrow button examines the SelCount property, and if a single item is selected, it moves the item to the other list with the commands of the previous list. If multiple items are selected, the arrow button scans the list backward, copying and deleting each selected item.

Code 5.8: The Second Arrow Button

```
Private Sub Command2_Click()
Dim i As Integer
```

```
If List2.SelCount = 1 Then
  List1.AddItem List2.Text
  List2.RemoveItem List2.ListIndex
ElseIf List2.SelCount > 1 Then
  For i = List2.ListCount - 1 To 0 Step -1
    If List2.Selected(i) Then
      List1.AddItem List2.List(i)
      List2.RemoveItem i
    End If
  Next
End If

End Sub
```

The code for the ListDemo application contains all the logic you will need in your ListBox manipulation routines. It shows how to:

- Maintain sorted lists
- Add and remove items
- Transfer items between lists
- Handle multiple selected items

Before we leave the topic of the ListBox control, let's examine one more powerful technique: using the ListBox control to maintain a list of keys to an array or random access file with records of related information.

Indexing with the ListBox Control

A key property of the ListBox control is the ItemData property, which is an array similar to the List array, but instead of containing strings that appear in the control, it contains numbers. Each item displayed on a ListBox control has two entries: a string, given by the list's List(i) property; and a number, given by the ItemData(i) property (*i* is the index of the item in the list).

The ItemData property can store any type of numeric information associated with each item, as long as this information need not be displayed on the list. If you maintain a list of employee names, the List() array can hold names, and the ItemData() array can hold the salary of each employee. Each employee can be accessed by name, but his or her salary can appear in a TextBox control on the same Form.

The real value of the ItemData property, however, is not for storing additional pieces of information along with the item. If you want to store more information than is visible on the list, you probably want to store more information than just a number. Suppose you need to maintain a list of names and addresses. Storing each entry in a ListBox control isn't practical. The control would have to be very wide to accommodate the entire string with each person's name, address, city, phone numbers, and so on.

A more practical approach is to store the names of the persons in the ListBox control and use the names as keys to access the elements of an array in which the rest of the information is stored. Each record is stored in an array element, which should match one of the items in the ListBox control. If the item's ItemData property is set to the index of the corresponding array element, you can access the array records instantly.

The same approach would also work with random access files, only this time the value of the ItemData property would be the number of the matching record. The KeyList application demonstrates this technique.

VB5 at Work: The KeyList Application

KeyList, shown in Figure 5.8, maintains a list of books, indexed by ISBN. It could be a list of names and addresses, a price list, or any other collection of related items. The application is simple and doesn't justify the design of a database. To save space and time, the information is stored in an array and saved to a disk file between sessions.

FIGURE 5.8

The KeyList application uses the ListBox control to maintain indexed information.

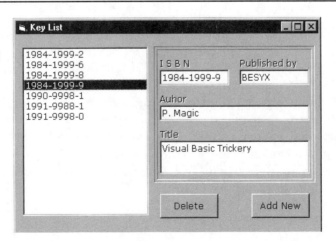

The array is a convenient storage mechanism for a few hundred entries, but it can't be sorted easily. Inserting each item in the proper array element requires massive copying. To insert a new item in the array's first element, you would have to copy all the items to the next array position. In general, you should avoid sorting whenever possible, especially if it has to be repeated at run time.

> **WARNING**
>
> The ListBox control is frequently used as an array, especially if you need to maintain sorted items. You can even hide the control by setting its Visible property to False and use it in your application as an array. It provides the same functionality and can maintain its items sorted at all times. Sorting is an especially intensive operation and should be avoided.

The KeyList application uses a ListBox control to maintain a sorted list of items. We could have stored all the information in the ListBox control, but this is hardly practical. The list will be used for storing the keys—the data items used in recalling the information—which are the books' ISBN numbers. The remaining fields can be stored in an array.

Figure 5.9 shows how the keys are stored in the ListBox control and the matching data in the array. The ItemData array points to the appropriate elements in the Data Array, which may contain a large number of fields.

All you need is a way to connect the ISBN numbers to the corresponding information in the array. This link is provided by the ListBox control, with its ItemData property. The ItemData property is an array of numbers, one per list item. Each item in the list has a value (what is displayed on the list) that can be accessed via the List property, and a related value that isn't displayed on the List but that can be accessed with the ItemData property.

The first element in the list is List1.List(0), and the related information is stored in the array element, whose index is given by the property List1.ItemData(0). The List's Sorted property is set to True so that the user sees the keys sorted and can easily locate any item in the List. The fields that correspond to each key, though, are appended to the array. As a programmer, you don't have to worry about maintaining the elements of the array in any order. As long as you can instantly access the array element that corresponds to the selected key in the List control, it's as if the array is sorted too.

FIGURE 5.9

The ItemData array links the items of a ListBox control to the elements of an array or to the records in a random access file.

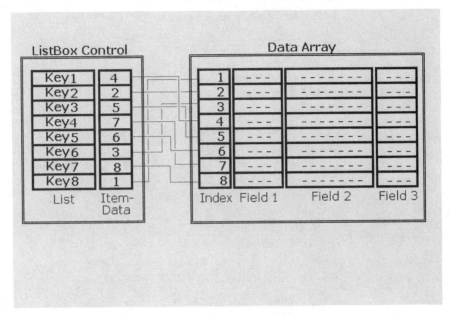

KeyList Code: Behind the Scenes

Now that we have looked briefly at the technique for maintaining sorted keys in the KeyList application, let's look at the code that created it. To add a new entry, the user must click on the Add New button, in which case the program lets the user enter data in the various fields. When done, the user clicks on the OK button to commit the changes. (You don't see this button in Figure 5.8 because it appears only while the user is entering a new entry, an action signaled to the program with the click of the Add New button.) The new record will be added to the array *DataArray()*, which is declared as follows:

```
Dim DataArray(999, 3) As String
```

The element *DataArray(i, 0)* holds the ISBN of the book, the element *DataArray(i, 1)* holds the publisher, the element *DataArray(i, 2)* holds the author of the current title, and the element *DataArray(i ,3)* holds the book's title. The *i* parameter is the index stored in the List's ItemData() property.

Code 5.9: The OK Button

```
Private Sub OKButton_Click()

    Key = Trim(Text1.Text)
    If Key = "" Then
        MsgBox "Key field must be non-empty"
        Exit Sub
    End If

    position = BSearch(Trim(Text1.Text))
    If position >= 0 Then
        reply = MsgBox("Key exists. Replace existing record?", vbYesNo)
        If reply = vbYes Then
            List1.RemoveItem position
        Else
            Text1.SetFocus
            Exit Sub
        End If
    End If

    ArrayIndex = ArrayIndex + 1
    List1.AddItem Key
    List1.ItemData(List1.NewIndex) = ArrayIndex
    DataArray(ArrayIndex, 1) = Text2.Text
    DataArray(ArrayIndex, 2) = Text3.Text
    DataArray(ArrayIndex, 3) = Text4.Text

    List1.ListIndex = List1.NewIndex
    ShowButtons

End Sub
```

The program reads the data entered by the user in the various fields, searches the list with the BSearch() function (explained in the following section) to see if an entry with this key exists, and then inserts the key in the ListBox control and stores the other fields in the DataArray() array. Because the List's Sorted property is True, the item is automatically inserted in its proper position in the list.

The *ArrayIndex* variable is global and points to the last element of the array. Each time a new element is added, the *ArrayIndex* variable is incremented by one. The value of the *ArrayIndex* property is stored in the ItemData array, in the position that corresponds to the newly added element. The following expression:

```
List1.NewIndex
```

is the index of the newly added element in the list. This expression is used to access the element of the ItemData array that corresponds to this item in the following statement:

```
List1.ItemData(List1.NewIndex) = ArrayIndex
```

The List's ItemData() array holds the keys to the array, and retrieving a book's title or author is a trivial task once you have its ISBN. Each time the user clicks on an item in the list, the program extracts the item's ItemData property and uses it as an index to access the title's fields in the DataArray() array.

Code 5.10: The List's Click Event Handler

```
Private Sub List1_Click()

  If List1.ListIndex < 0 Then
    Text1.Text = ""
    Text2.Text = ""
    Text3.Text = ""
    Text4.Text = ""
    Exit Sub
  End If
  ItemIndex = List1.ItemData(List1.ListIndex)
  Text1.Text = List1.List(List1.ListIndex)
  Text2.Text = DataArray(ItemIndex, 1)
  Text3.Text = DataArray(ItemIndex, 2)
  Text4.Text = DataArray(ItemIndex, 3)

End Sub
```

If no item has been selected in the list, the program clears the contents of the various fields (so that the program won't crash if the user clicks on the space of an empty item). The *ItemIndex* variable gets the value of the item's ItemData property and uses it to access the DataArray() where the remaining fields are stored.

Searching a Sorted List

There's one more interesting technique in this application. As the user types characters in the ISBN field, the program selects the item in the ListBox control that matches the partial entry of the ISBN field. This is a standard operation of the ListBox control. If the ListBox control has the focus and the user types characters, the matching item in the control is selected automatically.

This sorting function is duplicated in the ISBN TextBox control for two reasons:

- **Convenience**   When the user types characters in the TextBox control, he or she can see the string and edit it.

- **Practicality**   The algorithm that implements the search is practical, and it's likely that you will use it in your applications.

Searching for a specific item in a sorted arrangement of data is a common operation, and it can be implemented efficiently with a *Binary Search algorithm*. The Binary Search algorithm starts by comparing the desired element with the middle element of the sorted list (or array). If it's alphabetically or numerically larger than the middle element of the list, the first half of the list is rejected without further consideration. It can't be located in the first half of the list. If the opposite is true, the lower half of the list is rejected. The same process continues with the selected half of the list. Another half is rejected again, and the algorithm continues until it finds a single element, which should be the desired one. If not, the element is not in the list. Figure 5.10 shows the steps in locating an item in a sorted list with 16 items. The items rejected at each step are marked with a gray border.

FIGURE 5.10

Locating an item in a sorted list with 16 elements takes 4 comparisons.

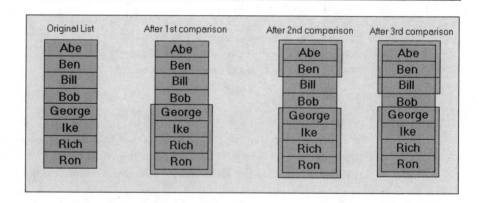

Suppose you have a list with 1024 elements. After the first comparison, 512 elements will be rejected. Of the 512 remaining elements, 256 will be rejected with the second comparison. After the third comparison, only 128 of the initial 1024 elements will be left. If this process continues, the size of the list will be reduced to 64 elements, then to 32, then to 16 and so on down to a single element. It will take only 10 comparisons to reduce the 1024 elements to the desired one. The Binary Search algorithm exploits the sorted list and is extremely efficient.

The Implementation of the BSearch() Function

The burden of sorting the elements to be searched often lies with the programmer, but with a flexible tool such as a sorted ListBox control, maintaining a sorted list at all times is also trivial. Combining a sorted list of keys maintained by a ListBox control and the Binary Search algorithm is a powerful approach that can be used in situations in which you would normally deploy database techniques. The database objects (discussed in Chapter 11, *Database Programming with Visual Basic*) require significant overhead, which isn't worthwhile for a small application such as KeyList.

As the user edits the contents of the ISBN TextBox, the Change event occurs with every character typed, and the following code is executed:

```
Private Sub Text1_Change()

position = BSearch(Trim$(Text1.Text))
If position >= 0 Then
  List1.ListIndex = position
  List1_Click
Else
  Text2.Text = ""
  Text3.Text = ""
  Text4.Text = ""
End If

End Sub
```

The code calls the BSearch() function with the text in the Text1 TextBox control. The BSearch() function searches the ListBox control for an item that partially matches its argument. If the item is found, the function returns its position in the list. If not, it returns the value -1. If the item is found, the program selects it in the list and calls the ListBox control's Click event, to update the contents of the other TextBox controls in the data-entry section of the Form.

Code 5.11: The BSearch() Function

```
Function BSearch(KeyField) As Integer
Dim Lower, Upper, Middle
Lower = 0
Upper = List1.ListCount - 1

While 1
  Middle = Fix((Lower + Upper) / 2)
```

```
     If Upper < Lower Then
       BSearch = -1
       Exit Function
     End If
     If StrComp(KeyField, List1.List(Middle)) > 0 Then
       Lower = Middle + 1
     Else
       If StrComp(KeyField, List1.List(Middle)) < 0 Then
         Upper = Middle - 1
       Else
         BSearch = Middle
         Exit Function
       End If
     End If
Wend

End Function
```

The *Upper* and *Lower* variables delimit the section of the list that may contain the desired element. The items before *Lower* and after *Upper* have already been rejected. When the function starts, the *Lower* variable is set to the position of the first item, and the *Upper* variable is set to the position of the last item. The position of the middle element is then calculated (variable *Middle*), and the key field is compared with the middle element. If the key field is smaller than the middle item, the upper half of the list is rejected, by adjusting the value of the *Upper* variable. (The list is sorted in ascending order, that is, the "a" character shows up in the list before the "g.") If the key field is larger than the middle item, the lower half of the list is rejected by adjusting the value of the *Lower* variable.

The ComboBox Control   The ComboBox control is similar to the ListBox control in the sense that it contains multiple items of which the user may select one, but it takes less space on-screen. The ComboBox is practically an expandable ListBox control, which can enlarge when the user wants to make a selection and retract after the selection is made. Normally, the ComboBox control displays one line with the selected item. The real difference, however, between ComboBox and ListBox controls is that the ComboBox control allows the user to enter more than one choice.

Three types of ComboBox controls are available in Visual Basic 5. The value of the control's Style property, whose values are shown in Table 5.3, determines which box is used.

TABLE 5.3 The Styles of the ComboBox Control

VALUE	DESCRIPTION
0	(Default) DropDown Combo. The control is made up of a drop-down list and a text box. The user can select an item from the list or type a new one in the text box.
1	Simple Combo. Includes a text box and a list that doesn't drop down. The user can select from the list or type in the text box.
2	DropDown List. This style is a drop-down list, in which the user can select one of its items.

The Combos project in this chapter's folder on the CD (see Figure 5.11) demonstrates the three styles of the ComboBox control. If you are not familiar with the ComboBox control, open the Combos project and experiment with it; you will soon recognize a common element of the Windows interface.

FIGURE 5.11

The Combos project demonstrates the various styles of the ComboBox control.

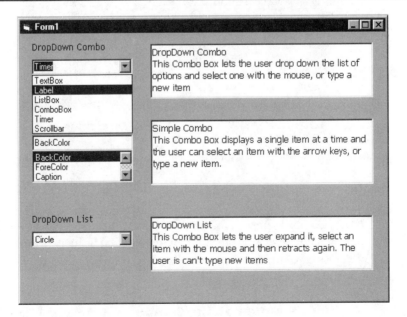

Most of the properties and methods of the ListBox control also apply to the ComboBox control. The AddItem property adds items to a ComboBox, and the

RemoveItem property removes items from a ComboBox. To access the items of the control, you can use the List array, and the current selection in the control is given by its Text property.

You can also use the ItemData property to maintain sorted lists of keys, as you will see in the KeyCombo example shortly. You can even set the control's Multi-Select property to 1 (Simple) or 2 (Extended) to allow the user to select multiple items in a ComboBox control. To find out whether an item has been selected, use the Selected property as before.

VB5 at Work: The KeyCombo Application

The KeyCombo application, shown in Figure 5.12, is similar to the KeyList application you saw earlier, but KeyCombo maintains three indexed lists, and the user can recall records based on any one key. Each record has four fields, three of them being potential keys.

FIGURE 5.12

The KeyCombo application maintains a list of records, indexed by three keys (SSN, VISA #, and AMEX #).

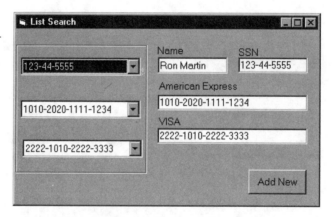

KeyCombo is perfect for incorporating into a larger payment tracking application. Customers can be recalled by their Social Security number, their American Express card number, or their VISA card number. All three keys are unique, and the information at hand will do.

Adding a New Item to KeyCombo   The KeyCombo application uses each control's ItemData array to store the index of the array element (or record number, in the case of a random access file) in which the matching record is stored.

When a new record is committed to the database, the following code goes into action. The OK button appears when the user adds a new record.

Code 5.12: The OK Button

```
Private Sub OKButton_Click()

  Key = Trim(Text1.Text)
  If Key = "" Then
    MsgBox "Key field must be non-empty"
    Exit Sub
  End If

  ArrayIndex = ArrayIndex + 1
  Combo1.AddItem Text2.Text
  Combo1.ItemData(Combo1.NewIndex) = ArrayIndex
  If Text3.Text <> "" Then
    Combo2.AddItem Text3.Text
    Combo2.ItemData(Combo2.NewIndex) = ArrayIndex
  End If
  If Text4.Text <> "" Then
    Combo3.AddItem Text4.Text
    Combo3.ItemData(Combo3.NewIndex) = ArrayIndex
  End If

  DataArray(ArrayIndex, 0) = Text1.Text
  DataArray(ArrayIndex, 1) = Text2.Text
  DataArray(ArrayIndex, 2) = Text3.Text
  DataArray(ArrayIndex, 3) = Text4.Text

  Combo1.ListIndex = Combo1.NewIndex
  Combo2.ListIndex = Combo2.NewIndex
  Combo3.ListIndex = Combo3.NewIndex
  ShowButtons

  Text1.SetFocus
End Sub
```

After ensuring that the name field is not empty, the program adds the corresponding fields to the three ComboBox controls. The SSN field is inserted in the Combo1 control, the VISA # field is inserted in the Combo2 control, and the AMEX # is inserted in the Combo3 field. The *ArrayIndex* variable is the index of the element where the new record will be added in the array DataArray(). This number is stored in each ComboBox control's ItemData array.

NewIndex is the index of the newly added item in a ComboBox control; so the expression ItemData(Combo3.NewIndex) matches the location of the new record in the data array. The fields are stored in the data array. The last few lines cause the keys of the newly added record to appear in the edit box of the ComboBox controls.

Selecting an Existing KeyCombo Item

When the user selects an item in one of the ComboBox controls, the program retrieves the matching record from the array and displays its fields in the data entry section of the Form.

Code 5.13: The Combo1 Control's Click Event

```
Private Sub Combo1_Click()

  If Combo1.ListIndex < 0 Then
    Text1.Text = ""
    Text2.Text = ""
    Text3.Text = ""
    Text4.Text = ""
    Exit Sub
  End If

  ItemIndex = Combo1.ItemData(Combo1.ListIndex)
  Text1.Text = DataArray(ItemIndex, 0)
  Text2.Text = DataArray(ItemIndex, 1)
  Text3.Text = DataArray(ItemIndex, 2)
  Text4.Text = DataArray(ItemIndex, 3)

End Sub
```

The event handlers for the other two ComboBox controls are identical.

The KeyCombo application is meant to be used for data retrieval only; it's not a data-entry application. The Add New button was included to help you enter some data and test the program, which is why the application lacks a Delete button. The ComboBox controls with the alternative keys need not be visible at run time. You might want to provide command buttons that make one of the combo boxes visible, according to the user's needs. Another improvement would be to replace the TextBox controls with combo boxes so that the user can either select an existing item or type a new one.

The ScrollBar and Slider Controls

The ScrollBar and Slider controls let the user specify a magnitude by scrolling a selector between its minimum and maximum values. In some situations, the user doesn't know in advance the exact value of the quantity to specify (in which case, a TextBox would suffice), and your application must provide a more flexible mechanism for specifying a value, along with some type of visual feedback.

The vertical scroll bar that lets you move up and down a long document is a typical example of the use of a ScrollBar control. In the past, users had to supply line numbers to locate the section of the document they wanted to view. With a highly visual operating system, however, this is no longer an option.

The scroll bar, along with visual feedback, are the prime mechanisms for repositioning your view in a long document or in a large picture that won't fit entirely in its window. When scrolling a document or an image up and down to locate the area of interest, the user doesn't know or care about line numbers or pixel coordinates. With the scroll bar, the user looks for something of interest. The visible part of the document provides the visual feedback. The example in Figure 5.13 was created with the ScrolPic application.

FIGURE 5.13

The ScrollBar controls in this window bring the desired part of the image into view and also provide a clue to the image's dimensions.

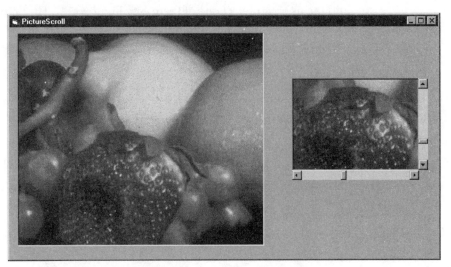

On the Mastering Visual Basic 5 CD-ROM: ScrolPic

The ScrolPic application shown in Figure 5.13 is in this chapter's folder on the CD. The ScrolPic application displays a large picture in a small PictureBox control and lets the user scroll around the image until the desired part is located.

You have probably noticed that the PictureBox control doesn't have a ScrollBars property; if it did, scroll bars would automatically attach to the image if it exceeds the control's dimensions. To display an image larger than the control's dimensions, you must simulate this feature through your code, and the ScrolPic application shows you how it's done.

The ScrolPic application will be explained in the next chapter, as it makes extensive use of graphics methods. Nevertheless, you might want to open the application to see how it uses the two scroll bars as navigational aids.

The Slider control is similar, but it doesn't cover a continuous range of values as the ScrollBar control does. The Slider control has a fixed number of tick marks, and the user can select one of them (see Figure 5.14). The ScrollBar control relies on some visual feedback outside the control itself to help the user position its indicator to the desired value; the Slider control forces the user to select a value from a range of valid values.

FIGURE 5.14

The Slider control lets the user select one of several discrete values.

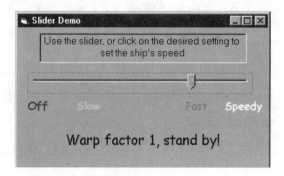

The tick marks on the Slider control make it easier for the user to locate the desired value. In short, the ScrollBar control is used when the exact value to be specified isn't as important as its effect on another object or data element. The Slider control is used when you would otherwise provide a TextBox control, in which the user could type a numeric value. If the value your application expects is a number in a specific range, such as an integer between 0 and 100, or is a value between 0 and 5 inches in steps of 0.1 inches (0.0, 0.1, 0.2 inches and so on up to 5 inches), use the Slider control. The Slider control is preferable to the TextBox control in similar situations, because there's no need for data validation on your part, and the user can specify a numeric value with the mouse.

The ScrollBar Control

The ScrollBar control is a long stripe with an indicator that lets the user select a value between the two ends of the control. The ScrollBar control comes in two versions: horizontal and vertical. Other than their orientation, there are no differences between the versions. The left (or bottom) end of the control corresponds to its minimum value. The other end is the control's maximum value. The current value of the control is determined by the position of the indicator, which can be scrolled between the minimum and maximum values. The basic properties of the ScrollBar control, therefore, are properly named Min, Max, and Value (see Figure 5.15).

Min   The control's minimum value

Max   The control's maximum value

Value   The control's current value, specified by the scroll box's position

FIGURE 5.15

The various items of the ScrollBar control

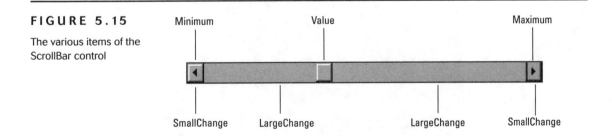

The Min and Max properties are positive integer values, which means the valid range of values for a ScrollBar control is 0 to 32655. To cover a range of negative

numbers or nonintegers, you must supply the code to map the actual values to integer values. For example, to cover a range from 2.5 to 8.5, set the Min property to 25, set the Max property to 85, and divide the control's value by 10. If the range you need is from -2.5 to 8.5, set the Min property to 0 and the Max property to 110 (25 + 85). This time you would not only divide the result by 10, you would also have to subtract 2.5 from it, to map the control's zero value to -2.5.

TIP

By default, scroll bars can be used to specify positive integers in the range 0 to 32655. To use them to specify negative or fractional numbers, you must use a little math in your code.

VB5 at Work: The Colors Application

Figure 5.16 shows another example that demonstrates how the ScrollBar control works. The Colors application lets the user specify a color by manipulating the value of its primary components (red, green, and blue) through scroll bars. Each scroll bar corresponds to the value of one of the primary colors; the minimum value is 0, and the maximum value is 255.

FIGURE 5.16

The Colors application demonstrates the use of the ScrollBar control.

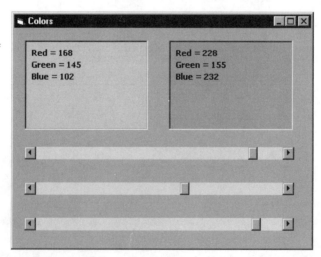

NOTE If you are not familiar with color definition in the Windows environment, see the section "Color Manipulation" in Chapter 7, *Advanced ActiveX Controls*.

As the scroll bar is moved, the corresponding color is displayed, and the user can easily specify a color without knowing the exact values of its primary components. All the user needs to know is whether the desired color contains too much red or too little green; with the help of the scroll bars and the immediate feedback from the application, the user can easily pinpoint the exact value. Notice that this "exact value" is of no practical interest; only the final color counts.

Scroll bars and slider bars have minimum and maximum values that can be set with the Min and Max properties. The indicator's position in the control determines its value, which is set or read with the Value property. All ScrollBar controls in the Colors application have a minimum value of 0 and a maximum value of 255. The initial value of the control is set to 128 (the middle of the range). Before looking at the code for the Colors application, let's examine the control's events.

The ScrollBar Control's Events

The user can change the ScrollBar control's value in three ways:

- By clicking on the two arrows at its ends. The value of the control changes by the amount specified with the SmallChange property.

- By clicking on the area between the indicator and the arrows. The value of the control changes by the amount specified with the LargeChange property.

- By scrolling the indicator with the mouse.

You can monitor the changes on the ScrollBar's value from within your code with two events: Change and Scroll.

- **Change** The Change event occurs every time the user changes the indicator's position and releases the mouse button. While the indicator is being moved, the Change event isn't triggered. For instance, if the user clicks on the indicator's button and holds down the mouse button while moving the mouse back and forth, no Change event is triggered. The Change event occurs only when the mouse button is released.

- **Scroll**   The Scroll event occurs continuously while the indicator is moving. This lets you update other controls on the Form from within your code as the user moves the indicator with the mouse. After the mouse button is released, the control stops triggering Scroll events and triggers a single Change event, because the control's value has changed. In most situations, you should program both events to react to user actions.

Scroll and Change Events in the Colors Application

The Colors application demonstrates the difference between the two events. The two PictureBox controls, which display the color designed with the three scroll bars, react differently to the user's actions. The first PictureBox is updated from within the Scroll event, which occurs constantly as the user moves the indicator of a scroll bar. The second PictureBox is updated from within the Change event, which occurs after the indicator is moved to another position.

As the user moves the indicator with the mouse, the first PictureBox displays the current color and provides immediate feedback to the user. The other PictureBox doesn't follow the changes. When the mouse button is released, a Change event occurs, and the second PictureBox is updated. At this point, both PictureBoxes display the color specified by the three scroll bars.

If the user attempts to change the color value by clicking on the two arrows of the scroll bars or by clicking in the area to the left or to the right of the indicator, only the second PictureBox is updated. The user doesn't slide the scroll bar, and therefore no Scroll event is generated. Open the Colors project and experiment by changing the values of the ScrollBar controls with the two techniques. The two PictureBoxes can have different colors if you set a color value by clicking on the arrows of the scroll bars.

The conclusion from this experiment is that you must program both the Scroll and the Change events to provide continuous feedback to the user. If this feedback requires too many calculations, which would slow down the reaction of the Scroll event, program only the Change event. This event may not take place continuously, but it will take place after the ScrollBar's value has changed, unlike the Scroll event, which occurs only during the sliding of the control.

The Slider Control Demo

The Slider control is similar to the ScrollBar control, but it lacks the *granularity* of the ScrollBar control. Suppose you want the user of an application to supply a value in a specific range, such as the speed of a moving object. Moreover, you don't want to allow extreme precision; you need only a few settings, such as slow, fast, and very fast. A Slider control with 3 or 4 stops, such as the one shown in Figure 5.17 (the same as Figure 5.14) will suffice. The user can set the control's value by sliding the indicator or by clicking on either side of the indicator.

> **NOTE**
>
> Granularity is the degree of detail, or accuracy, desired for a given magnitude and is usually imposed by the quantity you're measuring. In measuring distances between buildings, a granularity on the order of a foot is adequate. In measuring (or specifying) the dimensions of a building, the granularity should be on the order of millimeters. The Slider control lets you set the type of granularity that's necessary for your application. You can do the same with a scroll bar, but not without some extra calculations.

FIGURE 5.17

The Slider control is used to specify a value from a set of available values.

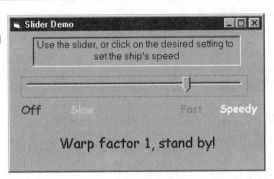

As with the ScrollBar control, SmallChange and LargeChange properties are available. SmallChange is the smallest increment by which the slider value can change. The user can only change the slider by the SmallChange value by sliding the indicator (unlike the ScrollBar control, there are no arrows at the two ends of the Slider control). To change the slider's value by LargeChange, the user can click on either side of the indicator.

The Slider on the Form in Figure 5.17 (also see the Slider project on the CD) has its Min property set to 1, its Max property set to 5 (that is, five stops), and its TickStyle set to 3 (sldNoTricks). The code behind the control's Change event sets the caption of the Label control at the bottom of the Form.

Code 5.14: The Slider Control's Change Event

```
Private Sub Slider1_Change()

  Select Case Slider1.Value
    Case 1: Label6.Caption = "Are we moving yet?"
    Case 2: Label6.Caption = "We're moving at 400 mph"
    Case 3: Label6.Caption = "We're cruising at 1000 mph"
    Case 4: Label6.Caption = "Warp factor 1, stand by!"
    Case 5: Label6.Caption = "Warp factor 9!"
  End Select

End Sub
```

In the place of the tick marks under the Slider control are Label controls, which indicate the desired speed. In addition, each Label's Click event has also been programmed to change the position of the Slider control:

```
Private Sub Label2_Click()

  Slider1.Value = 2

End Sub
```

This simple subroutine enables you to make the Label a functional element of the program's interface.

VB5 at Work: The Inches Application

Figure 5.18 demonstrates another situation that calls for a Slider control. The Form in Figure 5.18 is an element of a program's user interface that lets the user specify a distance between 0 and 10 inches and in increments of 0.1 inches. As the user slides the indicator, the current value displays on a Label control, above the Slider. If you open the Inches application, you will notice that there are more stops than there are tick marks on the control. This is made possible with the TickFrequency property, which determines the frequency of the visible tick marks.

FIGURE 5.18

This Slider control lets users specify a distance between 0 and 10 inches in increments of 0.1 inches. The tick marks correspond to half and whole inches.

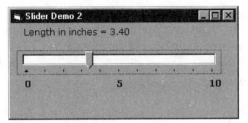

You may specify that the control has 50 stops (divisions) but that only 10 of them will be visible. The user can, however, position the indicator on any of the 40 invisible tick marks. You can think of the visible marks as the major tick marks and the invisible ones as the minor tick marks. If the TickFrequency property is 5, only every fifth mark will be visible. The slider's indicator, however, will stop at all tick marks.

TIP

When using the Slider control on your interfaces, you should set the TickFrequency property to a value that helps the user select the desired setting. Too many tick marks are confusing and difficult to read. Without tick marks, the control doesn't look professional. You might also consider placing a few labels to indicate the value of selected tick marks, as I have done in the examples.

The slider in the Inches application was designed with the following settings:

```
Min = 0
Max = 50
SmallChange = 1
LargeChange = 10
TickFrequency = 5
```

The slider needs to cover a range of 10 inches in increments of 0.1 inches. To set the SmallChange property to 1, you have to set LargeChange to 10. Moreover, the TickFrequency is set to 5, so there will be a total of 10 divisions (corresponding to half and whole inches). The numbers below the tick marks were placed there with properly aligned Label controls.

Inches Code   The Label's contents need to be updated as the Slider's value changes. This is signaled with two events (which don't occur simultaneously): the Change event, which occurs every time the value of the control changes , and the Scroll event, which occurs as the user slides the control's indicator. While the Scroll event takes place, the Change event doesn't, so you must program both events if you want to update the Label at all times. The code is the same and quite simple:

```
Private Sub Slider1_Scroll()

    Label1.Caption = "Length in inches = " & Format(Slider1.Value /
➡5,"#.00")

End Sub
```

This single line of Visual Basic code must be inserted into the control's Change event handler as well.

VB5 at Work: The TextMargin Application

To see the Slider control in use, here is a segment of another application, the RTFPad application, which is covered in Chapter 7, *Advanced ActiveX Controls*. The Form shown in Figure 5.19 contains a RichTextBox control and two sliders. (The RichTextBox control will be explained in Chapter 7. All you need to know about the control to follow the code is that the RichTextBox control is similar to a TextBox control, but provides many more editing and formatting options. Two of the control's properties we use in this example are the SelIndent and SelHanging-Indent properties.

- **SelIndent** specifies the amount by which the currently selected paragraph(s) is indented from the left side of the control.

- **SelHangingIndent** specifies the amount of the hanging indention (that is, the indention of all paragraph lines after the first line).

The two sliders above the RichTextBox control let the user manipulate these two indentions. Because each paragraph in a RichTextBox control is a separate entity, can be formatted differently. The upper slider controls the paragraph's indention, and the lower slider controls the paragraph's hanging indention.

You can open the TextMargin application in this chapter's folder on the CD. Enter a few paragraphs of text and experiment to see how the sliders control the appearance of the paragraphs.

FIGURE 5.19

The two Slider controls let the user format the paragraphs in a Rich-TextBox control.

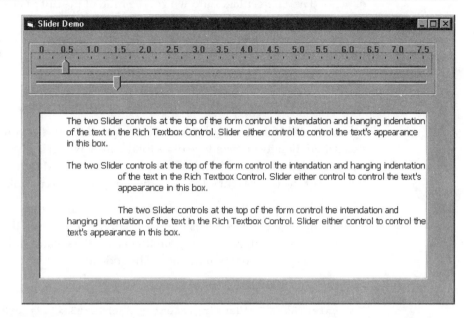

To create the Form shown in Figure 5.19, the left edge of the RichTextBox control must be perfectly aligned with the sliders' indicators at their leftmost position. When both sliders are at the far left, the SelIndent and SelHangingIndent properties are both zero. As each slider's indicator is scrolled, these two properties change value, and the text is reformatted instantly. All the action takes place in the Slider controls' Scroll event. Here's the code of the Slider1 control, which controls the paragraph's indention:

```
Private Sub Slider1_Scroll()

    RichTextBox1.SelIndent = RichTextBox1.RightMargin * (Slider1
➡.Value / Slider1.Max)
    Slider2_Scroll

End Sub
```

The paragraph's hanging indention is not the distance of the text from the left edge of the control, but the distance of the paragraph from the leftmost character of the first line. That's why every time the paragraph's indention changes, the program calls the Scroll event of the second slider to adjust the hanging indention, even though the second slider hasn't been moved. The hanging indention is expressed as a percentage, and we get the ratio of the difference between the two controls and their maximum value. This difference can become negative too, in which case the hanging indention is to the left of the normal indention. Remove the following line:

```
Slider2_Scroll
```

from the Slider1 control's Scroll event and see what happens.

Since the slider's tick marks do not correspond to physical units, we set the text's indention to a percentage of its total width, which is given by the Right-Margin property of the RichTextBox control. The RightMargin property is the distance of the text's right edge from the left side of the control.

This percentage is the same as the percentage of the slider's value divided by its maximum value. As soon as the SelIndent property is set, the entire paragraph is indented accordingly. The program then calls the second slider's Scroll event, which adjusts the hanging indention. The code for this event is shown here:

```
Private Sub Slider2_Scroll()

    RichTextBox1.SelHangingIndent = RichTextBox1.RightMargin *
    ➥((Slider2.Value - Slider1.Value) / Slider2.Max)

End Sub
```

The numbers (which don't correspond to any real units, but you could easily map them to inches, centimeters, or any other unit) are Label controls, carefully placed on the Form.

The Common Dialogs Control

A rather tedious, but quite common task in nearly every application is to prompt the user for filenames, font names and sizes, or colors to be used by the application. Designing your own dialog boxes for this purpose would be a hassle, not to mention that your applications wouldn't have the common look and feel of all Windows applications. Have you noticed that all Windows applications use some standard dialog boxes for such common operations as selecting a font or opening a file? Figure 5.20 shows a couple of examples. These dialog boxes are built into the operating system, and any application can use them.

FIGURE 5.20

The File Open and Font
common dialog boxes

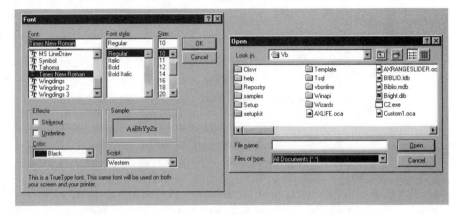

If you ever want to display a File Open dialog box or a Font dialog box, don't start designing one. It's already there, and all you have to do to use it is to place a Common Dialogs control on your Form and call the appropriate method. The ShowOpen method, for instance, invokes the File Open dialog box; the ShowColor method invokes the Color dialog box.

Using the Common Dialogs Control

The Common Dialogs control is peculiar in that it's not displayed on the Form at run time. It provides its services to the application, but it need not be displayed, just like the Timer control. The Common Dialogs control provides common Windows dialog boxes, such as the following:

- Open

- Save As

- Color

- Font

- Print

- Help

You will see many examples of the Common Dialogs control in the following chapters. This section explores the basic properties and methods of the control and especially the Flags property, which modifies the default behavior of each common dialog box.

To call upon the services of the Common Dialogs control, you must first place an instance of the control on the Form. To do this, you click on the control's icon on the toolbar.

If the Common Dialogs control's icon isn't on your toolbar, follow these simple steps:

1. Right-click on the toolbar, and from the pop-up menu select Components.

2. When the list of controls installed on your system appears, check the Microsoft Common Dialog Control - 5.0 option.

3. Click on OK.

After the control is placed on the Form, you can't adjust its size because the Common Dialogs control remains hidden at run time. You can, however, set several properties to adjust the appearance of any of the dialog boxes it can display, such as the initial font in the Font dialog box or a default filename in the Open or Save As dialog boxes.

To display a common dialog box from within your code, you must assign the proper value to the control's Action property. The Action property acts as a method; after you assign a value to it, the corresponding common dialog box displays. The values of the Action property are listed in Table 5.4.

TABLE 5.4   The Values of the Common Dialogs Control's Action Property

VALUE	DESCRIPTION
1	Displays the Open dialog box
2	Displays the Save As dialog box
3	Displays the Color dialog box
4	Displays the Font dialog box
5	Displays the Printer dialog box

An alternate (and preferred) way of invoking the previous dialog boxes is to use the more descriptive methods instead of numeric values, as shown in Table 5.5.

TABLE 5.5   The Names of the Methods for Displaying Specific Dialog Boxes

METHOD	ACTION
ShowOpen	Displays the Open dialog box
ShowSave	Displays the Save As dialog box
ShowColor	Displays the Color dialog box
ShowFont	Displays the Font dialog box
ShowPrinter	Displays the Print or Print Options dialog box
ShowHelp	Displays the Windows Help engine

After you assign a value to the Action property or call the equivalent method, the corresponding dialog box appears on-screen, and execution of the program is suspended until the dialog box is closed. Using the Open and the Save dialog boxes, for example, the user can traverse the entire structure of his or her hard disk and locate the desired filename.

When the user clicks on the Open or Save button, the control is returned to the application, which can read the name of the file selected by the user (Property FileName) and use it to open the file or to store the current document there.

Here is the sequence of statements used to invoke the File Open dialog box and retrieve the selected filename:

```
CommonDialog1.ShowOpen
fileName = CommonDialog1.FileName
```

The variable *fileName* is the full path name of the file selected by the user; you can store the current document in it. You can also set the FileName property to a file-name that is displayed when the common dialog box is first opened. The user can click on the Open button to open the preselected file or choose another file.

```
CommonDialog1.FileName = "C:\Documents\Doc1.doc"
CommonDialog1.ShowOpen
fileName = CommonDialog1.FileName
```

Similarly, you can invoke the Color dialog box with the following statements:

```
CommonDialog1.ShowColor
Color=CommonDialog1.Color
```

The dialog box sets the FileName and Color properties, and your application simply reads them. Each common dialog box has a number of properties that let you adjust its appearance or function, which you can set before opening it (most of these properties are optional). Some properties are common to nearly all the common dialog boxes, and the CancelError is one of them.

Canceling the Action

Each dialog box has a Cancel button, which should signal to your application the user's intention to halt the current operation. The Cancel action can be reported to your application by means of an error. To specify whether an error is generated when the user clicks on the Cancel button, set the CancelError property to True. If you don't want to handle this situation through an error handler, set the Cancel-Error property to False and examine the value of the FileName or Color property. If the user has canceled the operation, this value will be an empty string.

If you set the CancelError property to True, you must also provide an error handler that will detect this condition and act accordingly. All common dialog boxes return the same error, which is error number 32755 (constant cdlCancel). Your error handler must examine the error number and, if it's 32755, halt the operation. Here's how you can open the Open common dialog box and detect whether the user has canceled the operation.

Code 5.15: Checking for the Cancel Operation

```
On Error Goto NoFile
CommonDialog1.CancelError=True
CommonDialog1.ShowOpen
Fname=CommonDialog1.Filename
{more commands}
Exit Sub

NoFile:
     If Err.Number=32755 Then
     Exit Sub
     Else
          MsgBox "Unknown error in opening file " & Fname
     End If
```

Displaying Text in the Title Bar

The second common property is the DialogTitle property, which returns or sets the string displayed in the title bar of the dialog box.

Flags Property

A third property of all the common dialog boxes is Flags, which you use to adjust the function of each common dialog box. The values of this property, however, vary, depending on the specific common dialog box being opened. These values are discussed in the following sections devoted to each type of dialog box.

VB5 at Work: The CDBox Application

The Flags property of the Common Dialogs control may take on a large number of values, and remembering them is out of the question. When programming the Common Dialogs control, you should have a reference at hand.

In this chapter's folder on the CD-ROM, you will find the CDBox application, which lets you experiment with the various settings of the common dialog boxes, see what each property does, and determine which flag combinations you might need for a specific application.

The CDBox application is based on a Tab control, with one tab per common dialog box. The tab for the Color common dialog box, shown in Figure 5.21, contains a list of all the flags you can set in the Color common dialog box as well as the value of the Color property. Each tab will be explained in the following section, as we examine each common dialog box.

The Color Common Dialog Box

The Color common dialog box, shown in Figure 5.21, is one of the simplest dialog boxes. It has a single property, Color, which returns the color selected by the user or sets the initially selected color when the user opens the dialog box.

Before opening the Color dialog box with the ShowColor method, you can set a number of flags through its Flags property, whose values are shown in Table 5.6. To combine multiple flags, add their values or use the OR operator.

FIGURE 5.21

The Color common
dialog box

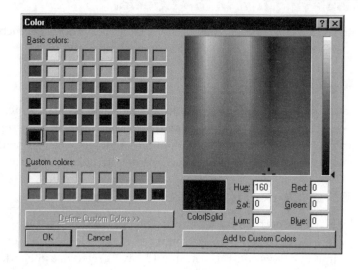

TABLE 5.6   The Flags Constants for the Color Common Dialog Box

CONSTANT	VALUE	DESCRIPTION
cdCClFullOpen	&H2	Displays the full dialog box, including the Define Custom Colors section
CdlCCHelpButton	&H8	Displays a Help button in the dialog box
cdlCCPrevent-FullOpen	&H4	Hides the Define Custom Colors section (preventing the user from defining custom colors)
cdlCCRGBInit	&H1	Sets the value of the color initially selected when the dialog box is opened.

The Color page of the CDBox application lets you set (or reset) the various flags and the value of the color that is initially selected in the Color dialog box. You can specify this value in decimal or hexadecimal format (the latter is more common). The Show Dialog Box button displays the Color common dialog box. When you select a color and then exit the Color dialog box, the PictureBox control at the bottom is filled with the selected color (see Figure 5.22). In addition, the color's value is displayed in the two TextBox controls under the Color Value heading, in decimal and hexadecimal format.

FIGURE 5.22

The Color tab of the
CDBox application

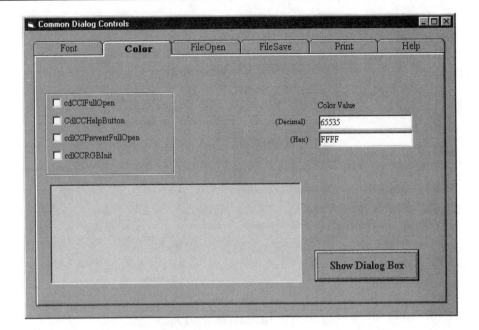

The Font Common Dialog Box

The Font common dialog box lets the user review and select a font and its size
and style (see Figure 5.23). To open the Font dialog box, set the Action property to
4, or invoke the ShowFont method of the Common Dialogs control.

After the user selects a font, its size and style, and possibly some special effects
(color or the underline attribute), and then clicks on OK, the Common Dialog control returns the attributes of the selected font through the following properties:

- **Color**   The selected color. To use this property, you must first set the Flags
  property to cdlCFEffects.

- **FontBold**   It's True if the bold attribute was set.

- **FontItalic**   It's True if the italic attribute was set.

- **FontStrikethru**   It's True if the strikethrough attribute was set. To use this
  property, you must first set the Flags property to cdlCFEffects.

FIGURE 5.23

The Font common
dialog box

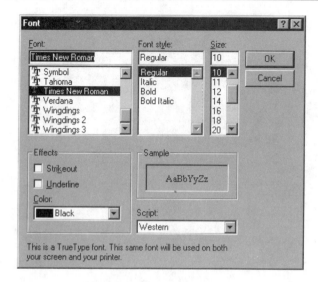

- **FontUnderline**   It's True if the underline attribute was set. To use this
  property, you must first set the Flags property to cdlCFEffects.

- **FontName**   Returns the selected font name.

- **FontSize**   Returns the selected font size.

When the Font common dialog box is closed, the values of these properties are
updated to match the settings specified by the user in the dialog box. You can also
set the value of any of the previous properties before calling the ShowFont
method, to specify the initial settings of the Font dialog box.

You may have noticed that some properties require that the cdlCEffects flag is
set. This flag displays a few additional settings that are considered special effects,
such as strikethrough, underline, and the color of the font.

> **NOTE**
>
> If you attempt to call the Font dialog box by invoking only the ShowFont
> method, you'll get an error message stating that no fonts are installed.
> To open the Font dialog box, you must first set the Flags property to
> cdlCFScreenFonts, cdlCFPrinterFonts, or cdlCFBoth, which determine
> which fonts will be displayed (screen fonts only, printer fonts only,
> or both).

Using the Flags Property with the Font Dialog Box

The CDBox Form shown in Figure 5.24 provides checkmarks for every type of flag you can set with the Font common dialog box. The Flags property of the Font common dialog box can take on any of the values shown in Table 5.7.

FIGURE 5.24

Switch to the Font tab of the CDBox application to experiment with the various settings of the Font common dialog box.

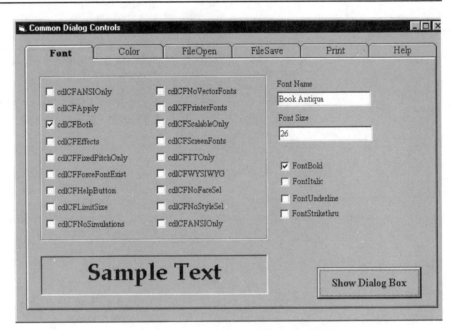

TABLE 5.7   The Flags Constants for the Font Common Dialog Box

CONSTANT	VALUE	DESCRIPTION
cdlCFANSIOnly	&H400	Specifies that the dialog box display only the fonts that use the Windows character set. If this flag is set, the user won't be able to select a font that contains only symbols, such as Wingdings.
cdlCFApply	&H200	Enables the Apply button in the dialog box.

TABLE 5.7   The Flags Constants for the Font Common Dialog Box (continued)

CONSTANT	VALUE	DESCRIPTION
cdlCFBoth	&H3	Displays both printer and screen fonts in the dialog box. (You must also set the hDC property to specify the current printer.)
cdlCFEffects	&H100	Specifies that the dialog box let the user set the strikethrough, underline, and color effects.
cdlCFFixedPitchOnly	&H4000	Specifies that the dialog box display only monospaced (fixed-pitch) fonts. These fonts are commonly used for program lists.
cdlCFForceFontExist	&H10000	Specifies that an error message box appear if the user attempts to select a font or style that doesn't exist.
cdlCFHelpButton	&H4	Displays a Help button in the dialog box.
cdlCFLimitSize	&H2000	Specifies that the dialog box display only font sizes within the range specified by the Min and Max properties.
cdlCFNoSimulations	&H1000	Specifies that the dialog box doesn't display simulated fonts.
cdlCFNoVectorFonts	&H800	Specifies that the dialog box doesn't display vector-font selections.
cdlCFPrinterFonts	&H2	Causes the dialog box to list only the fonts supported by the printer, specified by the hDC property.
cdlCFScalableOnly	&H20000	Specifies that the dialog box display only fonts that can be scaled.
cdlCFScreenFonts	&H1	Causes the dialog box to display only the screen fonts supported by the system.
cdlCFTTOnly	&H40000	Specifies that the dialog box display only TrueType fonts.
cdlCFWySIWyG	&H8000	Specifies that the dialog box display the fonts supported by the printer and on-screen. If this flag is set, the cdlCFBoth and cdlCFScalableOnly flags should also be set.
cdlCFNoFaceSel	&H80000	No font name selected.

TABLE 5.7   The Flags Constants for the Font Common Dialog Box (continued)

CONSTANT	VALUE	DESCRIPTION
cdlCFNoSizeSel	&H200000	No font size selected.
cdlCFNoStyleSel	&H100000	No style selected.

When the Font common dialog box is first opened, the font name, size, and attributes of the font selected the last time the same dialog box was opened are displayed. If you want these fields to be empty when the user opens this dialog box, set the Flags property to the following value:

```
CommonDialog1.Flags = cdlCFNoFaceSel OR cdlCFNosizeSel OR
➥cdlCFNoStyleSel
```

This line displays the Font dialog box without an initial font, size, or style selection.

The FileOpen and FileSave Common Dialog Boxes

FileOpen and FileSave (see Figure 5.25) are the two most widely used common dialog boxes. Nearly every application prompts the user for a filename. Windows 95 provides two highly customizable common dialog boxes for this purpose. The two dialog boxes are nearly identical, and most of their properties are common; so let's look at the properties of both.

FIGURE 5.25

The FileSave common dialog box

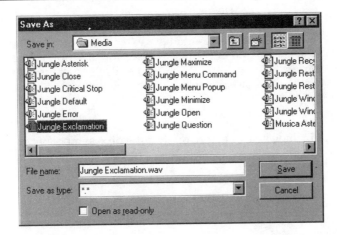

When a File common dialog box is opened, it rarely displays all the files in any given folder. Usually the number of files displayed is limited to the ones that the application recognizes so that users can easily spot the file they want. The Filter property determines which files appear in the File Open or File Save dialog box.

It is also standard for the Windows 95 interface not to display the extensions of files. Figure 5.25 shows the Save As dialog box of Microsoft Word. The Save As Type ComboBox contains the various file types recognized by the application. The various file types are described in plain English and not with their extensions, only a long, descriptive name (Windows distinguishes files using invisible extensions, however).

The extension of default file type for the application is described by the DefaultExt property, and the list of the file types displayed in the Save As Type box is described by the Filter property. Both the DefaultExt and the Filter properties are available in the control's Properties window at design time. At run time, you must set them manually from within your code.

- **DefaultExt**   Sets the default extension of the dialog box. Use this property to specify a default filename extension, such as TXT or DOC, so that when a file with no extension is saved, the extension specified by this property is automatically appended to the filename.

- **Filter**   The Filter property is used to specify the type(s) of files that are displayed in the dialog box's file list box. To display text files only, set the Filter property to Text | *.txt. The pipe symbol separates the description of the files (which is what the user sees) from the actual extension (which is how the operating system distinguishes the various file types).

TIP   If you want to display multiple extensions, such as BMP, GIF, and JPG, use a semicolon to separate extensions with the Filter property. The string "Images|*.BMP;*.GIF;*.JPG" displays all the files of these three types when the user selects Images in the Files of Type box.

Don't include spaces before or after the pipe symbol because these spaces will be displayed with the description and filter values. In the FileOpen dialog box of an image-processing application, you will probably provide options for each image file type, as well as an option for all images:

```
CommonDialog1.Filter = "Bitmaps|*.BMP|GIF Images|*.GIF|JPEG
➥Images|*.JPG|All Images|*.BMP;*.GIF;*.JPG"
```

The FileOpen dialog box has four options (see Figure 5.26) that determine what appears in the Files of Type box.

- **FilterIndex**   When you specify more than one filter for a dialog box, the filter specified first in the Filter property becomes the default. If you want to use a filter value other than the first one, use the FilterIndex property to determine which filter is displayed as the default. This property determines which of a number of alternate filters will become the default when the Open or Save dialog box is opened. The index of the first filter is 1, and there's no reason to ever set this property to 1. If you want to use the Filter property value of the previous example and set the FilterIndex property to 2, the Open dialog box will display GIF files by default.

- **FileTitle**   This property returns the name of the file to be opened or saved. The FileTitle property does not include the path name.

- **InitDir**   This property sets the initial directory (folder) whose files are displayed the first time the Open and Save dialog boxes are opened. Use this property to display the files of the application's folder or to specify a folder in which the application stores its files by default. If you don't specify an initial folder, it will default to the last folder where the dialog box opened or saved a file. It is also customary to set the initial folder to the application's path, with the following statement:

```
CommonDialog1.InitDir = App.Path
```

- **MaxFileSize**   This property returns or sets the maximum size of the filename opened using the CommonDialog control. Its default value is 256, which is plenty for any reasonable filename. Normally you won't use this property unless you allow the user to select multiple files; in that case, you must allocate enough memory to store the names of the selected files. See the description of the flags of this common dialog box in Table 5.8 to find out how you can allow multiple file selection in the Open and Save common dialog boxes.

FIGURE 5.26

Switch to the FileOpen tab of the CDBox application to experiment with the various settings of the File common dialog box.

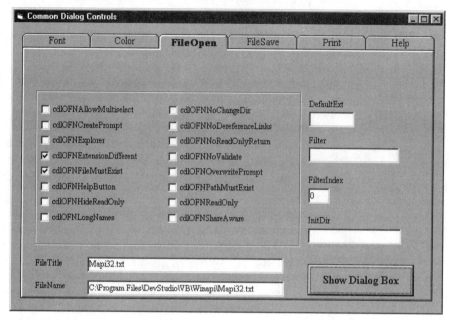

TABLE 5.8 The Flags Constants for the FileOpen and FileSave Common Dialog Boxes

CONSTANT	VALUE	DESCRIPTION
cdlOFNAllowMultiselect	&H200	Permits multiple file selection. The user can select more than one file at run time by pressing the Shift key and using the Up and Down arrow keys to select the desired files. On return, the FileName property returns a string containing the names of all selected files, delimited by spaces.
CdlOFNCreatePrompt	&H2000	Prompts the user to create a file that doesn't currently exist. This flag automatically sets the cdlOFNPathMustExist and cdlOFNFileMustExist flags.
CdlOFNExplorer	&H80000	Uses the Explorer-like Open a File dialog box template (works with Windows 95 and Windows NT 4).

TABLE 5.8   The Flags Constants for the FileOpen and FileSave Common Dialog Boxes (cont.)

CONSTANT	VALUE	DESCRIPTION
CdlOFNExtensionDifferent	&H400	Indicates that the extension of the returned filename is different from the extension specified by the DefaultExt property. This flag isn't set if the DefaultExt property is Null, if the extensions match, or if the file has no extension. This flag value is set by the Common Dialogs control, and the application must examine it when the dialog box is closed.
cdlOFNFileMustExist	&H1000	Specifies that the user can enter only names of existing files in the File Name text box. If this flag is set and the user enters an invalid filename, a warning is displayed. This flag automatically sets the cdlOFNPathMustExist flag.
cdlOFNHelpButton	&H10	Displays the Help button in the dialog box.
cdlOFNHideReadOnly	&H4	Hides the Read Only checkbox.
cdlOFNLongNames	&H200000	Allows long filenames.
cdlOFNNoChangeDir	&H8	Forces the dialog box to set the current directory to what it was when the dialog box was opened. Use this flag to force the user of the application to use a predetermined folder for storing the files.
cdlOFNNoDereferenceLinks	&H100000	Do not de-reference shortcuts. By default, choosing a shortcut causes it to be de-referenced by the shell.
cdlOFNNoReadOnlyReturn	&H8000	Disables the selection of files that have the Read Only attribute set and won't be in a write-protected directory. This attribute won't allow the user to save to a file on a CD-ROM drive.
cdlOFNNoValidate	&H100	Normally, the File Open dialog box validates filenames. To skip this validation step, set this flag value.
cdlOFNOverwritePrompt	&H2	Causes the Save As dialog box to generate a message box if the selected file already exists. The user must confirm the intention to overwrite a file before the file is overwritten.

TABLE 5.8 The Flags Constants for the FileOpen and FileSave Common Dialog Boxes (cont.)

CONSTANT	VALUE	DESCRIPTION
cdlOFNPathMustExist	&H800	Specifies that the user can enter only valid paths. If this flag is set and the user enters an invalid path, a warning message is displayed.
cdlOFNReadOnly	&H1	Checks the Read Only checkbox the first time the dialog box is opened. This flag also indicates the state of the Read Only checkbox on exit. Test this flag to find out whether the user wants to open a file as read-only.
cdlOFNShareAware	&H4000	Specifies that sharing violation errors will be ignored.

To specify that the user must select an existing file only (in other words, the user will not be allowed to type a nonexisting filename in the File Name field), set the Flags to cdlOFNFileMustExist, with the following statement:

```
CommonDialog1.Flags = cdlOFNFileMustExist
```

To set multiple flags, combine their values with the OR operator, as in:

```
CommonDialog1.Flags = cdlOFNFileMustExist OR cdlOFNLongNames OR
➥cdlOFNExplorer
```

You can also add the values instead of using OR.

Each value sets certain bits in the Flags property; when multiple flags are combined with the OR operator, all corresponding bits are set. To test for a flag value, you must use AND with the flag's corresponding value or constant. To find out the status of the Read Only checkbox, use a structure such as the following:

```
If CommonDialog1.Flags AND cdlOFNReadOnly Then
       {open file for input}
Else
       {open file for random access}
End If
```

The Print Common Dialog Box

The Print common dialog box enables users to select a printer, set certain properties of the printout (number of copies, pages to be printed, and so on), and set up a specific printer (see Figure 5.27).

FIGURE 5.27

The Print common
dialog box

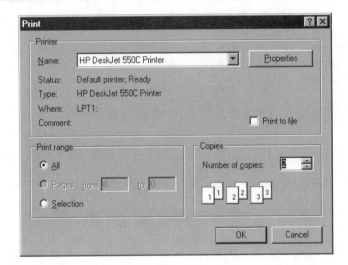

To open the Print dialog box, set the Action property of the Common Dialogs control to 5, or invoke the ShowPrinter method of the Common Dialogs control. After the user selects a printer and clicks on OK, the Common Dialogs control returns the printer name and the attributes of the desired printout to the calling program through the following properties:

- **Copies** Specifies the number of copies to print

- **FromPage** Specifies the page to start printing

- **ToPage** Specifies the page to stop printing

- **hDC** Specifies the device context for the selected printer

When the Print common dialog box is closed, the VB application reads the values of these properties to determine the settings specified by the user.

You can also set the value of any of the previous properties before calling the ShowPrinter method so that initial settings will appear when the dialog box is first opened. The Flags property of the Print common dialog box enables you to specify these initial settings. These values are shown in Table 5.9.

TABLE 5.9 The Flags Constants for the Print Common Dialog Boxes

CONSTANT	VALUE	DESCRIPTION
cdlPDAllPages	&H0	Returns or sets the state of the All Pages option button.
cdlPDCollate	&H10	Returns or sets the state of the Collate checkbox.
cdlPDDisable-PrintToFile	&H80000	Disables the Print to File checkbox.
cdlPDHelpButton	&H800	Causes the dialog box to display the Help button.
cdlPDHidePrintToFile	&H100000	Hides the Print to File checkbox.
cdlPDNoPageNums	&H8	Disables the Pages option button and the associated edit control.
cdlPDNoSelection	&H4	Disables the Selection option button.
cdlPDNoWarning	&H80	Prevents a warning message from being displayed when there is no default printer.
cdlPDPageNums	&H2	Returns or sets the state of the Pages option button.
cdlPDPrintSetup	&H40	Causes the system to display the Print Setup dialog box rather than the Print dialog box.
cdlPDPrintToFile	&H20	Returns or sets the state of the Print to File checkbox.
cdlPDReturnDC	&H100	Returns a device context for the printer selection made in the Printer dialog box. If this flag is set, the device context is returned in the dialog box's hDC property.
cdlPDReturnDefault	&H400	Returns the name of the default printer.
cdlPDReturnIC	&H200	Returns an information context for the printer selected in the dialog box. An information context provides a fast way to get information about the device without creating a device context. The information context is returned in the dialog box's hDC property.

TABLE 5.9 The Flags Constants for the Print Common Dialog Boxes (continued)

CONSTANT	VALUE	DESCRIPTION
cdlPDSelection	&H1	Returns or sets the state of the Selection option button. If neither cdlPDPageNums nor cdlPDSelection is specified, the All option button is automatically selected.
cdlPDUseDevMode-Copies	&H40000	If a printer driver doesn't support multiple copies, setting this flag disables the Number of Copies control in the Print dialog box. If a driver does support multiple copies, setting this flag indicates that the requested number of copies is stored in the Copies property.

To experiment with the various settings of the Print common dialog box, you can use the Print tab of the CDBox application, shown in Figure 5.28.

FIGURE 5.28

Switch to the Print tab of the CDBox application to experiment with the various settings of the Print common dialog box.

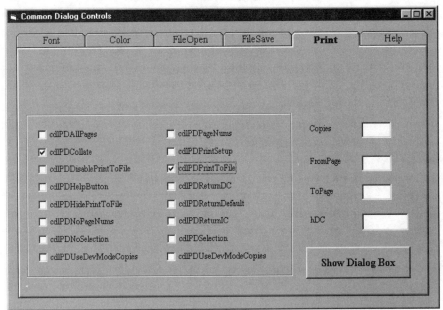

The Help Common Dialog Box

The Help common dialog box is as simple to use as the other ones, but you must first prepare your help files. I won't discuss how to build Help files in this book;

you can purchase many specialized tools for this task. If you don't have your own help files, you can use one that comes with an application, such as Visual Basic. Visual Basic's help file is called VB5. You don't have to specify an extension or a path; WinHelp knows where the Help files are located.

The basic properties of the Help common dialog box are the following:

- **HelpFile** Specifies the filename of a Windows Help file that will be used to display online help. This file must be supplied by your application, but for the purposes of learning the Help common dialog box, you can use any Help files already on your hard drive.

- **HelpCommand** Sets or returns the type of help requested. The values of this property are listed in Table 5.10. The constants listed in Table 5.10 look like flags, but they are actually parameters for the HelpCommand property. You can combine multiple commands by using the OR operator or by adding them together.

- **HelpContextID** Sets or returns a context number for an object. This ID is a number that tells WinHelp where in the Help file it will find the pages describing the specific topic. If you've created a Windows Help file for your application, Visual Basic searches the Help file for the topic identified by the current context ID when a user opens the Help common dialog box (by pressing the F1 key, for instance).

- **HelpKey** Sets or returns the keyword that identifies the requested Help topic. To use this property, you must also set the HelpCommand property to cdlHelpKey.

TABLE 5.10 The Values of the Common Dialogs Control's HelpCommand Property

CONSTANT	VALUE	DESCRIPTION
cdlHelpCommand	&H102&	Executes a Help macro.
CdlHelpContents	&H3&	Displays the Help contents topic as defined by the Contents option in the [OPTION] section of the HPJ file.
cdlHelpContext	&H1&	Displays Help for a particular context. When using this setting, you must also specify a context using the HelpContext property.

TABLE 5.10 The Values of the Common Dialogs Control's HelpCommand Property(cont.)

CONSTANT	VALUE	DESCRIPTION
cdlHelpContext-Popup	&H8&	Displays in a pop-up window a particular Help topic identified by a context number defined in the [MAP] section of the HPJ file.
cdlHelpForceFile	&H9&	Ensures that WinHelp displays the correct Help file. If the correct Help file is currently displayed, no action occurs. If the incorrect Help file is displayed, WinHelp opens the correct file.
cdlHelpHelpOnHelp	&H4&	Displays Help for using the Help application itself.
CdlHelpIndex	&H3&	Displays the index of the specified Help file. An application should use this value only for a Help file with a single index.
CdlHelpKey	&H101&	Displays Help for a particular keyword. When using this setting, you must also specify a keyword using the HelpKey property.
cdlHelpPartialKey	&H105&	Displays the topic found in the keyword list that matches the keyword passed in the dwData parameter if there is one exact match. If more than one match exists, the Search dialog box with the topics listed in the Go To list box is displayed. If no match exists, the Search dialog box is displayed. To display the Search dialog box without passing a keyword, use a long pointer to an empty string.
CdlHelpQuit	&H2&	Notifies the Help application that the specified Help file is no longer in use.
CdlHelpSetContents	&H5&	Determines which contents topic is displayed when a user presses the F1 key.
CdlHelpSetIndex	&H5&	Sets the context specified by the HelpContext property as the current index for the Help file. Used with Help files with more than one index.

You can use the CDBox application to experiment with some of the Windows Help files (see Figure 5.29). They are all located in the Help folder under the Windows folder, and you need specify only their name in the Help File box. If you set the cdlHelpIndex flag, the Index tab of the Help file is opened automatically. Or you can check the cdlHelpKey flag and supply a key, such as "text," in the Help Key box. The Help dialog box opens the specified Help file, locates the topic, and takes you there.

FIGURE 5.29

Switch to the Help tab of the CDBox application to experiment with the various settings of the Help common dialog box.

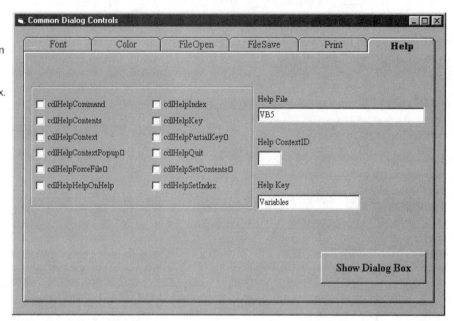

Certain flag combinations may be invalid and will cause a run-time error. For example, you can't hide the Print to File CheckBox in the Print dialog box and then set the Print to File option. The CDBox application will display the error message generated by Visual Basic (its number in parentheses, followed by its description). Even so, some errors don't have a description, and you must experiment with the settings to figure out exactly what went wrong.

The File Controls

The DriveListBox, DirListBox, and FileListBox (see Figure 5.30) are independent of one another, and each can exist on its own.

FIGURE 5.30

Three File controls are used in the design of Forms that let users explore the entire structure of their hard disks.

- **DriveListBox**   Displays the names of the drives within and connected to your PC. The basic property of this control is the Drive property, which sets the drive to be initially selected in the control or returns the user's selection.

- **DirListBox**   Displays the folders of the current drive. The basic property of this control is the Path property, which is the name of the folder whose sub-folders are displayed in the control.

- **FileListBox**   Displays the files of the current folder. The basic property of this control is also called Path, and it is the path name of the folder whose files are displayed.

The three File controls are not tied to one another. If you place all three of them on a Form, you can see the names of all the drives in the DriveListBox and select one of them, and you can see the names of all the folders under the current folder and select one of them as well. Each time you select a folder in the DirListBox by double-clicking on its name, its subfolders are displayed. Similarly, the FileList-Box control will display the names of all files in the current folder. Selecting a drive in the DriveListBox control, however, doesn't affect the contents of the DirListBox.

To connect the File controls, you must assign the appropriate values to their basic properties. To force the DirListBox to display the folders of the selected drive in the DriveListBox, you must make sure that each time the user selects another drive, the Path property of the DirListBox control matches the Drive property of the DriveListBox. The following is the minimum code you must place in the DriveListBox control's Change event:

```
Private Sub Drive1_Change()

  Dir1.Path = Drive1.Drive

End Sub
```

Similarly, every time the current selection in the DirListBox control changes, you must set the FileListBox control's Path property to point to the new path of the DirListBox control:

```
Private Sub Dir1_Change()

  File1.Path = Dir1.Path

End Sub
```

This is all it takes to connect the three File controls and create a Form that lets users traverse all the disks on their computers. Although the DriveListBox control displays all the drives and the DirListBox control displays all the subfolders, in most cases you will want to limit the files displayed in the FileListBox. To do this, use the control's Pattern property, which lets you specify which files will be displayed with a file-matching string such as "*.TXT" or "1997*.XLS".

It's also customary to display a list of available file-matching specifications in a ComboBox control, where the user can select one of them. The ComboBox control shown in Figure 5.31 is populated when the Form is loaded and when its selection is changed. The new file pattern is assigned to the Pattern property of the File control.

Changes in the ComboBox control are reported to the application with two distinct events: Change (the user enters a new file pattern) and Click (the user selects a new pattern from the list with the mouse). Both events contain the following line of code:

```
File1.Pattern = Combo1.Text
```

FIGURE 5.31

The ComboBox control below the ListBox control lets you specify a pattern, which will be used to populate the FileList control with filenames that match the pattern.

But why bother with the File controls when you can use the FileOpen and FileSave controls? The answer is that sometimes you want to build your own, custom applications that manipulate disk files. In Chapter 10, *Recursive Programming*, you will be introduced to the FileScan application, which scans a folder, including its subfolder, to locate specific files and then processes them. This application can't be implemented with the standard common dialog controls.

A program that scans the hard disk relies on the contents of these controls, and when it switches to a specific folder, it expects to find the names of the files in this folder in a FileListBox control. The ScanFolder application examined in Chapter 10 is a good example of the use of these controls, not only as elements of a user interface, but as functional elements of an application.

CHAPTER

SIX

6

Drawing and Painting with Visual Basic

One of the most interesting and fun parts of a language, and consequently of a program, is its graphics elements. Visual Basic provides many tools for manipulating graphics, and this chapter explores them.

In general, graphics fall into two major categories: vector and bitmap. Vector graphics are generated with graphics commands such as line and circle drawing commands. Bitmap graphics are images that can be displayed on various controls and processed on a pixel by pixel basis. The difference between vector and bitmap graphics is that vector graphics are not tied to a specific resolution. They are generated with commands and can be displayed at various resolutions. Figure 6.1 shows an interesting curve that was designed with the Spiral application, which we will explore later in the chapter. The vector image on the left was generated with drawing commands, and the image on the right is the equivalent bitmap. Figure 6.2 shows a detail of the same curve. The curve designed with drawing commands (the vector image) looks just as good when enlarged, whereas the bitmap reveals its blocklike structure. The drawing can be easily generated at the new resolution, but the bitmap can only be enlarged. And as you know, you can't blow up an image without some loss in quality.

FIGURE 6.1

The image on the left was created with drawing commands, and the image on the right is its bitmap. The two images appear to be identical.

Vector   Bitmap

This chapter explores both types of graphics as well as the Visual Basic tools for manipulating them. Despite their inherent limitations, bitmap graphics are quite useful, and much more common than vector graphics. For example, you can't create the image of a landscape with graphics commands. On the other hand, it doesn't make sense to display the bitmap of a circle when a simple Circle command can produce the same image faster and cleaner. Both types of graphics have their place, and you can mix them to produce the desired result.

FIGURE 6.2

When enlarged, the drawing retains its detail, but the bitmap reveals its structure.

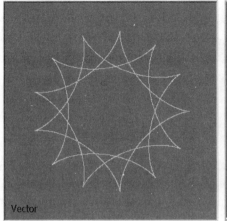
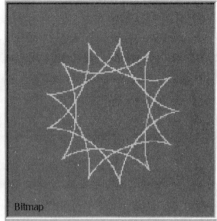

Form, PictureBox, and ImageBox Controls

You can place graphics on three controls:

- Form
- PictureBox
- ImageBox

The main difference between these three controls is that the ImageBox control was designed specifically for displaying bitmaps. The other two controls provide drawing methods, which let you design graphics at run time.

First, we'll look at the methods for loading graphics on the various controls, which is simpler than creating graphics from scratch. Vector drawings (generated with Visual Basic's methods, which we'll explore in the second part of the chapter) are not loaded. They are generated on the fly. Basically, you can place graphics on controls in two ways: at design time and at run time. To load a graphic (bitmap or icon) on a control at design time, you assign its filename to the Picture property of the control in the Properties window. To change the image displayed at run time, you can't directly assign a filename to the Picture property. Instead, you must use the LoadPicture() function, which is described shortly.

If the graphic is assigned to a control at design time, it is stored along with the application. One of the files that the Visual Basic editor generates for each Form in a project has the extension FRX. This is where the image (the actual bitmap) is stored. As a consequence, the size of the application will increase. The alternative is to load the graphic at run time with the LoadPicture() function. This reduces the size of the FRX file, but your application must make sure the file is available at run time.

Sizing Images

When an image is loaded on a Form or a PictureBox, you must make sure it will fill the available space—unless you let the user select the graphic at run time. Graphics are usually placed on ImageBox or PictureBox controls. The ImageBox is good for displaying graphics and uses fewer resources than PictureBox controls. The PictureBox control provides methods for drawing at run time and is much more flexible than the ImageBox control. As a consequence, the PictureBox control uses more resources. Each control provides a different property for controlling the appearance of the picture displayed.

The PictureBox Control   If the AutoSize property is True, the control is resized to the dimensions of the image it contains. If the AutoSize property is False, only the part of the image that can fit on the control is displayed.

The ImageBox Control   If the Stretch property is True, the image is resized to fill the control's area. Unless the control's dimensions have the same aspect ratio as the image's dimensions, the image is distorted as it's resized. If the Stretch property is False, the ImageBox control behaves like a PictureBox with its AutoSize property set to True. Figure 6.3 shows two ImageBox controls, both containing the same image. Notice how the image is resized in the ImageBox control whose Stretch property is True.

Loading and Saving Images

To load a graphic on a control at run time, use the LoadPicture method, like this:

```
Form1.Picture = LoadPicture(fileName)
```

FIGURE 6.3

The Stretch property of
the ImageBox control

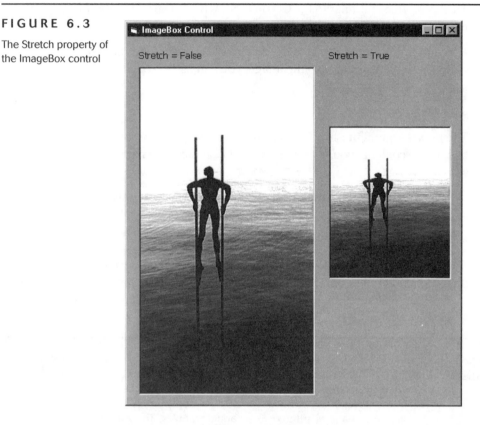

The *fileName* variable is the name of the file containing the graphic. This file can have the extension BMP (bitmap), GIF (Graphics Interchange Format), JPG (Joint Photographic Experts Group), DIB (Device Independent Bitmap), WMF (Windows MetaFile), EMF (Enhanced MetaFile), or ICO (icons). At present, Visual Basic doesn't support other types of graphic files.

If you use the LoadPicture method without an argument, the current picture is unloaded (along with any drawing or printing painted onto the control or Form with the Circle, Line, PSet, or Print commands). Using LoadPicture with no file-name specified clears the control. To remove a graphic from a PictureBox (or any control that can display graphics), issue the following command:

```
Picture1.Picture = LoadPicture( )
```

This technique is similar to the Cls method, which clears any drawing or printing from a Form or a control.

If your application processes the displayed image during the course of its execution and you want to save the image, you can use the SavePicture statement. Its syntax is as follows:

```
SavePicture picture, filename
```

The *picture* argument is the Picture property of the PictureBox or ImageBox control whose contents you want to save, and *filename* is the name of the file that will store the image.

To save the contents of the Picture1 control to a file, you must use a statement such as the following:

```
SavePicture Picture1.Picture, "c:\tmpImage.bmp"
```

The SavePicture method saves images in BMP format only, even if the original image loaded on the control was a GIF image. In addition, the SavePicture statement saves the entire image on the control, even if part of it is invisible.

WARNING If you use the SavePicture statement to save the contents of a PictureBox control, you can end up with an empty BMP file if the AutoRedraw property of the control is False. If you plan to save the contents of a PictureBox control to a file, be sure that its AutoRedraw property is set to True before loading any image or otherwise creating graphics. The AutoRedraw property is an important property of controls that can display images, and we will look at it in detail at the end of the chapter.

The SavePicture statement supports only BMP files, even if the original image loaded on the control came from a GIF or a JPG file. When prompting the user with the FileOpen common dialog box to select an image file to open, you can use the extensions BMP, GIF, or JPG. In the corresponding FileSave common dialog box, though, you can specify only the BMP (or DIB) extension.

Setting Picture and Image Properties

Another related property is the Image property, which is a pointer to a structure in memory where the bits of the image are stored. Unlike the Picture property, the

Image property is read-only and is used to pass bitmaps to API functions, as you will see in Chapter 12, *The Windows API*. Another difference between the Image and Picture properties is that the bitmap returned by the Picture property is the one saved along with the other Form elements in the FRX file and doesn't include any shapes drawn on top of the bitmap at run time. The PicImg application, shown in Figure 6.4, demonstrates the basic difference between the two properties.

FIGURE 6.4

The PicImg application demonstrates the difference between the Picture and Image properties.

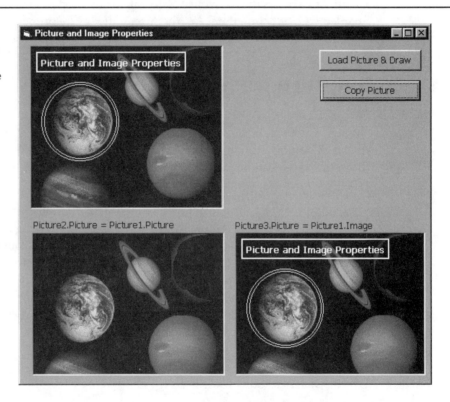

Clicking on the Load Picture & Draw button loads the Planets.bmp image on the PictureBox control in the upper half of the window and draws a couple of shapes over the bitmap with Visual Basic's drawing commands. Clicking on the Copy Picture button copies the contents of the top PictureBox on the other two PictureBox controls. The bitmap is copied on the left PictureBox control with the following command:

```
Picture2.Picture = Picture1.Picture
```

The same bitmap is copied on the other PictureBox with this command:

```
Picture3.Picture = Picture1.Image
```

Through the Picture property, you can copy only the bitmap loaded with the LoadPicture method. On the other hand, the Image property copies everything on the control, including the shapes. The Image property points to the persistent bitmap, which consists of the shapes drawn while the AutoRedraw property is True. Any shapes drawn while the AutoRedraw property is False will not be copied with either method. Another use of the Image property is to copy the image of a control to the Clipboard, as you'll see in the next section.

Exchanging Images through the Clipboard

Whether you use bitmap images or create graphics from scratch with the Visual Basic drawing methods, sooner or later you'll want to exchange them with other Windows applications. To do so, you use the Clipboard and its SetData and GetData methods, which are described in this section.

The ImgCopy application, shown in Figure 6.5, demonstrates how to use the Clipboard to exchange data with other applications. Clicking on the Load Image button loads the Planets.bmp image on the top PictureBox control, and clicking on the Draw on Image button draws a couple of shapes on top of the control's bitmap. The other two buttons copy the first PictureBox control's image to the Clipboard and paste the contents of the Clipboard on the second PictureBox control. The code behind the first two command buttons is straightforward. We used similar code in the PicImg application.

Using SetData   To copy the contents of a control to the Clipboard, you use the SetData method:

```
Clipboard.SetData Picture1.Image, vbCFBitmap
```

The *vbCFBitmap* argument is a built-in constant that corresponds to the bitmap format (which is one of the formats the Clipboard object can handle). The first argument of the SetData method specifies the bitmap to be copied, and it can be either the Picture or the Image property of the control. If you use the Picture property, any shapes drawn on the control at run time won't be copied.

FIGURE 6.5

The ImgCopy application uses the Clipboard to exchange images with any Windows application that can handle them.

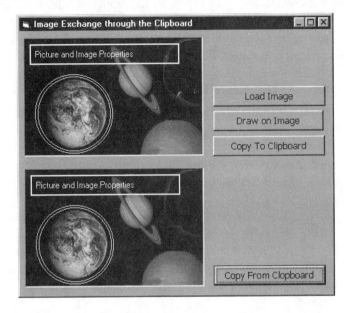

TIP

Before copying a bitmap to the Clipboard, you must clear its contents with the Clear method. If you attempt to copy a bitmap to the Clipboard without clearing its current contents, nothing will happen. The Clipboard's contents can't be overwritten.

Code 6.1: The Copy to Clipboard Button Code

```
Private Sub Command1_Click()

    Clipboard.Clear
    Clipboard.SetData Picture1.Image, vbCFBitmap

End Sub
```

Whatever has been copied to the Clipboard with the SetData method is available to any application in the Windows environment. If you start an image-processing application after copying the contents of the first PictureBox to the Clipboard, the application's Paste command will be enabled, indicating that the Clipboard's contents can be pasted on the current document.

Using GetData()   The Paste from Clipboard button uses the GetData() method to retrieve data from the Clipboard. The code behind this button checks the contents of the Clipboard, and if the Clipboard contains an image, it is copied onto the second PictureBox control.

Code 6.2: The Paste from Clipboard Button

```
Private Sub Command2_Click()

    If Clipboard.GetFormat(vbCFBitmap) Then
        Picture2.Picture = Clipboard.GetData()
    Else
        MsgBox "The clipboard doesn't contain image data"
    End If

End Sub
```

The Paste from Clipboard button pastes the Clipboard's contents on the PictureBox control, regardless of which application placed them there. The ImgCopy application can exchange images with other applications via the Clipboard.

Coordinate Systems

Visual Basic provides two basic methods for drawing shapes on controls and a method for displaying text:

- **Line**   Draws lines and boxes
- **Circle**   Draws circles and ellipses
- **Print**   Displays text strings

(A third method, Point, turns on and off individual pixels, and we'll explore this method in a later section.)

Before using any of these methods to draw something, you must know the dimensions of the control you are about to draw on and the units it uses. First, you must understand coordinates and coordinate systems and how they are used in drawing.

Coordinates describe the position of the individual pixels on the screen or of the points on a piece of paper in the printer. The coordinate system is similar to a city map. Each square on the map has its own unique address: a combination of a column and a row number. The row number is the horizontal coordinate, also called the X coordinate. The column number is the vertical coordinate, also called the Y coordinate. Any point on the Form can be identified by its X and Y coordinates, and we refer to it as the point at coordinates (X, Y) or simply the point (X, Y). An example is shown in Figure 6.6. The values along the X axis in the coordinate system of Figure 6.6 go from 0 to 100, and the values along the Y axis go from -50 to 50. Any pair of numbers in the ranges 0 to 100 and -50 to 50 specifies a point on the Form.

FIGURE 6.6

Any point on a Form can be identified by a pair of numbers, which are the point's X and Y coordinates.

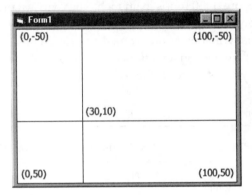

The coordinate values start at 0, and the point with the smallest coordinates is the *origin of the coordinate system*. In Visual Basic, the origin of the coordinate system is the upper left corner of the control or Form. The X coordinates increase to the right, and the Y coordinates increase downward. Each coordinate is a number, and it may or may not correspond to a meaningful unit. The letter and number coordinates on a city map don't correspond to meaningful units. They are arbitrary. The coordinates on a topological map, though, correspond to physical distances (kilometers, miles, and so on). It all depends on the intended application.

For example, if you want to draw a plan for your new house, you need to use a coordinate system in inches or centimeters so that there will be some correspondence between units and the objects you draw. If you are going to draw some nice geometrical shapes, any coordinate system will do. Finally, if you are going to display and process images, a coordinate system that uses pixels as units would be desired.

Visual Basic supports several coordinate systems, including a user-defined coordinate system, which lets you set up your own units. If you are familiar with computer graphics in older languages or operating systems, you probably expected that the most common coordinate system is based on pixels. Pixels are not the best units for all applications, however. If you use pixels to address a control's contents, you are tied to a particular resolution. If the monitor's resolution is increased, your designs are going to look different. Even the aspect ratio may not be the same, and the circles will become ellipses.

Visual Basic's default coordinate system uses a unit called *twip*, which equals 1/20 of a point. A point is a typographical measure of unit; there are 72 points in an inch and, therefore, 1440 twips in an inch. The twip is a precise unit of measurement, probably more precise than we need today. It does, however, allow us to draw shapes that will look good even when printed on a 1,200 dpi laser printer. But because twips are not convenient in all situations, Visual Basic provides the eight coordinate systems listed in Table 6.1.

TABLE 6.1 The Visual Basic Coordinate Systems

VALUE	DESCRIPTION	CONSTANT NAME	DIMENSION
0	User-defined coordinate system	vbUser	
1	Twips	vbTwips	1,440 twips per inch
2	Points	vbPoints	72 points per inch
3	Pixels	vbPixels	
4	Characters	vbCharacters	120 twips wide, 240 twips high
5	Inches	vbInches	
6	Millimeters	vbMillimeters	
7	Centimeters	vbCentimeters	

To change the default coordinate system, assign the appropriate value to the ScaleMode property. If you set ScaleMode to Inches, distances on the control must be specified in inches. In this case, two points that are one unit apart are one inch from each other. You can also specify decimal distances such as 0.1, which corresponds to 1/10 of an inch. Changing the ScaleMode property doesn't resize or otherwise affect the control. It simply changes the density of the grid you use to address the points on the control.

If none of the pre-defined coordinate systems suits your needs, you can create your own. Suppose you want to implement a game board with 12 squares along the X axis and 8 squares along the Y axis. The pieces of the game can only rest on a square of the grid, so you don't need the precision of units such as twips or pixels. You can set up a coordinate system that extends from 0 to 11 in the horizontal direction and from 0 to 7 in the vertical direction. If the game board is 32 by 32 squares, you set up a coordinate system that extends 32 units in both directions. The size of the PictureBox control doesn't change. There is, however, enough space for 32 by 32 squares, and each square is addressed with integer coordinates. To set up a user-defined coordinate system, you can use the Scale method or the Scale-related properties, which are explained next.

Scale Properties and Methods

Now we can look at the properties and methods that relate to the control's position and the coordinate system. Basically, there are two groups of properties: those that control the size and position of the control, and those that affect (and are affected by) the choice of coordinate system.

Width and Height Properties   These two properties determine the actual dimensions of the control and are always expressed in the units of the container of the control. Suppose you are placing a PictureBox control on a Form whose coordinate system is the default, twips. The Width and Height properties of the PictureBox control are expressed in twips. If you change the control's coordinate system, the values of these two properties will not change. If you resize the control on the Form by dragging its handles with the mouse, the Width and Height properties will change value to reflect the new size of the control. The Width and Height properties will also change value if you change the container's coordinate system, to reflect the control's dimensions in the new coordinate system.

Left and Top Properties   The Left and Top properties are the coordinates of the control's upper left corner, and they are expressed in the container's coordinate system. If you change their value, the control is repositioned. They also change value if you change the container's coordinate system, to reflect the control's position in the new coordinate system.

ScaleMode Property   The ScaleMode property sets (or returns) the control's current coordinate system. Set this property to one of the values in Table 6.1, earlier in this chapter, to establish a new coordinate system. If you set this property to zero (User), you must also set the ScaleWidth and ScaleHeight properties. Conversely, if you set the ScaleWidth and/or ScaleHeight properties, the ScaleMode property is reset to zero.

ScaleWidth and ScaleHeight Properties   These two properties are the control's inner dimensions in units of the current coordinate system. Changing the coordinate system doesn't change the size of the control, but does change the number of units that can fit along the two axes of the control. For example, a PictureBox control placed on a Form that is 2880 twips wide and 2880 twips tall is approximately 2 inches wide and 2 inches tall. Its Width and Height properties are 2880. If you change the Form's coordinate system to Inches, the control won't be resized, but its ScaleWidth and ScaleHeight properties will become 2 (inches). Where the X coordinate of the control's middle point in the previous coordinate system was 1440, it is now 1. You can also assign values to these properties, in which case you are switching automatically to a user-defined coordinate system (the ScaleMode property is reset to zero).

ScaleLeft and ScaleTop Properties   ScaleLeft and ScaleTop are the coordinates of the upper left corner of the control in a user-defined system of coordinates. Coordinate systems need not start at zero. ScaleLeft is the minimum value an X coordinate can assume. The maximum X coordinate is ScaleLeft+ScaleWidth. Suppose you want to draw an object with dimensions 12×10, but you want the X coordinate to start at 100 and the Y coordinate to start at 300. This coordinate system must be defined as follows:

```
Form1.ScaleWidth = 12
Form1.ScaleHeight = 10
Form1.ScaleLeft = 100
Form1.ScaleTop = 300
```

The X coordinates in this system extend from 100 to 112, and the Y coordinates extend from 300 to 310.

Scale Method   Using the Scale method is the most convenient way to set up a user-coordinate system. It has the following syntax:

```
Form1.Scale (X1, Y1) - (X2, Y2)
```

The coordinates of the upper left corner of the control are *(X1, 1)*, and *(X2, Y2)* are the coordinates of the lower right corner. The Scale method tells Visual Basic that the horizontal dimension of the control is (X2 - X1) units and that the vertical dimension is (Y2 - Y1) units. This is the address space of the control and does not affect its external dimensions.

To set up the game board mentioned earlier, you can call the Scale method as follows:

```
Form1.Scale (0, 0) - (11, 7)
```

The previous statement is equivalent to the following assignments:

```
Form1.ScaleTop = 0
Form1.ScaleLeft = 0
Form1.ScaleWidth = 11
Form1.ScaleHeight = 7
```

(Of course, setting any of the Scale properties resets the ScaleMode to zero , so you don't have to explicitly set the ScaleMode.)

TIP

Setting any of the ScaleWidth, ScaleHeight, ScaleTop, and ScaleLeft properties or calling the Scale method resets the ScaleMode property to zero (user-defined).

All properties that begin with the prefix *Scale* use the user-defined coordinate system. Setting any of these properties switches you to a user-defined coordinate system and sets the ScaleMode Property to zero but does not reposition or rescale the control or the Form. Similarly, every time you issue a Scale command such as Picture1.Scale (0, 0) - (11, 7), these four properties change value according to the Scale command's arguments.

ScaleX, ScaleY Methods   On occasions, you'll want to express the control's new size in a given coordinate system, without changing the container's coordinate system. Let's say the Form's coordinate system is 1 (twips) and you want to place a PictureBox on it, with dimensions 1.20 x 2.00 inches exactly. First, calculate how many twips correspond to 1.20 and 2.00 inches, and then assign these values to the control's Width and Height properties. Given that there are 1440 twips in an inch, mapping inches to twips is straightforward. Visual Basic, however, provides the ScaleX and ScaleY methods to convert units between any two coordinate systems.

Both methods have the identical syntax, which is:

```
Form1.ScaleX (width, fromscale, toscale)
```

The *width* argument is the number of units you want to convert, *fromscale* is the coordinate system from which the units will be converted, and *toscale* is the coordinate system into which the units will be converted.

Suppose you want to make the Picture1 control 200 pixels wide by 140 pixels tall. The Form on which the PictureBox lies has the default coordinate system, twips. The Width and Height properties of the Picture1 control, therefore, must be expressed in twips. To convert 200 pixels to twips, use the following statement:

```
WidthTwips = Form1.ScaleX(200, vbPixels, vbTwips)
```

Similarly, to convert the height of 140 pixels to twips, use the following statement:

```
HeightTwips = Form1.ScaleY(140, vbPixels, vbTwips)
```

And then use the results to set the control's size:

```
Picture1.Width = WidthTwips
Picture1.Height = HeightTwips
```

Since the Form's coordinate system is twips, you can omit the last argument of the ScaleX and ScaleY methods. You can resize the Picture1 control with the following statements:

```
Picture1.Width = Form1.ScaleX(200, vbPixels)
Picture1.Height = Form1.ScaleY(140, vbPixels)
```

TwipsPerPixelX, TwipsPerPixelY Properties   These two properties apply to the Screen object, and they return the number of twips per pixel for an object measured horizontally (TwipsPerPixelX) or vertically (TwipsPerPixelY).

CurrentX, CurrentY Properties   A basic concept in drawing with Visual Basic methods is the current point. Visual Basic allows you to draw shapes, a line for instance, without specifying a starting point. If the starting point isn't specified, the current point becomes the line's starting point. After the line is drawn, its endpoint becomes the current point. The properties CurrentX and CurrentY set or read the coordinates of the current point in the units of the current coordinate system.

VB5 at Work: The COORDS Application

To help you visualize the various coordinate systems and the related properties, use the COORDS application, shown in Figure 6.7. The option buttons on the left side of the Form set the ScaleMode of the PictureBox control on the right side. The PictureBox control has fixed dimensions, but you can easily change its coordinate system by clicking on one of the option buttons. Each time you set a new coordinate system, the coordinates of the PictureBox control's opposite corners are updated. Set a coordinate system, place the pointer over the PictureBox, and then move it around while holding down the left mouse button. As the pointer slides over the control, its coordinates are displayed.

FIGURE 6.7

The COORDS application

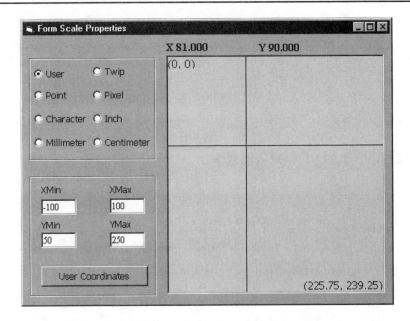

315

You can also set your own coordinate system by supplying the proper values in the four TextBox controls in the lower left segment of the window. You can use both positive and negative coordinates and then slide the pointer over the PictureBox to see its coordinates.

The most interesting part of the COORDS application's code is in the Picture-Box control's MouseMove event. You can open the COORDS application with the Visual Basic editor to find out how it works. You can also interrupt the application and move or resize the PictureBox control by setting its Top, Left, Height, and Width properties. The code for the application manipulates the control's Scale properties only, and you can't change the control's position with these properties.

Code 6.3: The Twip Option Button

```
Private Sub Option2_Click()

    Label1.Caption = "X " & Format$(Picture1.ScaleX(currX,
    ➡Picture1.ScaleMode, 1), "#.000")
    Label2.Caption = "Y " & Format$(Picture1.ScaleY(currY,
    ➡Picture1.ScaleMode, 1), "#.000")
    Picture1.ScaleMode = 1
    ShowSize

End Sub
```

First, you display the current coordinates in their new units, then you change the coordinate system, and finally you call the ShowSize subroutine, which displays the minimum and maximum coordinate values on the PictureBox control. Many of the methods used in this example are explained later in the chapter, so you might want to come back to this example later and examine its code.

The Drawing Methods

Now we can look at the drawing methods of Visual Basic, which are the following:

- **Print**   Displays a string

- **Line**   Draws lines and boxes

- **Circle**   Draws circles and arcs

- **Point**   Retrieves the color value of a point

- **PSet**   Sets the color of a point

The Print method has nothing to do with your printer; it draws text on a Form or a control. The Line and Circle methods accept many arguments that extend Visual Basic's drawing capabilities. With the Line and Circle methods, you can draw elaborate geometric shapes such as ellipses, filled shapes, pie charts, and so on. The Point and PSet methods manipulate pixels and are used frequently in image-processing applications and for drawing curves, which must be plotted point by point.

Drawing Text

The simplest drawing method is the Print method, which draws text on a Form or a PictureBox control, starting at the current point. The text is drawn in the control's current font and size, and after it is drawn, the current point is moved to the end of the text.

TIP

> Keep in mind that long lines of text don't wrap automatically when the control's right edge is reached. Your code must take care of breaking long lines of text into smaller ones before drawing them.

TextWidth, TextHeight Methods   Two methods commonly used to align text on a Form or a PictureBox control are TextWidth and TextHeight. These methods accept a string as argument; TextWidth returns the string's width, and TextHeight returns the string's height. Notice also that they apply only to the Form. If you are drawing on a PictureBox control and you want to align the text using the TextWidth and TextHeight properties, you must set the Form's Font property to the same value as the control's Font property. Only then will the values returned by the TextWidth and TextHeight properties be correct for the PictureBox control.

VB5 at Work: The TxtPrint Application

The TxtPrint application (see Figure 6.8) demonstrates how to use the Print method along with the TextWidth and TextHeight properties to draw text on a Form. To place a string in the middle of the Form, you must first calculate the Form's middle point: (Form1.Width/2, Form1.Height/2). You must then subtract one-half of the text's width from the X coordinate and one-half of the text's height from the

Y coordinate. Setting the current point to these coordinates and then issuing the Print command centers the text on the Form:

```
Form1.CurrentX = (Form1.Width - TextWidth("Centered Text")) / 2
Form1.CurrentY = (Form1.Height - TextHeight("Centered Text")) / 2
Form1.Print "Centered Text"
```

You can open the TxtPrint application in Visual Basic's editor to examine the rest of the code.

FIGURE 6.8

The TxtPrint application demonstrates how to use the TextWidth and TextHeight properties to align text on a Form with the Print method.

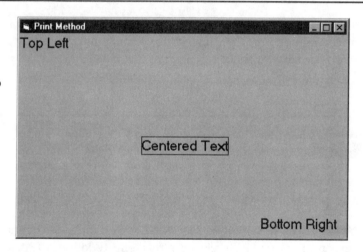

Drawing Lines

The method for drawing lines is called Line, and it has the following syntax:

```
Line[Step] (X1, Y1) - [Step] (X2, Y2) ,[color], [B][F]
```

The coordinates of the line's starting point are *X1, Y1*, and *X2, Y2* are the coordinates of the ending point. The following statement demonstrates the simplest form of the method:

```
Line (X1, Y1) - (X2, Y2)
```

The coordinates of the line's endpoints are expressed in the units of the control's coordinate system. The thickness of the line is determined by the DrawWidth property, and its style, by the DrawStyle property, whose settings are shown in

Table 6.2. If the width of the line is greater than 1 pixel, the settings 1 through 4 are identical to setting zero—that is, you cannot draw dashed or dotted lines that are thicker than 1 pixel.

TABLE 6.2   The Values of the DrawStyle Property

CONSTANT NAME	VALUE	DESCRIPTION
vbSolid	0	Solid (the default)
vbDash	1	Dash
vbDot	2	Dot
vbDashDot	3	Dash-Dot
vbDashDotDot	4	Dash-Dot-Dot
vbInvisible	5	Transparent
vbInsideSolid	6	Inside Solid

The meaning of each property is obvious, except for the last value, InsideSolid. When drawing with a line width larger than 1 pixel, Visual Basic splits the width of the line on both sides of the specified coordinates. If you set the DrawStyle property to 6 (Inside), the shape (line, box, or circle) will be drawn entirely within the specified coordinates.

The following short program draws lines of different styles on the Picture Box Picture1:

```
Private Sub Picture1_Click( )

Hstep = Picture1.ScaleHeight / 6
For i% = 1 to 6
        Picture1.DrawStyle = i% - 1
        Picture1.Line (.1 * Picture1.ScaleWidth, Hstep * i%) - (.0
        ➡*Picture1.ScaleWidth, Hstep * i%)
Next

End Sub
```

Specifying the Shape's Color

The ForeColor property of the Picture Box or Form determines the color of the line (or circle). You can, however, draw lines in different colors by specifying the optional argument *color*, available with the Line and Circle methods. The following statements show how the color argument is used:

```
Line (10, 10) - (100, 100), RGB(255, 0, 0)
Line (10, 10) - (100, 100), &H0000FF
Line (10, 10) - (100, 100), QBColor(3)
RedColor# = RGB(255, 0, 0)
Line (10, 10) - (100, 100), RedColor#
```

All three examples draw a red line from (10, 10) to (100, 100), regardless of the current setting of the ForeColor property. The method's *color* argument can be any valid color expression. (The section "Specifying Colors," later in this chapter, discusses the various ways to express colors in Visual Basic.) Normally, the line's color is determined by the control's ForeColor property. The *color* argument of the Line method overwrites this setting for the current line. If you draw another line, without specifying a color argument, it will be drawn in the control's Foreground color.

Using Relative Coordinates (The Step Option)

With the Step option of the Line method, you can define the second endpoint of the line relative to the first endpoint. In other words, the Step option defines a point not in terms of its coordinates, but in terms of its distance from the line's first endpoint. The coordinates we have used so far are absolute because they specify a unique point on the screen as measured from the control's upper left corner. The coordinates following the Step option are relative. The difference between the two types of coordinates is their origin. Absolute coordinates are always measured from the origin (ScaleLeft, ScaleTop), and relative coordinates are measured from the current position, wherever this might be. The following statement:

```
Line (100, 100) - (300, 200)
```

draws a line that starts at point (100, 100) and extends 100 units down and 200 units to the right from its starting point.

The following command:

```
Line (100, 100) - Step (300, 200)
```

draws a line from the same starting point, but this one extends 200 units down and 300 units to the right. The two numbers following the Step option are not the coordinates of the second endpoint, but its distance from the current point. You can also use the Step keyword in front of the Line method's first argument, in which case the line's starting point is defined relative to the current point (CurrentX, CurrentY).

Relative coordinates are used frequently in drawing closed shapes, because it is easier to define an endpoint in terms of its distance from the previous one. Suppose you want to draw a box with dimensions 100×300, with its upper left corner at the point (100,400). You can draw this box in absolute coordinates, with the following commands:

```
Line (100,400) - (200,400) ' Line to the right along the X axis
Line (200,400) - (200,700) ' Line down along the Y axis
Line (200,700) - (100,700) ' Line to the left along the X axis
Line (100,700) - (100,400) ' Line to the starting point
```

For each of the previous commands, you calculate the absolute coordinates of each corner of the frame by adding the appropriate dimensions to the previous endpoint. It is much easier, however, to draw the same box with relative coordinates. Here's how:

```
Line (100, 300) - Step (100, 0)
Line - Step(0,300)
Line - Step(-100,0)
Line - Step(0,-300)
```

You must define the starting point in absolute coordinates, but for the remaining points, it makes sense to use relative coordinates. Notice that you need not even define the first endpoint of each side, since it coincides with the second endpoint of the previous side. Following the Step option is the distance of the next corner of the box from the previous one.

Drawing Boxes

Visual Basic offers an even more convenient way to draw boxes: the B (Box) option of the Line method. If you include this option, you can draw a box whose upper left corner is defined by the first coordinate pair and whose lower right corner is defined by the second coordinate pair. The last four commands in the previous example could be replaced with the following line:

```
Line (100,400) - (200,700), , B
```

You must type the two consecutive commas if you omit the color argument; if you don't, Visual Basic assumes that B is a variable name specifying the color of the box. As you may have guessed, there is an even easier way to draw a box on the screen using relative coordinates. All we wanted was a rectangle with known dimensions and its upper left corner fixed at point (100, 400). Here's the command to do just that:

```
Line (100, 400) - Step (100, 300), , B
```

Here, you specify the coordinates of the upper left corner and the dimensions of the box. The advantage of the last command is that you don't have to perform any calculations; you simply type the dimensions of the box, which is what you usually know.

NOTE The Line method accepts one more option that can be used only along with the B option. If you want to fill the box, use the F (Fill) option immediately after the B option. There is no comma between the B and the F options. It might be easier to think of the two options as being the B (for box) and BF (for filled box) options, since you cannot use the F option alone. The FillColor property determines the color used for the filling. The BF option overwrites the current setting of the FillColor property for a single box, just as the color argument overwrites the ForeColor property of the control or Form for a single line.

Filling Shapes

Closed shapes can also be filled with various patterns, depending on the setting of the FillStyle property. By default, closed shapes are transparent. To draw solid or hatched shapes, you set the FillStyle property, which can take any of the values shown in Table 6.3.

TABLE 6.3   The Values of the FillStyle Property

CONSTANT	VALUE	DESCRIPTION
vbFSSolid	0	Solid
vbFSTransparent	1	Transparent (the default)
vbHorizontalLine	2	Horizontal Line
vbVerticalLine	3	Vertical Line
vbUpwardDiagonal	4	Upward Diagonal
vbDownwardDiagonal	5	Downward Diagonal
vbCross	6	Cross
vbDiagonalCross	7	Diagonal Cross

NOTE   If the FillStyle property is set to any value other than 1 (transparent), any closed shape is automatically filled with the specified pattern. The FillColor property determines the color used for drawing the pattern.

The effect of the FillStyle property in drawing filled shapes is shown in Figure 6.9. Each circle is filled with a different pattern and a different color. If the FillStyle property of a PictureBox control or Form is set to any value other than 1 (transparent), all the boxes and circles you draw on the control will be filled with the corresponding pattern. Moreover, the color used for drawing the pattern is given by the FillColor property. The FillColor property is the color with which the shape will be filled if the FillStyle is 0 (solid) or the color of the lines in the pattern.

If the FillStyle property is 1 and you still want to draw boxes filled with a solid color, use the BF option of the Line method. This option overwrites the FillStyle temporarily, and subsequent boxes are filled according to this property's setting. The Circle method does not have an equivalent option for drawing filled circles.

FIGURE 6.9

The various values of the FillStyle property applied to boxes and circles

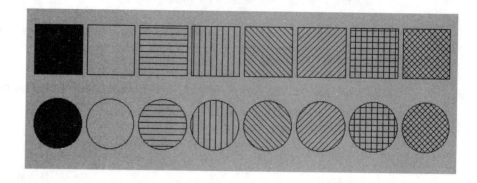

Using the Circle Method

The Circle method draws circles, arcs, and ellipses. The method's complete syntax is as follows:

```
Circle [Step] (X, Y), radius, [color] ,[start] ,[end] ,[aspect]
```

The coordinates of the circle's center are X and Y, and R is its radius. These are the only mandatory arguments, and both are expressed in units of the current coordinate system.

Drawing Circles

The simplest form of the Circle method is Circle (X,Y), R. The following statement:

```
Circle (Form1.ScaleWidth / 2, Form1.ScaleHeight / 2), Form1
➥.ScaleHeight / 3
```

draws a circle at the center of the Form1 Form. Its radius equals one-third of the Form's height. If the Form is taller than it is wide, part of the circle may be invisible.

As with the Line command, the Step option makes the coordinates of the center relative to the current point. Unlike the Line method, the Circle method does not allow you to use the current point as the center of the circle and omit its coordinates. To draw a circle centered at the current point, use the following command:

```
Circle Step (0, 0), R
```

You must specify the relative coordinates, even if they are zero.

You specify the radius of the circle in the units of the horizontal axis. With most coordinate systems, you could use the units of the horizontal or the vertical axis; however, in a user-defined coordinate system, the units of the horizontal and vertical axes might be different. The circle won't be distorted in any way, but you must be aware of this detail when defining the length of the radius, because it will affect the size of the circle.

Some Tips about Circles

If you set a coordinate system such as the following:

```
Form1.Scale (0, 0) - (100, 1000)
```

and then draw a circle with a radius of 50 units, the circle fills the Form.

If the coordinate system is defined as follows:

```
Form1.Scale (0, 0) - (1000, 100)
```

a circle with the same radius is only 1/10 of the Form's width (its radius being 1/20 of the Form's width). The circle won't be distorted, but the choice of radius will affect its size.

Drawing Ellipses

By including the aspect argument, you can also use the Circle method to draw ellipses. *Aspect* is the ratio of the vertical to the horizontal radius of the ellipse and can be an integer or a floating-point number; it can even be less than 1, but it cannot be a negative number. If the aspect is smaller than 1, the ellipse extends horizontally and is squeezed in the vertical direction. If the aspect is larger than 1, the ellipse extends vertically. Figure 6.10 shows how the aspect ratio is defined. The two ellipses of Figure 6.10 and their bounding boxes were drawn with the following statements:

```
SideX = 1
SideY = 0.75
Side = 2000
Form1.DrawWidth = 2
Form1.Line (100, 100)-Step(Side * SideX, Side * SideY), , B
XC = 100 + Side * SideX / 2
```

```
YC = 100 + Side * SideY / 2
Form1.DrawWidth = 1
Form1.Circle (XC, YC), Side / 2, , , , SideY / SideX

SideX = 0.75
SideY = 1
Form1.DrawWidth = 2
Form1.Line (3000, 100)-Step(Side * SideX, Side * SideY), , B
XC = 3000 + Side * SideX / 2
YC = 100 + Side * SideY / 2
Form1.DrawWidth = 1
Form1.Circle (XC, YC), Side / 2, , , , SideY / SideX
```

FIGURE 6.10

The aspect ratio determines how the circle is distorted to produce an ellipse.

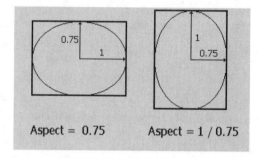

Drawing Arcs

In addition, you can use the Circle method to draw arcs. The arguments *start* and *end* specify the arc's starting and ending angles in radians.

> **TIP**
>
> Remember that a full circle contains 360 degrees, which correspond to 2*pi radians (pi = 3.14159625...). To convert an angle of D degrees to radians, use the formula 2 * pi * D / 360 or pi * D / 180.

The arc's starting and ending angles are measured counterclockwise. Negative angles do not reverse the direction of the arc. They simply tell Visual Basic to draw the arc as if they were positive numbers and then connect the endpoint that corresponds to the negative angle with the center of the circle. As you may have guessed, this technique is used for drawing pie charts.

Because circles (and connected arcs) are closed shapes, they are automatically filled with the pattern specified with the FillStyle property and take on the color specified with the FillColor property. For a discussion of these two properties, see the section "Filling Shapes," earlier in this chapter.

The PieChart application uses the Circle method to draw pie charts with connected arcs, as shown in Figure 6.11. Because a connected arc is a closed shape, it can also be filled with a pattern or a solid color, as specified by the FillStyle and FillColor properties. The PieChart application lets you select whether the pie's slices will be filled with a pattern or a solid color or will simply be hollow. The PieChart application also serves as an example of how to use the FillStyle and FillColor properties to fill closed shapes.

FIGURE 6.11

The PieChart application uses connected arcs to draw the pie's wedges.

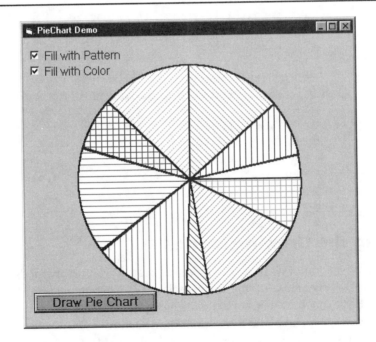

The program generates 10 random numbers in the range 20 to 100, stores them in the PieData() array, and then calculates the arc that corresponds to each number. Because the total must be a full circle (2 * pi), each element of the PieChart() array corresponds to an arc of 2 * pi * PieData(i) / Total. Each slice's starting angle is the ending angle of the previous slice, and its ending angle is the starting angle plus the angle corresponding to its element in the PieData() array.

Code 6.4: The PieChart Application

```
Private Sub Command1_Click()
Dim PieData(10) As Integer

    Form1.Cls
    For i = 0 To 9
        PieData(i) = 20 + Rnd() * 100
        Total = Total + PieData(i)
    Next

    Form1.DrawWidth = 2
    For i = 0 To 9
        arc1 = arc2
        arc2 = arc1 + 6.28 * PieData(i) / Total
        If Check1.Value Then
            Form1.FillStyle = 2 + (i Mod 5)
        Else
            Form1.FillStyle = 0
        End If
        If Check2.Value Then
            Form1.FillColor = QBColor(8 + (i Mod 6))
        Else
            Form1.FillColor = QBColor(9)
        End If
        Form1.Circle (Form1.ScaleWidth / 2, Form1.ScaleHeight / 2),
        ➥Form1.ScaleHeight / 2.5, , -arc1, -arc2
    Next
End Sub
```

Using the Drawing Modes

When you draw shapes with Visual Basic's graphics methods, by default the pixels that make up the shape replace any existing pixels on the control. Visual Basic can, however, combine the new pixels with the existing ones in various ways, depending on the settings of the control's DrawMode property. The settings of this property are shown in Table 6.4. Most of them correspond to logical operators such as AND, OR, and NOT. The default DrawMode setting is 13 (Copy Pen), which transfers the new pixels onto the control, replacing the underlying pixels. Setting 4 (Not Copy Pen) works the same way, except that it reverses the color of the pixels being drawn. Setting 9 combines the new pixels with the existing ones with the logical operator AND. As you can see, there are many ways to combine the color of the new pixels with the existing ones.

TABLE 6.4 The Values of the DrawMode Property

VALUE	NAME	MEANING
vbBlackness	1	Draws in black color
vbNotMergePen	2	Inverse of setting 15 (Merge Pen)
vbMaskNotPen	3	Combination of the colors common to the background color and the inverse of the drawing color
vbNotCopyPen	4	Inverse of setting 13 (Copy Pen)
vbMaskPenNot	5	Combination of the colors common to both the drawing color and the inverse of the background color
vbInvert	6	Inverse of the drawing color
vbXorPen	7	Combination of the colors in the background color and in the drawing color, but not in both
vbNotMaskPen	8	Inverse of setting 9 (Mask Pen)
vbMaskPen	9	Combination of the colors common to the drawing color and the display
vbNotXorPen	10	Inverse of setting 7 (Xor Pen)
vbNop	11	Output remains unchanged (Nop)
vbMergeNotPen	12	Combination of the control's background color and the inverse of the drawing color
vbCopyPen	13	Color specified by the ForeColor property
vbMergePenNot	14	Combination of the drawing color and the inverse of the background color
vbMergePen	15	Combination of the drawing color and the background color
vbWhiteness	16	Draws in white color

We will return to the topic of the drawing mode in the section "The Paint-Picture Method," in which you will find an application that allows you to experiment with the various settings. First, however, let's explore an especially interesting and useful drawing mode, XOR.

Using the XOR Operator

One of the most practical settings of the DrawMode property is 7 (vbXorPen). With this setting, the values of the new pixels are combined with the existing ones by means of the XOR operator. The bits are combined as shown in Table 6.5.

TABLE 6.5 Combining Bits with the XOR Operator

BIT 1	BIT 2	RESULT
0	0	0
0	1	1
1	0	1
1	1	0

The result of the operation is 1 only if the bits are different. If they are the same (either both 0 or both 1), the result is 0. Let's see how the XOR operator works. In the Immediate Execution window (if it's not visible, choose View ➤ Immediate Window), enter the following statements (press Enter after each Print statement to see the result):

```
print 184 XOR 45
        149
print 149 XOR 45
        184
print 149 XOR 184
45
```

As you can see, the number 184 is XORed with the value 45, and the result is a new number (149). When the result is XORed with one of the two original numbers again, it yields the other number. This is a unique property of the XOR operator, which makes it useful in many situations, including cryptography. Indeed, at the heart of every encryption algorithm, you will find the XOR operator. Let's run a small experiment with characters. As you know, characters are represented by numbers, which you can find with the Asc() function. Here are a few experiments with characters and the XOR operator:

```
print asc("d") XOR 88
60
```

```
print chr$(60)
<
print chr$(60 XOR 88)
d
```

When the character "d" is XORed with the number 88, it becomes the character "<". If the new character is XORed with 88, it becomes the original character. Repeating this process for every character in a text file encrypts the text. To recover the original text, you must XOR each character of the encrypted text with the key. The number 88 in the previous example is the key (something like an encryption password). Without the key, you'll find it difficult to recover the original text. More secure encryption algorithms use long encryption keys or other variations on this technique, but they are all based on this unique property of the XOR operator.

Now, how does this relate to Visual Basic graphics? If the XOR operator can mask and then reveal a number, why not use it to do the same with a line? If you draw a line in XOR mode, you will see a line superimposed over the existing pixels. If you draw another line on top of the first one, the line will disappear, revealing the underlying pixels. The XOR drawing mode has an interesting property: The first time you draw a shape on the screen, it is displayed on top of everything else—the colors change, but not the shape. If you draw the same shape again, the net result is to remove the shape without affecting the background (see Figures 6.12 and 6.13).

FIGURE 6.12

When you draw a solid rectangle over an image in XOR mode, its pixels change color, but you can still make out the original shape.

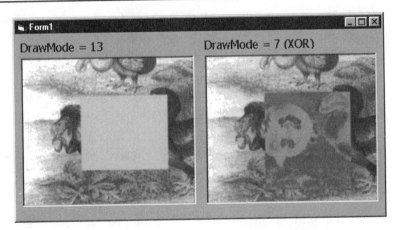

FIGURE 6.13

When you draw another solid rectangle on top of the previous one in XOR mode, the underlying pixels are revealed.

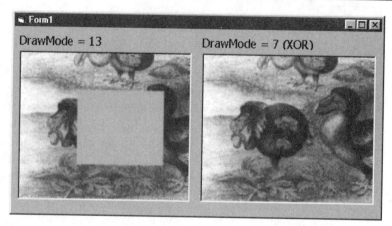

The two PictureBox controls on the Form shown in Figures 6.12 and 6.13 have the same dimensions and display the same image. They differ only in the setting of their DrawMode property, which is 13 (the default) for the first one and 7 (vbXorPen) for the second one. Figure 6.12 shows the result of drawing a solid rectangle on both of them. Figure 6.13 shows the result of drawing the same rectangle again. Nothing changed in the first PictureBox, but the rectangle was removed from the second control.

Drawing Rubber Lines

The most common example of the XOR drawing mode is in drawing rubber lines. A *rubber line* is a line with one of its endpoints fixed on the screen and the other moving around, following the movement of the pointer.

Using rubber lines, you can verify the final position of a line (and practically every other shape) before you commit it to the screen. You have seen this tool in action in just about any drawing application you have used, and now you'll learn how to incorporate this technique in your applications.

To implement a rubber line feature in an application, you must make use of the three mouse events:

- MouseDown
- MouseMove
- MouseUp

The *MouseDown event* signals the starting point of the rubber line. The coordinates of this point must be stored in two Form-wide variables, which we'll call Xstart and YStart. Set the DrawMode to 7 (XOR) so that you can continuously erase the previous line.

As long as the pointer is moving, Visual Basic generates *MouseMove events*. With each MouseMove event, you must erase the previous line and draw a new one from the starting point to the current point. To be able to erase the old line, you must store the coordinates of the old ending point in two more Form-wide variables, *XOld* and *YOld*. The MouseMove handler must draw two lines, one between the points (Xstart, Ystart) to (XOld, YOld) and another from the same starting point to the current point. The first line erases the previous rubber line, and the second becomes the current rubber line, which is erased with the next MouseMove event.

When the mouse button is released, you must draw the last line in COPY_PEN mode. First, however, you must erase the previous line, from (XStart, YStart) to (XOld, YOld), by drawing another line on top of it in XOR mode. Therefore, the *MouseUp event handler* must change the drawing mode momentarily to COPY_PEN and draw a line between the original point (Xstart, Ystart) and the point where the button was released (X, Y).

VB5 at Work: The Rubber Application

The Rubber application implements the technique just described and lets you draw rubber lines on a Form. Run it and press the left mouse button at the starting point of the line. When you move the mouse around without releasing the button, the second endpoint of the line follows the movement of the mouse. Every time you move the mouse, a new line is drawn between the starting point and the current position of the pointer. This line is called a rubber line because it can swing, shrink, and stretch as needed to follow the mouse; it's as if you had a rubber band attached to the starting point on one end and to the mouse pointer on the other end.

Once you decide on the exact placement of the line, release the mouse button; the last rubber line is committed on the Form.

Code 6.5: The Rubber Application

```
Dim XStart, YStart As Single
Dim XOld, YOld As Single
```

```
Private Sub Form_MouseDown(Button As Integer, Shift As Integer, X
➥As Single, Y As Single)

    If Button <> 1 Then Exit Sub
    XStart = X
    YStart = Y
    XOld = XStart
    YOld = YStart
    Form1.DrawMode = 7

End Sub

Private Sub Form_MouseMove(Button As Integer, Shift As Integer, X
➥As Single, Y As Single)

    If Button <> 1 Then Exit Sub
    Form1.Line (XStart, YStart)-(XOld, YOld)
    Form1.Line (XStart, YStart)-(X, Y)
    XOld = X
    YOld = Y

End Sub

Private Sub Form_MouseUp(Button As Integer, Shift As Integer, X As
➥Single, Y As Single)

    If Button <> 1 Then Exit Sub
    Form1.DrawMode = 13
    Form1.Line (XStart, YStart)-(XOld, YOld)
    Form1.Line (XStart, YStart)-(X, Y)

End Sub
```

It's easy to modify this application so that it draws rubber rectangles or even rubber circles. You'll see how this technique is used in the context of a drawing application in the next section.

VB5 at Work: The Draw Application

The Draw application (see Figure 6.14) demonstrates just about every method and technique presented in this chapter. It's a simple application that lets the user draw various shapes, such as lines, boxes, and circles, and even display text. All the shapes are drawn in rubber mode. The menus of the application let the user set the drawing parameters, such as the drawing or filling color, the width of the shapes, the style of the lines, and so on. The File menu contains commands for storing the drawings in BMP files and loading images from disk files (images that were saved earlier with the Draw application or images in BMP format).

FIGURE 6.14

The Draw application can become your starting point for a custom drawing application.

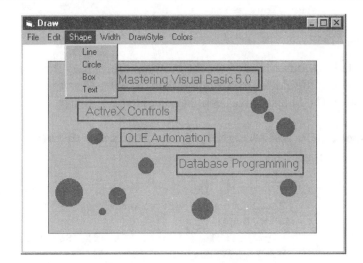

The Edit menu contains the usual Copy, Cut, and Paste commands that manipulate rectangular sections of the drawing. The parts of the drawing being copied are not transferred to the Clipboard, though. They are saved temporarily on an invisible PictureBox control, from which they can be pasted back within the same document (you'll see shortly why we aren't using the Clipboard for the Copy and Paste operations).

Drawing Rubber Shapes

The application's listing is too long to print in its entirety, so we will focus on its most important aspects. Let's start with the code for drawing rubber shapes. When the user selects the shape to be drawn from the Shape menu, the program sets the *Shape* global variable to LINE, CIRCLE, BOX, or TEXT. This variable is used in the MouseDown, MouseUp, and MouseMove event handlers as explained earlier. In the MouseDown event, the program stores the starting coordinates of the rubber shape in the variables *Xstart* and *YStart*. These are the coordinates of a line's first endpoint, a box's upper left corner, or a circle's center.

Code 6.6: The MouseDown Event

```
If Button = 1 Then
        XStart = X
        YStart = Y
        XPrevious = XStart
        YPrevious = YStart
        Form1.DrawMode = 7
End If
```

In the MouseMove event, the program draws the rubber shape by erasing the shape at the old coordinates and then drawing another one at the new coordinates. The MouseMove event handler is a Case switch.

Code 6.7: The MouseMove and MouseUp Events

```
    Select Case Shape
        Case "LINE":
            Form1.Line (XStart, YStart)-(XPrevious, YPrevious)
            Form1.Line (XStart, YStart)-(X, Y)
        Case "CIRCLE":
            Form1.Circle (XStart, YStart), Sqr((XPrevious - XStart)
            ➥^ 2 + (YPrevious - YStart) ^ 2)
            Form1.Circle (XStart, YStart), Sqr((X - XStart) ^ 2 +
            ➥(Y - YStart) ^ 2)
        Case "BOX":
            Form1.Line (XStart, YStart)-(XPrevious, YPrevious), , B
            Form1.Line (XStart, YStart)-(X, Y), , B
    End Select
    XPrevious = X
    YPrevious = Y
```

In the MouseUp event, the program draws the final shape in CopyPen ➥mode.

```
    Form1.DrawMode = 13
    Select Case Shape
        Case "LINE":
            Form1.Line (XStart, YStart)-(X, Y)
        Case "CIRCLE":
            Form1.Circle (XStart, YStart), Sqr((X - XStart) ^ 2 +
            ➥(Y - YStart) ^ 2)
        Case "BOX":
            Form1.Line (XStart, YStart)-(X, Y), , B
    End Select
```

Drawing Text

Unlike printing the standard shapes, printing the text requires a few extra steps. When the user selects Text from the Shape menu, the program prompts for the string to be printed on the Form. It then waits for the user to click the mouse on the Form and move it around. As the pointer moves, the text follows the movement of the pointer and is printed on the Form when the user releases the mouse button.

> **WARNING**
>
> Visual Basic's drawing commands combine the pixels of the new shapes with the existing ones, except for the Print method, which overwrites the underlying pixels, regardless of the setting of the DrawMode property.

The Print method isn't affected by the drawing mode, so you can't count on the XOR drawing mode to erase the text. The Draw application does the trick by placing the text on a transparent, borderless Label control. As the user moves the pointer around on the Form, the program moves the Label by changing its Left and Top properties. When the mouse is released, the program calls the Print method to print the text on the Form.

The process just described is implemented in the Text command and in the MouseDown and MouseUp events. The Text command of the Shape menu executes the code in Code 6.5.

Code 6.8: The Text Command

```
Private Sub DrawText_Click()
Dim DrawString As String

    DrawString = InputBox("Enter string")
    Label1.Caption = DrawString
    PrintText = True

End Sub
```

The PrintText variable is global, and we will use it in the Form's mouse events.

The Form's MouseDown event executes the code in Code 6.9.

Code 6.9: The MouseDown Event

```
If PrintText Then
        Label1.ForeColor = Form1.ForeColor
        Label1.Visible = True
        Label1.Left = X
        Label1.Top = Y
        Exit Sub
End If
```

Notice that the Label control used for moving the text around is invisible, except when needed.

Finally, in the MouseUp event, the program calls the Print method to place the string at the current location on the Form and hide the Label control again.

Code 6.10: The MouseUp Event

```
    If PrintText Then
        Form1.AutoRedraw = True
        Form1.CurrentX = X
        Form1.CurrentY = Y
        Form1.Print Label1.Caption
        Label1.Visible = False
        PrintText = False
        Exit Sub
    End If
```

Although the text is drawn in the current drawing color, the Draw application doesn't have a menu option for changing the font, its size, and style. You can easily add this feature to the program, as long as you change the font of both the Label control and the Form. The Label's text is displayed while the user moves the string around to its final position, where it's printed in the Form's font with the Print method.

Using the Copy Command

When choosing the Copy or the Cut command, the user can select a rectangular area of the drawing with the mouse. A rubber rectangle is drawn around the selection as the user presses the button and moves the mouse . As soon as the user releases the button, the program copies the selected area of the bitmap to a hidden PictureBox control with the PaintPicture method. The Clipboard's SetData method doesn't provide any arguments that let you specify which part of the image will be copied. This method transfers the entire bitmap to the Clipboard. To copy part of the image, you must first move it to a "local Clipboard," which is what the PictureBox control is. It's the program's internal clipboard, in which bitmaps are stored between Copy and Paste operations. The Copy operation is implemented from within the Form's Mouse events, as follows:

1. In the MouseDown event, the program sets the rectangle's starting coordinates. It also resets temporarily the DrawWidth property to 1 (pixel).

2. In the MouseMove event, the program draws a rubber rectangle, which encloses the area to be copied.

3. In the MouseUp event, finally, the rectangular area is transferred to the PictureBox control, with the following statements:

```
If X > XStart Then X1 = XStart Else X1 = X
If Y > YStart Then Y1 = YStart Else Y1 = Y
Picture1.PaintPicture Form1.Image, 0, 0, Abs(X - XStart), Abs
➡Y - YStart), X1, Y1, Abs(X - XStart), Abs(Y - YStart), &HCC0020
CopyBMP = False
CopyWidth = Abs(X - XStart)
CopyHeight = Abs(Y - YStart)
```

The two If statements ensure that the proper segment of the bitmap is copied, even if the user started the selection from its lower left corner. The *CopyWidth* and *CopyHeight* global variables hold the dimensions of the rectangle being copied so that later the program will paste only this area of the hidden PictureBox control. Picture1 is the name of a hidden container, where copied images (or parts of images) are stored with the Copy command and retrieved with the Paste command.

TIP

Visual Basic doesn't provide the means for copying part of an image to the Clipboard. To exchange pictorial data with other Windows applications, you must copy the segment of the image you want to copy to a PictureBox control, resize the control to the dimensions of the copied bitmap, and only then use the SetData method of the Clipboard object to copy the bitmap to the Clipboard.

Using the Paste Command

The Paste operation is simpler. When the user selects the Paste command, the program waits until the mouse button is pressed and then moves the bitmap to be pasted around, following the movement of the pointer. The pasted bitmap is drawn in XOR mode until the user releases the mouse button, and then the program copies the bitmap in XopyPen mode. This process is also implemented from within the Form's mouse events.

Further Improvements

The Draw application is a functional application that you can use as a starting point for many custom applications. Because it can draw on top of bitmaps, you can use it to annotate drawings and graphics, such as fax images. You could also specify the font for printing text and add an Undo feature. To implement an Undo command, temporarily store the drawing in another hidden PictureBox control after each drawing operation. When the user selects the Undo command, copy this PictureBox control's contents on the Form.

You can even implement a hierarchical Undo by tracking the drawing commands. For this, you must set up a structure in which each command is stored. This structure could be a list, such as the following:

```
Form1.DrawWidth = 3
Load "c:\drawings\cards.bmp"
Form1.Line (143, 193) - (302, 221), , B
Form1.FillColor = 134745&
Form1.Copy (0, 0) - (150, 100)
```

In other words, you must encode all the operations and save their descriptions in a list. If the user wants to undo an operation, you can present this list, let the user delete certain entries or change their order, and then clear the Form and execute all the commands in the list. This requires quite a lot of coding, but in principle it's a straightforward process. The problem with this application is that the rubber shapes assume strange colors, depending on the values of the underlying pixels. This is a side effect of the XOR drawing mode, which isn't a problem when drawing shapes over a solid background but becomes a problem if you draw on top of bitmaps. We will fix this problem later in the chapter, after we look at the AutoRedraw property and the Refresh method. The QDraw application is identical to the Draw application, but it uses a more robust method for drawing rubber shapes.

Drawing Curves

The Line and Circle methods are sufficient for drawing bar graphs or pie charts, but how about drawing interesting, mathematically defined curves, like the ones shown in Figures 6.15 and 6.16? To graph curves, you must provide the code that plots every single point of the curve. As you can guess, drawing curves isn't going to be nearly as fast as drawing lines, but Visual Basic isn't slow when it comes to drawing curves.

FIGURE 6.15

The graph of the function exp(2/t)*sin(2*t)

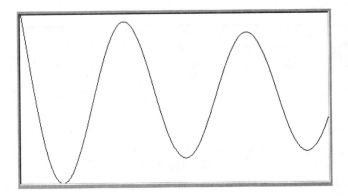

FIGURE 6.16

The graph of another function, this time the cos(3*t)*sin(5*t)

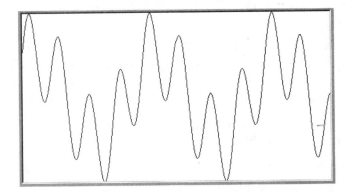

Suppose you want to plot a function, such as exp(2/t)*sin(2*t), for the values of *t* from 1 to 10. The *t* variable is the time and will be mapped to the X axis. We must clearly set up a user-defined scale mode that extends from 1 to 10 along the

X axis. But how about the vertical axis? We must either guess or calculate the minimum and maximum values of this function in the range 1 to 10 and only then set up the scale.

To plot the function, you calculate the function at consecutive X values and turn on the point that corresponds to this value. The first question is, At how many points along the X axis, must you calculate the function? The function must be evaluated at each pixel along the X axis. If you evaluate the function at more points, some will map to the same pixel. If you evaluate the function at fewer points, gaps will appear between successive points on the graph.

TIP

To draw a curve, you must calculate and display each and every point along the curve. To speed up applications that draw mathematically defined curves, compile them for execution speed.

Since you are going to calculate the function at every pixel along the X axis, you must map the pixels to the corresponding values of the *t* variable. Let's assume that the *t* variable goes from XMin to XMax. Let's also assume that there are XPixels along the X axis. The following loop scans all the pixels along the X axis and calculates the value of the time variable at each pixel:

```
For i = 0 To XPixels
    t = XMin + (XMax - XMin) * i / XPixels
Next
```

The variable *t* starts at *XMin*. When *i* reaches its maximum value, *XPixels*, the variable *t* becomes *XMax*. This loop goes through all the pixels along the X axis and calculates the value of the *t* variable that corresponds to each pixel. All you have to do now is calculate the function for each value of the time variable.

Let's write a function that calculates the function for any given value of the independent variable:

```
Function FunctionEval1(ByVal X As Double) As Double

    FunctionEval1 = Exp(2 / X) * Cos(2 * X)

End Function
```

The function FunctionEval1() accepts as argument the value of the independent variable, calculates the function at this point, and returns the value of the function.

Let's now modify the main loop so that it plots the function:

```
For i = 0 To XPixels
    t = XMin + (XMax - XMin) * i / XPixels
    Picture1.PSet (t, FunctionEval1(t))
Next
```

This loop does the plotting. In essence, it breaks the plot in as many points as there are pixels along the X axis, calculates the value of the function at each point, and then turns on the corresponding pixel. Now that you have a technique for mapping the values of the variable *t* to pixel values, creating the actual plot is straightforward.

And how about the value of the variable *XPixels*? You can switch the PictureBox control's ScaleMode property to 3 (pixels) temporarily, use the ScaleWidth property to find out the control's horizontal resolution, and then set up a user-defined coordinate system that is appropriate for the plot:

```
Picture1.ScaleMode = 3
XPixels = Picture1.ScaleWidth - 1
```

The last step is to figure out the dimensions of the user-defined coordinate system for each function you want to plot. Use a loop similar to the one that produces the plot, only this time, instead of plotting the function, track its minimum and maximum values:

```
For i = 1 To XPixels
    t = XMin + (XMax - XMin) * i / XPixels
    functionVal = FunctionEval1(t)
    If functionVal > YMax Then YMax = functionVal
    If functionVal < YMin Then YMin = functionVal
Next
```

After the completion of the loop, the variables *YMin* and *YMax* hold the minimum and maximum values of the function in the range *XMin* to *XMax*. To set up the coordinate system for the specific function, you can call the Scale method with the following arguments:

```
Picture1.Scale (XMin, YMin) - (XMax, YMax)
```

You've now seen all the important pieces of the code for plotting functions. Let's put it all together to build the application shown in Figure 6.17. The application is called Graph, and you will find it on this book's CD. The Draw First Function and Draw Second Function buttons plot the two functions mentioned earlier, and the Draw Both Functions button draws them both.

FIGURE 6.17

The Graph application
draws mathematically
defined curves.

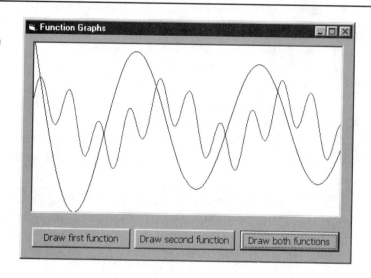

Code 6.11: The Draw First Function Button

```
Private Sub Command1_Click()
Dim t, functionVal As Double
Dim XMin, XMax, YMin, YMax As Double

YMin = 1E+101: YMax = -1E+101
XMin = 2 : XMax = 10
Picture1.Cls
Picture1.ScaleMode = 3
XPixels = Picture1.ScaleWidth - 1

' Calculate Min and Max for Y axis
For i = 1 To XPixels
    t = XMin + (XMax - XMin) * i / XPixels
    functionVal = FunctionEval1(t)
    If functionVal > YMax Then YMax = functionVal
    If functionVal < YMin Then YMin = functionVal
Next

' Set up a user defined scale mode
Picture1.Scale (XMin, YMin)-(XMax, YMax)

' Plot the function
For i = 0 To XPixels
    t = XMin + (XMax - XMin) * i / XPixels
```

```
    Picture1.PSet (t, FunctionEval1(t))
Next

End Sub
```

The Draw Second Function button's code is identical, only instead of calling the FunctionEval1() function, it calls the FunctionEval2() function, which calculates a different function:

```
Function FunctionEval2(ByVal X As Double) As Double

    FunctionEval2 = Cos(3 * X) * Sin(5 * X)

End Function
```

The actual graph of the function is shown in Figure 6.18. The problem with the code so far is that there are gaps between successive points of the function. To "close" these gaps, you can replace the PSet method, which turns on a single pixel, with the Line method, to draw a line segment from the last point to the new one. In other words, drawing the line segments between successive points on the control will close the gaps you see in the plot of Figure 6.18.

FIGURE 6.18

The function of Figure 6.15 is drawn by turning on isolated points.

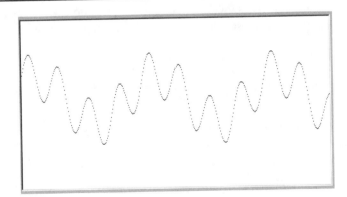

If you replace the line that turns on the pixels with the following one:

```
Picture1.Line -(t, FunctionEval1(t))
```

the plot of the same function will look like Figure 6.15. The solid line is much more suitable for plotting functions. Notice that the coordinates of the Line method are relative to the current point, which is the second endpoint of the previous line segment drawn. The previous Line method draws a line segment that joins two adjacent points on the plot. In the application's code, the lines that use the PSet method to turn on isolated pixels are commented out.

The Graph application is the core of a data-plotting application. You can supply your own functions and add features such as axis numbering, major and minor ticks along the axes, legends, and so on. Add color, graph multiple functions at once, and in general use the Graph application as a starting point for a custom data-plotting application. The code behind the Draw Both Functions button, for instance, plots both functions, each in a different color. The user-defined coordinate system is based on the values of the first function only.

VB5 at Work: The Spiral Application

The Spiral application demonstrates how to draw complicated, mathematically defined curves with Visual Basic's methods. It is a computer rendition of an old toy that made drawing curves literally a child's game. The actual toy consists of two plastic circles, dented along their circumference. The large circle remains fixed on a piece of paper while the smaller one slides around the larger one with the help of a pen. The pen is inserted in a small hole somewhere off the center of the smaller circle. The dents around the circumference of the two circles help the user keep them in touch as the outer circle slides around the inner one. As the outer circle moves around the inner one, the pen leaves intricate patterns on the paper.

If you find this description complicated, open the Spiral application and draw a few curves. The curves shown in Figures 6.19 and 6.20 are the traces left by a point fixed on a small circle that rotates around a bigger circle. The operation of the program is really simple to understand after spending a minute with it.

The curves drawn with this toy can be described mathematically. If the diameters of the two circles are R1 and R2 and the pen is fixed at a point that is r units from the smaller circle's center, as shown in Figure 6.21, the following equations describe the curve:

```
X = (R1 + R2) * Cos(t) - (R2 + r) * Cos(((R1 + R2) / R2) * t)
Y = (R1 + R2) * Sin(t) - (R2 + r) * Sin(((R1 + R2) / R2) * t)
```

The t variable is the angle of rotation and increases with time. Each complete rotation of the small circle around the large one takes 360 degrees (or 2 * pi radians). One complete rotation of the outer circle, however, doesn't complete the curve. The smaller circle must rotate many times around the inner circle to produce the entire curve. The exact number of rotations depends on the ratio of the radiuses of the two circles.

This application uses a quick-and-dirty algorithm to figure out how many rotations are required to complete a curve. If the ratio of the two radiuses is an integer, the algorithm works. If the ratio is not an integer, the algorithm may not recognize the end of the curve on time and will continue drawing over the existing curve. In this case, you can always click on the Clear Graph button to stop the drawing.

FIGURE 6.19

The Spiral application draws interesting, mathematically defined curves.

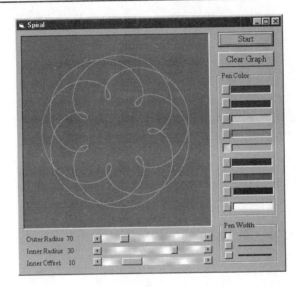

FIGURE 6.20

Another pattern made up of two spiral curves

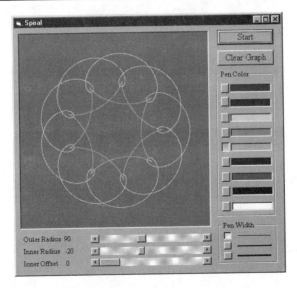

FIGURE 6.21

The spiral curve is generated by the trace of a point on the smaller circle, which slides around the larger one.

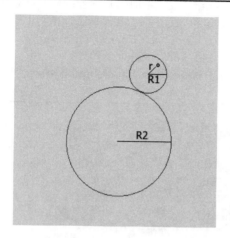
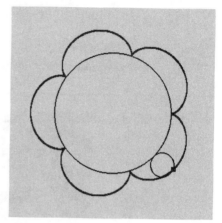

To plot the actual curve, you can turn on the pixel at (X, Y), or you can draw a line segment from the previous point to the new one. The complete code for drawing the spiral curves of Figures 6.19 and 6.20 is shown next.

Code 6.12: The Spiral Application

```
Sub DrawRoullette()
Dim R1, R2, r, pi

R1 = Form1.HScroll1.Value
R2 = Form1.HScroll2.Value - 80
If R2 = 0 Then R2 = 10
r = Form1.HScroll4.Value
pi = 4 * Atn(1)

Dim loop1, loop2
Dim t, X, Y As Double
Dim Rotations As Integer

If Int(R1 / R2) = R1 / R2 Then
    Rotations = 1
Else
    Rotations = Abs(R2 / 10)
    If Int(R2 / 10) <> R2 / 10 Then Rotations = 10 * Rotations
End If

For loop1 = 1 To Rotations
    If BreakNow Then
        Form1.Command1.Caption = "Start"
```

```
      BreakNow = False
      Exit Sub
   End If

   For loop2 = 0 To 2 * pi Step pi / (4 * 360)
      t = loop1 * 2 * pi + loop2
      X = (R1 + R2) * Cos(t) - (R2 + r) * Cos(((R1 + R2) / R2) * t)
      Y = (R1 + R2) * Sin(t) - (R2 + r) * Sin(((R1 + R2) / R2) * t)
      Form1.Picture1.PSet (Form1.Picture1.ScaleWidth / 2 + X,
      ➥Form1.Picture1.ScaleHeight / 2 + Y), PenColor
   Next
   DoEvents
Next
Form1.Command1.Caption = "Start"
BreakNow = False

End Sub
```

The program consists of two nested looops. The inner loop draws the trace of a complete rotation of the small circle around the large one. The outer loop determines how many times the small circle must rotate around the large one to produce a closed curve.

Experiment with the Spiral application. Try various combinations of the inner and outer radiuses by adjusting their values with the corresponding scroll bar. You will notice that the inner radius can assume negative values too. The negative values correspond to a small circle that slides inside the larger one. The last scroll bar controls the position of the pen in the small circle. It is the distance of the pen from the center of the smaller circle. For points on the circumference of the smaller circle, set the last scroll bar to zero.

Manipulating Pixels

The first half of this chapter explored the methods and techniques for drawing shapes. There are only three shape drawing methods, but when coupled with the various properties of the PictureBox control or the Form object, they are quite powerful and quite flexible. The examples you've now seen illustrate how far you can go with Visual Basic's drawing methods.

The second half of the chapter explores Visual Basic's two methods for manipulating pixels: PSet and Point. PSet turns on pixels, and Point reads their values. As are their drawing counterparts, the methods for manipulating pixels are quite flexible, and you can do a lot with them.

In the last section of this chapter, you will see how image-processing applications work, and you'll learn how to implement your own image-processing techniques in Visual Basic. The Image application isn't as fast or as elaborate as professional image-processing applications, but you can use it to experiment.

Let's begin by examining how computers manipulate color and then look at Visual Basic's function for specifying color values.

Specifying Colors

You have seen how the Color common dialog box is used to specify any color. To the computer, though, the specification of a color is more complicated. If you attempt to specify a color value through the common dialog box, you will see three boxes—Red, Green, and Blue—whose values change as you move the cross-shaped pointer over the color spectrum. These are the values of the three basic colors that computers use to specify colors. Any color that can be represented on a computer monitor can be specified by means of the red, green, and blue colors. By mixing percentages of these basic colors, you can design almost any color.

The model of designing colors based on the intensities of their red, green, and blue components is called the RGB model (Red Green Blue model), and it's a fundamental concept in computer graphics. If you are not familiar with this model, this section might be well worth reading. Every color you can imagine can be constructed by mixing the appropriate percentages of the three basic colors. Each color, therefore, is represented by a triplet (Red, Green, Blue), in which Red, Green, and Blue are three bytes that represent the basic color components. The smallest value, 0, indicates the absence of color. The largest value, 255, indicates full intensity, or saturation. The triplet (0, 0, 0) is black, because all colors are missing, and the triplet (255, 255, 255) is white. Other colors have various combinations: (255, 0, 0) is a pure red, (0, 255, 255) is a pure cyan (what you get when you mix green and blue), and (0, 128, 128) is a mid-cyan (a mix of mid-green and mid-blue tones). The possible combinations of the three basic color components are $256 \times 256 \times 256$, or 16,777,216 colors.

NOTE   Each color you can display on a computer monitor can be defined in terms of three basic components— red, green, and blue.

Notice that we use the term *basic colors* and not *primary colors*, which are the three colors used in designing colors with paint. The concept is the same; you mix the primary colors until you get the desired result. The primary colors used in painting, however, are different. They are the colors red, blue, and yellow. Painters can get any shade imaginable by mixing the appropriate percentages of red, blue, and yellow paint. On a computer monitor, you can design any color by mixing the appropriate percentages of red, green, and blue.

The process of generating colors with three basic components is based on the RGB Color Cube, shown in Figure 6.22. The three dimensions of the color cube correspond to the three basic colors. The cube's corners are assigned each of the three primary colors, their complements, and the colors black and white. Complementary colors are easily calculated by subtracting the color values from 255. For example, the color (0, 0, 255) is a pure blue tone. Its complementary color is (255-0, 255-0, 255-255), or (255, 255, 0), which is a pure yellow tone. Blue and yellow are complementary colors, and they are mapped to opposite corners of the cube. The same is true for red and cyan, green and magenta, and black and white. If you add a color to its complementary, you get white.

FIGURE 6.22

Color specification with the RGB Cube

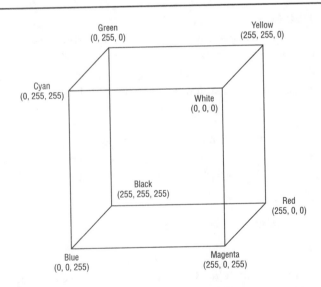

Notice that the components of the colors at the corners of the cube have either zero or full intensity. As you move from one corner to another along the same edge of the cube, only one of its components changes value. For example, as you move from the green to the yellow corner, the red component changes from 0 to 255. The other two components remain the same. As you move between these two corners, you get all the available tones from green to yellow (256 in all). Similarly, as you move from the yellow to the red corner, the only component that changes is the green, and you get all the available shades from yellow to red. This range of similar colors is called *gradient*.

Although you can specify more than 16 million colors, you can't have more than 256 shades of gray. The reason is that a gray tone, including the two extremes (black and white), is made up of equal values of all three primary colors. You can see this on the RGB Cube. Two gray shades lie on the cube's diagonal that goes from black to white. As you move along this path, all three basic components change value, but they are always equal. The value (128, 128, 128) is a mid-gray tone, but the values (127, 128, 128) and (129, 128, 128) aren't gray tones, although they are too close for the human eye to see the difference. That's why it's wasteful to store grayscale pictures using 16-million color True Color file formats. A 256-color file format stores a grayscale just as accurately and more compactly. Once you know an image is grayscale, you needn't store all three bytes per pixel. One value is adequate (the other two components have the same value).

The RGB() Function   For defining colors, Visual Basic provides the RGB() function, which accepts three arguments: RGB(Red, Green, Blue). With the RGB() function, you can define any color imaginable. I mentioned earlier that the triplet (255, 255, 0) is a pure yellow tone. To specify this color value with the RGB() function, you can use a statement such as the following:

```
newColor = RGB(255, 255, 0)
```

The *newColor* variable is a long integer (a long integer is made up of four bytes). It can be assigned to any color property. To change the Form's background color to yellow, you can assign the *newColor* variable to the BackColor property, like this:

```
Form1.BackColor = newColor
```

or you can combine both statements into one like this:

```
Form1.BackColor = RGB(255, 255, 0)
```

In Chapter 5, *Basic ActiveX Controls,* you saw the Colors application, which uses the RGB() function to design any color. You can open this application to see how it translates the values of the three scroll bars to RGB values. It simply plugs the values of the scroll bars into the RGB function and assigns the result to the PictureBox control's BackColor property.

Specifying Gradients

Another interesting application of the RGB() function is to generate gradients. When you move from one to another corner on the same side of the RGB cube (as from red to black or from green to blue), one or more components change value. The colors along the path that connects any two points in the RGB cube form a gradient.

To specify a gradient, you must call the RGB() function many times, each time with a slightly different argument. Suppose you want to fill a rectangle with a gradient. Because there's no function to produce the gradient, you must draw vertical or horizontal lines with slightly different colors and cover the area of the rectangle. Figure 6.23 shows the ClrGrads application, which lets you specify the starting and ending colors of the gradient (with the two narrow PictureBox controls on either side of the Form) and then it generates linear and circular gradients.

FIGURE 6.23

The ClrGrads application generates a linear and a circular gradient between any two user-specified colors.

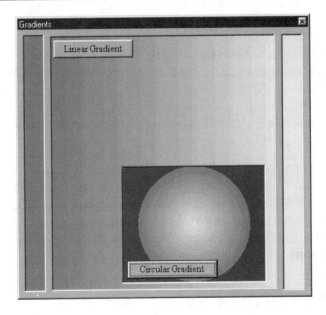

The starting color is the triplet (startRed, startGreen, startBlue), and the ending color is (endRed, endGreen, endBlue). If the rectangle's width in pixels is PWidth, you must write a loop that increments the red component by the increment redInc (which is (endRed - startRed)/PWidth) at a time, the green component by (endGreen - startGreen)/PWwidth, and the blue component by (endBlue - startBlue)/PWidth. Following is the complete code for painting the rectangle with a gradient.

Code 6.13: The ClrGrads Application

```
PWidth = Picture1.ScaleWidth
redInc = (EndRed - StartRed) / PWidth
greenInc = (EndGreen - StartGreen) / PWidth
blueInc = (EndBlue - StartBlue) / PWidth

For ipixel = 0 To PWidth - 1
    newColor = RGB(StartRed + redInc * ipixel, StartGreen +
    ➥greenInc * ipixel, StartBlue + blueInc * ipixel)
    Picture1.Line (ipixel, 0)-(ipixel, Picture1.Height - 1),
    ➥newColor
Next
```

This code draws as many vertical lines as there are pixels along the PictureBox. Each new line's color will be quite similar to the color of the previous line, with its three components adjusted by the amount *redInc*, *greenInc*, and *blueInc*. The values of the increments were chosen so that the first line has the gradient's starting color and the last line has the gradient's ending color. With variations on this technique, you can design vertical, diagonal, and even circular gradients. For a circular gradient, draw circles, starting with the outer one and then decrease the radius at each step. You will see this technique in the Gradients application, later in the chapter.

The code in the ClrGrad applications for generating gradients is straightforward, but it requires that you supply the color components of the starting and ending colors. Although this may be feasible in some applications, it would be best to let the user select two colors and then generate the gradient between them. The tricky part is extracting the three basic color components from a color value, a topic covered in the following section.

What's in a Color Value?

The RGB() function combines the three color components to produce a color value, which is a long number, but Visual Basic lacks a function that would return the three color components from a color value. Suppose the user selects a color value from the Color common dialog box, and your application needs to know its color components. In an image-processing application, such as the one later in this chapter, you want to read pixel values, isolate their red, green, and blue color components, and then process them separately. The Gradient application must calculate the three basic components of the starting and ending colors selected by the user with the help of the Color common dialog box. It is necessary, therefore, to write a function that extracts the red, green, and blue color components from any color value.

To do so, you must first look at how the three color components are stored in a long integer. A long integer is made up of four bytes, three of which store the values of the red, green, and blue components. The red component is in the least significant byte, the second least significant byte is the green color, and the third least significant byte is the blue color. The most significant byte is zero.

The long integer that corresponds to the triplet (64, 32, 192) is 12591168. This number bears no similarity to the original numbers. If you represent the color components with their hexadecimal values, the RGB triplet is (40, 20, C0). If you place these numbers next to one another, the result is the hexadecimal format of the long number. If you get the hexadecimal representation of the number 12591168 (with the Hex() function), the value is C02040. The last two digits correspond to the red component, the next two digits correspond to the green component, and the two most significant hexadecimal digits correspond to the blue value.

When you place the decimal values of the color components next to one another, the result bears no resemblance to the long integer value they represent. If you place the hexadecimal values of the color components next to one another, you get the hexadecimal representation of the long integer that corresponds to the color value. And this explains why hexadecimal numbers are used so frequently in specifying color values. The following three statements extract the values of the three color components from a color value, stored in the *pixel&* variable:

```
pixel& = Form1.Picture1.Point(j, i)
red = pixel& Mod 256
green = ((pixel& And &HFF00FF00) / 256&)
blue = (pixel& And &HFF0000) / 65536
```

The *i* and the *j* are the coordinates of the point whose value we're examining. Since the red value is stored in the least significant byte of the number, it is the remainder of dividing the number by 256.

To extract the next most significant byte, you must set the byte in front and after it to zero. This is done by combining the number with the hex number 00FF00 using the AND operator. If you type this number, though, Visual Basic truncates it to FF00 automatically, because the leading zeros make no difference. But when Visual Basic ANDs the two numbers, it takes into consideration the last two bytes (the length of the number FF00) and does not AND the high order byte. To force Visual Basic to AND all the digits, you must use the number FF00FF00. The high order byte of the color value is zero anyway, so it doesn't make any difference what value it's ANDed with. The green value is stored in the results' second least significant byte. To reduce it to a byte value, divide it by 256. Finally, you do something similar with the third byte from the right. You AND the color value with FF0000 to zero the other bytes and then divide the result by 65536 (which is 256 * 256).

If you are not familiar with hexadecimal number operations, print the intermediate results to see why this technique works. Let's start with the color value 12591168. If you AND it with FF00FF00, the result is 12591104. The hexadecimal format of this number is 002000. The byte 20 is there already, but it must be shifted down to the least significant byte position, which is what happens when it's divided by 256. The result is the value of the green color component. To extract the blue value, the color value is ANDed with FF0000. The result of the operation 12591168 AND FF0000 is 12582912 in decimal format, and C00000 in hexadecimal. The blue component's value is there, but this time it must be shifted to the right by two bytes, which is accomplished by dividing it with 65536.

There's also another technique to extract the color components from a color value, which is conceptually simpler, but a bit slower. If you take the hexadecimal representation of the original color value, the values of all three color components are there. All you have to do is extract them with string manipulation functions. The hexadecimal format of the number 12591168 is the string "C02040". The red color component is the value of the hexadecimal number formatted with the two rightmost digits of the number. The green component is the value of the hexadecimal number formatted with the next two digits, and the red component is the value of the hexadecimal number formatted with the two leftmost digits of the number. Here's the equivalent code:

```
n$ = Hex(Form1.Picture1.Point(j, i))
red = Val("&H" & Right(n$, 2))
green = Val("&H" & Mid$(n$, 3, 2))
blue = Val("&H" & Mid$(n$, 5, 2))
```

Now you can write three functions, GetRed(), GetGreen(), and GetBlue(), which accept as an argument a color value and return the value's red, green, and blue components. Here's the code for the three functions that extract a color's basic components:

```
Function GetRed(colorVal As Long) As Integer
    GetRed = colorVal Mod 256
End Function

Function GetGreen(colorVal As Long) As Integer
    GetGreen = ((colorVal And &HFF00FF00) / 256&)
End Function

Function GetBlue(colorVal As Long) As Integer
    GetBlue = (colorVal And &HFF0000) / (256& * 256&)
End Function
```

With the help of these functions, you can extract the color components of the gradient's starting and ending colors, calculate the increment, and use that to generate and display the desired gradient. Following is the complete code behind the Linear Gradient button.

Code 6.14: The Linear Gradient Button

```
Private Sub Command1_Click()
Dim newColor As Long
Dim ipixel, PWidth As Integer
Dim redInc, greenInc, blueInc As Single
Dim color1 As Long, color2 As Long

    color1 = StartColor.BackColor
    color2 = EndColor.BackColor

    StartRed = GetRed(color1)
    EndRed = GetRed(color2)
    StartGreen = GetGreen(color1)
    EndGreen = GetGreen(color2)
    Blue = GetBlue(color1)
    EndBlue = GetBlue(color2)

    PWidth = Picture1.ScaleWidth

    redInc = (EndRed - StartRed) / PWidth
    greenInc = (EndGreen - StartGreen) / PWidth
    blueInc = (EndBlue - StartBlue) / PWidth
```

```
For ipixel = 0 To PWidth - 1
    newColor = RGB(StartRed + redInc * ipixel, StartGreen +
    ➥greenInc * ipixel, StartBlue + blueInc * ipixel)
    Picture1.Line (ipixel, 0)-(ipixel, Picture1.Height - 1),
    ➥newColor
Next

End Sub
```

The code behind the Circular Gradient button is quite similar, but instead of drawing lines, it draws circles of varying colors. First, it draws the largest circle; then it draws all the successive circles, each having a radius smaller than that of the previous circle by one pixel. You can try other types of gradients on your own, such as diagonal gradients or off-center circular gradients. You can also use this technique to fill your Forms or certain controls with gradients when a Form is loaded. Grayscale gradients make quite interesting backgrounds. They have a subtle effect and add a nice three-dimensional look to your application's user interface.

The FrmGrad application, shown in Figure 6.24, is a variation of the ClrGrads application. (The buttons on the Form don't do anything; they simply show how to use the gradient as a backdrop on a Form.) The Form shown in Figure 6.24 has a gradient as background, which is generated as the program loads. The code is nearly identical to that presented earlier in the ClrGrads application and is executed from within the Form's Resize event so that the gradient is adjusted each time the user changes the Form's size. The FrmGrad Form won't look as nice on systems with 256 colors, because the current palette doesn't contain all the colors required by the gradient.

Using the PaintPicture Method

So far, you've seen the Visual Basic methods for manipulating individual pixels. Manipulating an entire image pixel by pixel is a slow process. In some situations, you may need a quick way to copy an image or part of an image from one container to another. Windows provides a powerful mechanism for moving pixels around, know as BitBlt (pronounced bit blit). BitBlt stands for Bit Block Transfers and is nothing but highly optimized code for moving bits around in memory. VB programmers can access the services of the BitBlt routines, which are built into the operating system, via the PaintPicture method. The PaintPicture method allows you to copy a rectangular area of pixels from one object (a PictureBox or

Form) onto another. Moreover, the source pixels need not replace the pixels at the destination control. They can be combined with them in various ways, yielding interesting effects.

FIGURE 6.24

This Form's background gradient is generated on the fly, in the Resize event handler.

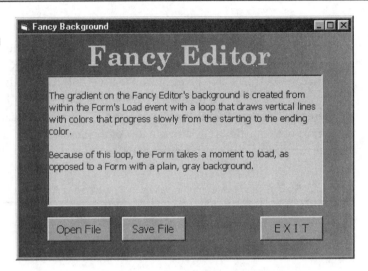

The syntax of the PaintPicture method is as follows:

```
Picture1.PaintPicture picture, DestX, DestY, DestWidth, DestHeight,
↦SourceX, SourceY, SourceWidth, SourceHeight, RasterOp
```

This method accepts a number of arguments, but their use is straightforward:

- The *picture* argument is the source of the transfer. It is the Picture property of a PictureBox, an ImageBox, or a Form, whose contents will be transferred to the Picture1 control.

- *DestX* and *DestY* are the coordinates of the transfer's destination. The rectangle can be transferred anywhere on the destination control.

- *DestWidth* and *DestHeight* are the dimensions of this area.

- *SourceX* and *SourceY* are the coordinates of the upper left corner of the rectangular area to be transferred and are also the dimensions of the rectangle.

- *RasterOp* specifies how the pixels being transferred will be combined with the existing pixels at the destination.

> **NOTE**
>
> If the *SourceWidth* and *SourceHeight* arguments don't match the *DestWidth* and *DestHeight* arguments, the area being copied will be stretched accordingly to fill its destination.

The most common operation is to replace existing pixels with the pixels being transferred. But the PaintPicture method lets you combine the source with the destination pixels using the logical operators AND, OR, XOR, and NOT. For example, you can OR the source pixels with the inverse (NOT) of the destination pixels. Or you can replace the destination pixels with the inverse of the source pixels. In all, there are 256 ways to combine source and destination pixels, but you will never need most of them. Table 6.5 shows a few of the *RasterOp* argument's values, which you may find useful in your applications.

T A B L E   6 . 6   The Most Common Values for the *RasterOp* Argument

CONSTANT	VALUE	DESCRIPTION
vbDstInvert	&H00550009	Inverts the destination bitmap
vbMergePaint	&H00BB0226	Combines the inverse of the source bitmap with the destination bitmap using the OR operator
vbNotSrcCopy	&H00330008	Copies the inverse of the source bitmap to the destination
vbNotSrcErase	&H001100A6	Combines the source and destination bitmaps using the OR operator and then inverts the result
vbSrcAnd	&H008800C6	Combines the source and destination bitmaps using the AND operator
vbSrcCopy	&H00CC0020	Copies the source bitmap to the destination bitmap
vbSrcErase	&H00440328	Combines the inverse of the destination bitmap with the source bitmap using the AND operator
vbSrcInvert	&H00660046	Combines the source and destination bitmaps using the XOR operator
vbSrcPaint	&H00EE0086	Combines the source and destination bitmaps using the OR operator

The values of the constants are given in hexadecimal because this is how they appear in Microsoft's documentation. Use the constants listed in the first column of the table. The value vbSrcCopy overwrites the existing pixels at the destination and is the one you'll be using most often. To copy the contents of the Picture1 PictureBox to the Picture2 control, use the following statement:

```
Picture2.PaintPicture Picture1.Picture 0, 0, _
Picture2.ScaleWidth, Picture2.ScaleWidth, _
0, 0, _
Picture1.ScaleWidth, Picture1.ScaleWidth, _
VbSrcCopy
```

This rather lengthy statement copies the pixels of the Picture1 control onto the Picture2 control. If the two controls don't have the same dimensions, the image will be distorted to cover the entire destination control. If you don't want the image to be distorted during the transfer, replace the arguments Picture2.Scale-Width and Picture2.ScaleHeight with Picture1.ScaleWidth and Picture1.Scale-Height. If the destination PictureBox is smaller than the source PictureBox, only part of the image will be displayed. If it's larger, the image won't fill it entirely. But in either case, the image won't be distorted during the process, because the width and height arguments are the same on both the source and the destination.

To best understand how to use the various settings of the RasterOp argument and what effect they have on the destination bitmap, experiment with the various settings and images. In this chapter's folder on the CD, you will find the PaintPic application, which lets you combine two bitmaps with the various raster operators, as well as with the remaining arguments of the PaintPicture method.

VB5 at Work: The PaintPic Application

The PaintPic application, shown in Figure 6.25, lets you combine the pixels of the source (left) and destination (right) PictureBox controls with the various values of the RasterOp argument of the PaintPicture method. The 8 sliders let you set the origin of the rectangle to be copied, its dimensions, the destination coordinates of the transfer, and its dimensions on the destination PictureBox control.

You can copy the entire source image or part of it and place it anywhere on the destination control. You can also specify different dimensions on the two controls to see how the PaintPicture method distorts the image's dimensions during the transfer. Also, try the various settings for the raster operator with different images.

FIGURE 6.25

Use the PaintPic application to experiment with the arguments of the PaintPicture method.

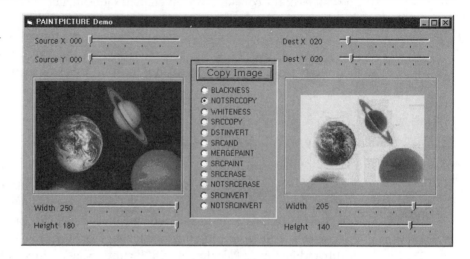

Notice that since most raster operations combine the source with the destination pixels, the result of the transfer depends on the destination control's current contents. The vbSrcInvert operation, for instance, merges the pixels of the source image with the destination pixels using the XOR operator. If you copy the source image again with the same setting, you will get the original contents of the destination image. That's because the XOR operator works like a toggle that merges the two images and then restores the original. The first time it's actually encrypting the original image. The second time it reveals it.

You can also experiment with successive transfers of the same image with different settings for the raster operation. Some settings will yield interesting effects, especially if you slide each successive image by one or two pixels. Finally, you can set the destination PictureBox control's background color to black or white by checking the Blackness or Whiteness CheckBox. You can also reset the destination PictureBox control's background color by right-clicking on it.

Flipping an Image with PaintPicture

Another interesting application of the PaintPicture method is to flip an image as it copies it. If the image's width is negative, the image flips horizontally; if the image's height is negative, the image flips vertically. If both width and height are negative, the image flips in both directions. The negative sign in the width of the destination, for example, tells the PaintPicture method to copy the pixels to the left of the origin (the same is true for the height of the destination). Thus, the pixels are copied to the left of the destination control's left edge. The entire image is copied outside the destination control. To compensate, set the origin to the other corner of the destination. Figure 6.26 shows the PicFlip application, which uses the PaintPicture method to flip an image as it copies it.

FIGURE 6.26

The PicFlip application flips an image using the PaintPicture method.

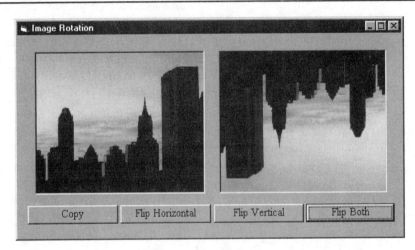

First, let's look at the code of the Copy button in the PicFlip application. The Copy button transfers the source image to the destination.

Code 6.15: The Copy Button

```
Private Sub Command3_Click()

        Picture2.PaintPicture Picture1.Picture, 0, 0, _
        Picture1.ScaleWidth, Picture1.ScaleHeight, 0, 0, _
        Picture1.ScaleWidth, Picture1.ScaleHeight, &HCC0020

End Sub
```

Compare the Copy button code with the code of the Flip Horizontal button.

Code 6.16: The Flip Horizontal Button

```
Private Sub Command1_Click()

        Picture2.PaintPicture Picture1.Picture, 0, 0, _
        Picture1.ScaleWidth, Picture1.ScaleHeight, Picture1
        ➥.ScaleWidth, _
        0, -Picture1.ScaleWidth, Picture1.ScaleHeight, &HCC0020

End Sub
```

Notice that in order to flip the image horizontally, the destination's X origin is not 0, but the image's width and the destination width are the negative of the actual width. The code behind the Flip Vertical button is similar, but instead of the X coordinate and the width of the image, it inverts the Y coordinate and the height of the image. The Flip Both button inverts both the X and Y coordinates and the width and height of the destination.

Processing Images

Images are arrays of pixels, much like a PictureBox control. When an image is displayed on a PictureBox or Form control, each one of its pixels is mapped to a pixel on the Picture Box or Form. As you will see, image processing is nothing more than simple arithmetic operations on the values of the image's pixels. The Image application we will build to demonstrate the various image-processing techniques is slow compared with professional image-processing applications, but it demonstrates the principles of image-processing techniques and can be a starting point for custom applications.

My approach will be simple and practical, and I'll demonstrate the basic concepts of image processing with examples. We will build a simple image-processing application that can read BMP, GIF, and JPG image files, process them, and then display the processed images. There are simpler ways to demonstrate Visual Basic pixel-handling methods, but image processing is an intriguing topic, and I hope many readers will use this application to experiment with image-processing techniques.

An image is a two-dimensional array of pixels that are represented by one or more bits. In a black and white image, each pixel is represented by a single bit. The most common types of images are those with 256 colors; each pixel is represented by a byte. The best quality images, however, use three bytes per pixel, one for each basic color component (red, green, and blue). These images are called true color images because their colors are not approximated.

Images composed of 256 colors are based on a palette; that's why they are sometimes called palette images. The program that created the image selected the 256 colors that best describe the image and stored them in a palette, along with the image. Each pixel in the image is represented by a byte, which is a pointer to the pixel's color in the palette. If the original image happens to contain more than 256 colors, some of them must be approximated with the existing colors.

A total of 256 colors is sufficient for describing a typical image. Even if some of the colors must be approximated, the quality of the image is relatively good. Most pages on the World Wide Web contain no more than 256 colors, and they look fine. The problem with palettes isn't with the image, but with the computers that display them. If your computer can display true color, it will display any number of images, even when opened at the same time. But systems that can display only 256 colors at a time will have a problem.

For example, if the original image contains 256 colors, the processing algorithm will most likely introduce additional colors that aren't present in the palette. Because the computer can't display more than 256 colors, some of them must be approximated. The Image application works best on true color systems. It will also work on systems capable of displaying palette images, but some of the colors may not look quite right.

Because images are two-dimensional arrays of integers, their processing is nothing more than simple arithmetic operations on these integers. Let's look at a simple technique, the inversion of an image's colors. To invert an image, you must change all pixels to their complementary colors—black to white, green to magenta, and so on (the complementary colors are on opposite corners of the RGB cube, shown in Figure 6.22, earlier in this chapter).

To calculate complementary colors, you subtract each of the three color components from 255. For example, a pure green pixel whose value is (0, 255, 0) will be converted to (255-0, 255-255, 255-0) or (255, 0, 255), which is magenta. Similarly, a mid-yellow tone (0, 128, 128) will be converted to (255-0, 255-128, 255-128) or (255, 127, 127), which is a mid-brown tone. To invert an image's colors, you set up two loops that scan the image's pixels and invert the colors of the pixels. The result is the negative of the original image (what you would see if you looked at the negative from which the picture was obtained).

Other image-processing techniques are not as simple, but the important thing to understand is that, in general, image processing is as straightforward as a few arithmetic operations on the image's pixels. After we go through the Image application, you will probably come up with your own techniques and be able to implement them.

VB5 at Work: The Image Application

The application we develop in this section is called Image and is shown in Figure 6.27. It's not a professional tool, but it can be easily implemented in Visual Basic and will give you the opportunity to explore various image-processing techniques on your own. To process an image with the Image application, choose File ➢ Open to load it to the PictureBox control and then select the type of processing from the Process menu. Using the Image application, you can apply the following effects to an image:

- **Smooth** reduces the amount of detail.

- **Sharpen** brings out the detail.

- **Emboss** gives the image a raised (embossed) look.

- **Diffuse** gives the image a painterly look.

- **Custom Filter** allows the user to specify the effect to be applied to the image.

FIGURE 6.27

The Image application demonstrates several image-processing techniques, all implemented with Visual Basic.

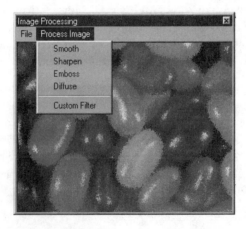

In the following few pages, I will explain how each algorithm works and how it is implemented in Visual Basic.

How the Image Application Works   Let's start with a general discussion of the application's operation before we get down to the actual code. Once the image is loaded on a PictureBox control, you can access the values of its pixels with the Point method, which returns a long integer representing each pixel's color. The basic color components must be extracted from this long integer value and used to implement the algorithms. This is a time-consuming step, and for most algorithms, it must be performed more than once for each pixel. To speed up the processing, I chose to read the values of all the pixels when the image is loaded and store them in an array. This trick also allow us to apply multiple processing techniques to the same image, without having to read the value of each pixel again and again. In effect, it introduces a delay while the image is loaded, to speed up the rest of the application.

The array that stores the values of the pixels is called *ImagePixels()* and is declared as follows:

```
Global ImagePixels(2, 500, 500) As Integer
```

The largest image you can process with the Image application can't exceed these dimensions. Of course, you can either change the dimensions of the array or abandon the array altogether and read the pixel values from the PictureBox, as needed. The application will run slower overall, but it will be able to handle any size image you throw at it.

There are two options for reading the image's pixels into the ImagePixels() array:

- Using the Point method

- Reading the pixels directly from the file

The Point method, which is simpler and is used in the Image application, reads the pixel values directly off the PictureBox. Most image-processing applications use the other option, reading the pixels directly from the file. This technique is faster, but you have to supply different routines for each image type. Visual Basic currently supports three image types: BMP, GIF, and JPG. Instead of learning the file structure for all three types of images and implementing a different routine for each one, we'll let Visual Basic read the image into a PictureBox control and then read the control's pixels with the Point method.

Reading the Pixel Values The code behind the Open command of the File menu is shown next. The program calls the File Open common dialog box, which lets the user select an image and then loads the image on the PictureBox. The PictureBox's ScaleMode property is set to 3 (pixels), and its AutoSize property is set to True, so we can find out the image's dimensions from the PictureBox's dimensions. If either of the image's dimensions exceeds 500, the program ends with a message. If the image's dimensions are smaller, the program proceeds by reading the pixel values into the ImagePixels array. The value returned by the Point method is a long integer, which contains all three color components, but can't be used in any operation as is. You must first extract the three color components with the GetRed(), GetGreen(), and GetBlue() functions.

Once extracted, the color components are stored in the appropriate elements of the ImagePixels array. The first index in the array corresponds to a color component (0 for red, 1 for green, 2 for blue), the second index corresponds to the pixel's column, and the third index corresponds to the pixel's row. While the image's pixels are read, the program updates a ProgressBar control that acts as a progress indicator. The ProgressBar control is updated after reading an entire row of pixels from the PictureBox control.

Code 6.17: The Open Command

```
Private Sub FileOpen_Click()
Dim i, j
Dim red As Integer, green As Integer, blue As Integer
Dim pixel&
Dim PictureName

CommonDialog1.Action = 1
PictureName = CommonDialog1.filename
If PictureName = "" Then Exit Sub
Picture1.Picture = LoadPicture(PictureName)
Form1.Refresh

X = Picture1.ScaleWidth
Y = Picture1.ScaleHeight
If X > 500 Or Y > 500 Then
    MsgBox "Image too large to process. Please try loading a smaller
    ➡image."
    X = 0
```

```
        Y = 0
        Exit Sub
End If

Form1.Width = Form1.ScaleX(Picture1.Width + 6, vbPixels, vbTwips)
Form1.Height = Form1.ScaleY(Picture1.Height + 30, vbPixels, vbTwips)
Form1.Refresh

Form3.Show
Form3.Refresh

    For i = 0 To Y - 1
        For j = 0 To X - 1
            pixel& = Form1.Picture1.Point(j, i)
            red = pixel& Mod 256
            green = ((pixel& And &HFF00) / 256&) Mod 256&
            blue = (pixel& And &HFF0000) / 65536
            ImagePixels(0, i, j) = red
            ImagePixels(1, i, j) = green
            ImagePixels(2, i, j) = blue
        Next
        Form3.ProgressBar1.Value = i * 100 / (Y - 1)
    Next
    Form3.Hide

End Sub
```

> **NOTE** Since the valid range for color values is the same as the value range of the Byte data type, why didn't we declare the ImagePixels array as an array of bytes? Visual Basic handles integers more efficiently than bytes, so we gave up some memory for speed. You can modify the declaration of the ImagePixels array to save memory.

Smoothing Images

Now we are ready to look at the image-processing techniques. One of the simplest and most common operations in all image-processing programs is the smoothing operation. The smoothed image contains less abrupt changes than the original image and looks a lot like the original image seen through a semitransparent glass. Figure 6.28 shows an image and its smoothed version, obtained with the Image application.

FIGURE 6.28

Smoothing an image reduces its detail, but in many cases makes the image less "noisy" and "busy."

Original Image   Blurred Image

The smoothing operation is equivalent to low-pass filtering. Just as you can cut off the sound's high frequencies in your stereo with the help of an equalizer, you can cut off the high frequencies of an image. If you are wondering what the high frequencies of an image are, think of them as the areas with abrupt changes in the image's intensity. These are the areas that are mainly affected by the blurring filter.

To smooth an image, you must reduce the large differences between adjacent pixels. Let's take a block of 9 pixels, centered on the pixel we want to blur. This block contains the pixel to be blurred and its 8 immediate neighbors. Let's assume that all the pixels in this block are green, except for the middle one, which is red. This pixel is drastically different from its neighbors, and for it to be blurred, it must be pulled toward the average value of the other pixels. Taking the average of a block of pixels is, therefore, a good choice for a blurring operation. If the current pixel's value is similar to the values of its neighbors, the average won't affect it significantly. If its value is different, the remaining pixels will pull the current pixel's value toward them. In other words, if the middle pixel is green, the average wouldn't affect it. Being the only red pixel in the block, though, it's going to come closer to the average value of the remaining pixels. It's going to assume a green tone.

Here's an example with numbers. If the value of the current pixel is 10 and the values of its 8 immediate neighbors are 8, 11, 9, 10, 12, 10, 11, and 9, the average value of all pixels will be (8+11+9+10+12+10+11+9+10)/9=10. The pixel under consideration happens to be right on the average of its neighboring pixels. The results would be quite different if the value of the center pixel was drastically different. If the center pixel's value were 20, the new average would be 11. Because the neighboring pixels have values close to 10, they pulled the "outlier" toward them. And this is how blurring works. By taking the average of a number of pixels, you force the pixels with values drastically different from their neighbors to get closer to them.

Another factor affecting the amount of blurring is the size of the block over which the average is calculated. We used a 3×3 block in our example, which yields an average blur. To blur the image even more, use a 5×5 block. Even larger blocks will blur the image to the point that useful information will be lost. The actual code of the Smooth operation scans all the pixels of the image (excluding the edge pixels that don't have neighbors all around them) and takes the average of their red, green, and blue components. It then combines the three values with the RGB function to compute the new value of the pixel.

Code 6.18: The Smooth Operation

```
Private Sub ProcessSmooth_Click()
Dim i, j As Integer

    For i = 1 To Y - 2
        For j = 1 To X - 2
            red = ImagePixels(0, i - 1, j - 1) + ImagePixels(0, i -
            ➥1, j) + ImagePixels(0, i - 1, j + 1) + _
            ImagePixels(0, i, j - 1) + ImagePixels(0, i, j) +
            ➥ImagePixels(0, i, j + 1) + _
            ImagePixels(0, i + 1, j - 1) + ImagePixels(0, i + 1, j)
            ➥+ ImagePixels(0, i + 1, j + 1)

            green = ImagePixels(1, i - 1, j - 1) + ImagePixels(1, i
            ➥- 1, j) + ImagePixels(1, i - 1, j + 1) + _
            ImagePixels(1, i, j - 1) + ImagePixels(1, i, j) +
            ➥ImagePixels(1, i, j + 1) + _
            ImagePixels(1, i + 1, j - 1) + ImagePixels(1, i + 1, j)
            ➥+ ImagePixels(1, i + 1, j + 1)
```

```
               blue = ImagePixels(2, i - 1, j - 1) + ImagePixels(2, i -
            ➥1, j) + ImagePixels(2, i - 1, j + 1) + _
               ImagePixels(2, i, j - 1) + ImagePixels(2, i, j) +
            ➥ImagePixels(2, i, j + 1) + _
               ImagePixels(2, i + 1, j - 1) + ImagePixels(2, i + 1, j)
            ➥+ ImagePixels(2, i + 1, j + 1)

               Picture1.PSet (j, i), RGB(red / 9, green / 9, blue / 9)
        Next
        Picture1.Refresh
    Next

End Sub
```

In the code, I used a 3 × 3 block, but you can change a few numbers in the code to blur the image with an even larger block. The pixels involved in the calculations are the neighboring pixels on the same, previous, and next rows, and the pixel being processed is always at the center of the block. You may notice that the code is quite verbose. I could have avoided the very long line that adds the color components with a couple of For…Next loops, but I chose this verbose coding over the more compact version to speed up the computations. Setting up loop counters would have introduced some small additional delays, which we can do without. The program is slow as it is, and every trick counts. Visual Basic is not the most efficient language for this type of operation, but it surely is the most convenient.

Sharpening Images

Since the basic operation for smoothing an image is the addition, the opposite operation will result in sharpening the image. The sharpening effect is more subtle than smoothing, but more common and more useful. Nearly every image published, especially in monochrome publications, must be sharpened to some extent. For an example of a sharpened image, see Figure 6.29. Sharpening an image consists of highlighting the edges of the objects in it—which are the very same pixels blurred by the previous algorithm. Edges are areas of an image with sharp changes in intensity between adjacent pixels. The smoothing algorithm smoothed out these areas; now we want to pronounce them.

The difference between two adjacent pixels will be zero or a very small number if the pixels are in a smooth area of the image; if the pixels are on an edge, the difference between two adjacent pixels will be a large value (perhaps negative). If the difference is zero, the two pixels are nearly identical, which means that there's nothing to sharpen. We are at a "flat" area of the image. (Consider an image with a constant background. There's no detail to be brought out on the background.) If the two pixels happen to be on an edge, their values will differ, and the difference will have a significant value. This is an area of the image with some degree of detail, which can be stressed.

FIGURE 6.29

The sharpening operation brings out detail that isn't evident in the original image.

Original Image   Sharpened Image

The difference between adjacent pixels isolates the areas with detail and completely flattens out the smooth areas. The question now is how to bring out the detail without leveling the rest of the image. How about adding the difference to the original pixel? Where the image is flat, the difference is negligible, and the processed pixel will be practically the same as the original one. If the difference is significant, the processed pixel will be the original plus a value that is proportional to the magnitude of the detail. The sharpening algorithm can be expressed as follows:

```
new_value = original_value + 0.5 * difference
```

If you simply add the difference to the original pixel, the algorithm brings out too much detail. You usually add a fraction of the difference, and a 50% factor is common.

Code 6.19: The Sharpening Algorithm

```
Private Sub ProcessSharpen_Click()
    Dim i, j
    Dim Dx, Dy
    Dx = 1
    Dy = 1
    Dim red, green, blue

    For i = 1 To Y - 2
        For j = 1 To X - 2
            red = ImagePixels(0, i, j) + 0.5 * (ImagePixels(0, i, j)
            - ImagePixels(0, i + Dx, j - Dy))
            green = ImagePixels(1, i, j) + 0.5 * (ImagePixels(1, i,
            j) - ImagePixels(1, i + Dx, j - Dy))
            blue = ImagePixels(2, i, j) + 0.5 * (ImagePixels(2, i,
            j) - ImagePixels(2, i + Dx, j - Dy))
            If red > 255 Then red = 255
            If red < 0 Then red = 0
            If green > 255 Then green = 255
            If green < 0 Then green = 0
            If blue > 255 Then blue = 255
            If blue < 0 Then blue = 0
            Picture1.PSet (j, i), RGB(red, green, blue)
        Next
        Picture1.Refresh
    Next

End Sub
```

The variables *Dx* and *Dy* express the distances between the two pixels being subtracted. You can subtract adjacent pixels on the same row, adjacent pixels in the same column, or diagonally adjacent pixels, which is what I did in this subroutine. Besides adding the difference to the original pixel value, this subroutine must check the result for validity. The result of the calculations may exceed the valid value range for a color value, which is 0 to 255. That's why you must clip the value if it falls outside the valid range.

Using the Emboss Special Effect

What do you think would happen to the processed image if you take the difference of adjacent pixels only? The flat areas of the image would be totally leveled, and only the edges would remain visible. The result would be an image like the image on the right in Figure 6.30. This effect clearly stresses the edges and flattens the smooth areas of the image. By doing so, it gives the image depth. The processed image looks as if it is raised and illuminated from the right side. This effect is known as *emboss* or bas relief.

FIGURE 6.30

The Emboss special effect

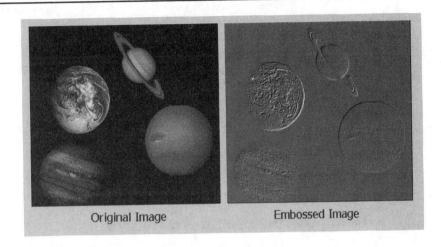

Original Image   Embossed Image

The actual algorithm is based on the difference between adjacent pixels. For most of the image, however, the difference between adjacent pixels is a small number, and the image will turn black. The Emboss algorithm adds a constant to the difference to add some brightness to areas of the image that would otherwise be dark. The algorithm can be expressed as follows:

```
new_value = difference + 128
```

As usual, you can take the difference between adjacent pixels in the same row, adjacent pixels in the same column, or diagonally adjacent pixels.

Code 6.20: The Emboss Algorithm

```
Private Sub ProcessEmboss_Click()
    Dim i, j
    Dim Dx, Dy
    Dx = 1
    Dy = 1
    Dim red, green, blue
```

```
For i = 1 To Y - 2
    For j = 1 To X - 2
        red = Abs(ImagePixels(0, i, j) - ImagePixels(0, i - Dx,
        ➥j - Dy) + 128)
        green = Abs(ImagePixels(1, i, j) - ImagePixels(1, i -
        ➥Dx, j - Dy) + 128)
        blue = Abs(ImagePixels(2, i, j) - ImagePixels(2, i - Dx,
        ➥j - Dy) + 128)
        Picture1.PSet (j, i), RGB(red, green, blue)
    Next
    Picture1.Refresh
  Next

End Sub
```

The variables *Dx* and *Dy* determine the location of the pixel being subtracted from the one being processed. Notice that the pixel being subtracted is behind and above the current pixel. If you set the *Dx* and *Dy* variables to -1, the result is similar, but the processed image looks engraved rather than embossed.

Using the Diffuse Special Effect

The Diffuse special effect is different from the previous ones, in the sense that it's not based on the sums or the differences of pixel values. The Diffuse special effect uses the Rnd() function to introduce some randomness to the image and give it a painterly look, as demonstrated in Figure 6.31.

FIGURE 6.31

The Diffuse special effect gives the image a painterly look.

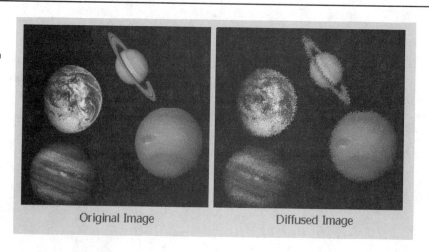

Original Image   Diffused Image

This time we won't manipulate the values of the pixels. Instead, the current pixel will assume the value of another one, selected randomly in its 5×5 neighborhood. The pixel whose value is assigned to the current pixel is selected randomly, with the help of the Rnd() function.

Code 6.21: The Diffuse Algorithm

```
Private Sub Diffuse_Click()
    Print Now
    Dim i, j
    Dim Rx, Ry
    Dim red, green, blue

    For i = 2 To Y - 3
        For j = 2 To X - 3
            Rx = Rnd * 4 - 2
            Ry = Rnd * 4 - 2
            red = ImagePixels(0, i + Rx, j + Ry)
            green = ImagePixels(1, i + Rx, j + Ry)
            blue = ImagePixels(2, i + Rx, j + Ry)
            Picture1.PSet (j, i), RGB(red, green, blue)
        Next
        DoEvents
    Next

End Sub
```

Implementing Custom Filters

The last operation on the Process menu is a versatile technique for implementing many filters. The Custom Filter command leads you to another Form, shown in Figure 6.32. You can use this Form to specify the size of the block over which the calculations will be performed, and it can be 3×3 or 5×5. Imagine that this block is centered over the current pixel. The coefficients for each cell of this block are multiplied by the underlying pixel values, and all the products are added together. Let's call this sum SP (sum of products). The sum of the products is then divided by the Divide factor, and finally the Bias is added to the result. Here's the code that processes an image with a custom filter, as specified in the Custom Filter window.

FIGURE 6.32

The Custom Filter
specification Form of
the Image application

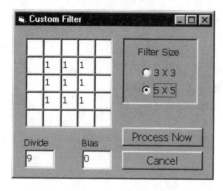

Code 6.22: The Custom Filter Command

```
Private Sub ProcessCustom_Click()
    Dim RedSum, GreenSum, BlueSum
    Dim red, green, blue As  Integer
    Dim fi, fj As Integer
    Dim i, j As Integer
    Dim Offset As Integer

    Form2.Show 1    ' wait for user to define filter
    If FilterCancel = True Then Exit Sub

    If FilterNorm = 0 Then FilterNorm = 1

    If Form2.Option1.Value Then
        Offset = 1
    Else
        Offset = 2
    End If
    For i = Offset To Y - Offset - 1
        For j = Offset To X - Offset - 1
            RedSum = 0: GreenSum = 0: BlueSum = 0
            For fi = -Offset To Offset
                For fj = -Offset To Offset
                    RedSum = RedSum + ImagePixels(0, i + fi, j + fj)
                    ➥* CustomFilter(fi + 2, fj + 2)
                    GreenSum = GreenSum + ImagePixels(1, i + fi, j +
                    ➥fj) * CustomFilter(fi + 2, fj + 2)
```

```
                    BlueSum = BlueSum + ImagePixels(2, i + fi, j +
                    ➥fj) * CustomFilter(fi + 2, fj + 2)
                Next
            Next
            red = Abs(RedSum / FilterNorm + FilterBias)
            green = Abs(GreenSum / FilterNorm + FilterBias)
            blue = Abs(BlueSum / FilterNorm + FilterBias)
            Picture1.PSet (j, i), RGB(red, green, blue)
        Next
        DoEvents
    Next

End Sub
```

The subroutine reads the values of the various controls on Form2 (the filter's Form) and uses them to process the image as described. The custom filter is the slowest one, but it's quite flexible.

To understand how this filter works, let's implement the smoothing algorithm as a custom filter. The smoothing algorithm adds the values of the current pixel and its 8 neighbors and divides the result by 9. If you set all the coefficients in the filter to 1, the sum of the products will be the sum of all pixel values under the filter's block. Multiplying each pixel by 1 won't change their values, and so the sum of the products will be the same as the sum of the pixel values. To calculate the average, you must divide by 9; so set the Divide field on the Custom Filter Form to 9. The Bias field should be 0. If you apply this Custom Filter to the image, it will have the same effect on the image as the smoothing algorithm. The values of all 9 pixels under the block are added, their sum is divided by 9, and the result, which is the average of the pixels under consideration, is assigned to the center pixel of the block. The same process is repeated for the next pixel on the same row, and so on, until the filter is applied to every pixel of the image.

Let's look at one more example of Custom Filter, this time one that uses the Bias field. The Emboss algorithm replaces each pixel with its difference from the one on the previous row and column and then adds the bias 128 so that the embossed image won't be too dark. To implement the Emboss algorithm as a Custom Filter, set the coefficients as shown in Figure 6.33.

FIGURE 6.33

FIGURE 6.33

The coefficients of the
Custom Filter Form for
the Emboss filter

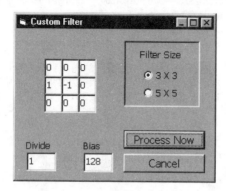

The pixel to the right of the current pixel is subtracted from the current pixel, and the bias 128 is added to the result, which is exactly what the actual algorithm did.

Using Edge Detection Filters   You can use another type of custom filter to extract the edges of an image. Because an image contains both horizontal and vertical edges, two types of edge detection filters detect the corresponding types of edges:

- Horizontal

- Vertical

The horizontal edge detection filter detects and extracts horizontal edges by subtracting a row of pixels above the center pixel from the corresponding pixels below the center pixel. The vertical edge detection filter subtracts columns of pixels instead of rows, and its definition is shown in Figure 6.34. Figure 6.35 shows the result.

FIGURE 6.34

A vertical edge
detection filter

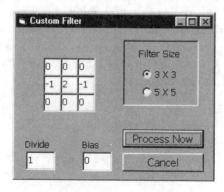

FIGURE 6.35

The result of applying the filter of Figure 6.34 to an image

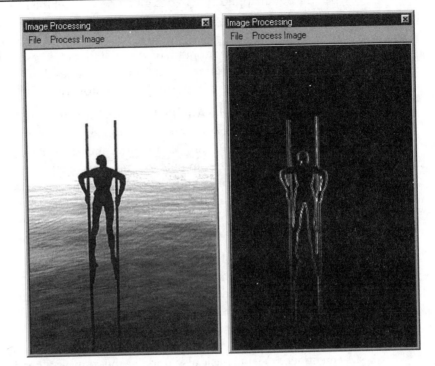

Optimization Issues

If you open the Spiral application and experiment with it, you will see that the application has a major flaw. If you switch to another application and then return to the Spiral window, the curve is erased. This isn't really a problem with the application; it's a thorny issue in drawing with Visual Basic. You can overcome it in several ways, but first you must understand how Visual Basic handles graphics.

One of the most important properties affecting VB graphics is AutoRedraw, which has two possible settings—True and False. When you draw on a control with its AutoRedraw property set to False, every shape appears instantly on the screen. This is how the SpiroGr application works. This setting has two problems. First, the drawing disappears when the window is covered by another one. Any shapes placed on a control while its AutoRedraw property is False are not stored permanently, and that's why Windows can't refresh the control. Which leads us to the second problem: Since Windows doesn't maintain a permanent copy of the control's contents, it can't save them with the SavePicture method.

Open the Spiral application in design mode, and set the PictureBox control's property to True. Although earlier you could watch the curve slowly being drawn, now you must wait until Visual Basic completes the drawing to see the curve on the control. The program now is half the fun to watch, not to mention that if you didn't know better, you'd think that it doesn't work. So, what's the problem with this setting of the AutoRedraw property?

When you draw with the AutoRedraw property set to True, Visual Basic draws in a special area of memory called a *device context*. A device context is a copy of the actual picture on the Picture Box or Form, and Visual Basic uses it to update the image of the actual object from time to time. The contents of the device context are transferred to the control under two circumstances:

- Whenever Visual Basic gets a chance

- When you instruct Visual Basic to do so with the Refresh method

The Refresh method refreshes the contents of the control to which it's applied, including any graphics. If you apply the Refresh method to the Form object, the entire window is refreshed. To refresh the contents of a PictureBox control, apply the Refresh method to the control, like this:

```
Picture1.Refresh
```

As mentioned, Visual Basic also updates the controls when it gets a chance, and this happens whenever the application isn't busy executing code. When the DrawRoulette subroutine is executing, Visual Basic doesn't get a chance to do anything else. When the subroutine ends and Visual Basic waits for an external event, it gets a chance to redraw the controls. That's why you don't see anything on the screen until the entire curve has been calculated.

When to Refresh

As you can see, the setting of the AutoRedraw property can seriously affect your application. If you set it to False, users are able to watch the progress of the drawing, as they should. But you don't have a permanent copy of the drawing, which means you can't save it in a file, and if the user switches to another application, the control will be cleared, and you will have to repeat the drawing. It looks as if we have a no-win situation here, but there are ways to overcome the problem.

One solution is to draw with AutoRedraw set to True and to refresh the control frequently. How about refreshing the control after each point is plotted? You can try this by inserting the following statement right after the Line method in the DrawRoulette() subroutine:

```
Picture1.Refresh
```

This statement causes the program to refresh the PictureBox control so often that it will behave as if its AutoRedraw property is set to False. Run the program now, and you'll see that this approach is out of the question. The program is too slow. This is the penalty of refreshing controls frequently.

How about refreshing the control after each rotation of the outer circle around the inner one? Simply remove the Refresh statement you just inserted in the code, insert it between the two loops, and run the program again. The DoEvents statement between the two loops has the same effect. It interrupts the program and gives Windows the chance to refresh the screen. (This statement was placed there to give the program a chance to process external events, such as the click of a command button.) The curve is drawn in pieces, a rather unnatural progression. This approach is quite useful in other situations, but it's not as helpful here. When you process an image, for instance, you can refresh the image one row at a time. This is what we did in the image-processing application. But the Spiral application requires a more complicated approach.

You can refresh the PictureBox control more frequently, and you might try another interesting approach, which is to draw on two identical PictureBox controls:

- A visible control that has its AutoRedraw property set to False (so that all points appear as they are plotted).

- An invisible control that has its AutoRedraw property set to True. The curve is always available to your code.

If you want to save the curve as a bitmap to a disk file, use the Picture property of the invisible PictureBox.

The other problem you must cope with is the update of the visible control when its contents are cleared because the user has switched to another window. This condition is signaled to your application by the Paint event. Therefore, every time the application receives a Paint event, the program must copy the contents of the invisible PictureBox control onto the visible one. This approach combines all the benefits of the True setting of the AutoRedraw property, and at the same time the curve is always visible, even while it's being drawn.

Spirals Revised

The Spirals1 application implements the technique described here. The Picture2 control is invisible and has its AutoRedraw property set to True. It also has the exact position and dimensions as the visible Picture1 control. The DrawRoulette() routine draws on both controls.

Code 6.23: The Revised DrawRoulette() Subroutine

```
Form1.Picture1.PSet (Form1.Picture1.ScaleWidth / 2 + X, Form1.Picture1
➥.ScaleHeight / 2 + Y), PenColor
Form1.Picture2.PSet (Form1.Picture2.ScaleWidth / 2 + X, Form1.Picture2
➥.ScaleHeight / 2 + Y), PenColor
```

When the program receives the Paint event, the contents of the Picture2 control are copied on the Picture1 control.

Code 6.24: The Paint Event

```
Private Sub Form_Paint()

    Picture1.Refresh
    Picture1.PaintPicture Picture2.Image, 0, 0, Picture2.Width,
    ➥Picture2.Height, 0, 0, Picture2.Width, Picture2.Height,
    ➥&HCC0020

End Sub
```

The Refresh method seems unnecessary, but the program won't work without it. Run the Spirals1 application, watch its behavior, and compare it with the Spirals application. You gain all the convenience of the immediate refreshing of the Picture control, and at the same time, the contents of the control are persistent.

Of course, the Spirals1 application requires a few more additional lines. For example, when the user changes the pen's width, you must change the Draw-Width property for both PictureBox controls. Likewise, when the Clear Graph button is clicked, the program must clear both PictureBox controls. Other than that, the code of the two applications is identical.

Transparent Drawings

The AutoRedraw property isn't a cause of problems only. Here's an interesting application of the AutoRedraw property. Since everything you draw while the AutoRedraw Property is set to False appears on the control but doesn't update the internal copy, you can manipulate the AutoRedraw property at run time to draw on layers that can be instantly removed from the control. Figure 6.36 shows the TRGrid application, which turns on and off a grid over the contents of a PictureBox control. The grid is drawn while the AutoRedraw property is False and can be easily removed with a single call to the Refresh method. The Refresh method copies the contents of the device context to the control. Because the grid is not saved in the device context, it disappears when the control is refreshed. Click on the two buttons at the bottom of the Form to superimpose a linear or polar grid on top of the image.

FIGURE 6.36

The grid on top of this PictureBox can be removed with a call to the control's Refresh method because it's drawn with AutoRedraw set to False.

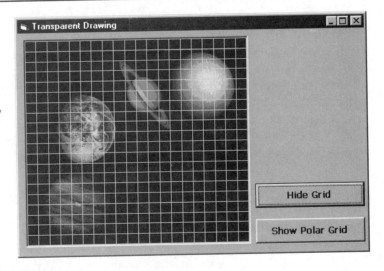

Code 6.25: The Show Linear Grid

```
Sub DrawLinearGrid()

    GridLines = 20
    Picture1.AutoRedraw = False
    GridSpaceX = Int(Picture1.ScaleWidth / GridLines)
    GridSpaceY = Int(Picture1.ScaleHeight / GridLines)
```

```
For i = 0 To GridLines + 1
    Picture1.Line (GridSpaceX * i, 0)-(GridSpaceX * i,
    ➥Picture1.Height - 1)
    Picture1.Line (0, GridSpaceY * i)-(Picture1.Width - 1,
    ➥GridSpaceY * i)
Next

End Sub
```

To remove the grid, you must either reload the graphic, to overwrite the contents of the Picture Box, or refresh the contents of the control with the Refresh method. The RemoveGrid subroutine that removes the grid from the Picture Box couldn't be simpler:

```
Picture1.Refresh
```

The trick is in the second line of the ShowGrid() subroutine:

```
Picture1.AutoRedraw = False
```

Everything drawn after this command (in other words, everything drawn while the AutoRedraw property is False) is ignored when Visual Basic updates the contents of the control because it is not part of the device context. This simple technique allows you to display all kinds of graphics on top of an image and then remove them with a Refresh command, as if they were drawn on a transparency over the actual image. You can even assign different colors to different users and let them annotate the same drawing (the image of a received fax, for instance, or a technical drawing).

Better Rubber Shapes

In the Draw application, you saw how to draw rubber shapes and in general how to temporarily place elements on a background without disturbing it, with the help of the XOR drawing mode. The problem with this approach is that the rubber shapes assume strange colors. The XOR drawing mode has the unique property of being reversible, but it also has a serious side effect. A better approach is to draw the rubber shape in copy mode (DrawMode=13), but switch to AutoRedraw= False mode. Then, instead of erasing the previous rubber shape as we did before, you can refresh the control. With each refresh, the rubber shape is erased, revealing the background, which is drawn with AutoRedraw set to True.

The QDraw application (see Figure 6.37) works just like the Draw application presented earlier, but it uses the technique just described to draw rubber shapes. The rubber shapes don't change color, and they are much more convincing. The QDraw application is identical to the Draw application, but instead of switching to the XOR mode to draw rubber shapes and erasing the previous rubber shape from within the MouseMove event, it turns off the AutoRedraw property and then uses the Refresh method to erase the previous shape. If you open the QDraw application and examine its code, you will see that only a few lines were changed.

FIGURE 6.37

The QDraw application can draw shapes over a bitmap without resorting to the XOR mode, which means that the underlying pixels don't affect the color of the shape.

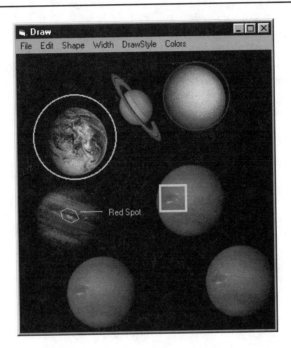

The Case switch that draws rubber shapes in the MouseMove event in the revised application is where most changes are found.

Code 6.26: The Case Switch

```
Select Case Shape
        Case "LINE":
                'Form1.Line (XStart, YStart)-(XPrevious, YPrevious)
                Form1.Refresh
```

```
          Form1.Line (XStart, YStart)-(X, Y)
     Case "CIRCLE":
          'Form1.Circle (XStart, YStart), Sqr((XPrevious - XStart)
          ➥^ 2 + (YPrevious - YStart) ^ 2)
          Form1.Refresh
          Form1.Circle (XStart, YStart), Sqr((X - XStart) ^ 2 + (Y
          ➥- YStart) ^ 2)
     Case "BOX":
          'Form1.Line (XStart, YStart)-(XPrevious, YPrevious), , B
          Form1.Refresh
          Form1.Line (XStart, YStart)-(X, Y), , B
End Select
```

Notice that the line that used to erase the previous line in XOR mode is commented out. Its function is now accomplished with a call to the Form's Refresh method.

PART II

Advanced Visual
Basic

CHAPTER
SEVEN

7

Advanced ActiveX Controls

- ■ The RichTextBox control

- ■ The MSFlexGrid control

This chapter explores a few of the more advanced AcitveX controls that you will find useful in building elaborate applications such as word processors, spreadsheets, and so on. In the following pages, you will find out how to use the RichTextBox control to build a word processor and how to use the MSFlexGrid control to build a spreadsheet application.

The controls presented in this chapter are more complicated than the ones of the previous chapter, in the sense that they have more properties and methods, which make them much more flexible. This chapter will show you:

- **The RichTextBox control,** the core of a word processor, wrapped as an ActiveX control.

- **The MSFlexGrid control,** the core of a spreadsheet application, also wrapped as an ActiveX control.

The RichTextBox control provides all the functionality you need to build a word processor, and the MSFlexGrid control provides all the functionality you need to build a spreadsheet application.

> **NOTE**
> You may be wondering, Why not use the Microsoft Office application and VBA and control them from within a Visual Basic application? The answer is that many of your users may not have Microsoft Office installed on their systems. Also, why put up with the monstrous functionality of the Office applications when a sleek, quick-loading, fast-executing VB application will do the trick?

The RichTextBox Control

The RichTextBox control is nothing less than the core of a full-blown word processor. For an example of what you can do with it, see Figure 7.1. It provides all the functionality of a TextBox control, it gives you the capability to mix different fonts, sizes, and attributes, and it gives you precise control over the margins of the text. You can even place images in your text on a RichTextBox control (but you don't have the kind of control over the embedded images that you have with Word 97, for example).

FIGURE 7.1

The RTFPad application uses the functionality of the RichTextBox control to implement a word processor.

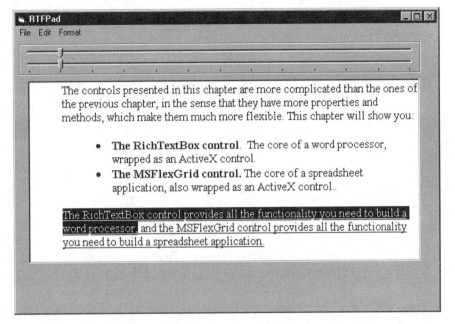

The fundamental property of the Rich Textbox control is its TextRTF property. The RichTextBox control has a Text property that is similar to the Text property of the TextBox control; it is the text currently displayed by the control. This property returns (or sets) the text of the control; however, it doesn't contain formatting information.

As mentioned, you can use the RichTextBox control to specify the text's formatting. You can apply different indention to different paragraphs, any font, size, or style to selected words, and so on. Formatting information is stored along with the control's text, but you can't access it via the Text property. The TextRTF property, however, returns (or sets) the text, along with any formatting information.

RTF stands for *Rich Text Format*, which is a standard for storing formatting information along with the text. The beauty of the RichTextBox control is that you, the programmer, need not supply the formatting codes. The control provides simple properties that turn the selected text into bold, change the alignment of the current paragraph, and so on. The RTF code is generated internally by the control and is used to save and load formatted files. It is possible to create elaborately formatted documents without knowing the RTF language.

> **NOTE**
> The WordPad application that comes with Windows is based on the RichTextBox control. You can easily duplicate every bit of WordPad's functionality with the RichTextBox control, as you will see in the section "VB5 at Work: The RTFPad Application."

The RTF Language

A basic understanding of the RTF format, its commands, and how it works will certainly help you in understanding how the RichTextBox control works. RTF is a document formatting language that uses simple commands to specify the formatting of a document. These commands, or tags as they are called, are ASCII strings, such as \par (the tag that marks the beginning of a new paragraph) and \b (the tag that turns on the bold style). And this is where the value of the RTF format lies. RTF documents don't contain special characters and can be easily exchanged among different operating systems and computers, as long as there is an RTF-capable application to read the document. Let's see an RTF document in action.

Open the WordPad application (choose Start ➤ Programs ➤ Accessories ➤ WordPad), and enter a few lines of text, as shown in Figure 7.2. Select a few words or sentences, and format them differently with any of WordPad's formatting commands. Then save the document in RTF format. Choose File ➤ Save As, select Rich Text Format, and then save the file as Document.rtf. If you open this file with a text editor, such as Notepad, you'll see the actual RTF code that produced the document.

> **NOTE**
> You can find the RTF file of the document shown in Figure 7.2 in this chapter's folder on the CD.

FIGURE 7.2

The formatting you've applied to the text using WordPad's commands is stored along with the text in RTF format.

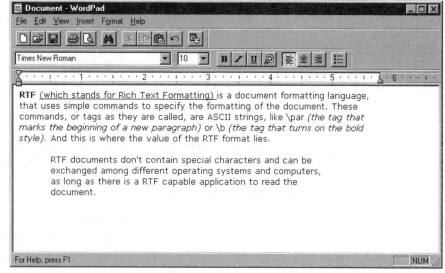

Code 7.1: The RTF Code for the Document in Figure 7.2

```
{\rtf1\ansi\deff0\deftab720{\fonttbl{\f0\fswiss MS Sans Serif;}
   {\f1\froman\fcharset2
Symbol;}{\f2\fswiss\fprq2 Verdana;}{\f3\froman Times New Roman;}}
{\colortbl\red0\green0\blue0;}
\deflang1033\pard\plain\f2\fs20\b RTF\plain\f2\fs20  \plain\f2\
   fs20\ul (which stands for
Rich Text Format) \plain\f2\fs20 is a document formatting language
   that uses simple
commands to specify the formatting of the document. These commands,
   or tags as they are
called, are ASCII strings, like \\par \plain\f2\fs20\i (the tag
   that marks the beginning of
a new paragraph) \plain\f2\fs20 or \\b \plain\f2\fs20\i (the tag
   that turns on the bold style). \plain\f2\fs20 And this is where
   the value of the RTF format lies.
\par
```

```
\par \pard\li720\ri1109\plain\f2\fs20 RTF documents don't contain
    special characters and can be exchanged among
different operating systems and computers, as long as there is an
    RTF-capable application to read the document.
\par \pard\plain\f3\fs20
\par }
```

As you can see, all formatting tags are prefixed with the slash (\) symbol. To display the \ symbol itself, insert an additional slash. Paragraphs are marked with the \par tag, and the entire document is enclosed in a pair of curly brackets. The \li and \ri tags, followed by a numeric value, specify the amount of the left and right indention. If you assign this string to the TextRTF property of a Rich-TextBox control, the result will be the document shown in Figure 7.2, formatted exactly as it appears in WordPad.

RTF is similar to HTML (Hypertext Markup Language), and if you are familiar with HTML, a few comparisons between the two standards will provide helpful hints and insight into the RTF language. Like HTML, RTF was designed to create formatted documents that can be displayed on different systems. The RTF language uses tags to describe the document's format. For example, the tag for italics is \i, and its scope is delimited with a pair of curly brackets. The following RTF segment displays a sentence with a few words in italics:

```
{{\b RTF} (which stands for Rich Text Format) is a {\i document
    formatting language} that uses simple commands to specify the
    formatting of the document.}
```

The following is the equivalent HTML code:

```
<B>RTF</B> (which stands for Rich Text Format) is a <I>document
    formatting language</I> that uses simple commands to specify
    the formatting of the document.
```

The familiar <B> and <I> tags of HTML are equivalent to the \b and \i tags of RTF. RTF, however, is much more complicated than HTML. It's not nearly as easy to understand an RTF document as it is to understand an HTML document because RTF was meant to be used internally by applications. As you can see in the RTF segment presented earlier, RTF contains information about the font being used, its size, and so on. Just as you need a browser to view HTML documents, you need an RTF-capable application to view RTF documents. WordPad, for instance, supports RTF and can both save a document in RTF format and read RTF files.

You're not expected to supply your own RTF code to produce a document. You simply select the segment of the document you want to format and apply the corresponding formatting command from within your word processor. Fortunately, the RichTextBox control isn't any different. It doesn't require that you, the developer, or the users of your application understand RTF code. The RichTextBox control does all the work for you, hiding the low-level details.

VB5 at Work: The RTFDemo Application

The RTFDemo application, shown in Figure 7.3, demonstrates the principles of programming the RichTextBox control. The large box in the upper section of the Form is a RichTextBox control, where you can type text as you would with a regular TextBox.

FIGURE 7.3

The RTFDemo application demonstrates how the RichTextBox control handles RTF code.

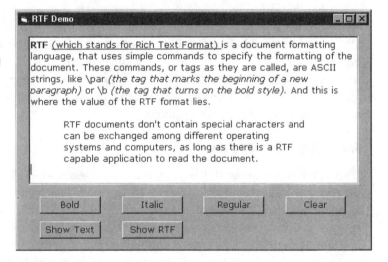

You use the buttons on the first row to set styles for the selected text. The Bold button turns on the bold attribute for the selected text, the Italic button turns on the italic attribute, and the Regular button restores the regular style of the text. All three buttons set (or reset) the value of a property, which is SelBold (for the bold attribute) and SelItalic (for the italic attribute). By setting one of these properties to True, the corresponding attribute is turned on for the selected text. To turn off an attribute, assign the value False to the corresponding property. Here's the code behind the Bold button:

```
RichTextBox1.SelBold = True
```

Here's the code behind the Italic button:

```
RichTextBox1.SelItalic = True
```

The Regular button's code contains the following two lines:

```
RichTextBox1.SelBold = False
RichTextBox1.SelItalic = False
```

The Clear button clears the contents of the control by setting its Text property to an empty string:

```
RichTextBox1.Text = ""
```

The two buttons on the second row demonstrate the nature of the RichTextBox control. Select a few words on the control, turn on their bold and/or italic attribute, and then click on the Show Text button. You'll see on-screen a message box that contains the control's text. No matter how the text is formatted, the control's Text property is the same. This is the text you would copy from the control and paste into a text-editing application that doesn't support formatting commands (such as Notepad, for example).

RTF Code in RTFDemo

If you click on the Show RTF button, you'll see the actual RTF code that produced the formatted document in Figure 7.3. The message box with the RTF code is shown in Figure 7.4. This is all the information the RichTextBox control requires to render the document. As complicated as it may look, it isn't difficult to produce. You simply manipulate a few properties (the recurring theme in Visual Basic programming), and the control does the rest: It generates the RTF code that describes the document and then renders it to produce the document shown in Figure 7.3.

In programming the RichTextBox control, you'll rarely have to worry about inserting actual RTF tags in the code. The control is responsible for generating the RTF code and for rendering the document.

On rather rare occasions, you may have to supply RTF tags. You will see an example of this in Chapter 10, *Recursive Programming*; the DirMap application produces RTF code on the fly. You don't have to know much about RTF tags,

FIGURE 7.4

The RTF code that produced the formatted document shown in Figure 7.3.

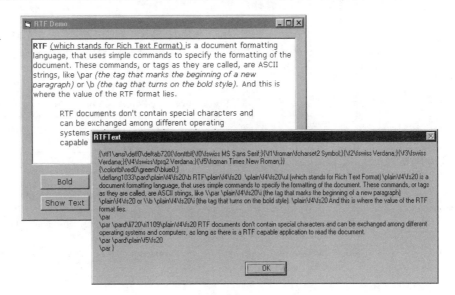

though. Simply format a few words with the desired attributes using the RTFDemo application (or experiment with the Immediate Execution window), copy the tags that produce the desired result, and use them in your application. If you are curious about RTF, experiment with the RTFDemo application.

The RTFPad Application

One of the most interesting applications on the book's CD-ROM is the RTFPad application, which is a word-processing application that is discussed in detail later in this chapter.

RTFPad resembles the Windows WordPad application. This application duplicates much of the functionality of WordPad but is included in this book to show you how the RichTextBox control is used.

The RTFPad application can become your starting point for writing custom word-processing applications (a programmer's text editor with color coded keywords, for example).

Text Manipulation Properties

The Rich TextBox control's properties for manipulating selected text start with the prefix *Sel*. The most commonly used properties related to the selected text are shown in Table 7.1.

TABLE 7.1   The Rich TextBox Control's Properties for Manipulating Selected Text

PROPERTY	WHAT IT MANIPULATES
SelText	The selected text
SelStart	The position of the selected text's first character
SelLength	The length of the selected text
SelBold, SelItalic, SelUnderline, SelStrikethru, SelColor, SelFontName, SelFontSize	Various font attributes of the selected text
SelIndent, SelRightIndent, SelHangingIndent	The indention of the selected text
SelRTF	The RTF code of the selected text

SelText, for example, represents the selected text. To assign the selected text to a variable, use the following statement:

```
SText=RichTextbox1.SelText
```

RichTextbox1 is the name of the control. You can also modify the selected text by assigning a new value to the SelText property. The following statement:

```
RichTextbox1.SelText=UCase(RichTextbox1.SelText)
```

converts the selected text to uppercase. If you assign a string to the SelText property, the selected text in the control is replaced with the string. The following statement:

```
RichTextbox1.SelText="Revised string"
```

replaces the current selection on the RichTextbox1 control with the string "Revised string". If no text is selected, the statement inserts the string at the location of the pointer. It is possible, therefore, to insert text automatically by assigning a string to the SelText property.

To simplify the manipulation and formatting of the text on the control, two additional Properties—SelStart and SelLength—report the position of the first selected character in the text and the length of the selection. You can also set the values of these properties to select a piece of text from within your code. One obvious use of these properties is to select (and highlight) the entire text (or a segment of the text):

```
RichTextBox1.SelStart=0
RichTextBox1.SelLength=Len(RichTextBox1.Text)
```

> **NOTE**
>
> The SelText property is similar to the Text property. The difference is that SelText applies to the current selection instead of to the entire text of the control.

The RichTextBox Control's Methods

The first two methods of the RichTextBox control you should learn about are SaveFile and LoadFile.

- **SaveFile** saves the contents of the control to a disk file.

- **LoadFile** loads the control from a disk file.

The syntax of the SaveFile method is as follows:

```
RichTextBox1.SaveFile(filename, filetype)
```

The *filename* argument is the full path name of the disk file where the contents of the control will be saved, and *filetype* determines how the control's contents will be saved. The filetype argument, which is optional, can have one of two values, as shown in Table 7.2.

TABLE 7.2   The Two File Types the RichTextBox Control Can Recognize

CONSTANT	VALUE	TYPE	DESCRIPTION
rtfRTF	0	(Default) RTF	The RichTextBox control saves its contents as an .RTF file. This is equivalent to saving the value of the TextRTF property to a disk file.

TABLE 7.2   The Two File Types the RichTextBox Control Can Recognize (continued)

CONSTANT	VALUE	TYPE	DESCRIPTION
rtfText.	1	Text	The RichTextBox control saves its contents as a text file. This is equivalent to saving the value of the control's Text property.

Similarly, the LoadFile method loads a text file or an RTF file to the control. Its syntax is identical to the syntax of the SaveFile method:

```
RichTextBox1.LoadFile(filename, filetype)
```

The *filetype* argument is optional. Saving and loading files to and from disk files is as simple as presenting a File Save or File Open common dialog control to the user and then calling one of the SaveFile or LoadFile methods with the filename returned by the common dialog box.

> **NOTE**   You can also use the RichTextBox control to display nicely formatted instructions to the user. To specify the RTF file to be loaded on the control at design time, you can assign its path name to the control's FileName property. In addition, you can capture the control's KeyPress event and suppress any keystroke, to prevent the user from changing the control's contents.

Advanced Editing Features

The RichTextBox control provides all the text-editing features you expect to find in a text-editing application. You can use the arrow keys to move through the text, you can use Ctrl+C to copy text, and you can use Ctrl+V to paste text. To facilitate the design of advanced text-editing features, the RichTextBox control provides the Span and UpTo methods. Both of these interesting methods operate similarly, and their syntax is nearly identical.

- **Span** selects text in a RichTexBox control based on a set of specified characters.

- **UpTo** moves the pointer up to, but not including, the first character that is a member of the specified character set.

Here's a simple example of a situation in which you might resort to these methods to add some advanced editing features to your application. Many text editors provide special keystrokes that either let the user select an entire word or sentence or move the pointer to the end of a word or a sentence. The Span and UpTo methods provide the exact same capabilities.

You use the Span method to specify the characters that signal the end of the selection. Similarly, you use the UpTo method to specify the characters that identify the position to which the pointer will be moved. When you call the Span method, the RichTextBox control starts searching, from the current position, for one of the characters in the specified character set. The first character found causes the search to stop, and the text from the pointer's location to the position of the character found is selected. When you call the UpTo method, the pointer is moved to the position of the first character found instead of selecting a range of text.

The Span method has the following syntax:

```
RichTextBox1.Span characterset, forward, negate
```

UpTo has a similar syntax:

```
RichTextBox1.UpTo characterset, forward, negate
```

The *characterset* argument is a string variable or constant that contains all the characters that mark the end of the selection or the new position of the pointer. The *forward* argument is a boolean variable that determines the direction of the search:

- **True** causes a forward search, from the current position of the pointer to the end of the text.

- **False** causes a backward search.

The *negate* variable is usually False and means that the search should locate one of the characters specified in the *characterset* variable. If you want to search for all characters *except for a few*, you can specify the characters you want to exclude from the search and set the *negate* argument to True. To implement a "select whole word" and "select sentence" feature in your text-editing application, capture the KeyUp event and check for the key pressed.

Selecting Words and Sentences

Suppose you want to select the current word when Ctrl+W is pressed and the current sentence when Ctrl+S is pressed. First, you must check the status of the

Control key, and if it is pressed, check the status of the W and S keys. If the W key was pressed, call the Span method to select everything from the pointer's location to the end of the word. If the S key was pressed, call the Span method to select everything from the pointer's location to the end of the sentence. You must also supply the characters that commonly mark the end of a word or a sentence. See Figure 7.5 for an example of how this works.

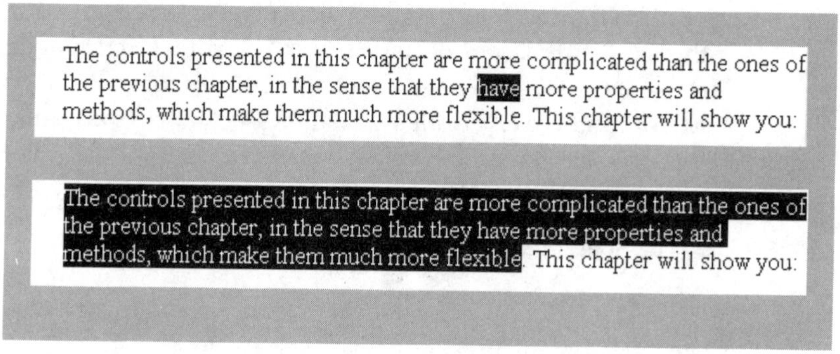

FIGURE 7.5

These two paragraphs show how Ctrl+W selects the word and Ctrl+S selects the sentence.

If the pointer is in the middle of a word, this technique selects only the characters from the pointer's location to the end of the word. Selecting part of a word or a sentence is not a practical operation; we usually want to select an entire word or sentence. And we obviously can't expect the user to position the pointer at the beginning of a word or a sentence. The user rests the pointer on a word and wants to select it with a single keystroke. To do this, you have to call the Span method twice, once to select the characters that belong to the word to the left of the pointer and again to select the characters to the right. In the first call of the function, you must set the *forward* argument to False (to search backward), and in the second call, you must set the *forward* argument to True (to search forward). This is what the first segment of the following code does.

Code 7.2: The Ctrl+W and Ctrl+S Key Combinations

```
Private Sub RichTextBox1_KeyUp(KeyCode As Integer, Shift As
    Integer)

' Select word, or sentence
    If Shift = vbCtrlMask Then
        Select Case KeyCode
            ' If Ctrl+S:
            Case vbKeyS
```

```
            RichTextBox1.Span ".?!", False, True
            SelectionStart = RichTextBox1.SelStart
            ' Select to the end of the sentence.
            RichTextBox1.Span ".?!", True, True
            ' Extend selection to include punctuation.
            SelectionEnd = RichTextBox1.SelStart + RichTextBox1
         ➡.SelLength
            RichTextBox1.SelStart = SelectionStart
            RichTextBox1.SelLength = SelectionEnd - SelectionStart

        ' If Ctrl+W:
        Case vbKeyW
            ' Select to the end of the word.
            RichTextBox1.Span " ,;:.?!", False, True
            SelectionStart = RichTextBox1.SelStart
            ' Select to the end of the word
            RichTextBox1.Span " ,;:.?!", True, True

            SelectionEnd = RichTextBox1.SelStart + RichTextBox1
         ➡.SelLength
            RichTextBox1.SelStart = SelectionStart
            RichTextBox1.SelLength = SelectionEnd - SelectionStart

        End Select
    End If

' Move pointer by word or sentence
    If Shift = (vbCtrlMask Or vbShiftMask) Then
        Select Case KeyCode
        Case vbKeyS
            ' Move pointer to end of sentence.
            RichTextBox1.UpTo ".?!", True, False
        Case vbKeyW
            ' Move pointer to end of word.
            RichTextBox1.UpTo " ,;:.?!", True, False
        End Select
    End If

End Sub
```

This subroutine is used in the RTFPad application to implement this editing feature. The Ctrl+W keystroke selects the current word, and the Ctrl+S keystroke selects the current sentence; and Ctrl+Shift+W moves the pointer to the end of the current word, and Ctrl+Shift+S keystrokes moves the pointer to the end of the current sentence. Notice the similarities between the Span and UpTo methods. You can open the RTFPad application in this chapter's folder on the CD, enter some text in the control, and see how these keystrokes behave.

TIP

The same technique can be used to select keywords in a programmer's editor. In HTML programming, for example, all tags are enclosed in a pair of angle brackets (< and >). You can use the Span method to select an entire tag (everything from the opening < symbol to the closing > symbol). Or you can highlight the arguments of a function, which are enclosed in parentheses. The Span method is a great tool for implementing advanced editing features for programmers' editors.

Searching in a RichTextBox Control

The Find method locates a string in the control's text and is similar to the InStr() function. You can use InStr()with the control's Text property to locate a string in the text, but the Find method is optimized for the RichTextBox control and supports a couple of options not supported by the InStr() function. The syntax of the Find method is as follows:

```
RichTextBox1.Find(string, start, end, options)
```

The *string* argument is the string you want to locate in the RichTextBox control, *start* and *end* are the starting and ending locations of the search (use them to search for a string within a specified range only), and *options* is the sum of one or more of the constants listed in Table 7.3.

TABLE 7.3   The Search Options of the RichTextBox Control's Find Method

CONSTANT	VALUE	DESCRIPTION
rtfWholeWord	2	Determines whether only whole words (if True) or a fragment of a word (if False) will be matched.
rtfMatchCase	4	Determines whether the match will be case sensitive (if True) or not (if False).
rtfNoHighlight	8	Determines whether the matched string will be highlighted in the control.

To combine multiple options, you can add their values, or you can combine them with the OR operator. All the arguments of the Find method are optional except for the string to be matched. If you omit them, they take on their default values; the search will not be case sensitive, the entire text will be searched, and the matching text is highlighted. If you specify only the *start* argument, the search is performed on the text from the start location to the end of the text. Likewise, if you specify only the *end* argument, the search is performed on the text from the first character up to the end of the text.

The RTFPad application's Find command demonstrates how to use the Find method and its arguments to build a Find & Replace dialog box that performs all the types of text-searching operations you might need in a text-editing application. The code is identical to the code of the Search & Replace dialog box of the Notepad application presented in Chapter 5, *Basic ActiveX Controls,* and it's explained in the section "Search and Replace Operations."

Text Formatting Properties

The RichTextBox control provides a number of properties for setting the appearance of the text in the control. Through the formatting properties, you can format the text in any of the ways possible through a word-processing application such as WordPad. This section discusses all the text formatting properties of the RichTextBox control and how they are used.

Font Properties and Attributes

The following properties apply user-specified font, size, and attributes to the selected text. They can also be used to read the settings from within your code.

SelFontName, SelFontSize Properties

To change the font and size of the selected text, use these properties. The following statements render the selected text in Verdana font, 24 points:

```
RichTextBox1.SelFontName = "Verdana"
RichTextBox1.SelFontSize = 24
```

You must supply the name of a font that exists on the client computer; if you do not, a similar font will be substituted. Use the Font common dialog box (discussed in Chapter 5, *Basic ActiveX Controls*) to let the user select one of the available fonts as well as the desired attributes.

SelBold, SelItalic, SelUnderline Properties   You can read the value of these properties to check the formatting of the selected text from within your code, or you can set them to change the formatting accordingly. The following statements:

```
RichTextbox1.SelBold=True
RichTextbox1.SelItalic=True
```

turn on the bold and italic attributes of the selected text. If no text is selected, the attributes are set for the character at the current location of the pointer. By setting the character-formatting properties accordingly (usually with the click of a button or a menu command), the user is in effect changing the style of the selected text.

The character-formatting properties are frequently used as toggles. Every time the user clicks on a Bold button (or selects Bold from the application's menu), the following code is executed:

```
RichTextbox1.SelBold=NOT RichTextbox1.SelBold
```

If the selected text is in bold, it's turned back to normal; if it's normal, it's turned to bold. As you have noticed, there is no property to reset the text style to normal. To do so, you must manually set all three properties to False:

```
RichTextbox1.SelBold=False
RichTextbox1.SelItalic=False
RichTextbox1.SelUnderline=False
```

SelCharOffset Property   This property determines whether the selected characters appear on, above, or below the text baseline. Normally, text appears on the baseline. You can raise characters above their baseline to create superscripts (you must also reduce the text's font size by a point or two) or place it below the baseline to create subscripts. To lower the selected text, assign a negative number to the SelCharOffset property. This value must be expressed in twips (a twip is 1/20 of a point, and there are 72 points in an inch).

> **NOTE**   Twips is a peculiar unit of length, used extensively in the Windows environment. A twip is 1/20 of a point, or 1/1440 of an inch. To raise selected characters 1 point above the baseline, use the statement `RichText-Box1.SelCharOffset = 20`. To lower the selected text by 1/20 of an inch, use the statement `RichTextBox1.SelOffset = -72`.

Text Alignment Properties

The next group of properties control (or return) the alignment and indention of the selected text in the RichTextBox control.

SelAlignment Property   Use this property to read or change the alignment of one or more paragraphs. It can have one of the values shown in Table 7.4.

TABLE 7.4   The Alignment Values of the RichTextBox Control

VALUE	DESCRIPTION
0	Left-aligns selected paragraph(s); the default
1	Right-aligns selected paragraph(s)
2	Centers selected paragraph(s)

NOTE

The user doesn't have to actually select the entire paragraph to be aligned. Placing the pointer anywhere in the paragraph or selecting a few characters in the paragraph will do, because there is no way to align only part of a paragraph.

SelIndent, SelRightIndent, SelHangingIndent Properties   You set the indention of the selected text with these properties.

When designing applications with the RichTextBox control, the most meaningful values for the container's ScaleMode property are points, inches, and millimeters. Setting the values of the indention properties is rather trivial, but designing a user interface that will enable the user to intuitively and conveniently set these properties isn't.

- **SelIndent** sets (or returns) the amount of the text's indention from the left edge of the control.

- **SelRightIndent** sets the indention of the right side of the text from the right margin.

- **SelHangingIndent** specifies the distance between the left edge of the first line of the selected paragraph(s) (including any indention specified by the SelIndent property) and the left edge of subsequent lines in the paragraph(s).

The hanging indention can also be negative, in which case the first line of text extends to the left farther than the rest of the paragraph. Figure 7.6 shows three possible combinations of the left and hanging indention, all made possible with the two slider controls above the text.

SelBullet Property   You use this property to create a list of bulleted items. If you set the SelBullet property to True, the selected paragraphs are formatted with a bullet style, similar to the <UL> tag in HTML. To create a list of bulleted items, select them with the pointer, and then assign the value True to the SelBullet property. To change a list of bulleted items back to normal text, select the items, and then assign the value False to the SelBullet property.

The paragraphs formatted with the SelBullet property set to True are also indented from the left by a small amount. To change the value of the indention, use the BulletIndent property, whose syntax is as follows:

```
RichTextBox1.BulletIndent = value
```

You can also read the BulletIndent property from within your code to find out the bulleted items' indention. Or you can use this property, along with the SelBullet property, to simulate nested bulleted items. If the current selection's SelBullet property is True and the user wants to apply the bullet format, you can increase the indention of the current selection.

VB5 at Work: The RTFPad Application

Creating a functional, even fancy, word processor based on the Rich Textbox control is quite simple. The challenge is to provide a convenient interface that lets the user select text, apply attributes and styles to it, and then set the control's properties accordingly. This chapter's application does just that. It's called RTFPad, and you can find it in this chapter's folder on the CD.

The RTFPad application (see Figure 7.7) is based on the TextPad application, developed in Chapter 5, *Basic ActiveX Controls*. It contains the same text-editing commands and some additional text-formatting commands that can only be implemented with the RichTextBox control, and they allow you to mix font styles in the text. This section examines the code and discusses a few topics unique to this application's implementation with the RichTextBox control.

FIGURE 7.6

Various combinations of the SelIndent and SelHangingIndent properties produce interesting paragraph formatting.

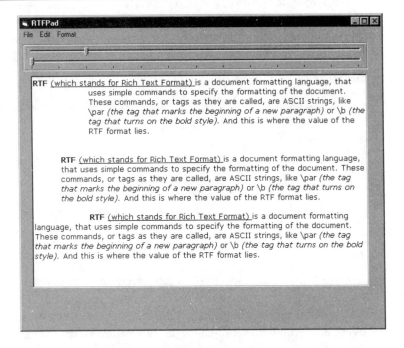

FIGURE 7.7

The RTFPad application is a word processor based on the RichTextBox control.

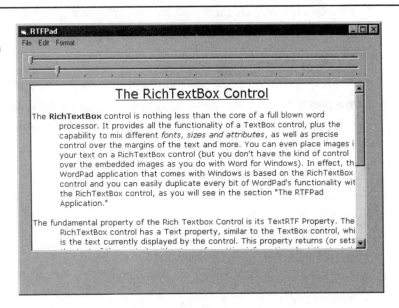

The two slider controls above the RichTextBox control manipulate the indention and hanging indention of the text. We have already explored this arrangement in the Slider control discussion in Chapter 5, but let's review the operation of the two Slider controls. Every time they are scrolled, the following code is executed:

```
Private Sub Slider1_Scroll()

    RichTextBox1.SelIndent = RichTextBox1.RightMargin * (Slider1
➥.Value / Slider1.Max)
    Slider2_Scroll

End Sub

Private Sub Slider2_Scroll()

    RichTextBox1.SelHangingIndent = RichTextBox1.RightMargin *
➥((Slider2.Value - Slider1.Value) / Slider2.Max)

End Sub
```

The Slider1 control sets the text left indention, as a percentage of the control's width (same percentage as the control's value compared with the maximum value). After setting the text's left indention, the code of the other control's Scroll event is executed, to set the hanging indention. When the user changes the hanging indention, the Slider1_Scroll subroutine isn't called from within the Slider2 control's code because there's no reason to adjust the overall indention.

Enter some text in the control, select one or more paragraphs, and check out the operation of the two sliders. Unfortunately, there's no Slider control that has indicators for setting both left and right values and thus control both margins.

The File Menu   The File menu contains the usual Open and Save commands, which are implemented with the LoadFile and SaveFile methods. Here is the implementation of the Open command in the File menu.

Code 7.3: The Open Command

```
Private Sub FileOpen_Click()
Dim txt As String
Dim FNum As Integer

On Error GoTo FileError:
    CommonDialog1.CancelError = True
    CommonDialog1.Flags = cdlOFNFileMustExist
    CommonDialog1.DefaultExt = "RTF"
```

```
        CommonDialog1.Filter = "RTF Files|*.RTF|Text Files|*.TXT|All
    ➥Files|*.*"
        CommonDialog1.ShowOpen

        RichTextBox1.LoadFile CommonDialog1.filename, rtfRTF
        OpenFile = CommonDialog1.filename

        Exit Sub

FileError:
        If Err.Number = cdlCancel Then Exit Sub
        MsgBox "Unknown error while opening file " & CommonDialog1
    ➥.filename
        OpenFile = ""
End Sub
```

The *OpenFile* variable is global and holds the name of the currently open file. It is set every time a new file is successfully opened and used by the Save command to automatically save the open file, without prompting the user for a filename.

The Edit Menu   The Edit menu's commands are quite simple. Instead of the SelText property, they use the control's SelRTF command to move information to the Clipboard and back so that the copied text carries its formatting information with it. If you aren't familiar with the Clipboard's method, all you need to know to follow this example are the SetText method, which copies a string to the Clipboard, and the GetText method, which copies the Clipboard's contents to a string variable.

The Find command in the Edit menu opens the dialog box shown in Figure 7.8, with which the user can perform various search (whole word or case-sensitive match or both) and replacement operations. The code behind the command buttons on this form is quite similar to the code for the Find & Replace dialog box of the TextPad application, with one basic difference. It uses the control's Find method and the options of this method that aren't available with the InStr() function.

FIGURE 7.8

The Search & Replace dialog box of the RTFPad application

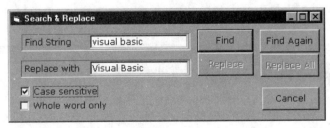

Code 7.4: The Find Button

```
Private Sub FindButton_Click()
Dim FindFlags As Integer

    Position = 0
    FindFlags = Check1.Value * 4 + Check2.Value * 2
    Position = Form1.RichTextBox1.Find(Text1.Text, Position + 1, ,
    ➥ FindFlags)
    If Position >= 0 Then
        ReplaceButton.Enabled = True
        ReplaceAllButton.Enabled = True
        Form1.SetFocus
    Else
        MsgBox "String not found"
        ReplaceButton.Enabled = False
        ReplaceAllButton.Enabled = False
    End If

End Sub
```

The *FindFlags* variable takes its value from the CheckBox controls that determine the type of match. When a checkbox is checked, its value is 1. The code multiplies the control's value by 4 or 2 to set the *rtfWholeWord* and *rtfMatchCase* options. This value is passed as the last argument of the Find method.

The search starts with the first character of the text and moves forward. To implement a "backward search" option, add another CheckBox on the Find Form and adjust the start and end arguments of the Find method accordingly.

The Format Menu   The Format menu lets the user set the font, size, and attributes of the selected text. The first command of the Format menu is Font, and it opens the Font common dialog box, in which the user can select the font, size, and attributes of the currently selected text. Although the font doesn't change frequently in a document, the attributes do, and the application shouldn't force the user to open the Font common dialog box just to turn a word into bold or italics. That's why the font attributes are also implemented as commands on the Format menu.

NOTE   If you'd like certain variables set in the Font common dialog box when the user opens it, you need to set a number of flags. Chapter 5, *Basic ActiveX Controls*, lists all the flags related to the Font common dialog box and shows you how to set these flags in your code.

The Bold, Italic, Underline, and Regular commands on the Format menu turn on and off the corresponding attribute. Not only that, but a checkmark next to one of these commands indicates the attribute of the current selection. If the user has selected a word that appears in bold in the text or if the pointer rests on a word in bold, the Bold command is checked (a little checkmark appears next to its name).

If part of the selection is bold and part isn't, the SelBold property returns neither True nor False. It returns Null to indicate that the selection isn't uniform. You must always check the values of the properties SelItalic, SelBold, and SelUnderline for Null values. You will see an example of how these properties are used to read the attributes of the selected text in the section "The SelChange Event," later in this chapter.

The first function of the Bold, Italic, and Underline commands is quite simple: to turn on the corresponding attribute of the selected text. If the selected text isn't bold, selecting the Bold command turns on the bold attribute for this text. If the selected text is bold already, this command turns off the bold attribute. The second function of these buttons, namely the indication of the attributes of the selected text, is a bit more complicated.

The RTFPad application must track the user's actions through the SelChange event, which is triggered every time the current selection changes. From within this event, we must examine the values of the SelBold, SelItalic, and SelUnderline properties and set (or reset) the checkmark in front of the corresponding menu command. The three font attribute commands are implemented with code from within two events: the menu command's Click event, and the RichTextBox control's SelChange event.

Code 7.5: The Bold Command

```
Private Sub FormatBold_Click()

    FormatBold.Checked = Not FormatBold.Checked
    RichTextBox1.SelBold = FormatBold.Checked

End Sub
```

First, the program switches the current state of the menu command (if it's checked, it unchecks it; if it's unchecked, it checks it). It then turns on or off the bold attribute of the selected text, according to the recently updated state of the Bold command.

The SelChange Event   To be able to set the status of the various commands of the Format menu, you must be able to detect when the user changes the current selection. This action is reported to your application by the control's SelChange event. In the RichTextBox control's SelChange event, the program does the opposite. It examines the attribute of the selected text and sets the command state accordingly.

Code 7.6: The SelChange Event

```
Private Sub RichTextBox1_SelChange()

    If Not IsNull(RichTextBox1.SelBold) Then FormatBold.Checked =
    ➥RichTextBox1.SelBold
    If Not IsNull(RichTextBox1.SelItalic) Then FormatItalic.Checked
    ➥= RichTextBox1.SelItalic
    If Not IsNull(RichTextBox1.SelUnderline) Then FormatUnderline
    ➥.Checked = RichTextBox1.SelUnderline

End Sub
```

Notice the use of the IsNull() function. If part of the selected text has an attribute turned on and part of it has the same attribute turned off, the SelBold property is neither True nor False. Instead, it's undefined, and the program must check for this condition. If the SelBold property, for example, is not undefined, the Bold command is checked or unchecked, depending on the value of the property.

If the SelBold attribute is not defined, the menu command doesn't change. (You could replace the Bold title with another string, such as "mixed," indicating that the corresponding attribute is not uniform for the current selection.)

These attribute menu commands are best implemented with tri-state buttons, such as the SSRibbon control. When the selected text is bold, for example, and the bold button is pressed, the text is reset to regular, and if the current selection's bold attribute is undefined, the corresponding button should assume a third (grayed) appearance.

When the user clicks on the Bold button, RTFPad should turn the bold attribute on and off. This feature is relatively easy to implement, except perhaps for designing the pictures for the three states (on, off, mixed) of the command buttons. Visual programming requires some artistic talent; your programming abilities won't help you much here.

You've learned basically everything there is to know about the RichTextBox control. The RichTextBox control will provide the basic functionality of a word-processing application. Adding more features to your editor is as simple as setting the values of its various properties.

The MSFlexGrid Control

One of the most impressive new controls added to Visual Basic 5 is the MSFlex-Grid control. As you can guess by its name, the MSFlexGrid control is a descendant of the old Grid control, which is still available for compatibility reasons, but if you're going to develop any new applications that require a spreadsheet-like control, you should consider the new MSFlexGrid control.

NOTE
> The MSFlexGrid control provides all the functionality for building spreadsheet applications, just as the RichTextBox control provides all the functionality for building word-processing applications. Once you master its basic properties, writing spreadsheetlike applications for displaying data is a question of setting its properties.

The MSFlexGrid control is an extremely useful tool for displaying information in a tabular form. In effect, it's a simple spreadsheet that you can place on your Forms to present nicely organized data to the user. Figure 7.9 shows a Grid control displaying financial data. At first glance, it looks a lot like a spreadsheet. It's made up of cells arranged in rows and columns, which may contain text (including numbers) or graphics, and each row and column can have its own width and height. The first row and column are fixed and contain titles.

The scroll bars give the user easy access to any part of the control. Although all the cells can scroll, the fixed cells always remain visible.

TIP
> The grid shown in Figure 7.9 was created with the Grid1 application, which you can find in this chapter's folder on the CD. The Grid1 application demonstrates the basic properties of the MSFlexGrid control and is discussed below.

FIGURE 7.9

The MSFlexGrid control looks very much like an Excel spreadsheet. The title was placed on the Form, but everything else, including the scroll bars, belongs to the control.

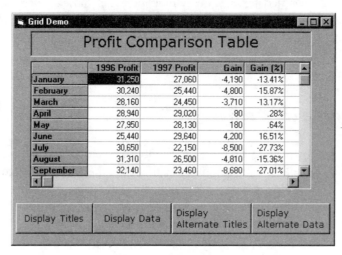

Despite external similarities, the MSFlexGrid control is not a spreadsheet, in the same sense that the Textbox control is not a word processor. Although it could become the basis for building a spreadsheet, this is not the purpose for which the MSFlexGrid control was designed. It was meant for displaying information in tabular form and not for data entry.

Most of the properties of this control pertain to the placement of the data and their appearance; there are no properties or events for the immediate editing of the cells' contents. However, it's not too difficult to take control of the KeyPress event to capture keystrokes and add data-entry capabilities to the control, as you will see in the section "The FlexGrid Application," later in this chapter.

NOTE   The MSFlexGrid control doesn't directly support data-entry operations, but by capturing the keyboard events, you can easily add data-entry capabilities to the control.

Basic Properties

Let's review the basic properties of the control by examining its operation. The grid's cells can contain text, numbers, or images. You can assign a value to a cell in several ways, and all methods require that you first select the cell by means of its address on the grid and assign the desired value to its Text property.

The address of a cell is given by its Row and Col properties, whose values start at zero. Row zero is the fixed title row, and column zero is the fixed title column. To address the first non-fixed cell in the grid of Figure 7.9, you use the following statements:

```
Grid.Row = 1
Grid.Col = 1
```

After you specify the cell's address, you can examine its contents with a statement such as:

```
CellValue = Grid.Text
```

or set its contents with a statement such as:

```
Grid.Text = "January"
```

This method of reading or setting cell values requires too many statements for a such a simple task and is probably available for compatibility with the old Grid control. The simplest way to address a cell on the grid is by means of the TextMatrix property, which has the following syntax :

```
Grid.TextMatrix(row, col)
```

The *row* and *col* arguments are the cell's coordinates in the grid. To extract the value of the first editable cell, use a statement such as:

```
CellValue = Grid.TextMatrix(1, 1)
```

The names of the months and the corresponding profit figures of the grid shown in Figure 7.9, earlier in this chapter, were assigned with the following loop (part of the Grid1 application):

```
Private Sub Command1_Click()
Dim irow As Integer

    For irow = 1 To 12
        Grid.TextMatrix(irow, 1) = MonthNames(irow)
        Grid.TextMatrix(irow, 2) = Format$(Profit97(irow), "#,###")
        Grid.TextMatrix(irow, 3) = Format$(Profit96(irow), "#,###")
        Grid.TextMatrix(irow, 4) = Format$(Grid.TextMatrix(irow, 3)
        ➥- Grid.TextMatrix(irow, 2), "#,###")
```

```
        Grid.TextMatrix(irow, 5) = Format$(100 * (Grid.TextMatrix
        ➡(irow, 3) - Grid.TextMatrix(irow, 2)) / Grid.TextMatrix
        ➡(irow, 2), "#.##") & "%"
    Next

End Sub
```

The array *MonthNames()* holds the names of the months. Notice that the contents of the last two columns (Gain and Gain [%]) are calculated.

A third way to access the cells of the grid is by means of the TextArray property, which is similar to the TextMatrix property but uses a single index to address a cell. It has the following syntax:

```
Grid.TextArray(cellindex)
```

To calculate the *cellindex* argument, which determines the location of the desired cell, multiply the desired row by the Cols property and add the desired column. The following statement calculates the value of the *cellindex* argument, given its row (*row*) and column (*col*) number:

```
cellindex = row * Cols + col
```

The TextArray property is less convenient than the TextMatrix property because you have to convert the actual address of the desired cell to a single number. Use the TextArray property to assign values to the grid's cells if the values are already stored in a one-dimensional array.

Displaying Row and Column Titles

The cells of the first row and column have a gray background because they were meant to be used as titles for the corresponding columns and rows. The unique feature of these cells is that they don't scroll along with the rest of the cells, so the titles always remain visible. You can change the number of the title rows and columns with the FixedCols and FixedRows properties.

FixedCols, FixedRows Properties   The most common value for these two properties is one, which translates into one fixed row and one fixed column. Another characteristic of the title row and column is that clicking on one of their cells selects the entire row or column (see Figure 7.10). Clicking on the very first fixed cell of the grid, in its upper left corner, selects the entire grid. This behavior can be changed by setting the AllowBigSelection property to False. Its default value is True, and it allows the user to select entire rows and columns, even the entire spreadsheet.

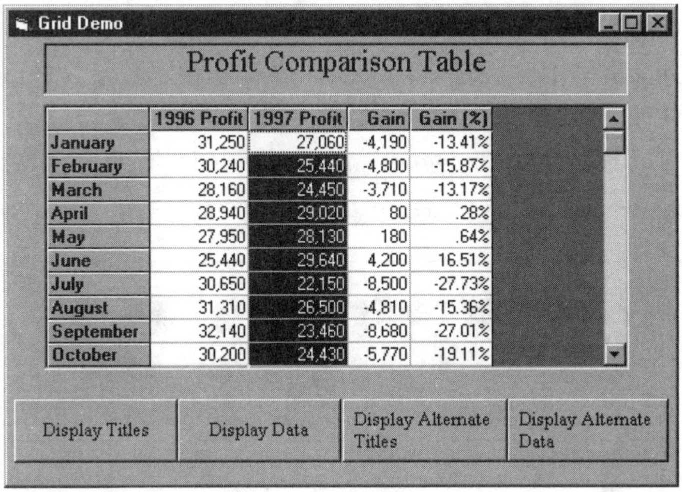

FIGURE 7.10

Clicking on a column's header automatically selects the entire column.

The fixed row and column contain titles that can be assigned with any of the methods mentioned earlier (other than their different background color and the fact that they don't scroll, the fixed cells aren't any different from the other cells of the grid) or with the help of the FormatString property.

FormatString Property   This property can be assigned a string variable that sets up the control's column width, alignments, and fixed row and column text. The FormatString property is made up of segments separated by pipe characters (|). The text between two pipes defines a new column or row, and it can contain text and the alignment characters shown in Table 7.5.

TABLE 7.5   The Alignment Characters

THE CHARACTER	WHAT IT DOES
<	Left-aligns the column
^	Centers the column
>	Right-aligns the column

The text becomes the column's header, and its width defines the width of the column. You can also use the FormatString property to set up the alignment of rows. The semicolon (;) denotes that the following text applies to the next row. The text becomes the row's header, and the longest string defines the width of the fixed column. Successive row titles are separated with the pipe symbol as column titles.

Figures 7.11, 7.12, and 7.13 demonstrate the use of the FormatString property to set up a grid with a fixed row, column, or both.

The header row of Figure 7.11 was created with the following format string:

```
s$ = "<Country  |^Athletes   |^ Gold  |^Silver |^Bronze"
```

FIGURE 7.11

The titles on the fixed row of this grid were placed there with a format string.

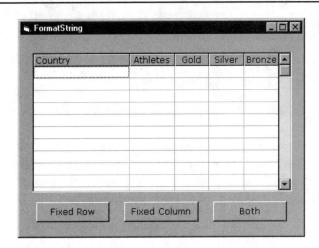

Successive column headers were separated by the pipe character, and some spaces in front and behind the titles were inserted to leave some space between the headers and the cell dividers.

The header column of Figure 7.12 was created with a similar format string:

```
s$ = ";  | Country |Athletes|Gold|Silver|Bronze"
```

This string starts with the semicolon, which indicates that the following entries are row headers. After the semicolon, the pipe symbol is used to delimit each row's header.

In the grids in Figures 7.11 and 7.12, the user is expected to enter the country names, along with the other information. The grid in Figure 7.10 displays the headers of the previous examples, as well as the country names; the user need

FIGURE 7.12

The titles on the fixed
column of this grid were
placed there with a
format string.

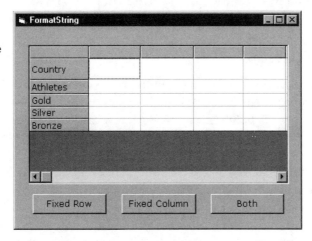

supply only the numeric data. This grid's headers were set up with a format
string that is a combination of the two previous format strings:

```
s$ = "<Country  |^Athletes   |^ Gold  |^Silver |^Bronze ;| Argentina
    | Belgium | Denmark | Equador | France | Germany"
```

FIGURE 7.13

The titles on the fixed
column of this grid were
placed there with a
format string.

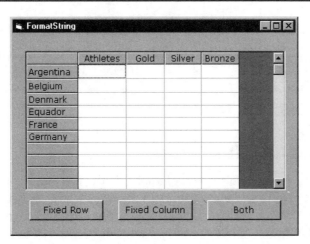

Notice again that there's only one semicolon in the string, denoting that the
following entries are row headers. The country names are separated by the pipe
symbol, and the longest country name determines the width of the fixed column.

Each column in the grid may have its own width, which is controlled by the ColWidth property. To set the width of the first column (the title column), use the following statement:

```
Grid1.ColWidth(0)=500
```

The width's value is expressed in twips, and as mentioned earlier, there are 20 twips in a point. The previous statement sets the width of the first column to approximately 25 points. Likewise, each row can have a different height, which is controlled by the RowHeight property, whose syntax is quite similar.

AllowUserResizing   The user can change the width of columns and height of rows at run time by dragging the column and row separators with the mouse. If you place the mouse over a dividing line between two columns (or rows) and in the title section of the grid, it assumes the shape of a double arrow, indicating that it can be dragged to resize a row or column of cells. To disable row and/or column resizing, set the AllowUserResizing property to one of the values shown in Table 7.6.

TABLE 7.6   The Values of the AllowUserResizing Property

CONSTANT	VALUE	DESCRIPTION
FlexResizeNone	0	The user can't resize the cells (the default).
FlexResizeColumns	1	The user can resize columns only.
FlexResizeRows	2	The user can resize rows only.
FlexResizeBoth	3	The user can resize columns and rows.

Working with Multiple Cells

One of the most useful aspects of a spreadsheet is the ability to select multiple cells and perform certain operations on them, such as copying, pasting, and formatting. Unfortunately, you can't insert formulas for calculated fields in an MSFlexGrid control, but you can perform simpler, yet useful, operations such as sorting the grid's rows, as you will see later in the section "Sorting the Grid."

The user can select a range of cells with a click-and-drag operation over multiple cells. By clicking on a fixed column (or row) cell, the user can select the entire column (or row). The selected range is always a rectangle, and the coordinates of the first selected cell (where the mouse button was pressed) are given by the properties Row and Col. The coordinates of the last selected cell (where the mouse button was released) are given by the properties RowSel and ColSel.

These two pairs of coordinates specify a rectangle that encloses all the selected cells. Moreover, the selected range is highlighted. If you set these properties, you can select a range from within your code. The following statements select the month names on the grid in Figure 7.9, earlier in this chapter:

```
Grid.Row = 1
Grid.Col = 0
Grid.RowSel = 12
Grid. ColSel = 0
```

All the selected cells appear in reverse background color, except for the first select cell. This one is distinguished from the rest because it also happens to be the active cell, which is the cell that was clicked on when the click-and-drag operation started. You can also restrict the way cells are selected with the SelectionMode property, whose settings are shown in Table 7.7.

TABLE 7.7 The Values of the SelectionMode Property

VALUE	CONSTANT	DESCRIPTION
0	flexSelectionFree	Allows selections to be made normally, spreadsheet-style.
1	flexSelectionByRow	Forces selections to be made by rows.
2	flexSelectionByColumn	Forces selections to be made by columns.

The simplest operation you can perform on a range of cells is the assignment of an initial value to them. Normally, the value assigned to the control's Text property applies to the active cell. The property FillStyle, however, determines whether a value is assigned to the active cell or to the entire range of selected cells. The FillStyle property is a property of the control, and its values are shown in Table 7.8.

TABLE 7.8 The Values of the FillStyle Property

VALUE	CONSTANT NAME	DESCRIPTION
0	flexFillSingle	Changes affect only the active cell. (default value)
1	flexFillRepeat	Changes affect all selected cells.

The same property can be used to specify whether other cell properties, such as cell alignment or background color, for instance, will be applied to the active cell or to an entire range of cells.

Clip Property   This property holds the contents of the selected cells on the grid. Values of adjacent cells on the same row are delimited by a tab character (Chr$(9)), and successive rows are delimited by a new line character (Chr$(13)). Chr$(9) is the tab character, and Chr$(13) is the carriage return character. The most common operation of the Clip property is to transfer data to and from the Clipboard. The following statement:

```
Clipboard.SetText Grid.Clip
```

transfers the values of the selected cells to the Clipboard, where they are stored as text. To paste these cell values to another area of the control, first select the destination of the paste operation and then use the following statement:

```
Grid.Clip = Clipboard.GetText
```

Observe that the contents of the Clipboard, are pasted only on the selected cells, that is, on the cells that are part of the current Clip property. If the number of selected cells is larger than the number of cells in the Clip property, some cells won't be affected. On the other hand, if there are fewer selected cells than the Clipboard's entries, some of the Clipboard's data will not end up in the Grid.

> **NOTE**   The Clip property is all you need to implement the Copy, Cut, and Paste operations in an application that uses the MSFlexGrid control. However, you must make sure that enough cells have been selected to accommodate all the data on the Clipboard before you actually paste them.

The MSFlexGrid control doesn't provide any method for storing its contents to a disk file, similar to the SaveFile and LoadFile methods of the RichTextBox control. The simplest way to store the contents of an entire grid to a disk file is to use the Clip property. First, select the entire grid, and then write the Clip property (which by now holds the contents of the entire grid) to a file. The following statements store the current grid to the Grid.GRD file (the extension is arbitrary, and no file type known to me uses it):

```
Open "Grid.GRD" For Output As #1
Write #1, Grid.Clip
Close #1
```

This method is used in the FlexGrid application to implement the Save and Save As commands.

You can also prepare data to append to a spreadsheet from within another application. First, create a long string with data, using the Tab character to delimit successive values on the same row and the carriage return character to delimit successive columns. Then assign this string to the MSFlexGrid control's Clip property.

Cell Appearance and Alignment

Another group of properties relate to the font, style, and color of the cells. With the MSFlexGrid control, you have the flexibility to control the appearance of individual cells. Here are your choices:

- **CellFontBold** and **CellFontItalic** set the style of the text in the selected cells. To change the style of multiple cells, you first select the cells and then set the FillStyle property to flexFillRepeat.

- **CellFontName** sets the font to be used in rendering the text in the selected cells.

- **CellFontSize** sets the font's size in points.

- **CellFontWidth** sets the width of the selected cell(s) in points.

When you change the font's width, its height remains the same, as specified with the CellFontSize property (or whatever font size you specified at design time in the control's Properties window).

CellFontSize, CellFontWidth Properties   To find out how these properties affect the appearance of the text on an MSFlexGrid control, experiment with the FontSize application in the Grid folder on the CD (shown in Figure 7.14). The two ComboBoxes at the bottom of the form let you set the size of both properties in points.

FIGURE 7.14

The FontSize application demonstrates the difference between the CellFontSize and CellFontWidth properties.

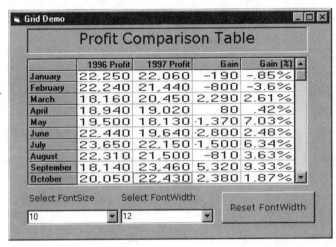

As you changze the CellFontSize property, both the width and height of the characters change. Change the CellFontWidth property, and only the width of the characters changes. In general, you do not need to set the width of the text without taking into consideration its height. If you have a large amount of data to display, you can set both the CellFontSize and CellFontWidth properties to squeeze more data in the available area, by making the numbers narrow yet still easy to read.

CellForeColor, CellBackColor Properties   To change the color of the text or the background color in the selected cell(s), use these properties. The value of these properties can be an RGB color value or a QBColor value. A few more color-related properties include:

- **BackColorBgk**   Returns or sets the background color of various elements of the control (the area outside the grid)

- **ForeColorFixed**   Returns or sets the foreground color of the fixed rows and columns

- **BackColorFixed**   Returns or sets the background color of the fixed rows and columns

- **ForeColorSel**   Returns or sets the foreground color of the selected cells

- **BackColorSel**   Returns or sets the background color of the selected cells

You will see how these properties are used in the FlexGrid application, discussed later in the chapter. The FlexGrid application allows the user to select a range of cells and set their foreground and background colors, independently of the rest of the grid.

CellAlignment Property   Each cell in the grid can also be aligned differently using this property. You can use it to set the alignment of the active cell or the range of selected cells (as long as the FillStyle property was set to True, of course), and it can take on one of the values listed in Table 7.9.

TABLE 7.9   The Values of the CellAlignment Property

VALUE	DESCRIPTION
0	Left Top
1	Left Center
2	Left Bottom
3	Center Top
4	Center Center
5	Center Bottom
6	Right Top
7	Right Center
8	Right Bottom
9	General (Left Center for strings, Right Center for numbers)

As you can see, the cell's contents can be aligned both vertically and horizontally. To align a range of cells from within your code, follow these steps:

1. Select the range by setting the Row, Col, SelRow, and SelCol properties to the appropriate values.

2. Be sure that the FillStyle property is True.

3. Assign one of the values in Table 7.9 to the CellAlignment property.

ColAlignment Property   If you want to align an entire column, you can use this property instead. It is an array with one element per column. Its syntax is as follows:

```
MSFlexGrid1.ColAlignment(column) = value
```

The *column* argument is the number of the column whose alignment you want to set. The ColAlignment property may take on any of the values of the Table 7.8, earlier in this chapter. The following statement:

```
MSFlexGrid1.ColAlignment(0)= 4
```

centers the text in the first (most likely fixed) column, regardless of the current selection. Notice that there is no RowAlignment property to set the alignment of the cells of an entire row.

Sorting the Grid

Nearly every application you will develop with the MSFlexGrid control will require a sorting feature, especially if the user is allowed to enter data. The control's Sort property does just that. Sort is not a method, as you might expect, but a property. Each time the Sort property is set to a value, the selected rows of the grid are sorted according to selected criteria. If no rows are selected, the entire grid is sorted.

Sort Property   Before setting this property, you must select one or more columns, which are the *keys* used in the sorting. The keys are the values according to which the rows of the grid are sorted, and they must be the elements of one or more rows. If you select a single column, the rows are sorted according to the entries of this column. If you select multiple columns, their entries are combined to create the sort key. If you set the Col property to 1 and the ColSel property to 3, the entries in the first column are the primary sorting keys. If two or more rows have the same primary key, they are sorted according to their values in the second column, and if these keys are identical, the same cells in the third column are used as keys.

TIP

The columns used in the sorting process must be adjacent. In other words, the columns used as sorting keys can be selected only with the Col and ColSel properties. Moreover, the order of the selection doesn't matter, because the key columns are used from left to right. Whether you specify Col = 1 and ColSel = 3 or specify Col = 3 and ColSel = 1, the rows are sorted according to the content of column 1, then column 2, and then column 3.

The syntax of the Sort property is as follows:

```
MSFlexGrid1.Sort = value
```

The variable *value* can be one of the values shown in Table 7.10.

T A B L E 7. 10 The Values of the Sort Property

VALUE	DESCRIPTION
0	None
1	Generic Ascending (the control guesses whether text is string or number)
2	Generic Descending
3	Numeric Ascending (strings are converted to numbers)
4	Numeric Descending
5	String Ascending, case-insensitive
6	String Descending, case-insensitive
7	String Ascending, case-sensitive
8	String Descending, case-sensitive
9	Custom; uses the Compare event to compare rows

If the Sort property is set to 4, for example, the rows are sorted according the numeric value of the selected column(s). The Sort menu of the FlexGrid application (discussed later in this chapter) contains commands for all types of sorting operations, as shown in Figure 7.15. When an option from this menu is selected, the code assigns the appropriate value to the Sort property, and the (selected) rows are sorted instantly.

FIGURE 7.15

This menu structure contains commands for sorting a grid's rows in all available ways.

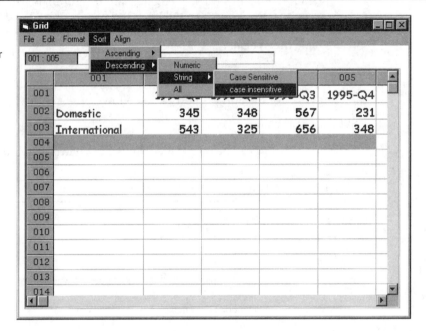

Sort's Custom Setting (9) and Compare Event   All but the last value of the Sort property are self-explanatory. When Sort is set to Custom, the program must specify the order of the columns through a series of Compare events. The Compare event is peculiar in that it's triggered a number of times. It is triggered as many times as there are rows in the grid, and it practically prompts your program to specify which of two columns will appear first.

The first Compare event determines the order of the first and second rows. When the first two columns are in place, the Compare event is triggered for the second and third rows, then for the third and fourth rows, and so on. As you can imagine, the Custom value of the Sort property is slow compared with the other values, but it is the most flexible value. Custom allows you to sort rows according to any criteria and to use nonadjacent columns as sorting keys.

The syntax of the Compare event is as follows:

```
Sub MSFlexGrid1.Compare(row1, row2, cmp)
```

In this event's handler, your code must decide how the rows *row1* and *row2* will be sorted and set the *cmp* argument according to one of the values in Table 7.11.

TABLE 7.11 The Custom Values of the Sort Property

VALUE	DESCRIPTION
-1	Row1 appears before row2.
0	Both rows are equal, or either row can appear before the other.
1	Row1 appears after row2.

The Compare event arranges two rows at a time, so once the Sort property is set to 9, it is triggered many times. The first time it's triggered, the row1 argument is 1, and the row2 argument is 2 (assuming that the first row is fixed). The second time it is triggered, the two arguments are 2 and 3, the third time, they are 3 and 4, and so on up to the rows Rows-1 and Rows. Depending on the type of sorting you want to achieve, you may have to set the Sort property to 9 several times, and your code will become really slow.

TIP

A trick to avoid the Compare event for unusual sorts is to create an invisible column that contains all the sorting keys and to use this column as the sorting key. Set this column's width to 1 pixel (or twip), and it will be practically invisible. This invisible column is usually the last one in the grid.

The various sorting options are demonstrated by the FlexGrid application, whose Sort menu contains the commands for sorting rows in all possible ways.

Merging Cells

Another useful operation you may want to perform on a grid's data is to merge cells with identical data. Figure 7.16 shows a grid with duplicate data, and Figure 7.17 shows the same grid after certain cells were merged. The MSFlexGrid control provides a mechanism for merging adjacent cells automatically if their contents happen to be identical.

FIGURE 7.16

This grid's appearance can be greatly improved if certain cells are merged.

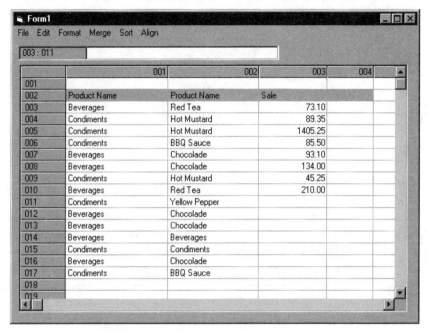

MergeCells Property   This property determines whether adjacent cells will be merged and can take one of the values shown in Table 7.12.

TABLE 7.12 The Values of the MergeCells Property

VALUE	DESCRIPTION	PURPOSE
0	Never (default value)	Prohibits the merging of cells.
1	Free	Merges cells in both rows and columns.
2	Restrict rows	Merges cells across rows.
3	Restrict columns	Merges cells across columns.
4	Restrict both	Similar to free merging. Merges cells only if the cells to be merged are next to other cells that have been merged already.

FIGURE 7.17

The cell-merging mechanism of the MSFlexGrid control enables you to present tabular data in appealing formats.

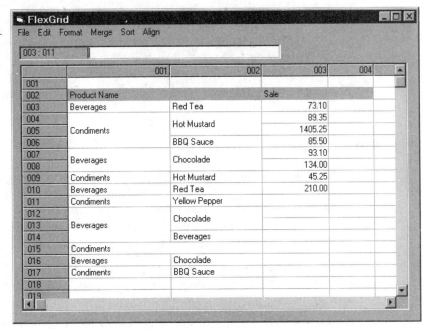

MergeRow(), MergeCol() Properties   Setting the MergeCells property to True does not necessarily merge the cells. For a cell to be merged, it must belong to a row or to a column, with its MergeRow() or MergeCol() property set to True. The MergeRow() and MergeCol() properties are arrays that determine whether the cells of any given row or column can be merged. In other words, you can specify the rows and columns whose cells will be merged and through the MergeRow() and MergeCol() properties have absolute control over the appearance of your grid. To merge consecutive cells on the first column of the grid, use the following settings:

```
Grid1.MergeCells = 3
Grid1.MergeCol(1) = True
```

Likewise, if you want to merge consecutive cells that have identical contents on the grid's first three rows, use the following settings:

```
Grid1.MergeCells = 2
Grid1.MergeRow(1) = True
Grid1.MergeRow(2) = True
Grid1.MergeRow(3) = True
```

NOTE

The Merge menu of the FlexGrid application in this chapter's folder on the CD enables you to experiment with the various settings of the MergeCells, MergeRow0, and MergeCol0 properties. Ideally, these properties should be set by the application for specific data on the grid and should not rely on the user to select the rows and/or columns to merge.

Data Entry

The MSFlexGrid control is an extremely useful tool for displaying data, but it lacks a basic capability: The user cannot edit a single cell. This limitation can be easily overcome with the help of an edit control, namely the TextBox control. The grid itself provides a few properties and events that make the task of combining the MSFlexGrid control with the TextBox control simple.

There are two approaches to editing a grid's cells. The first is to place a TextBox control on the Form. Each time the user clicks on a cell, copy the contents of the active cell to the TextBox control, and let the user edit it. This simple approach is used in the FlexGrid application later in this chapter. The second approach is a bit more elegant, but also more complicated in terms of coding: Place a TextBox control, with the exact dimensions of the cell being edited, right on top of the cell. The user gets the impression of editing a cell directly on the grid.

To integrate the TextBox control with the MSFlexGrid control, use the CellWidth, CellHeight, CellTop, and CellLeft properties of the grid, which determine the current cell's dimensions and placement on the grid. These properties were missing from the old Grid control and were introduced to accommodate data-entry operations. If you assign the location and size properties of the current cell to the TextBox control, the TextBox control is placed on top of the current cell.

After the text control is placed exactly on top of the cell, the contents of the current cell are copied to the TextBox. When the user moves to another cell by clicking on it, the TextBox's contents are copied to that cell, and then the TextBox control is placed over it.

VB5 at Work: The GridEdit Application

The GridEdit application, shown in Figure 7.18, implements the technique just described. The Form of the application contains an MSFlexGrid control and a TextBox control.

FIGURE 7.18

The GridEdit application simulates data-entry operations on a grid by combining the MSFlexGrid control with a TextBox control.

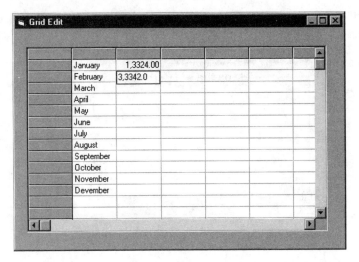

Figure 7.19 shows the GridEdit application at design time. The TextBox control will remain practically invisible at runtime. Because it will be moved from cell to cell, users won't be able to distinguish it from the underlying cell.

Coding GridEdit

Now you are ready to code the application, but you must first select the events to code. The two events that signal the change of the active cell are CellEnter and CellExit. No matter how the focus is moved from one cell to another, these events will take place. It's a good idea, therefore, to place your code behind them.

The CellEnter Event   This event takes place every time a new cell is activated. This event's handler will:

- Clear the contents of the TextBox control.

- Place the TextBox control over the active cell and resize it to fit the cell.

- Assign the contents of the active cell to the TextBox control's Text property.

- Move the focus to the TextBox control.

FIGURE 7.19

The GridEdit application at design time. The TextBox control, partially overlapping the Grid control, is seamlessly integrated with the active cell at runtime.

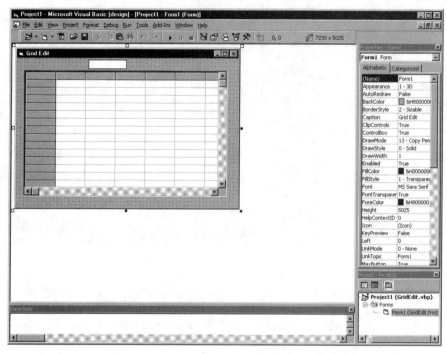

These instructions are translated directly to code with the following lines:

```
Grid1.Row = Grid1.MouseRow
    Grid1.Col = Grid1.MouseCol
' clear contents of current cell
    Text1.Text = ""
' place Textbox over current cell
    Text1.Visible = False
    Text1.Top = Grid1.Top + Grid1.CellTop
    Text1.Left = Grid1.Left + Grid1.CellLeft
    Text1.Width = Grid1.CellWidth
    Text1.Height = Grid1.CellHeight
' passing cell's contents to Textbox
    Text1.Text = Grid1.Text
' move focus to Textbox
    Text1.Visible = True
    Text1.SetFocus
```

When the user leaves the active cell by moving the focus to another cell, the application must copy the TextBox control's contents to the active cell. The MouseLeave event contains a single line of code:

```
Private Sub Grid1_LeaveCell()
    Grid1.Text = Text1.Text
End Sub
```

If you program the two events as explained, the application won't work as expected. What happens when the user clicks on a fixed cell? If a cell in the fixed row is clicked, the entire column is selected. The user can still edit the fixed cell (the column's title), but all the cells in the column remain selected. This isn't what a data-entry operator expects to see when entering data, so we must change this behavior of the program. One solution is to disable multiple selections by setting the AllowBigSelection property to False.

The other approach is to disable the editing of the fixed cells from within the code. To do this, you must check the MouseCol and MouseRow properties to see if the user clicked on a fixed cell (these two properties return the current mouse position in row and column coordinates). If the user did click on a fixed cell, you must exit the subroutine. The active cell won't change, but the user will be able to select an entire row or column as usual.

Code 7.7: The CellEnter Event

```
Private Sub Grid1_CellEnter()

' Make sure the user doesn't attempt to edit the fixed cells
    If Grid1.MouseRow = 0 Or Grid1.MouseCol = 0 Then
        Text1.Visible = False
        Exit Sub
    End If
    Grid1.Row = Grid1.MouseRow
    Grid1.Col = Grid1.MouseCol
' clear contents of current cell
    Text1.Text = ""
' place Textbox over current cell
    Text1.Visible = False
    Text1.Top = Grid1.Top + Grid1.CellTop
    Text1.Left = Grid1.Left + Grid1.CellLeft
    Text1.Width = Grid1.CellWidth
    Text1.Height = Grid1.CellHeight
' passing cell's contents to Textbox
```

```
    Text1.Text = Grid1.Text
' move focus to Textbox
    Text1.Visible = True
    Text1.SetFocus
End Sub
```

When the user is done editing the current cell and moves to another one, the application must copy the text from the TextBox control to the cell just edited. This is done by a single line of code from within the MSFlexGrid's LeaveCell event:

```
Private Sub Grid1_LeaveCell()

    Grid1.Text = Text1.Text

End Sub
```

If you run the application as is, two more problems will surface. First, what happens when the Form is first loaded? The code of the CellEnter event must also be executed when the Form is loaded.

Code 7.8: The Form's Load Event

```
Private Sub Form_Load()

    Grid1.Row = 1
    Grid1.Col = 1

End Sub
```

Notice that we didn't have to explicitly call the control's CellEnter subroutine. Setting a cell's address from within the code causes the CellEnter event to be executed.

The code presented so far is the absolute minimum required for a functional data-entry application based on the MSFlexGrid control. A serious limitation is that the user can't change the active cell with the help of the keyboard. When the user presses the Enter key, for example, the focus should move to the next cell on the same column or row. No such luck. The arrow keys don't even work.

It's relatively easy to adjust the code to add more features that will facilitate data-entry operations, and I've omitted them from the example. The GridEdit application's code demonstrates the basic principles of adding data-entry capabilities to the MSFlexGrid control. The properties and methods discussed so far will allow you to add advanced editing features to your application.

VB5 at Work: The FlexGrid Application

The FlexGrid application demonstrates most of the methods and properties of the MSFlexGrid control. FlexGrid is a functional spreadsheet application with data-entry capabilities that you can easily customize for your specific needs. The application's Form is shown in Figure 7.20.

FIGURE 7.20

The FlexGrid application is a functional spread-sheet application based on the MSFlexGrid control.

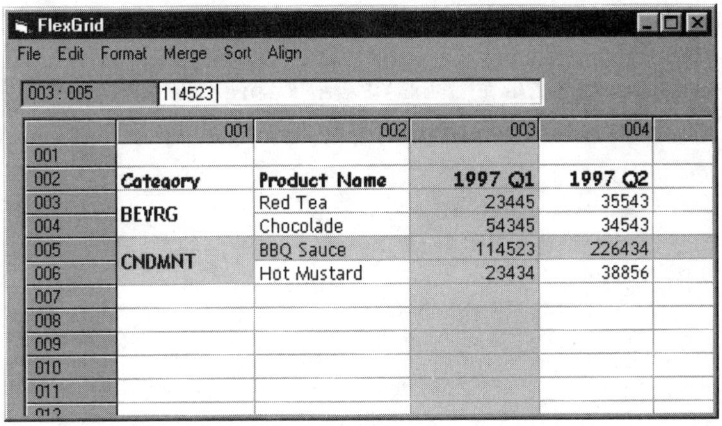

The top-level menus of hte FlexGrid application are as follows:

- **File** contains the usual Open and Save commands.

- **Edit** contains commands for exchanging information with the Clipboard.

- **Format** contains commands for setting the appearance of individual cells (font, text color, and background color) and formatting for numeric values.

- **Merge** contains commands for merging cells in all possible ways.

- **Sort** enables you to sort selected rows in all possible ways.

- **Align** contains commands for left-aligning, right-aligning, and centering the contents of selected cells.

Data Entry in FlexGrid

The code for data entry in FlexGrid uses a technique different from the one described earlier in GridEdit. GridEdit adds data-entry capabilities to the MSFlexGrid control using a TextBox control that is placed over the cell being edited. In the FlexGrid application, the data-entry mechanism relies on a TextBox control above the grid.

Each time the user selects a cell to edit, the program copies the contents of this cell to the TextBox control, where the editing takes place. When the user is done, the contents of the TextBox control are copied to the original cell, the contents of the next cell are copied to the TextBox, and the process is repeated. The data-entry mechanism is implemented in the MSFlexGrid control's EnterCell and LeaveCell events.

Code 7.9: The EnterCell and LeaveCell Events

```
Private Sub Grid_EnterCell()

    Label1.Caption = Grid.TextMatrix(Grid.Col, 0) & " : " & Grid
    ➥.TextMatrix(0, Grid.Row)
    Text1.Text = Grid.Text
    Text1.SetFocus
    Text1.SelStart = 0
    Text1.SelLength = Len(Text1.Text)

End Sub

Private Sub Grid_LeaveCell()

    Grid.Text = Text1.Text

End Sub
```

On entering a new cell, the program updates the Label control with the coordinates of the newly selected cell and then copies its contents to the TextBox. It also selects the text in the control. On leaving the cell, the program copies the TextBox control's text to the original cell. This code works nicely, but it requires the user to select the next cell with the mouse.

To simplify the data-entry process, some code has been added in the TextBox's KeyPress event. When the user presses Enter, the TextBox control's contents are copied to the corresponding cell, and the focus moves to the next cell on the same column. If this cell is the last one in the current column, the focus moves to the first cell of the next column. Or, you can move the focus to the next cell on the same row, and when the end of the row is reached, move to the next row. In other words, Enter signals the user's intention to commit the changes in the current cell and edit the next one.

You can add more lines in the same event handler to let the user move to other cells with different keystrokes. You can use the Tab key, for instance, to move to the next cell on the same row, or you can use the up and down arrow keys to move to the previous or next cell in the same column. The other two arrow keys are needed for editing the text and can't be used for navigation purposes. Here's the TextBox control's KeyPress event handler as implemented in the FlexGrid application.

Code 7.10: The KeyPress Event Handler

```
Private Sub Text1_KeyPress(KeyAscii As Integer)
Dim SRow, SCol As Integer

    If KeyAscii = 13 Then 'Enter Key = 13
        Grid.Text = Text1.Text
        SRow = Grid.Row + 1
        SCol = Grid.ColSel
        If SRow = Grid.Rows Then
            SRow = Grid.FixedCols
            If SCol < Grid.Cols - Grid.FixedCols Then SCol = SCol + 1
        End If

        Grid.Row = SRow
        Grid.Col = SCol
        Grid.RowSel = SRow
        Grid.ColSel = SCol
        Text1.Text = Grid.Text
        Text1.SetFocus
        KeyAscii = 0
    End If

End Sub
```

Saving and Loading Data

The MSFlexGrid control doesn't provide any methods for storing or loading its contents to and from a disk file. To implement the Open, Save, and Save As commands in the File menu, you can select the entire spreadsheet, copy it to a string variable, and then save it with the Write statement. To load an existing file to the grid, use the Input statement.

After the entire grid has been selected, the Clip property holds the values of all cells in the grid, and the problem of saving them to a disk file is reduced to writing a string variable to the file. The grid's data are stored in files with the extension GDT (for Grid DaTa) so that the FileOpen and FileSave dialog boxes can use a default extension unique to this application.

Code 7.11: The Save As Command

```
Private Sub FileSaveAs_Click()
Dim allCells As String
Dim FNum As Integer
Dim curRow, curCol As Integer

    curRow = Grid.Row
    curCol = Grid.Col
On Error GoTo FileError
    CommonDialog1.DefaultExt = "GDT"
    CommonDialog1.ShowSave
    EditSelect_Click
    allCells = Grid.Clip
    FNum = FreeFile
    Open CommonDialog1.filename For Output As #FNum
    Write #FNum, allCells
    Close #FNum
    OpenFile = CommonDialog1.filename

    Grid.Row = curRow
    Grid.Col = curCol
    Grid.RowSel = Grid.Row
    Grid.ColSel = Grid.Col
    Exit Sub

FileError:
    If Err.Number = cdlCancel Then Exit Sub
    MsgBox "Unknown error while opening file " & CommonDialog1
    ➥.filename
    OpenFile = ""

End Sub
```

As you can see, most of the lines set up the FileSave common dialog box. The code that actually extracts the data and writes them to the file consists of a few lines that select the entire grid (by calling the Select All command of the Edit menu), assign the Clip property to the *allCells* variable, and then write to a disk file. The Save command uses the *openFile* global variable to save the grid's contents without prompting the user for a filename. (The FreeFile() function returns the next available file handle and is described in Appendix A.)

The Open command is quite similar. It reads the string variable from the disk file, selects the entire grid, and then assigns the *allCells* variable to the control's Clip property.

The Edit Menu   The application's Edit menu contains the usual Cut, Copy, and Paste commands, which manipulate the control's Clip property. The Copy command extracts the selected cells from the grid via its Clip property and assigns them to the Clipboard with the SetText method as follows:

```
Private Sub EditCopy_Click()
Dim tmpText As String
    tmpText = Grid.Clip
    Clipboard.Clear
    Clipboard.SetText tmpText

End Sub
```

The Paste command does the opposite. It extracts the data from the Clipboard with the GetText method and then assigns them to the grid as follows:

```
Private Sub EditPaste_Click()
Dim tmpText As String

    tmpText = Clipboard.GetText
    Grid.Clip = tmpText

End Sub
```

Problems with Paste   As implemented in the preceding code, the Paste command has a rather serious drawback: The copied cells are pasted in the selected range only. In other words, the user must select a range (whose dimensions should match the dimensions of the range of cells currently in the Clipboard) and then issue the Paste command.

To improve the Paste command, your program must first examine the string that holds the Clipboard's contents. Successive cell values are separated by a Tab character (Chr$(9)), and successive columns are separated by a new line character (chr$(13)). Your program must first select a range with as many columns as there are cells in a row and as many rows as there are rows in the Clipboard's string and then assign the variable to the Clip property.

The Format Menu   The FlexGrid's Format menu contains the following commands:

- **Font** lets the user specify the font attributes of the selected cell(s) through a Font common dialog box.

- **Text Color** lets the user specify the text color for the selected cell(s).

- **Cell Color** lets the user specify the background color for the selected cell(s).

Also included is a group of commands for formatting numeric data. To apply the desired format to the selected cells, select one of these commands:

###	Formats 1802.5 as 1802
###.00	Formats 1802 as 1802.00
#,###.00	Formats 1802.5 as 1,802.50
$#,###.00	Formats 1802.5 as $1,802.50

These commands call the FormatCells() subroutine with the proper argument, and the subroutine scans the entire range of selected cells and formats their contents with the Format$() function:

```
Sub FormatCells(formatString)
Dim irow, icol As Integer

   For irow = Grid.Row To Grid.RowSel
      For icol = Grid.Col To Grid.ColSel
         Grid.TextMatrix(irow, icol) =
➥Format$(Grid.TextMatrix(irow, icol), formatString)
      Next
   Next

End Sub
```

The Sort and Align Menus   The Sort menu contains a number of nested commands that let the user specify all types of possible sorting methods with the MSFlexGrid control, except for the Custom sort. Through the Sort menu's commands, you can sort the rows of the grid as strings or numbers, in ascending or descending rows. Moreover, the sorting process can be case-sensitive or case-insensitive.

Implementing the Sort menu is simple. Each command in this menu assigns the appropriate value to the MSFlexGrid control's Sort property (see Table 7.9, earlier in this chapter, for a list of these values and how they affect the sorting process).

The Sort command relies on the user to select the columns with the keys. To sort all the rows in the grid, select all the key columns by clicking on their fixed cells. To sort a range of rows only, select the cells in the column(s) with the sorting keys and the rows to be sorted.

The code behind the command Sort | Descending | Numeric consists of a single line:

```
Private Sub DescNumeric_Click()

    Grid.Sort = 4

End Sub
```

The grid's rows will be sorted according to the values of the cells in the selected column(s). If part of a column has been selected, only the selected rows will be sorted (see Figure 7.21).

FIGURE 7.21

Rows 2 through 8 on this spreadsheet are sorted, and rows 10 through 17 are not. To partially sort the grid, select only the rows you want to sort in the key column.

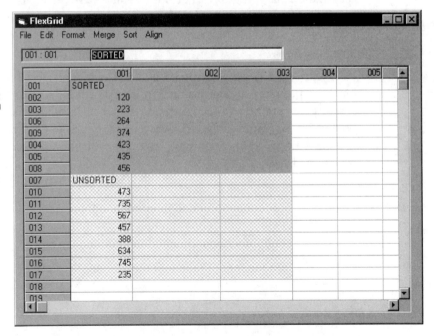

The Align menu contains the commands that let the user left-align, right-align, and center selected cells. After the alignment property for a cell is set, it remains in effect even if the cell's contents are edited. The same is true for the font attributes of the cell, but not for the number formatting commands.

Improvements

FlexGrid has most of the functionality you'll need to write complicated spreadsheet applications. For instance, you can easily add data-processing capabilities to the application. Inserting formulas won't be easy, but you can calculate the average of a range of cells or normalize them. The code for formatting a range of numeric values, which scans the range of the selected cells, is the structure you need. Instead of formatting the cells' contents, add their values and divide the sum by the number of selected cells. Or you can fill a column with a function of the values of the cells to its left.

A few commands that automatically fill a range of cells are also quite common. You can implement a command that reads the value of a cell and fills the following cells in the same column with the initial value incremented by a user-supplied step. These values can also be dates. The user can supply the initial day and an increment in days, and your program can fill the following cells with the appropriate dates.

As you've seen here, you can easily add functionality to the FlexGrid control for many practical situations that require a gridlike structure for displaying or entering data, but don't need something such as Excel. If you need the data-processing capabilities of Excel, especially data processing with formulas, or if you need a built-in programming language, you should look into more specialized spreadsheet controls.

Using Multimedia Elements to Enhance Applications

- Images

- Wipes

- Waveform Audio

- MIDI

- MCI commands

- Video for Windows

What catches your eye when you check out an application, especially a game, is multimedia. The images, sounds, and animation that enhance the application's user interface make the application more approachable to the average user and more fun. In other words, the "eye candy." You can achieve highly desirable effects by combining some or all the following:

- Cool graphics

- Great sounds

- Dynamic animation

- Stunning digital video

This chapter explores the basic tools and the techniques you need to incorporate these elements into your applications. Although these exciting elements can add a lot to your application, it must also contain quality content and functionality. But even a not-so-great application looks attractive when enhanced with multimedia elements.

Enhancing Applications with Images

Most of the information you need in order to include images in your application is covered in Chapter 6, *Drawing and Painting with Visual Basic*. You will, however, find a useful technique in this chapter, namely how to use the PaintPicture method to create smooth transitions (or wipes) between images.

Graphics come in many flavors and will be in some kind of format, depending on their original source. Depending on what you plan to do with them, you might need to do some conversion before you can actually use them. Also, the way you store images depends on what you intend to do with them. If you want your images to be accessed on the Internet, you should probably consider reducing their size by compressing them. If the users of your application will have True Color displays, you can use high-resolution, true-color images.

Image Quality

The resolution of your screen can profoundly affect the image that you display. Each individual pixel on the screen corresponds to a value in the computer's video memory. The number of pixels and color values that can be displayed on a computer monitor are the system's resolution. There are three types of resolution:

- Horizontal

- Vertical

- Color

For example, a screen that has a resolution of 800 × 600 has 600 lines of pixels along its horizontal axis, and each line contains 800 pixels. An image's resolution is the number of pixels in the image; image resolution is not related to screen resolution. The only connection is that, if the image is too large for a given monitor resolution, the image won't be displayed in its entirety. In general, size your images so that they will fit nicely on a monitor with resolution of 800 × 600. The lowest common denominator is 640 × 480, but this screen size is gradually being abandoned. Most systems sold today, even notebooks, have a screen resolution of 800 × 600.

The *color resolution* refers to the number of colors in an image and is not related to screen resolution or the size of an image. The more colors an image contains, the smoother it looks. As with the physical resolution of the image, the more colors it contains, the more disk space it requires for storage and the more time it takes to load. Screen resolution and color resolution are independent of each other, but usually one helps the other. Games are usually displayed on low-resolution monitors (or a small area of the screen) because updating too many pixels is an enormous computational burden (and games are not normally played on top-of-the-line computers). To make up for the low resolution, game designers use many colors.

True Color and Palettes

Obviously, a true-color image yields the highest quality, but what if the computer can't display all the colors in the image? As you probably know, many systems can display only 256 colors. To address a larger number of users, your applications should not fall apart when executed on these systems. Multimedia systems, however, support true color, and it's not unreasonable to request that your application is run on systems that support more than 256 colors.

Systems that can't display more than 256 colors use a palette of 256 colors. Only colors present in this palette can be displayed. Since the 256 colors aren't fixed, there's an optimal palette for each image. This palette contains the 256 colors that best describe that image. If you display another image with similar colors, Visual Basic won't have a problem displaying it, because most of the colors it contains are already on the palette or can be approximated.

If you attempt to display another image with drastically different colors, though, Visual Basic has three choices:

1. Create a common palette with the colors of both images.

2. Switch the appropriate palette, depending on which image has the focus.

3. Use halftone patterns to approximate the colors of both images.

> **NOTE**   A halftone consists of tiny, evenly spaced spots of variable diameter that, when printed (on screen or on paper), visually blur together to appear as shades of gray. On the monitor, you can't have dots of variable diameter, so it's the number of dots of each color placed next to each other that produce an approximate color.

The display method used depends on the setting of the Form's PaletteMode property, which can take one of the values shown in Table 8.1.

TABLE 8.1   The Values of the PaletteMode Property

VALUE	TYPE	DESCRIPTION
0	Halftone	Halftone patterns are used to accommodate the colors of both images.
1	UseZOrder	The palette of the image in front of the ZOrder is used for rendering the colors of both images.
2	Custom	A user-specified palette is used for rendering the colors of both images.

PaletteMode 0   When PaletteMode is 0, Visual Basic uses halftone patterns to display the colors of all images, as best as it can, every time a new image is loaded. All images are displayed with approximate colors, and none is displayed as it would appear on its own.

PaletteMode 1   When PaletteMode is 1, Visual Basic uses the palette of the image in front of the ZOrder for all the images on the Form. This setting allows you to control from within your application which image will be displayed with its colors, without regard for the other images (whose colors may change drastically).

PaletteMode 2   When PaletteMode is 2, you can assign the palette that will be used to render the colors of all images on the Form. This is equivalent to changing the ZOrder of the various images, with one exception. The common palette can belong to an image that isn't even displayed. You can use a generic palette with many colors (such as the palettes that come with Visual Basic) for all the images. Again, the image whose colors are closest to the palette's colors will be displayed best.

> **NOTE**
>
> PaletteMode is a Form property and determines how the images on the Form or on the Form's controls will be displayed. PictureBox and ImageBox controls don't have a PaletteMode or Palette property.

VB5 at Work: The Palettes Application

To demonstrate the PaletteMode and Palette properties, I have included the Palettes application, shown in Figure 8.1. The Load Image buttons above the PictureBox controls let you load a new image to the corresponding PictureBox. You should try both true-color and palette images.

The three option buttons at the bottom of the Form set the PaletteMode property of the Form. After setting the mode, you can click on one of the two images. If the PaletteMode is set to 1 (ZOrder), the image you clicked is brought to the front of the ZOrder. If the PaletteMode is 2 (Custom), the palette of the image you clicked on is assigned to the Form's Palette property so that both images are rendered with this palette. Experiment with the various settings and various types of images to understand how Visual Basic handles multiple palettes and true-color images on systems capable of displaying only 256 colors.

FIGURE 8.1

The Palettes application lets you experiment with the settings of the PaletteMode property.

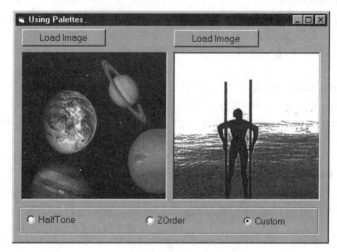

The three OptionButton controls form an array.

Code 8.1: The Click Event Handler Code for the OptionButton Controls

```
Private Sub Palette_Click(Index As Integer)

    Form1.PaletteMode = Index
    Form1.Refresh

End Sub
```

The other subroutine worth mentioning here is the PictureBox control's Click event handler.

Code 8.2: The Click Event Handler Code for the PictureBox Control

```
Private Sub Picture1_Click()

    If Form1.PaletteMode = 1 Then
        Picture1.ZOrder 0
        Picture2.ZOrder 1
    End If
    If Form1.PaletteMode = 2 Then
        Form1.Palette = Picture1.Image
    End If

End Sub
```

The action of this subroutine depends on the setting of the PaletteMode property. To text the Palettes application, set your computer's display to 256 colors. On a true-color system, all images are displayed in their original colors. If the PaletteMode is 1 (ZOrder), the code moves the PictureBox control to the front of the ZOrder. If PaletteMode is 2 (Custom), the palette of the control that was clicked becomes the Form's palette, and both images are rendered with this palette. You can load the palettes that come with Visual Basic (the files Bright.dib, Rainbow.dib, and Pastel.dib) in one of the PictureBox controls and then apply this palette to another image. You can also add a third PictureBox control or assign an image to the Form to see how Visual Basic handles multiple images with different palette requirements.

Image Formats

A graphics file is the format in which graphics data are stored. Because programs try to find an optimal method for storing their data, a graphics file format can be complex. Three factors are taken into account:

1. The speed at which the image data can be accessed

2. The total disk space required

3. The applications that can access the image data

An important aspect of all image file formats is compression. Images can be easily compressed because they contain a lot of redundant information. A long stripe of blue pixels, for instance, need not be stored as a sequence of identical numbers. The most common compression algorithms store the value of one pixel and how many times this value is repeated. This type of compression is called *Run Length Encoding* (RLE). RLE coding isn't the most efficient compression scheme, however; its basic benefit is speed. RLE compressed images can be easily and quickly decompressed.

Other file formats deploy more complicated, and certainly more efficient, compression schemes. The more complicated the algorithms used for image compression, the more calculations they require, which means additional loading time.

Below is a description of the most common formats used in today's applications.

Windows Bitmap

The Microsoft Windows Bitmap (BMP) is a standard bitmap storage format used in the Windows environment, in OS/2 (which is a strict superset of Windows), and in some DOS-based programs. This format supports color depths of 1-bit, 4-bit, 8-bit, 16-bit, and 24-bit. Color depths of 1 and 4 bits correspond to monochrome and 16 color images, which you really shouldn't use in multimedia applications. Eight-bit images contain a palette with the 256 colors that best describe the image. Twenty-four–bit images use true color, as discussed in Chapter 6, *Drawing and Painting with Visual Basic*. In between palettes and true color is another image quality referred to as *high color*. Sixteen-bit images contain 64K colors, and they use 5 bits to represent the color's green and blue components and 6 bits for the red component. For most practical purposes, they are good as true-color images.

The two basic types of bitmaps are:

- Device-dependent (BMP)
- Device-independent (DIB)

Device-dependent bitmaps (BMPs) are tied to the output display because the bits of the bitmap and the pixels of the output display device are closely corre-lated. Device-independent bitmaps (DIBs), however, are not tied to a particular display device because they represent the appearance of the image. For purposes of this discussion, BMPs and DIBs are equivalent.

The JPEG format (Joint Photographic Experts Group) supports true-color and palette images and can achieve a higher degree of compression. It allows variable levels of compression and is lossy because it discards a little information in order to achieve a high degree of compression.

Graphics Interchange Format

CompuServe designed the Graphics Interchange Format (GIF, pronounced "JIFF") mainly for a fast exchange of bitmapped images between computers. GIF files are relatively small, but displaying them is slow. This format is great for use on the Internet or on electronic bulletin board systems. GIF is one of the most stable image file standards even though it only supports images that have 256 or fewer colors. Most of the images you will find on the World Wide Web are stored in GIF format.

TIP Because GIF files are compressed by nature, running a file compression utility, such as WinZIP or PKZIP, on them does not result in smaller files.

Microsoft Windows Icon Image

Microsoft Windows Icon Image (ICO) is the format of all Windows icons. Icons are usually stored as resources in a program. An icon image consists of a bitmapped image and a mask to make up the transparent parts of the picture. (The mask is a color, usually the background color, that is ignored when the image is rendered. Every pixel painted with the mask color lets the underlying bitmaps show through.) An icon is typically 32 × 32 pixels and is composed of 16 colors. When you minimize an application, its icon appears on the screen. A smaller version is displayed on the task bar in Windows 95.

To create or edit icons, you use an icon editor. ImagEdit is the icon editor that comes with the Professional Edition of Visual Basic 5.0. For an example of what you can do with it, see Figure 8.2. IconMagic is an adequate shareware program for creating or editing icons.

FIGURE 8.2

Creating cursors (and icons) with the ImagEdit utility

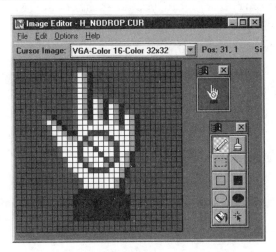

Microsoft Windows Cursor Image

Microsoft Windows Cursor Image (CUR) is the format of all Windows cursors. CUR is a special bitmap that indicates the current position of the mouse. You can define your own custom cursors or use any of the predefined Windows cursors. You can also use ImagEdit to edit cursors. Cursors are important in giving users feedback about the status of your application. For example, if your program is busy with a task, display a wait cursor, such as the hourglass. Then, when the operation is complete, reset the hourglass to the standard cursor. Whichever cursors you decide to use, keep them simple and intuitive for the user.

In Visual Basic, you can use custom cursors to set the mouse pointer. By creating your own cursors, you can make your application unique and also show the current state of the user's actions in a more meaningful fashion. Visual Basic uses the MousePointer property to set the cursor and to load icons. When loaded, the icons are converted to the CUR format.

> **NOTE**
>
> An animated cursor is a special type of cursor. It consists of sequences of static cursors that are played back in rapid succession to produce a small animation. Visual Basic, however, does not support animated cursors; nor does it support color cursors.

To load a custom cursor or icon, you must use both the MousePointer and the MouseIcon properties. Follow these steps:

1. Set the MousePointer property to "99-Custom."

2. Load the icon into the MouseIcon property, or add the following statement to your Form:

```
Form1.MouseIcon =
LoadPicture("c:\vb\graphics\cursors\wait08.cur")
```

Windows Metafile

The Microsoft Windows Metafile (WMF) format is used for storing vector data. Visual Basic doesn't provide any methods for storing information in Metafiles, but you can still assign them to the Picture property of the controls that can display images.

Table 8.2 summarizes the formats discussed above.

TABLE 8.2 Common Windows Image Formats

FILE FORMAT	FILE TYPE	EXTENSION
Windows Bitmap	Bitmap	BMP, DIB
JPEG	Bitmap	JPG

TABLE 8.2   Common Windows Image Formats (continued)

FILE FORMAT	FILE TYPE	EXTENSION
Graphics Interchange Format	Bitmap	GIF
Windows Icon	Bitmap	ICO
Windows Cursor	Bitmap	CUR
Windows Metafile	Vector	WMF

Image Compression

Compression means making files smaller by removing repetitive patterns of data so that it can be stored in fewer bits and thus take up less disk space. Depending on what you intend to do, you need to consider speed and compression ratio. Because graphics data usually require a lot of disk space, compression is important. Regardless of the platform your application is running on, you must use some compression method. You need to fit graphics data on the disk and sometimes in a block of memory.

TIP   When you assign an image to a Form or a PictureBox control, the bitmap is stored along with the Form (in the corresponding FRX file, as explained in Chapter 2, *Visual Basic Projects*). Visual Basic uses the original file format to store the bitmap. If it's a BMP file, it is stored as a BMP bitmap. If the original file was in JPG format, Visual Basic stores the bitmap in JPG format. Therefore, you should try to assign compressed image formats to the Picture property at design time.

In developing today's applications, you must be familiar with the major types of compression and how they are used.

Types of Compression

The term *codec* is shorthand for *compressor/decompressor* and refers to the program that compresses and decompresses an image (or other types of information, for that matter). Data that is not compressed is sometimes referred to as *raw data* or *unencoded data*. The term *compression ratio* refers to the ratio of uncompressed data to compressed data and is shown as, for example, 2:1. In this case, the amount of uncompressed data is twice the amount of compressed data. The higher the ratio, the better the compression scheme. Notice that the compression ratio refers to the amount of bytes required to store the information, not to the information itself. The two types of compression methods are lossy and lossless.

Lossy Compression   This method discards any data that the compression method decides is not needed, and original data is lost when the file is decompressed. Although lossy compression methods achieve better ratios than lossless methods, their use depends on the type of image your application uses. For example, you would not want to use the lossy method for program files or medical X rays. The lost data would be significant. Using the lossy method is, however, an excellent choice for graphics on a Web page or in printed media. In general, the information lost through lossy compression becomes evident only when the image is enlarged. If the image isn't going to be enlarged or processed in other ways, any artifacts introduced by lossy compression go practically unnoticed by the human eye.

Lossless Compression   This method re-records the data a file contains in a more compact fashion. No data is lost when the file is decompressed. Let's assume you have a picture of the ocean. A large portion of the image consists of blue tones, and a number of adjacent pixels have identical color. Instead of repeating the same color value, say 12 times, you can replace these 12 values with the number 12 followed by the color value. When the decompressor sees the number 12 followed by a color value, it generates 12 identical color values. Another compression trick is to take the differences of adjacent pixels. On the average, an image's pixels in any given area have similar values. Instead of storing their absolute values, you store their differences, which have small sizes and can be represented with fewer bits than the original color values.

Although compression might not be an issue in business applications, it plays an important role in developing Web pages for the Internet or an intranet, on which lengthy images translate into prolonged download times.

Image-Processing Tools

No matter what types of images you use in your applications, an image-processing application is a must-have tool. At the least, you will need to resize images, change their format, control their color content, and so on. You can also use image-processing software to produce striking images that will greatly enhance your user interfaces. A few of the products you should check out are discussed next.

Paint Shop Pro

This is definitely one of the best shareware programs out there. It supports 35 file formats—26 bitmap formats and 9 vector formats. It can even convert multiple file formats simultaneously, using a batch file option.

You can download Paint Shop Pro from the following URL:

`http://www.shareware.com`

PhotoShop

This is a powerful and popular commercial application. Although it is expensive, it is probably worth the investment if you intend to do some serious artwork. PhotoShop comes packed with powerful features and plug-ins, which are programs developed to enhance and extend the standard program. Some of the most impressive plug-ins for PhotoShop are published by Adobe and can be used for highly unusual special effects.

Microsoft Image Composer

Although Microsoft Image Composer is an application for creating images for on-screen display on Web sites, you can also use it to create and edit your images. It doesn't support as many formats as Paint Shop Pro (the default file type used by Image Composer is MIC), but it does support most of the common ones.

A powerful tool is the warps feature, which allows you to distort a sprite's appearance. A *sprite* is an element of an image, similar to a shape of drawing applications. An important distinction between a drawing application and an image-processing application is that drawings are made up of simpler entities, such as boxes, circles, and other shapes. A drawing program allows you to edit individual entities. Traditional image-processing applications handle bitmaps, and you can't edit individual parts of the bitmap. Microsoft Image Composer uses sprites, which are equivalent to the shapes of drawing applications. You can place sprites (small bitmaps) together to create a new image, but maintain the ability to edit individual sprite. The warp options include Bulge, Escher, Mesa, Vortex, Radial Sweep, and Spike Inversion, as shown in Figure 8.3.

FIGURE 8.3:

The Image Composer
environment

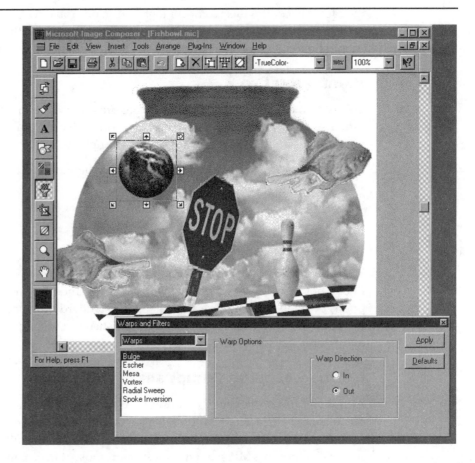

Image Composer accepts plug-ins, such as Kai's Power Tools and KPT Convolver. Impressionist is a plug-in that allows you to apply and modify various artistic styles on a sprite. Examples include a cave-painting effect, a crayon stroke effect, a spatter effect, and a detailed, soft pencil effect. The Impressionist plug-in also provides 17 artistic style groups, including Chalk, Charcoal, Crayon, Paint, Pencil, Pointillist, and Watercolor.

You can download Microsoft Image Composer from Microsoft's Web site at the following URL:

```
http://www.microsoft.com/imagecomposer/start.htm
```

VB5 at Work: The Wipes Application

All the information you need to use images effectively from within your Visual Basic applications is covered in Chapter 6, *Drawing and Painting with Visual Basic*. As mentioned earlier, however, there is an interesting multimedia type of application I saved for this chapter. In some situations, you will want to display a number of images in a sequence, like a slide show. Because computer-controlled slide shows are popular, I developed the Wipes application, which demonstrates the basic concepts.

The Wipes application, shown in Figure 8.4, displays an image on a PictureBox control with a smooth transition, or wipe. It can bring the image from the left or display it in stripes starting from the middle. Also included is a special type of wipe that stretches the image outside its destination and progressively resets it to its original size. The program uses a single image to demonstrate the various transitions, and in your own application, you can probably keep the PictureBox control with the source image hidden. Each time you want to wipe another image, you must load it in the hidden PictureBox and activate the code of one of the buttons or similar code that performs another type of wipe.

FIGURE 8.4

The Wipes application demonstrates how to use the PaintPicture method to set up a slide show on your computer.

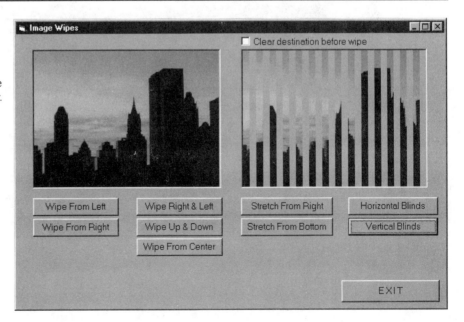

The transitions are achieved by moving blocks of pixels from one PictureBox control to the other with the PaintPicture method. The techniques are simple, and you can come up with numerous transitions of your own. The basic idea is to copy blocks of pixels from the source image to the destination. By controlling the shape of the block and its origin and destination, you can create all types of transitions.

Let's look at the wipe that displays an image progressively from left to right. The code behind the Wipe from Left button copies a vertical stripe from the source to the destination image and increases the stripe's width at each step. The first time it copies a stripe that is one pixel wide and that extends from the top to the bottom of the PictureBox control. It then increases the width of the stripe and copies it again, and so on, until the entire destination is covered. Figure 8.5 shows how this works.

FIGURE 8.5

A few stages of the Wipe from Left wipe

Code 8.3: The Wipe from Left Button's Click Event Handler

```
Private Sub WipeLeft_Click()
Dim X

  If ClearDestination.Value Then Picture2.Picture = LoadPicture()
  For X = 1 To Picture1.ScaleWidth
    Picture2.PaintPicture Picture1.Picture, 0, 0, _
    X, Picture1.ScaleHeight, 0, 0, X, _
    Picture1.ScaleHeight, &HCC0020
  Next

End Sub
```

In Code 8.3, X is the width of the stripe being copied. Its initial value is 1 (a one-pixel wide stripe), which is incremented by 1 until the value equals the control's width. ClearDestination is the CheckBox above the destination PictureBox, which lets the user specify whether the destination PictureBox will be cleared before a new transition or not.

The Stretch wipes copy a stripe of the original image, only the destination's width and height are not the same as the source dimensions. Instead, the stripe is stretched to fill the entire destination. In the first step, the destination image is filled with the first column of pixels of the source image. The destination is then filled with the first two columns of pixels, and so on, until the entire source image is copied on the destination.

Code 8.4: The Stretch from Right Wipe

```
Private Sub StretchRight_Click()
Dim X

  If ClearDestination.Value Then Picture2.Picture = LoadPicture()
  For X = 1 To Picture1.ScaleWidth Step 3
    Picture2.PaintPicture Picture1.Picture, 0, 0, _
    Picture1.ScaleWidth, Picture1.ScaleHeight, 0, 0, X, _
    Picture1.ScaleHeight, &HCC0020
  Next

End Sub
```

Figure 8.6 shows how the Stretch from Right effect works. During the first stages, a small vertical stripe of the original image covers the entire destination picture box. This small stripe becomes increasingly wider, until the entire source image is copied to the destination picture box.

FIGURE 8.6

A few stages of the
Stretch from Right wipe

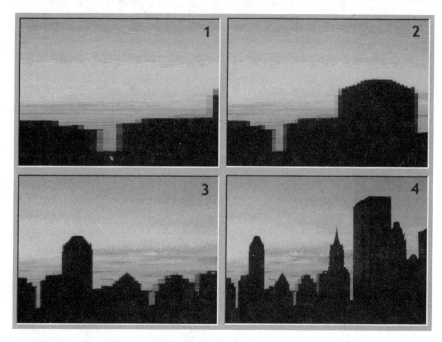

Code 8.5: The Stretch from Bottom Wipe

```
Private Sub StretchBottom_Click()
Dim X

  If ClearDestination.Value Then Picture2.Picture = LoadPicture()
  For X = 1 To Picture1.ScaleHeight Step 3
    Picture2.PaintPicture Picture1.Picture, 0, 0, _
    Picture1.ScaleWidth, Picture1.ScaleHeight, 0, 0, _
    Picture1.ScaleWidth, X, &HCC0020
  Next

End Sub
```

The OpCode value used with the PaintPicture method (the method's last argument) has the default value and could be omitted. You can try different values to create additional special effects with the Wipes application.

To understand how the Wipe from Center effect works (see Figure 8.7), imagine that the two images are square. The wipe starts by copying the middle pixel, then it copies a 3 × 3 block centered around the pixel at the middle of the source image, then it copies a 5 × 5 block, and so on until the destination is filled.

FIGURE 8.7

A few stages of the Wipe from Center effect

Because most images aren't square, the first block isn't a single pixel, but a row or column of pixels. The number of pixels is chosen so that after the initial block is copied, the following blocks are 2 pixels wider and taller than the previous one, and they approach all four edges at the same speed.

Code 8.6: The Wipe from Center Effect

```
Private Sub WipeCenter_Click()
Dim PWidth, PHeight As Integer
Dim i As Integer

    If ClearDestination.Value Then Picture2.Picture = LoadPicture()
    If Picture1.ScaleWidth > Picture1.ScaleHeight Then
      PWidth = Picture1.ScaleWidth - Picture1.ScaleHeight
      PHeight = 1
    ElseIf Picture1.ScaleWidth < Picture1.ScaleHeight Then
```

```
        PWidth = 1
        PHeight = Picture1.ScaleHeight - Picture1.ScaleWidth
      Else
        PWidth = 1
        PHeight = 1
      End If

      For i = 1 To Picture1.ScaleWidth - PWidth
        Picture2.PaintPicture Picture1.Picture, _
        Int((Picture1.ScaleWidth - PWidth) / 2), _
 Int((Picture1.ScaleHeight - PHeight) / 2), _
        PWidth, PHeight, _
        Int((Picture1.ScaleWidth - PWidth) / 2), _
 Int((Picture1.ScaleHeight - PHeight) / 2), _
        PWidth, PHeight, &HCC0020
        PWidth = PWidth + 1
        PHeight = PHeight + 1
      Next

End Sub
```

The wipes that use blinds are a bit more complicated. The Horizontal Blinds wipe draws multiple stripes of equal size at equal distances from each other. With each iteration, the stripes get taller, until they touch each other. The program starts by calculating the number of stripes required to cover the entire destination. Each stripe is one pixel tall and grows to *StripeHeight* pixels. Therefore, the number of stripes required to cover the destination is as follows:

```
StripeHeight = 20
Stripes = Fix(Picture1.ScaleHeight / StripeHeight)
```

A double loop then begins. The outer loop is repeated as many times as the maximum number of pixels in each stripe (which is given by the *StripeHeight* variable). The inner loop copies stripes of pixels and is repeated *Stripes* times. With each iteration, the stripe's width is increased by one pixel.

Code 8.7: The Horizontal Stripes Effect

```
Private Sub Horizontal_Click()
Dim Stripes As Integer
Dim i, j As Integer
Dim StripeHeight As Integer
```

```
If ClearDestination.Value Then Picture2.Picture = LoadPicture()
StripeHeight = 20
Stripes = Fix(Picture1.ScaleHeight / StripeHeight)
On Error Resume Next
For j = 1 To StripeHeight
  For i = 0 To Stripes
    Picture2.PaintPicture Picture1.Picture, 0, i * StripeHeight,
    ➥Picture1.ScaleWidth, j, 0, i * StripeHeight, Picture1
    ➥.ScaleWidth, j, &HCC0020
  Next
Next

End Sub
```

Figure 8.8 shows how the Vertical Blinds special effect works. During the first stages, a few thin vertical stripes are copied from the source to the destination picture box. These stripes become increasingly wider, until they cover the entire destination picture box.

FIGURE 8.8

A few stages of the Vertical Blinds wipe

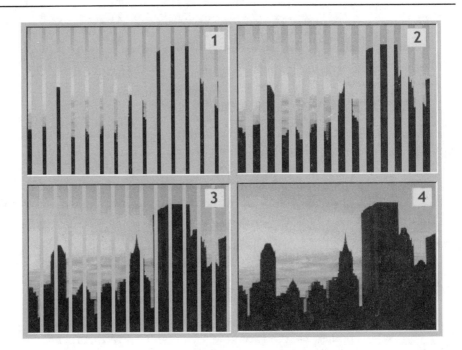

Enhancing Applications with Sound

Besides including great-looking pictures, you can enhance an application with sounds. You can add two types of sounds to your applications:

- Recorded sounds (files with the extension WAV)
- Synthesized, or MIDI, sounds (files with the extensions MID)

You can also control the CD player to play back tracks from an audio CD, but this technique is used almost exclusively with programs (mostly games) that require the presence of a CD in the CD-ROM drive.

> **TIP**
>
> Many developers will consider adding sound capabilities to their application after everything else is in place. If you want to make sounds an integral part of your application, incorporate them early in the development cycle and find ways to make them part of the application's user interface. Later in this chapter, you will learn how to use sound to provide audio messages to the users of your applications.

Using Waveform Audio

This is the format used for digitized sounds, which are stored in files that have the extension WAV. If you have a sound card and a microphone, you can record your own sounds. You can also use the WAV files included on the CD for the purposes of this chapter's examples. You will find some useful sound files, such as the names of the days and months, numbers, and more. In the following sections, you'll see how to use sound files to add audio features to your applications.

Sound quality depends on two major factors:

- The sampling rate
- The number of bytes allocated to each sample

The *sampling rate* is the number of audio samples taken per second. The more samples, the more accurately you can later reconstruct the original sound but also the more disk space the file consumes. The sampling rate varies from 8KHz (8,000 samples per second) to more than 40KHz (40,000 samples per second).

Lower sampling rates can only be used with voice. Sounds taken at 8,000 samples per second are equivalent to telephone quality. You can recognize the speaker, but that's about it. A sampling rate of 11,025 samples per second is a good trade-off between storage requirement and quality, but it's still low quality. The most common sampling rate for digitizing human speech is 22,050 samples per second (known as radio quality).

The highest sampling rate you can achieve with a sound card (and play back on a sound card) is 44,100 samples per second. This sampling rate yields the best possible sound quality and is known as CD quality. As you can easily calculate, sounds taken at this sampling rate consume four times as much disk space as telephone quality sounds.

The second factor that determines quality is the *number of bytes allocated to each sample*. Each sample represents the intensity of the sound at any given instance in time. Sound samples are represented as integers in the computer's memory. If you allocate one byte to each sample, there are 256 levels of intensity. The smallest value, zero, corresponds to silence, and the largest value, 255, corresponds to the sound's maximum intensity. If you use an integer to represent each sample, you have more than 30,000 levels of intensity. Thus, the samples are represented more accurately in the computer's memory. As you can also easily calculate, this sound will take twice as much disk space as a sample represented by a byte.

TIP

There are remarkable similarities between sounds and images. The sampling rate corresponds to an image's resolution, and the sampling accuracy corresponds to the number of colors. Raising the sampling rate is equivalent to scanning an image with more dots per inch. Raising the sampling accuracy (representing a sample with an integer instead of a byte) is equivalent to raising an image's color resolution (true color instead of a 256-color palette).

One other factor that affects the quality of digitized sound is whether the sound is digitized in mono or in stereo. A stereo recording has two separate channels, which means twice the samples (and twice the disk space) of a mono recording.

Sounds as well as images can be compressed. If you surf the Web, you are familiar with the various sound compression schemes, such as RealAudio. Even Windows 95 includes codecs for sound files. One of them, the TrueSpeech codec, can squeeze sounds sampled with 1 byte per sample down to 1 bit per sample. To see the codecs installed on your system, follow these steps:

1. Choose Start ➤ Programs ➤ Accessories ➤ Multimedia ➤ Sound Record.

2. In the Sound Recorder dialog box, choose File ➤ Open, and select a WAV file.

3. Choose File ➤ Properties to open the Properties for Sound dialog box, as shown in Figure 8.9.

FIGURE 8.9

The sound codecs can be located in the Sound Selection window of the Properties for Sound dialog box.

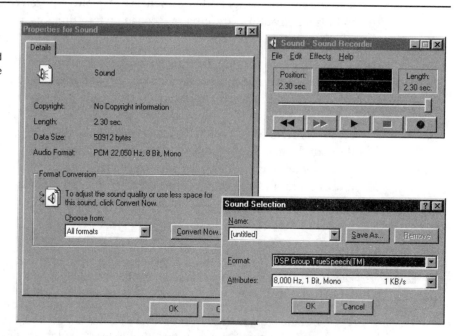

4. Click on the Convert Button to open the Sound Selection window.

5. Click on the Format drop-down list arrow to see a list of the codecs installed on your system.

In general, computers can handle sound files easily, and there's no need to compress sound files unless you are going to place them on the Web or unless you have many large files to distribute with your application.

Using MIDI

MIDI (pronounced "middy") is an acronym for Musical Instrument Digital Interface, a serial interface standard that can connect music synthesizers, musical instruments, and computers. A MIDI file doesn't contain the sound; it contains instructions as to how the sound can be constructed—notes and durations that describe a tune. With the help of the appropriate hardware, these instructions are translated into sounds.

As described earlier, a WAV file stores digitized sound; a WAV file is a pictorial representation of the original sounds. You can think of the WAV file as the image of a printed page (much like a fax), and you can think of the MIDI file as the textual information that corresponds to the fax. The pictorial representation of the page may take 100 times as much disk space as the text file with the fax's contents. Using MIDI files reduces storage requirements to a minimum.

To record sound files (and edit them to some extent), you can use the Sound Recorder application that comes with Windows. For more advanced sound processing tools, you can resort to a couple of excellent shareware applications such as CoolEdit, which is available from:

```
ftp:syntrillium.com
```

and GoldWave, which is available from:

```
http://web.cs.mun.ca/~chris3/goldwave/goldwave.html
```

Using the MCI Control

The Media Control Interface, or MCI, was introduced as part of the Multimedia Extensions provided with Windows 3.0. MCI is now part of the Windows operating system. Basically, MCI is designed to communicate with a plethora of device types, including waveform audio, MIDI, CD audio, and MPEG video. It does so by communicating with device drivers, which interpret MCI commands into the device's command set, thus driving the device.

MCI is part of several high-level multimedia services provided by Windows. You can easily access these services through Visual Basic controls.

MCI can communicate with devices in two ways:

- By sending text commands to the device driver (through the string interface)
- By sending commands directly to the devices

Because the string interface is much easier to use, this discussion is limited to it.

About MCI Device Types

MCI device types can be simple or compound. *Simple MCI devices* do not require a data file for playback. Videodisc players and CD audio players are simple device types. These devices are called simple because they stream the data from an external source to an output. The computer is hardly involved in the process.

On the other hand, *compound MCI devices* require a data file for playback, and the computer *is* involved in the process. MIDI sequencers and waveform audio players are compound device types. To play back an audio file, for instance, the samples must be decompressed and then fed to the audio card, with the appropriate timing information. Table 8.3 lists all the MCI devices that respond to the common set of commands.

TABLE 8.3   Currently Defined Device Types

DEVICE TYPE	DESCRIPTION
animation	Animation device
cdaudio	CD audio player
dat	Digital audio tape player
digitalvideo	Digital video in a window
waveaudio	Audio device that plays digitized waveform files
videodisc	Videodisc player
vcr	Videotape recorder or player
sequencer	MIDI sequencer
scanner	Image scanner
overlay	Overlay device
other	Undefined MCI device

MCI devices recognize plain, English-like commands, such as play, stop, resume, and so on. To send a command to an MCI device, you use the mciSendString() function. The mciSendString() function passes an MCI command to the MCI device, which executes the command and reports back a return code. If all went well, the return code is zero. If not, the return code is a number that indicates the error that occurred. The error code isn't very helpful. It is possible to retrieve the description of the error by passing the code to the mciGetErrorString() function. This function will return an error description such as "The command was carried out" or "The file cannot be played back on the specified MCI device."

The basic syntax of all MCI commands contains a verb, an object, and a modifier. The verb describes the action to take place, such as "play" or "stop." The object is the device on which the verb, acts. For example, to play back the file Months.wav, you issue the following MCI commands:

```
open months.wav type waveaudio alias months
play months
close months
```

This command sequence requests that the Months.wav file be opened on the waveaudio device with the alias *months*. The file is then played back and finally closed. When the file is closed, the device is free to play back another file. In the second MCI command, *play* is the verb, and *months* is the object.

The modifier (if any) determines how the waveform will be played back. For example, you can request that only a section of the sound file be played back. If you want to play back the name of the first month only, you can use the from and to modifiers:

```
play months from 0 to 1200
```

This command plays back only the first 1200 samples of the months file, which presumably correspond to the spoken word "January." The parameters from and to are the command's modifiers (they modify the default behavior of the command).

Executing MCI Commands

The MCI commands are simple to understand and use. They are actually simpler than Visual Basic's commands. But passing these commands to the MCI interface isn't quite as simple. To issue an MCI command, you use the mciSendString() function. The mciSendString() function is an API function (see Chapter 12, *The*

Windows API, for a detailed discussion). To use this function in a Visual Basic application, you first declare it as follows:

```
Declare Function mciSendStringA Lib "MMSystem" _
(ByVal mciCommand As String, ByVal returnString As String, _
ByVal returnLength As Integer, _
ByVal callBack As Integer ) As Long
```

NOTE The suffix A at the end of an API function name is a convention introduced with Win32 to differentiate between 16-bit and 32-bit functions. For more information, see the introduction in Chapter 12.

Because you can't use callback functions with Visual Basic, the last argument in the above declaration will always be zero. The *mciCommand* argument is a string that holds the MCI command (the string "play," for instance). The *returnString* argument holds a string with a response from the MCI device. Some MCI commands request information from the MCI interface, such as the characteristics of an audio file or the current track on an audio CD or an AVI file. This information is returned via the *returnString* argument. The *returnLength* argument, is the length of the *returnString* argument. The value returned by the mciSendString() function is a long integer, indicating the success of the operation (if it's zero) or the reason for its failure (if it's positive).

To use the mciSendString() function to send commands to an MCI device, follow these steps:

1. Declare the mciSendString() function.

2. Declare the argument *returnString* as String * 255.

3. Call the mciSendString() function.

    ```
    Dim errorCode As Integer
    Dim returnStr As Integer
    Dim returnCode As Integer

    errorCode = mciSendStringA("play months", returnStr, 255, 0)
    ```

You must examine the code returned by the function, which indicates the success or failure of the call. You should actually pass this value to the mciGetErrorString() function, which will translate this number to an actual error message. We will discuss the mciGetErrorString() function shortly, but let's first look at the MCI commands you can use to control the MCI devices.

VB5 at Work: The MCITest Application

As you read the following sections, you can experiment with the MCITest application, shown in Figure 8.10, which lets you type plain MCI commands, passes them to the MCI interface, and displays the string returned by the MCI interface.

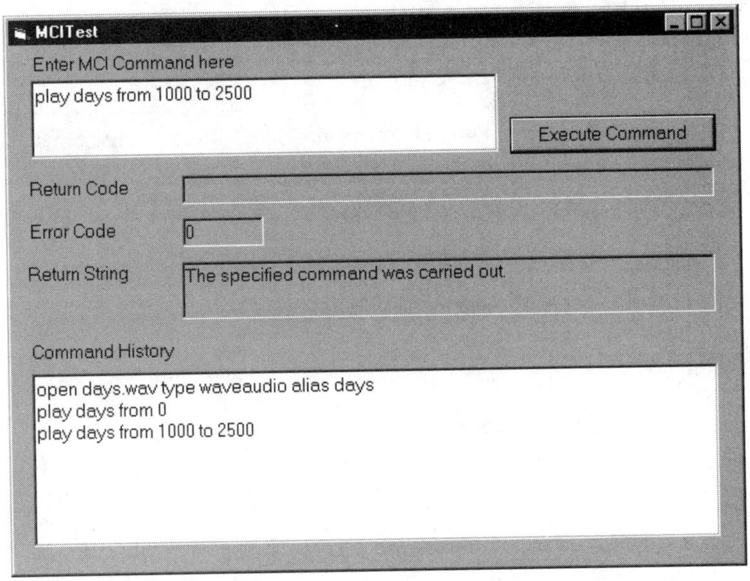

FIGURE 8.10

The MCITest application lets you issue MCI commands directly to the various MCI devices.

Enter the MCI commands you want to pass to the MCI interface in the Enter MCI Command Here text box, and then click on the Execute Command button. The MCI command is executed, and the result of the operation is displayed in the Return Code, Error Code, and Return String boxes. Error Code is the value returned by the mciSendString() function, and Return Code is the error message that corresponds to this value. Return String is the value of the mciSendString() function's *returnString* argument.

If the MCI command executed successfully, it is added in a separate line in the Command History text box at the bottom of the Form. You can select any command from the Command History text box with the mouse, copy it by pressing

Ctrl+C, and then paste it in the Enter MCI Command Here text box by pressing Ctrl+V.

Now let's look at the various MCI commands for controlling the MCI devices. Their number is small, but most accept many arguments, and their functions differ depending on the device to which they apply. The open command, for example, opens any MCI device, but it accepts different arguments, depending on whether it's used to open a MIDI file or animation device. Table 8.4 summarizes the most commonly used MCI commands.

TABLE 8.4   Commonly Used MCI Command Strings

COMMAND	DESCRIPTION
capability	Requests information about the capabilities of a device
close	Closes a device
info	Requests information about a device
open	Opens and initializes a device for use
pause	Pauses playing or recording on a device
play	Begins playing on a device
record	Begins recording on a device
resume	Resumes playing or recording on a paused device
seek	Changes the current position in the media
set	Changes control settings on the device
status	Requests information about the status of a device
stop	Stops playing or recording on a device

Opening a Device

Before you can use a device, you must initialize it by using the open command. The open command loads the driver into memory and sets a device ID for future use with other MCI commands. The amount of memory dictates the number of devices that you can have open. The open command has the following arguments:

- **alias** *alias*   An alias by which you can refer to the device.

- **shareable**   Allows applications to share a common device.

- **type** *devicename*   Identifies the MCI device name when device refers to a media element instead of to the MCI device name.

The following sample command string opens the audio CD device and sets an alias for it:

```
open cdaudio alias CD
```

The following commands may refer to this device by its alias. If you are opening a compound device, you must also specify the file that will be associated with the device:

```
open c:\vb\apps\audio\Months.wav type waveaudio alias months
```

The Months.wav file is opened as *months*, and its alias is used to refer to it in subsequent MCI commands. For example, to play back the sound file, use the following command:

```
play months
```

Retrieving Information about Devices

You can get information from an open device by using the capability, status, and info commands. For example, the following string determines if the cdaudio device can play:

```
capability cdaudio can play
```

If you pass this command string to an MCI device, it returns True if the cdaudio device can play.

The capability Command   You can use the following arguments with the capability command:

can eject	*can play*	*can record*
can reverse	*can save*	*compound device*
device type	*has audio*	*has video*
inputs	*outputs*	*uses files*
uses palettes		

To find out if an open device can play backward, for example, use the argument *can reverse*. The MCI interface's response is returned via the *returnString* argument of the mciSendString() function. If you issue the following command:

```
capability cd has video
```

with the MCITest application, the response will be False.

The info Command   You can use the following arguments with the info command:

- *input*   The device's input (for the waveaudio device, it will be Microsoft Sound Mapper)

- *output*   The device's output

- *file*   The file associated with the device (applies to compound devices only)

- *product*   The name of the hardware device that corresponds to the MCI device

The status Command   The type of status information you can receive depends on the device. Following are some common arguments for the status command:

- *channels*   Number of channels in an audio device.

- *bitspersample*   Bits per sample for a waveaudio device.

- *mode*   Returns the "not ready," "paused," "playing," "seeking," or "stopped" string, depending on the current activity of the device.

- *position*   Returns the current position in the open file. The position is reported in the current time format (see the discussion of the Set command later in this chapter).

- *ready*   Returns True if the device is ready.

- *length*   Returns the total number of frames in an animation or the total number of samples in a WAVE file.

- *window handle*   Returns the handle of the window that is used for animation playback.

The "status days position" MCI string requests the current location in the Days.wav file (which was opened with the alias days, as you can see in the history list). This location is reported in the Return Code box (see Figure 8.11).

FIGURE 8.11

If the MCI command requests information about a device, the response is displayed in the Return Code box.

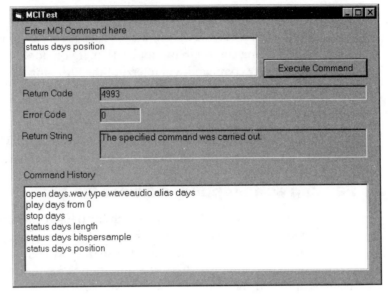

Playing a File

Once a device is open, playback can begin with the play command. If no arguments are set, the device plays until the command is stopped or until the end of the file is reached. The following command starts playback on the audio cd device:

```
play cdaudio
```

You can use three arguments with the play command:

- *from*
- *to*
- *wait*

The *from* and *to* arguments specify the starting and ending locations of the segment to be played back. The file Days.wav, for instance, contains the names of the days of the week. To play back the name of a specific day, you use the following command:

```
play days from 0 to 1000
```

485

This command plays the first 1000 milliseconds (1 second) from the beginning of the file.

When you use the *wait* argument, the MCI device waits for the playback to end before relinquishing control to the application. If you don't specify the wait argument, another play command will interrupt the file being played. The following statement:

```
play days wait
```

plays the open file with the alias days and waits until the playback is complete. The wait argument ensures that the entire sound will be heard.

Pausing and Stopping a Device

You pause playback on an MCI device with the pause command and stop playback with the stop command. To start a paused device again, you use the resume command. To start a stopped device, you use the play command. Issue the following commands with the MCITest application to see how the pause, stop, and resume commands behave:

```
play cdaudio
pause cdaudio
resume cdaudio
stop cdaudio
play cdaudio
```

Setting Device Properties

You use the set command to establish various properties of MCI devices. The form of the set command is similar to that of the capabilities command. The device name and an argument follow the name of the command. You can use the following arguments with the set command for all compound devices (some arguments may not apply to all devices):

- *audio all off*   Turns off the audio

- *audio left off*   Turns off the left audio channel

- *audio right off*   Turns off the right audio channel

- *video off*   Turns off the video playback on an animation device

- *audio all on*   Turns on both audio channels

- *audio left on*   Turns on the left audio channel

- *audio right on*   Turns on the right audio channel

- *video on*   Turns on the video playback on an animation device

- *time format*   Returns or sets the measurement unit for the file

The most important argument of the set command is the *time format* argument, which sets the measurement format of a file (if it's a compound device) or the medium (if it's a simple device). The value of the time format depends on the device. For waveaudio devices, the time format can be *milliseconds, bytes*, or *samples*. For animation devices, the time format can be either *milliseconds* or *frames*. The MCI command:

```
set months time format samples
```

sets the time format for the file Months (opened with the waveaudio device) to samples. If you use the seek command (see the following section for details about the seek command) to move the current pointer in the file, you must specify the new location samples:

```
seek months to 3000
```

Likewise, if you request the file's total length with the command:

```
status months length
```

the length is reported in samples.

Audio CD devices use the tms format, which stands for *track, minutes, seconds*. To select a tune on an audio CD, you specify the track number, as follows:

```
seek cd to 3:00:00
```

This command moves the current pointer to the beginning of the third track. To skip part of the tune, use a statement such as the following:

```
seek cd to 3:01:00
```

which positions the current pointer 60 seconds after the beginning of the third track.

Other Common Commands

Some other useful MCI commands are cue, delete, record, and seek, which give the programmer more control over the function of the various devices.

The cue Command   This command sets up a waveform device so that it can be ready to play or record with minimal delay. You can use two arguments with the cue command: *input* and *output*. The following MCI command:

```
cue waveaudio input
```

prepares the waveaudio device for recording.

The delete Command   This command deletes part of a waveform file, and you can use two arguments with it: *from* a *position* and *to* a *position*. *Position* must be expressed in the current time format. To delete the current sound, use a statement such as the following:

```
delete wave
```

in which wave is the alias of the device.

The record Command   Use this command to start recording on a device. It can take the following arguments: *insert, from, to,* or *overwrite.*

The save Command   Use this command to save a recorded file. The save command follows the record command, as shown here:

```
open waveaudio alias recwave
record recwave from 0 to 3000
save recwave c:\sounds\noise.wav
close recwave
```

Notice that the waveaudio device can be opened without a filename. In this example, you open the waveaudio device for recording with the alias *recwave*. The file is specified later, when the recorded sound is saved on disk.

The seek Command   To move to a new position in a waveform file, you use the seek command with the arguments *to, to start,* or *to end.* If the time format for the waveaudio device is milliseconds, the statements:

```
seek wave to 4000
record wave overwrite
```

skip the first four seconds in the sound and start recording, overwriting the samples that follow.

VB5 at Work: The PlayDays Application

PlayDays is a simple application that demonstrates the mciSendString() function call with the waveaudio device, which is the most common multimedia device.

The application uses the open and play commands to open and play the names of the days of the week that are stored in the Days.wav file. The MCI command that actually plays back the names is the play command with the *from* and *to* arguments. Be sure that Days.wav is in your current directory. To hear the name of a day, click on its button, as shown in Figure 8.12.

FIGURE 8.12

The PlayDays
application

The code of the application is straightforward, except for figuring out the starting and ending locations of each day's name in the Days.wav file. For this, you must use a sound-processing application that lets you select segments of the audio and play them back. To illustrate, I use CoolEdit, an excellent shareware application for processing sounds and for producing new sounds.

You can use CoolEdit, shown in Figure 8.13, to select a section of an audio file and play it back. The selected sound segment in Figure 8.13 corresponds to the word *Monday* in the file. In the lower right corner of the window, the program reports the starting and ending locations of the selected segment in milliseconds. By default, the program reports these locations in samples, but you can click on the corresponding boxes to see these values in milliseconds. (Or you can change the time format of the device to specify them in samples.)

FIGURE 8.13

Use a sound-processing application (CoolEdit is the one shown in the figure) to find out the starting and ending locations of each word in a sound file.

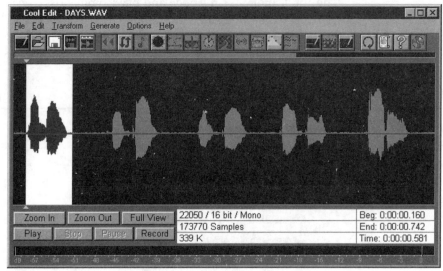

The word *Monday* starts at 160 milliseconds and ends at 750 milliseconds approximately. The MCI command to play back the word *Monday* is as follows:

```
play days.wav from 150 to 750
```

You can easily spot the remaining words in the file and extract their starting and ending locations. Then, use these values with the *from* and *to* parameters of the play command.

Code 8.8: The PlayDays Application

```
Option Explicit

    Private Declare Function mciSendStringA Lib "WinMM" _
        (ByVal mciCommand As String, ByVal returnStr As String, _
        ByVal returnLength As Integer, ByVal callBack As Integer) As
        ➥Long
```

```
Private Sub Play_Click(Index As Integer)
    Dim errorCode As Integer
    Dim returnStr As Integer
    Dim cmd As String * 255

    cmd = "open " & App.Path & "\days.wav type waveaudio alias days"
    errorCode = mciSendStringA(cmd, returnStr, 255, 0)

    If Index = 0 Then errorCode = mciSendStringA("play days from 150
    ➥to 850 wait", returnStr, 255, 0)
    If Index = 1 Then errorCode = mciSendStringA("play days from
    ➥1200 to 1900 wait", returnStr, 255, 0)
    If Index = 2 Then errorCode = mciSendStringA("play days from
    ➥2200 to 2900 wait", returnStr, 255, 0)
    If Index = 3 Then errorCode = mciSendStringA("play days from
    ➥3100 to 4000 wait", returnStr, 255, 0)
    If Index = 4 Then errorCode = mciSendStringA("play days from
    ➥4300 to 4900 wait", returnStr, 255, 0)
    If Index = 5 Then errorCode = mciSendStringA("play days from
    ➥5100 to 5800 wait", returnStr, 255, 0)
    If Index = 6 Then errorCode = mciSendStringA("play days from
    ➥6100 to 6800 wait", returnStr, 255, 0)

End Sub
```

The mciGetErrorString() Function   If you run the PlayDays application and hear no sound, you won't be able to easily locate the mistake. It could be that you don't have a waveaudio device installed or that the waveaudio device didn't find the audio file or something else. The mciSendString() function returns a code that indicates if the function completed successfully. If no error occurred, the function returns a code of 0. If an error did occur, you can use the mciGetError-String() function to get information about the error code. The mciGetErrorString() function accepts the value returned by the mciSendString() function and returns a string that describes the error in English.

You can declare the 32-bit version of the function as follows:

```
Declare Function mciGetErrorStringA Lib "winmm" _ (ByVal errorCode
➥As Long, ByVal errorString As String, _ ByVal returnLength As
➥Integer) As Integer
```

The *errorCode argument* is the value returned by mciSendString(), *errorString* contains the error message on return, and *returnLength* is the length of the *errorString* variable.

Usually, you call the mciSendString() function to send a command to the MCI interface and then examine the return value with the mciGetErrorString() function, as shown here:

```
Dim returnStr, errorStr As String * 255
errorCode = mciSendStringA("play audio", returnStr, 255, 0)
returnCode = mciGetErrorStringA(errorCode, errorStr, 255)
MsgBox errorStr
```

VB5 at Work: The MCITest Application

Now, let's look at the code of the MCITest application (see Figures 8.10 and 8.11, earlier in this chapter), which is quite straightforward. Each time the user clicks on the Execute Command button, the program reads the MCI command from the text box, sends it to the MCI interface with the mciSendString() function, and displays the function's return code, the string that corresponds to the return code, and the return string. If the MCI command executed successfully (the error code returned by the mciSendString() function was zero), the MCI command is added to the Command History box.

The Command History is maintained in a TextBox control, and, as mentioned earlier, you can copy any command from it and paste it in the Enter MCI Command Here box. Moreover, you can edit the contents of the Command History box. You can change the order of the commands and delete commands, but you shouldn't edit their arguments. You can use the MCITest application to generate a sequence of MCI commands to carry out a task, determine the correct sequence of MCI commands and their arguments, and copy them into your application.

Code 8.9: The Execute Command Button

```
Private Sub Command1_Click()

    errorCode = mciSendStringA(MCIcommand.Text, returnStr, 255, 0)
    ➡MCIerror.Caption = errorCode
    returnCode = mciGetErrorStringA(errorCode, errorStr, 255)
    MCIcode.Caption = returnStr
    MCIstr.Caption = errorStr
```

```
If errorCode = 0 Then History.Text = History.Text & MCIcommand.Text
➡& Chr$(13) & Chr$(10)
```

End Sub

The *MCIerror, MCIcode,* and *MCIstr* entries are the names of the Label controls, in which the corresponding return codes and messages are displayed. In the Form's declaration section, the usual MCI functions are declared:

```
Private Declare Function mciSendStringA Lib "WinMM" (ByVal
➡MCIcommand As String, ByVal returnStr As String, ByVal
➡returnLength As Integer, ByVal callBack As Integer) As Long

Private Declare Function mciGetErrorStringA Lib "WinMM" (ByVal
➡error As Long, ByVal buffer As String, ByVal length As Integer) As
➡Integer
```

The mciSendCommand0 Function

The MCI command message interface gives you lower-level access to multimedia devices than the command string interface does. However, it is also more difficult to use than the command string interface. Windows does not need to parse the command strings into command messages. By providing the messages directly, Windows can speed up the time required to process the commands.

To pass a message directly to an MCI device, use the mciSendCommand() function as follows:

```
Declare Function mciSendCommandA Lib "WinMM" (ByVal deviceID As
➡Integer, ByVal message As Integer, ByVal param1 As Long, param2 As
➡Any ) As Long
```

The *deviceID* argument is an integer that specifies the device ID, and *message* is another integer that specifies the command to be carried out. The *param1* argument is a Long value that contains the various arguments, and *param2* is a data structure that contains the information needed by the command. If the command requests information about the device, the information is reported back via the *param2* data structure.

Table 8.5 lists the basic MCI command messages, which are the same as the MCI commands but have different names. See the Win32 Software Development Kit for the specific structure that needs to be passed with each command.

TABLE 8.5 The Basic MCI Command Messages

COMMAND	DESCRIPTION
MCI_CLOSE	Closes the device
MCI_OPEN	Initializes the device
MCI_PLAY	Starts transferring data to device
MCI_PAUSE	Pauses playing
MCI_STOP	Stops playing or recording
MCI_GETDEVCAPS	Obtains the capabilities of a device
MCI_INFO	Obtains information from a device
MCI_STATUS	Obtains status information from a device
MCI_LOAD	Loads data from a file
MCI_RECORD	Starts recording
MCI_RESUME	Resumes playing on a paused device
MCI_SAVE	Saves data to a file
MCI_SEEK	Seeks forward or backward
MCI_SET	Sets the operating state of a device

VB5 at Work: The PlayWave Application

The PlayWave application demonstrates how to set up the data structures and call the mciSendCommand() function to play a WAVE file. The application contains a Command button that calls the PlayWave() subroutine:

```
Private Sub Sound_Click()

  PlayWave App.Path & "\howareu.wav"

End Sub
```

You may have to adjust the path name of the sound file.

The PlayWave() subroutine initializes the data structures needed for calling the mciSendCommand() function. Let's start with the declarations, constant definition, and data types.

Code 8.10: The mciSendCommand Function and Its Data Types

```
Private Declare Function mciSendCommandA Lib "WinMM" _
    (ByVal wDeviceID As Long, ByVal Message As Long, _
    ByVal dwParam1 As Long, dwParam2 As Any) As Long

  Const MCI_OPEN = &H803
  Const MCI_CLOSE = &H804
  Const MCI_PLAY = &H806
  Const MCI_OPEN_TYPE = &H2000&
  Const MCI_OPEN_ELEMENT = &H200&
  Const MCI_WAIT = &H2&

  Private Type MCI_WAVE_OPEN_PARMS
    dwCallback As Long
    wDeviceID As Long
    lpstrDeviceType As String
    lpstrElementName As String
    lpstrAlias As String
    dwBufferSeconds As Long
  End Type

  Private Type MCI_PLAY_PARMS
    dwCallback As Long
    dwFrom As Long
    dwTo As Long
  End Type
```

Finally, here's the code of the PlayWave() subroutine, which initializes the data structures and calls the MCISendCommand() function.

Code 8.11: The PlayWave() Subroutine

```
Sub PlayWave(WaveFile As String)

  Dim errorCode As Integer
  Dim returnStr As Integer
  Dim errorStr As String * 256
  Dim MCIWaveOpenParms As MCI_WAVE_OPEN_PARMS
  Dim MCIPlayParms As MCI_PLAY_PARMS
```

```
MCIWaveOpenParms.dwCallback = 0
MCIWaveOpenParms.wDeviceID = 0

MCIWaveOpenParms.lpstrDeviceType = "waveaudio"
MCIWaveOpenParms.lpstrElementName = WaveFile

MCIWaveOpenParms.lpstrAlias = 0
MCIWaveOpenParms.dwBufferSeconds = 0
' Open the device
errorCode = mciSendCommandA(0, MCI_OPEN, MCI_OPEN_TYPE Or
➥MCI_OPEN_ELEMENT, MCIWaveOpenParms)

If errorCode = 0 Then
  MCIPlayParms.dwCallback = 0
  MCIPlayParms.dwFrom = 0
  MCIPlayParms.dwTo = 0
' Play the wave file
  errorCode = mciSendCommandA(MCIWaveOpenParms.wDeviceID, MCI_PLAY,
  ➥MCI_WAIT, MCIPlayParms)
' and close the device
  errorCode = mciSendCommandA(MCIWaveOpenParms.wDeviceID,
  ➥MCI_CLOSE, 0, 0)
End If
End Sub
```

The mciSendCommand() function has four parameters as discussed above. The default waveaudio device's ID is 0. The MCI_OPEN_TYPE specifies a device type name that is defined in the *lpstrDeviceType* member of the MCI_WAVE_OPEN_PARMS structure. The MCI_PLAY_PARMS structure contains the information required for the file's playback. This structure only indicates the position to play from and the position to play to. The device id, *wDeviceID*, in the MCI_WAVE_OPEN_PARMS structure is used for the first parameter. To close the device, you use the MCI_CLOSE command again with the same *wDeviceID*.

More API Sound Functions

The mciSendString() and mciSendCommand() API functions are the two most important functions for playing audio files. There are, however, three more API functions for manipulating sounds: MessageBeep(), sndPlaySound(), and PlaySound().

MessageBeep() You use the MessageBeep function to play a sound associated with one of Windows' alert events:

- Asterisk

- Critical Stop

- Default Beep

- Question

- Exclamation

- Windows Exit

- Windows Start

You can assign any sound stored in your system to these events through the Sounds program in the Control Panel. If you double-click on the Sounds icon in the Control Panel, you will see the window shown in Figure 8.14.

FIGURE 8.14

The Sounds Properties window

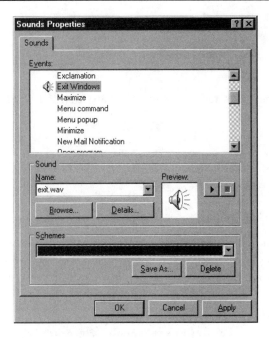

The syntax of the PlayBeep() function is as follows:

```
Private Declare Function MessageBeep Lib "User32" (ByVal alertLevel
➥As Integer) As Integer
```

The *alertLevel* argument is an integer that identifies an alert level.

The PlayBeep application, shown in Figure 8.15, shows you how to play a few of the sounds assigned to the Windows standard events.

FIGURE 8.15

The PlayBeep
application

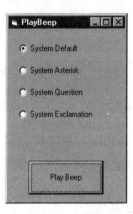

The events demonstrated in this example are identified by the following constants:

- MB_OK

- MB_ICONQUESTION

- MB_ICONEXCLAMATION

- MB_ICONASTERISK

You use one of these constants as the argument for MessageBeep(). The sample program shows you how to declare the function and set up the constants. The function returns a non-zero value if successful; otherwise, it returns zero.

Code 8.12: The PlayBeep Application

```
Private Declare Function MessageBeep Lib "User32" (ByVal alertLevel
➥As Integer) As Integer
```

```
Const MB_OK = 0
Const MB_ICONQUESTION = &H30
Const MB_ICONASTERISK = &H40
Const MB_ICONEXCLAMATION = &H20

Private Sub Play_Click()

  If SndOption(0) = -1 Then MessageBeep (MB_OK)
  If SndOption(1) = -1 Then MessageBeep (MB_ICONASTERISK)
  If SndOption(2) = -1 Then MessageBeep (MB_ICONQUESTION)
  If SndOption(3) = -1 Then MessageBeep (MB_ICONEXCLAMATION)

End Sub
```

sndPlaySound()   The sndPlaySound() function can play any waveform file. Its syntax is as follows:

```
Function sndPlaySound(ByVal nameString As String, ByVal flags As
➥Integer) As Integer
```

This function takes two arguments: (1) the name of the WAVE file to be played (*nameString*), and (2) a list of options, which can be a combination of the constants listed in Table 8.6.

TABLE 8.6   The Flags of the sndPlaySound() Function

FLAG	DESCRIPTION
SND_ASYNC	The sound plays asynchronously, which means the function returns immediately. If this parameter is not specified, the function starts the playback and returns control to the calling program. The sound continues playing.
SND_LOOP	The sound plays repeatedly. To stop the playback, call sndPlaySound() without a filename and with the SND_ASYNC and SND_LOOP parameters.
SND_SYNC	The sound plays synchronously, which means that the function returns control to the calling program only after the sound is finished playing.
SND_MEMORY	Specifies that the waveform sound is in memory (it can be placed there with other API functions).
SND_NOSTOP	Indicates that the function does not play the sound it is already playing.
SND_NODEFAULT	If the sound is not found, the function returns and does not play the default Windows sound.

To declare the function and the constants that correspond to its flags argument, include the following lines in your application:

```
Option Explicit

Private Declare Function sndPlaySoundA Lib "WinMM" _ (ByVal
➥nameString As String, ByVal flags As Integer) As Integer

Const SND_ASYNC = &H1
Const SND_LOOP = &H8
Const SND_MEMORY = &H4
Const SND_NODEFAULT = &H2
Const SND_NOSTOP = &H10
Const SND_SYNC = &H0
```

To play a WAVE file, call the function with the file's name and the appropriate flags combination:

```
Dim errorCode As Integer

errorCode = sndPlaySoundA("hello.wav", SND_SYNC Or SND_NODEFAULT)
```

PlaySound()   The PlaySound() function is similar to sndPlaySound(). In addition to the SND_ASYNC, SND_SYNC, and SND_NODEFAULT flags, this function provides the additional flags that are described in Table 8.7.

TABLE 8.7   The Additional Flags of the PlaySound() Function

FLAG	DESCRIPTION
SND_ALIAS	The sound name is in the system registry.
SND_RESOURCE	The sound name is a resource name.
SND_FILENAME	The sound name is the filename of a WAVE file.
SND_NOWAIT	If the device is busy, the function should fail.

To use the sndPlay() function, type the following declaration and define its flags as constants:

```
' Function declaration
Private Declare Function PlaySound Lib "WinMM" _ (ByVal
➥nameString As String, ByVal handle As Integer, _ ByVal flags As
➥Integer) As Integer
```

```
' Constant declaration
  Const SND_ALIAS = &H10000
  Const SND_FILENAME = &H20000
  Const SND_RESOURCE = &H40004
  Const SND_NOWAIT = &H2000
  Const SND_SYNC = &H0
  Const SND_NODEFAULT = &H2

  errorCode = PlaySound("hello.wav", 0, SND_SYNC)

  If errorCode <> 0 Then
    {process error}
  End If
```

Adding Voice Messages to Applications

A great way to enhance all types of applications with multimedia elements is to add audio messages. Windows provides the Sounds utility, with which you can associate sounds and system events. You can easily add voice and other audio messages to your applications. The messages can be simple greetings, dates, or number readouts.

The first example, the ReadNums application, is a number-reading utility that can be used as a proofing tool. For example, you can design a program that reads out long sequences of numbers such as the contents of a spreadsheet. The second example, the ReadDate application, is a utility that reads out the current date.

VB5 at Work: The ReadNumb Application

In this example, we again use the mciSendString() function to play back individual words within a single WAVE file. We use the *from* and *to* parameters of the play MCI command to play selected portions of the sound file. The example prompts the user to enter numbers with the InputBox() function and then reads out the number. You can easily modify the application to accept input from a grid, a text file, or any other source.

The ReadNums application (see Figure 8.16) uses the Numbers.wav file, which contains the basic sounds needed to read out any number (the numbers 1 through 20, 30, 40, and so on up to 90, and the sounds hundred and thousand). The application can handle positive numbers up to 9,999, but you can easily modify the code to handle negative numbers, as well as numbers outside this range.

FIGURE 8.16

The ReadNums applica-
tion reads out user-
supplied numbers.

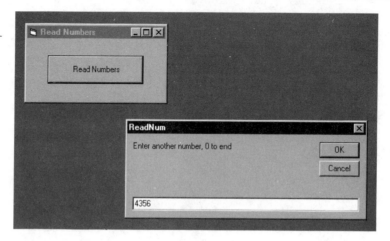

The application's complete code is given next. The comments along with the
code will help you understand how the program works, although it's fairly
straightforward. First, it reads the thousands as if they were single numbers and
then the word *thousand*. It then reads the hundreds followed by the word *hundred*,
and finally it reads the rest of the numbers, which are smaller than 100.

Code 8.13: The ReadNums Application

```
'This is the routine to read numbers
Private Sub ReadNum(number)

  Dim errorCode As Integer
  Dim returnStr As Integer
  Dim returnCode As Integer
  Dim errorStr As String * 256
  Dim tenth As Integer
  Dim leftover As Integer
  Dim hundred As Integer
  Dim thousand As Integer

  If number < 20 Then      'Reads unique numbers
    ReadSingle (number)
  ElseIf number < 100 Then  'Reads numbers less than 100
    tenth = number / 10
    ReadTenths (tenth * 10)
    leftover = number - (tenth * 10)
```

```
      If leftover > 0 Then
        ReadSingle (leftover)
      End If
  ElseIf number < 1000 Then  'Reads numbers between 100 and 999

      hundred = number / 100
      ReadSingle (hundred)
      errorCode = mciSendStringA("play numbers.wav from 28000 to
    ➥29000 wait", returnStr, 255, 0)

      leftover = number - (hundred * 100)
      If leftover > 0 Then
        tenth = leftover / 10
        If tenth > 0 Then ReadTenths (tenth * 10)
        leftover = number - (hundred * 100) - (tenth * 10)
        If leftover > 0 Then
          ReadSingle (leftover)
        End If
      End If
  Else              'Reads number between 1000 and 9999
      thousand = number / 1000
      ReadSingle (thousand)
      errorCode = mciSendStringA("play numbers.wav from 29000 to
    ➥30500 wait", returnStr, 255, 0)
      leftover = number - (thousand * 1000)

      If leftover > 0 Then
        hundred = leftover / 100
        If hundred > 0 Then
          ReadSingle (hundred)
          errorCode = mciSendStringA("play numbers.wav from 28000 to
          ➥29000 wait", returnStr, 255, 0)
        End If

        leftover = number - (thousand * 1000) - (hundred * 100)
        If leftover > 0 Then
          tenth = leftover / 10
          If tenth > 0 Then ReadTenths (tenth * 10)
          leftover = number - (hundred * 100) - (tenth * 10)
          If leftover > 0 Then
            ReadSingle (leftover)
          End If
        End If
      End If
  End If
```

```
      End If

   End Sub
```

The ReadSingle() module reads numbers 1 through 19. The ReadTenths() procedure reads the numbers 20, 30, 40, 50, 60, 70, 80, and 90.

The ReadDate application, which you can find in this chapter's folder on the CD, is quite similar. It uses the words in the files Days.wav, Months.wav, and Years.wav to read out dates. You can open the project in Visual Basic's editor and examine it. We will use the procedures of these applications in Chapter 15, *Visual Basic and the Web*, to build an ActiveX control that reads out numbers and dates.

Enhancing Applications with Video

To really extend your application to another level, you can add digitized video and animation. Digitizing video is fairly straightforward, but it requires a video capture board. Animation can be produced with the appropriate software on a PC. Whether you digitize video or produce animation with software, the result is usually an AVI (Audio-Video Interleaved) file, which can be played back with the ActiveX Movie control on any Windows 95 system.

Several types of digital video formats are on the market today. The native format for the Windows operating system is Microsoft's Video for Windows. The other formats include Apple Computer's QuickTime for Windows and MPEG.

Video can be stored in 8-bit, 16-bit, and 24-bit format. As you might expect, storing video in 24-bit format is not practical since the image can be large. Video is also stored at a certain frame size; currently, the standard frame size is 320 × 240, or quarter-screen. The only limitations are the playback rate and available disk space.

We normally view movies and television at 30 frames a second, which is full-motion video. Playback at 15 frames a second, however, is sufficient for computer applications. Playback at higher rates requires special, and expensive, hardware.

Using Video for Windows

To solve the problems of playing video from Windows, Microsoft invented the Video for Windows format, which was introduced in Windows 3.1. Now

Windows 95 ships with a 32-bit version that allows for the playback of 320×240 video. Video for Windows can play back AVI files without hardware support. If you purchase a video capture card, you will get VidCap and VidEdit, two utilities for capturing and editing video. The package allows for playing back, capturing, and editing video.

The AVI format of Video for Windows means that audio and video information is interleaved on the track of the CD-ROM, which enables playback of synchronized sound and video.

To sustain an acceptable frame rate, Video for Windows must compress the digitized video a great deal. Windows 95 comes with several video compression schemes. To see the available compression schemes, follow these steps:

1. Choose Start ➤ Settings ➤ Control Panel.

2. Double-click on Multimedia, and then select the Advanced tab.

3. Double-click on the Video Compression Codecs folder. Windows displays the Multimedia Properties window shown in Figure 8.17.

The video codecs include Cinepak, Indeo, Video 1, and RLE.

FIGURE 8.17

The video compression codecs for Windows 95

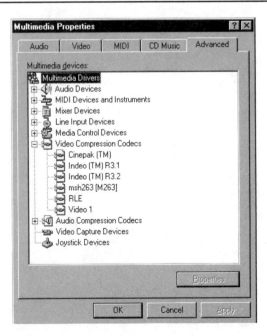

Using MPEG

MPEG (Motion Picture Experts Group) video is now possible on the PC and is already being used by professionals. MPEG is the most efficient codec for video compression and will probably emerge as the new standard for video compression. Until recently, MPEG compressed video couldn't be played back without the aid of dedicated hardware. The speed of the Pentium processor and the Windows built-in support for MPEG software-only playback will lead to the replacement of AVI by the MPEG standard. MPEG playback cards are fairly inexpensive, but they are still required for anything more than stamp-size, jerky video playback. The problem with MPEG is that capturing video in this format requires expensive hardware, which isn't found on most PCs. When software-only MPEG playback becomes available, new possibilities for high-quality multimedia presentations will emerge, and MPEG recording prices will drop significantly.

CHAPTER
NINE

9

The Multiple Document Interface

- Built-in MDI capabilities

- Parent and child Forms

- The Window menu

- The Arrange property

- Objects and instances

- The QueryUnload event

The Multiple Document Interface (MDI) was designed to simplify the exchange of information among documents, all under the same roof. With an MDI application, you can maintain multiple open windows, but not multiple copies of the application. Data exchange is easier when you can view and compare many documents simultaneously.

You almost certainly use Windows applications that can open multiple documents at the same time and allow the user to switch among them with a mouse click. Microsoft Word is a typical example, although most people use it in Single Document Mode (SDI). Each document is displayed in its own window, and all document windows have the same behavior. The main form, or MDI Form, is not duplicated, but it acts as a container for all other windows, and it's called the *parent window*. The windows in which the individual documents are displayed are called *child windows* (or document windows). When you reposition the parent window on the desktop, its child windows follow. Child windows, however, exist independently of the parent window. You can open and close child windows as you want, and child windows can even have different functions. For example, you can open a few text windows and a few graphics windows next to one another, although this is rare.

Figure 9.1 shows Word in MDI mode. The application's main window contains five documents, three of them in custom size windows and two of them minimized. The menus and the toolbars of the parent window apply to all the child windows. In reality, the menu bar of the MDI Form contains the menu of the active child Form.

Paint Shop Pro is a popular MDI application (see Figure 9.2), and most mail applications display each message in a separate window and allow the user to open multiple messages. Most of the popular text editors (NotePad excluded) are MDI applications too.

MDI Applications: The Basics

An MDI application must have at least two Forms, the *parent* Form and one or more *child* Forms. Each of these Forms has certain properties. There can be many child Forms, which are contained within the parent Form, but there can be only one parent Form.

FIGURE 9.1

Using Word in
MDI mode

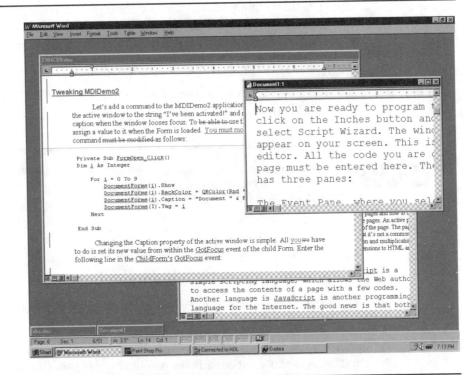

FIGURE 9.2

PaintShop Pro, one of the
most popular shareware
applications, uses the
MDI user interface.

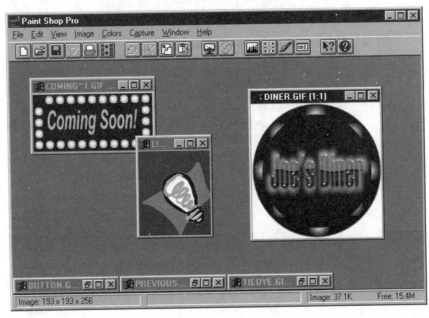

The parent Form may not contain any controls. While the parent Form is open in design mode, the icons on the Toolbox aren't disabled, but you can't place any control on the Form. The parent Form can, and usually does, have its own menu.

To create an MDI application, follow these steps:

1. Start a new project, and then choose Project ➤ Add MDI Form to add the parent Form.

NOTE   After you add an MDI Form to your application, the Add MDI Form command in the Project menu is disabled. The reason: You can't have a second MDI Form in the same application.

2. Set the Form's caption to MDI Window.

3. Choose Project ➤ Add Form to add a regular Form.

4. Make this Form the child Form by setting its MDIChild property to True. To denote that this is a child Form, set its Caption property to MDI Child Form.

Visual Basic automatically associates this new Form with the parent Form. This child Form cannot exist outside the parent Form; in other words, it will only be opened within the parent Form.

MDI Built-in Capabilities

You just created an MDI application. It doesn't do much, but if you run the project now, you will see two Forms, one inside the other, as shown in Figure 9.3. Simply make Form1 the application's startup Form. (Open the project's Properties window, and set Form1 as the Startup Object. If the Startup Object is the MDI Form, the child window won't be displayed by default, and you must load it from within the application code.) The child Form is contained entirely within the parent Form and exists only in the context of its parent Form. If you close or minimize the parent Form, the child Form is also closed or minimized.

Use the mouse to move the child Form around and change its size. If you click on the child Form's Maximize button, the two Forms are combined into one, as shown in Figure 9.4.

FIGURE 9.3

The framework of an MDI application with a single child Form

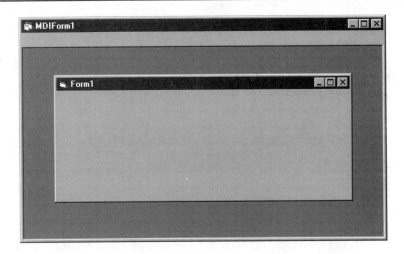

FIGURE 9.4

The MDI application shown in Figure 9.3, after the child window was maximized

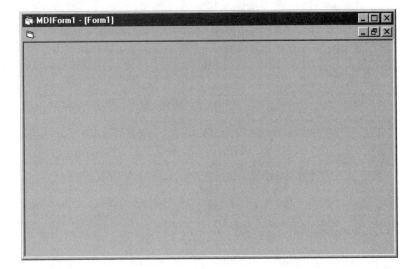

Notice that the window's caption is now the parent Form's caption, followed by the caption of the child Form. You can also move the child Form outside the parent Form, in which case the appropriate scroll bars are attached to the parent Form. In addition, both the child window and the MDI Form have a Control menu (which you can open by clicking on the icon in the upper left corner) and their own Minimize, Normal, and Close buttons (in the upper right corner).

NOTE

Later in this chapter, when you start to create MDI applications, you'll learn that naming parent and child windows is important to maintaining the Windows GUI guidelines. The most important rule for parent and child windows is that the parent Form's caption is usually the name of the application; the captions of the child Forms are the names of the documents in each one of them.

Clicking on the child Form's Minimize button reduces the child Form to an icon, but always within the parent Form. You will never see a child Form's icon on the Desktop's status bar. To restore the minimized Form to its original size, double-click on the icon. A child window is usually minimized instead of being closed to make room for other documents. In short, the child Form behaves like a regular Form on the Desktop, only its desktop is the parent window.

I have just demonstrated the basic operations of an MDI application without writing a single line of code. These capabilities are built into the language and are available to your applications through the settings of certain properties.

To see how useful and powerful MDI applications can be, let's add a second child Form to the application and throw in a few commands. Follow these steps:

1. Add one more Form to the project and make it an MDI child Form by setting its MDIChild property to True.

2. Set the Form's Caption property to MDI Child 2.

If you run the application now, you won't see the second child Form. This makes perfect sense because you must be able to open and close child Forms under program control.

3. To display the second From, you need to add the following line behind a menu command or in the MDI Form's Load event so that both Forms display when the MDI Form is loaded:

```
Form2.Show
```

In a later example, you'll see how to design menus for MDI applications with commands for opening and closing child Forms.

If you run this small MDI program now, its main window will look much more like an MDI application, thanks to its two child Forms. You can add more child Forms and open them when the MDI Form is loaded with the Show method.

Parent and Child Menus

MDI Forms can contain no objects other than child Forms, but MDI Forms do have their own menus. There's also a peculiarity about the MDI menus, because most of the operations of the application have meaning only if there is at least one child Form open. The MDI Form usually has a menu with a couple of commands for loading a new child Form and quitting the application. The child Form can have any number of commands in its menu, depending on the application. When the child Form is loaded, the child Form's menu replaces the original menu on the MDI Form. To see this in action, design an MDI Form with a simple menu.

VB5 at Work: The MDIDemo1 Form

Start a new project, add an MDI Form, and design a menu that has the following structure:

- **MDIMenu**   Menu caption
  - **MDIOpen**   Opens a new child Form
  - **MDIExit**   Terminates the application

Then design the following menu for the child Form:

- **ChildMenu**   Menu caption
  - **Child Open**   Opens a new child Form
  - **Child Save**   Saves the document in the active child Form
  - **Child Close**   Closes the active child Form

You don't need to add any code to the previous menus at this point. If you run this application now (it's the MDIDemo1 application on the CD), you will see the child Form's menu on the MDI Form's menu bar (see Figure 9.5). If you close the child Form, however, the original menu of the MDI Form will replace the child Form's menu. The reason for this behavior should be obvious. The operations available through the MDI Form are quite different from the operations of the child windows. Moreover, each child Form shouldn't have its own menu.

FIGURE 9.5

When a child Form is loaded, its menu becomes the application's menu.

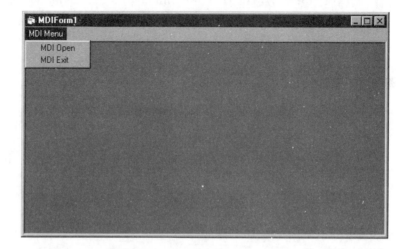

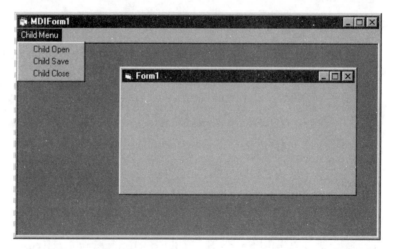

A different menu on the container (the MDI Form) and a different menu on the individual child Forms would confuse the user. You should be aware of this idiosyncrasy when designing menus for MDI applications. The common practice is to attach a limited menu to the MDI Form, which is repeated in the child Form's menu. You will see an example of MDI menu design in the section "MDIEditor" later in this chapter.

The Window Menu   A few more features are built into MDI Forms. These features are not available through properties, but with a minimum of coding you can include them in your programs. As you already know, all MDI applications in the Windows environment have a submenu called Window that contains two groups of commands, as shown in Figure 9.6.

FIGURE 9.6

Visual Basic maintains the Window submenu.

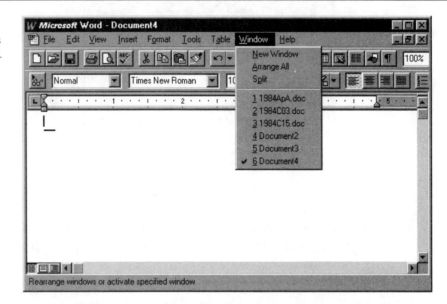

The first group of commands positions the child windows on the MDI Form, and the second group consists of the captions of the open child windows. With the commands on this menu, you can change the arrangement of the open windows (or the icons of the minimized windows) and activate any child window.

Let's begin with the list of windows, which is maintained by the MDI Form. Follow these steps:

1.   Select a child Form in the Project window and design a menu for this window.

2.   Add a single command named Window.

3.   Check the WindowList checkbox in the Menu Editor, as shown in Figure 9.7.

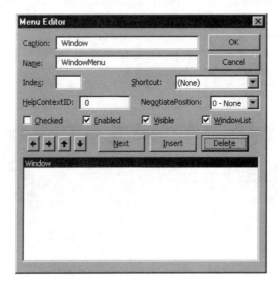

FIGURE 9.7

The Window menu
shown in Figure 9.6 is
implemented with a
single command in the
Menu Editor

You have just told the MDI application to maintain a list of all child windows
that appear on the Form and display their names in the Window menu. The active
child window is denoted with a checkmark next to its entry in the menu. Even the
separator between the two groups of commands is placed there automatically.

> **WARNING**
>
> You can add the Window menu to the MDI Form, but only if the child windows don't have their own menus. If the child windows have a menu, this menu takes over the MDI Form's menu when the child Form is loaded.

The Arrange Property   The commands for the arrangement of the windows
on the MDI Form require a bit of programming. Windows offers three ways for
arranging the windows on an MDI Form. You can cascade them, tile them vertically, or tile them horizontally. Of course, the user can resize and move the windows around, and the automatic placement comes in handy when the MDI Form
becomes messy and the user can no longer easily locate the desired window. The
placement of the child windows on the Form is controlled with the Arrange property, which can take one of the values shown in Table 9.1.

TABLE 9.1   The Values of the MDI Form's Arrange Property

CONSTANT	VALUE	DESCRIPTION
vbCascade	0	Cascades all child Forms
vbTileHorizontal	1	Tiles all child Forms horizontally
vbTileVertical	2	Tiles all child Forms vertically
vbArrangeIcons	3	Arranges the icons for minimized child Forms at the bottom of the MDI Form

The Arrange property isn't available at design time and is usually set by the commands in the Window menu. The first three values in Table 9.1 concern the arrangement of the windows when they are in normal state; the last value concerns the arrangement of the icons of minimized windows. As the user minimizes and maximizes the windows, it is possible for the icons to end up in the four corners of the MDI Form, some of them even outside the Form's visible area.

When the Arrange property is set to 3, the icons are placed next to one another in the lower left corner of the MDI Form. This property acts as a method in the sense that it causes an action when it's set. To see how the Arrange property works, design a menu as shown in Figure 9.6. Don't do anything about the list of child windows; just check the WindowList checkbox in the Menu Edit window. The code behind each one of the first four commands doesn't do anything more than set the MDI Form's Arrange property. The code for the Cascade command, for example, follows.

Code 9.1: The Cascade Command

```
Private Sub WindowCascade_Click()

  MDIForm1.Arrange vbCascade

End Sub
```

The subroutines for the remaining commands are similar. Run the application, and check out all the features that are already built in to the MDI Form (or open the MDIDemo2 application from the CD). Move the child windows around, minimize and maximize them, arrange the windows and their icons on the MDI Form, and switch from one to the other with the help of the Window menu's commands.

With just a few lines of code, you can create a good deal of functionality. By the way, the name of this menu need not be Window (any menu name will do). This is the name used by all Windows applications, however, and you'd better stick with it.

You have probably noticed a problem with this approach. Do you have to design a separate child Form for each document you need to display on the MDI Form? And, even worse, do you have to refer to each child window with a different name? It would be so much easier if you could declare an array of child Forms and access them with an index. Actually, this is the way child Forms are handled, and this is the next topic to explore.

Objects and Instances

A fundamental concept in the design of MDI applications is that of an object and its instances. All the controls you use in building an application's user interface are control objects. Forms are objects too, and they are called Form objects. Visual Basic is an object-oriented language, and most of the development consists of manipulating the values of objects or invoking the methods of the various objects to perform certain tasks. An *object* is the instance of a control or a Form. It is actually possible to create new objects and delete existing ones at run time, from within your code.

To help you handle objects from within your code, Visual Basic allows the declaration of variables that represent objects. These variables are called *object variables*, and they allow you to manipulate objects (create new instances or delete existing instances) just as you would manipulate any other type of variable. For example, you can design a single Form object and create multiple instances of this Form from within your code. You can even declare an array of object variables and manipulate them through the application.

The Form you design is the prototype. An instance of a Form is a copy that inherits all the properties of the original but that exists in your application independently of the original. On an MDI Form, all child Forms are usually instances of one basic Form. They have the same behavior, but the operation of each one doesn't affect the others. When a child Form is loaded, for example, it will have the same background color as its prototype (but you can change it from within your code by setting its BackColor property). The most common approach in designing MDI applications is to design a single child Form, which will be used as the prototype for as many child Forms as you want to place on the MDI form. Here's how it's done.

An MDI Form can contain a number of child Forms, and you could start by designing each one of them. The first one might be called DocumentForm1, the second, DocumentForm2, and so on. Unfortunately, this setup requires much programming effort to handle individual Forms, compared with an array of Forms, with a structure such as DocumentForm(). As with control arrays (discussed in Chapter 2, *Visual Basic Projects*), you need design only the first element of the array. With this index structure, each child Form can be accessed by an index. The maintenance of the child Forms is simplified. The application in Figure 9.8 shows an MDI Form with three child Forms, all members of the DocumentForms() array.

To create a Form that can be used as a prototype, follow these steps:

1. Start a new project, add an MDI Form, as usual, and set its Caption to MDI Example.

2. Add a new Form to the project, and set its MDIChild property to True.

3. Set other properties of the child Form (such as its background color) and even add a few controls.

When you're done, you can use this Form as a prototype and declare an array of child Forms, with a statement such as the following:

```
Global DocumentForms(9) As New ChildForm
```

FIGURE 9.8

The child windows of this application were not designed separately. They are elements of an array of Forms.

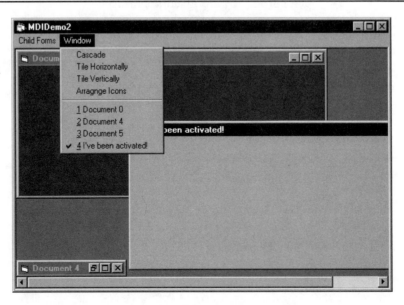

ChildForm is the name of the child Form. This declaration must appear in a module or be a form-wide declaration. Each element of the *DocumentForms()* array is a child Form's name.

To change the Caption property of the third child Form, use the following statement:

```
DocumentForms(2).Caption = "Document #3"
```

The name of the *DocumentForm()* array followed by an index value is equivalent to the name of the child Form.

The keyword New tells Visual Basic to create 10 new instances of the Form ChildForm. The one you designed doesn't exist until it's loaded. The ChildForm Form you see in the Project window is just the prototype. The next example illustrates the difference between the ChildForm Form and the array of child Forms.

Loading and Unloading Child Forms

Let's design a menu that will load and unload the child Forms. This section's application is called MDIDemo2, and you will find it in this chapter's folder on the CD. This menu, shown in Figure 9.8, earlier in this chapter, has two commands on the first level, Child Forms and Window. The Window menu is identical to that in Figure 9.8. The Forms command leads to a submenu with two commands:

- **Open Forms**   Opens all child Forms
- **Close Forms**   Closes all open child Forms

Code 9.2: The Open Forms and Close Forms Commands

```
Option Explicit
Dim DocumentForms(10) As New ChildForm

Private Sub FormsClose_Click()
Dim i As Integer

  For i = 0 To 9
    Unload DocumentForms(i)
  Next

End Sub

Private Sub FormOpen_Click()
Dim i As Integer

  For i = 0 To 9
```

```
    DocumentForms(i).Show
    DocumentForms(i).BackColor = QBColor(Rnd * 14 + 1)
    DocumentForms(i).Caption = "Document " & Format(i)
  Next

End Sub
```

VB5 at Work: The MDIDemo2 Application

The preceding code segment is all there is to the MDIDemo2 application, short of the code for the Window menu, which does not need to be presented here.

The Open Forms event loads all 10 child Forms and assigns a different background color and caption to each one as it is loaded. The Close command closes the Forms. If you run the application now, you will see 11 child Forms—the original ChildForm (the one with caption Form1), which is loaded automatically, and the 10 child Forms of the DocumentForms() array.

You can rearrange the child Forms on the MDI window, minimize and maximize them as usual, and close them by clicking on their Close button. You can also choose Forms ➤ Close Forms to close them all. If you do so, the original child Form remains on the MDI window. This window isn't part of the array. It is the first child window, which Visual Basic loads automatically each time the MDI Form is loaded. You can modify this default behavior by changing the Startup Form in the project's Properties window. To do so, right-click on the project's name, select Project Properties, and change the value of the Startup Object box.

By default, the Startup Object is the first child Form, but because a child Form can't exist on its own, the MDI Form is loaded first, in which the child Form is displayed. Select the MDI Form in the Startup Object ComboBox control, and run the application again. This time, the MDI Form appears without any child Forms. To display a child Form, you must Load it explicitly from within your code.

> **NOTE** Notice that the MDI Form's menu didn't change this time, because a child Form doesn't have its own menu. If it did, this menu would have replaced the MDI Form's menu. In this case, menus that you want to remain always visible, such as the Window menu, must be designed on the child Form.

Tracking the Active Window　Another useful keyword in working with MDI and child Forms is the Me keyword, which refers to the active child Form. If you consider that the MDI Form is the desktop environment for its child Forms, the Me keyword is equivalent to the Screen object's ActiveForm property (which is the active Form). Me is the active child Form in an MDI Form, and you can address any of its properties through the Me property.

In most situations, however, you want to know the index of the active child Form in your code. For example, you can't find out whether a specific child Form is open with the Me keyword. Visual Basic doesn't report the index of the active window, so you must design a way to track it. The solution is to use the Form's Tag property. Every time a new child Form is loaded, you can store its index in the Form's Tag property:

```
DocumentForms(i).Tag = i
```

When the Form is unloaded, Visual Basic resets its tag (you needn't worry about resetting it). When the Form is loaded, you can use the Form's Tag property to find the index of the active child Form and access its properties and methods.

Tweaking MDIDemo2   Let's add a command to the MDIDemo2 application that changes the caption of the active window to the string "I've been activated!" and resets it to the original caption when the window looses focus. To use the Tag property to keep track of the active window, as described in the previous section, you must assign a value to it when the Form is loaded. You modify the Open Forms command as follows:

```
Private Sub FormOpen_Click()
Dim i As Integer

  For i = 0 To 9
    DocumentForms(i).Show
    DocumentForms(i).BackColor = QBColor(Rnd * 14 + 1)
    DocumentForms(i).Caption = "Document " & Format(i)
    DocumentForms(i).Tag = i
  Next

End Sub
```

Changing the Caption property of the active window is simple. All you have to do is set its new value from within the GotFocus event of the child Form. Enter the following line in the ChildForm's GotFocus event:

```
Private Sub Form_GotFocus()
  Me.Caption = "I've been activated!"

End Sub
```

The Me keyword is equivalent to DocumentForms(i), in which *i* is the index of the active window. Instead of tracking the active window's index, use the Me keyword.

Similarly, the caption must be reset each time the window loses the focus. But this time you have to know the index of the active window in the Document-Forms() array, which is given by its Me.Tag property. The LostFocus event handler is again only a single line:

```
Private Sub Form_LostFocus()

    Me.Caption = "Document " & Format(Me.Tag)

End Sub
```

Now that you know the basics of an MDI application, it's time to put this information to use by looking at a functional MDI application. In the following section, we are going to convert the TextPad application of Chapter 5, *Basic ActiveX Controls*, to an MDI editor that will open multiple documents at once.

VB5 at Work: The MDIPad Application

Chapter 5 walked you through the development of the TextPad application, which you are now going to convert to an MDI application. Why? An MDI application lets you open and edit multiple documents simultaneously. You can also copy information from one window and paste it into another, and you can arrange multiple documents on-screen so that you can view any other document while editing the active one. All this is possible without invoking multiple instances of the application. Figure 9.9 shows the TextPad application, and Figure 9.10 shows the MDIPad application.

FIGURE 9.9

The TextPad application

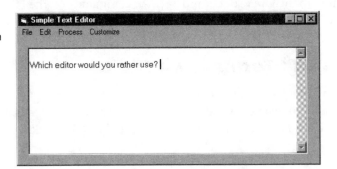

FIGURE 9.10

The MDIPad
application

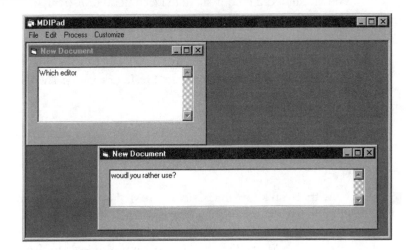

To convert TextPad to an MDI application, follow these steps:

1. Open the TextPad project and save it in a different folder.

2. Select the Editor Form and rename it to Editor.

3. Set its MDIChild property to True. (This becomes the child Form in which the documents will be opened and processed.)

4. Choose Project ➤ Add MDI Form to add the MDI Form and set its Caption property to MDIPad.

5. Run the application now to see how it works.

The child Form's menu appears in the MDI Form's menu bar, and all its commands work as before. The code refers to the Editor TextBox control of the Form1 Form, and it still works. You can even open and save the active window's document with the Open, Save, and Save As commands on the File menu, resize the child Form, and do everything you could do with the TextPad application.

Adding Child Forms to MDIEditor

The modified TextPad application isn't an MDI application yet. For one thing, you can't open a new child Form. The Open command loads another document in the child Form, and if you close the child Form by clicking on its Close button, you won't be able to open it again. Some programming is needed to convert a regular application to an MDI application.

Let's start by adding multiple child Forms. Add a module to the application, and in its declaration section add these lines:

```
Global DocumentForms(10) As New Form1
Global OpenFile(10) As String
Global currentDocument As Integer
```

The *DocumentForms()* array tracks the active document. The *OpenFile()* array has the same role as the *OpenFile* variable of the TextPad application: It holds the names of the documents open in each child Form. *OpenFIle()* is used by the Save command of the File menu to save the active window's contents to the text file from which they were read.

When a new file is opened, its name is stored in this array. When a new document is created, the corresponding entry in the *OpenFile()* array is blank. The *currentDocument* variable is the index of the active window in the *DocumentForms()* array. Each time the focus is moved to a new child window, the *currentDocument* variable is updated with the following code:

```
Private Sub Form_GotFocus()

  currentDocument = Me.Tag

End Sub
```

To continue updating the TextPad application, you must now create a new File menu for the MDI Form. This menu will contain the following commands:

- **New** opens a new child window.
- **Open** opens an existing document in a new child window.
- **Exit** terminates the application.

NOTE Notice the lack of a Save command? The MDI Form's menu is visible only if no documents are open. Therefore, the Save and Save As commands won't be of any use in the MDI Form's File menu. Moreover, there's no need to attach the Edit, Format, and Customize menus to the MDIForm.

Programming the New Command

Start the Menu Designer for the MDI Form and create the File menu with the commands New, Open, and Exit. Now include the following code for the New menu command.

Code 9.3: The New Command

```
Private Sub MDINew_Click()
Dim windex As Integer

  windex = FindFree()
  If windex = -1 Then
    MsgBox "You must close one of the documents before another one
can be opened"
    Exit Sub
  End If

  Load DocumentForms(windex)
  DocumentForms(windex).Caption = "New Document"
  DocumentForms(windex).Tag = windex
  DocumentForms(windex).Show

End Sub
```

The New command doesn't clear the contents of the active child window, as was the case with the TextPad application. Instead, it opens a new, blank child window. As you can see in this code, before the New command can create a new child window, it must first find out if a child Form is available. This is done with the *FindFree()* function, which returns the index of the first available child Form. If all 10 child Forms are open, the program prompts the user to close one of the open windows and try again. If a free child window is found, the program does the following:

1. Loads the corresponding element of the DocumentForms() array

2. Sets its caption to New Document

3. Sets its tag to its index in the DocumentForms() array

4. Displays the window

Later in the program, the window's caption will be set to this file's name if the user saves its document to a disk file.

Programming the Open Command

The Open command's code is longer, but not drastically different from the Open command of the TextPad application. Like the New command, it doesn't display the file in the active child window. Instead, it loads a new child Form and displays the file in it.

Code 9.4: The Open Command

```
Private Sub MDIOpen_Click()
Dim FNum As Integer
Dim txt As String
Dim windex As Integer

  windex = FindFree()
  If windex = -1 Then
    MsgBox "You must close one of the" & _
" documents before another one can be opened"
Exit Sub
  End If

  Load DocumentForms(windex)
  DocumentForms(windex).Show
  currentDocument = windex
On Error GoTo FileError
  CommonDialog1.CancelError = True
  CommonDialog1.Flags = cdlOFNFileMustExist
  CommonDialog1.DefaultExt = "TXT"
  CommonDialog1.Filter = "Text files|*.TXT|All files|*.*"
  CommonDialog1.ShowOpen
  FNum = FreeFile
  Open CommonDialog1.filename For Input As #1
  txt = Input(LOF(FNum), #FNum)
  Close #FNum
  DocumentForms(currentDocument).Editor.Text = txt
  OpenFiles(currentDocument) = CommonDialog1.filename
  DocumentForms(currentDocument).Tag = OpenFile(currentDocument)
  DocumentForms(currentDocument).Caption =
OpenFiles(currentDocument)
  Exit Sub

FileError:
  If Err.Number = cdlCancel Then Exit Sub
```

```
MsgBox "Unknown error while opening file " & CommonDialog1.filename
OpenFiles(currentDocument) = ""
End Sub
```

The Open command first opens a new child window (as does the New command) and then prompts the user with the FileOpen common dialog box to select a file to open. The child window's caption is set to the file's name, which is also stored in the corresponding element of the *OpenFile()* array. Every instance of the *OpenFile* variable in the program must be replaced with *OpenFiles(currentDocument)*. This is the name of the file in which the document of the current child window must be saved. The Save and Save As commands are implemented similarly: There's no need to list the corresponding code here.

Programming the Exit Command

The Exit command of an MDI application is a bit more complicated than a simple End statement. See the code behind this command in the section "Ending an MDI Application" later in this chapter.

Differences between TextPad and MDIPad

Some commands of the MDI Form's menu have a different function than the commands with the same name on the child Form's File menu. In the TexPad application, the New command cleared the contents of the editor. In the MDI version of the application, the New command opens a new, empty child window. Likewise, the Open command in the TextPad application reads a file into the editor. In the MDI version of the application, the Open command reads a file into a new child window. The differences in the operation of most MDI applications need to be kept in mind as you convert applications from SDI to the MDI model. You can't simply duplicate the code of the New and Open commands of the equivalent SDI application to its MDI version.

The problems arising out of the different behavior of the New and Open commands in the two types of applications can be overcome easily by duplicating the code of the MDI Form's File menu. Simply copy the code behind the New and Open commands of the MDI Form's menu to the equivalent subroutines of the child Form.

Regardless of these differences, you managed to get the File commands to work in the MDI application, which represent the most important differences between single and multiple window applications. The next task is to ensure that the rest of the program references the Editor TextBox of the current child Form.

In the TextPad application, the program references this TextBox as Form1.Editor. The name of the child Form is no longer Form1; it's *DocumentForms(currentDocument)*, in which *currentDocument* is the index of the active window in the DocumentForms() array. Replace all instances of *Form1* in the code with *DocumentForms (currentDocument)*, and this is all it takes. Even the Find & Replace Form's code will reference the correct window in the MDI Form. The *Form1* variable is also referenced in the child Form's Resize event.

Ending an MDI Application

In most cases, and certainly for the examples in this book, ending an application with the End statement isn't necessarily the most user-friendly approach. Before you end an application, you must always offer your users a chance to save their work. Ideally, you should maintain a True/False variable whose value is set every time the user edits the open document (the Change event of many controls is a good place to set this variable to True) and reset every time the user saves the document (with the Save or Save As commands).

This simple setup doesn't require too much code, but it's one of the finishing touches that the examples have avoided (the objective is to demonstrate the core of various applications, not provide truly professional applications). The error-catching code required is totally unrelated to the point we're trying to make, and it would make our examples too lengthy. In a real-world application, however, these "details" can make all the difference for your application's future.

Handling unsaved data in normal applications is fairly simple. There's only one document to deal with. But in an MDI application, you have to cope with several situations:

- The user closes a child window by clicking on its Close button. You should detect this condition and provide the same code you would use with a single Form application.

- The user quits a single document only. This situation is easy to handle (it's just like a normal application).

- The user closes the MDI Form. If the MDI Form is closed, all the open documents will close with it! If losing the edits in a single document is bad, imagine losing the edits in multiple documents.

Terminating an MDI application with the End statement is unacceptable. One approach would be to go through all child Forms, examine whether they are open, and for each open document, prompt the user accordingly. This is possible, but it takes a lot of programming, and you may have guessed there's a simpler way, which we'll explore next.

Using QueryUnload to Protect Data   The MDI mechanism provides a better solution, via the QueryUnload event. This event is triggered when a child window is unloaded. If the entire MDI Form is unloaded, the QueryUnload event is triggered for each open child Form and gives your code a chance to cancel the action. The QueryUnload event's syntax is as follows:

```
QueryUnload(cancel As Integer, unloadmode As Integer)
```

The application can set the *cancel* argument to halt the termination process. If you set the *cancel* argument to True in your code, the child Form won't be unloaded, which in turn prevents the unloading of the MDI Form.

The *unloadmode* argument tells you which event caused the QueryUnload event, according to the values in Table 9.2.

TABLE 9.2   The Values of the QueryUnload's *unloadmode* Argument

CONSTANT	VALUE	DESCRIPTION
vbFormControlMenu	0	The user clicked on the Form's Close button or selected Control ➤ Close.
vbFormCode	1	The Unload statement is invoked from within the code.
vbAppWindows	2	Windows itself is shutting down.
vbAppTaskManager	3	The application was shut down through the Task Manager.
vbFormMDIForm	4	The MDI Form is closing.

As you can see, the QueryUnload event is triggered even if Windows itself is shutting down. If you program the QueryUnload event of the child Forms, you can rest assured that the users of your application won't lose any data unless their computer crashes or they reset it. You can examine the value of this argument from within your code to find out why the Form is being unloaded and act accordingly. On certain occasions, you may want to handle the situation differently, depending on the external event that caused the Form to unload, but the process is practically the same. Offer your user a chance to save the data, discard the data, or cancel the program's termination altogether (see Figure 9.11).

To use the QueryUnload event, you must unload the child Form from within its Exit menu command. Here's the code behind the End command of the MDIEditor's File menu.

Code 9.5: The End Command

```
Private Sub FileExit_Click()

    Unload MDIForm1
    End

End Sub
```

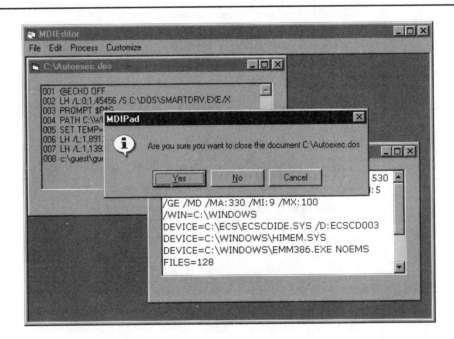

FIGURE 9.11

If you shut down the MDIPad application, you'll be prompted to save each and every open document.

Notice that this is the Exit command of the child Form's File menu. The MDI Form's File menu is visible only if no child windows are open, in which case there's nothing to save and a single End statement will suffice. To terminate the MDI application, first unload the MDI Form and then End the application.

Unloading the MDI Form triggers a QueryUnload event for all its child Forms. In each child Form's Unload event, you can prompt the users accordingly and give them a chance to save their data, discard the data, or cancel the operation. Here's how you can handle this event in the MDIEdit application.

Code 9.6: The QueryUnload Event

```
Private Sub Form_QueryUnload(Cancel As Integer, UnloadMode As
Integer)
Dim reply As Integer

  reply = MsgBox("Are you sure you want to close the document " &
➥Me.Tag, _
  vbYesNoCancel + vbInformation)
  If reply = vbCancel Then
    Cancel = True
  ElseIf reply = vbYes Then Exit Sub
  Else
    FileSaveAs_Click
  End If

End Sub
```

These few lines of code enable the user of the application to discard unsaved data, cancel the operation, or save any unsaved data with a call to the child Form's FileSave_Click subroutine.

Handling the unloading of multiple Forms in a single point in your code is a great convenience, because you can make the process of terminating the application as simple or as complicated as you wish for all child Forms. For instance, you can create temporary files with unsaved information in case the user decides that the discarded information was too valuable.

CHAPTER

TEN

10

Recursive Programming

- Understanding the basics

- Performing a binary search

- Creating a custom File Manager

- Creating a custom Explorer

- Exploring the stack and recursive programming

- Determining when to use recursive programming

This chapter is slightly different from the previous ones in that it doesn't describe Visual Basic techniques. Instead, it introduces a powerful technique for implementing efficient, compact programs. *Recursion* is a special topic in computer programming, but one of the least understood by beginners and even by some advanced programmers. It's surrounded by an aura of mystery, and most BASIC programmers ignore it. The truth is, recursive programming is no more complicated than any other programming approach, once you understood how it works and when to use it.

Some readers may think that the material in this chapter is of little use to the average programmer. They are probably right, but there is some valuable information in this chapter. Toward the end of it, you will learn how to write applications that scan an entire folder, including its subfolders. The DirMap application is a customized Windows Explorer that you can incorporate in your applications even if you don't quite understand how it works.

Basic Concepts

Recursive programming is used for implementing algorithms, or mathematical definitions, that are described *recursively*, that is, in terms of themselves. A recursive definition is implemented by a procedure that calls itself and is called a recursive procedure.

Code that calls functions and subroutines to accomplish a task, such as the following segment, is quite normal:

```
Function MyPayments()
{other statements}
CarPayment = CalculatePayment(CarCost, Interest, Duration)
MonthlyCost = MonthlyCost + CarPayment
HomePayment = CalculatePayment(Mortgage, Interest, Duration)
MonthlyCost = MonthlyCost + HomePayment
{more statements}
End Function
```

In the preceding code, the MyPayments() function calls the CalculatePayment() function twice to calculate the monthly payments for a car and home loan. There's nothing puzzling about this piece of code because it's "linear." Here's what it does:

1. The MyPayments() function suspends execution each time it calls the CalculatePayment() function.

2. It waits for the CalculatePayment() function to complete its task and return a value.

3. It then resumes execution.

But what if, as in the following, a function calls itself?

```
Function DoSomething(n As Integer) As Integer
{other statements}
      value = value - 1
      if value = 0 Then Exit Function
      newValue = DoSomething(value)
{more statements}
End Function
```

If you didn't know better, you'd think that this program will never end. Every time the DoSomething() function is called, it gets into a loop by calling itself again and again, and it never exits. In fact, this is a clear danger with recursion. It is not only possible, but quite easy for a recursive function to get into an endless loop. A recursive function must exit explicitly. In other words, you must tell a recursive function when to stop calling itself and exit. The condition that causes the DoSomething() function to end is met when *value* becomes zero.

Apart from this technicality, you can draw a few useful conclusions from this example. A function performs a well-defined task. When a function calls itself, it has to interrupt the current task to complete another, quite similar task. The DoSomething() function can't complete its task (whatever this is) unless it performs an identical calculation. And it does so by calling itself.

Recursion in Real Life

Does this ever happen in everyday life? It does, and here's a familiar example. Suppose you're viewing a World Wide Web page that describes a hot new topic. The page contains a term you don't understand, and the term is a hyperlink. When you click on the hyperlink, another page that defines the term is displayed. This definition contains another term you don't understand. The new term is also a hyperlink, so you click on it, and a page containing its definition is displayed. Once you understand this definition, you click on the Back button to go back to the previous page, read and understand the definition, and then go back to the original page.

The task at hand is understanding a document, a description, and a definition. Every time you run into an unfamiliar term, you interrupt the current task to accomplish another, identical task—understand another definition.

The process of looking up a definition in a dictionary is similar and epitomizes recursion—interrupting one task to perform another, identical task. For example, you've looked up the phrase *Active Web pages* and find that they "contain ActiveX controls." You don't know what an ActiveX control is, so you look up that term and see the following definition:

ActiveX Controls are the elements used to build Active Web pages.

This is a sticky situation. You must either give up your attempt to understand what Active Web pages are or look up the definitions elsewhere. Going back and forth between two definitions isn't going to take you anywhere. This is the endless loop mentioned earlier.

Because this situation can arise easily in recursive programming, you must be sure that your code contains conditions that will cause the recursive procedure to stop calling itself. In the example of the DoSomething() function, this condition is as follows:

```
If value = 0 Then Exit Function
```

The code decrements the value of the variable *value* by one until it eventually reaches zero, in which case the sequence of recursive calls ends. Without such a condition, the recursive function calls itself indefinitely. Once the DoSomething() function ends, the suspended instances of the same function resume their execution and terminate.

Now, let's look at a few practical examples and see these concepts in action.

A Simple Example

I'll demonstrate the principles of recursive programming with a trivial example, the calculation of the factorial of a number. The factorial of a number, denoted with an exclamation mark, is described recursively as follows:

```
n! = n * (n-1)!
```

The factorial of n (read as n factorial) is the number n multiplied by the factorial of $(n-1)$, which in turn is $(n-1)$ multiplied by the factorial of $(n-2)$ and so on, until we reach 0! which is 1 by definition.

Here's the process of calculating the factorial of 4:

```
4! = 4 * 3!
   = 4 * 3 * 2!
   = 4 * 3 * 2 * 1!
   = 4 * 3 * 2 * 1 * 0!
   = 4 * 3 * 2 * 1 * 1
   = 24
```

For the mathematically inclined, the factorial of the number *n* is defined as follows:

```
n! = n * (n-1)!      if n is greater than zero
n! = 1               if n is zero
```

The factorial is described in terms of itself and is a prime candidate for recursive implementation. The Factorial application, shown in Figure 10.1, lets you specify the number whose factorial you want to calculate in the box on the left and displays the result in the box on the right. To start the calculations, you click on the Factorial button.

FIGURE 10.1

The Factorial application

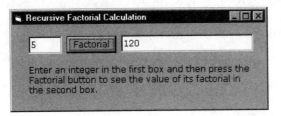

Here's the factorial() function that implements the previous definition:

```
Function factorial(n As Integer) As Double

  If n = 0 Then
    factorial = 1
  Else
    factorial = factorial(n - 1) * n
  End If

End Function
```

The recursive definition of the factorial of an integer is implemented in a single line:

```
factorial = n * factorial(n-1).
```

The function can be described in English as follows: As long as the argument of the function is not zero, the function returns the product of its argument times the factorial of its argument minus one. With each successive call of the factorial() function, the initial number is decremented by one, and eventually *n* becomes zero and the sequence of recursive calls ends.

So, what happens when this sequence of recursive calls ends? Each time the factorial() function calls itself, the calling function is suspended temporarily.

When the called function terminates, the most recently suspended function resumes execution. To calculate the factorial of 10, you call the factorial() function with the argument 10, as follows:

```
MsgBox "The factorial of 10 " & factorial(10)
```

The execution of the function factorial(10) is interrupted when it calls factorial(9). This function is also interrupted when factorial(9) calls factorial(8), and so on. By the time factorial(0) is called, ten instances of the function are suspended and waiting for the function they called to finish. When that happens, they resume execution.

Let's watch this happen by adding a couple of lines to the factorial() function. Open the Factorial application and add a few statements that print the function's status in the Immediate Execution window, as shown next:

```
Function factorial(n As Integer) As Double

Debug.Print "Starting the calculation of " & n & " factorial"
  If n = 0 Then
    factorial = 1
  Else
Debug.Print "Calling factorial(n) with n=" & n - 1
    factorial = factorial(n - 1) * n
  End If
Debug.Print "Done calculating " & n & " factorial"

End Function
```

Watching the Algorithm

The Print statements are commented out in the Factorial application. You can remove the apostrophes from in front of them and then run the application to watch the sequence of function calls while the factorial of a number is being calculated.

The first Print statement tells us that a new instance of the function has been activated and gives the number whose factorial it's about to calculate. The second Print statement tells us that the active function is about to call another instance of itself and shows which argument it will supply to the function it's calling. The last Print statement informs us that the factorial function is done. Here's what you'll see in the Immediate Execution window if you call the factorial function with the argument 4:

```
Starting the calculation of 4 factorial
Calling factorial(n) with n=3
Starting the calculation of 3 factorial
Calling factorial(n) with n=2
Starting the calculation of 2 factorial
Calling factorial(n) with n=1
Starting the calculation of 1 factorial
Calling factorial(n) with n=0
Starting the calculation of 0 factorial
Done calculating 0 factorial
Done calculating 1 factorial
Done calculating 2 factorial
Done calculating 3 factorial
Done calculating 4 factorial
```

This list of messages is lengthy, but it's worth examining the sequence of events. The first time the function is called, it attempts to calculate the factorial of 4. It can't complete its operation and calls factorial(3) to calculate the factorial of 3, which is needed to calculate the factorial of 4. The first instance of the factorial() function is suspended until factorial(3) returns its result.

Similarly, factorial(3) doesn't complete its calculations because it must call factorial(2). So far, there are two suspended instances of the factorial() function. In turn, factorial(2) calls factorial(1), and factorial(1) calls factorial(0). Now, there are four suspended instances of the factorial() function, all waiting for an intermediate result before they can continue with their calculations. Figure 10.2 shows this process.

When factorial(0) completes its execution, it prints the following message and returns a result:

```
Done calculating 0 factorial
```

This result is passed to the most recently interrupted function, which is factorial(1). This function can now resume operation and print another message indicating that it finished its calculations.

As each suspended function resumes operation, it passes a result to the function from which it was called, until the very first instance of the factorial() function finishes the calculation of the factorial of 4. Figure 10.3 shows this process. (In the figure, factorial is abbreviated as *fact*.)

FIGURE 10.2

Watching the progress of the calculation of a factorial in the Immediate Execution window

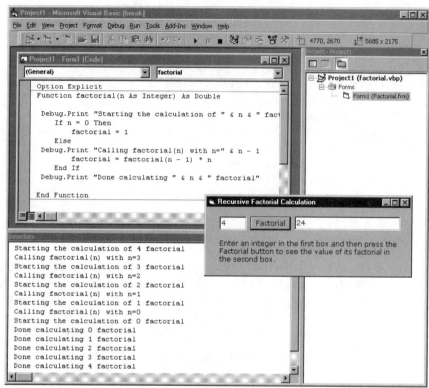

FIGURE 10.3

The process of the recursive calculation of the factorial of 4. The arrows pointing to the right show the direction of recursive calls, and the ones pointing to the left show the propagation of the result.

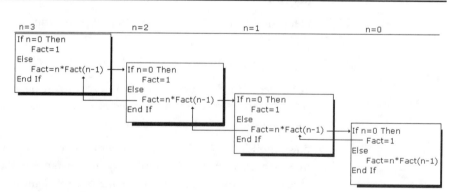

What Happens When a Function Calls Itself

If you are totally unfamiliar with recursive programming, you're probably uncomfortable with the idea of a function calling itself. Let's take a closer look at what happens when a function calls itself. As far as the computer is concerned, it doesn't make any difference whether a function calls itself or another function. When a function calls another function, the calling function suspends execution and waits for the called function to complete its task. The calling function then resumes (usually by taking into account any result returned by the function it called). A recursive function simply calls itself instead of another one.

Let's assume that the factorial in the previous function was implemented with the following line:

```
factorial = n * factorial1(n-1)
```

and that factorial1() is identical to factorial(). When the factorial() function calls factorial1(), its execution is suspended until factorial1() returns its result. A new function is loaded into the memory and executed. If the factorial() function is called with 3, the factorial1() function calculates the factorial of 2.

Similarly, the code of the factorial1() function would be the following:

```
factorial1 = n * factorial2(n-1)
```

This time the function factorial2() is called to calculate the factorial of 1. The function factorial2() calls in turn factorial3(), which calculates the factorial of zero. The factorial3() function completes its calculations and returns the result 1. This is in turn multiplied by 1 to produce the factorial of 1. This result is returned to the function factorial1(), which completes the calculation of the factorial of 2 (which is 2 times 1). The value is returned to the factorial() function, which now completes the calculation of 3 (3*2, or 6).

A Recursive Function and the Operating System

You can think of a recursive function calling itself as the operating system supplying another identical function with a different name. And this is what happens, more or less. Each time your program calls a function, the operating system does the following:

1. Saves the status of the active function

2. Loads the new function in memory

3. Starts executing the new function

If the function is recursive—in other words, if the new function is the same as the one currently being executed—nothing changes. The operating system saves the status of the active function somewhere and starts executing it as if it were another function. Of course, there's no reason to load it in memory again because the function is already there.

When the newly called function finishes, the operating system reloads the function it interrupted in memory and continues its execution. I mentioned that the operating system stores the status of a function every time it must interrupt it to load another function in memory. The *status information* includes the values of its variables and the location at which execution was interrupted. In effect, after the operating system loads the status of the interrupted function, the function continues execution as if it were never interrupted. We'll return to the topic of storing status information later in this chapter in the section "The Stack Mechanism."

Fibonacci Numbers

Another recursive mathematical definition is that of the Fibonacci numbers, which are defined as follows:

```
f(n) = f(n-1) + f(n-2)
```

A Fibonacci number is the sum of the last two Fibonacci numbers. The first Fibonacci number is 0, and the second Fibonacci number is 1. Thus, the third Fibonacci number is 1 (0+1), the fourth Fibonacci number is 2 (1+2), the fifth Fibonacci number is 5 (2+3), and so on. The *n*th Fibonacci number can be calculated with the following function, which is a direct translation of the mathematical definition into Visual Basic code:

```
Function Fibonacci(N As Integer) As Integer

    If N = 0 Then
Fibonacci = 0
    Elseif N = 1 Then
Fibonacci = 1
    Else
        Fibonacci = Fibonacci(N-1) + Fibonacci(N-2)
    End If

End Function
```

Recursion by Mistake

Recursion isn't as complicated as you may think. Here's an example of a recursive situation you may have run into without knowing it. Figure 10.4 shows a simple application that fills the background of a Picture box with a solid color. Instead of setting the control's BackColor property, though, it draws vertical lines from one end of the control to the other. Every time the New Color button is clicked, the PictureBox control is filled slowly with vertical lines. The color of the lines is chosen randomly. This application is quite similar to the ClrGrads application of Chapter 6, *Drawing and Painting with Visual Basic*, which fills the background of the control with a gradient. I used a solid color in this example to simplify the code.

FIGURE 10.4

Click on the New Color button before the program has a chance to fill the control to watch a recursive behavior.

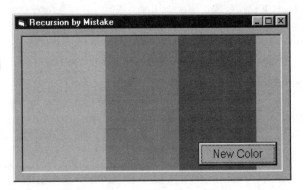

Code 10.1: The New Color Button Code

```
Private Sub Command1_Click()
RGBColor = Rnd * 16000000
For i = 0 To Picture1.Width
    Picture1.Line (i, 0)-(i, Picture1.Height), RGBColor
    DoEvents
Next

End Sub
```

VB5 at Work: The Recurse Application

You will find the Recurse application on the book's CD in this chapter's folder. Load it and run it. Click on the New Color button, and the program starts filling the picture box with a random color from left to right. Because the control's ScaleMode is twips, the progress of the drawing is slow, even on a fast Pentium. Suppose the program starts filling the picture box with red. Before the program has a chance to complete its operation, click on the New Color button again. The subroutine Command1_Click() is interrupted, and the program starts filling the control with a new color, perhaps fuchsia. Interrupt the process again. This time, yellow kicks in and starts filling the control from left to right. Let this operation complete.

As soon as the picture box is filled with yellow, the interrupted process continues. The program completes the drawing of the fuchsia lines, and it doesn't start drawing from the left edge of the control. It picks up from where it was interrupted. When the fuchsia color reaches the right edge of the control, red kicks in! Can you see what's going on here? Each time you click on the New Color button, the Command1_Click() subroutine is interrupted, and a new copy of the same subroutine starts executing. The interrupted (or suspended) instance of the subroutine doesn't die. It waits for a chance to complete, which it gets when the newer instance of the subroutine completes its task.

This recursion is made possible by the DoEvents() statement placed in the loop's body. Without it, you wouldn't be able to interrupt the subroutine and invoke another instance of it. Normally, you wouldn't use the statement DoEvents(), to avoid the very behavior you witnessed in this example.

I need to mention one important aspect of recursion here. The *RGBColor* variable is local, and it maintains its value while the subroutine is interrupted. Visual Basic stores the values of the local variables of the interrupted procedures and recalls them when the procedure gets a chance to complete. This is possible because each new copy of the procedure that starts executing has its own set of local variables.

Binary Search: A Recursive Implementation

The examples used to introduce the concepts of recursive programming are quite interesting—if you are mathematically inclined, that is. But most people aren't, so let's look at a couple of practical examples. We'll return to the Binary Search algorithm we explored in Chapter 5, *Basic ActiveX Controls*, and implement it with a recursive function.

The Binary Search algorithm searches a list of ordered (sorted) entries to locate any given item. This algorithm starts by comparing the desired item with the middle entry of the list. Because the entries are sorted, depending on the outcome of the comparison, half the list will be rejected. If the desired element is above the middle element of the list, the lower half of the list can be rejected. The search continues in the upper half, and the process is repeated. The desired element is located somewhere in the upper half of the list, and the algorithm now compares the desired element with the middle element of the upper half of the list. Depending on the outcome of this comparison, one half of the already reduced list is rejected again, and the process is repeated until we are left with a single element, which is the desired element. If it isn't, you know that the element you are looking for does not belong to the list.

The idea behind the Binary Search algorithm is to halve the list at each iteration and reach the location of the desired element quickly. If you start with a list of 1024 items, after the first comparison you'll be left with 512 elements, after the second comparison you'll be left with 256 elements, after the third comparison you'll be left with 128 elements, and so on. It will take only 10 comparisons to narrow down to the item you want. The definition of the Binary Search algorithm is recursive in nature and can be easily and efficiently implemented with a recursive function.

The BSearch() Function

Following, in plain English, is a description of the function BSearch(), which implements the Binary Search algorithm:

1. Find the list's middle element.

2. Compare the desired element with the list's middle element.

3. If the desired element is found, the task is finished.

4. If the desired element is larger than the list's middle element,

   - Reject the lower half of the list.

   Else

   - Reject the upper half of the list.

5. If the list to be searched has one or no elements, quit. The element isn't in the list.

6. Search the remaining list.

The last test is essential; without it, the search would never end. If the list's size is reduced to a single element, you know that this element is the desired one or that the desired element does not exist. Here's the implementation of the BSearch() function in Visual Basic.

Code 10.2: The BSearch() Function

```
Function BSearch(lower As Integer, upper As Integer, KeyField As
String) As Integer
Dim middle As Integer

  middle = Fix(lower + upper) / 2
  If DataArray(middle) = KeyField Then
    BSearch = middle
    Exit Function
  End If

  If lower >= upper Then
    BSearch = -1
    Exit Function
  End If

  If KeyField < DataArray(middle) Then
    upper = middle - 1
  Else
    lower = middle + 1
  End If
  BSearch = BSearch(lower, upper, KeyField)

End Function
```

The BSearch() function is a straightforward coding of the verbal explanation of the algorithm. Here's what it does:

1. First, it calculates the index of the list's middle element and compares the list's middle element with the desired element (*KeyField*).

2. If both elements are the same, the desired element is located and the search need not continue. The function returns the index of the desired element in the list.

3. If both elements are not the same, the values of the two limits of the array are compared.

4. If the upper limit is equal to or less than the lower limit (that is, if the list has been reduced to a single element), the desired element is not in the list, and instead of an index, the function returns the value -1.

5. If the end of the list has not been reached, the function compares the desired element with the current entry and shortens the array accordingly by changing the values of the *upper* and *lower* variables, which are the indices delimiting the section of the array in which the desired element resides.

Figure 10.5 shows the BSearch application of Chapter 5, *Basic ActiveX Controls*, only this time the BSearch() function is implemented recursively. The new BSearch application (in this chapter's folder on the CD) demonstrates how to use the BSearch() function presented earlier in this section to search for an item in a sorted list.

FIGURE 10.5

The revised BSearch application uses a recursive implementation of the Binary Search algorithm.

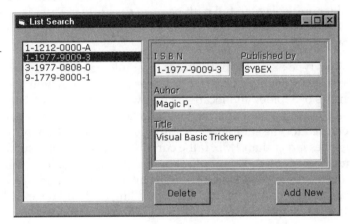

Recursive functions are also used in certain, very efficient searching and sorting algorithms that I won't go into in this book. They are rather advanced, and with all the programming tools that Visual Basic provides, it's doubtful that you'll ever need them. Instead, we'll look at a more practical example and at an application that I believe most readers will find quite useful.

A Custom File Manager

The examples of recursive functions we looked at so far haven't convinced you of the usefulness of recursion. The factorial of a number can be easily calculated with a For...Next loop, and the Binary Search algorithm has been implemented nonrecursively earlier in this book. So, what good is recursion after all?

The answer is the FileScan application, which can't be implemented nonrecursively. I hope that the previous examples helped you understand the principles of recursive programming and that you're ready for some real recursion. We will design an application, similar to the Windows Explorer, that scans an entire folder, including its subfolders. As the application scans the files and subfolders of a folder or an entire volume, it can locate files by name, size, and date; it can also move files around and, in general, perform all the operations of the Windows Explorer, plus any other custom operation you might require. Much of the functionality of this application is provided by Windows Explorer, but as you will see shortly, this application is highly customizable, and it can serve as your starting point for many file operations that Windows Explorer doesn't provide. For example, your custom Explorer could expand all the subfolders each time you open a folder or display the full path name of each folder. Later in the chapter, you will see an application that generates a list of all the files in a folder, including its subfolders, organized by folder.

This type of application is ideal for implementing with a recursive function, because its operation is defined recursively. Suppose you want to scan all the entries of a folder and locate the files whose size exceeds 1Mb, or suppose you want to count them. If an entry is another folder, the same process must be repeated for the subfolder. The program must switch to this folder and locate all the files larger than 1Mb. If the current folder contains a subfolder, the process must be repeated. This application calls for a recursive function, because every time it runs into a subfolder, it must interrupt the scanning of the current folder and start scanning the subfolder by calling itself. If you spend some time thinking about the implementation of this algorithm, you'll conclude that there's no simple way to do so nonrecursively.

Describing a Recursive Procedure in Words

When you're about to write a recursive procedure, it's helpful to start with a verbal description of the procedure. For the FileScan application, we need a subroutine (since it's not going to return any result) that scans the contents of a folder. Let's call it ScanFolder(). The ScanFolder() subroutine must scan all the entries of the initial folder and process the files in it. If the current entry is a file, it must act upon the file, depending on its name or size. If the current entry is a folder, it must scan the contents of this folder. In other words, it must interrupt the scanning of the current folder and start scanning the subfolder. And the most efficient way to scan a subfolder is to call itself. Here's the *ScanFolder()* function in pseudocode:

```
Sub FileScan()
Process files in current folder
```

```
If current_folder contains subfolders
For each subfolder
            Switch to subfolder
            FileScan()
       Next
       Move to parent directory
End If
```

Translating the Verbal Description to Code

Now, let's translate this description to actual code. Because we need access to each folder's files and subfolders, we'll use a DriveListBox control, a DirListBox control, and a FileListBox control, as shown in Figure 10.6.

FIGURE 10.6

The FileScan application scans the files and sub-folders of any folder on your disk, performing a custom operation on each file along the way.

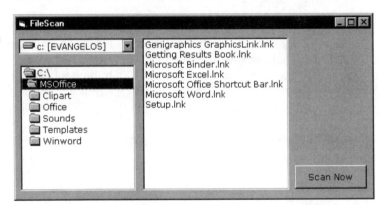

Using the File Controls

The three file controls (DriveListBox, DirListBox, and FileListBox) are connected with the following subroutines.

When the user selects a different drive from the DriveListBox control, the program switches to the new drive and updates the contents of the DirListBox control.

Code 10.3: The DriveListBox

```
Private Sub Drive1_Change()

    ChDrive Dir1.Path
```

```
    Dir1.Path = Drive1.Drive
    Dir1.Refresh

End Sub
```

Likewise, when the user selects a folder in the DirListBox control, the program switches to the selected folder and updates the contents of the FileListBox.

Code 10.4: The DirListBox

```
Private Sub Dir1_Change()

  ChDir Dir1.Path
  File1.Path = Dir1.Path

End Sub
```

Since we are only scanning folders, we needn't display the FileListBox control on the Form, but I decided to include it so that the user can watch the progress of the scanning process.

The subfolders of a given folder are displayed in a DirListBox control (Dir1) and are accessed with the help of the Dir1.List array. The first subfolder is Dir1.List(0), the second subfolder is Dir1.List(1), and so on. Similarly, you can access the files of the current folder through the File1.List() array. After the user selects the folder to be scanned in the DirListBox control and clicks on the Scan Now button, the program starts scanning.

Code 10.5: The Scan Now Button

```
Private Sub Command1_Click()

    ChDrive Drive1.Drive
    ChDir Dir1.Path
    InitialFolder = CurDir
    totalFiles = 0
  ScanFolders
  MsgBox "There are " & totalFiles & " under the " & InitialFolder &
  ➥" folder"

End Sub
```

(The global variable *InitialFolder* is used later in the code to determine whether we have exhausted all the subfolders of the current folder and must end the process.)

The ScanFolders() Subroutine

Now, let's look at the actual code of the ScanFolders() subroutine. The number of subfolders in the current folder is given by the number of entries in the DirList-Box control, which is *Dir1.ListCount*. If this number is positive, the program scans each subfolder with a For...Next loop. With each iteration, it switches to the next subfolder, updates the contents of the DirListBox and FileListBox controls, and calls itself to scan the new folder.

This process is repeated as long as there are subfolders to be scanned. When a folder without subfolders is reached, the If statement is skipped, and the Scan-Folders() subroutine moves to the parent folder and returns. The ScanFolders() subroutine doesn't do any real processing. It simply counts the total number of files in the folders visited (with the following statement:

totalFiles = totalFiles + File1.ListCount.

First, ScanFolders()updates the File Control, and then it adds the number of files in the current folder to the *totalFiles* global variable. Finally, it moves up to the parent directory and exits. When an instance of the ScanFolders() subroutine terminates, the most recently suspended instance of the subroutine resumes, by scanning the remaining entries of the current folder.

Code 10.6: The ScanFolders() Subroutine

```
Sub ScanFolders()
Dim subFolders As Integer

  totalFiles = totalFiles + File1.ListCount
  subFolders = Dir1.ListCount
  If subFolders > 0 Then
    For i = 0 To subFolders - 1
      ChDir Dir1.List(i)
      Dir1.Path = Dir1.List(i)
      File1.Path = Dir1.List(i)
      Form1.Refresh
      ScanFolders
    Next
  End If
  File1.Path = Dir1.Path
  MoveUp
End Sub
```

At first, the program processes the files in the current folder. The processing in this example consists of counting the files, but as you will see shortly, you can insert many types of custom file processing here.

The variable *subFolders* holds the number of subfolders in the current folder. If that number is positive (that is, if the current folder contains subfolders), the ScanFolders() function scans each one of them by calling itself. If some of these folders happen to contain subfolders of their own, they are scanned by another call to the same subroutine.

The For...Next loop scans all the subfolders of the current folder by switching to each subfolder (with the ChDir command). Once in a subfolder, the program changes the contents of the Directory and File List controls. The Form1.Refresh statement updates the contents of all controls on the Form so that they reflect the contents (subfolders and files) of the current folder. The program then calls the ScanFolders() subroutine again, to scan the entire folder.

The MoveUp()Subroutine

The subroutine MoveUp() is called every time the program finishes scanning the files and subfolders of the current folder to back up to the parent folder. The current folder's parent folder is Dir1.List(-2). Likewise, Dir1.List(-1) is the name of the current folder. The MoveUp() subroutine first makes sure that the program is not at the folder where it started. If so, it doesn't move to the parent folder. If the program is at a subfolder, it moves to the parent folder.

Code 10.7: The MoveUp() Subroutine

```
Sub MoveUp()

  If Dir1.List(-1) <> InitialFolder Then
    ChDir Dir1.List(-2)
    Dir1.Path = Dir1.List(-2)
  End If

End Sub
```

If you run the FileScan application, you can watch the folder names in the DirListBox control and the current folder's files in the FileListBox control. In a real application, you don't want to display the name of the folder visited and its files, so these controls should be invisible. But while trying to understand the program's operation, it might be helpful to watch the folder-scanning process through the changing contents of these two controls on the Form.

A Custom Explorer

All the features of the FileScan application are built into Windows Explorer. FileScan is an interesting example of recursive programming, but why duplicate functionality that's already available for free? The FileScan application is highly customizable. In the previous section you saw how you can count all the files of a given folder, including those in its subfolders. You can add many more useful features to the FileScan application, which aren't available through Windows Explorer.

For example, you can implement a version of the Find utility that locates files and/or folders based on criteria that aren't available through the Find utility. A limitation of the Find utility is that you can't specify exclusion criteria. For instance, you can't find all the files whose size exceeds 1Mb and are not system files (EXE, DLL, and so on) or images (BMP, TIF, JPG, and so on). You can modify the FileScan application to handle all types of file selection or rejection criteria by designing the proper user interface.

Mapping a Folder

Here's another customization idea for the FileScan application. Did you ever have to prepare a hard copy of your hard disk's structure? (If you'll ever have to submit the contents of an entire CD to a publisher, this utility will save you a good deal of work.) As far as I know, there is no simple way to do it. You can, however, easily modify the FileScan application so that it prints the contents of a folder, including its subfolders, to a text box. Figure 10.7 shows the DirMap application, which does exactly that. The structure of a user-specified folder is printed on a RichTextbox control so that folder names can be displayed in bold and stand out. The contents of the text box can be copied and pasted in any other document or used in a mail message.

The code of the DirMap application is quite similar to the code of the FileScan application, with the exception of a few additional lines that create the output shown in the lower half of the Form.

Code 10.8: The Map This Folder Button

```
Private Sub Command1_Click()

    currentDepth = 1
    InitialFolder = CurDir
    DirStructure = "{"
```

FIGURE 10.7

The DirMap application
generates a text file with
the structure of any
given folder.

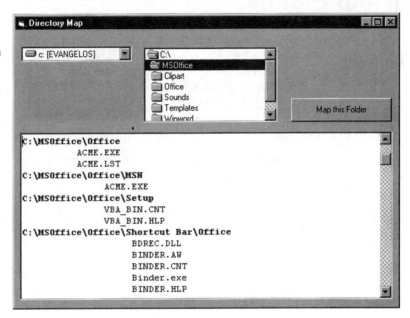

FIGURE 10.7

The DirMap application
generates a text file with
the structure of any
given folder.

```
DirStructure = DirStructure & "{\b " & DoubleSlashes(Dir2.List(-1))
➥ & "}" + newLine
Screen.MousePointer = ccHourglass
ScanFolders
DirStructure = DirStructure & "}"
RichTextBox1.TextRTF = DirStructure
Screen.MousePointer = ccDefault

End Sub
```

The *DirStructure* Variable   The *DirStructure* variable is a long string variable that holds the RTF description of the contents of the RichTextBox control. This string is being built slowly as the program scans each folder along the way. Folder names are displayed in bold, and filenames are displayed in regular font, but indented from the right according to their level within the parent folder.

The \b tag in RTF causes everything that appears within a pair of curly braces to appear in bold. Folder names are printed as {\b c:\windows\desktop}, and when rendered in the RichTextBox control, they appear in bold. Files in the first directory level are indented by 5 spaces, files in the second directory level are indented by 10 spaces, and so on. Everything placed in the *DirStructure* string must be enclosed in a pair of curly brackets so that when assigned to the TextRTF property of the RichTextBox control it will be interpreted as RTF code, and not be simply displayed as is.

The pointer's icon is then switched to an hourglass, indicating that the process will take a while. Depending on the total number of files under the folder you are mapping, the program may get quite slow. The *DirStructure* variable can grow large because it holds the entire contents of the RichTextBox control. Although Visual Basic 5 doesn't impose any practical limitations on the variable's length (a string variable can hold as many as 2 million characters), appending more characters at the end of a long string introduces delays. Visual Basic reallocates space for the *DirStructure* variable continuously, which grows all the time, and this causes the delay.

An alternative is to append the filenames not to a memory variable, but to a disk file, and then open the file and read its contents into the RichTextBox control. Or, if you don't care about displaying folder names in bold, you could abandon the RichTextBox control and use a plain TextBox control; instead of updating the *DirStructure* variable, append each new filename directly to the TextBox control. If the folder being mapped is of moderate size, the approach I chose here works well, and I think the benefit of richly formatting the folder structure offsets the less than optimal execution speed.

The ScanFolders() subroutine is the same as before, with the addition of the lines that append the file and folder names to the *DirStructure* variable.

Code 10.9: The Revised ScanFolders() Subroutine

```
Sub ScanFolders()
Dim subFolders As Integer
Dim txtLine As String

  txtLine = ""
  For j = 0 To File1.ListCount - 1
    txtLine = txtLine & Space(currentDepth * 5) + File1.List(j) &
    ➡newLine
  Next
  DirStructure = DirStructure & txtLine

  subFolders = Dir2.ListCount
  If subFolders > 0 Then
    currentDepth = currentDepth + 1
    For i = 0 To subFolders - 1
'msgbox "moving from " & CurDir & " to " & Dir1.List(i)
```

```
            DirStructure = DirStructure & "{\b " & DoubleSlashes
        ➥(Dir2.List(i)) & "}" & newLine
            ChDir Dir2.List(i)
            Dir2.Path = Dir2.List(i)
            File1.Path = Dir2.List(i)
            ScanFolders
        Next
        currentDepth = currentDepth - 1
        DoEvents
    End If
    MoveUp
    File1.Path = Dir2.Path
End Sub
```

Every time this subroutine visits a new folder, it prints the names of all the files in it, with the first For...Next loop. Likewise, every time it switches to another folder, it prints its name in bold with the line:

```
DirStructure = DirStructure & "{\b " & DoubleSlashes(Dir2.List(i))
➥& "}" & newLine
```

The newLine constant is defined as follows:

```
Const newLine = "{\par }"
```

Notice that the Chr$(10)+Chr$(13) combination won't cause a line break in a RichTextBox control. The DoubleSlashes() function replaces the slashes in the path name with two slashes. The slash is a special character in RTF; to cause the RichTextbox control to print a slash instead of interpreting a slash, you must prefix the slash with another slash.

Hidden Controls in the DirMap Application

Figure 10.8 shows the window of the application at design time. Notice that the Form contains a second DirListBox control and a FileListBox control, which remain invisible at run time. The FileListBox control is where the program looks for the current folder's files. There's no reason for the user to watch its contents change a dozen times a second as new folders are mapped, so I chose to hide it from the user. The other DirListBox control is where the current folder's subfolders are displayed. Again, once the user selects the folder to be mapped, there's no reason for him or her to watch the names of the various subfolders as the program scans a folder.

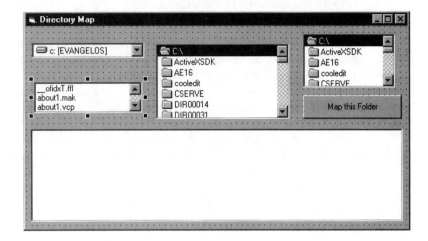

FIGURE 10.8

The Directory Map application

The user selects the folder to be mapped in the visible DirListBox control. The program uses the hidden DirListBox control for its own purposes and lets the visible DirListBox control display the selected folder. The two DirListBox controls are kept in sync from within the Change events of the visible controls. As a new drive or folder is selected, both DirListBox controls are updated.

Code 10.10: The File Controls

```
Private Sub Dir1_Change()

    ChDir Dir1.Path
    Dir2.Path = Dir1.Path
    File1.Path = Dir2.Path

End Sub

Private Sub Drive1_Change()

    ChDrive Drive1.Drive
    Dir1.Path = Drive1.Drive
    Dir2.Path = Drive1.Drive

End Sub
```

Further Customization

Another customization idea is to process selected files with a specific application. Suppose your DownLoad folder is full of ZIP files you have downloaded from various sources. Unzipping these files in the DownLoad folder would be a disaster. Ideally, you should create a separate folder for each ZIP file, copy a single ZIP file there, and then unzip it. You can do this manually, or you can let a variation of the FileScan application to do it for you. All you need is a small program that creates the folder, moves the ZIP file there, and then unzips it with PKUNZIP. (Of course, any zipping/unzipping utility will work in a similar manner.) You could even write a DOS batch file, such as the following, to process the ZIP files:

```
md c:\Shareware\%2
copy %1 c:\Shareware\%2\
del %1
pkunzip c:\Shareware\%1
```

 TIP A batch file is a program that can be started with the Shell function. To start the PKUNZIP application from within Visual Basic, use a statement such as `Shell("pkunzip c:\zipfiles\*.ZIP")`.

If this batch file is named Mvfiles.bat, you can call it with two arguments, like this:

```
MVFILES CuteUtility.zip CuteUtility
```

The first argument is the name of the ZIP file to be moved and unzipped, and the second argument is the name of the folder where the ZIP file will be moved and unzipped. You can modify the FileScan application so that every time it runs into a ZIP file, it calls the Mvfiles.bat program with the appropriate arguments and lets it process the ZIP file.

The Stack Mechanism

Now that you have seen examples of recursive programming and have a better understanding of this powerful technique, let's look at the mechanism that makes recursion possible. I mentioned earlier that each time a procedure (function or subroutine) calls another, its status must be stored in memory so that it can later resume execution. The status of an interrupted procedure includes the location of the line where it was interrupted and the values of the local variables the moment it was interrupted. This information is enough for a procedure to resume operation and never be aware that it was interrupted.

Stack Explained

The area of memory in which the procedure's status is stored is called the *stack*. The stack is a protected area of the system's memory that is handled exclusively by the operating system. The stack memory is regular memory, but the operating system handles it differently from the way it handles the rest of memory. For one thing, programs can't grab any byte from the stack. The items in this memory are stacked on top of one another, and only the topmost item can be extracted.

Each time a program places a value on the stack, the new item is placed at the top of the stack. When a program reads a value from the stack, it can only read the item on top, which is the item that was placed on the stack most recently. This type of memory organization is called Last-In-First-Out, or LIFO. The item that was placed on the stack last is the first to be read from it. And this is exactly the mechanism used to pass arguments between procedures.

Recursive Programming and the Stack

If you are not familiar with the role of stack in the computer's operation, the following discussion will probably help you understand a little better the mechanics of recursion. The stack is one of the oldest models used in programming, and it's still as useful and as popular as ever. In fact, it's an important part of the operating system, and microprocessors provide special commands for manipulating the stack. Fortunately, you won't have to worry about the stack, since it's handled exclusively by the operating system and your favorite programming language. The description of the stack you'll find in this section is a bit simplified. The goal is to explain how recursive procedures work, and I don't want to get too technical.

Suppose the recursive procedure is a subroutine and accepts no arguments, similar to the ScanFolders() subroutine. When the ScanFolders() subroutine calls itself, it must first store its status on the stack so that it can later resume. One component of the subroutine's status is the line that was executing when the program was interrupted. The ScanFolders() subroutine calls itself from within a loop. When it resumes, it should be able to continue with the remaining loops, not start all over again. The loop's counter, i, is part of the subroutine's status, and it must also be stored on the stack, along with all the information that makes up the function's status.

The ScanFolders() subroutine's status is stored on top of the stack, and the same subroutine starts executing again with a fresh set of local variables (a new loop counter, for example). When this copy of the ScanFolders() subroutine calls itself again, its status is stored on the stack, on top of the status of the previously interrupted subroutine. As more instances of the same subroutine are called, the status of each is stored on top of the previously interrupted subroutine's status. Eventually, the active ScanFolders() subroutine terminates, and the most recently interrupted one takes over. Its status is on the top of the stack. The operating system removes the values of its local variables from the stack so that the subroutine can resume execution.

What's left on the top of the stack now is the status of the subroutine that must resume execution when the active subroutine terminates. When these values are removed from the stack, the status of another interrupted function surfaces on the stack, and so on. This simple mechanism allows procedures to interrupt each other and track their status without any complicated operations. Each procedure finds its status on the stack, as if no other information was ever placed on top of it.

Passing Arguments through the Stack

The same mechanism is used to pass arguments from one procedure to another. Suppose your program calls the function Payment(Amount, Interest), which expects to read two arguments—the loan amount and an interest rate—and return the monthly payment. As you know so well by now, you must also supply the arguments in this order: first the amount, then the interest. The calling program leaves its status and the two arguments on the stack, in the same order: first its status (the values of its local variables), then the value of the *Amount* argument, and finally the value of the *Interest* argument. When the Payment() function takes over, it retrieves the two arguments from the top of the stack: first the value of the last argument, then the value of the first argument. After the removal of these two values from the stack, the status of the calling procedure is at the top of the stack. When the Payment() function finishes, it leaves its result on the top of the stack and relinquishes control to the calling procedure.

The calling procedure removes the value from the top of the stack (the result of the Payment() function) and uses it for its own purposes. It then removes the values of the local variables (its status) so that it can resume execution. As you can see, the LIFO structure is ideal for exchanging data between procedures.

Suppose the Payment() function calls another function. Again, the arguments of the new function are placed on the stack, where the new function will find them. When the other function returns, it leaves its result on the top of the stack where the Payment() function will find it and remove it from the stack. It also finds its status information on the stack. No matter how many functions are called in such a nested manner, the information required is always at the top of the stack.

The only requirement when passing arguments through the stack is that they are placed there in the order they are needed. The procedure being called has no other means to decipher which value corresponds to which argument. That's why these arguments are also known as *positional arguments*. Many Visual Basic functions now support named arguments, and you can pass to them arguments in any order, as long as you provide both the name and the value of the argument. Even these procedures use the stack mechanism to pass the named arguments, but the mechanics are a bit more complicated. The basic idea is the same: The information is always placed on top of the stack, and when it's read, it's also removed from the stack. In this way, each procedure is guaranteed to find the information it left on the stack, the moment it needs it.

A Real-Life Example

Imagine that you were so disciplined and organized that you could place every document you use in your office on top of a document stack. Every time you're interrupted by a visitor or a phone call, you leave the document you were working with on top of this paper stack, remove another document from your filing cabinet, place it in front of you, and work with it. When you're done, you take the document in front of you and place it back in the filing cabinet (or if you're interrupted again you place this document on the stack and retrieve another one from the filing cabinet).

What you now have in front of you is the document you were working with when you were interrupted. When you're done with this document, you put it back where it belongs, and another document surfaces on the stack—the document you were working with before you were interrupted. Work with this document, revise it, put it away, and there you have another document, from an even earlier interruption. If you can maintain this type of organization, you'll never waste time looking for documents. Everything will be in its filing cabinet, and most of the time the document you need will be right in front of you. Fortunately, we're not as simplistic as our computers and need not be so rigid. But you have to agree that this type of memory organization makes perfect sense for keeping track of interrupted tasks on your computer.

Some Special Issues in Recursive Programming

Recursion is not a technique that most programmers commonly use. Only a few situations call for recursive programming, and, unfortunately, these programs can't be implemented otherwise. The following sections discuss the dangers of recursion and give you a few hints to help you recognize a procedure that calls for recursive programming.

It's Easy to Write a Never-Ending Program

If you forget to specify an exit condition, a few statements that stop the procedure from calling itself, you'll end up with a never-ending program, something like an endless loop. If this happens, your computer will run out of memory for storing the intermediate results, and the program will end with the error message of Figure 10.9. The memory available for storing intermediate results between procedure calls is limited, and it's easy to exhaust it.

FIGURE 10.9

The "Out of Stack Space" error message

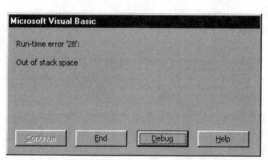

The stack isn't used only for recursive procedures. Each time a function is called, the status of the one that's interrupted, along with the arguments of the function being called, are stored on the stack. It's practically impossible to run out of stack space with regular procedures; to do so, you would have to call several hundred procedures, one from within the other. You can run out of stack space with recursive procedures, though, because you don't have to write several hundred routines—only one that calls itself and doesn't provide an exit mechanism.

Knowing When to Use Recursive Programming

Another issue is knowing *when* to use recursion. The recursive nature of many problems isn't obvious, so it may take a while to get the hang of it. (We humans aren't trained to think recursively. Once you've established the recursive nature of a problem, the recursive algorithm will follow quite naturally.) An algorithm that in the middle of carrying out a task has to start (and complete) an identical task is a prime candidate for recursive implementation. Consider the Binary Search algorithm, which rejects half the original list and then has to do the same with the other half. Or consider a procedure for scanning the contents of a folder. First, it counts the files. If the folder has subfolders, the same process must be repeated for each subfolder.

If you find yourself nesting loops in many levels or if you're trying to set up conditions to exit these loops prematurely, your code would probably benefit from a recursive implementation. Recursion bears some resemblance to iteration, and in many situations, you can implement a recursive algorithm with a loop. The factorial algorithm, for instance, can be easily implemented with a For...Next loop. But there are situations in which iterations won't help.

Try It!

If you're interested in recursion and would like to experiment a little, here's a problem that can be solved both recursively and nonrecursively. Write a program that accepts a phone number and produces all possible 7-letter combinations that match the phone number (vanity numbers, as they are called). This is not a trivial task, no matter how you look at it.

CHAPTER
ELEVEN

11

Database Programming with Visual Basic

- ■ Working with Databases and database management systems

- ■ Using the Data control and data-bound controls

- ■ Manipulating RecordSets

- ■ Using SQL statements

- ■ Using advanced data-bound controls

- ■ Mapping databases

If there is one topic that's too big to fit in a single chapter, it's database programming. This chapter, therefore, is an introduction to the basic concepts of database programming with Visual Basic. It's primarily for those who want to set up small databases and for those familiar with other database management systems, such as dBase. If you are familiar with database programming in other environments, the information in this chapter will help you get up to speed quickly in database programming with Visual Basic.

> **NOTE**
>
> The applications in this chapter use the sample databases BIBLIO and NWIND, which come with the Professional Edition of Visual Basic. The names of the databases are hardcoded in many of the examples. In particular, the databases are expected to reside in the default folder that is created during installation. If you didn't install Visual Basic to its default folder, you must change the name of the database to match its location on your system. You must change the DatabaseName property of the Data control (if the application uses the Data control) or the path of the database in the OpenDatabase() method in the code (if the application opens the database directly). Because you can't change these settings on the CD, you must first copy the sample applications to a folder on your hard disk and then run or modify them.

Databases and Database Management Systems

Nearly all business applications need to store large volumes of data, organized in a format that simplifies retrieval. This is accomplished with a database management system (DBMS), a mechanism for manipulating tabular data with high-level commands. The database management system hides low-level details, such as how data are stored in a database, and frees the programmer to concentrate on managing information, rather than on the specifics of manipulating files or maintaining links among them.

Visual Basic provides a wealth of tools for creating and accessing databases on both individual machines and networks. The two major tools are:

- The Data control
- The Data Access object

The *Data control* gives you access to databases without any programming. You can set a few properties of the control and use regular controls such as text boxes to display the values of the fields in the database. This is the no-code approach to database programming, which is implemented quite nicely in Visual Basic. But as you can guess, this approach can't take you far. Sooner or later, you will have to write code.

The *Data Access object* is a structure of objects for accessing databases through your code. All the functionality of the Data control is also available to your code, through the Data Access object (DAO).

Just what is a database? In its basic sense, a database is simply a grouping of related information, organized for easy processing and retrieval. The actual data in a database is stored in *tables*, which are similar to random access files. Data in a table is made up of *columns* and *rows*. The rows contain identically structured pieces of information, which are equivalent to the records of random access files. A *record* is a collection of values (called fields).

FIGURE 11.1

A pictorial representation of a database and the structure of tables

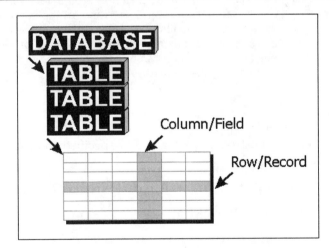

RecordSets

RecordSets are objects that represent collections of records from one or more tables. In database programming, RecordSets are the equivalent of variables in regular programming. You can't access the tables of a database directly. The only way to view or manipulate records is via RecordSet objects. A RecordSet is constructed of columns and rows and is similar to a table, but it can contain data from multiple tables. The contents of the grid shown in Figure 11.2 come from a single table, and they form a RecordSet. Such records are the result of queries, such as all the customers and the total of their invoices in a given month.

FIGURE 11.2

The Products table of the NWIND database. The selected row is a record of the Products table.

ID	ProductName	SupplierID	egoryID	QuantityPerUnit	UnitPrice
1	Chai	1	1	10 boxes x 20 bags	18
2	Chang	1	1	24 - 12 oz bottles	19
3	Aniseed Syrup	1	2	12 - 550 ml bottles	10
4	Chef Anton's Cajun Seasoning	2	2	48 - 6 oz jars	22
5	Chef Anton's Gumbo Mix	2	2	36 boxes	21.35
6	Grandma's Boysenberry Spread	3	2	12 - 8 oz jars	25
7	Uncle Bob's Organic Dried Pears	3	7	12 - 1 lb pkgs.	30
8	Northwoods Cranberry Sauce	3	2	12 - 12 oz jars	40
9	Mishi Kobe Niku	4	6	18 - 500 g pkgs.	97
10	Ikura	4	8	12 - 200 ml jars	31

NOTE

One way to think of RecordSets is as object variables. They store the results of queries or an entire table of the database, just as a numeric variable stores numbers. The contents of a RecordSet, however, have a more complicated structure (they are made of rows and columns), and each cell on this grid can be of a different type. To access the contents of the RecordSet, you use its properties and methods.

A RecordSet, therefore, is a view of some of the data in the database, selected from the database according to user-specified criteria. The three types of RecordSets are:

- **DynaSets,** which are updatable views of data

- **SnapShots,** which are static (read-only) views of data

- **Tables,** which are direct views of tables

DynaSets and SnapShots are usually created with SQL (Structured Query Language) statements. We will look at SQL statements shortly, but all you need to know about SQL statements for now is that they are commands that you use to specify criteria for recalling data from a database. DynaSets are updated every time users change the database, and changes you make to the corresponding RecordSet are reflected in the underlying tables. SnapShots are static views of the same data. A SnapShot contains the records requested the moment the SnapShot was generated (changes made to the underlying tables are not reflected in SnapShots), and you can't update SnapShots.

The DynaSet is the most flexible and powerful type of RecordSet, although a few operations (such as searches) may be faster with the Table type of RecordSet. The Table type, however, requires a lot of overhead. The least flexible RecordSet type, the SnapShot, is the most efficient in terms of overhead. If you don't need to update the database and simply want to view records, prefer the SnapShot type.

There's also a variation of the SnapShot type, the *forward-only SnapShot*, which is even more limited that the SnapShot type, but is faster. Forward-only Snap-Shots let you move forward only. You can use them in programming situations in which you want to scan a number of records and process them sequentially (use their values in a calculation, copy selected records to another table, and so on). By not providing any methods to backstep in the records, this RecordSet type requires the least overhead of all.

The Table type of RecordSet is a reference to a table in the database. The Table is faster that the other types of RecordSets, it is always in sync with the table's data, and it can be used to update the database. But the Table is limited to a single table. In addition, when accessing a table through a Table type of RecordSet, you can take advantage of the Table's indices to perform very fast searches.

The Data Control

RecordSets are the foundation of database programming. Let's look at an example that will help you visualize RecordSets and explore the Data control. The Data1 application, shown in Figure 11.3, is nothing less than a front end for an existing table in a database.

FIGURE 11.3

The Data1 application lets you browse a table's rows without writing a single line of code.

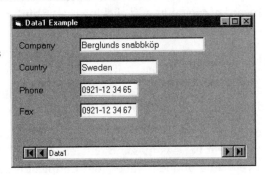

VB5 at Work: The Data1 Application

To build this application, follow these steps:

1. Start a new Standard EXE project and design a Form like the one shown in Figure 11.3. Start by drawing a Data control at the bottom of the Form. The Data control is your gateway to the database.

2. With the Data control selected, locate its DatabaseName property in the Properties window, and then click on the ellipsis button to open the Open dialog box.

3. Select the NWIND database that comes with Visual Basic.

4. Locate the RecordSource property and drop down the list of available entries. You'll see all the tables in the NWIND database. Select the Customers table.

5. Place four text boxes on the Form, as shown in Figure 11.3.

6. Select the first text box, and in the Properties window locate its DataSource property. Set it to Data1.

7. Set the DataField property of the text box to CompanyName. The DataField property is a drop-down list with the names of all fields in the Customers table.

8. Set the DataSource property of the other three text boxes to Data1, and set the DataField property to Country, Phone, and Fax.

Now run the application. The text boxes will display the values of the corresponding fields of the Customers table in the NWIND database. Using the Data control's buttons, you can move through the records (rows) of the table. Clicking on the leftmost button displays the first record of the table, and clicking on the button next to it displays the previous record. Clicking on the rightmost button displays the last record of the table, and clicking on the button next to it displays the next record.

Not only can you navigate through the table's records with the Data control, you can also edit its fields. Change the value of a field, move to the next record, and then come back to the previous record. The changes you made to the record are saved to the database, and now you see the updated value of the record.

You should also attempt to enter invalid data in the table's fields. The program won't allow you to enter invalid values and will let you know why. If you attempt to enter a very long phone number, for example, the application displays a message indicating that the entry is too long for the field and gives you a chance to correct the value. The field was obviously declared with a limited length in the definition of the database. It is actually the database management system that issues the warning, not Visual Basic and certainly not the application. You have yet to enter a single line of code.

Figure 11.4 shows the relationship among the TextBox controls on the Form, the Data control, and the database. The controls on the Form can't see the database directly. Instead, they see the database through the Data control. The Data control, in turn, sees a RecordSet, which happens to be a table of the database. You'll learn later how to specify other types of RecordSets for the Data control.

FIGURE 11.4

The Data control sees one row of the RecordSet and updates the data-bound controls on the Form with the value of the specific field.

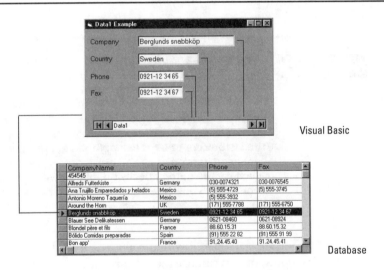

The Data Control's Properties

The most important properties of the Data control are:

- **DatabaseName,** which specifies the database to be used

- **RecordSource,** which specifies the part of the database seen by the control

At any given time, the Data control is positioned at a single row (record) of its RecordSet. The user can move to any other record with the help of the navigation buttons on the Data control.

The text boxes see a field in the current row. Each time the Data control is repositioned in its RecordSet, the text boxes are updated. If the data in a text box changes, the new value is written to the database when the Data control is repositioned. The TextBox controls are connected to a field of the RecordSet through the Data control, and they are called *data-bound* (they have been bound to a field in the RecordSet).

The most important properties of a data-bound control are:

- **DataSource,** which is the name of a Data control through which they are bound to a Data control

- **DataField,** which is the name of a field in the RecordSet that the control displays and updates

NOTE   The controls are bound to a specific field, and they are called data-bound. There are other controls that you can bind to the Data control's RecordSet. If you want to prevent users of the application from editing the contents of the table, you can use Label controls. If the table contains Boolean fields (that have the values True/False only), you can bind them to CheckBox controls. Some common controls aren't data-bound. The ListBox control, for example, isn't data-bound. Microsoft provides an enhanced version of the ListBox control, the Databound ListBox control, which can be automatically populated with the values of a column in the RecordSet. You'll see later how to use this control in your applications.

You can set the following properties of the Data control from the Properties window, or you can use them from within your code to manipulate the control.

EOF   The EOF (End Of File) property returns a True/False value that indicates whether the current record position is after the last record in a RecordSet object.

BOF   The BOF (Beginning Of File) property returns a True/False value that indicates whether the current record position is before the first record in a RecordSet object.

BOFAction   This property sets or returns a value indicating what action the Data control should take when the BOF property is True, which can be one of the actions in Table 11.1.

TABLE 11.1   The Values Returned by the BOFAction Property

CONSTANT	VALUE	ACTION
vbBOFActionMoveFirst	0	(Default) Repositions the control on the first record.
vbBOFActionBOF	1	Moves past the beginning of a RecordSet and lands on an invalid record. At the same time, it triggers the Data control's Validate event for the first record. You'll see later how to handle this situation.

EOFAction   This property sets or returns a value indicating what action the Data control takes when the EOF property is True, which can be one of the actions in Table 11.2.

TABLE 11.2   The Values Returned by the EOFAction Property

CONSTANT	VALUE	ACTION
vbEOFActionMoveLast	0	(Default) Repositions the control on the last record.
vbEOFActionEOF	1	Moves past the end of a RecordSet and lands on an invalid record. At the same time, it triggers the Data control's Validate event for the last record. You'll see later how to handle this situation.
vbEOFActionAddNew	2	Adds a new blank record to the RecordSet, which the user can edit. The new record is written to the database when the user repositions the Data control.

ReadOnly   This property returns or sets a value that determines whether the control's RecordSet is opened for read-only access.

RecordsetType   This property returns or sets a value indicating the type of RecordSet object you want the Data control to create. It can have one of the values shown in Table 1.3.

TABLE 1.3   The Values of the RecordsetType Property

CONSTANT	VALUE	DESCRIPTION
vbRSTypeTable	0	A Table type of RecordSet
vbRSTypeDynaset	1	(Default) A DynaSet type of RecordSet
vbRSTypeSnapshot	2	A SnapShot type of RecordSet

Options   This property sets one or more characteristics of the RecordSet object and can have one of the values shown in Table 11.4.

TABLE 11.4   The Values of the Options Property

CONSTANT	VALUE	DESCRIPTION
dbDenyWrite	1	In a multiuser environment, other users can't make changes to records in the RecordSet.
dbDenyRead	2	In a multiuser environment, other users can't read records (Table type of RecordSet only).
dbReadOnly	4	The user of the application can read but can't make changes to records in the RecordSet.
dbAppendOnly	8	The user of the application can add new records to the RecordSet, but can't read existing records.
dbInconsistent	16	Updates can apply to all fields of the RecordSet, even if they violate the join condition (applies to RecordSets based on SQL queries).
dbConsistent	32	(Default) Updates apply only to those fields that don't violate the join condition (applies to RecordSets based on SQL queries).
dbSQLPassThrough	64	When using Data controls with an SQL statement in the RecordSource property, sends the SQL statement to an ODBC database, such as a SQL Server or an Oracle database, for processing.

TABLE 11.4   The Values of the Options Property (continued)

CONSTANT	VALUE	DESCRIPTION
dbForwardOnly	256	The RecordSet object supports forward-only scrolling.The only Move method allowed is MoveNext. This option cannot be used on RecordSet objects manipulated with the Data control.
dbSeeChanges	512	Generates a trappable error if another user is changing data you are editing.

Bookmark   This property is a Variant that identifies a row in the RecordSet. Each row has its own, unique bookmark that isn't related to the record's order in the RecordSet. Save the Bookmark property to a variable so that you can return to this record later by assigning the variable to the Bookmark property.

The Data Control's Methods

The built-in functionality of the Data control, which is impressive indeed, can be accessed through an application's code with the Data control's methods. The simplest methods are the navigation methods, which correspond to the actions of the four buttons on the control, and they are as follows:

- **MoveFirst**   Repositions the control to the first record
- **MoveLast**   Repositions the control to the last record
- **MovePrevious**   Repositions the control to the previous record
- **MoveNext**   Repositions the control to the next record

You can use these methods to implement navigation buttons. However, you must take care of two special cases: (1) what happens when the Data control is positioned at the first or last record and (2) what happens when the Previous button is clicked while the Data control is on the first record, and what happens when the Next button is clicked while the Data control is on the last record.

VB5 at Work: The Data2 Application

The Data2 application is similar to the Data1 application, but this time we'll use a different database. The BIBLIO database, which also comes with Visual Basic, is a database of book titles, publishers, and authors. We will look at the structure of this database later in the chapter, but in this application we are going to build a front end for navigating through the Titles table, which contains Title, ISBN, Description, Subject, and Comments fields, among others. The Form of the Data2 application is shown in Figure 11.5.

FIGURE 11.5

The Data2 application uses the methods of the Data control to implement the four navigation buttons.

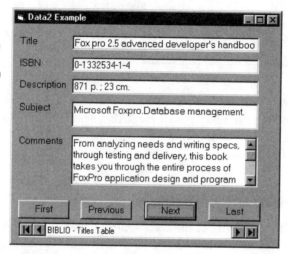

Designing the Form is straightforward. Follow these steps:

1. Place a Data control and connect it to the BIBLIO database by setting its DatabaseName property to the path of the database on your system and setting its RecordSource property to the Titles table.

2. Place the data-bound controls on the Form and bind them to the Data control by setting their DataSource property to Data1 and their Datafield properties to the fields they display.

The code behind the First and Last buttons is simple. It calls the corresponding navigation method of the control.

Code 11.1: The First and Last Buttons

```
Private Sub firstBttn_Click()
    Data1.Recordset.MoveFirst
End Sub

Private Sub LastBttn_Click()
```

```
        Data1.Recordset.MoveLast
End Sub
```

The code behind the other two buttons is a bit more complicated, as it takes into consideration the EOF property of the control.

Code 11.2: The Next Button's Click Event

```
Private Sub NextBttn_Click()
    Data1.Recordset.MoveNext
    If Data1.Recordset.EOF Then
        MsgBox "You are on the last record"
        Data1.Recordset.MoveLast
    End If
End Sub
```

The program moves to the next record, and then it examines the EOF property. If EOF is True, we have landed on a record after the last one. The program displays a message to let the user know that the last record has been reached and then moves to the last record.

NOTE
Landing on a record beyond the last one isn't catastrophic. It's a blank record, which you can let the user edit and then append to the table. A problem will arise, however, if the Next button is clicked again. Attempting to move even further beyond this record will cause a run-time error. That's why we must handle this situation as soon as we hit the EOF=True condition. You will also notice that the fields are blank while the message is displayed. Normally, you should display the message after moving to the last valid record. I used this order here to demonstrate that after the last record in the RecordSet there's indeed a blank record.

The code behind the Previous button is quite similar. It calls the MovePrevious method, and instead of the EOF property, it examines the BOF property of the Data control.

Code 11.3: The Previous Button

```
Private Sub PreviousBttn_Click()
    Data1.Recordset.MovePrevious
    If Data1.Recordset.BOF Then
        MsgBox "You are on the first record"
```

```
        Data1.Recordset.MoveFirst
    End If
End Sub
```

The Find Methods

In addition to the navigation methods, the Data control provides four methods for finding records in the RecordSet. One of the basic operations you perform on databases is locating specific records. The following methods locate records:

- **FindFirst**   Finds the first record that meets the specified criteria

- **FindLast**   Finds the last record that meets the specified criteria

- **FindNext**   Finds the next record that meets the specified criteria

- **FindPrevious**   Finds the previous record that meets the specified criteria

These methods can locate any record in the RecordSet, based on any user-specified criteria. The syntax of all these methods is the same and is as follows:

```
RecordSet.FindFirst criteria
```

The *criteria* entry is a string expression specifying a relation between field values and constants. The following statement:

```
Data1.RecordSet.FindFirst "State='NY'"
```

locates the first record in the RecordSet in which the state is NY. Notice that literals within the *criteria* string are delimited with single quotes. The user-specified criteria can be more complicated and can combine values of multiple fields with logical and relational operators. For example, the following statement:

```
Data1.RecordSet.FindFirst "InvoiceDate > '12/31/1996' AND Invoice
>= 1000'"
```

locates the first invoice issued in 1997 with a total of $1,000 or more.

In addition to the usual relational operators, you can use the LIKE operator, which allows you to locate records that match a pattern. For example, to locate any book in the BIBLIO database with SQL in its title, use the following Find method:

```
RecordSet.FindFirst "Title LIKE '*SQL*'"
```

The string *SQL* is a pattern that allows any number of characters to appear before and after SQL. In other words, it matches titles such as *SQL: An Introduction*, *Mastering SQL*, or *The SQL Handbook*.

How the Find Methods Search

The search performed by the Find methods is case-insensitive. Thus, the argument *SQL* matches SQL, , sql, and SqL. To change the default search mode, use the following statement to make comparisons case-insensitive:

```
Option Compare Text
```

Use the following statement to make comparisons case-sensitive:

```
Option Compare Binary
```

The Option Compare statement must appear in the Form's declarations or in a module.

When a Find method is called, Visual Basic locates a record that matches the criteria and repositions the Data control to this record. In your code, however, you must first examine the value of the NoMatch property, which is set to False if a record was found, and True otherwise. The following code segment shows how the Find methods are used:

```
Data1.Recordset.FindFirst "City='Berlin'"
If Data1.Recordset.NoMatch Then
    MsgBox "No such record found"
Else
    MsgBox Data1.Recordset.Fields("Country")
End If
```

This code segment searches for the first record whose City field has the value Berlin. If no such record is found, the program displays a message. If it's found, the program displays the value of the field Country.

VB5 at Work: The FindDemo Application

The FindDemo application demonstrates how to use the Find methods on a RecordSet. You can actually include this little utility in a larger application to implement a general Find feature. The application is shown in Figure 11.6. The first ComboBox control lets you select a table, and the second ComboBox control lets you select a field. You can then type a search argument for the operation in the Search Value text box and click on the buttons to locate the records that meet the specified criteria.

FIGURE 11.6

The FindDemo application demonstrates the Find commands.

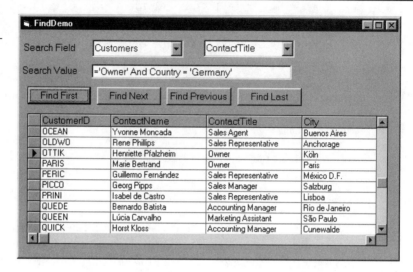

As you can see in Figure 11.6, it is possible to specify additional fields in the search argument, beyond the one selected in the ComboBox. Any strings in the Search Value field must be enclosed in single quotes. Alternatively, you can write a small procedure that replaces any double quotes found in the string with single quotes.

If you run the FindDemo application, you'll see columns that are different from the ones shown in Figure 11.6. If you place the pointer on the dividing line between two columns in the data-bound Grid control, it turns into a double arrow, indicating that you can resize the column. To prepare Figure 11.6, I eliminated some columns with meaningless data by setting their width to zero and resized other columns to display the columns with the data of interest (contact names and cities).

The Form of the FindDemo application contains a data-bound Grid control and a hidden Data control. The data-bound Grid control is discussed later in this chapter. For purposes of this example, all you need to know is that this control can be bound to a Data control and can display the Data control's RecordSet in a tabular arrangement. The code that populates the two ComboBox controls accesses the values of the fields through code, and this will be explained in the section "Accessing Fields in RecordSets" later in this chapter.

Code 11.4: The Find First Button

```
Private Sub firstBttn_Click()
On Error GoTo SQLError
    Data1.Recordset.FindFirst GenerateSQL()
    If Data1.Recordset.NoMatch Then
        MsgBox "No such record found"
    End If
    Exit Sub

SQLError:
    MsgBox Err.Description

End Sub
```

The Generate SQL() Function   Most of the application's code handles potential errors. The program uses the search argument returned by the Generate-SQL() function to call the FindFirst method and then examines the value of the NoMatch property. If no matching records are found, the program displays a message and exits the subroutine.

The GenerateSQL() function generates the search argument for all Find operations. The value returned by the GenerateSQL() function is used with the Find methods. After calling the FindFirst method, the program examines the NoMatch property. If it's True, the program displays a message. If a record matching the criteria was found, the Data control is automatically repositioned at this record.

The code of the GenerateSQL() function extracts the text from the txtsearchValue text box, appends it to the selected field, and returns a string that can be used as an argument with the Find methods.

Code 11.5: The GenerateSQL() Function

```
Private Function GenerateSQL() As String
    GenerateSQL = cmbFields.Text & " " & txtsearchValue
End Function
```

Relational Concepts

The databases described and used so far are *relational* because they are based on relations among the tables. The foundation of a relational database system is to break the data into multiple tables that are related by common information (keys).

Suppose you are designing a database for storing invoices. This database should have a table with customer names, product names, and prices and, of course, a table for the invoices. Each invoice that is issued to a customer contains a number of products. Instead of storing product names and customer names in the invoice, you store numbers that uniquely identify the customers and the products. These numbers are the *keys* that connect rows in one table to rows in another table. The keys establish relationships among the tables and make it possible to break the information into separate tables and avoid duplicating information.

> **NOTE** The relational database model was created in 1970 by Dr. E. Codd of IBM, who also created the query language that became SQL.

Let's look at a few basic concepts of the relational model, and then we'll develop some applications to demonstrate these principles.

The Primary Key

In a relational database system, each record has a unique identifier that is used to indicate the record and to relate it to other records in other tables. Often, a close inspection of your data will reveal something already in the data that makes each record unique; frequently, this can become the primary key. This type of primary key is called *composite*. For example, in an employees database, an employee's Social Security number is a composite primary key.

When there is not an apparent field or set of fields that can be used to form a composite primary key, Visual Basic's database management system (the JET engine, as it's known) can automatically generate a unique numeric key for each record. This type of key is made by adding a field to your table and setting it to the AutoNumber field type. An AutoNumber field automatically increments by one whenever a new record is added. This ensures that the key is unique, although the key may not necessarily mean anything. As long as all tables refer to the same record with the same key, the key need not be meaningful. Sometimes an auto-numbered primary key can be made to fit a business purpose, for example, using an auto-numbered field for an invoice number.

Regardless of the type of primary key, it is wise to *always* make the primary key of a table a field of the type long (a standard Visual Basic data type, as explained in Chapter 3, *Visual Basic, the Language*). By doing so, you greatly simplify design of other tables.

Foreign Key

A field (column) in a table that stores a value which relates it to another table is called a *foreign key*. For example, a field in an Invoices table that stores the customer number is a foreign key. The same value in the Customers table is the primary key. A foreign key should be of the same type as the primary key of the table to which it is relating.

Indices

Indices are structures that determine the order of the records in a table. Normally, data aren't maintained in any special order in the table. In most practical situations, though, you want to access them in a specific order. When you print a list of customers, you want them in alphabetic order. If you print mailing labels, you probably want customers' names ordered according to their ZIP codes. In general, the type of processing you want to perform determines the order in which a table's rows should be furnished, and it is common for a table to be furnished in different orders for different operations.

Rearranging the rows of a table each time the application needs them in a different order is out of the question. This would take too much time. The solution is to maintain small tables, called indices, that dictate the order in which records will be read from the table. The index file doesn't contain any of the information that appears in the table itself. It contains only the numbers that determine the order of the records.

Suppose that the fifth record in a table should appear first when the table's rows are requested in alphabetic order. The first element of the index file contains the value 5, so when the database supplies the rows of the specific table, it retrieves the fifth element first.

NOTE   In Chapter 5, *Basic ActiveX Controls,* we looked at an application that used the List's ItemData property to maintain sorted data with the help of a ListBox control. The index files are similar to the elements of the ItemData property.

A table can have more than a single index. The indices of all tables in a database are maintained by the JET engine, and you need not do anything more than specify the fields on which the index will be based.

When Shouldn't I Index?

When a record is updated, the indexes must be updated as well. This obviously increases the amount of time needed to update a record. Indexes also increase the amount of storage space and consequently increase both the time and media needed for routine backups. So, even though maintaining multiple indices for each table, just in case, sounds like a good idea, there's a performance penalty for the index files, and you should specify additional indices only as needed for the proper operation of the database. Too many indices, especially with very large tables that must updated frequently, will degenerate performance.

Using the Visual Data Manager

The Visual Data Manager is a Visual Basic tool for designing databases. Although it's rather crude, you can use the Visual Data Manager to create and modify tables, to implement security, and to experiment with SQL. When you open an existing database, the Visual Data Manager displays a database window listing the tables and properties of that database. Figure 11.7 shows the Visual Data Manager window with the BIBLIO database open in design mode. We'll look at the structure of the BIBLIO database shortly, but first let's explore the basic operations of the Visual Data Manager application.

FIGURE 11.7

Examining and modifying a database's structure with the Visual Data Manager

To create new tables, right-click in the database window to open the context menu, and select New Table. In the Table Structure dialog box that appears, create your fields.

Each time you add a new field to the table, by clicking on the Add Field button, the Add Field dialog box opens, as shown in Figure 11.8.

The Add Field dialog box has the options shown in Table 11.5. Some of the options are disabled in the figure and may not be readable. Follow the steps outlined to open the Add Field dialog box and see all the options on it.

TABLE 11.5 The Options in the Add Field Dialog Box

OPTION	WHAT IT IS
Name	The name of the field.
Ordinal Position	The position of the field within the field roster.
Type	The field type. A field can have the usual types of any variable, plus two additional types: Binary and Memo. Binary fields store binary data, such as sounds and images. Memo fields store long segments of text. The size of Memo fields is not specified during the design of the database. (Text fields have a predetermined length for efficiency.)
Validation Text	The text to be displayed if an attempt is made to place invalid data into the field.

TABLE 11.5   The Options in the Add Field Dialog Box (continued)

OPTION	WHAT IT IS
Validation Rule	Simple rules used to validate the values entered for the field
Default Value	The initial value for the field whenever a record is created.
Fixed Length	The field must have a fixed length.
Variable Length	The field can have variable length.
AutoIncrement	If a field is going to be used as a key, you can set its type to Long and check this box. Each time a new record is added to the table, this field is assigned a value, which is by one larger than the value of the same field in the last record.
Allow Zero Length	Check this box if a blank string is a valid value for the field.
Required	Check this box if the field can't be omitted. In a table with invoices, for example, the customer ID is a required field and so is the date.

FIGURE 11.8

Adding tables to a database and fields to tables with the Visual Data Manager

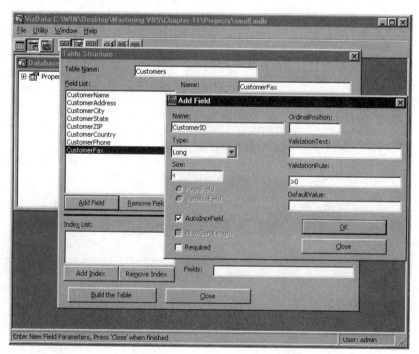

Specifying Indices with the Visual Data Manager

You can also use the Visual Data Manager to manage indexes within a database. At the bottom of the database window is a list of the indexes currently in the database. Click on the Add Index button to open the Add Index To dialog box, as shown in Figure 11.9. The Add Index To dialog box has the options listed in Table 11.6.

FIGURE 11.9

The Add Index To dialog box

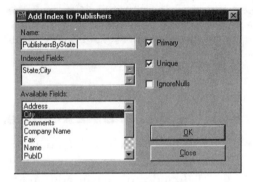

TABLE 11.6 The Options in the Add Index To Dialog Box

OPTION	WHAT IT DOES
Name	The name of the index. As a programmer, you will only use the name of the index when you are programming a Table type of RecordSet. In query situations, the RushMore technology automatically uses index information to optimize queries.
Indexed Fields	A list of the fields on which the table is indexed, separated by semicolons.
Available Fields	A list box of the available fields. Clicking on one will add it to the list of index fields.
Primary	Check this box to indicate whether the index's field should be considered the primary key for the table.
Unique	Check this box if you want to force unique values for the field. If you are indexing the Customers table on the customer's name field, this index need not be unique. There can be two customers with the same name. The index based on the customer's ID, though, must be unique. Two customers can't have the same key, even if they have the same name.

TABLE 11.6   The Options in the Add Index To Dialog Box (continued)

OPTION	WHAT IT DOES
IgnoreNulls	This property indicates whether any of the fields used in the index can contain a NULL value. If it's set to False and the Required property is True, a run-time error is generated if the corresponding field is Null.

> **NOTE**
>
> **Null is a special value, described in Chapter 3, *Visual Basic, the Language*. A field is Null if it hasn't been initialized (in other words, if it contains nothing). It's common to test field values against the Null value before using them in operations.**

Entering Data with the Visual Data Manager

In addition, you can use the Visual Data Manager for data-entry. Double-clicking on the name of a table in the Database window opens the table in data-entry mode, as shown in Figure 11.10, and you can edit, add, and delete records.

FIGURE 11.10

You can also use the Visual Data Manager for data entry.

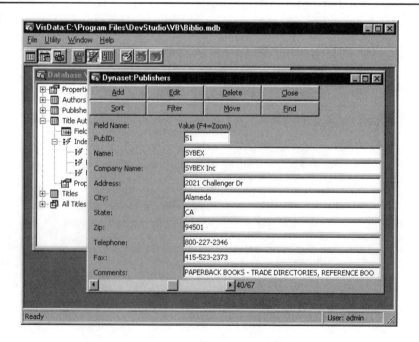

You will learn how to implement these operations from within your code in the following sections, but first we must look at the basic concepts of database design by exploring the structure of the BIBLIO database.

The Structure of the BIBLIO Database

One of the two sample databases that comes with Visual Basic is called BIBLIO. The BIBLIO database has a simple structure, almost trivial, but it demonstrates many of the topics we covered so far. You can open the BIBLIO database with the Visual Data Manager and explore its structure.

The BIBLIO database contains book titles, authors, and publishers, and it's made of four tables, as shown in Figure 11.11. Instead of showing the names of the fields of each table, this figure shows some of the data they contain, and it shows only the fields needed to demonstrate the relationships among the tables. The field names are displayed as column headings.

FIGURE 11.11

The structure of the BIBLIO database

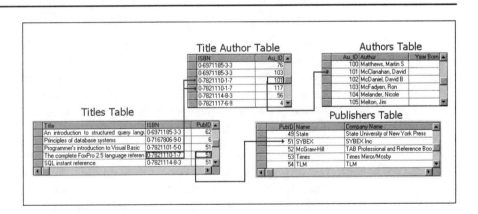

The first rule in database design is to avoid data duplication. Storing author names along with the titles would violate this rule because an author may have written more than one book. In this case, you would have to repeat the same author name in more than one row of the Titles table. Author names are stored in a separate table, the Authors table. The same is true for publishers. Since each publisher appears in many books, you shouldn't store information about publishers in the Titles table. Why repeat the publisher's address with each title?

So far, we have established the reasons for the presence of three tables in the database. But the BIBLIO database has a fourth table. Each book can have more than one author, and an author's name may appear with more than a single title. Think about this for a moment. Storing multiple author names, even author IDs for each title, would require a field for each author. This field would be analogous to the PubID field, but because a book might have multiple authors, you would have to provide a number of fields for storing Author IDs (AuthorID1, AuthorID2, and so on). It is clear that authors can't be handled like publishers.

The Title Author table sits between the Titles and Authors tables and connects them with a pair of fields, which are the Title's ISBN and the Author's ID. When you want to see a specific title's author, you will do the following:

1. Locate the desired title in the Titles table.

2. Read the Title's ISBN and use it as a key to locate the matching rows in the Title Author table.

3. For each of the matching rows in the Title Author table, read the author's ID and use it as a key to locate the author's name in the Authors table.

If you are not familiar with database programming, this procedure may sound complicated, but it isn't (perhaps you should just get used to it). Later in this chapter, you'll see two ways to search for specific records with keys. The technique just described won't work efficiently unless there's a quick way to locate a record based on the value of a specific field. And this can be accomplished with the proper indexing of the tables.

As you can see, the indices are an essential part of database design. The Title Author table, for example, must be indexed on the ISBN field. If you want to be able to search in the opposite direction (given an author's name, locate the books on which this name appears), you should also index the Title Author table on the AuID field. Obviously, the Authors table must be indexed on the AuID file, since the information in the Title Author table is the author's ID, not his or her name. The Publishers table must be indexed on the PubID field so that you can go quickly from a title to its publisher.

Data Validation

You have seen in the first example of this chapter that the Data control can also be used for editing records. Database applications, however, should have the means to validate user input before attempting to save data to the database. The Data control provides a few properties and supports a few events that let you validate the input before committing it to the database.

The Validate Event

The validation of input takes place in the Data control's Validate event, whose declaration is as follows:

```
Private Sub object_Validate (action As Integer, save As Integer)
```

The *action* entry is an integer indicating the operation that caused this event to occur and can have one of the values shown in Table 11.7.

TABLE 11.7   The Values of the Action Argument of the Validate Event

CONSTANT	VALUE	DESCRIPTION
vbDataActionCancel	0	Cancel the operation when the Sub exits.
vbDataActionMoveFirst	1	MoveFirst method.
vbDataActionMovePrevious	2	MovePrevious method.
vbDataActionMoveNext	3	MoveNext method.
vbDataActionMoveLast	4	MoveLast method.
vbDataActionAddNew	5	AddNew method.
vbDataActionUpdate	6	Update operation (not UpdateRecord).
vbDataActionDelete	7	Delete method.
vbDataActionFind	8	Find method.
vbDataActionBookmark	9	The Bookmark property has been set.

TABLE 11.7 The Values of the Action Argument of the Validate Event (continued)

CONSTANT	VALUE	DESCRIPTION
vbDataActionClose	10	The Close method.
vbDataActionUnload	11	The Form is being unloaded.

The value vbDataActionCancel can be set from within code to cancel the operation that triggered the Validate event. For example, if the user changes the data on a data-bound control and then clicks on the Move Next button of the control, you can reject the changes from within your code and cancel the Move Next operation.

The *save* argument is a Boolean expression specifying whether bound data has changed. You can set this argument to False to reject the changes.

The Error Event

Another useful event in data validation operations is the Error event. When you update records in a database, the JET engine ensures that the data entered don't invalidate the rules incorporated in the design of the database. For example, if an index requires that a specific field be unique, it won't update the record if the value entered has already been used. If a field exceeds its maximum length, the changes will also be rejected. In other words, the JET engine performs some data validation on its own. It also performs any validation steps you specified in the Validation Rule field, in each table's design.

If the data violates rules specified in the design of the database, a run-time error is generated. Before the error message is displayed, the Error event is generated. You can find out the condition that generated the error and handle it from within your code.

The declaration of the Error event is as follows:

```
Sub Error (dataerr As Integer, response As Integer)
```

The *dataerr* entry is the error number, and *response* is an integer that you can set from within the event to specify how the error will be handled. The *response* argument can take one of the values shown in Table 11.8. You must handle the error from within the Error event and then set the *response* argument to 0 to prevent the run-time error.

TABLE 11.8   The Values of the Response Argument of the Error Event

CONSTANT	VALUE	DESCRIPTION
vbDataErrContinue	0	Continue
vbDataErrDisplay	1	(Default) Display the error message

Entering Data

The Data control is a great tool for browsing tables and editing their contents, but how about entering new information or deleting existing records? These actions require a few lines of code. Nothing extreme, but you can't rely on the no-code approach of the Data control for data entry. To write data-entry applications, you use the following methods:

- **AddNew**   Appends a record to the table

- **Delete**   Deletes the current record

- **Update**   Writes the current record to the database

- **Refresh**   Reloads the data from the database (refreshes the RecordSet)

> **NOTE**
>
> It is also possible to use the Data control for data entry. To do so, set the EOFaction of the Data control to 2-Add New. Every time the user is at the last record and clicks on the Next button, the Data control displays a new empty record, which can be filled and written to the database. The method is not intuitive (to say the least), and it doesn't reflect the way in which professional data-entry applications are written.

The AddNew Method   To add a new record to a table, you call the AddNew method of the control's RecordSet (it must be a Table type of RecordSet). A new blank record is appended at the end of the RecordSet, and the Data control is positioned at this record. The user can now enter data in the data-bound controls.

The Update and Refresh Methods   When the user signals an intention to commit the new record to the database (by clicking on OK or moving to a new record), you call the Update method of the control's RecordSet. To reject the data, call the Refresh method, which refreshes the RecordSet by reading it from the database. Since the newly appended record hasn't been committed to the database, it is lost when the RecordSet is refreshed.

The Delete Method   To delete a record, call the Delete method of the control's RecordSet. The current record is removed from the RecordSet, but only after the JET engine checks any relations that might be affected. If the database enforces certain references, you won't be able to remove a record that's referenced by another one. I'm not going to discuss referential integration at length in this book, but let's see how the JET engine maintains the integrity of the references in a database.

Referential Integrity

The NWIND database, which also comes with Visual Basic, enforces the integrity of certain relations. To see how this works, follow these steps:

1.   Using the Visual Data Manager, open the NWIND database, and double-click on the Orders table, which contains all the invoices.

2.   Select an invoice and make a note of the customer ID to whom the invoice was issued.

3.   Close this table, and double-click on the name of the Customers table to open it in data-entry mode.

4.   Select the customer whose ID appeared in the invoice, and click on Delete. The JET engine displays the error message shown in Figure 11.12.

   This error message tells you that the customer you are trying to delete is referenced in another table and can't be removed.

   If a relation is important for the integrity of the database, you can ask the JET engine to enforce it. Enforcing referential integrity is one of the most important features of a database management system. Without it, your program would have to ensure that important relations are enforced (not a simple task).

FIGURE 11.12

Some relations can be enforced by the JET engine itself.

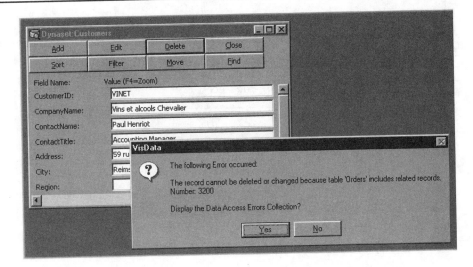

Although you can enforce certain references from within your code, the best way to implement this feature is by incorporating referential integrity in the database itself. You can't use the Visual Data Manager for this purpose, but if you use a more advanced tool for designing databases, such as Microsoft Access, you can specify which relations must be enforced by the system, and this information is stored in the database itself.

VB5 at Work: The DEntry Application

Now we are ready to build a real data-entry application, with add and delete features, as shown in Figure 11.13. When the user clicks on the Add Record button, the application calls the AddNew method and hides the two buttons on the Form. In their place, it displays the usual OK and Cancel buttons. The user can commit the new record to the database by clicking on OK or reject it by clicking on Cancel. In either case, the OK and Cancel buttons are hidden, and the Add Record and Delete Record buttons are displayed again.

The Form of the DEntry application contains a Data control, whose RecordSet is the Titles table of the BIBLIO database. The text boxes are all bound to the Data control, and they display the Title, ISBN, Description, Subject, and Comments fields of the table.

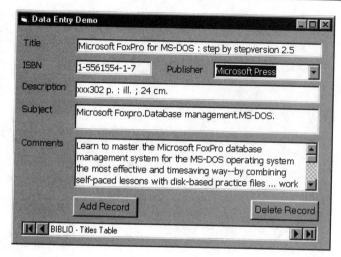

FIGURE 11.13

The DEntry application demonstrates the basic data-entry methods of the Data control.

As you recall from the discussion of the structure of the BIBLIO database, each record in the Titles table has a key that links the title to a publisher. Instead of providing a text box, in which the user can type the ID of the title's publisher, we provide a ComboBox control with the names of all publishers; the user can select one of the publishers by name. This control isn't the usual Visual Basic Combo-Box control. It's a data-bound ComboBox control, and we will look at it in the section "Advanced Data-Bound Controls," later in the chapter.

To build this application, follow these steps:

1. Add a Data control to the Form and set its DatabaseName property to the path of the BIBLIO database and its RecordSource property to the Titles table.

2. Place the five text boxes you see on the Form in Figure 11.13 and bind them to the Data1 Data control. Set each text box's DataField property to the appropriate field of the table.

3. Now, create four command buttons and set their Name and Caption properties as shown in Table 11.9.

TABLE 11.9   The Name and Caption Properties for the Command Buttons

CAPTION	NAME
Add Record	AddBttn
Delete Record	DelBttn
OK	OKBttn
Cancel	CancelBttn

4. Position the buttons on the Form so that the OK and Add Record buttons coincide and so that the Cancel and Delete buttons coincide.

Now you are ready to program the application.

Code 11.6: The Add Button's Click Event

```
Private Sub AddBttn_Click()
    HideButtons
    Data1.Recordset.AddNew
End Sub
```

The HideButtons subroutine hides the Add Record and Delete Record buttons and displays the other two buttons. The AddNew button appends a new blank record at the end of the RecordSet and repositions the Data control at this record. The user can enter new data in the text box controls and then click on OK to write the changes to the database.

Code 11.7: The OK Button's Click Event

```
Private Sub OKBttn_Click()
On Error GoTo CancelUpdate
    Data1.Recordset.Update
    ShowButtons
    Exit Sub

CancelUpdate:
    MsgBox Err.Description
    Data1.Recordset.CancelUpdate
    ShowButtons
End Sub
```

The Update method commits the temporary record to the database. The ShowButtons subroutine then hides the OK and Cancel buttons and displays the other two buttons.

> **WARNING**
>
> If an error occurs while the database is being updated (an error triggered most likely by the JET engine), the operation must be canceled. Because the Update method has been called already, it's too late to call the Refresh method. Instead, you must call the CancelUpdate method.

The Cancel button deletes the temporary record (the one displayed) by calling the Refresh method and then hides the OK and Cancel buttons.

Code 11.8: The Cancel Button's Click Event

```
Private Sub CancelBttn_Click()
    Data1.Refresh
    ShowButtons
End Sub
```

Code 11.9: The Delete Button's Click Event

```
Private Sub DelBttn_Click()
On Error Resume Next

    Data1.Recordset.Delete
    If Not Data1.Recordset.EOF Then
        Data1.Recordset.MoveNext
    ElseIf Not Data1.Recordset.BOF Then
        Data1.Recordset.MovePrevious
    Else
        MsgBox "This was the last record in the table"
    End If
End Sub
```

The Delete method deletes the current record. After a delete operation, the RecordSet isn't moved to another record automatically. Instead, it remains on the deleted record until a Move button is pressed. The code moves to the next record, unless the record deleted was the last one, in which case it moves to the previous record. If the deleted record was the only record in the table, the program displays a message and remains on the current record.

The ShowButtons and HideButtons subroutines manipulate the Visible properties of the buttons. In addition, they hide and display the Data control so that the user can end a data-entry operation with only the OK or Cancel button.

Code 11.10: The ShowButtons Subroutine

```
Sub ShowButtons()

    AddBttn.Visible = True
    DelBttn.Visible = True
    OKBttn.Visible = False
    CancelBttn.Visible = False
    Data1.Visible = True

End Sub
```

If you open the DEntry application with Visual Basic, you will a few more interesting subroutines. In the Data control's Error event, for example, the program displays the error message and cancels the update operation. This may happen if the user edits the current record and enters invalid information in one of the fields.

Code 11.11: The Data Control's Error Event

```
Private Sub Data1_Error(DataErr As Integer, Response As Integer)
    MsgBox Err.Description
    Response = 0
    Data1.Recordset.CancelUpdate
End Sub
```

In the Data control's Validate event, the program finds out whether any data-bound control has been changed, and if so, it prompts the user as to whether it should save the changes to the table.

Code 11.12: The Validate Event

```
Private Sub Data1_Validate(Action As Integer, Save As Integer)
Dim reply

    If txtTitle.DataChanged Or txtISBN.DataChanged Or
    ➥txtDescription.DataChanged Or txtSubject.DataChanged
    ➥Or txtComments.DataChanged Then
        reply = MsgBox("Record has been changed. Save?", vbYesNo)
        If reply = vbNo Then
            Save = False
```

```
          End If
      End If
End Sub
```

Typically, the code behind the Validate event takes into consideration the value of the *Action* argument and reacts according to the action that caused the error.

Accessing Fields in RecordSets

The data-bound controls can display the fields of the current record in the RecordSet of a Data control, but you must also be able to access the fields' values from within the application. The field values can be accessed via the Fields object of the RecordSet. The following expression:

```
recordset.Fields
```

represents the fields (columns) of the RecordSet. The *recordset* variable represents a RecordSet (it could be a Data control's RecordSet property, Data1.RecordSet, or a *RecordSet* variable).

You access individual fields through the field's name or through the field's ordinal position in the table. If the Data1 Data control is connected to the Titles table of the BIBLIO database, you can access the Title field of the current record with either of the following statements:

```
bookTitle = Data1.Recordset.Fields(0)
bookTitle = Data1.Recordset.Fields("Title")
```

Two more properties of interest are the RecordCount property of the RecordSet object (which returns the number of records in the RecordSet) and the Count property of the Fields object (which returns the number of fields in the Record-Set's row). These two properties are actually the dimensions of the RecordSet. The number of rows in the RecordSet of the Data1 Data control is:

```
Data1.RecordSet.RecordCount
```

and the number of columns in the same RecordSet is:

```
Data1.RecordSet.Fields.Count
```

VB5 at Work: Scanning a RecordSet

Let's develop a short application to demonstrate how you can scan the records in a RecordSet and process their fields. The processing is quite trivial: We will place the rows of a RecordSet on a ListBox control. However, the code demonstrates how to scan a RecordSet and extract specific fields.

To build this application, follow these steps:

1. Start a new project and place a ListBox control and a Data control on it, as shown in Figure 11.14.

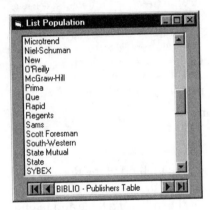

FIGURE 11.14

This application loads the fields of a RecordSet to a ListBox control.

2. Set the Data control's Visible property to False. You can't use the Data control to navigate through the RecordSet, since all the records will be in the ListBox control.

3. Set the DatabaseName and RecordSource properties of the Data control to any table of the BIBLIO or NWIND database.

4. Now, enter the following code in the Form's Load event:

```
Private Sub Form_Load()
Dim i As Integer

    Data1.Refresh
    Data1.Recordset.MoveLast
    Data1.Recordset.MoveFirst
    For i = 1 To Data1.Recordset.RecordCount
        List1.AddItem Data1.Recordset.Fields(1)
```

```
        Data1.Recordset.MoveNext
    Next
End Sub
```

TIP

If you run this application, the ListBox control is populated with the entries of the second field in the table. This code segment is meant to be used in a larger application and not on its own, of course. In the Section "Advanced Data-Bound Controls," later in this chapter, you will learn about the data-bound ListBox control, which can be populated automatically. The Refresh method causes the Data control to read the RecordSet from the database, and you should call it before using the Data control's properties. When a RecordSet is first created or refreshed, it doesn't know how many records it has. Actually, it thinks it has one record (the first one). If the user clicks on the Next button, the RecordSet thinks it has two records, because it hasn't seen the other ones yet. To find out the number of records, you must visit the last record with the MoveLast method. After calling this method, you can use the RecordCount property to find out the number of rows in the RecordSet.

The Seek Method   The Seek method of the RecordSet object can instantly locate a record in a table, based on the value of an index field. The Seek method is extremely fast because it uses the index of a table and in effect locates an item in a sorted list. The Seek method has the following syntax:

```
Seek operator key
```

The *operator* argument is one of the following relational operators:

- = (equal)
- \> (larger than)
- < (less than)
- \>= (greater or equal)
- \>= (less or equal)

The *key* argument is the value to be compared with the key field of the index. If the index is made up of a single field, *key* is a single value. If the index is made up of multiple fields, the *key* argument may contain multiple values, separated by commas.

For example, if the Customers table is indexed according to its ZIP field, you can seek the first customer in California with the following statement:

```
Data1.Recordset.Seek "=", "CA"
```

The Seek method is much faster than the Find method, but it's not as flexible. If you frequently need to locate records based on a specific field's value, create an index on this field and use the Seek method. You can use the Find method to perform all types of searches involving multiple fields and the LIKE operator, but it's not nearly as fast as the Seek method.

VB5 at Work: The ManyTbls Application

The ManyTbls application (see Figure 11.15) demonstrates the use of the Seek method to quickly locate records based on their primary keys. This application combines all the tables in the BIBLIO database to display the titles, along with their authors, publishers, and related data (comments and descriptions).

NOTE If you are familiar with SQL, you have already realized that this application can be implemented without resorting to the Seek method. In essence, you don't need to write a single line of code; just an SQL statement. This example was meant to demonstrate the use of the Seek method. We will revise the ManyTbls application later in the chapter, and you will see how to implement it with a single SQL statement.

As the user navigates through the titles with the navigation buttons of the TITLES Data control, the program displays the next or previous title in the first text box and the book's Comments and Description fields in their corresponding text boxes. These text boxes are bound directly to the Data control on the Form.

To display the publisher of the title, the application uses the PubID field of the Titles table as a key to the Publishers table, where it locates (using the Seek method) the record with the same PubID.

FIGURE 11.15

The ManyTbls application displays all the titles in the BIBLIO database, along with their authors and publishers, which are stored in different tables.

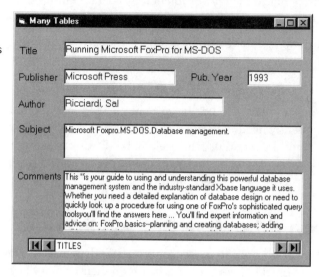

To display the author of the title, the application uses the ISBN field to locate the matching record in the Title Author table. When the record that corresponds to the current title is found, the program uses the Au_ID field as a key to the Authors table to locate the primary author's name.

These actions must take place within the Data control's Reposition event, which is triggered every time the user clicks on one of the navigation buttons to move to another record in the Titles table. The applications uses all four tables in the database, and you must therefore use four RecordSets, one for each table. The Form of the application at design time contains four Data controls, as shown in Figure 11.16, but only one of them is visible at run time.

To design the ManyTbls application, follow these steps:

1. Start a new project and place the Label and TextBox controls you see in Figure 11.16.

2. Place four Data controls on the Form: TITLES, PUBLISHERS, AUTHORISBN, and AUTHORS. Set their DatabaseName property to the path of the BIBLIO database.

3. Each Data control sees a different table of the database, so you must set the RecordSource property of each control according to Table 11.10.

FIGURE 11.16

The ManyTbls applica-
tion at design time

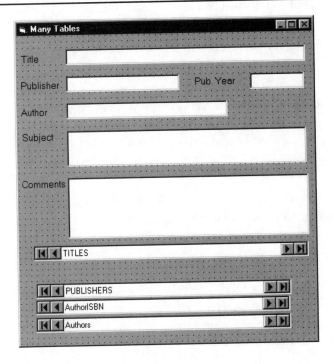

TABLE 11.10   The RecordSource Settings for the Data Control on the ManyTbls Form

DATA CONTROL NAME	RECORDSOURCE SETTING
TITLES	Titles
PUBLISHERS	Publishers
AUTHORISBN	Title Author
AUTHORS	Authors

4. Now bind the text boxes to the corresponding fields of the Data controls on
   the Form.

   - Bind the text box in which the title is displayed to the Title field of the
     TITLES Data control

- Bind the text box in which the publisher is displayed to the Publisher field of the PUBLISHERS Data control

- Bind the text box in which the author is displayed to the Author field of the AUTHORS Data control

Bind the remaining text boxes to the corresponding fields of the proper Data control. You can open the ManyTbls project in Visual Basic's IDE and examine how the various data-bound controls are bound to the Data controls. At this point, you can combine any title with any author and any publisher because the three Data controls are not connected and can be positioned at will in the corresponding tables.

We are going to use the Seek method of the Data control to connect the controls, so we must use the primary indices of the tables. This must take place when the Form is loaded.

5. Enter the following code in the Form's Load event:

```
Private Sub Form_Load()

    PUBLISHERS.Refresh
    AUTHORISBN.Refresh
    AUTHORS.Refresh

    PUBLISHERS.Recordset.Index = "PrimaryKey"
    AUTHORISBN.Recordset.Index = "ISBN"
    AUTHORS.Recordset.Index = "PrimaryKey"

End Sub
```

To open an index file for a table-type RecordSet, you must assign the name of the index to the Index property of the RecordSet. Once the Index property has been set, all Seek operations on the RecordSet will use this index.

6. Enter the following code in the TITLES Data control's Reposition event:

```
Private Sub TITLES_Reposition()

    PUBLISHERS.Recordset.Seek "=", TITLES.Recordset.Fields
    ➟("PubID")
    If PUBLISHERS.Recordset.NoMatch Then lblPublisher.Caption =
    ➟"****"
    AUTHORISBN.Recordset.Seek "=", TITLES.Recordset.Fields
    ➟("ISBN")
    If AUTHORISBN.Recordset.NoMatch Then
```

```
        lblAuthor.Caption = "***"
        Exit Sub
    End If
    AUTHORS.Recordset.Seek "=", AUTHORISBN.Recordset.Fields
    ➥("Au_ID")

End Sub
```

All the action takes place in the Reposition event. Each time the user repositions the Data control in the RecordSet, the program does the following:

1. It uses the Seek method on the PUBLISHERS RecordSet to locate the record whose PubID field matches the PubID field of the title displayed.

2. If no such record exists, it prints asterisks in the text box where the publisher's name would normally appear. If a matching record is found, the program doesn't do anything. The Seek method repositions the PUBLISHERS Data control to the row of the Publishers table with the title's publisher, and the corresponding data-bound text box is updated automatically.

3. The program then locates the record of the Title Author table whose ISBN field is the same as the current book's ISBN. If no such record exists, it prints asterisks and exits the subroutine. If a matching record is found, its Au_ID field becomes the key for the last seek operation, which locates the record in the AUTHORS table, whose Au_ID field matches the Au_ID field located in the Title Author table.

The Seek method is fast; the fields on the Form are updated instantly. Even with large files, this approach works well and doesn't introduce any significant delays. Notice that you can seek records in a RecordSet based on more than one index. Each Seek operation must be performed with a specific index, but you can change the current index by setting the Index property of the RecordSet to another value.

Displaying Multiple Authors

You may have noticed that this program displays only the primary author of each title. In an application such as this, you would probably have to display all the authors for each title.

You could, for example, add the author names in a ComboBox or ListBox control. You can easily adjust the program to display all author names if you consider that the second, third, and other authors of any title will appear right after the first matching record in the Title Author table. You can issue the MoveNext method on the AUTHORISBN RecordSet, and if its ISBN is the same as the current book's ISBN, the book has another author, and you can display it. If the ISBN field is different, the book has no more authors.

The Move methods of a RecordSet take into consideration the index of the RecordSet. For example, issuing the MoveNext method on a RecordSet with an index takes you to the next record in the index.

An Introduction to SQL

SQL, or Structured Query Language, is a nearly universal language used for database management. SQL is a *declarative language*, as opposed to a procedural language such as Visual Basic. In a declarative language, you specify *what* you want, not *how* to do it. You do not need to tell SQL *how* to access a database; you only need to tell it what you *want* from the database. In a procedural language, you must tell the language to some degree *how* to accomplish a given task.

TIP Procedural versus Declarative is the primary dividing line between a third-generation language (3GL) such as Visual Basic and a fourth-generation language (4GL) such as SQL. Whether SQL is a fourth-generation language is a tricky question. It was designed in the 1970s by Dr. E. F. Codd at IBM. At that time, languages were not even classified by generations.

We'll start by examining the structure of SQL statements and the keywords used in them, and then we'll look at numerous examples of SQL statements and develop a tool for retrieving data from databases with SQL statements.

The Format of SQL Statements

There are SQL statements for all types of operations you can perform on a database. You can use SQL statements to create a new database and to create and add tables and indices to it. You can use other SQL statements to update a database. SQL is a complete database manipulation language, but the most common use of SQL is retrieving data from databases. Retrieving data from a database is called querying the database, and the SQL statements for querying databases are called Select statements, because they begin with the SELECT verb.

The general format of a Select SQL statement is:

```
SELECT (field list) FROM (table list) WHERE (expression)
```

NOTE   The SQL keywords in this book appear in uppercase, but SQL is not case-sensitive. Using uppercase is a matter of style. It helps readers who are not familiar with SQL to spot the keywords and understand the components of a complicated SQL statement.

(field list)

This part of the statement is a list of fields to be included in the query, separated by commas. If the name of an element (field or table) contains a space, you must enclose the name in square brackets ([and]). For example, to include the Customer Name field in a query, you enter [Customer Name].

Prefix the full name of each field with the name of the table to which it belongs. This notation ensures that field names are unique, even if multiple tables have fields with the same name. For example, the full name of the Total field in the Customer Orders table is [Customer Orders].Total. If the field name Total doesn't appear in any other table, you can omit the table's name and refer to it as Total.

The output of a Select query contains the rows that match the criteria, plus a row of headers. The headers are by default the names of the fields. When you display the results of a query on a data-bound Grid control, the names of the fields are displayed as headers. To change the headers, use the AS keyword after the field name. This addition can be handy when a field name that is appropriate in the context of a table would be unclear from the context of a query consisting of several tables or would clash with the field name in another table involved in the query. For example, if you have a Total field in the Customer Orders table, you can display the header Order Total for this field with the following syntax:

```
[Customer Orders].[Total] AS [Order Total]
```

TIP   To select all the fields in a table, you can use the asterisk (*) instead of entering all the field names. For example, the following statement selects all the fields in the Orders table: SELECT * FROM Orders.

(table list)

This part of the statement is a list of all the tables on which the query is based. To retrieve fields from multiple tables, separate the field names with a comma. If your SQL statement is based on more than one table, it's a good idea to prefix the field names with the name of the table to which they belong.

When you select fields from multiple tables, you must tell the SQL engine how to combine the tables. If you specify only the names of the tables, the result of the query will contain all possible combinations of the fields in each table. To combine fields from multiple tables, you must create a so-called *join*, which is a fundamental concept in SQL Select statements that we will look at shortly.

(expression)

This part of the statement is a logical expression that is used to filter the data and report back a subset of the RecordSet. You can use most Visual Basic built-in functions and operators to form this expression as well as the following SQL-specific operators.

field_name BETWEEN value1 AND value2   Only rows in which the *field_name* is between *value1* and *value2* are returned. See the entry #date# for an example.

field_name IN(value1, value2, ...)   Only rows in which *field_name* is one of the values listed in parentheses are returned. You can specify any number of list elements inside the parentheses. The following statement retrieves customer records from certain cities:

```
SELECT Customers.CompanyName, Customers.ContactTitle,
Customers.City, Customers.Country  FROM Customers WHERE
```

```
UCase(customers.city) IN("BERLIN", "LONDON", "BERN", "PARIS")
ORDER BY Customers.Country
```

#date#   This operator specifies dates within an expression. Dates are always specified using the U.S. system of month / day / year. The following SQL statement retrieves all the orders placed in 1994 from the NWIND database:

```
SELECT Orders.ShipName, Orders.OrderDate , Orders.CustomerID
FROM Orders WHERE OrderDate BETWEEN #1/1/94# AND #12/31/94#
```

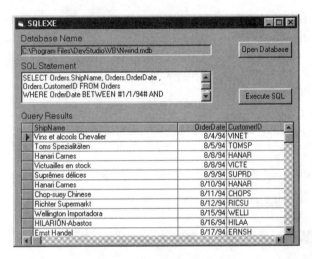

LIKE   The LIKE operator is one of the more powerful and complex of the SQL operators, and you can use it to select rows with a pattern string. To build the expression, use the special characters in Table 11.11.

TABLE 11.11   Special Characters for Use with the LIKE Operator

SYMBOL	USAGE	EXAMPLE
*	Any group of characters	Joh* locates John, Johnson, and John's.
?	Any single character	?t locates at and it.
#	Any single numeric digit	1234#67 locates 1234167, 1234267, 1234367, 1234467, and so on.
[ ]	Individual character in the brackets	[ai]t locates at and it, but not bt.

TABLE 11.11   Special Characters for Use with the LIKE Operator (continued)

SYMBOL	USAGE	EXAMPLE
[!]	Any character *not* in the brackets	[!a]t locates it but not at.
[-]	Any character within a range	[i-k]t locates it, jt, and kt, but not at or st.

ORDER BY (field list)   This operator orders the rows of the RecordSet according to the values of the specified fields. The following SQL statement creates a RecordSet of the names of all the customers in the Customers table of the NWIND database, sorted by country. Customers in the same country appear in the order of their city:

```
SELECT Customers.CompanyName, Customers.ContactName,
Customers.Country, Customers.City FROM Customers ORDER BY
Customers.Country, Customers.City
```

(The table name need not appear in front of the field names in this statement.)

The results of this statement are shown below:

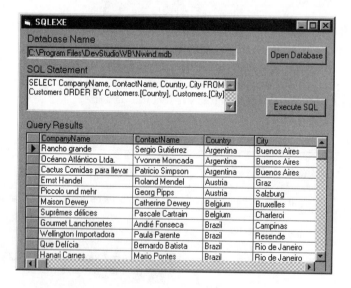

Joins in SQL

Joins specify how you connect multiple tables in a query, and there are three types of joins:

- Left Outer
- Right Outer
- Inner

A join operation combines all the rows of one table with the rows of another table. Joins are usually followed by a condition, which determines which records in either side of the join will appear in the RecordSet.

Left Outer Join   The Left Outer Join displays all the records in the left table and only those records of the table on the right that match certain user-supplied criteria. This join has the following syntax:

```
FROM (primary table) LEFT JOIN (secondary table) ON
➡(primary table).(field) (comparison) (secondary table).(field)
```

In a Left Outer Join, all records in the primary table are matched according to specified criteria with records from a secondary table. Records from the left table (the one whose name appears to the left of the Left Join keyword) are included even if they do not match any records in the secondary table.

Right Outer Join   The Right Outer Join is similar to the Left Outer Join, except that all the records in the table on the right are displayed and only the matching records from the left table are displayed. This join has the following syntax:

```
FROM (secondary table) RIGHT JOIN (primary table) ON (secondary
 table).(field) (comparison) (primary table).(field)
```

In a Right Outer Join, all records in the primary table are matched according to specified criteria with records from a secondary table. Records from the primary table are included even if they do not match any records in the first table.

Outer Joins return enormous RecordSets, and you should avoid using them. Inner Joins, on the other hand, are common, and most SQL statements are built with them.

Inner Join   The Inner Join returns the rows of both tables involved in the operation that match according to specified criteria. The Inner Join has the following syntax:

```
FROM (primary table) INNER JOIN (secondary table) ON (primary
➥table).(field) (comparison) (secondary table).(field)
```

Because Inner Joins are so useful, we'll look at a couple of examples in detail. In their simplest format, Inner Joins are similar to WHERE clauses. The following SQL statement combines records from the Titles and Publishers tables of the BIBLIO database if their PubID fields match. It returns a RecordSet with all the titles and their publishers:

```
SELECT Titles.Title, Publishers.Name FROM Titles, Publishers
➥WHERE Titles.PubID = Publishers.PubID
```

You can retrieve the same RecordSet using an Inner Join, as follows:

```
SELECT Titles.Title, Publishers.Name FROM Titles, Publishers,
➥INNER JOIN Titles ON Titles.PubID = Publishers.PubID
```

The results of this statement are shown below:

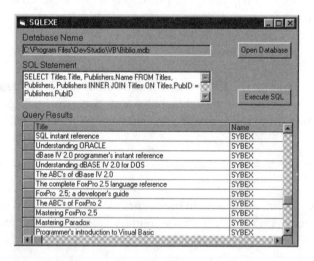

Let's look at a more complicated join operation. This time we are going to retrieve all titles, along with their authors and publishers, from the BIBLIO database. The following statement is quite complicated and represents a real-world situation:

```
SELECT Titles.Title, Titles.ISBN, Authors.Author, Titles.[Year
    Published], Publishers.[Company Name] FROM ((([title author]
    INNER JOIN Titles ON [title author].ISBN = Titles.ISBN) INNER
    JOIN Authors ON [title author].Au_ID = Authors.Au_ID) INNER
JOIN Publishers ON Titles.PubID = Publishers.PubID ORDER BY
    Titles.Title
```

The results of this statement are shown below:

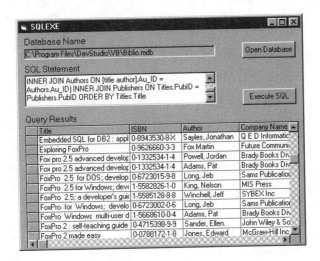

In this statement, brackets indicate the field names that contain spaces. Also, all field names are prefixed with the corresponding table's name, even though most field names are unique, to make the statement easier to read and understand.

The field list specifies the following fields:

- Titles.Title, the book's title

- Titles.ISBN, the book's ISBN

- Authors.Author, the book's author

- Titles.[Year Published], the book's publication year

- Publishers.[Company Name], the book's publisher

As you recall from our discussion of the BIBLIO database, four tables are involved, and our query requires data from all tables. Actually, no data from the Title Author table are displayed in the query's results, but this table links titles and authors (via the book's ISBN), and we must use it in the SQL statement.

The fields won't come directly from any single table. Instead, they come from a series of Inner Joins. The first Inner Join is as follows:

```
[title author] INNER JOIN Titles ON [title author].ISBN =
➥Titles.ISBN
```

This expression extracts (and matches) each title with its author's ID if the ISBNs on both tables match. In essence, you get an author ID for each title. Let's call this expression, which represents a RecordSet, Title-AuthorIDs. This RecordSet is placed in parentheses and joined with another RecordSet:

```
(Title-AuthorIDs INNER JOIN Authors ON [title author].Au_ID =
➥Authors.Au_ID)
```

This RecordSet joins the Author IDs of the previous RecordSet with actual author names. So far, we have created a RecordSet with author names and titles. Let's call it Titles-Authors. The last join operation joins the RecordSet that has author names and titles with the Publishers table as follows:

```
(Title-Author) INNER JOIN Publishers ON Titles.PubID =
➥Publishers.PubID
```

This time, the publishers' IDs must match. The final RecordSet contains titles, authors, and publishers, and our data will come from it.

The last keyword in this SQL statement, ORDER BY, determines the order in which the orders will be displayed.

Using SQL Statements

You now know the basic SQL statements, and you can extract data from a database with SQL statements using the SQLExec application. But how can you use SQL statements in your application?

SQL statements are basically RecordSet definitions. The RecordSet property of the Data control need not be a table's name. You can be more specific by identifying certain rows of the table or combining data from more than one table. The RecordSet that the SQL statement selects from the database is assigned to the

Data control, and the bound fields see the fields of this RecordSet. Let's look at a simple example.

The Data1 application, presented earlier in this chapter, displays a few fields from the Customers table in the NWIND database. The Data control's RecordSource property was set to the name of the Customers table, which you selected from a drop-down list. The list next to the name of the RecordSource property in the Properties window is a combo box, and you can also enter data in it.

Suppose you want the Data1 application to display customers from Germany only. To select part of a table, you supply the SQL statement that will create the corresponding RecordSet in the RecordSource property's field. Follow these steps:

1. Open the Data1 application and select the Data control.

2. In the Properties window, locate the RecordSource property and enter the following SQL statement (as shown in Figure 11.17):

   ```
   SELECT * FROM Customers WHERE Country = "Germany"
   ```

3. Now run the application and use the Data control's buttons to navigate through the customers of the NWIND database, whose country is Germany.

FIGURE 11.17

Set the RecordSource property to a SQL statement to retrieve a RecordSet that is part of a table or that combines multiple tables.

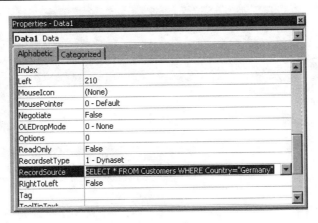

Because SQL statements are so common in databases, you can incorporate them in the design of the database itself. If you expand the list of the RecordSource property for a Data control connected to the NWIND database, you will see that the list contains more than table names. It contains the names of SQL queries that are stored in the database itself. The Category Sales for 1995 item, for example, is not a table name. It's the name of a query that returns sales for 1995, grouped according to product category. If you set the RecordSource property to this item, the resulting RecordSet's fields will appear in the list next to the DataField property of the data-bound controls. For the Categories Sales for 1995 query, the field names that can be displayed in data-bound controls are CategoryName and CategorySales.

Attaching Queries to a Database

Before we end this section of the chapter, we must look at the process of specifying queries with SQL statements and attaching them to the database. To get started, follow these steps:

1. Start the Visual Data Manager and open the BIBLIO database.

2. In the Database window, right-click on the All Titles query, and from the shortcut menu, select Design. Visual Data Manager displays another window containing the definition of the query, as shown in Figure 11.18.

FIGURE 11.18

In addition to tables, a database can contain queries, which are SQL statements that were incorporated into the design of the database.

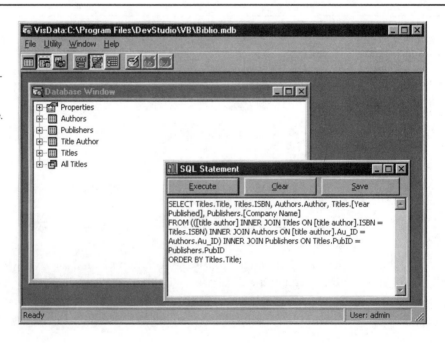

TIP

The Query icon is different from the Table icon, as you can see when you open the Database window.

The name of the query appears in the RecordSource property of a Data control connected to the BIBLIO database. We will use this query later to revise the ManyTbls application, but first let's look at the tools of the Visual Data Manager for building SQL queries.

Building SQL Queries

If you have found SQL difficult to learn, you'll be pleasantly surprised to find out that the Visual Data Manager can generate simple SQL statements with point-and-click operations. Right-click in the Database window of the Visual Data Manager, and from the context menu, select New Query to open the Query Builder window, as shown in Figure 11.19.

FIGURE 11.19

The Query Builder of the Visual Data Manager lets you build SQL statements with point-and-click operations.

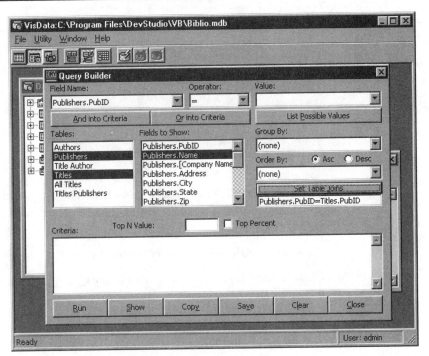

Let's use the Visual Data Manager to build a simple SQL statement. Follow these steps to create a query that retrieves all titles and their publishers:

1. Select the names of the Publishers and Titles tables by clicking on their names in the Tables list. The fields of the selected tables will appear in the Fields to Show list.

2. Now click on the names of the fields you want to include in the query (the RecordSet that this query will return). Click on the following field names: Titles.Title Titles.[Year Published] and Publishers.Name.

Now we'll get the difficult part of the SQL statement out of the way. Click on the Set Table Joins button to define the joins (in other words, to specify how the tables will be combined). The Visual Data Manager doesn't use the JOIN operator. It implements joins with the WHERE keyword, which means you can't rely on this tool to implement advanced queries.

3. In the Select Table Pair list, click on the names of the tables Titles and Publishers. The fields of the two tables will appear in the lists under the heading Select Fields to Join On, as shown in Figure 11.20.

FIGURE 11.20

The Join Tables dialog box of the Query Builder lets you easily specify Inner Joins with point-and-click operations.

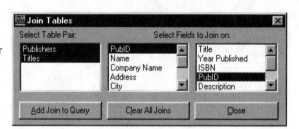

4. Now click on the PubID field in both lists. The Titles and Publishers tables are joined on the value of the PubID field. Records with matching PubID fields are joined.

5. Click on the Add Join to Query button to add the join to the query.

6. Click on the Close button to return to the Query Builder window. The query is defined.

7. Click on the Show button to display the SQL statement that implements the query, or click on the Run button to execute it. When prompted as to whether this is a SQLPassThrough Query, click on No. You will see a new Form with a Data control that lets you navigate through the retrieved records.

8. Click on the Save button to attach the query to the database. Visual Data Manager prompts you for the name of the query and attaches it to the database. The next time you connect a Data control to the database, you will see the query's name in the list of available RecordSource items.

You can use the Query Builder to specify selection criteria, which are also implemented with the WHERE keyword, to group and order the results of the query and to limit the size of the RecordSet to a number of records if it's too long.

To add selection criteria, for example, select a field name in the Field Name list, select the operator, and then specify a value in the Value box. If you don't remember the values of a specific field, click on the List Possible Values button, and the Visual Data Manager retrieves all the values of the specified list and displays them in the list, from which you can select one.

The SQL statements generated by the Query Builder are relatively simple and are adequate for simple queries (in case you were wondering why I chose such a simple example). For example, the Query Builder can't create multiple joins. However, you can always edit the SQL statement (by opening the query in design mode) and add more keywords to it. If you must create SQL statements, yet you don't feel comfortable with the language, you can use a more elaborate tool, such as Microsoft Access.

VB5 at Work: SQLTbls, ManyTbls Revised

The ManyTbls application combined all the tables of the BIBLIO database to display the titles, along with their authors and publishers. It used the Seek method to combine the tables, not because this was the most efficient implementation but to demonstrate the use of indices and the Seek method. Now, we are going to implement a similar application, but we'll use SQL statements to define the RecordSet with the fields we need. Follow these steps:

1. Open the ManyTbls application and save it as SQLTbls (change the name of the Form to SQLTbls too) and store it in a new folder.

2. Delete all the Data controls on the Form and place a new one on it. Name it TITLES and set its Caption property to Titles-Authors-Publishers.

3. Connect this control to the BIBLIO database by setting the DatabaseName property to the path name of the database on your hard disk.

4. Now, expand the RecordSource property list and select All Titles. This is the name of a SQL query stored in the database, and it returns the desired RecordSet (the titles with their authors and publishers).

5. Because this RecordSet is created with a SQL statement, it's a DynaSet-type RecordSet, so you must set the Data control's RecordSetType property to 1-DynaSet.

6. Now, adjust the DataSource and DataFields properties of the data-bound controls on the Form so that they see the corresponding fields of the RecordSet via the Data1 Data control. You must set their DataSource property to Data1 and their DataField properties to Title, Company Name, Year Published, and Author.

7. The last two fields of the ManyTbls application (Description and Comments) are not part of the All Titles query, so delete them from the Form. You can also change the query or create a new one that contains these fields, based on the All Titles query.

8. Now, delete all the code in the application, because you don't need it any longer.

The SQL statement, in effect, takes the role of the application's code. It does the same thing, only it's as compact and as efficient as it can be.

Advanced Data-Bound Controls

In this section we are going to look at two data-bound controls that are quite different from the ones we've used so far:

- The data-bound List control
- The data-bound Grid control

Unlike the other data-bound controls, these two can display fields from multiple rows. The data-bound List control is similar to the regular ListBox control and can be populated with an entire column of a RecordSet. The data-bound Grid control is similar to the Grid control and can display an entire RecordSet. Each row of the grid holds a row (record) of the RecordSet, and the RecordSet's columns correspond to the columns (fields) of the RecordSet.

These two data-bound controls aren't installed by default. To use them in your projects, you must first add them to the Toolbox. To do so, follow these steps:

1. Right-click on the Toolbox, and select Components to open the Components dialog box.

2. Check the Microsoft Data Bound Grid Control and the Microsoft Data Bound List Control boxes.

3. Click on the Close button to close the Components dialog box.

When you check the Microsoft Data Bound List Control checkbox, Visual Basic also adds the data-bound ComboBox control. It is similar to the data-bound List control and supports the same methods. The icons for the data-bound List, ComboBox, and Grid controls now appear in your Toolbox.

Using the Data-Bound List Control

The data-bound List control can be bound to a specific column of the RecordSet and is commonly used as a lookup table. Figure 11.21 shows how the data-bound List control can be used as a lookup table to simplify navigation in a RecordSet. This list contains the names of all products in the Products list of the NWIND database, which are loaded when the program starts. Each time you click on a new item, the program updates the data-bound controls on the Form to display the fields of the selected record.

The data-bound List control is different from the data-bound controls we have looked at thus far: It can connect to two data controls. It has the standard Data-Source/DataField properties, which are used just like any other data-bound control, and it has RowSource/ListField properties that determine how the control is populated:

- **RowSource** specifies the source (RecordSet or Data control) for populating the list.

- **ListField** specifies the field that will be used to fill the list.

FIGURE 11.21

The DBList application shows how to use the List control as a navigation tool in browsing applications.

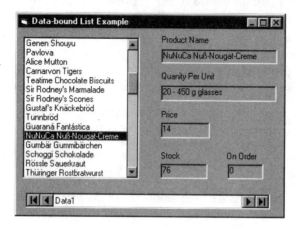

VB5 at Work: The DBList Application

The DBList application demonstrates the use of the data-bound List control as a navigation tool. The Form you see in Figure 11.21 contains a number of fields from the Products table in the NWIND database. Design the Form shown in Figure 11.21 by binding the various text boxes to their corresponding fields through a Data control, as if you were going to navigate through the list of products with the buttons on the Data control.

The problem with the Data control is that you can't really use it to navigate through a RecordSet, even if it's indexed, because you only see one record at a time. If you could place the key values in a ListBox control and use it as a navigation tool, you would have a much more convenient user interface.

Place a data-bound ListBox control on the Form, and set its RowSource property to the name of the Data1 Data control and its ListField property to the name of the field you want to display in the list. For the DBList application, this is the ProductName field.

If you run the application now, nothing will happen, because you haven't specified how the List control should react to the Click event. Basically, you want to reposition the Data control to the row of the RecordSet that has the matching ProductName field. To do this, insert the following code in the List control's Click event:

```
Private Sub DBList1_Click()
    Data1.Recordset.Bookmark = DBList1.SelectedItem
End Sub
```

The Bookmark property identifies a row in the RecordSet. By setting this property to a value, you are in effect forcing the Data control to be repositioned to the specified row. The control's SelectedItem property is not the text displayed in the edit box of the control, but the bookmark of the record to which the selected field belongs. This code repositions the Data control in the RecordSet and updates the data-bound labels on the Form.

Using the Data-Bound ComboBox Control

The ComboBox control is commonly used as a lookup table, as demonstrated in the DEntry application earlier in this chapter. To populate the list of the data-bound ComboBox control, you must set its RowSource property to a Data control, connected to the database and table from which the data will come.

The DEntry application contains a hidden Data control (named Data2) that is connected to the Publishers table of the BIBLIO database. The data-bound ComboBox control's ListField property is the name of the field that will be used to populate the list. In the DEntry application, this property is set to the Name field of the Publishers table. When the program starts, the data-bound ComboBox control is populated automatically with the names of the publishers in the database, as shown in Figure 11.22.

FIGURE 11.22

The data-bound ComboBox control on the Form of the DEntry application contains the names of all publishers in the database.

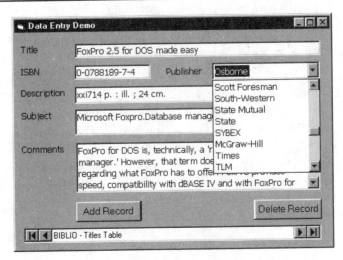

629

The data-bound ComboBox control has the usual DataSource and DataField properties, just like the other data-bound controls. In the DEntry application, we want the data-bound ComboBox control to operate as follows:

1. When the program starts, the control is populated with the names of all publishers.

2. When the user navigates through the Titles table, the ComboBox control picks up the publisher's ID from the Titles table, looks up this value in the Publishers table, and displays the Name field of the matching record in the edit box.

3. When appending a new record, the user specifies the book's publisher by selecting a name in the ComboBox control, but the control reports the matching ID to the first Data control.

This sounds like complicated behavior, but it's all built-in to the data-bound ComboBox control. You've already seen how the first behavior can be implemented with the help of the RowSource and ListField properties. The other two behaviors are typical of a data-bound control. We want to use the edit box of the data-bound ComboBox control as if it were a regular text box, bound to the PubID field of the Titles table. To achieve this, follow these steps:

1. Select the data-bound ComboBox control, and set its DataSource property to Data1 (the Data control that sees the Titles table).

2. Set the DataField property to the name of the field you want to update in the database, which is the PubID field.

The PubID field is also the field that should be displayed on the data-bound ComboBox control. But the user now sees the names of the publishers, and not their IDs, in the combo box.

The data-bound ComboBox has one more property, BoundColumn, which is the name of the field in its own RowSource that links the field displayed in the list with the actual field to which it is bound. The value of the BoundColumn property must be an index field so that the JET engine can locate it quickly. With the help of the DataSource, DataField, and BoundColumn properties, you can use the data-bound ComboBox control as a lookup table in your applications to let the user select meaningful field values, and at the same time store key values in the database. And all this, without a single line of code.

Using the Data-Bound Grid Control

The data-bound Grid control is one of the most flexible and powerful Visual Basic controls. If you have used Microsoft Access, you'll be familiar with this control. The data-bound Grid control looks a lot like the MSFlexGrid control (discussed in Chapter 7, *Advanced ActiveX Controls*), with two major differences:

- It is populated automatically from a RecordSet.

- It has built-in data-entry mechanisms with which you can edit the RecordSet (if it can be updated).

To fill the control with the data in a RecordSet, all you have to do is to set its DataSource property to a Data control. The grid is filled with the rows of the RecordSet. Because of the two-dimensional arrangement of the data on the control, you can really see the structure and contents of the entire RecordSet. I used this control to depict RecordSets in some of the figures at the beginning of this chapter. I also used this control to display the results of the SQL statements in the SQLExec application, which we are going to look at next.

VB5 at Work: The SQLExec Application

Earlier in this chapter, we used the SQLExec application to experiment with SQL statements. Now, we are going to build this application. Follow these steps:

1. Start a new Standard EXE project.

2. To add the data-bound Grid control to the Toolbox, right-click on the Toolbox, and select Components.

3. In the Components dialog box, check the Microsoft Data Bound Grid Control checkbox. We will also use the Common Dialog control in this project, so also check the Microsoft Common Dialog Control 5.0 checkbox and then click on the Close button.

4. Draw the controls you see on the Form shown in Figure 11.23. In addition to the visible controls on the Form, there is a Common Dialog control (which is invisible at run time) and a Data control (Data1), whose Visible property is set to False.

5. The TextBox control, on which the SQL statements are typed, is called txtSQL. Set its MultiLine property to True, and set its Scrollbars property to 2-Vertical.

FIGURE 11.23

The SQLExec application lets you query the database with SQL statements and displays the results on a data-bound Grid control.

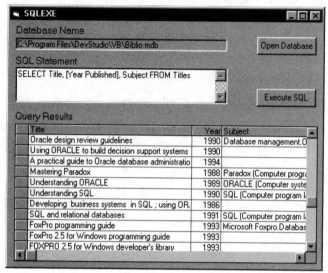

6. Now, you can program the buttons. The code for the Open Database button opens the File Open dialog box, in which you can select the database with which you want to work. The name of the database is displayed on the Label control next to the command button.

Code 11.13: The Open Database Button

```
Private Sub DBOpen_Click()
On Error GoTo NoDatabase
CommonDialog1.CancelError = True
CommonDialog1.Filter = "Databases|*.MDB"
CommonDialog1.ShowOpen

    Data1.DatabaseName = CommonDialog1.filename
    Data1.Refresh

    If Err = 0 Then
        Label1.Caption = CommonDialog1.filename
    Else
        MsgBox Err.Description
    End If
```

```
NoDatabase:
    On Error GoTo 0
End Sub
```

7. The Execute SQL button retrieves the SQL statement from the txtSQL text
    box and assigns it to the Data control's RecordSource property with the
    following statement (the Refresh method must be called to force the Data
    control to read the new data from the database and update the display):

```
Private Sub ExecuteSQL_Click()
On Error GoTo SQLError

    Data1.RecordSource = txtSQL
    Data1.Refresh
    Exit Sub

SQLError:
    MsgBox Err.Description

End Sub
```

The OnError statement traps any error in the SQL statement and displays it in
a message box. Assigning a new value to the control's RecordSource property
doesn't update the contents of the control. You must also call the Refresh method
of the Data control to force an update.

Mapping Databases

You design databases using special tools, the Visual Data Manager being one of
the simpler ones. These tools let you examine and modify the structure of the
database and in some cases enter data. You can also access the structure of a database from within an application, through a series of objects.

In this section, we will develop a utility that maps the structure of any database, and in the process, you'll see how these objects are used. These objects form
a hierarchy, starting with the Database object at the top, and each element in the
database is represented by a unique object that can be accessed as a property of
the Database object.

The Database Object

In the previous sections, we focused on the contents of a database. Now let's shift our attention to the structure of the database. Even if you know the structure of a database, in some situations you must access its table fields and indices from within your code. For example, you might need to know how many fields a particular table contains or how an index file is defined.

The DBStruct application, shown in Figure 11.24, demonstrates all the objects discussed in this section. First, I'll explain the objects that make up the database, and then we'll look at the implementation of the DBStruct application.

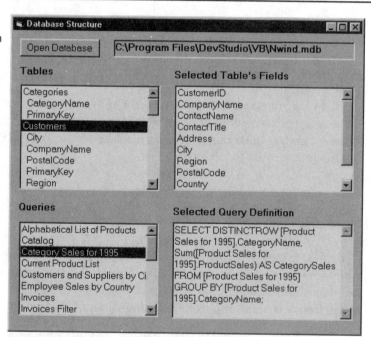

FIGURE 11.24

The DBStruct application can map any Access database.

The top-level object is the Database object, which represents the database. To create a Database object and assign a database to it, declare an object variable with a statement such as the following:

```
Dim DB As Database
```

The DB variable is assigned a Database object with the OpenDatabase function, which accepts the path name of an existing database as an argument and returns a Database object, as in the following:

```
Set DB = OpenDatabase(dbName)
```

The *dbName* argument is the path name of the database and could be the FileName property of the CommonDialog control. All the objects we explore in the following sections are properties of the Database object.

A table in a database is represented by the TableDef object, and a query is represented by the QueryDef object. Each of these objects has its own properties, such as the Name property (which is the table's or query's name) and the Count property (which returns the number of tables in the TableDef object and the number of queries in the QueryDef object).

The TableDef Object: The Tables' Definitions

A TableDef object represents the definition of a table in the Database object. All TableDef objects form a collection, the TableDefs collection. The number of tables is given by the property TableDefs.Count.

Each table in the database is represented by a TableDef object, whose most important properties are the following:

- **Count**   This property returns the number of rows in the table.

- **Fields**   Fields is another collection of Field objects. Each Field object represents a field in the table.

- **Indexes**   Indexes is another collection of Index objects. Each Index object represents an index of the table.

Assume that you have declared and opened a Database object with the following statements:

```
Dim DB As Database
Set DB = OpenDatabase(dbName)
```

To access the database's table definitions, use the expression DB.TableDefs, which is a collection of objects, one for each table. Through the members of this collection, you can access the properties of the tables in the database. The simplest way to access each table is to first declare a *TableDef* variable, as follows:

```
Dim tbl As TableDef
```

and then scan each element of the DB.TableDefs collection with a For Each ... Next structure, like this:

```
For Each tbl In DB.TableDefs
    Debug.Print tbl.Name
Next
```

This loop displays the names of the tables. You can also access a table's indices, as explained next.

A Table's Indices

Most tables in a database have at least one associated index file, sometimes more. To access the indices of a table, you use the Indexes property of the TableDefs object. Indexes is another collection of objects, one for each index of the table. The simplest way to access each index in a table is to first declare an Index object like this:

```
Dim idx As Index
```

and then scan each member of the Indexes collection with a For Each ... Next structure like this:

```
For Each idx In tbl.Indexes
    Debug.Print idx.Name
Next
```

The *tbl* entry is a TableDef object, declared as explained in the previous section. The following nested loop displays the names of all tables in the database, and under each table it displays the names of its indices :

```
For Each tbl In DB.TableDefs
    Debug.Print tbl.Name
    For Each idx In tbl.Indexes
        Debug.Print idx.Name
    Next idx
Next tbl
```

You can request the definition of each index with the Fields property, and you use the Unique property to determine whether a given index requires unique keys.

A Table's Fields

The most important property of the TableDefs object is the Fields property, which is another collection of objects, one for each field in the table. To access a table's fields, you first specify the table in the database that you want. You specify tables with an index value, which is 0 for the first table, 1 for the second table, up to DB.TableDefs.Count-1 for the last table. You can access the fields of the first table in the database through the object:

```
DB.TableDefs(0).Fields
```

Alternatively, you can use the table's name in place of the index. The following object represents all the fields in the Titles table of the BIBLIO database:

```
DB.TableDefs(Titles).Fields
```

To access each individual field in the Fields collection, declare a Field object variable and then scan the collection's members with a For Each ... Next structure. The following code segment prints the names and types of each field in the first table of the database:

```
Dim fld As Field

For Each fld In DB.TableDefs(0).Fields
    Debug.Print fld.Name, fld.Type
Next
```

The Type property returns an integer value that represents the type of the field. You must provide a short procedure that converts this number to a string such as "Integer", "String", and so on.

The other properties of the Fields object are:

- **OrdinalPosition**   The order of the fields in the table

- **AllowZeroLength**   A Boolean property indicating whether the field can be set to an empty string

- **Size**   The size of the field in bytes

- **Value**   The current value of the field

The QueryDef Object: The Queries' Definitions

In addition to tables, a Database can also contain query definitions. The queries that are commonly used on a database can be stored in the database and called by name. All the queries stored in a database can be accessed through the QueryDefs object, which is similar to the TableDef object. The QueryDef object is a collection of QueryDef objects, one for each stored query. You can access the following properties of the QueryDef object from within your code:

- **Count**   Returns the number of queries stored in a database

- **Name**   Returns the name of the query

- **SQL**   Returns the SQL statement of the query

The number of queries stored in a database is given by the following expression:

```
DB.QueryDefs.Count
```

To access all queries stored in a database, declare a QueryDef object variable as follows:

```
Dim qry As QueryDef
```

and then scan the elements of the QueryDefs collection with a For Each ... Next loop:

```
For Each qry In DB.QueryDefs
    Debug.Print qry.Name
Next
```

VB5 at Work: The DBStruct Application

The DBStruct application, shown in Figure 11.24 earlier in this chapter, lets you open any database and view the names of its tables, their structure, the queries stored in the database, and their definitions. The tables and queries of the database are displayed in the two lists on the left. Under each table's name you see the names of the indices for the table. Click on the name of a table to display its fields, and click on the name of a query to display its definition.

Let's start with the code of the Open Database button.

Code 11.14: The Open Database Button

```
Private Sub Command1_Click()
On Error GoTo NoDatabase
    CommonDialog1.CancelError = True
    CommonDialog1.Filter = "Databases|*.mdb"
    CommonDialog1.ShowOpen

' Open the database
    If CommonDialog1.filename <> "" Then
        Set DB = OpenDatabase(CommonDialog1.filename)
        Label1.Caption = CommonDialog1.filename
    End If
' Clear the ListBox controls
    FldList.Clear
    TblList.Clear

Dim tbl As TableDef
Dim idx As Index
Dim TName As String

Debug.Print "There are " & DB.TableDefs.Count & " tables in the
➥database"
' Process each table
    For Each tbl In DB.TableDefs
        ' EXCLUDE SYSTEM TABLES
        If Left(tbl.Name, 4) <> "MSys" And Left(tbl.Name, 4) <>
    "USys" Then
            TblList.AddItem tbl.Name
' For each table, process the table's indices
            For Each idx In tbl.Indexes
                TblList.AddItem "  " & idx.Name
            Next
        End If
    Next

Dim qry As QueryDef
Debug.Print "There are " & DB.QueryDefs.Count &
" queries in the database"
' Process each stored query
    For Each qry In DB.QueryDefs
        QryList.AddItem qry.Name
```

```
     Next

NoDatabase:

End Sub
```

Along with the filenames, the program displays the names of the indices for each table below the name of the corresponding table and indents them two spaces.

Let's look at the basic parts of this subroutine. The user-specified database is opened and assigned to the DB object variable. It then scans the members of the TableDefs object and appends the name of each table to the Tables list. Notice the following If structure:

```
If Left(tbl.Name, 4) <> "MSys" And Left(tbl.Name, 4) <> "USys"
```

> **NOTE**
>
> Along with the tables you specify when you design a database, Microsoft Access databases contain a few system tables. The JET engine uses these, and you need not manipulate them from within your code. Actually, you shouldn't. System table names begin with the prefixes *MSys* and *USys*. The program ignores these tables with the previous If statement.

After displaying the name of the current table, the program scans the indices of the table, with the help of the current table's Indexes object. After all table and index names are displayed, the program displays the names of all queries stored in the database.

When a table name is clicked in the Tables list, its fields are displayed in the Selected Table's Fields list. Likewise, when a query name is clicked, its definition (a SQL statement) appears in the Selected Query Definition text box.

Code 11.15: The Tables List Click Event Handler

```
Private Sub TblList_Click()
Dim fld As Field
Dim idx As Index

    If Left(TblList.Text, 2) = "  " Then Exit Sub
    FldList.Clear
    For Each fld In DB.TableDefs(TblList.Text).Fields
```

```
        FldList.AddItem fld.Name
    Next

End Sub
```

If the item that is clicked begins with two spaces, it's an index name, and the program doesn't react. If the item does not begin with two spaces, the program clears the ListBox control where the field names will be displayed and starts filling the list with each field's name. To access the names of the fields, the program scans the elements of the DB.TableDefs(TblList.Text).Fields collection. With each iteration, it appends the name of another field (fld.Name) to the list. You can also display the field's type with the Type property and the field's Size (in bytes) with the Size property.

When a query name is clicked, its definition appears in the multiline text box.

Code 11.16: The Queries List Box Click Event Handler

```
Private Sub QryList_Click()
Dim qry As QueryDef

    txtSQL.Text = DB.QueryDefs(QryList.ListIndex).SQL

End Sub
```

Notice that the objects of the TableDefs are accessed by the name of the table and QueryDefs objects are accessed by the name of the stored query. The alternative is to access them with an index. Since the system tables were omitted, the order of the tables in the Tables list is not the same as the order of the tables in the database; therefore, this method wouldn't work for this application.

PART III

Extending Visual Basic

CHAPTER

TWELVE

The Windows API

- Accessing the Win32 API from Visual Basic

- Passing arguments by value and by reference

- Determining Windows global memory

- Managing large data files

- Determining drive medium and free disk space

- Creating menus that incorporate bitmaps

- Changing menus at run time

- Detecting mouse movements

- Accessing the system

- Manipulating graphics

12

So far you have been programming within the limits of Visual Basic. You have been designing Forms and using Visual Basic statements to program the controls on the Forms. You've seen how far you can go with Visual Basic, and there's a lot you can do. Sometimes, however, you must get into the core of the operating system and access many of its functions. To do advanced programming, such as detecting mouse movements even when the mouse moves outside a Form, you need some additional functions. These functions are provided by the Win32 Application Programming Interface (API).

The Win32 API is a set of functions developed primarily for C programmers, but there is no reason you can't use it from within your VB applications. Many VB programmers resort to the Win32 API functions to accomplish what is simply impossible (or too complicated) from within Visual Basic.

The API functions aren't complicated, and they are not as exotic as VB programmers might think. The problem is that the API is documented for C programmers, and you may find it difficult to map the function and data type declarations from C jargon to Visual Basic.

All Win32 API functions are available from within the Visual Basic environment. The graphics methods of Visual Basic are masqueraded API functions. In Chapter 6, *Drawing and Painting with Visual Basic,* we looked at the PaintPicture method, which copies bitmaps from one control to another. The PaintPicture method was introduced with Visual Basic 4. Before that, VB programmers had to use the BitBlt() API function to achieve similar functionality. The BibBlt() function can copy pixels from anywhere on the Desktop, and you may have to use it in place of the PaintPicture method.

Many Windows applications use the API to some extent. Fortunately, Visual Basic hides a lot of the complexities of Windows programming from you while providing access to the API. This chapter will not attempt to explain all 1000 API functions, but only a few I think you will find useful.

The goal of this chapter is to introduce the basics of calling the API functions and to explain how to use the API viewer to add API function declarations to your code. Instead of quickly presenting many API functions, I will present a few useful ones and build small applications that use them. These applications demonstrate not only how to call the corresponding functions, but how to use them in the context of a Visual Basic application.

Basic Concepts

Before we dive into using API functions, let's go over the fundamental elements. The Win32 API consists of functions, structures, and messages that can be accessed to build Windows 95 and Windows NT applications.

The four functional categories of the Windows API are as follows:

- Windows Management (User)
- Graphics Device Interface (GDI)
- System Services (Kernel)
- Multimedia

The functions in these categories are implemented as DLLs (Dynamic Link Libraries) and can be called from any language. A DLL is loaded at run time and need not be linked to your application. Because the API functions are required for the proper operation of Windows itself, the DLLs are always available to your application.

Windows Management provides the essential functions to build and manage your applications. All the basic input and output of the system goes through this layer of the Win32 API, including mouse and keyboard input and all processing of messages sent to your application.

The *Graphics Device Interface* provides the functions you use to manage all supported graphical devices on your system, including the monitor and the printer. In addition, you can define fonts, pens, and brushes. The GDI provides support for the line and circle drawing operations and for bit-blit operations with the BitBlt() function (see the discussion of the PaintPicture method in Chapter 6, *Drawing and Painting with Visual Basic*, for details on bit-blit).

System Services provides functions to access the resources of the computer and the operating system. You will see how to call these functions to figure out the free resources on the system running your application.

The *Multimedia* functions allow you to play waveform audio, MIDI music, and digital video. You can achieve this with the MCI Command String and MCI Command Message interface, which were discussed in detail in Chapter 8, *Using Multimedia Elements to Enhance Applications*.

Accessing the Win32 API from Visual Basic

The only difference between Visual Basic functions and the Win32 API functions is that API functions must be declared before they can be used. In essence, you must tell Visual Basic the DLL in which an API function resides and the arguments it requires. You can then use it as you would use any other Visual Basic function.

Declaring API Functions

You declare the Win32 API functions with the Declare statement. One way is to enter the function along with the arguments, as in the following:

```
Declare Function mciSendStringA Lib "MMSystem" _
(ByVal mciCommand As String, ByVal returnString As Any, _
ByVal returnLength As Integer, _
ByVal callBack As Integer ) As Long
```

NOTE   **Long declarations such as this one are usually broken into multiple lines with an underscore character at the end of each line.**

The Win32 API function mciSendString is part of the MMsystem multimedia library (which is in the Mmsystem.dll file in the Windows/System folder). The A suffix indicates that it's the 32-bit version of the function; the mciSendString() function is its 16-bit counterpart. Because the two functions operate identically, I'll use the name mciSendString() in the text. Obviously, for Windows 95 (and Windows NT) you must use the 32-bit version of the function.

Nearly all API functions expect their arguments to be passed by value. Only arguments that must be modified by the function are passed by reference. By default, Visual Basic passes arguments by reference, so you must always precede the argument names with the ByVal keyword.

Using the API Viewer Application

You are not expected to remember the arguments of every API function (not even the function names), so it's assumed you will look them up in a reference. This reference is available from within Visual Basic's IDE, and it is the API Viewer, shown in Figure 12.1.

FIGURE 12.1

The API Viewer application

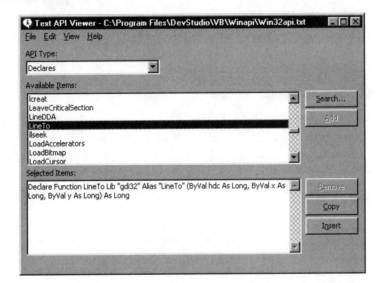

You can easily copy and paste any function into your Visual Basic programs. To do so, follow these steps:

1. Choose Add-Ins ➤ API Viewer. (If the command API Viewer doesn't appear in the Add-Ins menu, select Add-Ins Manager, and in the dialog box check VB API Viewer to add the API Viewer add-in to the Add-Ins menu.)

2. In the API Viewer window appears, choose File ➤ Load Text File or File ➤ Load Database File. The Load Database File loads faster (except for the first time, when the test file is converted to a database).

3. In the Available Items list box, select the function you want, and click on the Add button. API Viewer displays the selected function(s) in the Selected Items list box.

4. Select the functions you need for your application, and then click on the Copy button to copy the function's declaration to the Clipboard.

5. Open your application's Code Window and paste in the function declarations.

TIP

The Win32 Software Development Kit (SDK) provides full documentation for each function, including all structures and messages. The Microsoft Developer Network (MSDN) contains everything you need to develop Windows applications. For more information on the Microsoft Developer Network, visit the site at http://www.microsoft.com/msdn.

Windows Arguments

When using the Win32 API functions, you must supply the functions' declarations and their arguments. The Win32 API was written for programmers writing in the C or C++ language, so the documentation uses the C data structures, which you must map to their Visual Basic equivalents. Table 12.1 summarizes the C declarations and the corresponding Visual Basic data types.

TABLE 12.1   Visual Basic and C Data Types

C Declaration	Visual Basic Data Type	Argument Type
Integer	Integer	ByVal
Integer Pointer (LPINT)	Integer	ByRef
Long	Long	ByVal
Long Integer Pointer	Long	ByRef
String Pointer (LPSTR)	String	ByVal
Handle	Long	ByVal
Char	String	ByVal
Void Pointer	Any	ByRef

Passing Arguments by Value

To use API functions in your code, you must understand the two argument passing mechanisms, the ByVal and ByRef mechanisms. They are explained in detail in Chapter 3, *Visual Basic, the Language*, but I'm including an overview of Visual Basic's argument-passing mechanisms in this section.

When you pass arguments by value, you pass a copy of the argument to the called procedure. The procedure can change the value, but the change affects only the copy, and not the argument itself. Visual Basic uses the ByVal keyword to indicate that the argument is passed by value. Code 12.1 shows the AnySub procedure with the argument *anyNumber* passed by value. Within the AnySub procedure, the argument *anyNumber* is set to the value 10. When the program exits this procedure, however, *anyNumber* reverts to its assigned value.

Code 12.1: Passing Arguments by Value

```
Sub AnySub( ByVal anyNumber as Integer)

    anyNumber = 10

End Sub
```

If you call the AnySub() function with the following lines:

```
x=1
Call AnySub(x)
Debug.Print
```

The Print statement displays the value 1 in the Immediate window. The value 10 of the procedure's argument takes effect only while the AnySub() procedure executes, and not outside.

Passing Arguments by Reference

When you pass arguments by reference, you give the procedure access to the actual contents of the argument. The procedure to which it is passed has the actual memory address at which the argument resides and can permanently change the value of the argument. In Visual Basic, this is the default argument-passing mechanism. The AnySub() procedure in the following example changes the value of its argument permanently.

Coded 12.2: Passing Arguments by Reference

```
Sub AnySub( myInt As Integer )

    myInt = 20              'myInt is now 20

End Sub
```

If you call this subroutine with the following lines:

```
Dim x As Integer
. . .
x = 4
Debug.Print "Before calling AnySub x= " & x
Call AnySub(x)
Debug.Print "After calling AnySub x = " & x
```

the Print statements display the following lines in the Debug window:

```
Before calling AnySub x= 4
After calling AnySub x = 20
```

The changes made to the *x* variable in the AnySub() subroutine have a global effect, because the argument is passed by reference. If the called procedure has no reason to change the value of an argument, the argument must be passed by value. Some API functions store results in some of the arguments. These functions expect that their arguments are passed by reference. In C, these arguments are called pointers (they point to the memory location where the variable is stored).

Declaring 32-bit Functions and Structures

Some API functions use structures for their arguments. The MousePos application (you'll find it in the MousePos folder on the CD) demonstrates how to declare and use a simple structure. It uses the GetCursorPos() function to get the current mouse position when the mouse is clicked. Open this project now and follow along with the discussion.

1. Open the API Viewer (choose Add-Ins ➢ API Viewer).

2. In the API Viewer window, choose File ➢ Load Text File.

3. Select the file Win32api.txt, and in the Available Items list, double-click on the GetCursorPos entry.

4. The following declaration appears in the Selected Items list:

   ```
   Declare Function GetCursorPos Lib "user32" Alias "GetCursorPos"
   ➥(lpPoint As POINTAPI) As Long
   ```

The argument required for the function is a data structure named POINTAPI. As you can guess, this structure holds the coordinates of a point on the screen. Let's find the definition of the POINTAPI data structure with the API Viewer.

5. Select Types in the API Type drop-down list. The Available Items list is populated with all the data structures used by the API functions.

6. Locate the POINTAPI data structure and double-click on its name. Its definition appears in the Selected items list:

```
Type POINTAPI
    x As Long
    y As Long
End Type
```

7. Click on the Copy button to copy this definition (along with the declaration of the GetCursorPos function) into your application's Code window.

> **TIP**　Function declarations may appear anywhere, but it's customary to place them in a module so that they will be available from within any procedure.

Add a new module to the project and paste the selected declaration there. You will paste the following declarations from the API Viewer via the Clipboard:

```
Type POINTAPI
    x As Long
    y As Long
End Type
Declare Function GetCursorPos Lib "user32" Alias "GetCursorPos"
➥(lpPoint As POINTAPI) As Long
```

If you want to paste these declaration on a Form because they won't be used outside a single Form, prefix the declarations with the Private keyword.

Now you can use the GetCursorPos() function in your code. Suppose you want to know the location of the pointer in the Click event. Visual Basic's Click event doesn't report the coordinates of the point where the mouse was clicked, but you can find them with the GetCursorPos function. With the previous declarations in the application's Module, enter the following code in the Form's Click event:

```
Private Sub Form_Click()
Dim MouseLoc As POINTAPI
Dim retValue As Boolean

    retValue = GetCursorPos(MouseLoc)
```

```
Debug.Print "X Pos = " & MouseLoc.x
Debug.Print "Y Pos = " & MouseLoc.y

End Sub
```

The GetCursorPos() function returns the pointer's coordinates in pixels. The values you see in the Immediate window correspond to screen pixels. The origin is (0, 0) and corresponds to the pixel at the upper left corner of the screen. If the display is set to a resolution of 800 × 600, the pixel at the lower right corner of the screen is (799, 599). To actually click on that coordinate, you must move the Form to the lower right corner of the screen and then click on a pixel.

Accessing Memory and Files

Often, you will need to access Windows' memory. Accessing the system's memory can be useful when dealing with large files, such as bitmap files. When you know how to allocate memory, you can read in memory and manipulate large data files. You can use a rich set of Win32 API functions to access global memory and to manipulate data files. In addition, you can get information about the types of drives, directory structure, and free disk space—all of which are useful in determining whether your program will work correctly.

Determining Windows' Global Memory

One of the factors that may affect your application's performance the most is the amount of available memory. Windows applications can use more memory than is available in the system by using the Swap file. The MemStat application you will find in the following section lets you find out how much physical memory is available and how much free space is in the Swap file.

VB5 at Work: The MemStat Application

The MemStat application, shown in Figure 12.2, demonstrates how to obtain information about the current memory status from the system. Click on the Memory Status button to display the status of memory. The values depend on the number of applications that are running. Run the MemStat application, and then start other applications and monitor the use of memory on your system.

FIGURE 12.2

The Memory Status project

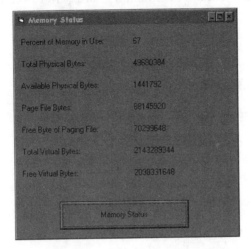

The Win32 API function that gets the current memory status from the system is GlobalMemoryStatus(). With the MemStat application open, follow along with the discussion.

First, using the API Viewer, copy all the necessary declarations for the function and its arguments. Find and copy the GlobalMemoryStatus() function and the data structure MEMORYSTATUS to a module in your application. Both are declared as follows:

```
Private Declare Sub GlobalMemoryStatus Lib "kernel32" (lpBuffer
    As MEMORYSTATUS)

Private Type MEMORYSTATUS
    dwLength As Long
    dwMemoryLoad As Long
    dwTotalPhys As Long
    dwAvailPhys As Long
    dwTotalPageFile As Long
    dwAvailPageFile As Long
    dwTotalVirtual As Long
    dwAvailVirtual As Long
End Type
```

Table 12.2 describes the members of the MEMORYSTATUS data structure. You must set the dwLength member, which is the size of the data structure, before passing the argument to the GlobalMemoryStatus() function. The function sets the other fields.

TABLE 12.2 The MEMORYSTATUS Data Structure

MEMBER	DESCRIPTION
dwLength	Size of MEMORYSTATUS structure
dwMemoryLoad	Percentage of memory in use
dwTotalPhys	Total number of bytes of physical memory
dwAvailPhys	Free number of bytes of physical memory
dwTotalPageFile	Total number of bytes in paging file
dwAvailPageFile	Free number of bytes in paging file
dwTotalVirtual	Total virtual bytes
dwAvailVirtual	Free virtual bytes

The Memory Status button reads the values of the fields of the MEMORYSTATUS structure set by the GlobalMemoryStatus() function and displays them in Label controls.

Code 12.2: The Memory Status Button

```
Private Sub Command1_Click()

    Dim memStat As MEMORYSTATUS
    memStat.dwLength = Len(memStat)
    Call GlobalMemoryStatus(memStat)

    Label1(0).Caption = memStat.dwMemoryLoad
    Label1(1).Caption = memStat.dwTotalPhys
    Label1(2).Caption = memStat.dwAvailPhys
    Label1(3).Caption = memStat.dwTotalPageFile
    Label1(4).Caption = memStat.dwAvailPageFile
    Label1(5).Caption = memStat.dwTotalVirtual
    Label1(6).Caption = memStat.dwAvailVirtual

End Sub
```

The ReadText Application

The ReadText application (shown in Figure 12.3) demonstrates the Win32 API functions that you can use to allocate, manipulate, and free system memory:

- GlobalAlloc()
- GlobalLock()
- CopyMemory()
- GlobalUnlock()
- GlobalFree()

FIGURE 12.3

The ReadText application

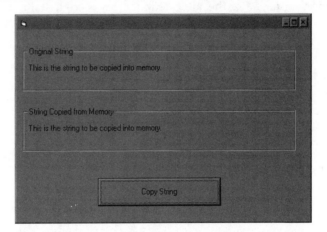

We are going to use these functions to copy a block of memory in the ReadText application. Before looking at the application's code, let's look at the steps you must follow:

1. Use the GlobalAlloc() function to allocate the required memory from the global heap.

2. After allocating the memory, you need to lock it with the GlobalLock() function. You pass the memory handle returned by the GlobalAlloc() function as an argument to the GlobalLock() function. The GlobalLock() function returns a pointer to the first byte of the memory block, which cannot be moved or destroyed.

3. Now you can copy the contents of the locked block of memory to another block.

4. After the memory is copied, you must unlock it with the GlobalUnlock() function, which accepts as an argument the handle you used to lock the memory block.

5. Finally, you can free the memory block with the GlobalFree() function.

VB5 at Work: The ReadText Application

The ReadText application copies a string from one variable to another, through the memory allocation and manipulation functions. The original string and its copy are also displayed on two labels. Code 12.3 shows how to use the functions described earlier. After the allocated memory is copied, it must be cleared, otherwise, you will quickly run out of memory. Use the functions GlobalUnlock() and GlobalFree() to clean up the used memory.

Code 12.3: The ReadText Application

```
Option Explicit

Const GMEM_MOVEABLE = &H2
Const GMEM_ZEROINIT = &H40

Private Declare Function GlobalAlloc Lib "kernel32" (ByVal
    wFlags As Long, ByVal dwBytes As Long) As Long
Private Declare Function GlobalLock Lib "kernel32" (ByVal
    hMem As Long) As Long
Private Declare Function GlobalFree Lib "kernel32" (ByVal
    hMem As Long) As Long
Private Declare Function GlobalUnlock Lib "kernel32" (ByVal
    hMem As Long) As Long
Private Declare Sub CopyMemory Lib "kernel32" Alias
    "RtlMoveMemory" (ByVal dest As Any, ByVal Src As Any, _
                      ByVal length As Long)

Private Sub Command1_Click()

  Dim origStr As String
  Dim copiedStr As String
  Dim strSize As Long
  Dim memHandle As Long
  Dim memPointer As Long
```

```
   origStr = "This is the string to be copied into memory."
   Label1.Caption = origStr
   strSize = Len(origStr)
   copiedStr = Space(strSize)
   memHandle = GlobalAlloc(GMEM_MOVEABLE Or GMEM_ZEROINIT, strSize)
   memPointer = GlobalLock(memHandle)
   Call CopyMemory(memPointer, origStr, strSize)
   Call CopyMemory(copiedStr, memPointer, strSize)
   Label2.Caption = copiedStr
   GlobalUnlock (memHandle)
   GlobalFree (memHandle)
End Sub
```

Managing Large Data Files

You sometimes will need to read in a large data file such as a bitmap file or even a text file. Just as you may need to copy large segments of memory, you may want to copy large files. To do so, you set the memory size according to the file size. Use the GlobalAlloc() and GlobalLock() functions to allocate and lock the system memory required to manipulate the data files. In this section, you'll see the steps required to read a large data file, such as a bitmap file, into memory and then write it out to disk. The name of the application is CopyBMP and you will find it on the CD.

VB5 at Work: The CopyBMP Application

First, use the CreateFile() function to open the file so that you can read in the data. The name of this function is somewhat misleading because it is used both to open an existing file and to create a new file. Its action depends on the flags passed with the *dwCreationDisposition* argument to the function. Here's how the function is declared:

```
Private Declare Function CreateFile Lib "kernel32" Alias "CreateFileA"
   (ByVal lpFileName As String, ByVal dwDesiredAccess As Long,
   ByVal dwShareMode As Long, ByVal lpSecurityAttributes As Any,
   ByVal dwCreationDisposition As Long, ByVal dwFlagsAndAttributes
   As Long,
   ByVal hTemplateFile As Long) As Long
```

Table 12.3 lists and describes the arguments for the CreateFile() function.

TABLE 12.3 Arguments for the CreateFile() Function

ARGUMENT	DESCRIPTION
lpFileName	Name of file to open for reading or writing.
DwDesiredAccess	Type of access, usually GENERIC_READ or GENERIC_WRITE.
DwShareMode	Specifies how the file can be shared.
LpSecurityAttributes	Pointer to security descriptor.
DwCreationDisposition	Specifies how to create the file. It can be one of the following flags: CREATE_NEW, CREATE_ALWAYS, OPEN_EXISTING, OPEN_ALWAYS, TRUNCATE_EXISTING.
DwFlagsAndAttributes	Specifies the file attributes. The flags are: FILE_ATTRIBUTE_ARCHIVE, FILE_ATTRIBUTE_COMPRESSED, FILE_ATTRIBUTE_HIDDEN, FILE_ATTRIBUTE_NORMAL, FILE_ATTRIBUTE_OFFLINE, FILE_ATTRIBUTE_READONLY, FILE_ATTRIBUTE_SYSTEM, FILE_ATTRIBUTE_TEMPORARY.
HtemplateFile	Specifies a handle to a file with attributes to copy. This value is NULL.

The next step is to use the GetFileSize() function to get the size of the file so that you can allocate the appropriate memory with the GlobalAlloc() and Global-Lock() functions. After allocating memory, you can read the bitmap file into memory, using the ReadFileLong function, which is declared as follows:

```
Private Declare Function ReadFileLong Lib "kernel32" Alias
    "ReadFile" (ByVal hFile As Long,
  lpBuffer As Long, ByVal nNumberOfBytesToRead As Long,
    lpNumberOfBytesRead As Long,
  ByVal lpOverlapped As Any) As Long
```

The ReadFileLong() function reads data from a file starting at the position of the file pointer lpBuffer. The file pointer is adjusted by the number of bytes read. The hFile parameter is the handle to the file that was opened with the CreateFile() function. Table 12.4 describes the rest of the arguments for the ReadFileLong()

function (the same arguments are also used by the WriteFileLong() function, which I'll describe shortly).

TABLE 12.4 Arguments for the ReadFileLong() and WriteFileLong() Functions

ARGUMENT	DESCRIPTION
hFile	Identifies the file to read. The file must be created with the GENERIC_READ flag.
LpBuffer	Points to the memory location into which the data is read.
NnumberOfBytesRead	Specifies the file size in bytes.
LpNumberOfBytesRead	Pointer to number of bytes read.
LpOverlapped	Points to a structure if the file was created with the FILE_FLAG_OVERLAPPED flag. In our example, the value is NULL.

Next, you must create a new file to write the data just read into memory. You use the CreateFile() function as before, but this time you pass the CREATE_ALWAYS flag, which tells the system to create the file even if it already exists. You can also use the CREATE_NEW flag to create a new file.

Now, you write the data to the newly opened file. The WriteFileLong() function writes data to a file starting at the file pointer position lpBuffer. As with the Read-FileLong() function, you will need to pass in the handle to the file, the memory location to write from, the number of bytes to write, a pointer to indicate the number of bytes written, and the pointer to the structure for the FILE_FLAG _OVERLAPPED flag. Table 12.4, earlier in this section, describes these arguments. The function itself is declared as follows:

```
Private Declare Function WriteFileLong Lib "kernel32" Alias
    "WriteFile" (ByVal hFile As Long,
    lpBuffer As Long, ByVal nNumberOfBytesToWrite As Long,
    lpNumberOfBytesWritten As Long, ByVal lpOverlapped As Any)
    As Long
```

Finally, close the file with the CloseHandle() function. The CloseHandle() function must be passed the handle that was returned by the call to the corresponding CreateFile() function. Here's the declaration of the CloseHandle() function:

```
Private Declare Function CloseHandle Lib "kernel32" (ByVal
➥hObject As Long) As Long
```

Of course, you must free up the allocated memory with calls to GlobalUnlock() and GlobalFree(), in that order.

The CopyBMP application (see Figure 12.4) demonstrates how to copy large bitmap files into memory and then back to a disk file with the API functions presented in this section. When you click on the Copy Image button, you are prompted to select a BMP file in the standard File Open dialog box. The file is then read into memory and displayed in the top PictureBox. Via a message box, the application informs you that the file has been copied into memory prompts you to enter the name of the file in which to save the bitmap, and then saves the bitmap. After the bitmap is copied, the program loads the new image file to the bottom PictureBox.

FIGURE 12.4

The CopyBMP application reads large BMP files into memory and copies them back to a new disk file.

Code 12.4: The CopyBMP Application

```
Option Explicit

Const GMEM_MOVEABLE = &H2
Const GMEM_ZEROINIT = &H40
Const GENERIC_READ = &H80000000
Const GENERIC_WRITE = &H40000000
Const OPEN_EXISTING = 3
Const FILE_ATTRIBUTE_NORMAL = &H80
Const CREATE_NEW = 1
Const CREATE_ALWAYS = 2

Private Declare Sub CopyMemory Lib "kernel32" Alias _
    "RtlMoveMemory" (ByVal dest As Any, ByVal Src As Any, _
    ByVal length As Long)

Private Declare Function GlobalAlloc Lib "kernel32" _
    (ByVal wFlags As Long, ByVal dwBytes As Long) As Long

Private Declare Function GlobalLock Lib "kernel32" _
    (ByVal hMem As Long) As Long

Private Declare Function GlobalFree Lib "kernel32" _
    (ByVal hMem As Long) As Long

Private Declare Function GlobalUnlock Lib "kernel32" _
    (ByVal hMem As Long) As Long


Private Declare Function CreateFile Lib "kernel32" Alias _
    "CreateFileA" _
    (ByVal lpFileName As String, ByVal dwDesiredAccess As Long, _
    ByVal dwShareMode As Long, ByVal lpSecurityAttributes As Any, _
    ByVal dwCreationDisposition As Long, ByVal _
    dwFlagsAndAttributes As Long, _
    ByVal hTemplateFile As Long) As Long

Private Declare Function ReadFileLong Lib "kernel32" Alias _
    "ReadFile" (ByVal hFile As Long, _
    lpBuffer As Long, ByVal nNumberOfBytesToRead As Long, _
    lpNumberOfBytesRead As Long, _
    ByVal lpOverlapped As Any) As Long

Private Declare Function WriteFileLong Lib "kernel32" Alias _
    "WriteFile" (ByVal hFile As Long, _
```

```
        lpBuffer As Long, ByVal nNumberOfBytesToWrite As Long, _
        lpNumberOfBytesWritten As Long, ByVal lpOverlapped As Any)
        As Long

Private Declare Function GetFileSize Lib "kernel32"
        (ByVal hFile As Long, _
        lpFileSizeHigh As Long) As Long

Private Declare Function CloseHandle Lib "kernel32"
        (ByVal hObject As Long) As Long

Dim filePointer As Long

Private Sub Command1_Click()

        Dim memHandle As Long
        Dim memPointer As Long
        Dim fileName As String
        Dim retValue As Long
        Dim nBytes As Long
        Dim fileSize As Long

        Dim origStr As String
        Dim strSize As Long
        Dim textStr As String

On Error GoTo noFileName

        CommonDialog1.cancelerror = True
        CommonDialog1.showopen
        fileName = CommonDialog1.fileName
        Picture1.Picture = LoadPicture(fileName)
        filePointer = CreateFile(fileName, GENERIC_READ Or _
    GENERIC_WRITE, 0&, 0&, OPEN_EXISTING, _
    FILE_ATTRIBUTE_NORMAL, 0&)

        fileSize = GetFileSize(filePointer, 0)

        memHandle = GlobalAlloc(GMEM_MOVEABLE Or _
    GMEM_ZEROINIT, fileSize)
        memPointer = GlobalLock(memHandle)

        retValue = ReadFileLong(filePointer, _
    ByVal memPointer, fileSize, nBytes, 0&)
```

```
    CloseHandle (filePointer)

    MsgBox "Image copied. Click on OK to save it on disk."

    'New file
    CommonDialog1.showopen
    fileName = CommonDialog1.fileName
    filePointer = CreateFile(fileName, GENERIC_READ Or _
    GENERIC_WRITE, 0&, 0&, CREATE_ALWAYS, _
FILE_ATTRIBUTE_NORMAL, 0&)
    retValue = WriteFileLong(filePointer, ByVal memPointer, _
    fileSize, nBytes, 0&)

    CloseHandle (filePointer)
    GlobalUnlock (memHandle)
    GlobalFree (memHandle)
    Picture2.Picture = LoadPicture(fileName)
    Exit Sub
noFileName:

End Sub
```

Determining Drive Medium and Free Disk Space

This section describes the functions you use to determine a drive's medium type and its free disk space and the functions you use to find the Windows directory and the current directory:

- GetDriveType()
- GetDiskFreeSpace()
- GetWindowsDirectory()
- GetCurrentDirectory()

These functions add capabilities that are normally not available with Visual Basic. You can, for example, determine if a certain drive is a CD-ROM drive and determine the amount of free space on a disk drive.

GetDriveType()   This function determines the drive type and is declared as follows:

```
Private Declare Function GetDriveType Lib "kernel32" Alias _
    "GetDriveTypeA" (ByVal nDrive As String) As Long
```

You pass the drive that you want to check with the nDrive argument, and the function returns a long value, which describes the type of the drive. Table 12.5 lists and describes the values.

TABLE 12.5   The Values For Drive Types

VALUE	DESCRIPTION
0	Drive type cannot be determined.
1	There is no root directory.
DRIVE_REMOVABLE	Drive can be removed, for example, a ZIP drive.
DRIVE_FIXED	Drive cannot be removed, for example, drive C.
DRIVE_REMOTE	Drive is remote, for example, a network drive.
DRIVE_CDROM	Drive is CD-ROM drive.
DRIVE_RAMDISK	Drive is a RAM drive.

VB5 at Work: The Drives Application

The Drives application (see Figure 12.5) uses drive C. Click on the Get Drive and Directories Info button to display information about your current hard drive. You can experiment with this function by opening this project and substituting another drive. Many of the functions described in this section are used in the Drives application.

GetDiskFreeSpace()   This function gets specific information about a disk, including the amount of free space. It also returns the number of sectors per cluster, the number of bytes per sector, the total number of free clusters on the disk,

FIGURE 12.5

The Drives application

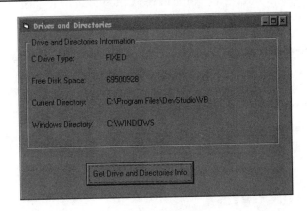

and the total number of clusters. The free disk space is calculated by taking the product of the bytes per sector, sectors per cluster, and the number of free clusters. Here's how you declare the function:

```
Private Declare Function GetDiskFreeSpace Lib "kernel32" Alias _
    "GetDiskFreeSpaceA" (ByVal lpRootPathName As String, _
    lpSectorsPerCluster As Long, lpBytesPerSector As Long, _
    lpNumberOfFreeClusters As Long, _
    lpTtoalNumberOfClusters As Long) As Long
```

The arguments of this function have intuitive names, and you'll see how they are used in the FileInfo application, later in this chapter. To find out the free space on drive C, use the following statements:

```
    retValue = GetDiskFreeSpace("c:\", Sectors, Bytes, _
    freeClusters, totalClusters)
    Label6.Caption = Sectors * Bytes * freeClusters
```

The total free space is calculated as the product of free clusters, times the sectors per cluster, times the bytes per sector.

GetCurrent Directory()   Use this function to retrieve the current directory in which your program is running. This function expects two arguments, the buffer length and the buffer in which the path name will be stored. The function is declared as follows:

```
Private Declare Function GetCurrentDirectory Lib "kernel32" _
    Alias "GetCurrentDirectoryA" (ByVal nBufferLength As Long, _
    ByVal lpBuffer As String) As Long
```

When the function returns, you can read the value of the lpBuffer argument to find out the current path.

GetWindowsDirectory() Use this function to find where Windows is installed on the hard drive. You may need this information to install any initialization files or help files in the Windows directory. Its arguments are identical to the arguments of the GetCurrentDirectory() function, and it is declared as follows:

```
Private Declare Function GetWindowsDirectory Lib "kernel32" _
    Alias "GetWindowsDirectoryA" (ByVal lpBuffer As String, _
    ByVal nSize As Long) As Long
```

Other File Functions

Sometimes you want information about a file such as its path, attributes, or size. The FileInfo application on the CD (see Figure 12.6) demonstrates how to retrieve information about a file using API functions.

FIGURE 12.6

The FileInfo application

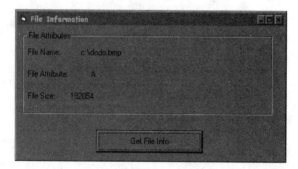

VB5 at Work: The FileInfo Application

This application uses the following functions:

- GetFullPathName()
- GetFileAttributes()
- GetFileSize()

GetFullPathName()   This function obtains the full path name of a file, and its declaration is as follows:

```
Private Declare Function GetFullPathName Lib "kernel32" Alias
"GetFullPathNameA" _
  (ByVal lpFileName As String, ByVal nBufferLength As Long, ByVal
lpBuffer As String, _
  ByVal lpFilePart As String) As Long
```

In the FileInfo application, the GetFullPathName() function returns the path for the file selected by the user in a standard File Open dialog box. It accepts as an argument the name of the file whose full path you want and returns the path of the filename in the *filePath* variable.

GetFileAttributes()   This function returns a flag that indicates the status of the file—read-only, hidden, normal, and so on. It is similar to the Visual Basic GetAttr() function and its declaration is as follows:

```
Private Declare Function GetFileAttributes Lib "kernel32" Alias
  "GetFileAttributesA" _
  (ByVal lpFileName As String) As Long
```

Table 12.6 lists the attributes that a file can have. The FileInfo application demonstrates the use of this function.

TABLE 12.6   File Attributes

VALUE	DESCRIPTION
FILE_ATTRIBUTE_ARCHIVE	File is archived; for example, it is marked for backup or removal.
FILE_ATTRIBUTE_COMPRESSED	File is compressed.
FILE_ATTRIBUTE_DIRECTORY	Name is a directory.
FILE_ATTRIBUTE_HIDDEN	The file or directory is hidden; that is, you can't see it in a normal listing.
FILE_ATTRIBUTE_NORMAL	File has no other attributes.
FILE_ATTRIBUTE_READONLY	File is read-only.
FILE_ATTRIBUTE_SYSTEM	File is part of the operating system.

GetFileSize()   To determine the file size, first open the file using the Create-
File() function (described in the section "Managing Large Data Files") with the
OPEN_EXISTING flag to indicate that the file already exists. You can now use the
GetFileSize() function to return the file size in bytes. Of course, you must close
the file with the CloseHandle() function when you are done.

Code 12.5: The File Information Project

```
Option Explicit

Private Declare Function GetFileAttributes Lib "kernel32" Alias
   "GetFileAttributesA" _
   (ByVal lpFileName As String) As Long

Private Declare Function GetFullPathName Lib "kernel32" Alias
   "GetFullPathNameA" _
   (ByVal lpFileName As String, ByVal nBufferLength As Long,
    ByVal lpBuffer As String, _
   ByVal lpFilePart As String) As Long

Private Declare Function CreateFile Lib "kernel32" Alias
   "CreateFileA" _
   (ByVal lpFileName As String, ByVal dwDesiredAccess
   As Long, _
   ByVal dwShareMode As Long, ByVal lpSecurityAttributes
   As Any, _
   ByVal dwCreationDisposition As Long, ByVal
     dwFlagsAndAttributes As Long, _
   ByVal hTemplateFile As Long) As Long

Private Declare Function GetFileSize Lib "kernel32" _
   (ByVal hFile As Long, lpFileSizeHigh As Long) As Long

Private Declare Function CloseHandle Lib "kernel32" _
   (ByVal hObject As Long) As Long


Const FILE_ATTRIBUTE_ARCHIVE = &H20
Const FILE_ATTRIBUTE_COMPRESSED = &H800
Const FILE_ATTRIBUTE_DIRECTORY = &H10
Const FILE_ATTRIBUTE_HIDDEN = &H2
Const FILE_ATTRIBUTE_NORMAL = &H80
Const FILE_ATTRIBUTE_READONLY = &H1
Const FILE_ATTRIBUTE_SYSTEM = &H4
Const GENERIC_READ = &H80000000
```

```
Const OPEN_EXISTING = 3
Const GENERIC_WRITE = &H40000000

Private Sub Command1_Click()

  Dim retValue As Long
  Dim filePath As String * 255
  Dim attrFlag As Long
  Dim attrStr As String
  Dim fileName As String
  Dim filePointer As Long
  Dim fileSize As Long

  fileName = "c:\dodo.bmp"

  'Get full path for file name
  retValue = GetFullPathName(fileName, 255, filePath, 0)
  Label15.Caption = filePath

  'Get file attributes
  attrFlag = GetFileAttributes(fileName)

  If (attrFlag And FILE_ATTRIBUTE_ARCHIVE)
  Then attrStr = "A"
  If (attrFlag And FILE_ATTRIBUTE_COMPRESSED)
  Then attrStr = attrStr & "C"
  If (attrFlag And FILE_ATTRIBUTE_DIRECTORY)
  Then attrStr = attrStr & "D"
  If (attrFlag And FILE_ATTRIBUTE_HIDDEN)
  Then attrStr = attrStr & "H"
  If (attrFlag And FILE_ATTRIBUTE_NORMAL)
  Then attrStr = attrStr & "N"
  If (attrFlag And FILE_ATTRIBUTE_READONLY)
  Then attrStr = attrStr & "R"
  If (attrFlag And FILE_ATTRIBUTE_SYSTEM)
  Then attrStr = attrStr & "S"

  Label16.Caption = attrStr

  'Get file size
  filePointer = CreateFile(fileName, GENERIC_READ Or
   GENERIC_WRITE, 0&, 0&, OPEN_EXISTING, _
              FILE_ATTRIBUTE_NORMAL, 0&)
```

```
fileSize = GetFileSize(filePointer, 0&)
Label7.Caption = fileSize

CloseHandle (filePointer)

End Sub
```

Forms and Windows

This section describes Win32 API functions that you can use to extend the usual Visual Basic functions to enhance your Forms, windows, and menus. Using these functions, you can create menus that incorporate bitmaps and dynamically change menu items. You can also use these functions to track the mouse and manipulate windows.

Creating Menus with Bitmaps

The menus you create with Visual Basic can contain only regular text. Using several Win32 API functions, however, you can modify the menu to contain bitmap graphics. The process is a little time-consuming, but well worth it. The MenuBMP application (see Figure 12.7) creates a menu with bitmaps at run time.

FIGURE 12.7

The MenuBMP application

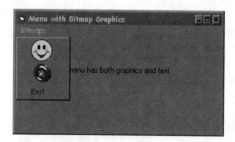

VB5 at Work: The MenuBMP Application

This application uses the following functions:

- GetMenu()

- GetSubMenu()

- CreateCompatibleBitmap()

- SelectObject()

- ModifyMenu()

To manipulate menus with API functions, you must obtain the menu's handle. Menus are objects, and as such they have a handle that identifies them to the operating system (just as Forms, bitmaps, and so on). In effect, you can manipulate the menus of other application that are running at the time by obtaining the handle of their menu.

To obtain a menu's handle, use the GetMenu() function, which is declared as follows:

```
Private Declare Function GetMenu Lib "user32" (ByVal hwnd As Long)
    As Long
```

The *hWnd* argument is the handle of the Form whose menu you want to manipulate. To obtain the handle of the current Form's menu, use the following expression:

```
MenuHandle = GetMenu(Me.hWnd)
```

First-level menus contain submenus that are identified by their order in the main menu. Submenus also have handles, which can be obtained with the GetSubMenu() function:

```
Private Declare Function GetSubMenu Lib "user32" _
    (ByVal hMenu As Long, ByVal nPos As Long) As Long
```

The *hMenu* argument is the menu handle returned by the GetMenu() function, and *npos* is the position of the submenu. If *nPos* is zero, the GetSubMenu() function returns the handle of the first submenu, which, most likely, is the File menu.

After you retrieve the handle of a submenu, you can modify it with the ModifyMenu() function, which is declared as follows:

```
Private Declare Function ModifyMenu Lib "user32" Alias
    "ModifyMenuA" _
    (ByVal hMenu As Long, ByVal nPosition As Long,
    ByVal wFlags As Long,_
    ByVal wIDNewItem As Long, ByVal lpString As Any) As Long
```

This function can change a menu entry, and it requires some explanation. The *hMenu* argument is the handle of the submenu, retrieved by the GetSubMenu() function. The *nPosition* argument identifies the menu item to be changed.

If the MF_BYCOMMAND flag in the wFlags argument is set, this argument refers to the ID of the command to be changed. If the MF_BYPOSITION flag is set, this argument specifies the position of the item in the submenu. The *wFlags* argument is a combination of flags, described in Table 12.7.

TABLE 12.7   Menu Flags

VALUE	DESCRIPTION
MF_BITMAP	The menu item is a bitmap. The bitmap should remain in memory while it's used in the menu.
MF_BYCOMMAND	The menu entry is specified by the command ID of the menu.
MF_BYPOSITION	The menu entry is specified by its position in the submenu. The position of the first item is zero.
MF_CHECKED	Displays a checkmark next to the specified menu item.
MF_DISABLED	Disables the specified menu item.
MF_ENABLED	Enables the specified menu item.
MF_GRAYED	Disables the specified menu item and draws it in gray (instead of making it invisible).
MF_MENUBARBREAK	Places the specified item on a new column with a vertical bar, which separates the columns.
MF_MENUBREAK	Places the specified item on a new column.
MF_POPUP	Places a pop-up menu at the specified item location.
MF_SEPARATOR	Places a separator line at the specified item's location.
MF_STRING	Places a string at the specified item location.
MF_UNCHECKED	Clears the checkmark in front of the specified item (if it was checked).

To assign a bitmap to a menu item, you set the MF_BITMAP flag in the *wFlags* argument of the ModifyMenu() function. Modifying the menu is relatively simple. Specifying the bitmap to be assigned in the place of the item's caption, though, isn't simple.

To assign a bitmap to a menu item, you create a device context (a memory area in which a bitmap can be stored) with the CreateCompatibleCD() function. The bitmap comes from an image (a BMP file) that is first loaded on a hidden Picture-Box control. The bitmap on the hidden PictureBox control is copied to the device context with the CreateCompatibleBitmap() function. When the bitmap is selected into the device context, you can assign it to a menu item, as if it were a string. The next listing shows how the bitmaps were added to the menu of the MenuBMP application.

Code 12.6: The MenuBMP Application

```
Option Explicit

Private Declare Function GetMenu Lib "user32" (ByVal hwnd As
    Long) As Long

Private Declare Function GetSubMenu Lib "user32" (ByVal hMenu As
    Long, _
    ByVal nPos As Long) As Long

Private Declare Function GetMenuItemID Lib "user32" (
    ByVal hMenu As Long, _
    ByVal nPos As Long) As Long

Private Declare Function ModifyMenu Lib "user32" Alias
    "ModifyMenuA" _
    (ByVal hMenu As Long, ByVal nPosition As Long,
    ByVal wFlags As Long, _
    ByVal wIDNewItem As Long, ByVal lpString As Any) As Long

Private Declare Function CreateCompatibleDC Lib "gdi32"
    (ByVal hdc As Long) As Long

Private Declare Function CreateCompatibleBitmap Lib "gdi32"
    (ByVal hdc As Long, _
    ByVal nWidth As Long, ByVal nHeight As Long) As Long

Private Declare Function SelectObject Lib "gdi32"
    (ByVal hdc As Long, _
    ByVal hObject As Long) As Long

Private Declare Function BitBlt Lib "gdi32"
    (ByVal hDestDC As Long, _
    ByVal x As Long, ByVal y As Long, ByVal nWidth As Long,
    ByVal nHeight As Long, _
```

```
    ByVal hSrcDC As Long, ByVal xSrc As Long, ByVal ySrc As
    Long, ByVal dwRop As Long) _
    As Long

Private Declare Function DeleteDC Lib "gdi32"
(ByVal hdc As Long) As Long

Const SRCCOPY = &HCC0020
Const MF_BYPOSITION = &H400&
Const MF_BITMAP = &H4&


Private Sub Exit_Click(Index As Integer)
  Unload Me
End Sub

Private Sub Form_Load()

  Dim Width As Integer
  Dim Height As Integer
  Dim hTmpDC As Long
  Dim hMenuID As Long
  Dim hBitmap As Long
  Dim retValue As Long
  Dim tmpID As Long
  Dim fileName As String
  Dim menuPos As Integer
  Dim menuID As Long

  'Set menu position and file name
  menuPos = 0
  fileName = "c:\face03.ico"
  Picture1.Picture = LoadPicture(fileName)

  Width = Picture1.Width / Screen.TwipsPerPixelX
  Height = Picture1.Height / Screen.TwipsPerPixelY

  'Get handle to menu
  hMenuID = GetSubMenu(GetMenu(Me.hwnd), menuPos)

  'Create device context to store bitmap
  hTmpDC = CreateCompatibleDC(Picture1.hdc)

  'Create the bitmap for the picture
  hBitmap = CreateCompatibleBitmap(Picture1.hdc, Width,
  Height)
```

```
'Select bitmap into temporary dc
tmpID = SelectObject(hTmpDC, hBitmap)

'Copy contents from picture control to DC
retValue = BitBlt(hTmpDC, 0, 0, Width, Height, _
 Picture1.hdc, _
          0, 0, SRCCOPY)

'Deselect bitmap
tmpID = SelectObject(hTmpDC, tmpID)

'Modify the menu
menuID = GetMenuItemID(hMenuID, menuPos)
retValue = ModifyMenu(hMenuID, menuPos, MF_BYPOSITION
Or MF_BITMAP, _
          menuID, hBitmap)

'Second menu item
menuPos = 1
fileName = "c:\donuts.ico"

  'Create the bitmap for the picture
hBitmap = CreateCompatibleBitmap(Picture1.hdc,
Width, Height)

  'Select bitmap into temporary dc
tmpID = SelectObject(hTmpDC, hBitmap)

retValue = BitBlt(hTmpDC, 0, 0, Width, Height, _
 Picture1.hdc, _
          0, 0, SRCCOPY)

tmpID = SelectObject(hTmpDC, tmpID)

menuID = GetMenuItemID(hMenuID, menuPos)
retValue = ModifyMenu(hMenuID, menuPos,
MF_BYPOSITION Or MF_BITMAP, _
          menuID, hBitmap)

  'Clean up
retValue = DeleteDC(hTmpDC)

End Sub
```

Changing Menus at Run Time

At times, you will want to change the menus dynamically. The MenuMod application, which is based on the MenuBMP application, shows how this can be done.

VB5 at Work: The MenuMod Application

The MenuMod application lets you switch the menu items from bitmaps to text and back. The application has the same menu as the MenuBMP application, plus a third item, whose caption is Display Graphics (when the menu displays text) and Display Text (when the menu displays graphics). The Click event handler for this menu item calls the DisplayTextMenu() or DisplayBitmapMenu() function to switch the menu between text and graphics. In the ModifyMenu() procedure, you use the MF_STRING flag to change the menu item to text, and you use the MF_BITMAP flag to change the menu item to graphics.

Code 12.7: The MenuMod Application

```
Private Sub DisplayTextMenu()

  Dim hMenuID As Long
  Dim menuID As Long
  Dim menuPos As Integer
  Dim retValue As Long

  'Get handle to menu
  hMenuID = GetSubMenu(GetMenu(Me.hwnd), 0)

  menuPos = 0
  menuID = GetMenuItemID(hMenuID, menuPos)
  retValue = ModifyMenu(hMenuID, menuPos, MF_BYPOSITION Or
MF_STRING, _
            menuID, "Happy Face")

  menuPos = 1
  menuID = GetMenuItemID(hMenuID, menuPos)
  retValue = ModifyMenu(hMenuID, menuPos, MF_BYPOSITION Or
MF_STRING, _
            menuID, "Donut")

End Sub
Private Sub DisplayBitmapMenu()
```

```
Dim Width As Integer
Dim Height As Integer
Dim hTmpDC As Long
Dim hMenuID As Long
Dim hBitmap As Long
Dim retValue As Long
Dim tmpID As Long
Dim fileName As String
Dim menuPos As Integer
Dim menuID As Long

'Set menu position and file name
menuPos = 0
fileName = "c:\face03.ico"
Picture1.Picture = LoadPicture(fileName)

Width = Picture1.Width / Screen.TwipsPerPixelX
Height = Picture1.Height / Screen.TwipsPerPixelY

'Get handle to menu
hMenuID = GetSubMenu(GetMenu(Me.hwnd), menuPos)

'Create device context to store bitmap
hTmpDC = CreateCompatibleDC(Picture1.hdc)

'Create the bitmap for the picture
hBitmap = CreateCompatibleBitmap(Picture1.hdc, Width, Height)

'Select bitmap into temporary dc
tmpID = SelectObject(hTmpDC, hBitmap)

'Copy contents from picture control to DC
retValue = BitBlt(hTmpDC, 0, 0, Width, Height, Picture1.hdc, _
          0, 0, SRCCOPY)

'Deselect bitmap
tmpID = SelectObject(hTmpDC, tmpID)

'Modify the menu
menuID = GetMenuItemID(hMenuID, menuPos)
retValue = ModifyMenu(hMenuID, menuPos, MF_BYPOSITION Or
MF_BITMAP,
          menuID, hBitmap)

'Second menu item
menuPos = 1
```

```
fileName = "c:\donuts.ico"
Picture1.Picture = LoadPicture(fileName)

 'Create the bitmap for the picture
hBitmap = CreateCompatibleBitmap(Picture1.hdc, Width, Height)

'Select bitmap into temporary dc
tmpID = SelectObject(hTmpDC, hBitmap)

retValue = BitBlt(hTmpDC, 0, 0, Width, Height, Picture1.hdc, _
         0, 0, SRCCOPY)

tmpID = SelectObject(hTmpDC, tmpID)

menuID = GetMenuItemID(hMenuID, menuPos)
 retValue = ModifyMenu(hMenuID, menuPos, MF_BYPOSITION Or
MF_BITMAP,
            menuID, hBitmap)

 'Clean up
 retValue = DeleteDC(hTmpDC)

End Sub
```

Detecting Mouse Movements

A common event in event-driven programming is the MouseMove event, which lets you monitor the movement of the mouse. The MouseMove event reports the coordinates of the mouse as it moves on a Form. In some situations, you want to monitor the coordinates of the point from within the Click event, which doesn't report the coordinates of the pointer when the button was clicked. To find out the location of the mouse at any time, you use the GetCursorPos() function. It has the following syntax:

```
Private Declare Function GetCursorPos Lib "user32" (lpPoint As
    POINTAPI) As Long
```

NOTE See the introductory example in this chapter for the arguments of the GetCursorPos() function.

VB5 at Work: The MouseMov Application

The MouseMov application (see Figure 12.8) uses a tracking loop to track the mouse, but also releases control to Windows with the DoEvents statement. This allows Windows to process other events such as ending the program when the user clicks on the Stop button. Without the DoEvents statement, we would not be able to stop the program.

FIGURE 12.8

The MouseMov application tracks the mouse location, even outside the application's Form.

You use the GetCursorPos() function to determine the current mouse position. The function returns a *POINTAPI* variable, which you use for the WindowFromPoint() function. The WindowFromPoint() function gets the window handle, given the point of the mouse. When the program has the window handle, it can proceed to get the class name of the window. The GetClassName() function returns the name of the window's class, and the program displays this name in the label box. If the name is SysListView32, the mouse is over the Windows Desktop. Otherwise, the mouse is over some other window.

The main portion of the code is the tracking loop. The code gets the current mouse position and uses this information to get the window handle and the class name. The class name is then displayed and updated each time the mouse moves over a new window.

Code 12.8: The MouseMov Application

```
Option Explicit

Private Declare Function GetCursorPos Lib "user32" (1pPoint As
    POINTAPI) As Long
```

```
Private Declare Function WindowFromPoint Lib "user32" (ByVal
    xPoint As Long, _
  ByVal yPoint As Long) As Long

Private Declare Function GetClassName Lib "user32" Alias
    "GetClassNameA" _
    (ByVal hwnd As Long, ByVal lpClassName As String, ByVal
    nMaxCount As Long) As Long

Private Type POINTAPI
    X As Long
    Y As Long
End Type

Private gStop As Boolean

Private Sub Command1_Click()

  Dim mousePT As POINTAPI
  Dim prevWindow As Long
  Dim curWindow As Long
  Dim X As Long
  Dim Y As Long
  Dim className As String
  Dim retValue As Long

  'Track mouse here
  If Command1.Caption = "Start" Then
    Command1.Caption = "Stop"

    gStop = False
    prevWindow = 0

    'Track until user stops
    Do
      'Stop tracking
      If gStop = True Then Exit Do

      Call GetCursorPos(mousePT)

      X = mousePT.X
      Y = mousePT.Y

      'Get window under mouse
      curWindow = WindowFromPoint(X, Y)
```

```
      If curWindow <> prevWindow Then

         className = String$(256, " ")
         prevWindow = curWindow

         retValue = GetClassName(curWindow, className, 255)
         className = Left$(className, InStr(className, vbNullChar) - 1)

         If className = "SysListView32" Then
           Label1.Caption = "The mouse is over the desktop."
         Else
           Label1.Caption = "The mouse is over " & className
         End If

      End If
      DoEvents
    Loop

  'Stop tracking the mouse
  Else
     Command1.Caption = "Start"
     gStop = True
  End If

End Sub

Private Sub Form_QueryUnload(Cancel As Integer, UnloadMode As
➥Integer)
  gStop = True
End Sub
```

Keeping a Window on Top

You have often seen applications that keep a window on top regardless of
whether the window is active. Microsoft Word does this with its Find window.
This is done with a single call to the SetWindowPos() API function, which is
declared as follows:

```
Private Declare Function SetWindowPos Lib "user32"
   (ByVal hwnd As Long,
  ByVal hWndInsertAfter As Long, ByVal x As Long,
   ByVal y As Long,
   ByVal cx As Long, ByVal cy As Long, ByVal wFlags As Long) As Long
```

The *hWnd* argument is the handle of the window, *x* and *y* are the coordinates of the window's upper left corner, and *cx* and *cy* are the window's width and height. The *hWndInsertAfter* argument is the handle of a window, after which the hWnd window is in the window list. It can also be one of the values shown in Table 12.8

TABLE 12.8 The Values of hWnd

VALUE	WHAT IT DOES
HWND_BOTTOM	Places the window at the bottom of the window list.
HWND_TOP	Places the window at the top of the z order.
HWND_TOPMOST	Places the window at the top of the list of windows.
HWND_NOTOPMOST	Places the window at the top of the list of windows, behind any topmost window.

The *wFlags* argument is an integer that contains one or more of the flags shown in Table 12.9.

TABLE 12.9 The Flags of the wFlags Argument

FLAG	WHAT IT DOES
SWP_DRAWFRAME	Draws a frame around the window.
SWP_HIDEWINDOW	Hides the window.
SWP_NOACTIVATE	Does not activate the window.
SWP_NOMOVE	Retains the window's current position (the *x* and *y* arguments are ignored).
SWP_NOREDRAW	The window is not redrawn automatically.
SWP_NOSIZE	Retains the window's current size.
SWP_NOZORDER	Retains window's current position in the window list.
SWP_SHOWWINDOW	Displays the window.

TIP

I'm not listing the values of the constants here. You can copy them from the API Viewer's window into your application. You should avoid hard-coding constant values in your code.

The sample application that demonstrates the SetWindowPos() function is called WinTop, and its listing is shown next.

Code 12.9: The WinTop Application

```
Option Explicit

Private Declare Function SetWindowPos Lib "user32" (ByVal hwnd
  As Long, _
  ByVal hWndInsertAfter As Long, ByVal x As Long, ByVal y
  As Long, _
  ByVal cx As Long, ByVal cy As Long, ByVal wFlags As Long)
  As Long

Const HWND_TOPMOST = -1
Const SWP_SHOWWINDOW = &H40

Private Sub Form_Load()

  Dim retValue As Long

  retValue = SetWindowPos(Me.hwnd, HWND_TOPMOST,
  Me.CurrentX, Me.CurrentY, _
        300, 300, SWP_SHOWWINDOW)
End Sub
```

You can use this technique to make the Search and Replace window of the TextPad (see Chapter 5, *Drawing and Painting with Visual Basic*) and RTFPad (see Chapter 7, *Advanced ActiveX Controls*) applications. This window always remains on top and is visible even when the user switches to the editor's Form.

Accessing the System

The API functions described in this section let you look at other running applications from within your Visual Basic application and obtain information about an application and even its parent window.

Querying Other Applications

To query an application, you must be able to tell your program which application to query. One way to do this is by placing the mouse pointer over the other application's window. The Query application (see Figure 12.9) demonstrates how to spy on other active applications and uses the GetCursorPos() and SetWindowPos() functions.

VB5 at Work: The Query Application

The window of the Query application displays information about the current active window and retrieves information about the parent window of the active window.

This program uses the following functions:

- SetWindowPos()

- GetCursorPos()

- WindowFromPoint()

- GetClassName()

- GetWindowText()

- GetParent()

FIGURE 12.9

The Query application

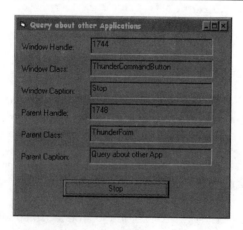

SetWindowPos()   The program keeps the window on top of other applications with the SetWindowPos() function call. The key element is the HWND _TOPMOST flag, which tells Windows to keep a particular window on top of the Z order. You track the mouse to see which window the mouse is over and obtain information about the window. This is accomplished with the GetCursorPos() and the WindowFromPoint() functions.

GetCursorPos(), WindowFromPoint()   The GetCursorPos() function returns the screen coordinates of the mouse pointer. These coordinates are then used by the WindowFromPoint() function to retrieve the name of the window that is visible at the pointer's coordinates. The declaration of the WindowFromPoint() function is:

```
Declare Function WindowFromPoint Lib "user32" (ByVal xPoint As
   Long, _
   ByVal yPoint As Long) As Long
```

The arguments *xPoint* and *yPoint* are a pair of coordinates, and the function returns a long integer, which is the handle of the window at the specified location (the window that would be brought on top of the Z order if the user clicked on the specific point).

GetClassName(), GetWindowText   To spy on other applications, you can use the GetClassName(), and GetWindowText() functions. The GetClassName() function obtains a window's class name, and the GetWindowText() function gets the window's title bar if there is one; if the window is a control, the text of the control is returned.

GetParent()   This function gets the window's parent window. The Query application uses all these functions to retrieve information about any other window that happens to be open.

Code 12.10: The Query Application

```
Option Explicit

Private Declare Function SetWindowPos Lib "user32"
   (ByVal hwnd As Long, _
   ByVal hWndInsertAfter As Long, ByVal X As Long,
   ByVal Y As Long, ByVal cx As Long, _
   ByVal cy As Long, ByVal wFlags As Long) As Long
```

```
Private Declare Function GetCursorPos Lib "user32"
   (lpPoint As POINTAPI) As Long

Private Declare Function WindowFromPoint Lib "user32"
   (ByVal xPoint As Long, _
   ByVal yPoint As Long) As Long

Private Declare Function GetParent Lib "user32"
   (ByVal hwnd As Long) As Long

Private Declare Function GetClassName Lib "user32"
   Alias "GetClassNameA" _
   (ByVal hwnd As Long, ByVal lpClassName As String,
   ByVal nMaxCount As Long) As Long

Private Declare Function GetWindowText Lib "user32"
   Alias "GetWindowTextA" _
   (ByVal hwnd As Long, ByVal lpString As String,
   ByVal cch As Long) As Long

Const HWND_TOPMOST = -1
Const SWP_SHOWWINDOW = &H40

Private Type POINTAPI
    X As Long
    Y As Long
End Type

Private gStop As Boolean

Private Sub Command1_Click()

  Dim mousePT As POINTAPI
  Dim prevWindow As Long
  Dim curWindow As Long
  Dim X As Long
  Dim Y As Long
  Dim tmpStr As String
  Dim retValue As Long
  Dim parentWnd As Long

  'Track mouse here
  If Command1.Caption = "Start" Then

    Command1.Caption = "Stop"
    gStop = False
    prevWindow = 0
```

```
    'Track until user stops
    Do
      'Stop tracking
      If gStop = True Then Exit Do

      Call GetCursorPos(mousePT)

      X = mousePT.X
      Y = mousePT.Y

      'Get window under mouse
      curWindow = WindowFromPoint(X, Y)

      If curWindow <> prevWindow Then

        tmpStr = String$(256, " ")
        prevWindow = curWindow

        retValue = GetClassName(curWindow, tmpStr, 255)
        tmpStr = Left$(tmpStr, InStr(tmpStr, vbNullChar) - 1)

        Text1(0).Text = curWindow
        Text1(1).Text = tmpStr

        retValue = GetWindowText(curWindow, tmpStr, 255)
        Text1(2).Text = tmpStr

        'Get parent window
        parentWnd = GetParent(curWindow)

        retValue = GetClassName(parentWnd, tmpStr, 255)
        tmpStr = Left$(tmpStr, InStr(tmpStr, vbNullChar) - 1)

        Text1(3).Text = parentWnd
        Text1(4).Text = tmpStr

        retValue = GetWindowText(parentWnd, tmpStr, 255)
        Text1(5).Text = tmpStr

      End If
      DoEvents
    Loop
  'Stop tracking the mouse
  Else
    Command1.Caption = "Start"
    gStop = True
  End If

End Sub
```

```
Private Sub Form_QueryUnload(Cancel As Integer, UnloadMode As
→Integer)
  gStop = True
End Sub

Private Sub Form_Load()

  Dim retValue As Long

  If Command1.Caption = "Start" Then

    gStop = False
    'Command1.Caption = "Stop"
    retValue = SetWindowPos(Me.hwnd, HWND_TOPMOST,
    Me.CurrentX, Me.CurrentY, _
              Me.Width,
    Me.Height, SWP_SHOWWINDOW)

  Else
    gStop = True
    Command1.Caption = "Start"
  End If

End Sub
```

Registry Functions

The Windows 95 Registry is a hierarchical database of settings used by Windows that includes information on users, system hardware configuration, and application programs. The Registry system replaces the old INI files used in previous versions of Windows.

You access the Registry using a program called Regedit. To run Regedit, follow these steps:

1. Choose Start ➤ Run.

2. In the Run window, type **regedit** and press Enter to open the Registry Editor window, as shown in Figure 12.10.

As you can see if you double-click on one of the items in the main Registry Editor window, the Registry stores data in an outline layout. The first item is usually referred to as the Registry *key*, and subsequent items are referred to as *subkeys*. The Registry keys are predefined to organize the data as follows:

- HKEY_CLASSES_ROOT holds OLE information about applications that have been installed or documents with particular filename extensions, such as TXT or DOC. In addition, it maintains the list of programs that can handle each file type.

FIGURE 12.10

The main Registry Editor window

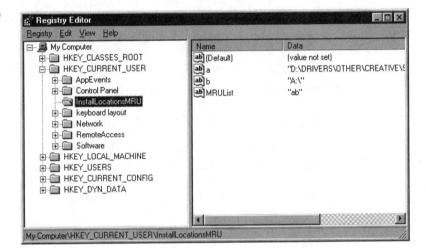

- HKEY_CURRENT_USER describes settings and configuration information about the user currently logged on to the computer.

- HKEY_LOCAL_MACHINE contains the settings for the hardware installed on the computer. The following are subkeys in the HKEY_LOCAL_MACHINE section:

  - HKEY_USERS contains profiles for all users who can log on to the machine. If only one person uses the machine, this key contains only the .Default subkey.

  - HKEY_CURRENT_CONFIG contains font and printer information.

  - HKEY_DYN_DATA contains dynamic information that should be read into the system's RAM, because it has to be available quickly to the operating system.

WARNING If you are not familiar with the Registry, you should not fool around with it. Ruining a few items in the Registry is a sure way to crash your machine. You can even disable the operating system itself.

You can browse the Registry Editor to find out the type of information stored by other applications. It's relatively safe to use the Registry to store information about your application. For example, you can store initialization information about an application in the Registry so that the next time it's run, it looks up the settings of the last time it was executed in the Registry. The list of most recently opened files, which you will find in nearly every Windows application, is stored in the Registry. While manipulating the Registry, be sure you don't touch other applications' entries. Manipulate only your own application's entries.

VB5 at Work: The Registry Application

The Registry application (see Figure 12.11) demonstrates how to create keys, store values, and get Registry data. It creates three subkeys under the HKEY_LOCAL_MACHINE key, where it stores the dimensions of the Form the last time it was executed:

- \Sybex\Mastering VB 5.0

- Window Width

- Window Height

FIGURE 12.11

The Using the Registry program

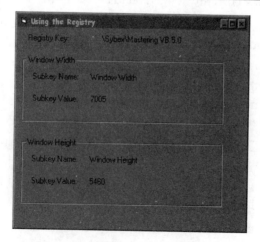

The program uses the Window Width and Window Height subkeys to store and retrieve the window width and height.

When the program first runs, it checks for values in Window Width and Window Height, with the RegQueryValueEx() function. If these subkeys contain values, the program simply retrieves them and sets the window width and height. If these subkeys do not contain values, there are no entries in the Registry. The program gets the current window width and height and stores that information in the Registry with the RegSetValueEx() function. The RegCreateKey() function creates the specified key; if the key already exists, this function opens the key.

If you resize the window, the program saves the new window width and height to the Registry in the QueryUnload method. The next time you run the program, the application window will open at this new size. As you can see, you can store you program initialization settings using the Registry and retrieve them when your application starts up.

Code 12.11: The Using the Registry Program

```
Option Explicit

Private Declare Function RegCreateKey Lib "advapi32.dll" Alias
    "RegCreateKeyA" _
        (ByVal hKey As Long, ByVal lpSubKey As String, phkResult
    As Long) As Long

Private Declare Function RegDeleteKey Lib "advapi32.dll" Alias
    "RegDeleteKeyA" _
        (ByVal hKey As Long, ByVal lpSubKey As String) As Long

Private Declare Function RegDeleteValue Lib "advapi32.dll" Alias
    "RegDeleteValueA" _
        (ByVal hKey As Long, ByVal lpValueName As String) As Long

Private Declare Function RegQueryValueEx Lib "advapi32.dll" Alias
    "RegQueryValueExA" _
        (ByVal hKey As Long, ByVal lpValueName As String, ByVal
    lpReserved As Long, _
        lpType As Long, lpData As Any, lpcbData As Long) As Long

Private Declare Function RegSetValueEx Lib "advapi32.dll" Alias
    "RegSetValueExA" _
```

```
     (ByVal hKey As Long, ByVal lpValueName As String, ByVal
Reserved As Long, _
     ByVal dwType As Long, lpData As Any, ByVal cbData As
Long) As Long

Const ERROR_SUCCESS = 0&
Const ERROR_BADDB = 1009&
Const ERROR_BADKEY = 1010&
Const ERROR_CANTOPEN = 1011&
Const ERROR_CANTREAD = 1012&
Const ERROR_CANTWRITE = 1013&
Const ERROR_REGISTRY_RECOVERED = 1014&
Const ERROR_REGISTRY_CORRUPT = 1015&
Const ERROR_REGISTRY_IO_FAILED = 1016&
Const HKEY_CLASSES_ROOT = &H80000000
Const HKEY_CURRENT_USER = &H80000001
Const HKEY_LOCAL_MACHINE = &H80000002
Const REG_SZ = 1

'Dim regKey As String
Const regKey = "\Sybex\Mastering VB 5.0"

Private Sub Form_Load()

    Dim retValue As Long
    Dim result As Long
    Dim keyID As Long
    Dim keyValue As String
    Dim subKey As String
    Dim bufSize As Long

    Label6.Caption = regKey

    'Create key
    retValue = RegCreateKey(HKEY_LOCAL_MACHINE, regKey, keyID)

    If retValue = 0 Then

    'Create width
    subKey = "Window Width"
    retValue = RegQueryValueEx(keyID, subKey, 0&,
➡REG_SZ, 0&, bufSize)

    'No value, set it
    If bufSize < 2 Then
     keyValue = Me.Width
```

```
      retValue = RegSetValueEx(keyID, subKey, 0&, _
      ➥REG_SZ, ByVal keyValue, Len(keyValue) + 1)
   Else

      keyValue = String(bufSize + 1, " ")

      retValue = RegQueryValueEx(keyID, subKey,
      ➥0&, REG_SZ, ByVal keyValue, bufSize)

      keyValue = Left$(keyValue, bufSize - 1)

      Me.Width = keyValue
   End If

   'Set values on form
   Label4.Caption = subKey
   Label5.Caption = Me.Width

   'Create height
   subKey = "Window Height"
   retValue = RegQueryValueEx(keyID, subKey, 0&,
   ➥REG_SZ, 0&, bufSize)

   If bufSize < 2 Then
     keyValue = Me.Height
     retValue = RegSetValueEx(keyID, subKey, 0&, _
     ➥REG_SZ, ByVal keyValue, Len(keyValue) + 1)
   Else

      keyValue = String(bufSize + 1, " ")

      retValue = RegQueryValueEx(keyID, subKey, 0&, REG_SZ, _
      ➥ByVal keyValue, bufSize)

      keyValue = Left$(keyValue, bufSize - 1)

      Me.Height = keyValue
   End If

   'Set values on form
   Label8.Caption = subKey
   Label7.Caption = Me.Height

  End If

End Sub
```

```
Private Sub Form_QueryUnload(Cancel As Integer,
➥UnloadMode As Integer)

  Dim keyValue As String
  Dim retValue As Long
  Dim keyID As Long

  retValue = RegCreateKey(HKEY_LOCAL_MACHINE, regKey, keyID)
  keyValue = Me.Width
  retValue = RegSetValueEx(keyID, "Window Width", 0&, _
➥REG_SZ, ByVal keyValue, Len(keyValue) + 1)

  keyValue = Me.Height
  retValue = RegSetValueEx(keyID, "Window Height", 0&, _
➥REG_SZ, ByVal keyValue, Len(keyValue) + 1)
End Sub
```

The Registry application works only on Windows 95 only, not on Windows NT 4.

Manipulating Graphics

Graphics attract users and are an important part of any application. A graphic can be a simple icon or a complex bitmap. This section describes some techniques for manipulating the display of bitmaps using the Win32 APIs. In this section, we'll look at the API graphics functions BitBlt() and StretchBlt() functions, which are more or less equivalent to the PaintPicture method of the graphics controls of Visual Basic. There is, however, an important difference: The PaintPicture method applies to a given control (PictureBox or Form), but the BitBlt() and StretchBlt() functions can copy pixels from anywhere on the Desktop. As a result, you can use them for applications in which the PaintPicture method is inadequate. For example, you can use the BitBlt() function to build a screen capture application.

The BitBlt Function

The BitBlt() function is used to blit, or copy, an image from a source to a destination object. The function transfers a rectangle of pixels from the specified source device context into a destination device context. Earlier in this chapter, the Menu-BMP application demonstrated the use of BitBlt(). Now, let's look at it in detail and compare it with the PaintPicture method provided with Visual Basic.

Declare the BitBlt() function as follows:

```
Declare Function BitBlt Lib "gdi32" Alias "BitBlt" (ByVal _
    hDestDC As Long, ByVal x As Long, ByVal y As Long, ByVal _
    nWidth As Long, ByVal nHeight As Long, ByVal hSrcDC As Long, _
    ByVal xSrc As Long, ByVal ySrc As Long, ByVal dwRop As Long) _
    As Long
```

Unlike the PaintPicture method, the BitBlt() function requires that you supply all the arguments. You must supply the starting X and Y coordinates, the height and width, and the starting coordinates of the source.

Before you can use the BitBlt() function, you must create a device context for the source and destination objects with the CreateCompatibleDC() and CreateCompatibleBitmap() functions. If you plan to use the BitBlt() function to copy from a PictureBox control, the control's device context is its hWnd property. However, the BitBlt function can be used with any device context, even with the device context of a bitmap loaded into memory.

With the exception of *hDestDC* and *hSrcDC*, the remaining arguments of the BitBlt() function are the same as those of the PaintPicture method. They specify the origin of the rectangle to be copied (the source arguments) and the origin and dimensions of the rectangle to which the pixels will be copied to (the destination arguments). The dimensions of the source and destination rectangles must be the same. Table 12.10, later in this chapter, lists the raster-operation codes for the *dwRop* argument. These codes define how the pixels of the source rectangle are combined with the pixels of the destination rectangle.

The StretchBlt Function

Another way to draw bitmaps is with the StretchBlt() function. With this function, you can copy a bitmap from a source rectangle into a destination rectangle, stretching or compressing the bitmap to fit the destination rectangle. Here's the declaration for StretchBlt():

```
Declare Function StretchBlt Lib "gdi32" Alias "StretchBlt" _
    (ByVal hdc As Long, ByVal x As Long, ByVal y As Long, ByVal _
    nWidth As Long, ByVal nHeight As Long, ByVal hSrcDC As Long, _
    ByVal xSrc As Long, ByVal ySrc As Long, ByVal nSrcWidth As _
    Long, ByVal nSrcHeight As Long, ByVal dwRop As Long) As Long
```

As you can see, StretchBlt() has all the arguments of the BitBlt() function plus two more arguments that specify the size of the source rectangle. StretchBlt() can compress a picture, stretch it backward, or turn it inside out by using different signs for the arguments. The raster-operation codes in Table 12.10 define how Windows combines the colors of the source and destination rectangle to achieve the final color.

TABLE 12.10 Raster-Operation Codes for BitBlt() and StretchBlt()

VALUE	DESCRIPTION
BLACKNESS	Fills in the destination rectangle with black.
DSTINVERT	Inverts the destination rectangle.
MERGECOPY	Merges the source rectangle with a pattern using the AND operator.
MERGEPAINT	Merges the inverted source rectangle with the destination rectangle using the OR operator.
NOTSRCCOPY	Copies the inverted source rectangle to the destination.
NOTSRCERASE	Combines the source and destination rectangle with the OR operator and inverts the final color.
PATCOPY	Copies a pattern to the destination rectangle.
PATINVERT	Combines a pattern with the destination rectangle using the XOR operator.
PATPAINT	Combines the colors of the pattern with the inverted source rectangle using the OR operator. The result is combined with the destination rectangle using the OR operator.
SRCAND	Combines the source and destination rectangles using the AND operator.
SRCCOPY	Copies the source rectangle into the destination rectangle.
SRCERASE	Combines inverted colors of the destination rectangle with the source rectangle using the AND operator.
SRCINVERT	Combines the source and destination rectangles using the XOR operator.
SRCPAINT	Combines the source and destination rectangle using the OR operator.
WHITENESS	Fills the destination rectangle with the color white.

These settings are also explained in Chapter 6, *Drawing and Painting with Visual Basic*. You can open the PaintPic application, discussed in Chapter 6, to experiment with various settings of the raster-operation codes. The PaintPic application uses the PaintPicture method, but the raster operations are the same.

Object Programming with Visual Basic

■ Extending Visual Basic with OLE

■ Understanding OLE terminology

■ Linking and embedding at design time

■ Linking and embedding at run time

■ Using OLE Container Control properties and methods

■ Writing OLE Server applications

Visual Basic is an object-oriented language and a highly successful one because it manages to hide many of the details of using and manipulating objects. The elements you use to build a user interface are objects, and you manipulate them via their properties and methods. By now, you are quite familiar with Visual Basic's object nature.

This chapter explores two more major aspects of Visual Basic's object nature:

- OLE (Object Linking and Embedding)

- ActiveX components

OLE (pronounced "oh-lay") lets Visual Basic applications access the functionality of other applications in the Windows environment. The controls you've used so far are built in to Visual Basic. They appear in the editor's Toolbox, and you can place them on Forms with point-and-click operations. Some objects in the Windows environment, however, aren't unique to Visual Basic and don't come with the language. Other applications provide these objects, and you can use them within your own applications.

A Word document is such an object, and you can incorporate Word documents in your applications. You don't have to know much about Word files, their contents, or how documents are stored on disk. You can still incorporate them in your applications, and when the need arises to edit them, you can momentarily borrow Word's menus and toolbars and display them in your own application. The user can then edit the document as if using Word—all from within your application's window. ActiveX components are like extensions to the operating system, available to any application that can access them.

ActiveX components are more or less the opposite. ActiveX components provide functionality to other applications. For example, you can create an object that offers certain services, such as custom calculations, or other operations you need to perform from within different environments (multiple VB applications, Microsoft Excel, and so on). Instead of limiting these services to a single application, you can access them from within many environments if you implement them as ActiveX components. ActiveX components are like extensions to the operating system, available to any application that can access them.

Extending Visual Basic with OLE

Object Linking and Embedding enables you to access the functionality of multiple applications from within a single programming environment. OLE is not another programming technique; it's a technology, rooted deeply in the Windows programming model. Instead of building with controls, as you've been doing so far in this book, in this chapter you will build applications by borrowing functionality from other applications.

You have learned how to build an application by manipulating the properties and calling on the methods of certain objects. Now, you'll learn how to develop applications using the properties and methods of other applications. You'll learn how to treat an entire application as an object and manipulate it. In the future, you won't have to implement your own spreadsheet application with Excel-like features or a word processor with Word-like features. You can use the real thing: Excel for your spreadsheets, Word for your documents, and so on. Of course, the users of your applications must have these other applications installed on their systems, but Office applications are quite common in business environments, and solutions developed around the Microsoft Office suite of applications are in high demand.

The essence of OLE is to build applications with available components. For example, the ListBox control is an available component that you can use to add a specific functionality to your applications. The ListBox control provides the functionality you need, but hides the details of its implementation. You don't have to know how the items are stored in the control or how the control maintains a sorted list of items. If you know the names of the control's properties and methods, you can use it in your applications and exploit its functionality without much difficulty. OLE allows you to do something similar with applications. If you know how to program Excel to carry out an operation (which presumably is not easy to accomplish with Visual Basic), through OLE you can instruct Excel to carry out this operation from within a Visual Basic application.

The topic of OLE could easily be the single topic of another book and is. For more information, see *Mastering OLE*, by Bryan Waters, and available from Sybex. This chapter presents the basic principles and some important aspects of OLE technology. In specific, you will learn:

- The basics of OLE (what OLE can do for the end user)

- How to work with embedded and linked objects

- OLE Automation (how to control other applications from within your own)

- How to create your own OLE containers

- How to create OLE servers and clients (which is how to expose the functionality of your own application so that other applications can use it)

What Is OLE?

Traditionally, software development tools have been uniform throughout, allowing little, if any, variation and component exchange with other tools. Programming environments were islands, somewhat isolated from other applications. Using structured programming techniques, you analyzed programming problems in terms of procedures and then implemented those procedures.

With the introduction of OLE, however, software development was significantly transformed from procedural to object-oriented programming. You no longer have to work with prepackaged tools. You can create self-contained modules, called *objects*, that greatly simplify programming, especially when building large applications. In the previous chapters, you learned how to use Visual Basic objects to build applications. With OLE, you can use both Visual Basic objects and objects exposed by other applications. As a result, your applications are no longer islands of functionality. They are an integral part of the operating system and the applications that run under it.

Component Software

The essence of OLE is *component software*. A component is an item (a control or an application) that someone else developed. You don't have to reinvent it to use it in your applications. If the component supports OLE, you can "borrow" its functionality for your own purposes. Microsoft Word, for example, comes with a powerful spell checker. Why buy another spell checker or write your own when you can borrow this functionality from Word?

The developer of component software sees a program as a combination of components working together to provide a common interface standard for OLE applications. For example, the functionality of a spreadsheet can be available in a word-processing document and vice versa. Or a Visual Basic application can borrow the functionality from both a word processor and a spreadsheet.

Compound Documents

A document that contains more than a single type of object is called a *compound document*. For example, a Word document that contains an Excel worksheet or an image is a compound document. In the past, there have been attempts to develop all-in-one applications that could handle text, numbers, images, communications, and every other aspect of computing upon which the average user relies. But they all failed. Until the advent of OLE technology.

The folks at Microsoft recognized the need of the average user to integrate favorite applications. They also understood that the all-in-one approach was not feasible, and they came up with OLE—a way for applications to exchange not only data but also functionality. OLE applications can communicate with one another so that end users can put together the pieces they need and create their own all-in-one software. The beauty of OLE is that the application that calls upon the services of another need not know much about it, short of how to accomplish the task, in the same sense that you, the VB programmer, need not know much about the operation of the RichTextBox or MSFlexGrid control, short of the properties and methods that let you manipulate them.

A Data-Centered Approach

For the user, this means a data-centered approach to a program rather than a product approach. All the user has to consider is *what* needs to be done, not *how* or *which application* should be used for the task at hand. For example, in a component software environment, the user does not have to work exclusively with a spreadsheet such as Microsoft Excel to manipulate numbers or with WordPerfect to manage text. Using an OLE application, the user has access to the functionality of a spreadsheet, a word processor, or a graphics application within one environment called a *container application*. As you will soon see, Visual Basic lets you build components that can share functionality with other applications, as well as applications that can host compound documents.

> **NOTE** Whereas traditionally structured applications focus on the *how* of processing data, OLE applications focus on the *what* of processing data. As you are learning OLE techniques, keep this simple principle in mind. It is the essence of OLE. It is what makes OLE useful for the end user, which must always be your goal. OLE programming may get complicated, but the end product must be a simple and easy-to-use application.

OLE Terminology

At this point, we would normally look at a few examples to demonstrate the items discussed so far, but before doing so, we must look at some OLE terms that we'll be using in this chapter. You may not quite understand all of them, but they will be illustrated later with examples. OLE has its own terminology, which we can't avoid, so this is as good a place as any to present it.

OLE Object

An item that has been *exposed*, or made available, by an OLE application is an OLE object. OLE servers are applications that expose different types (or classes) of objects that can be used in a container application (see the next section). As Figure 13.1 illustrates, Excel can expose a worksheet that can be inserted as is in a Word document.

FIGURE 13.1

An Excel worksheet is embedded in a Microsoft Word document.

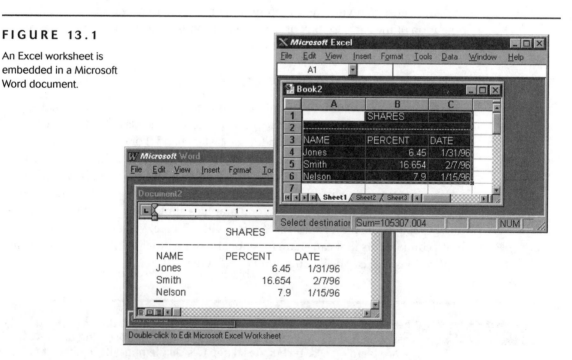

Container Application

This is an application that contains *linked* or *embedded* objects. A container is also an object itself. A good example of this in Visual Basic is the Form (FRM) object, which contains controls. The container is also referred to as a *client* because it uses the services of OLE servers.

Object Embedding

With this technique, you can insert an object from one application (the object application) into another application (the container application). The inserted object is a copy of the original and can be manipulated and stored separate and apart from the original object. For example, you can embed a range of cells from an Excel worksheet in a Word document. To edit the cells, you switch to Excel by double-clicking on the embedded Excel object. If the container application supports in-place editing, you'll see the menus of the server application right in the container application (see the section "In-Place Editing").

Server Application

This is the application that exposes the objects your VB application contacts. When your application must edit a document created by another application, it contacts the server application, which will be used to edit the document.

Object Linking

This technique is similar to embedding, except that the embedded data are also linked to the document from which they came. Changes to the object in the server are reflected automatically in the container application. Linking does not store the object but makes a reference to the object exposed by the server application. Each time you open the document that contains the linked object, the container application contacts the server application, which actually opens the most up-to-date version of the linked object. Linked objects are not copies. They *are* the originals, viewed from within different containers.

In-Place Editing

In-place editing is also known as in-place activation. The functionality of the server application is incorporated into the container application, thus enabling you to edit the object using the menus and tools of the server application. For example, if a Word document contains a range of cells from an Excel spreadsheet, double-clicking on the Excel object replaces the Word menus with the Excel menus. You can now edit the cells without switching to another application.

In-place editing is the most obvious manifestation of what was previously called "borrowing another application's functionality." For this to happen, both server and container applications must support OLE Automation (discussed next). When you select the embedded object, the menus and tools of the container application are replaced with the menus and tools of the server application.

OLE Automation

This method allows you to programmatically manipulate objects exposed by another application. It is also a standard that defines how code is shared between applications and how applications can be controlled from within other applications. For example, when you copy a range of cells from an Excel spreadsheet into a Word document, you embed the range of cells. With OLE Automation, your application can request that Excel perform some calculations and return the result to Word. For example, you can pass a table to Excel and request that Excel manipulate the numeric data in ways that are not possible with Word's tools and then return the processed data to Word.

OLE Drag-and-Drop

This method allows you to pick up objects that have been exposed in an application and place or drop them into your container application. For example, you can create an embedded object in a Word document by dragging-and-dropping a range of cells from an Excel worksheet.

An Example of Embedding and Linking

Let's look at an example of embedding and linking objects from a user's point of view. To create a compound document with WordPad, follow these steps:

1. Choose Start ➢ Programs ➢ Accessories ➢ WordPad.

2. Choose Insert ➢ Object to display the Insert Object dialog box, as shown in Figure 13.2.

3. Check the Create from File button, and then click on the Browse button.

4. In the Browse dialog box (which is identical to a File Open dialog box), select a bitmap image, and click on OK. The selected bitmap will be embedded in the WordPad document.

When you save the document, the bitmap is saved with it. WordPad is the container application that contains the bitmap object.

FIGURE 13.2

The Insert Object dialog box lets the user select an existing object (or create a new one) and embed or link it in the current document.

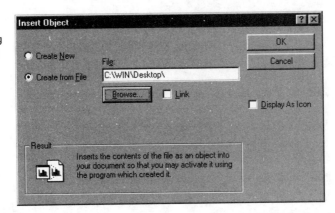

FIGURE 13.2

The Insert Object dialog box lets the user select an existing object (or create a new one) and embed or link it in the current document.

To edit the bitmap, simply double-click on the image. The operating system searches the Registry to find an application associated with bitmaps. The default application is Paint, which comes with Windows. If you haven't changed this setting, the Paint application starts, and its menus and toolbars appear in place of WordPad's menus (as shown in Figure 13.3). (If you did change it, that image-processing application starts.) You can edit the bitmap and then return to the main document by clicking somewhere outside the image. Paint is the server application that knows how to manipulate bitmaps.

The bitmap in the WordPad document and the bitmap in the disk file are two separate objects. You can change the disk file, even remove it from the disk, and the WordPad document won't be affected. What you have in the original document is a copy of the bitmap.

Furthermore, you can edit the embedded object in the same window that contains it. You don't need to understand which program created which object, nor do you have to work with that object in a separate window. You can remain in the window of the container application and edit the object without switching applications or windows. One benefit this approach is that it makes it easy to resize the object with respect to the surrounding text.

FIGURE 13.3

The menus and toolbar of the container application are replaced by those of the server application.

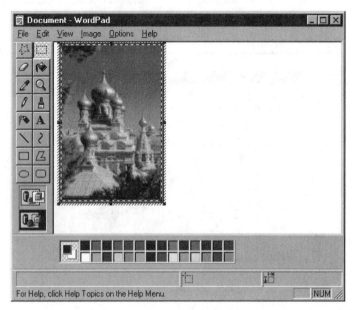

If you click on the Link checkbox in the Insert Object dialog box, the object in the WordPad document is linked to the original object. When linking an object, there will be only one object (bitmap file) in the system. WordPad will contain a reference to it, not a copy of the object. The same object can be linked to another document, perhaps with a different application. No matter how many documents make references to this object, there is a single object in the system. If this object is updated, all documents that reference this object will see its updated version (see Figure 13.4).

NOTE
If the object inserted in the container application is linked to the source object (the source file), you won't be able to edit it from within the container application. You will have to do so from within the server application. The essence of linking is that the user shouldn't be able to edit the object from within various applications. Only one copy of the object is on the computer, and it can be revised only from within the application that created it. As soon as the object is edited, any applications that contain links to this object are updated.

FIGURE 13.4

When you edit a linked object from with the server application, its linked image in the container application is updated as you edit the original object.

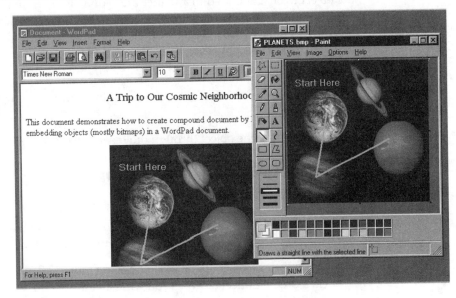

The OLE Container Control

Now, let's look at how you can exploit this technology from within your Visual Basic applications. To incorporate OLE functionality into your Visual Basic applications, you need the OLE Container control, which allows you to insert objects from other applications into your program. You can place only one object in the container control at a time, but you can have multiple OLE Container controls on the same Form, each one with its own object.

The OLE Container control is your door to the various objects available within the operating system that Visual Basic can't handle on its own: Word documents, sounds, bitmaps, Excel spreadsheets, and so on. You can embed objects in an OLE Container control at design time or at run time.

Object Linking and Embedding at Design Time

In this section we are going to create a simple OLE Container control to demonstrate object embedding at design time. Embed objects at design time if you know the object to be embedded in advance and you want to limit the users of the application to a specific object or type of object (a Word document, for example). It is also possible to link objects with the following techniques, but at design time you usually embed, rather than link documents. You can embed objects in two ways at design time:

- By pasting an existing object (or dragging-and-dropping the object on the control).

- By selecting the object through the Insert Object dialog box.

Embedding with Drag-and-Drop

To embed with drag-and-drop, follow these steps:

1. Start a new Visual Basic project, and double-click on the OLE icon in the Toolbox to place an OLE Container control on the Form.

2. In the Insert Object dialog box (show in Figure 13.2, earlier in this chapter), click on the Cancel button. (You want an empty OLE Container control of Form1 so that you can later drop an OLE object on it.)

3. In the OLE Container control's Properties window, change the SizeMode property to 1-Stretch (if it's a drawing that can be resized) or to 2-AutoSize (if it's text or a bitmap, which will look bad when resized) to adjust the size of the object or the container.

The settings of the SizeMode property are explained in Table 13.1.

TABLE 13.1   The Values for the SizeMode Property

VALUE	DESCRIPTION
Clip	The object is displayed in actual size. If it's larger than the OLE Container control, its image is clipped.
Stretch	The object's image is sized to fill the OLE Container control. The image may be distorted as the object is resized.
AutoSize	The control is resized to display the entire object.
Zoom	The object is resized to fill the OLE Container control as much as possible while still maintaining its original proportions.

4. Next, start an application that supports OLE and open a file. In this example, we will embed a Microsoft Word document in our OLE container by dragging-and-dropping the document from the source application (Word) into the OLE Container control.

5. With both Visual Basic and Word visible on your screen, drag the document (or part of it) onto the empty OLE Container Control.

TIP To drag part of a Word document and drop in into an OLE Container control, select it with the mouse. Then click somewhere on the selected paragraphs and start dragging. If the Visual Basic window isn't visible, press Alt+Tab to switch to it, *without releasing the mouse button*. When the Visual Basic Form is visible on the Desktop, drop the selection on the OLE Container. The selected text will be removed from the original object (the Word document). To embed a copy of the selected text, hold down the Control key as you drag the selection. Plain drag-and-drop operations move the source, even when you move a file on the Desktop. To make a copy, use the Control key while you drag-and-drop.

6. As you drag the object, an oblong appears under the pointer arrow. Drop this into the empty OLE Container control. After a few seconds, the Microsoft Word document will appear in your OLE Container control (see Figure 13.5).

Your Form now contains a Word document. When you run the application, the Word document is displayed in the OLE Container control. You can edit it with Word's menus and toolbars.

Class, SourceDoc, and SourceItem   Let's look at a few more basic properties of the OLE Container control. When you create an object on your Form, the Properties window contains the following information:

- The name of the application that produced the object (Class)

- The data or a reference to the data (SourceDoc)

- The image of the data (SourceItem—this applies to linked objects only. It specifies the data within the source file that are linked to the OLE control.)

FIGURE 13.5

The Microsoft Word document appears in the OLE Container control.

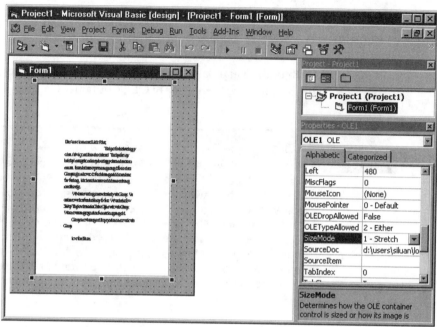

Examine the values of the Class, SourceDoc, and SourceItem properties in the Properties window. You can also embed an object by setting these properties of the OLE Container control:

- Class is the type of the embedded document.

- SourceDoc is the name of the file in which the object is stored.

- SourceItem describes the part of the document that was selected for embedding.

These properties are discussed later, but I mention them here so that you can watch their values as you embed and link objects at design time.

The OLETypeAllowed Property   Whether the source document is embedded or linked into the OLE Container control depends on the setting of the control's OLETypeAllowed property. Select the OLE control on the Form and scroll down to OLETypeAllowed property. Table 13.2 shows the valid values for this property. The default is 2-Either.

TABLE 13.2 The Values for the OLETypeAllowed Property

VALUE	CONSTANT	DESCRIPTION
0	vbOLELinked	Linked. The OLE Container control can contain only a linked object.
1	vbOLEEmbedded	Embedded. The OLE Container control can contain only an embedded object.
2	VbOLEEither	(Default) Either. The OLE Container control can contain either a linked or an embedded object.

Let's make a linked object by setting this property to 0 (Linked). The default setting of this property does not determine what kind of OLE type you are going to use, but rather what type can be used. The actual OLE type is indicated in the Insert Object dialog box. For example, if OLETypeAllowed is 2, the Create New and Create from File buttons and the Link Checkbox control are enabled in the Insert Object dialog box. If the OLETypeAllowed property is 0 (Linked), the Create New button is disabled (you can't link a nonexisting object). If you select 1 (Embedded), the Link checkbox is disabled.

Linking with the Insert Object Dialog Box

Drag-and-drop is only one way to embed or link objects in an OLE Container control. You can also do so through the Insert Object dialog box. Follow these steps:

1. Delete the OLE Container control in Form1, and create a new OLE Container control as you did earlier.

2. In the Insert Object dialog box, select the Create from File option button and check the Link checkbox, as shown in Figure 13.6.

As mentioned, the Link checkbox is sometimes disabled. This occurs when you have set OLETypeAllowed to 1 - Embedded. To make the Link checkbox available, set the OLETypeAllowed to 2 - Either.

3. Click on the Browse button to locate the file you want.

4. Place the file on the OLE Container control. You will see part of the linked file. To fit the entire object in the container, resize the control.

FIGURE 13.6

To link an object, check the Link checkbox in the Insert Object dialog box.

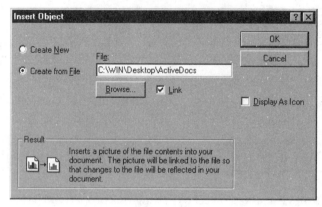

Depending on the setting of the SizeMode property, the image of the linked file may be distorted. The OLE Container control now contains a reference to the object, not a copy of the object, as with an embedded object. Whenever the server application changes the linked object, the object in your container will be updated.

> **NOTE**
>
> **When the inserted object is linked to the original, the container application does not hold any data. Even what you see in the container application is an image of the object you inserted, not a copy of the object's data, as happens with an embedded object.**

If the linked object is a Word document, it will appear in your OLE Container control as shown in Figure 13.7. You will notice that the SourceDoc property is now the *path\filename* of the linked object.

5. Keep the Visual Basic window open while you open the document in Word. Make some changes to the document, and watch the linked document in the Visual Basic window being updated in real time. You don't have to run the application for this to happen. Even in design mode, the linked document is updated in real time, as the original is being edited.

FIGURE 13.7

A Microsoft Word document embedded in an OLE Container control

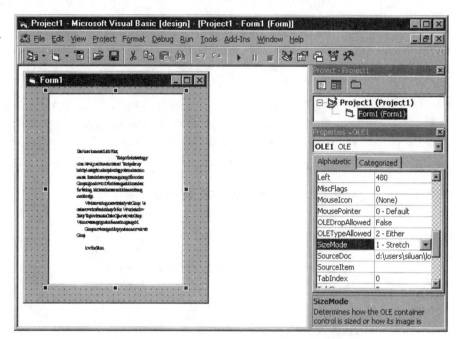

Saving and Retrieving Embedded Objects

Embedded objects are created by server applications, but are stored in your container application. Once an object is embedded, there is no connection between the contents of the OLE control and the original object. To edit the embedded object, you access the resources of the application that supplied the object. Moreover, data in an embedded object is not automatically saved. To save the embedded object and any changes made by the server application, you use the SaveToFile method. It has the following syntax:

```
OLE1.SaveToFile filenumber
```

The *filenumber* variable is a numeric expression specifying an open file's number. The number must correspond to a file opened in binary mode. The code below demonstrates how to prompt the user for a filename and save the embedded document in it with the SaveToFile method.

Code 13.1: Saving OLE Data

```
Private Sub mnuFileSaveas_Click()
    On Error GoTo Cancel
```

```
CommonDialog1.ShowSave        ' show Save As dialog
Open CommonDialog1.FileName For Output As #1      ' Open file
OLE1.SaveToFile (1)           ' Write to file No. 1
Close #1                      ' Close file
Cancel:
End Sub
```

To load an object that has been saved to a data file, use the ReadFromFile method. It syntax is similar to the syntax of SaveToFile. The following code demonstrates how to read the contents of an OLE container from a file (where they were stored earlier with the SaveToFile method).

Code 13.2: Reading OLE Data

```
Private Sub mnuFileOpen_Click()
    On Error GoTo Cancel
    CommonDialog1.ShowOpen        ' show Open dialog
    Open CommonDialog1.FileName For Input As #1      ' Open file
    OLE1.ReadFromFile (1)         ' Read file No. 1
Cancel:
End Sub
```

NOTE If the property OLEType is 0 (vbOLELinked), only the link information and an image of the data are saved to the specified file. If the property OLEType is 1 (vbOLEEmbedded), the object's data are saved by the SaveToFile method.

When you save an embedded file, the following information is saved:

- The name of the application that produced the object
- The object's data
- A metafile image of the object

When you save a linked file, the following information is saved:

- The name of the application that created the object
- The filename of the object
- A metafile image of the object

The data saved by the SaveToFile method is only accessible by the container application and only through the ReadFromFile method. Although these are Visual Basic methods that you can invoke from within your applications, you don't have to know anything about the object's native format.

Using In-Place Editing

If you run the application now, you will see the embedded or linked object right on your VB Form. The user of the application can actually edit the object by double-clicking on it. You can open the embedded object for editing in several ways, and I'll discuss them in the sections "Common OLE Container Control Properties" and "Common OLE Container Control Methods," later in this chapter. The simplest way to open the application that provided the embedded object and use its menus and toolbars to edit the object is to double-click on the object.

In-place editing, or in-place activation, is an enhancement to embedding objects in Visual Basic. With this feature, you can edit the embedded object within the OLE container. The functionality of the server application is incorporated into the container. In-place editing is available only if both the OLE Container control and the server application support OLE Automation. When you select the embedded object, the menus and toolbars of the server application replace the menus and toolbars of the OLE Container control (see Figure 13.8). In-place editing allows your container application to borrow the functionality of the embedded object's server application.

FIGURE 13.8

In-place editing the previous paragraph of this Word document on an OLE Container control in a Visual Basic application

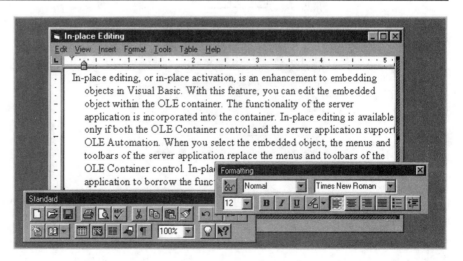

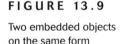

Some OLE-capable applications may not be able to display their toolbars for in-place editing of an object. This problem is specific to the applications and can't be fixed from within your VB application.

Embedding Multiple Objects

You can embed or link more than one object at design time, as long as you provide a separate OLE Container control for each object. In this example, you will embed a video clip. Follow these steps:

1. Place a second OLE Container control on the same Form.

2. In the Insert Object dialog box, click on the Create from File button, and then click on the Browse button to select a file to embed. For this example, select one of the sample video clips that comes with Windows.

3. Click on OK to embed the object. Figure 13.9 shows the video clip I embedded.

FIGURE 13.9

Two embedded objects on the same form

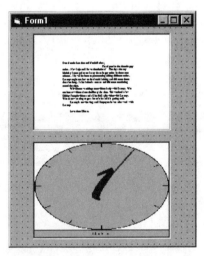

Now, run your application to see the video clip in action. You can also play the video clip using the pop-up menu. The VCR-style control panel will be displayed at the bottom of the video clip, as shown in Figure 13.10.

FIGURE 13.10

At run time, the control panel appears at the bottom of the window, indicating a media player.

The OLE Control's Shortcut Menu

Another way to embed objects in an OLE Container control is through the control's shortcut menu. Right-click on an OLE Container control at design time to display the shortcut menu shown in Figure 13.11. Use this menu to insert a new object or to edit the embedded document if the control already contains an object. To embed (or link) another object in an OLE Container control, first delete the existing object.

FIGURE 13.11

To display the OLE Container control's shortcut menu, right-click on the control at design time.

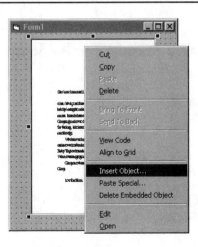

The commands on the shortcut menu depend on the state of the selected object. The shortcut menu in Figure 13.11 contains the Edit and Open commands since the selected object is a Word document. If the embedded object were a sound file, the shortcut menu would contain the Edit and Play commands. If the control doesn't contain an object (because you clicked on the Cancel button in the Insert Object dialog box), the Edit and Open commands, which depend on the control's contents, will be missing from the shortcut menu.

The shortcut menu of the OLE Container may contain some or all of the following commands:

- **Cut**   Copies the object in the container to the Clipboard and clears the container.

- **Copy**   Copies the object in the container to the Clipboard.

- **Paste**   Pastes an object from the Clipboard to the control.

- **Delete**   Removes the OLE object from the OLE control.

- **Insert Object**   Deletes the existing object and opens the Insert Object dialog box so that the user can insert a new or an existing object in the OLE Container control.

- **Paste Special**   Opens the Paste Special dialog box, which allows you to paste an object copied to the Clipboard from another OLE application. The Paste command embeds the object in the control; the Paste Special command creates a link to the object on the Clipboard. The Paste Special dialog box is similar to the Insert Object dialog box, except that its options apply to the object currently stored on the Clipboard.

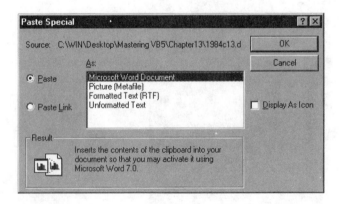

- **Create Link**   Appears only if the SourceDoc property of the OLE Container control is set; creates a linked object.

- **Delete Link**   Breaks a link and turns a linked object into an embedded object.

- **Create Embedded Object**   Appears if either the SourceDoc or the Class properties are set; creates an embedded object.

NOTE   To share your program with other users, the latter must have a copy of the application that created the file. If the OLE control contains a Word document, users of your application won't be able to view and edit the document unless they have Word installed on their system. Also, they must have a valid link (path name) to the linked file. Otherwise, when users run your program, only an image of the original data will be displayed.

Object Linking and Embedding at Run Time

In this section we are going to create linked and embedded objects at run time. This section's example is called OLERTime, and you will find it in this chapter's folder on the CD. The OLERTime application demonstrates how to:

- Insert an object

- Choose between linking and embedding

- Set the size of the container control or the size of the object

- Display information about the object

The OLERTime application demonstrates how to embed and link objects to an OLE Container control by opening the Insert Object dialog box from within your code. It does what you've been doing in the previous examples manually. Operations are performed from within the framework of a VB application, which lets the user select the object and set some basic properties of the object. The application's main Form is shown in Figure 13.12.

FIGURE 13.12

The OLERTime application's main window

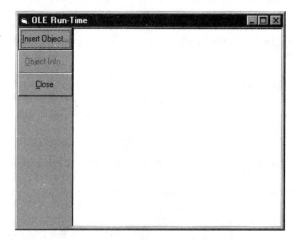

When you click on the Insert Object button, the application displays the Object Type dialog box (see Figure 13.13) in which you set the container's Stretch mode and the OLE type (link or embed). Then, click on OK to display the Insert Object dialog box; you can specify a new object or select an existing one.

FIGURE 13.13

The OLERTime application's Object Type dialog box

VB5 at Work: The OLERTime Application

To design the application, follow these steps:

1. Start a new Visual Basic project, and change the Form's name to frmOLE.

2. Save the Form as OLERTime.frm, and save the project as OLERTime.vbp.

3. Place an OLE Container control on the Form frmOLE.

4. In the Insert Object dialog box, click on Cancel to place an empty container on the Form.

5. Resize the OLE Container control, and place on it the command buttons shown in Figure 13.12, earlier in this chapter.

Now, you add the code to do the following:

- Display the second window (frmType) and activate the Insert Object dialog box

- Display information about the object

Open the Insert Object button's Click handler and enter the following:

```
Private Sub cmdInsObj_Click()
  frmType.Show
End Sub
```

The Object Info button displays information about the object that has been inserted in the container (you'll see shortly how the object is selected and inserted). The following code is executed when you click on the Object Info button (oleDisplay is the name of the OLE control).

Code 13.3: The Object Info Button

```
Private Sub cmdObjInfo_Click()
  Dim SourceText As String
  Dim TypeText As String
  Dim ItemText As Sring
  Dim MsgText As String
  SourceText = "The object's source file is " & oleDisplay
➥.SourceDoc
  TypeText = "The type of object is " & oleDisplay.Class
  ItemText = "The selected item is" & oleDisplay.SourceItem
  MsgText = SourceText & vbCrLf & TypeText & ItemText
  MsgBox MsgText, vbInformation, "Object Information"
End Sub
```

The carriage return character (vbCrLF) breaks the message into multiple, shorter lines. If the embedded (or linked) object is a Word document, the following information is displayed:

```
The object's source file is C:\My Documents\FileName
The type of object is Word.Document
```

(*FileName* will be replaced by the name of the file you actually embed in the OLE control.) Figure 13.14 shows what the Object Info button displays if a Word document is linked to the OLE Container control. The SourceItem is blank for a Word document.

FIGURE 13.14

The information reported by OLERTime for a linked bitmap

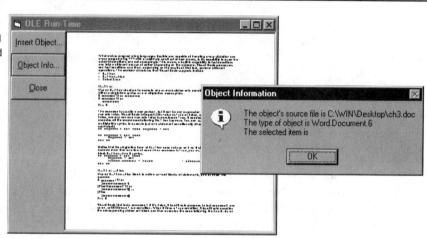

SourceDoc and Class Properties   The Object Info button displays the values of the SourceDoc and Class properties. The SourceDoc property is the name of the linked or embedded file. The Class property sets or returns the class name of an embedded object, which is its type. Other object types you will find on your computer are Excel spreadsheets (Excel.Sheet), Paint pictures, and the objects you'll create in the following sections of this chapter. If you create a new object from Microsoft Excel or Microsoft Word or another compatible OLE application, there will be no SourceDoc property because the embedded object is not yet a document that lives somewhere on the disk.

The SourceItem Property   The SourceItem property indicates the part of the embedded or linked document. In many cases, this property is undefined because the entire object is linked. You can, however, select part of some objects for embedding. You can't select part of a Word document or a bitmap, but you can select part of an Excel spreadsheet. If you select a range of cells, the SourceItem property might be something like "R1C1:R1C10." Because the OLERTime application allows you to select a file to be embedded and doesn't support drag-and-drop, the SourceItem property is empty.

When you click on the Insert Object button, the application displays a window that offers you a choice of data types. You can select Linked or Embedded. You can also determine the size of the object to be displayed by setting the size mode in the OLE properties windows. The choices are:

- Stretch the OLE Container control to fit the object (2-AutoSize)

- Stretch the object to fit the container (1-Stretch)

When you click on OK, the Insert Object dialog box opens, and you can select the data to insert.

Draw the command buttons, option buttons, and frames as shown in Figure 13.12, earlier in this chapter. Now add the following code for frmType.

Code 13.4: The frmType

```
Option Explicit
Private Sub cmdCancel_Click()
  Unload frmType
End Sub
```

This Sub procedure closes the application by unloading frmType.

Setting the Size of the OLE Container Control   Let's digress for a moment and set the size for the OLE Container control. When embedding objects in an OLE Container control at run time, you must take into consideration the size of the control, which the user can't change with the mouse. Let's declare the variables *OLEHeight* and *OLEWidth* so that the size of the control will be the size you selected at design time. Instead of hardcoding the height and width of the container control, we'll use *OLEHeight* and *OLEWidth*, which are more flexible. In the frmOLE Form's declaration section enter the following:

```
Public OLEHeight As Integer
Public OLEWidth As Integer
```

and in the Form's Load event add the following lines:

```
OLEHeight = oleDisplay.Height
OLEWidth = oleDisplay.Width
```

Now return to frmType and add the code to call the Insert Object dialog box after the user sets the desired options.

Code 13.5: Invoking the Insert Object Dialog Box

```
Private Sub cmdOK_Click()
  With frmOLE.oleDisplay
      .Height = frmOLE.OLEHeight
      .Width = frmOLE.OLEWidth
  End With
  If optStretchObject.Value = True Then
      frmOLE.oleDisplay.SizeMode = 1       ' Stretch
  Else
      frmOLE.oleDisplay.SizeMode = 2       ' AutoSize
  End If
```

and add the following line to hide the Form:

```
frmType.Hide
```

Finally, the following lines open the Insert Object dialog box and insert the object:

```
frmOLE.oleDisplay.InsertObjDlg
If frmOLE.oleDisplay.Class <> "" Then
    frmOLE.cmdObjInfo.Enabled = True
End If
Unload frmType
```

The Object Info button becomes enabled only if an object is inserted.

InsertObjDlg is a method of the OLE Container control that displays the Insert Object dialog box so that the user can create a linked or an embedded object by choosing its type and the application that provides the object. The user's choices are automatically assigned to the appropriate properties of the OLE control.

To size the container, follow these steps:

1. Run the application, and click on the Insert Object button to display the Object Type dialog box.

2. Click on one of the Size Mode buttons, and then click on one of the Object Type buttons. The Insert Object dialog box appears as shown in Figure 13.15.

FIGURE 13.15

The Insert Object dialog box shows the Create from File option button selected and displays the path to the data file.

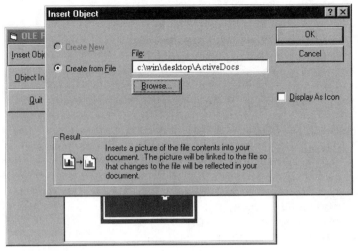

Code 13.6: The frmOLE Form

```
Option Explicit
Public OLEHeight As Integer
Public OLEWidth As Integer
Private Sub cmdClose_Click()
  Dim Quit As String
  Quit = MsgBox("Are you sure you want to quit? ",
  ➥vbYesNo + vbQuestion)
  If Quit = vbYes Then
    End
  End If
End Sub
Private Sub cmdInsObj_Click()
  frmType.Show
End Sub

Private Sub cmdObjInfo_Click()
  Dim SourceText As String
  Dim TypeText As String
  Dim MsgText As String
  SourceText = "The object's source file is " &
  ➥oleDisplay.SourceDoc
  TypeText = "The type of object is " & oleDisplay.Class
  MsgText = SourceText & vbCrLf & TypeText
```

```
      MsgBox MsgText, vbInformation, "Object Information"
End Sub
Private Sub Form_Load()
  OLEHeight = oleDisplay.Height
  OLEWidth = oleDisplay.Width
End Sub
```

Code 13.7: The frmType Form

```
Option Explicit
Private Sub cmdCancel_Click()
  Unload frmType
End Sub

Private Sub cmdOK_Click()
  With frmOLE.oleDisplay
    .Height = frmOLE.OLEHeight
    .Width = frmOLE.OLEWidth
  End With
  If optStretchObject.Value = True Then
    'SizeMode=
      '1-Stretch
      '2-Autosize
    .SizeMode = 1
  Else
    .SizeMode = 2
  End If

  If optTypeEmbedded.Value = True Then
      frmOLE.oleDisplay.OLETypeAllowed = 1      ' Linked
  Else
      frmOLE.oleDisplay.OLETypeAllowed = 0      'Embedded
  End If

  'Hide frmType
  frmType.Hide
  'Insert Object
  frmOLE.oleDisplay.InsertObjDlg
  If frmOLE.oleDisplay.Class <> "" Then
    frmOLE.cmdObjInfo.Enabled = True
  End If
  Unload frmType
End Sub
```

Try embedding various objects in the OLE control of the OLERTime Form and double-clicking to edit them.

Common OLE Container Control Properties

This section summarizes the properties and methods used in creating embedded and linked documents at run time. The same properties are set by Visual Basic when the object is inserted at design time with any of the methods already described.

Class   This property identifies the type of object held by the OLE container control. Run the OLERTime application, select various types of objects registered on your system, and then click on the Object Info button to view their Class property.

DisplayType   This property specifies whether the object displays with content (0) of the object or as an icon (1) of the OLE server. The related constants are:

- **vbOLEDisplayContent (0)**   Displays object's contents
- **vbOLEDisplayIcon (1)**   Displays object as an icon

OLETypeAllowed   This property determines the type of object you can create:

- 0-Linked
- 1-Embedded
- 2-Either

The type of object is determined in the Insert Object dialog box. The related constants are:

- **vbOLELinked (0)**   Object will be linked.
- **vbOLEEmbedded (1)**   Object will be embedded.
- **vbOLEEither (2)**   Object can be linked or embedded.

OLEDropAllowed   If this property is set to True, a user can drag-and-drop an object into the OLE Container control at run time. This has the same effect as copying an object onto the Clipboard and the application calling the Paste Special method on the OLE Container control.

SizeMode   This property determines how an object's icon or data image is displayed in the OLE Container control, and its settings are as follows:

- **vbOLESizeClip (0)**   The object is displayed in its actual size. If the object is larger than the OLE Container control, its image is clipped by the control's borders. This is the default.

- **VbOLESizeStretch (1)**   The object's image is sized to fill the OLE Container control. The image may not maintain the original proportions of the object.

- **VbOLESizeAutosize (2)**   The OLE Container control is resized to display the entire object.

- **VbOLESizeZoom (3)**   The object is resized to fill the OLE Container control as much as possible while maintaining its original proportions.

SourceDoc   When you create a linked object, this property determines which source file to link. When you create an embedded object, this property determines the file to use as a template.

SourceItem   This property is for linked objects only. It specifies the data to link within a file. For example, if you are linking a range of Excel worksheet cells, the SourceItem property specifies the range of cells that are linked.

OLEType   This property is read-only and returns the status of an object at run time. Its value is 0 for linked objects, 1 for embedded objects, and 3 if no object is inserted. The related constants are:

- **vbOLELinked (0)**   Object is linked in the OLE control.

- **vbOLEEmbedded (1)**   Object is embedded in the OLE control.

- **vbOLENone (3)**   The OLE Container control is empty.

AutoActivate   This property determines whether the contents of the OLE Container will be activated by a double-click or each time the focus moves to the control. The AutoActivate property can take the following values:

- **vbOLEActivateManual (0)**   The object isn't activated automatically. You use the DoVerb method to activate it.

- **VbOLEActivateGetFocus (1)**   The object is activated for editing each time the OLE Container control gets the focus.

- **VbOLEActivateDoubleclick(2)** This is the default value. The object in the OLE Container control is activated when the user double-clicks on the control.

- **vbOLEActivateAuto (3)** The object is activated based on its normal method of activation: either when the control receives the focus or when the user double-clicks on the control.

Common OLE Container Control Methods

To manipulate embedded or linked objects, in addition to the properties already mentioned, the OLE Container control provides the following methods.

CreateEmbed This method creates an embedded object. It has the following syntax:

```
CreateEmbed sourcedoc, class
```

The *sourcedoc* argument is the filename of a document used as a template for the embedded object. To create a new embedded document, supply a zero-length string ("") for the *sourcedoc* argument.

The *class* argument is an optional argument that specifies the name of the class of the embedded object. This argument is required only if the *sourcedoc* argument is omitted. To find out the registered classes, select the OLE Container control's Class property in the Properties window and click on the button with the ellipsis.

CreateLink This method creates a linked object from the contents of a file. It has the following syntax:

```
CreateLink sourcedoc, sourceitem
```

The *sourcedoc* argument is the file from which the object will be created, and *sourceitem* is the data within the file to be linked in the linked object. To link the contents of the OLE Container control to a range of Excel cells, for example, specify the file with the *sourcedoc* argument, and specify the range of cells to be linked with the *sourceitem* argument. The *sourceitem* argument can be a single cell, such as R10C12, or a range of cells, such as R1C1:R10C20. You can also specify a named range.

After the linked document is created, the SourceItem property is reset to a zero-length string, and its original value is appended to the SourceDoc property, which becomes something like the following:

```
"c:\data\revenus\rev1997.xls|R1C1:R20C25"
```

An easy way to determine the syntax of the two commands is to select the object you want to link (or a similar one) and then paste it with the Paste Special command on the OLE Container control at design time. After the object is linked, look up the value of the SourceDoc property and use it in your code.

DoVerb *verb* This method opens an object for an operation, such as editing. The optional *verb* argument can have one of the values in Table 13.3.

TABLE 13.3 The Values of the *verb* Argument

CONSTANT	VALUE	DESCRIPTION
vbOLEPrimary	0	Default action for the object.
vbOLEShow	-1	Opens the object for editing. This activates the application that created the document in the OLE Container.
vbOLEOpen	-2	Opens the object for editing. This activates the application that created the document in a separate window.
vbOLEHide	-3	For embedded objects, hides the application that created the object.
vbOLEUIActivate	-4	Activates the object for in-place editing and shows any user interface tools. If the object doesn't support in-place editing, an error occurs.
VbOLEInPlaceActivate	-5	When the user moves the focus to the OLE Container control, this action creates a window for the object and prepares the object to be edited.
VbOLEDiscardUndoState	-6	When the object is activated for editing, this method can discard all the changes that the object's application can undo.

InsertObjDlg   This method displays the Insert Object dialog box. The user's selections are reported to the application via the properties of the OLE Container control.

PasteSpecialDlg   This method displays the Paste Special dialog box. The user's selections are reported to the application via the OLE Container control's properties.

To find out the intrinsic constants you can use with the various methods and properties of the OLE Container control, use the Object Browser. Follow these steps:

1.   Choose View ➢ Object Browser.

2.   Select the Visual Basic object library, and then choose the Constants object to display the names of the constants under Methods/Properties.

OLE Automation

OLE Automation goes one step further than linking. When you link, you borrow the functionality of another application. When you use OLE Automation, you control the source document from within your application. Applications that support OLE Automation make available (or, in Microsoft's colorful terminology, *expose*) their objects to other applications. An object that Word exposes, for example, can be a sentence, a paragraph, or an entire document. An object that Excel exposes could be a macro, a range of cells, or an entire worksheet.

You can control exposed objects from your VB application via the properties and methods exposed by the source application. An important feature of Visual Basic 5 is that you can access the objects of an OLE Server application as well as use the functionality of the Server application. The benefit of OLE Automation is that you can work in a single environment, but use any OLE tools that are available from other applications.

If you have followed the examples in this chapter so far, you have enough tools and knowledge to explore further the power of Visual Basic 5 for creating OLE Automation applications. In this section, you will learn how to automate the OLE Container control and ask the Server application to perform certain actions on the embedded objects. The Discount application introduces the power of OLE Automation.

If you develop applications for Microsoft's Office environment, you can use OLE Automation to combine the features from multiple applications and create automated solutions. The pieces are there; all you have to do is put them together.

VB5 at Work: The Discount OLE Automation Application

The Discount application (see Figure 13.16) demonstrates how to access the functionality of Excel to perform calculations on data supplied by a VB application. You will find it in this chapter's folder on the CD. To test it, you must have Excel installed on your system.

FIGURE 13.16

The Discount OLE Automation application

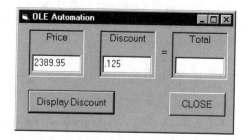

Using the Discount application, you enter a value and a discount, and then the application calculates the discounted price. In essence, it multiplies two numbers, but it passes the data to Excel and lets Excel do the calculations and return the result. This trivial operation doesn't require (or even justify) Excel's resources, but the goal is to demonstrate how to contact Excel and borrow any piece of its functionality you need for your application.

Begin a new project, change the Form's default name to frmAuto, and draw the controls shown in Figure 13.16. You will need to store the application's data in an Excel worksheet (details are in "The Excel Worksheet" section, later in this chapter).

The GetObject Method   In this application, you use the GetObject method to open an existing Excel worksheet, and then you use the Object property to access the cells of the worksheet. GetObject accesses an existing object in an application and allows you to manipulate that object from within your OLE Container control. The OLE Container control first loads Excel, which then opens the file.

When you call this method with a valid path and filename, OLE checks the registry to find out which application is associated with files that have the XLS extension. Since this extension applies to Excel, Excel is loaded with the file.

The GetObject method has the following syntax:

```
GetObject(pathname, class)
```

The *pathname* variable is the full path and name of the file to be retrieved, and *class* is a string representing the object class.

Some files may support more than one class of object and require that you specify the application to load with the file. Image files, for instance, are associated with a single application, but usually more than one application can handle them. To specify that an image file be opened with an image-processing application that isn't the default for the file's extension, you specify the object's Class property. The Discount application calls the GetObject method with the *pathname* argument only, as follows:

```
GetObject ("C:\accounts\Jun97.xls")
```

You could also use the following statement:

```
GetObject ("C:\accounts\Jun97.xls", "Excel.Sheet")
```

The CreateObject Method   An alternative to GetObject is the CreateObject method, which can create a new OLE Automation object. The CreateObject method has the following syntax:

```
CreateObject (class)
```

The *class* argument is the type of the object. The CreateObject method does not actually create a file on the disk for the object. You must use the SaveToFile method to save the file. To create a new Excel worksheet object, use the following statement:

```
CreateObject(Excel.Sheet)
```

How the Discount Application Works

Before you examine the code, run the Discount application and see how it works. Enter a value and a discount in the two TextBox controls, and click on the Display Discount button to see the discounted price that Excel returns.

All the application code is behind the Display Discount button. Let's follow the steps for contacting Excel from within the VB application.

First, declare an object variable in which to store the worksheet, as follows:

```
Dim XLSheet As Object
```

The object variable *XLSheet* plays the role of the OLE Container control. Since the user of the application need not edit the contents of the Excel worksheet (the application takes care of exchanging data with Excel), you don't need to place an OLE Container control on the Form. You must, however, create a variable in which to store the object.

To access the Excel worksheet, call the GetObject method, which contacts Excel and gets a worksheet object. The object is stored in the *XLSheet* variable:

```
Set XLSheet = GetObject("C:\My Documents\Disco.xls")
```

The *XLSheet* object represents an Excel worksheet. It is not a worksheet object. Instead, it's the means through which you access the Server application and request that it perform certain operations. Through the *XLSheet* object, you can access any of Excel's objects and menus. Each cell in Excel is addressed by its row and column number, as follows:

```
cells(2, 3)
```

Use this format to access a specific cell within Excel. To access the same cell from an external application through OLE Automation, you use the following expression:

```
XLSheet.Cells(2, 3).Value
```

Through the *XLSheet* object, you can access all Excel properties and methods and manipulate the current worksheet. In essence, you'll be "driving" Excel through this object.

Let's start by making Excel visible during the execution of the application. To do so, use the following statement:

```
XLSheet.Application.Visible = True
```

To place your data figures into specific cells in the worksheet, you must assign the Text property of the txtPrice TextBox to Cells(2, 3) and assign the Text property of the txtDiscount TextBox to Cells(3, 3), as follows:

```
XLSheet.Cells(2, 3).Value = txtPrice.Text

XLSheet.Cells(3, 3).Value = txtDiscount.Text
```

These two statements pass the data to Excel and place them in the proper cells.

Next, you must calculate the discount using the following statement:

```
XLSheet.Cells (4, 3).Formula = (=r2c3-(r2c3*r3c3))
txtResult.Text = XLSheet.Cells(4, 3)
```

Where did the (=r2c3-(r2c3*r3c3)) come from? To calculate the discounted price and display it in the cell (4, 3) from within Excel, you enter a formula in this cell. The formula is "the price minus the price times the discount rate." Excel formulas are preceded by an equals sign. The first statement assigns a formula to the cell (4, 3) of the current worksheet. As soon as you assign a formula to a cell, it's calculated, and the result is displayed in the cell. The next statement retrieves the calculated value from Excel and assigns it to the Text property of the txtResult TextBox control.

Here's what we have done so far:

- Created a new object through which we can access Excel
- Passed a few values from our VB application to Excel
- Instructed Excel to perform some calculations
- Extracted the results from Excel and used them in our VB application

Next, we'll add a command to save the contents of the current worksheet in the file Discount.xls. To save a file from within Excel, you use the Save or the Save As command. We'll do the same through the XLSheet object:

```
XLSheet.SaveAs "C:\My Documents\discount.xls"
```

Finally, you must close Excel with the following statement:

```
XLSheet.Application.Quit
```

and reset the object variable by setting it to Nothing, as follows:

```
Set XL = Nothing
```

It is important to close the OLE Server application when it's no longer needed and free its resources. In a real-world application, you would probably keep Excel open for as long as the user needs it (that is, as long as the user has more discounted prices to calculate). When the user switches to another application, you close the OLE Server application.

Microsoft Word and OLE

Microsoft Word does not fully support OLE. You can't use the GetObject method to access a Word document. To embed a Word document, you must use the CreateObject method to access WordBasic (the programming language of Word) and then issue a WordBasic command such as FileOpen, which opens a Word document. Here is the code:

```
Dim word As Object
Set word = CreateObject ("Word.Basic")
word.FileOpen Name:= "C:\Myfile.doc
```

Code 13.8: The Discount OLE Automation Application

```
Option Explicit

Private Sub cmdClose_Click()
  End
End Sub

Private Sub cmdMultiply_Click()
  Dim XLSheet As Object
  'Open Excel
  Set XLSheet = GetObject(App.Path & "\discount.xls", _
  "Excel.Sheet")
  'Make Excel visible
  XLSheet.Application.Visible = True
  'Equate the first two txt boxes to specific cells
  XLSheet.Cells(2, 3).Value = txtMultiplier1.Text
  XLSheet.Cells(3, 3).Value = txtDiscount.Text
  'Multiply the numbers and display result
  XLSheet.Cells(4, 3).Formula = "=r2c3-(r2c3*r3c3)"
  txtResult.Text = XLSheet.Cells(4, 3)
  XLSheet.SaveAs " App.Path & "\discount.xls"

  'Close Excel
  XLSheet.Application.Quit

  'Clear variable
  Set XLSheet = Nothing
End Sub
```

The Excel Worksheet

The Discount application requires that you set up an Excel worksheet to contain and process the data entered in the Discount application. To do so, follow these steps:

1. Open Excel, and then enter the data shown in Figure 13.17 in the default worksheet.

2. Save the worksheet as Discount.xls.

3. Set the value of the cell r3c4 to the following:

   ```
   =r2c3-(r2c3*r3c3)
   ```

4. Remove the corresponding line from the cmdMultiply_Click() subroutine.

FIGURE 13.17

The Excel worksheet is ready to receive input from the OLE Container control.

Excel Macros and Your OLE Automation Application

If you are familiar with Excel, you can develop really complicated macros to process your data. To simplify the development of OLE Automation applications, you can turn on the macro recorder and then perform the desired actions with menu commands. Excel records the commands that correspond to each and every action. You can then look up the macro and copy and paste its commands into your VB application, or you can invoke the Excel macro directly from within the VB application.

Writing Server Applications

So far in this chapter you have learned how to embed and link objects with the OLE Container control and how to us OLE Automation in applications. Now, you are going learn how to define your own objects with classes. Controls live on Forms, and OLE objects live in class modules. And like controls, OLE objects provide functionality that can be accessed via their properties and methods. Class modules are similar to modules, in the sense that they are invisible at run time and contain functions that can be called from any other place in the application. You can think of the Class module as a Form without controls and without a Form window at run time. Class modules contain data and procedure references that are unique to the object and that other applications can share

VB5 at Work: The CalcServer Server and the CalcClient Client Applications

Let's start by looking at the CalcServer application (the project is called CalcSrvr, and your will find it in this chapter's folder on the CD). CalcServer calculates the volume of a sphere and stores a message locally. These are simple operations that you could easily implement in any application, without resorting to server applications. So why implement the tasks as new objects?

The answer is that these two functions are not limited to one application or a number of applications. By implementing a new object, the two functions are available to all applications on the system. You can use the function that calculates the volume of a sphere from any VB application, even from within Excel. You don't have to locate the module with the definition of the function and load it in your project. All you need is a reference to the object, and you can then access its methods.

Running the Applications   Before we look at the code, let's run the applications. Follow these steps:

1. Open the CalcSrvr application in the CalcSrvr folder on the CD.

2. Choose File ➤ Make CalcServer.exe to create the Server application and register it on your system.

3. Open the CalcClnt application in the CalcSrvr folder on the CD and run the application. CalcClnt displays the Form shown in Figure 13.18.

4. Enter the radius of the sphere in the first text box, and then click on the Show Volume button to display the volume of a sphere with the specified radius.

5. Click on Create Message. The application prompts you to enter a message.

6. Enter a message, and then click on Display Message. The application displays the message you entered.

FIGURE 13.18

The CalcClnt application uses a server application to calculate the volume of spheres and store messages.

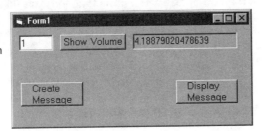

The Code for CalcClnt and CalcServer   Let's look now at the code of the application. Open the CalcClnt Form in design mode, and double-click on the Show Volume button.

Code 13.9: The Show Volume Button

```
Private Sub cmdSphere_Click()
    Dim sph As Object
    Set sph = CreateObject("CalcServer.Calc")
    lblSphere.Caption = sph.Sphere((txtSphere.Text))
    Set sph = Nothing
End Sub
```

TIP

Notice the double parentheses surrounding the argument of the Sphere method? The Sphere method expects a Double as an argument. The value of the TextBox control's Text property is a string. To match the available value and the argument value, you enclose the string with its own pair of parentheses. This tells Visual Basic to convert the argument to the proper type before passing it to the Sphere method. The outer parentheses delimit the method's argument and can't be omitted.

The *Sph* variable is assigned a new object, CalcServer.Calc, which is created with the CalcServer server. Sphere is a method of this object and calculates the volume of a sphere given its radius. The application passes the value entered by the user in the txtSphere text box to the Sphere method, which returns the volume of the sphere. After the volume is calculated and displayed in the lblSphere control, the application closes the Server application by setting the Sph object to Nothing.

> **NOTE**
>
> Sphere is a method of an object, not a function. You may have guessed already that the server implements it with a function, but for any application outside CalcServer, Sphere is a method of a properly declared object, not a function.

Code 13.10: The Create Message Button

```
Private Sub cmdCreateMessage_Click()
    Set MsgServer = CreateObject("CalcServer.Calc")
    MsgServer.Message = InputBox("Enter Message")
End Sub
```

Code 13.11: The Display Message Button

```
Private Sub cmdDisplayMessage_Click()
    MsgBox MsgServer.Message
End Sub
```

The Create Message button code creates another object, which is also based on the same server application (CalcServer.Calc). It then prompts the user to enter a message with the InputBox() function and stores the message in the Message property of the MsgServer object. Notice that this subroutine doesn't close the Server application, because another button on the same Form must read the value of the string.

The Display Message button code retrieves the value of the message from the server and displays it in a message box. The Server application isn't closed here either. The MsgServer remains open for the rest of the application. If you start the application now and click on the Display Message button, the run-time error message 91 is generated:

```
"Object variable or With block not set"
```

In our application, the *MsgServer* variable hasn't been set. CalcServer was meant to demonstrate the basic concepts of a server application and is far from perfect. You must first create a message and then view it.

NOTE

The MsgServer object remains open for as long as the application runs. The sph object is opened and closed as needed. That's why displaying the volume of the sphere takes a few seconds, but storing and retrieving the message is instantaneous (except for the first time you create a message).

The CalcClnt application demonstrates how server applications work. The CalcServer server application exposes properties and methods that you can use from within your applications. Obviously, there must be an executable file somewhere that Visual Basic uses to carry out the calculations. There is no code to calculate the volume of sphere in the CalcClnt application. When you created CalcServer.exe, not only was an EXE file created, but it was also registered in your system. You will see shortly how this happened.

We will come back to this application to discuss its code in more detail, but first let's build a simple server application.

Building a Simple Server

We will create a simple server that exposes two properties, stringProperty and integerProperty, which can set and read from within your code. We will build a quick-and-dirty server that exposes a few properties by declaring them as public variables, which can be accessed from any application. A poor approach, but it will demonstrate how to build a component that exposes its properties to other applications.

To create a server application with VB5, you can start a new ActiveX EXE or ActiveX DLL project. In VB5, the server application is an ActiveX component, which can be implemented as an EXE or as a DLL. We will implement an EXE file. The ActiveX EXE builds an independent component, or *out-of-process* server. This means that the server runs in its own process, with its own thread of execution. Because the server runs in its own process, the client can tell it to do something and then continue its own tasks while the server does the work.

If you create an ActiveX DLL instead, you are creating an *in-process* component. After a DLL is loaded into the memory, other processes can use it. The component need not be reloaded, as is the case with an ActiveX EXE component.

When you start an ActiveX EXE or ActiveX DLL project, Visual Basic adds a new class module. Open this class module and type the following lines in the general declarations section of the module:

```
Public integerProperty As Integer
Public stringProperty As String
```

Both *integerProperty* and *stringProperty* are public variables, which our server application will make available to other applications. Other applications will access these variables as properties of an object.

Let's also change the name of the class module. Select the module in the Project window, and set its Name property to PubClass. In addition, let's also call the project Class1. This project is in the Server1 folder on the CD.

The Class module has another property, called Instancing, that determines whether other applications can access your public class. It can have one of the values in Table 13.4.

TABLE 13.4 The Values of the Instancing Property

VALUE	DESCRIPTION
Private (1)	This is the default setting. The class module is private to the project to which it belongs. Other applications aren't allowed access to type library information about the class and cannot create instances of it.
PublicNotCreatable (2)	Other applications can use objects of this class only if your component creates the objects first. Other applications cannot use the CreateObject() function.
SingleUse (3)	Other applications can create objects from the class, but every object of this class that a client creates starts a new instance of your component.
GlobalSingle (4)	Similar to SingleUse, except that properties and methods of the class can be invoked as if they were simply global functions. This is what we are doing in our example.
MultiUse (5)	Allows other applications to create objects from the class. One instance of your component can provide any number of objects created in this fashion, regardless of how many applications request them.

TABLE 13.4   The Values of the Instancing Property (continued)

VALUE	DESCRIPTION
GlobalMultiUse (6)	Similar to MultiUse, only its properties and methods of the class can be invoked as if they were simply global functions.

Set the class module's Instancing property to 5 (MultiUse) so that any application can create instances of it. Then save the project's components and the project in its own folder. You will find this server in the Server1 folder on this book's CD.

To actually create the server and register it with your system, follow these steps:

1. Choose File ➢ Make Class1.exe.

2. Click on the Object Browser button to see your new class.

3. Select the class name in the left window (as shown in Figure 13.19) to see the properties it exposes.

FIGURE 13.19

The members of the PubClass class

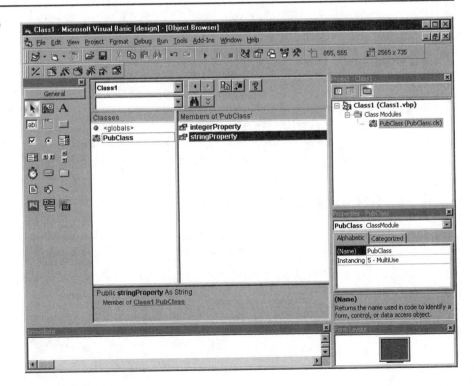

4. Click on a property to see its definition in the window above the Immediate Execution window.

Now, start a new Standard EXE project. Place a button on the Form and enter the following statement in its Click event:

```
Private Sub Command1_Click()
    Dim X As Object
    Set X = CreateObject("Class1.PubClass")
    X.stringProperty = "USA"
    X.integerProperty = 1234
    Debug.Print X.stringProperty
    Debug.Print X.integerProperty
End Sub
```

The X object variable is set to an object based on the Class1 server. After you create the variable, you can access the properties of the server.

The Class1 server application provides two properties (stringProperty and integerProperty) that any application can access. The important thing about the Class1 module is that it doesn't have to be included in the application that requires access to its variables. It's been registered once in the system, and any application can use it. Run the test application and watch the values of the properties displayed in the Immediate window.

This class, however, has a problem. Any application can access its properties and assign any value to them. Your server doesn't even get a chance to validate the values. Assign a value outside the valid range for integers to the integerProperty and see what happens. You'll get a run-time message that could have been easily avoided if the server had an opportunity to validate the input. There must be a better way to build servers, and the next section shows you how.

Building a Robust Server

Open the Class1 project again and rename the class module to PrvClass and save the project as Class2. (The modified server is in the Server1 folder on the CD.)

Open the module and change the definitions of the two variables to Private:

```
Private PintegerProperty As Integer
Private PstringProperty As String
```

PintegerProperty and *PstringProperty* are now private variables and can't be accessed from outside the module. The initial *P* differentiates them from the names of the actual properties. These two variables will hold the values of the two properties. But access to these variables will take place through the Property Let and Property Get procedures. In other words, outside applications will no longer be able to access two public variables in the class module. Instead, any value assignment will invoke a special procedure in the Class module, and the object will get a chance to validate the values or execute any other statements necessary.

Each time a client application attempts to set the value of one of the server's properties through the corresponding object (with a statement such as object-name.PropertyName), the Property Get procedure is executed. Enter the following procedures in the Class's code window:

```
Public Property Get stringProperty() As String

    stringProperty = PstringProperty

End Property

Public Property Get integerProperty() As Integer

    integerProperty = PintegerProperty

End Property
```

Whenever an application requests the value of either property, the corresponding Property Get procedure gets the value of the private variable that corresponds to the requested property and assigns it to the name of the property. In effect, the Property Get procedure isolates the variables from the outside application.

Likewise, each time an application sets the value of either property, the corresponding Property Let statement assigns the new value to the variable that corresponds to the requested property. This is where you can place any data-validation code. To enable outside applications to set the values of the properties, enter the following procedures in the Class's code window:

```
Public Property Let integerProperty(ByVal NewValue As Integer)

    PintegerProperty = NewValue

End Property
```

```
Public Property Let stringProperty(ByVal NewValue As String)

    PstringProperty = NewValue

End Property
```

Create the Class2.exe file, and then run the same client application as before. To access the values of the variables, declare an object variable as follows:

```
Dim X As Object
Set X = CreateObject("Class2.PrvClass")
```

and then use the structures X.stringProperty and X.integerProperty to access its properties. The Class's properties are accessed in the same way that the properties of any control are accessed.

Let's add some lines in the Property Let procedure to validate the values passed to the server. If this property should be positive, enter the following procedure definition:

```
Public Property Let integerProperty(ByVal NewValue As Integer)
On Error GoTo IntError

    If NewValue < 0 Then
        MsgBox "integerProperty can't be negative"
        Exit Property
    End If
    PintegerProperty = NewValue
    Exit Property

IntError:
    MsgBox "There was an error in assigning the value " & _
        NewValue & " to the integerProperty property"

End Property
```

Assign a negative value to the integerProperty property to see how the data-validation code handles negative values. The error handler is a good idea to include in every Property Let procedure, just in case.

You can also add methods to your class. A method is implemented as a Public procedure. The following procedure, for instance, displays the current date in a message box:

```
Public Sub ShowDate()
    MsgBox Date
End Sub
```

You will see more ways to implement methods in Classes in the examples that follow. In the next section, we look at the implementation of the CalcSserver Class module. Before we do so, however, let's summarize what's involved in building a server application.

- Properties are set with the Property Let procedure, which reads the value supplied by the outside application and assigns it to a private variable.

- Property values are read with the Property Get procedure, which reads the value of the corresponding private variable and then assigns it to the property name.

- Methods are implemented as Public subroutines and functions.

Coding Property Procedures

The Property Get procedure has a type, which is the type of the corresponding property. The Property Let procedure accepts as an argument the new value of the corresponding property. The two types in the definitions of the two procedures must match:

```
Property Let Color(newColor As Long)

...

End Property


Property Get Color() As Long

...

End Color
```

VB5 at Work: The CalcServer Application Revisited

Now we can look at the Calc Class module of the CalcServer application, which, as mentioned earlier, is in the CalcSrvr folder on the CD. To create it from scratch, start a new ActiveX EXE project and rename the Class module to Calc. In its Code window, enter the following declarations:

```
Private privateRadius As Double
Private privateMsg As String
```

The *privateRadius* and the *privateMsg* variables are private to the module, and they hold the values of the sphere's radius and the message supplied by the application. Add the Property Let and Property Get procedures for the *privateMsg* variable as follows:

```
Public Property Let Message(Msg)
    privateMsg = Msg
End Property

Public Property Get Message()
    Beep
    Message = privateMsg
End Property
```

The Beep statement demonstrates that the Property Get procedure is not restricted to the task of assigning a value to a variable. You can perform other actions from within this procedure as well.

The last step is to add a public function that will act as a method. Enter the following function definition in the Code window:

```
Public Function Sphere(Radius As Double) As Double
    Dim pi As Double
    pi = 3.14159265358979
    'Radius = InputBox("Enter the radius of the sphere")
    Sphere = (4 / 3) * pi * (Radius ^ 3)
End Function
```

The function's argument is a Double value, and the sphere's volume is also returned as a Double. Notice the line that is commented out. A Class method's code can prompt the user for input. As you will see shortly, a Class can provide its own user interface by displaying Forms on which the user can enter information.

Having entered the code for the Calc class module, your next step is to register the new class in the system registry (system.dat) as an object application. Up till now the system is not aware of the existence of the object application you have written. For the system to recognize your application, it is necessary to register it. To do so, follow these steps:

1. Choose Project ➤ CalcServer Properties to open the Project Properties dialog box, as shown in Figure 13.20.

2. Select the General tab, and fill in the information as shown in Figure 13.20.

FIGURE 13.20

The General tab of the Project Properties dialog box

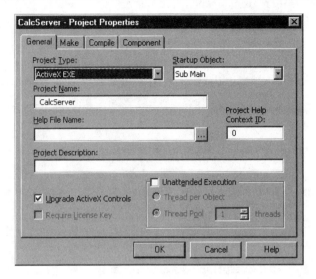

3. Select the Component tab, and set the Start Mode to ActiveX Component by checking the corresponding checkbox.

The Project Properties Dialog Box

Here are the options on the General tab of the Project Properties dialog box:

- **Project Type** Sets the project type. For the CalcServer application, the type is AxtiveX.

- **Startup Object** For an ActiveX component, this is None or Sub Main (if you have supplied an empty public Main subroutine).

- **Project Name** This is the component's name and identifies your Class to the Windows Registry and the Object Browser. This name should be unique and descriptive. The project name is the name of the type library for your component. The type library of the Object Browser contains the description of the objects and interfaces provided by your component. The project name is also used to qualify the names of classes. The full name of your class is a combination of the project name and the class name and is sometimes referred to as a *programmatic ID*.

- **Help File Name**   If the Class has an associated Help file, you supply its name here.

- **Project Help Context ID**   This is the context ID for the topic in the Help file that corresponds to your Class. This text is displayed when the user selects the class in the Object Browser and clicks on the Help button.

- **Project Description**   Descriptive text that is displayed in the References dialog box.

- **Upgrade ActiveX Controls**   Enables upgrading of the ActiveX controls.

- **Require License Key**   Enables licensing for a project that produces ActiveX components. A Visual Basic license file (VBL) is created when you build the file, which must be registered on the user's machine for the components to be used. Visual Basic license files are registered automatically by the SetUp Wizard.

- **Unattended Execution**   Indicates that the project is intended to run without user interaction. Unattended projects have no interface elements, and any run-time functions, such as message boxes, are redirected to an event log.

  - **Thread per Object**   Indicates that each instance of a class marked as Multiuse in the Instancing property will be created on a new and distinct thread. Each thread has a unique copy of all global variables and objects and will not interfere with any other thread.

  - **Thread Pool**   Indicates that each instance of a class marked as Multiuse in the Instancing property will be created on a thread from the thread pool. The choice of thread is determined in a round robin fashion. Each thread has a unique copy of all global variables, but multiple instances reside on a given thread and can potentially interfere with one another.

  - **Number of Threads**   Determines the maximum number of threads created for the thread pool. When the Instancing property is set to Multiuse, threads are created as needed up to the number set here.

Creating the ActiveX Component

To create the ActiveX component and register it with Windows 95, choose File ➤ Make. Visual Basic creates the EXE (or DLL) file and registers it for you. If you want to distribute this file along with your application, start the Application Setup Wizard, and create a setup file for the ActiveX component.

The CalcClnt application that contacts the CalcServer server application was explained earlier. Once you know the name of the server application, it's fairly straightforward to create an object of the same class. Simply declare an object variable, and then set it to the class's full name as follows:

```
Dim X As Object
Set X = CreateObject("CalcServer.Calc")
```

You can now reference the properties and methods of the new object through the X variable. But what if an object has too many properties and methods? You've seen that each Class's properties and methods are listed in the Object Browser, but only if the Class is in the Project window. How about the elements of servers that have been registered in your system already?

Referencing the Component in Other Projects

To view all registered servers, follow these steps:

1. Choose Project ➢ References to open the References dialog box shown in Figure 13.21. (This figure contains a few server names that aren't present in your system yet. The HTMLSrvr server application will be discussed later in the chapter.) This dialog box contains all the objects you can reference in your projects.

2. To select the objects of another application, check the checkbox next to the application's name.

To see all the classes and the members of your ActiveX component, follow these steps:

1. Start a new project (a Standard EXE), and choose Project ➢ References to open the References dialog box shown earlier in Figure 13.21.

2. Check the CalcServer checkbox.

3. Choose View ➢ Object Browser to open the Object Browser window, as shown in Figure 13.22.

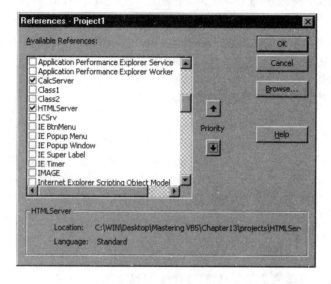

FIGURE 13.21

The References dialog box

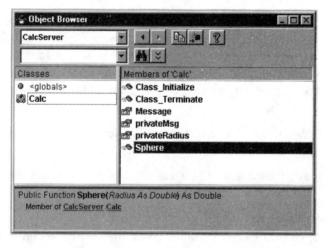

FIGURE 13.22

The Object Browser lists all the Classes and their members of your ActiveX component.

4. In the Classes window pane, select the Calc Class to display the properties and methods exposed by the Calc Class.

5. Select the Sphere method to display its syntax at the bottom of the Object Browser window. Any user who has installed your ActiveX component can access these members.

Accessing CalcServer through Excel

You can test the availability of your object application by calling it from within Excel. To do so, open Excel and create a macro module. Add these lines of code to the module window:

```
Option Explicit
Sub main()
Dim Solid As Object
Set Solid = CreateObject("CalcServer.Calc")
➥Sheets("Sheet1").select
Range("B1").Value = Solid.SphereVolume(Range("A1").Value)
End Sub
```

When you run this macro in Excel, the CalcServer calculates the volume of a sphere with radius equal to the value in cell A1. The result is displayed in cell B1.

OLE Auto-Registration

Most object-oriented applications register themselves automatically with the Windows 95 system Registry (System.dat). OLE Server applications provide information about the types of their objects, their file extensions, the service, and the path directory to the Server application. Microsoft Word for Windows 95 and Microsoft Excel 5.0, for example, automatically verify correct system registration at startup. Both applications install their corresponding Ole2.reg files into the \Windows\System folder. When Word is started, for example, it checks the Registry for the name of the Word executable and changes it if necessary throughout all of Word's registration. Word then matches the Winword7.reg file with the current Registry and makes any changes necessary.

In the Windows 95 environment, the Registry replaces the INI files that were used in earlier versions of Windows. To see what type of information is stored in the Registry about the CalcServer application, follow these steps:

1. Choose Start ➤ Run, and in the Open text box, type **RegEdit.**

2. In the Registry Editor window, choose Edit ➤ Find to open the Find dialog box, as shown in Figure 13.23.

FIGURE 13.23

Searching for the CalcServer entry in the system Registry

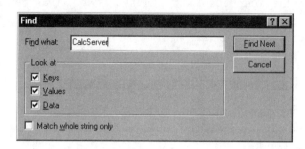

3. In the Find What text box, type **calcserver,** and click on the Find Next button. The registry address of the CalcServer application appears at the bottom of the Registry Editor window as:

```
My Computer\HKEY_CLASSES_ROOT\CalcServer.Calc.
```

4. Click on the plus sign preceding the name CalcServer.Calc to display its subkey, Clsid. The long number displayed in the windows on the right is used by the system to reference your server when an application contacts it. (See Figure 13.24.)

FIGURE 13.24

The entry for CalcServer is found in Hkey_ Classes_Root.

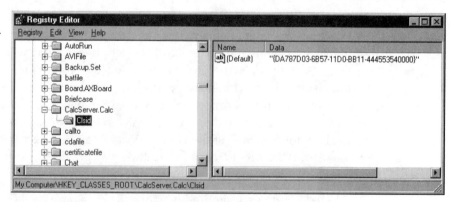

VB5 at Work: The HTMLServer Application

Our next example, HTMLServer, is a simple server application that converts plain text into HTML format, suitable for viewing with a browser. To build an HTML document, you must either provide the appropriate HTML code yourself or use an application such as Microsoft FrontPage. HTMLServer builds trivial HTML documents that have a simple structure, but if you are familiar with HTML (you will find an introduction to HTML in Part IV, *From the Desktop to the Web*), you can expand it to suit your needs. In this application, the user supplies the information that appears on the HTML page, and HTMLServer returns the HTML source code. Any application that needs to create HTML documents can contact the HTMLServer and retrieve the HTML source it needs.

When you use HTMLServer, you enter a title for the document, a few paragraphs of text, and a list of hyperlinks on the two Forms shown in Figure 13.25. The server then generates the appropriate HTML code and returns the page to the client application through its HTMLSourceCode property.

FIGURE 13.25

The HTMLServer application expects the user to enter the contents of the HTML document, in text format, in these two Forms.

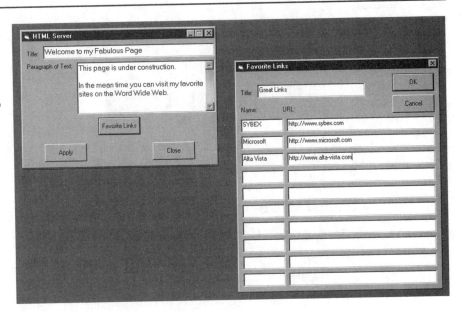

You are going to build two applications: an ActiveX component (the server) and a client application. The ActiveX component has a single property, the HTMLSource-Code property, which is read-only. It also has a method, the CreateSourceCode method, which invokes the server. To use the HTMLSrvr server, the client application must do the following:

1. Call the server's CreateSourceCode method. The server application presents two Forms. The first Form prompts the user to enter the page's text, as shown in the window on the left in Figure 13.25. The second Form prompts the user to enter a list of hyperlinks to be added on the Web page, as shown in the window on the right in Figure 13.25.

2. Retrieve the HTML source code by reading the server's HTMLSourceCode property and display the HTML source in its window, as shown in Figure 13.26.

FIGURE 13.26

The source code of the HTML document that corresponds to the document specified in the windows of Figure 13.23

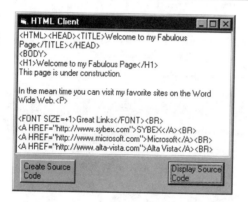

Let's start by building the ActiveX component, and then we'll look at how to access the services of the HTMLServer through the client application.

The HTMLServer Server

To create the HTMLServer application, follow these steps:

1. Start a new ActiveX EXE project. Visual Basic creates a new Class module in the project.

2. Change the Class module's default name to HTMLFile, and save it as HTMLFile.cls.

3. Open the Code window of the Class module, and enter the following code:

```
Option Explicit
Public Sub CreateSourceCode()

  frmHTML.Show

End Sub

Public Property Get SourceCode()

  SourceCode = frmHTML.SourceCode

End Property

Public Property Let SourceCode(NewValue)

  MsgBox "SourceCode is a read-only variable" , vbExclamation

End Property
```

The Property Let procedure for the SourceCode property shows another example of the types of operations you can perform from within a property procedure. This one displays a message when the user tries to change the value of a read-only property.

The CreateSource subroutine is the server's only method. This method doesn't do much; it simply shows the frmHTML Form, which is the server's user interface. Now create a new Form, name it frmHTML, and draw three command buttons on it as shown in the left window of Figure 13.25, earlier in this chapter. These buttons function as follows:

- **Favorite Links** (cmdLinks)   Adds your links to your page. It displays the HTMLLink Form, on which you can enter a number of URLs (Uniform Resource Locators).

- **Apply** (cmdApply)   Generates the HTML source code.

- **Close** (cmdClose)   Ends the server application and returns control to the client application.

You will also need to draw the Title (txtTitle) and Paragraph of Text (txtPara) text boxes and their corresponding labels. The txtTitle text box will hold the page's title, and txtPara will hold the page's text.

How It Works   The client application (to be built later) calls the HTML server, which displays the Form frmHTML containing a text box for the title of your Web page (txtTitle) and a text box for the main body of text (txtPara). Enter the title for your page and then enter the main body of your text. When you finish, click on the Favorite Links button to add your favorite URLs to your page. When you are done, simply close the server Form and return to the client application, in which you can display the HTML source code for the text you entered by clicking on the Show HTML Source button.

Code 13.12: The frmHTML Form

```
Option Explicit
Public LinksText As String
Public SourceCode As String
Private Sub cmdApply_Click()
  SourceCode = "<HTML><HEAD<TITLE>" _
    + txtTitle.Text + "</TITLE></HEAD>" _
    + vbCrLf + "<BODY>" + vbCrLf + _
    "<H1>" + txtTitle.Text + "</H1>" + _
    vbCrLf + txtPara.Text + "<P>" + _
    vbCrLf + vbCrLf + LinksText + _
    vbCrLf + vbCrLf + "</BODY></HTML>"
End Sub

Private Sub cmdClose_Click()
  Unload frmHTML
End Sub

Private Sub Form_Unload(Cancel As Integer)
  Select Case MsgBox("Are you sure you want to close?", _
    vbYesNo + vbDefaultButton2)
    Case 6
    Case 7
      Cancel = 1
  End Select
End Sub

Private Sub cmdLinks_Click()
  frmLinks.Show
End Sub
```

The variable *SourceCode* contains the HTML source code for your document. The data stored in txtTitle.Text—that is, the text you entered—is surrounded by a pair of TITLE and HEAD tags to create valid HTML source code for the page's title:

```
"</TITLE></HEAD>"   & txtTitle.Text  & "</TITLE></HEAD>"
```

The Form on which the favorite URLs are entered contains two control arrays—one for the friendly names of the hyperlinks, txtLinkName(), and one for the corresponding URLs, txtURL(). The application combines these arrays to generate the list of hyperlinks that appears at the bottom of the page as follows:

```
"<A HREF=" & Chr(34) & txtURL(x).Text & Chr(34) & ">" &
➥txtLinkName(x).Text & "</A><BR>" & vbCrLf
```

If txtURL(x) is:

```
"Microsoft"
```

and if txtLinkName(x) is:

```
"http://home.microsoft.com"
```

the previous line produces the following link:

```
<A HREF="http://home.microsoft.com>Microsoft</A>
```

Here's the code you must enter in the HTMLLinks Form's code window:

```
Private Sub Form_Load()
    frmHTML.Enabled = False
End Sub

Private Sub Form_Unload(Cancel As Integer)
    frmHTML.Enabled = True
    frmHTML.SetFocus
End Sub

Private Sub cmdCancel_Click()
    Unload frmLinks
End Sub

Private Sub cmdOK_Click()
    Dim x As Integer
    frmHTML.LinksText = "<FONT SIZE=+1>" + _
        txtTitle.Text + "</FONT><BR>" + vbCrLf
    For x = 0 To 9
        If txtLinkName(x).Text <> "" And _
```

```
                    txtURL(x).Text <> "" Then
                    frmHTML.LinksText = _
                        frmHTML.LinksText & _
                        "<A HREF=" & Chr(34) & _
                        txtURL(x).Text & Chr(34) & _
                        ">" & txtLinkName(x).Text & _
                        "</A><BR>" & vbCrLf
            End If
        Next x
        Unload frmLinks
    End Sub
```

Now register your object application as you did for CalcServer. Choose File ➤ Make HTMLServer.exe. The HTMLServer.exe file is built and registered in the Windows Registry. The server is ready. We are now going to build a client application to demonstrate how to contact the HTMLServer server application.

VB5 at Work: The HTMLClnt Application

The HTMLClnt application is also in the HTMLSrvr folder on the CD. To begin, follow these steps:

1. Open a new Standard EXE project.

2. Change the default name of the Form to frmHTMLClient.

3. Draw two command buttons on the Form as shown in Figure 13.26, earlier in this chapter. Name them cmdCreate and cmdDisplay.

4. Add a TextBox control and name it txtHTML.

5. Add the following code:

```
Option Explicit
Dim HTML As Object
Private Sub Form_Unload(Cancel As Integer)
    End
End Sub
```

When the user clicks on the Create Source Code button, the client application must contact the server and call its CreateSourceCode method, which causes the server to display the windows on which the page's contents will be entered.

Code 13.13: The Create Source Code Button

```
Private Sub cmdCreate_Click()
    Set HTML = CreateObject ("HTMLServer.HTMLFile")
    HTML.CreateSourceCode
End Sub
```

To view the HTML code produced by the server application, click on the Display Source Code button.

Code 13.14: The Display Source Code Button

```
Private Sub cmdDisplay_Click()
    txtHTML.Text = HTML.SourceCode
End
```

Notice that the object is not released until the application ends. As long as the HTMLClnt application is running, the server application is also open, waiting to be contacted.

VB5 at Work: The HTMLCln2 Application

The application HTMLCln2 is a variation of the HTMLClnt application, which not only displays the HTML source code, but also renders it on a WebBrowser control. The WebBrowser control is explored in the last part of this book, but for the purposes of this example, you can think of the WebBrowser control as Internet Explorer wrapped in a control. The HTMLCln2 application has the same structure as HTMLCln, plus an additional Form that displays the HTML code as it would appear in Internet Explorer.

The HTMLCln2 application displays the HTML source code as usual, and it also renders it on a WebBrowser control, as shown in Figure 13.27.

The Display Source Code button displays an additional Form with the WebBrowser control. To render the document on the control, the program saves the HTML source code in the file VBWeb.htm in the application's path and then passes this filename as an argument to the WebBrowser control's Navigate method. The two client applications differ in the Display Source Code button's Click handler.

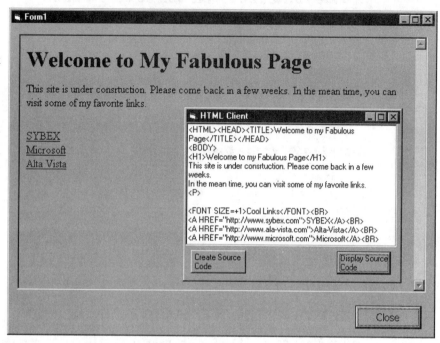

FIGURE 13.27

The HTMLCln2 application is similar to the HTMLCln application, but it also renders the HTML code produced by the server.

Code 13.15: The Display Source Code Button Code in HTMLCln2

```
Private Sub cmdDisplay_Click()
    txtHTML.Text = HTML.SourceCode
    Open App.Path + "\VBWeb.htm" For Output As #1
    Print #1, HTML.SourceCode
    Close #1

    WebForm.Show 1
    WebForm.WebBrowser1.Navigate App.Path + "\VBWeb.htm"

End Sub
```

If you are converting custom documents to HTML format frequently, consider developing an OLE server application to streamline the job. For example, you could create a server that contacts Excel, reads a range of cells, creates a table, and stores the corresponding HTML code in a file. Granted, a number of tools are available for automating HTML design, but for special applications, a custom HTML converter may be your best bet.

Building ActiveX Controls

- Using the ActiveX Control Interface Wizard

- Exploring the skeleton of the ActiveX control

- Designing Property Pages with the Wizard

- Building a generic control

- Developing an application with an ActiveX control

f there's one feature of Visual Basic 5 that attracts all kinds of developers, this is it. For the first time, you have a simple, easy-to-learn, and fun-to-use language for building an ActiveX control. An ActiveX control is what was formerly called an OLE control. You can think of ActiveX controls as extensions to the Visual Basic language. They are the objects that are represented on Visual Basic's Toolbox with a small icon and can be included on any Form.

The first question is, Why are they now called ActiveX controls? More than anything else, it's a question of marketing. OLE controls were synonymous with difficult, tricky C programming. A name such as ActiveX will certainly help the average VB programmer feel less intimidated. And, indeed, this feature of Visual Basic has been so well implemented that developing ActiveX controls is within the reach of the average VB programmer. It's not only that Visual Basic 5 can produce ActiveX controls, it's how easily it can do so. In addition, you can use ActiveX controls on Web pages, one of the fastest-growing arenas for Visual Basic program development.

Now, who should be developing ActiveX controls? If I have managed without ActiveX controls, why bother now? Indeed, many of you may not develop custom ActiveX controls for a while. But sooner or later, you will. If you come up with an interesting utility that can be used from within several applications, why not package it as ActiveX control? Besides, why not indulge in the latest, truly hot stuff? ActiveX controls are cool and will help you leverage your capabilities as a Visual Basic programmer. Being able to design components that can be used both on the Desktop and on the Internet is a great prospect for anyone who makes a living with Visual Basic.

This chapter starts by showing you how to convert one of the applications we developed earlier to an ActiveX control. We will develop our control the easy way, by using the tools that come with Visual Basic. We'll then look deeper at the peculiarities and idiosyncrasies of ActiveX controls.

The Gradient Custom Control

In Chapter 6, *Drawing and Painting with Visual Basic,* you saw the FrmGrad application, which covers the background of a Form with a smooth gradient between two colors. The application is shown in Figure 14.1. As a reminder, the program reads the values of the gradient's starting and ending colors and produces the color between them by increasing each of the starting color's basic components (red, green, and blue) by a small increment. (Of course, we're only interested in the background of the Form. The controls and titles you see in Figure 14.1 just demonstrate how you can use the gradient as a backdrop for a typical business application.)

FIGURE 14.1

The FrmGrad application is our starting point for building an ActiveX control.

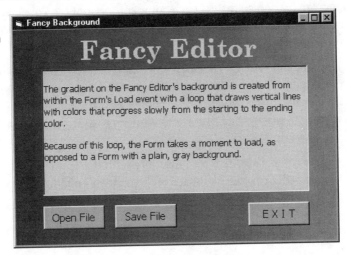

Code 14.1: The Core of the FrmGrad Application

```
startRed = 100
endRed = 220
startGreen = 20
endGreen = 180
startBlue = 180
endBlue = 20

PWidth = Form1.ScaleWidth

redInc = (endRed - startRed) / PWidth
greenInc = (endGreen - startGreen) / PWidth
blueInc = (endBlue - startBlue) / PWidth

For ipixel = 0 To PWidth - 1
    newColor = RGB(startRed + redInc * ipixel, startGreen +
    ➡greenInc * ipixel, startBlue + blueInc * ipixel)
    Form1.Line (ipixel, 0)-(ipixel, Form1.Height - 1), newColor
Next
```

You will find a detailed description of the program in Chapter 6, but here's a quick rundown of the listing. The program starts by setting the values of the gradient's two end colors. It then calculates the increment for each of the color components (redInc, greenInc, blueInc). The loop draws vertical lines of changing colors that generate the gradient on the control's background. Each successive line's color differs from the color of the previous one by a small shade. The increments are chosen so that, if each color component increases by the corresponding amount, when the other end of the form is reached, we will have also reached the gradient's ending color.

The problem with this approach is that you have to copy the same Form to each project in which you want to use this fancy background. Not to mention that you must specify colors by value. A far better approach is to create an ActiveX control that you can place on a Form in the same way that you place a shape control. Some benefits of implementing the background with the gradient include the following:

- The control's code won't interfere with the application code. Your application will not even be aware of the control's code.

- You can change the colors of the gradient in the Properties window by selecting them from a dialog box. No need to edit the code that produces the gradient.

- The control can cover only part of the Form. Moreover, you can place multiple controls with different gradients on the same Form (and group other controls on the various gradient controls).

- You can distribute the control easily, and other developers can use it.

The technique for drawing gradients has been tested in Chapter 6, and there is no reason to adjust it from one project to the other. Ideally, it should be packaged in a way that isolates its implementation details from the user and is a self-contained component. And this is exactly what an ActiveX control buys you. The Gradient control we develop next is a fancier Shape, or Frame, control that you can use to group controls. Unfortunately, just like the original application, the Gradient control won't look nice on 256-color systems. I'll give you some tips about how you can make this control work on systems that don't support more than 256 colors (but it will take a fair amount of extra work).

The Gradient Control's Specifications

All the associated files for the Gradient control are in the Gradient folder on the CD. The Gradient control doesn't have much of an interface. All you can do with it is place it on a Form and use it as a container for other controls. The values of the starting and ending colors must be supplied as properties. Let's call them StartColor and EndColor. In addition, this control draws vertical and horizontal gradients, so we'll introduce another property, the GradientDirection property, which will have one of the following values:

- 0 for a horizontal gradient

- 1 for a vertical gradient

This is the definition of our control. It's not going to have any methods. The gradient should display as soon as the control is loaded, and it is adjusted every time the control is resized.

You can design a control in two ways:

- With the help of the ActiveX Control User Interface Wizard

- Manually

In the first example, we will use the Wizard. Later, you will see how to design a control manually.

The ActiveX Control Interface Wizard

To start a new ActiveX control project, follow these steps:

1. Choose File ➢ New Project.

2. In the New Project window, select the ActiveX Control icon. Visual Basic creates a new project named Project1, which contains a UserControl named UserControl1.

The initial setup for an ActiveX control project is shown in Figure 14.2 (the names in the project window are different, and I'll show you immediately how to change them).

Let's rename the project and the control. These two names will be used to register your control in your system, so they should be meaningful. Follow these steps:

1. Select Project1 in the Project window, and when its properties appear, change the Name property to Custom1.

2. Select UserControl1 in the Project window, and when its properties appear, change the Name property to Gradient.

FIGURE 14.2

An ActiveX control
project contains a
User control instead
of a Form.

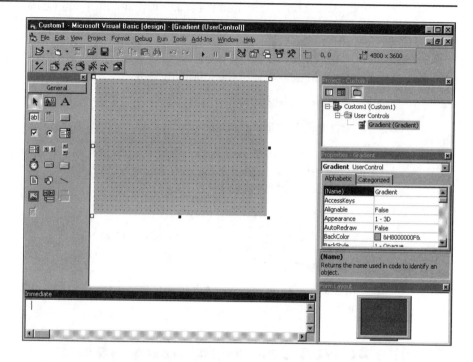

A new object was just introduced: the UserControl object. As you will soon see, the UserControl is the "Form" on which the custom control will be designed. It looks, feels, and behaves like a regular VB Form, but it's called a UserControl. UserControl objects have additional unique properties that don't apply to a regular Form, but in order to start designing new controls, think of them as regular Forms. Whereas the FrmGrad application draws vertical lines of progressively lighter or darker color on the Form to produce the gradient, the Gradient custom control draws lines on the UserControl object. Now, choose Add-Ins ➤ ActiveX Control Interface Wizard to open the Wizard. This Wizard will guide you through the steps of creating a new ActiveX control. It will create the control's interface (its properties, methods, and events) and prepare the basic code for it. You will have to provide only the code that draws the gradient and a few more features that can't be automated. The bulk of the work will be taken care of for you by the Wizard. The ActiveX Control Interface Wizard has six windows, which are explained next.

Introduction

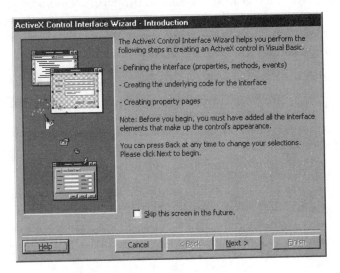

The first screen of the Wizard is introductory, and you can disable it in the future by checking the Skip This Screen in the Future checkbox. Click on the Next button to start the design of your control's user interface.

Selecting Interface Members

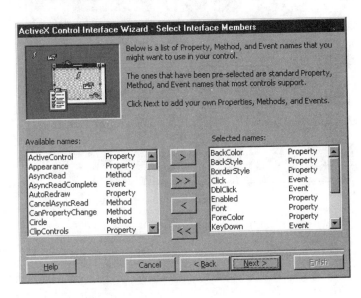

The next window of the Wizard prompts you to select the standard members of the control. On the left is a list of standard properties, methods, and events that you can include in your custom control. On the right is a list of common members of the user interface, already selected for you. Visual Basic suggests that your control should support these members.

The Gradient control won't have a BackColor property or a BackStyle property. The control's background will be filled with a gradient. It also won't have Font and ForeColor properties, because it doesn't display text. We won't include a Text or Caption property; instead, you can place transparent Label controls with text on top of the control. Remove these properties by selecting them with the mouse and clicking on the button that has a single left-pointing arrow.

To add a new member, select it from the left list and click on the button that has a single right-pointing arrow. It would be nice to add a 3-D look to our control, so let's add the Appearance property from the left list. The Select Interface Members window should now look like the one in Figure 14.3. Click on the Next button.

FIGURE 14.3

The Select Interface Members window with the Gradient control's members selected

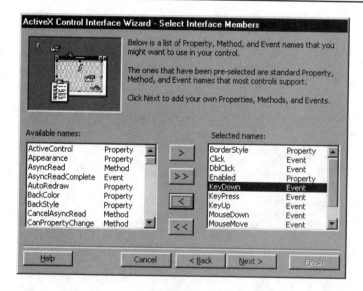

Creating Custom Interface Members

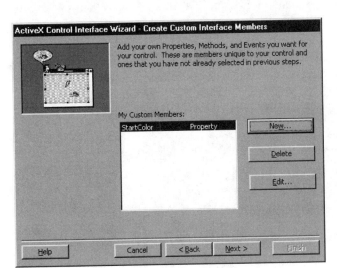

In this window, you add the properties, events, and methods that are unique to your custom control. Follow these steps:

1. Click on the New button to display the Add Custom Member window, as shown in Figure 14.4.

2. In the Name box, enter **StartColor** (which is the name of a property), and check the Property radio button.

3. Click on OK. The name of the first custom property is now displayed in the My Custom Member box of the Create Custom Interface Members window.

4. Repeat steps 1 through 3 to add the **End Color** and **GradientDirection** properties.

FIGURE 14.4

Specifying a new member in the Add Custom Member window. The StartColor member is a property.

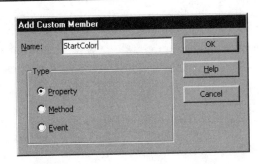

If you have misspelled any of the property names or if you want to delete one and re-enter it, use the Edit and Delete buttons. When you are done, click on the Next button.

Setting Member Mapping

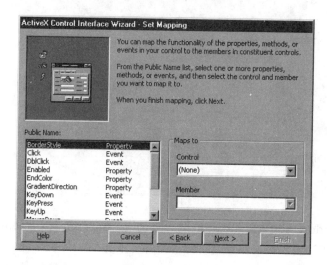

You use this window to map certain properties of your custom control to properties of the so-called constituent controls. A *constituent control* is a regular VB control that your custom control uses. Suppose your custom control contains a Label control, and you want the label's background color to become your control's background color (or foreground color, for that matter). In this window, you map the properties of the controls used by your custom control to the properties of any of the controls it uses. When calling one of the mapped members, the user thinks he or she is setting a control's properties, but in reality is setting a constituent control's member.

You must map all properties except the custom properties and the events to the UserControl. When the user clicks on the control, for instance, the Click event is passed to the host application, as if it were generated by the custom control. Any properties, methods, or events that you don't want to handle with your own code must be mapped to the UserControl object. To map properties, follow these steps:

1. From the Public Name list, select a property or an event.

2. Click on the Control drop-down list's down arrow, and select UserControl. The Wizard immediately selects the UserControl member with the same name, as shown in Figure 14.5.

3. Map all members of the new control (except for custom members) to the equivalent members of the UserControl object.

4. Click on the Next button.

FIGURE 14.5

The control's Click event is mapped to the UserControl object's Click event.

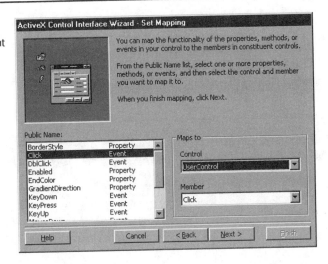

Setting Attributes

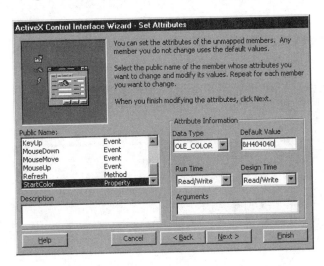

In this window, you set the attributes of the new members (or change the attributes of some default members, if you want, but this isn't recommended). The Wizard has declared all new properties as Variants, because it can't decipher their types from their names. Our StartColor and EndColor properties, however, are long values (they represent color).

To set attributes, follow these steps:

1. In the Public Name box, select StartColor.

2. Click on the Data Type drop-down arrow, and select OLE_COLOR, which is a special data type for representing colors.

NOTE
OLE_COLOR is not a general data type you can use in normal variable declarations in Visual Basic, and it has special meaning here. It places a color select dialog box that pops up every time the user tries to set up a new value for the StartColor property. If you set the StartColor property's data type to Long, the user of the control must type a long value (for example, &H00FF00 for green) in the Properties window.

Notice that you can set an initial value too. Let's make our gradients start with a dark gray tone.

3. In the Default Value box, enter the value **&H404040.** This is the value that is displayed by default in the Properties window for the Gradient control.

4. Repeat steps 1 through 3 for the EndColor property. Set its data type to OLE_COLOR and its initial value to a light gray shade such as &HC0C0C0.

The default gradient on the control will start with a dark gray tone and get lighter as it progresses.

TIP
Don't forget to supply a short description of each property in the Description box. These descriptions are displayed below the Properties window when the user selects a property. The standard members have a description already, but you must supply descriptions for your custom properties.

In the Arguments box, you supply the arguments of the events.

5. In the Public Name box, select the KeyPress event. Visual Basic places the arguments of the event in the Arguments box.

Each time you open a control's KeyPress event handler, Visual Basic supplies the argument. To create a new event (or method), you supply the definition of its arguments in this box. You will see examples of controls with methods in later sections.

Notice that the properties can have different design-time and run-time properties, which is the first really unique characteristic of a user control. If you think that the user of your control has no reason to change the gradient (its colors or direction) at run time, make these properties Read-Only at run time. In our example, we'll do something more interesting. We will redraw the gradient every time one of these properties is changed.

6. Finally, select the GradientDirection property and make it an integer. Its values will be 0 (for a horizontal gradient) and 1 (for a vertical gradient). Supply the initial value 0, and then click on the Next button.

Finishing

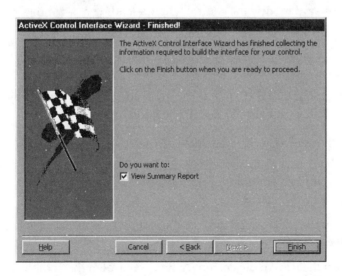

In this window, you are prompted to click on Finish to generate the control. Leave View Summary Report checked.

Your hard disk will spin for a few seconds, and you will see the summary report. Read the summary report (which basically tells you how to proceed) and close or save the editor window.

You have created the Gradient control. Not that it does much (you haven't entered the code for displaying the gradient yet), but you are ready to test its behavior as a control. At this point, your control has its own Properties page, and you can place it on your Forms.

There's nothing on the screen except a Form. This is the UserControl object, which for all intents and purposes is a Form. There's also a new icon in the Toolbox. This is your new control. The icon of a matrix with a pen on top is the default icon for all ActiveX controls. Let's first make sure the control works, and then we'll customize it. The ActiveX control's icon is disabled because you are still designing the control. The control won't be activated while it's being designed.

Testing Your New ActiveX Control

To test your new control, you would normally have to create an OCX file, start a new project, and then place the new custom control on a Form. To simplify development, Visual Basic lets you add a new project to the existing project. In this way, you can test and modify the control without loading a new project each time. The next steps are standard, and you will follow them every time you design an ActiveX control:

1. Choose File ➢ Add Project, to open the New Project window.

2. Select Standard EXE. A new project is added in the New Project window, with a default Form, as usual, named Form1.

3. Close the UserControl Design window by clicking twice on its Close button.

When the Form1 Form is selected, the custom control's icon in the Toolbox is enabled. From this point on, you can use the Gradient control just as you use any other VB control.

Now you can place an instance of the Gradient control on the Form1 Form. Follow these steps:

1. Select the icon of the custom ActiveX control in the Toolbox and draw the control as usual. The control is automatically named Gradient1, following the Visual Basic convention for naming controls.

2. With the control selected on the Form, locate the EndColor property in the Properties window and set it to a different color, as shown in Figure 14.6.

FIGURE 14.6

Setting a value for a custom color property through the Properties window

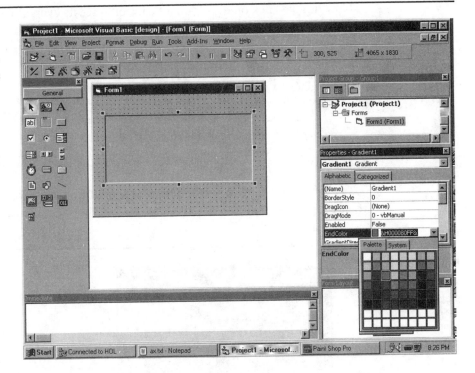

The StartColor and EndColor properties behave just like any other color property you can set from the Properties window. Remember the OLE_COLOR data type? Had you specified the Long data type for the StartColor and EndColor properties (after all, colors are represented as long values), you wouldn't have seen the nice color selection dialog box in Figure 14.6).

You can assign only valid values to the StartColor and EndColor properties. That's a nice feature, already built into the control. You can, however, set the GradientDirection property to an invalid value. As long as you specify an integer value, Visual Basic accepts it. You'll see what can be done about that shortly.

As you may have noticed already, ActiveX controls have an Appearance property that by default is 3-D, which gives the controls a 3-D type edge. But the Appearance property doesn't take effect unless the BorderStyle property is also set to the 1 - Fixed Single. The default value of the BorderStyle property is 0 - Flat (a rather peculiar choice, considering the effect it has on the Appearance property). Open the BorderStyle property and set it to 1 - Fixed Single.

Now double-click on the Gradient control to see its events. Your new control has its own events, and you can program them just as you would program the events of any other VB control. Enter the following code in the control's Click event:

```
Private Sub Gradient1_Click()
    MsgBox "My properties are " & _
      "StartColor = " & Gradient1.StartColor & Chr$(13) & _
      "EndColor = " & Gradient1.EndColor & Chr$(13) & _
      "GradientDirection = " & Gradient1.GradientDirection
End Sub
```

To run the control, press F5 and then click on the control. You will see the control's properties displayed in a message box, as shown in Figure 14.7.

FIGURE 14.7

The custom control's properties as they are displayed by the control itself

You can program other events too. There's nothing peculiar about programming the custom control. For the user, it's a regular control. VB has done quite a lot for us. It generated a working ActiveX control. Of course, we must still add the code that makes the control tick. Creating something that looks and feels like a control with point-and-click operations was quite a feat, but our final goal is to design something practical and useful.

The Skeleton of the ActiveX Control

Let's see how the Wizard did it. Switch to the Project Explorer window, and double-click on the name of the control to open it in design mode. Then, double-click on the UserControl to open the code pane and see the lines inserted by the Wizard.

Code 14.2: The ActiveX Control

```
Option Explicit
'Default Property Values:
Const m_def_StartColor = &H404040
Const m_def_EndColor = &HC0C0C0
Const m_def_GradientDirection = 0
'Property Variables:
Dim m_StartColor As OLE_COLOR
Dim m_EndColor As OLE_COLOR
Dim m_GradientDirection As Integer
'Event Declarations:
Event DblClick()
Event Click()
Event KeyDown(KeyCode As Integer, Shift As Integer)
Event KeyPress(KeyAscii As Integer)
Event KeyUp(KeyCode As Integer, Shift As Integer)
Event MouseDown(Button As Integer, Shift As Integer,
➥X As Single, Y As Single)
Event MouseMove(Button As Integer, Shift As Integer,
➥X As Single, Y As Single)
Event MouseUp(Button As Integer, Shift As Integer,
➥X As Single, Y As Single)

Public Property Get StartColor() As OLE_COLOR
    StartColor = m_StartColor
End Property

Public Property Let StartColor(ByVal New_StartColor As OLE_COLOR)
    m_StartColor = New_StartColor
    PropertyChanged "StartColor"
End Property

Public Property Get EndColor() As OLE_COLOR
    EndColor = m_EndColor
End Property
```

```
Public Property Let EndColor(ByVal New_EndColor As OLE_COLOR)
    m_EndColor = New_EndColor
    PropertyChanged "EndColor"
End Property

Public Property Get GradientDirection() As Integer
    GradientDirection = m_GradientDirection
End Property

Public Property Let GradientDirection(ByVal
New_GradientDirection As Integer)
    m_GradientDirection = New_GradientDirection
    PropertyChanged "GradientDirection"
End Property


'Initialize Properties for User Control
Private Sub UserControl_InitProperties()
    m_StartColor = m_def_StartColor
    m_EndColor = m_def_EndColor
    m_GradientDirection = m_def_GradientDirection
End Sub


'Load property values from storage
Private Sub UserControl_ReadProperties(PropBag As PropertyBag)
    UserControl.Enabled = PropBag.ReadProperty("Enabled", True)
    UserControl.BorderStyle = PropBag.ReadProperty
    ("BorderStyle", 1)
    m_StartColor = PropBag.ReadProperty("StartColor",
    m_def_StartColor)
    m_EndColor = PropBag.ReadProperty
    ("EndColor", m_def_EndColor)
    m_GradientDirection = PropBag.ReadProperty("GradientDirection",
    m_def_GradientDirection)
End Sub

'Write property values to storage
Private Sub UserControl_WriteProperties(PropBag As PropertyBag)
    Call PropBag.WriteProperty("Enabled",
    UserControl.Enabled, True)
    Call PropBag.WriteProperty("BorderStyle",
    UserControl.BorderStyle, 1)
    Call PropBag.WriteProperty("StartColor", m_StartColor,
    m_def_StartColor)
```

```
        Call PropBag.WriteProperty("EndColor", m_EndColor,
        ➥m_def_EndColor)
        Call PropBag.WriteProperty("GradientDirection",
        ➥m_GradientDirection, m_def_GradientDirection)
End Sub

Public Property Get Enabled() As Boolean
    Enabled = UserControl.Enabled
End Property

Public Property Let Enabled(ByVal New_Enabled As Boolean)
    UserControl.Enabled = New_Enabled
    PropertyChanged "Enabled"
End Property

Public Property Get BorderStyle() As Integer
    BorderStyle = UserControl.BorderStyle
End Property

Public Property Let BorderStyle(ByVal New_BorderStyle As Integer)
    UserControl.BorderStyle = New_BorderStyle
    PropertyChanged "BorderStyle"
End Property

Public Sub Refresh()
    UserControl.Refresh
End Sub

Private Sub UserControl_Click()
    RaiseEvent Click
End Sub

Private Sub UserControl_DblClick()
    RaiseEvent DblClick
End Sub

Private Sub UserControl_KeyDown(KeyCode As Integer,
➥Shift As Integer)
    RaiseEvent KeyDown(KeyCode, Shift)
End Sub

Private Sub UserControl_KeyPress(KeyAscii As Integer)
    RaiseEvent KeyPress(KeyAscii)
End Sub
```

```
Private Sub UserControl_KeyUp(KeyCode As Integer,
➡Shift As Integer)
    RaiseEvent KeyUp(KeyCode, Shift)
End Sub

Private Sub UserControl_MouseDown(Button As Integer,
➡Shift As Integer, X As Single, Y As Single)
    RaiseEvent MouseDown(Button, Shift, X, Y)
End Sub

Private Sub UserControl_MouseMove(Button As Integer,
➡Shift As Integer, X As Single, Y As Single)
    RaiseEvent MouseMove(Button, Shift, X, Y)
End Sub

Private Sub UserControl_MouseUp(Button As Integer,
➡Shift As Integer, X As Single, Y As Single)
    RaiseEvent MouseUp(Button, Shift, X, Y)
End Sub
```

It's quite lengthy, but not as complicated as it appears. Let's look at each section of the code in detail, starting with the declaration section:

```
Option Explicit
'Default Property Values:
Const m_def_StartColor = &H404040
Const m_def_EndColor = &HC0C0C0
Const m_def_GradientDirection = 0
```

Here are the definitions of a few constants that correspond to the values we specified in the Set Attributes window of the Wizard. These constants will be used later in the code as initial values for various properties. Notice that you don't have to run the Wizard to change these values. You can easily edit the control's code. Notice also that the names of the constants are based on the actual property names and that you can easily edit the code.

```
'Property Variables:
Dim m_StartColor As OLE_COLOR
Dim m_EndColor As OLE_COLOR
Dim m_GradientDirection As Integer
```

The next section defines three local variables, which are the properties we defined earlier through the Wizard. The control's properties are mapped to private variables in the control's code, because that's what they are. As is the case with an ActiveX component, what the applications perceive and access as properties from the outside are actually plain variables in the control. Later, you'll see how the control gets the values entered by the user in the Properties window (or the code at run time) and assigns them to these private variables. (Do you remember how you were manipulating the properties of your own OLE server in the previous chapter with the Property Let and Property Get procedures? The same approach works with ActiveX controls. But more on this later.)

```
'Event Declarations:
Event DblClick()
Event Click()
Event KeyDown(KeyCode As Integer, Shift As Integer)
Event KeyPress(KeyAscii As Integer)
Event KeyUp(KeyCode As Integer, Shift As Integer)
Event MouseDown(Button As Integer, Shift As Integer,
    X As Single, Y As Single)
Event MouseMove(Button As Integer, Shift As Integer,
    X As Single, Y As Single)
Event MouseUp(Button As Integer, Shift As Integer,
    X As Single, Y As Single)
```

The event declarations follow. These are the events we specified in the first two windows of the Wizard, and we mapped them to the UserControl object. Clicking on the custom control generates a Click event, which is reported to the application as if it were generated by the ActiveX control.

NOTE If the Click event wasn't mapped to the UserControl object, only the UserControl would see the Click event. If you want to perform a special action when the control is clicked, you program the Click event in the custom control's code window. This results in a standard behavior; however, the user won't be able to program the Click event.

In our custom control, we don't have any exclusive use for the Click event (and the other common mouse and keyboard events), so we are exposing them to the application that uses the ActiveX control.

Setting and Reading Property Values

Next, you see a number of subroutines, two for each property.

Code 14.3: The StartColor Property Subroutines

```
Public Property Get StartColor() As OLE_COLOR
    StartColor = m_StartColor
End Property

Public Property Let StartColor(ByVal New_StartColor As OLE_COLOR)
    m_StartColor = New_StartColor
    PropertyChanged "StartColor"
End Property
```

Each property is defined by two Public procedures:

- Property Get

- Property Let

The Property Let procedure is invoked every time the property is changed, either via the Properties window (at design time) or via code (at run time). The code that's executed when a property changes values consists of two lines. The first line gets the value supplied by the procedure's argument (which is the new value of the property) and assigns it to the private property that represents the property in the control. The rest of the code sees only the m_StartColor local property, not the actual property. The second line notifies Visual Basic that the property has changed value. The PropertyChanged method is important and must be included in the Property Let procedure, because this is how Visual Basic saves any changes made to the property at design time so that it will take effect at run time.

The Property Get procedure is invoked every time the program recalls the value of the property. This procedure reads the value of the *m_StartColor* private variable and assigns it to the StartColor property. There must be a Property Let and a Property Get procedure for each property, and they must include the lines shown here. They represent the minimum functionality of the mechanism for setting and reading property values.

Of course, you can add validation code here too. The GradientDirection property's value must be 0 or 1. As is, the custom control allows the user to enter any value in the Properties window for this property. Let's add some validation code in the Property Let procedure of the Gradient direction property. The validation code is simple: It rejects any values that are not 0 or 1.

Code 14.4: Validation Code for the Property Let Procedure

```
Public Property Let GradientDirection
     (ByVal New_GradientDirection As Integer)
    If New_GradientDirection < 0 Or
    ➥New_GradientDirection > 1 Then
        MsgBox "The GradientDirection property can be
        ➥either 0 or 1"
        Exit Property
    End If
    m_GradientDirection = New_GradientDirection
    PropertyChanged "GradientDirection"
End Property
```

The If statement tests the validity of the supplied value, and if the new value is outside the valid range (0 and 1), the attempt to set the property is rejected. Notice that the procedure is halted with the Exit Property statement (which is something like the Exit Sub or Exit Function statement).

Modify the Property Let procedure according to the previous listing, and then switch to the test Form (Form1). Select the control on the test Form, open the Properties window, and set the GradientDirection property to an invalid value (3 or 1000, for example). As soon as you attempt to change the property's value to an invalid setting, the control displays the warning and rejects the changes. You may be wondering now, How can I make this property display its valid settings only in a drop-down ListBox control, like other Visual Basic controls? It is possible, of course, but it takes a bit of code, and you'll see how shortly.

After the Property Let and Property Get procedures for all properties of the control comes some initialization code:

```
'Initialize Properties for User Control
Private Sub UserControl_InitProperties()
    m_StartColor = m_def_StartColor
    m_EndColor = m_def_EndColor
    m_GradientDirection = m_def_GradientDirection
End Sub
```

The statements of the InitProperties subroutine assign initial values to the private variables that represent the control properties. The constants m_def_ StartColor, m_def_EndColor, and m_def_GradientDirection were defined earlier in the program. When this control is placed on a Form, Visual Basic looks up the values of the *m_StartColor*, *m_EndColor*, and *m_GradientDirection* variables and uses them to assign the proper values to the entries of the Properties window.

Saving and Retrieving Property Values

Now come two interesting subroutines:

- ReadProperties
- WriteProperties

When you set some properties through the Properties window, the new values must be saved somewhere. The reason? So that the control won't forget them. An application may (and usually does) change the values of certain properties at run time. But when the application stops and you're back in design mode, the properties changed at run time must be reset to their values before the application started. *Not to their default values, but to whatever values you assigned to them at design time.*

Visual Basic provides a special object for storing all property values: the Property-Bag. The PropertyBag object exposes two methods, one for saving a property's value and one for reading a property's value. You, the control developer, need not know anything about how the values are stored. Visual Basic stores them, and when you request their values, it furnishes them. The two methods are properly named WriteProperty and ReadProperty.

The WriteProperty Method   The WriteProperty method has the following syntax:

```
WriteProperty propertyName, value, defaultValue
```

The *propertyName* variable is the name of the property (GradientDirection, for instance), *value* can be a literal (such as 1 or "some direction") but is nearly always the name of the private variable that holds the property value, and *defaultValue* is the property's default value.

> **NOTE** Why specify both a value and a default value in the WriteProperty method? Visual Basic compares the value to the default setting, and if that value and the default value are the same, Visual Basic doesn't save it. When you later request the property's value with the ReadProperty method, Visual Basic provides the same default value.

The ReadProperty Method   The ReadProperty method has the following syntax:

```
ReadProperty propertyName, defaultValue
```

The *propertyName* variable is the name of the property (GradientDirection, for instance), and *defaultValue* is the value stored earlier in the Property Bag object for this property. In the WriteProperties event's code, you must call the WriteProperty method once for each property. Likewise, in the ReadProperties subroutine, you must call the ReadProperty method once for each property. Here are the listings of the WriteProperties and ReadProperties events of the Gradient application as generated by the Wizard:

```
'Load property values from storage
Private Sub UserControl_ReadProperties(PropBag As PropertyBag)
    UserControl.Enabled = PropBag.ReadProperty("Enabled", True)
    UserControl.BorderStyle = PropBag.ReadProperty("BorderStyle", 1)
    m_StartColor = PropBag.ReadProperty("StartColor", m_def_StartColor)
    m_EndColor = PropBag.ReadProperty("EndColor", m_def_EndColor)
    m_GradientDirection = PropBag.ReadProperty("GradientDirection",
    ➡ m_def_GradientDirection)
End Sub

'Write property values to storage
Private Sub UserControl_WriteProperties(PropBag As PropertyBag)
    Call PropBag.WriteProperty("Enabled", UserControl.Enabled, True)
    Call PropBag.WriteProperty("BorderStyle",
UserControl.BorderStyle, 1)
    Call PropBag.WriteProperty("StartColor", m_StartColor, m_def_
    ➡StartColor)
    Call PropBag.WriteProperty("EndColor", m_EndColor, m_def_EndColor)
    Call PropBag.WriteProperty("GradientDirection",
m_GradientDirection, m_def_GradientDirection)
End Sub
```

Reporting Events

The last section of the code maps the various control's events to the equivalent events of the UserControl object. When the user clicks on the ActiveX control, Windows reports the Click event to the UserControl object. As a control developer, you can process the event from within the control (in which case, the application that uses the control doesn't see the Click event), you can pass it to the control (in which case, the application receives Click events for the control and the application programmer can program them), or you can do both (do something within your code and then pass them to the host application).

You pass an event to the application via the RaiseEvent method. The User-Control object's Click event is coded as follows:

```
Private Sub UserControl_Click()
    RaiseEvent Click
End Sub
```

The code for the remaining events is nearly identical.

The Wizard hasn't done anything terribly special; it simply inserted some straightforward code. With the exception of the ReadProperty and WriteProperty methods, everything else should be more or less familiar to most VB programmers. The ActiveX control, therefore, is slightly more complicated than a standard project. Now it's time to type in a few lines of code. After all, we must tell our control how to draw the gradient.

Drawing the Gradient

We now have a functional control, and it wasn't difficult to develop. Visual Basic created the skeleton of a working control. It hooks into the environment, its icon appears in the Toolbox, and we can use it in our projects just as we use any other control; it even manages its own Properties window. Now, it's time to make this control "click." We must add the code that's unique to this control: the code that paints its background.

Most of a custom control's code goes into the Paint event. This event is raised by Visual Basic every time a control must be redrawn, and we must supply the code to redraw it. What we are going to do now is copy the code we developed for the FrmGrad application in Chapter 6, *Drawing and Painting with Visual Basic*, and paste it into the custom control.

Code 14.5: Filling the Form with a Gradient

```
Dim newColor As Long
Dim ipixel, PWidth As Integer
Dim redInc, greenInc, blueInc As Single
Dim color1 As Long, color2 As Long
Dim startRed, startGreen, startBlue As Integer
Dim endRed, endGreen, endBlue As Integer
```

```
color1 = StartColor.BackColor
color2 = EndColor.BackColor

startRed = GetRed(color1)
endRed = GetRed(color2)
startGreen = GetGreen(color1)
endGreen = GetGreen(color2)
startBlue = GetBlue(color1)
endBlue = GetBlue(color2)

PWidth = Picture1.ScaleWidth

redInc = (endRed - startRed) / PWidth
greenInc = (endGreen - startGreen) / PWidth
blueInc = (endBlue - startBlue) / PWidth

For ipixel = 0 To PWidth - 1
➥newColor = RGB(startRed + redInc * ipixel,
➥startGreen + greenInc * ipixel,
➥startBlue + blueInc * ipixel)
➥Picture1.Line (ipixel, 0)-(ipixel,
➥Picture1.Height - 1), newColor
Next
```

We must also add the following three supporting functions that extract the basic components of a color value:

```
Function GetRed(colorVal As Long) As Integer
    GetRed = colorVal Mod 256
End Function

Function GetGreen(colorVal As Long) As Integer
    GetGreen = ((colorVal And &HFF00FF00) / 256&)
End Function

Function GetBlue(colorVal As Long) As Integer
    GetBlue = (colorVal And &HFF0000) / (256& * 256&)
End Function
```

First, copy the definitions of the three supporting functions and paste them somewhere at the beginning to the custom control's code pane. In the actual project, I copied the definitions of these functions after the control's declarations, under the heading SUPPORT FUCNTIONS.

Next, copy the statements of the subroutine and paste them in the UserControl's Paint event. You must, however, make a few changes. Basically, set the starting and ending colors to the values of the corresponding properties, and modify the code that produces the gradient by taking into consideration the setting of the GradientDirection property. Follow these steps:

1. Replace Picture1 with UserControl, because we are not painting a Picture Box control but the control's Form (the UserControl object).

2. Because the starting and ending values of the gradient are given by the properties m_StartColor and m_EndColor, replace the following lines:

```
color1 = StartColor.BackColor
color2 = EndColor.BackColor
```

with these lines:

```
color1 = m_StartColor
color2 = m_EndColor
```

3. Because our control isn't filled with horizontal lines only, replace the variable *PWidth* with the variable *PSize*. Replace the following line:

```
PWidth = Picture1.ScaleWidth
```

with the following lines:

```
If m_GradientDirection = 0 Then
        PSize = UserControl.ScaleWidth
    Else
        PSize = UserControl.ScaleHeight
End If
```

4. If the gradient's direction is 0, we must draw vertical lines. If it's 1, we must draw horizontal lines. The code that fills the control's background with a gradient takes into consideration the value of the *m_GradientDirection* variable, and it is as follows:

```
If m_GradientDirection = 0 Then
        For ipixel = 0 To PSize
            newColor = RGB(startRed + redInc * ipixel,
startGreen + greenInc * ipixel, startBlue + blueInc * ipixel)
            UserControl.Line (ipixel, 0)-(ipixel,
UserControl.Height - 1), newColor
        Next
    Else
```

```
              For ipixel = 0 To PSize
                  newColor = RGB(startRed + redInc * ipixel,
                  ➥startGreen + greenInc * ipixel, startBlue +
                  ➥blueInc * ipixel)
                  UserControl.Line (0, ipixel)-(UserControl.Width,
                  ➥ipixel), newColor
              Next
          End If
```

And you are done. Close the Control design window and switch to Form1. As soon as the Form is displayed, you will see the gradient being drawn. You almost have your new custom control. And it works nicely, with one small problem. The drawing of the gradient is slow. Filling the control with a gradient takes much longer than it did in the ClrGrads application. But this isn't a problem with the control.

The UserControl is nothing more than a Form on which you can draw. As such, it has a ScaleMode property, which by default is 1 (twips). We are actually drawing a line for each twip along the Form's width. You must go back to the UserControl and set its ScaleMode property to 3 (pixels). This will make the drawing of the background really swift, because the program will be drawing one line for each pixel along the horizontal axis of the control, which is all we need to fill the control. Implement this change and check out the new control. This time the gradient is drawn instantly. (Pentium Pro, right?)

Enumerated Properties

We now need to implement one last improvement in our control. We need to add some code that will display only valid values for the GradientDirection property so that the user won't be able to specify an invalid setting. Figure 14.8 shows the Properties window for the control when the GradientDirection property is selected.

FIGURE 14.8

Some custom properties may have limited values, which should be displayed in a drop-down list such as this one.

A data type that can hold a small number of values is called Enumerated type. The Integer, Double, and other numeric data types are generic and can represent all numbers. If your application uses a variable that may take on only a limited number of integer values, you can use the Enumerated data type. The Gradient-Direction property is such a variable. It can take only one of two integer values. The days of the week and the months of the year are also examples of Enumerated data types. To create such a data type, you must first declare the Enumerated type's values so that Visual Basic knows which ones are valid. Insert the following Enumerated type declaration at the beginning of the code, right after the Option Explicit statement:

```
Enum Directions
Horizontal
Vertical
End Enum
```

This declaration tells Visual Basic that any variable defined as *Directions* can have the value 0 or 1 (Enumerated types correspond to numeric values, starting with 0). The strings that appear in the declaration are synonyms of the corresponding numeric values, which will be displayed in the Properties window.

For this to happen, we must change the type of the GradientDirection property from Integer to Directions (the Enumerated type we just declared). The Gradient-Direction property shouldn't be an integer, but an Enumerated type. Open the GradGrp project group and implement the following changes:

1. At the beginning of the code insert the following type definition:

   ```
   Enum Directions
   Horizontal
   Vertical
   End Enum
   ```

2. Now, change the definitions of the GradientDirection property's Let and Get procedures so that their type is Directions and not Integer. Make the following changes to these two procedures:

   ```
   Public Property Get GradientDirection() As Directions
       GradientDirection = m_GradientDirection
   End Property

   Public Property Let GradientDirection(ByVal
   ➥New_GradientDirection As Directions)
   ```

```
        m_GradientDirection = New_GradientDirection
        PropertyChanged "GradientDirection"
        UserControl_Paint
    End Property
```

Notice that the validation code in the Property Let procedure is no longer needed because the user can't select an invalid value for this property in the Properties window. If you attempt to assign an invalid value to this property from within your code, the command will be ignored without any warnings or error messages. The property will simply not change value.

Testing the Finished Control

Let's test our control a little further. Select the control on the Form, and in the Properties window, change the settings of its unique properties: StartColor, EndColor, and GradientDirection. You can change them as before, but nothing happens because Visual Basic isn't raising the Paint event and our code isn't notified to repaint the control. To force the repainting of the control, resize it with the mouse. If you resize the control by dragging its handles, the gradient will be redrawn.

As you can see, you must invoke the Paint event every time a property is changed. The PropertyChanged method in the Property Let procedure doesn't call the Paint event, because it doesn't know where we inserted our code. We must add the following line:

```
UserControl_Paint
```

at the end of each property's Let Property procedure.

Code 14.6: The EndColor Property's Let Procedure

```
Public Property Let EndColor(ByVal New_EndColor As OLE_COLOR)
    m_EndColor = New_EndColor
    PropertyChanged "EndColor"
    UserControl_Paint
End Property
```

By invoking the Paint event every time a property changes values, we ensure that the control is redrawn with the new settings.

Now save all the files of the project and the project in its own folder. The project group consists of the UserControl and a project, which we used to test the behavior of our new control both at design and at run time. The Form1 Form is not part of the new ActiveX control. We used it to test the control as we were designing it. Let's see how the new control can be used with other projects.

Choose File ➤ Make Custom1.ocx. The OCX file is all your need to include the control in your projects. Then, save and close the project and start a new one. Follow these steps:

1. Start a new Standard EXE project, and add the new control to the Toolbox.

2. Right-click on the Toolbox, and from the shortcut menu, select Components to display the Components window shown in Figure 14.9.

FIGURE 14.9

Your new control appears in the Components window and can be added to any project.

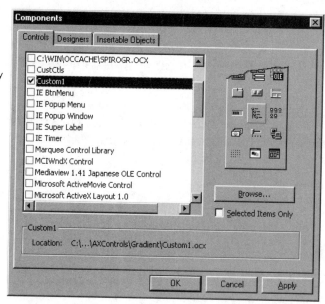

3. Check the Custom1 checkbox and click on OK. The Toolbox displays the custom control's icon.

If you use this icon to place a Gradient control on a Form, Visual Basic automatically names it Gradient1 (if it's the first control on the Form; the second will be named Gradient2, and so on).

4. Place the control on the Form, and set the gradient's colors and direction through the Gradient1 control's Properties window, as shown in Figure 14.10. (The project shown in Figure 14.10 is called GradForm, and you will find it on the CD in the same folder as the Gradient control.)

FIGURE 14.10

The Gradient control used on a new project, just like any other VB control

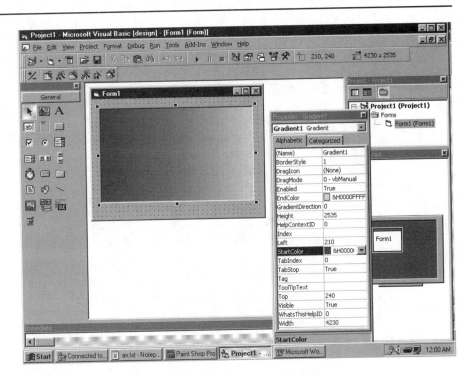

5. Now, open the Resize event and insert the following lines:

```
Private Sub Form_Resize()

    Gradient1.Top = 0
    Gradient1.Left = 0
    Gradient1.Width = Form1.ScaleWidth
    Gradient1.Height = Form1.ScaleHeight

End Sub
```

These lines resize the Gradient control every time the Form is resized to cover the entire area of the Form. If you run the application now, you will have a Form filled with a user-defined gradient. Not only that, but the inside of the Form has a three-dimensional look. To change the three-dimensional look to a flat one, set the control's BorderStyle property to zero.

6. Place a few more controls on the Form, as shown in Figure 14.11, and then run the application.

FIGURE 14.11

The Gradient custom ActiveX control in action

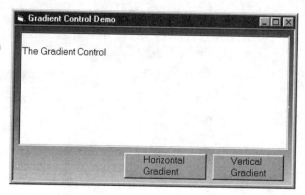

7. Resize the Form to see how it fills the Form with a gradient. You can add the following code behind the Horizontal Gradient and the Vertical Gradient buttons to change the direction of the gradient:

```
Private Sub HGrad_Click()

    Gradient1.GradientDirection = 0

End Sub

Private Sub VGrad_Click()

    Gradient1.GradientDirection = 1

End Sub
```

You can also add code to change the starting and ending colors from within the code. Simply assign the desired values to the properties Gradient1.StartColor and Gradient1.EndColor.

If you really test the new control, you will discover a few minor bugs or inconsistencies with other, comparable Visual Basic controls—you might actually discover a real bug we missed during our tests.

If the Gradient control is to be used as a background, it should also be able to act as a container. In other words, any controls drawn on the Gradient control should be dragged along with the control. This isn't the case, however. If you place a text box on the Gradient control, you can move the Gradient anywhere with the mouse, and the text box won't follow. Not to mention that you can move the text box outside the control. Normally, any control drawn on a container can be repositioned only within its container.

If you attempt to place a transparent label on the Gradient control, the Label won't show. It will always be underneath the control. Choosing Format ➤ Order ➤ Bring to Front or Bring to Back won't help. The Label control is hidden behind the Gradient control. The same will happen with several other controls such as the Shape and ImageBox control. The Gradient control covers controls that don't support user input. This won't happen with a TextBox or a Command Button control.

You can fix both problems by changing the ControlContainer property of the UserControl object. This property's default value is False, which means that the UserControl can't act as a container for other controls. To change this behavior, the next time you open the Gradient control project, set the control's Control-Container property to True. Doing so won't affect any existing properties, and it won't necessitate any changes in the rest of the code. The OCX file you will find on the CD includes this adjustment. Figure 14.12 shows the same Form as Figure 14.11, only this time a transparent label is on top of it.

FIGURE 14.12

The Gradient ActiveX control acting as a container with a transparent label overlaid

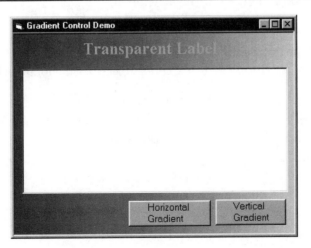

The Gradient control is an interesting design element, but it can't be used as a background for all controls. Many controls don't support a BackStyle property and can't be overlaid transparently on a gradient. (CheckBox and ComboBox are two common controls that can't be placed on a gradient, unless a little gray background doesn't bother you.)

Our custom control works fine, but there is one last improvement we must implement. The GradientDirection property takes two values, and we have included the necessary code for validating any user-supplied values for this property. It is customary in Visual Basic, though, that properties with a limited range of values display a list of their values in the Properties window.

Interacting with the Container

ActiveX controls are meant to be used as building blocks in application development. As such, they are sited on Forms or other controls that can act as containers. As an ActiveX control designer, you should be able to access the properties of a control's container and adjust the control's appearance according to the properties of the container. You will find two objects useful in designing custom controls: Extender and Ambient.

The Extender Object

The Extender object provides some of your control's basic properties, such as its Name, Width, and Height. The Extender object is also your gateway to certain properties of the *parent control*, the control on which the custom control is sited.

The Name Property   You can find out the Name of the container control and its dimensions. To access the Extender object, use the following construct:

```
UserControl.Extender.extProperty
```

The *extProperty* entry is an Extender property name. The name of the custom control is returned by the following expression:

```
UserControl.Extender.Name
```

NOTE
But do I really have to invoke the Extender object to find out the custom control's name from within the custom control? Isn't it an overkill? If you think about it, the control doesn't know its own name! The user can set the control's Name property at any time during the control's design, and to read this name from within the control's code, you must indeed call upon the services of the Extender object.

The Width and Height Properties   The Width and Height properties return the control's dimensions, as specified by the user, the Tag property, the Index property (if one exists), and in general all the properties of the custom control that are maintained for you by Visual Basic. Tag, Index, and the other properties aren't properties of the Extender object (although the syntax indicates that they are). They are properties of your custom control that can't be accessed directly. We didn't include any code for maintaining these properties, but they appear in the control's Properties window anyway. Because the UserControl object maintains them, you can't access them directly but must go through the Extender object.

The Parent Property   This property returns the object on which your control is sited. The UserControl.Extender.Parent object is one way of accessing the container control's properties. To find out the container control's dimensions, you can use the following statements:

```
PWidth = UserControl.Extender.Width
PHeight = UserControl.Extender.Height
```

You can use similar statements to read the container control's name (UserControl .Extender.Parent.Name), it's background (UserControl.Extender.Parent.BackColor), and so on.

TIP
Notice this important difference: UserControl.Extender.Name is the custom control's name (for example, Gradient1); UserControl.Extender .Parent.Name is the container's name (for example, Form1).

To experiment with a few of the Extender object's dimensions, insert the following lines in the Gradient UserControl's Click event, run the test Form, and click on the Gradient control:

```
Private Sub UserControl_Click()
Dim MT As String
    MT = "I'm a custom control. My name is " &
    ➥UserControl.Extender.Name
    MT = "I'm located at (" & UserControl.Extender.Left &
    ➥", " & UserControl.Extender.Left & ")"
    MT = MT & vbCrLf & " My dimensions are " &
    ➥UserControl.Extender.Width & " by " &
    ➥UserControl.Extender.Height
    MT = MT & vbCrLf & "I'm tagged as " &
    ➥UserControl.Extender.Tag
    MT = MT & vbCrLf & "I'm sited on a control named
    ➥" & UserControl.Extender.Object.Name
    MT = MT & vbCrLf & "whose dimensions are
    ➥" & UserControl.Extender.Parent.Width &
    ➥" by " & UserControl.Extender.Parent.Height
    MsgBox MT
    RaiseEvent Click
End Sub
```

You will see the message box shown in Figure 14.13. Notice that this message is displayed from within the custom control's Click event, not from the test application. Only after the message is displayed does the test application receive the Click event.

The Ambient Object

The Ambient object is similar to the Extender object, and the two actually overlap in some ways. The Ambient object gives your control's code hints about the control's environment, such as the container's background color, its font, and so on. The single most important property of the Ambient object is UserMode, which indicates whether the control is operating in design or run-time mode.

As you know from working with regular controls, all VB controls operate in design and run-time modes. Because our control behaves identically in both modes, there's no need to distinguish between the two. In designing custom ActiveX controls, however, you frequently need to differentiate between the two modes.

FIGURE 14.13

Use the Extender object to access certain properties of the custom control and its container.

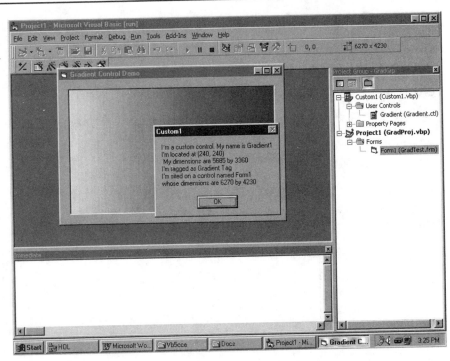

The UserMode Property This property is True when the control is operating in run-time mode and False when the control is operating in design mode. To see how this property works, let's display the text "Design Mode" while the control is in design mode. Open the Paint event's subroutine, and insert the following lines at the end of the Paint event's handler:

```
If Not Ambient.UserMode Then
        UserControl.CurrentX = 0
        UserControl.CurrentY = 0
        UserControl.Print "Design Mode"
End If
```

These statements determine whether the control is being used in design or run-time mode. In design mode, the string "Design Mode" is displayed in its upper left corner, as shown in Figure 14.14.

FIGURE 14.14

The "Design Mode" string is displayed in the control's upper left corner when it's open in design mode.

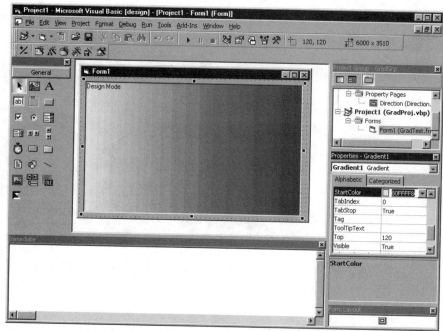

Other Properties of the Ambient Object   Other important properties of the Ambient object are ForeColor and BackColor, which report the colors of the container, and Font, which reports the current font on the container. Your code can look up these properties and initialize certain of the control's properties to match those of the container. For example, all controls placed on a Form assume by default the Form's font, size, and attributes.

If you include code to match your control's appearance with that of its environment, you should also use the AmbientChanged() event, which occurs each time one of the ambient properties changes (either through the Properties window or through the application). The AmbientChanged() event has a single argument, which is the name of the property that changed. Use this event to stay on top of changes in the control's container and to adjust the control's appearance or behavior accordingly.

Designing Property Pages

ActiveX controls can also have Property Pages. Property Pages are similar to the Properties window, in that they allow the developer (the programmer who is using your control in a VB project) to set the control's properties. Unlike the Properties window, however, the Property Pages offer a better and extremely flexible user interface, including instant visual feedback, for setting up a control.

Property Pages are basically design elements. Figure 14.15 shows the Property Pages for the TabStrip control. Through this interface, you can set up the TabStrip control in ways that are simply impossible through the Properties window. The properties you can set through the Properties window apply to the entire control, and you can't set the titles and appearance of the individual tabs, their number, and so on. The Property Pages for this control contain several pages (General, Color, Font, and Pictures) on which related properties are grouped.

FIGURE 14.15

The Property Pages of the TabStrip control

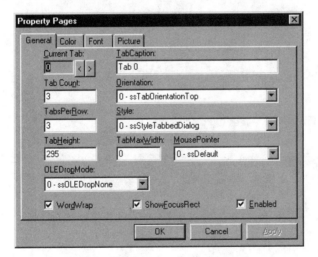

The design of Property Pages is greatly simplified by (what else?) the Property Page Wizard. Let's add some Property Pages to the Gradient control. Because this control has three properties—two Color properties and one Enumerated property—we will build two Property Pages, one for each category of properties.

Using the Property Page Wizard

To use the Property Page Wizard, follow these steps:

1. Open the Gradient application if it's not already the active project.

2. Choose Add-Ins ➤ Property Page Wizard, and step through the screens outlined in this section.

Introduction   This is an introductory window, which you can skip in the future by checking the Skip This Screen in the Future checkbox.

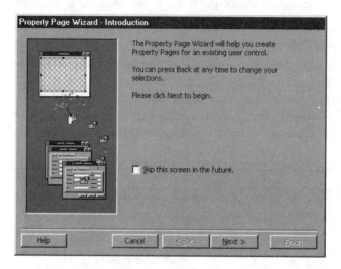

Selecting the Property Pages

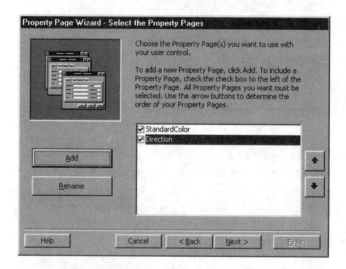

In this window, you select the Property Pages for your control. This window contains some (or all) of the standard Property Pages:

- Standard Color, which allows you to set color
- Standard Font, which allows you to set the font
- Standard Picture, which allows you to set Picture properties

For our control's Property Pages, we need the Standard Color page, plus a custom one, which we can add by clicking on the Add button. The Wizard prompts you to enter the name of the custom page. Enter **Direction**, and then click on the Next button.

Can you see why the Wizard selected the Standard Color page for us? Some of the control's properties were defined as OLE_COLOR type. If you don't want a Property Page for the color-related properties, clear the checkbox that precedes the property name. But we do need the page for specifying color, so leave this page checked. You can also rename the pages with the Rename button.

Adding Properties

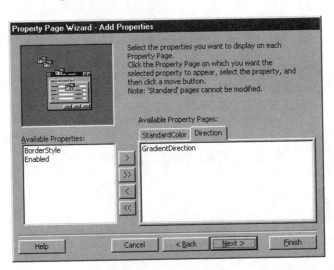

In this window, you specify the properties to be displayed in each Property Page. The Wizard has already assigned the color-related properties to the Standard Color page. Follow these steps:

1. Select the Direction tab.

2. Select the GradientDirection property from the list on the left and then click on the right-arrow button to add it to the Direction page.

3. Click on Next to display the last page of the Property Page Wizard, and then click on Finish.

Let's see what the Wizard has done for us. Follow these steps:

1. Switch to test mode, and right-click on the Gradient control

2. From the shortcut menu, choose Properties to display the two Property Pages shown in Figures 14.16 and 14.17.

FIGURE 14.16

The Color Property Page of the Gradient control

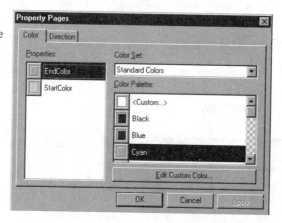

FIGURE 14.17

The Direction Property Page of the Gradient control

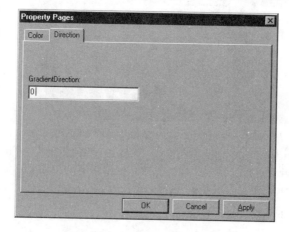

The Color page looks fine, but the Direction page needs drastic improvement. The Wizard just dumped a few controls on it, and you should not only fix their appearance, but provide the actual code as well.

The Color tab has a Properties list that contains the names of the color-related properties (they are the ones whose types are OLE_COLOR). Had you created more properties of the same type for the control, they would appear on the same page. To assign a new value to a color-related property, do one of the following:

- Select it and then chose a standard color from the Windows palette.

- Specify a custom color by clicking on the Edit Custom Color button.

The new color appears in front of the property's name in the Properties list. If you click on the Apply button, the gradient on the control is redrawn according to the new selection. The Direction page lets you specify the GradientDirection property's value by entering a value in a TextBox control.

NOTE Notice that you can set the colors on the control without explicitly calling the control's Paint event. Clicking on the Apply button sets the value of the StartColor and/or EndColor property, which activates the control's Property Let procedure. This procedure calls the Paint event. If the UserControl_Paint line isn't in the Property Let procedure, the control is not updated instantly, which has a disconcerting effect on the user. The Apply button does what it's supposed to do: It changes the value of the property. But if this change is not accompanied by some visual feedback, the user will be frustrated. So, you can't rely on the Wizard for the coding of the Apply button.

If you look at the Project window, you will see that the Wizard has added another item, a Property Page. This is the Direction Property Page. Double-click on it to open the page's Form in design mode. Notice that the OK, Cancel, and Apply buttons are not part of the Form. They belong to the TabStrip control, which displays the Property Pages at run time (this control isn't available to you and can't even be customized). Moreover, there is no Form for the Color Property Page. This is a standard Property Page, and you can't modify it (but you can create a new custom page for specifying colors if you really don't like the standard one).

Let's examine the code created by the Wizard for the Direction Property Page:

```
Option Explicit

Private Sub txtGradientDirection_Change()
    Changed = True
End Sub

Private Sub PropertyPage_ApplyChanges()
    SelectedControls(0).GradientDirection = txtGradientDirection.Text
End Sub

Private Sub PropertyPage_SelectionChanged()
    txtGradientDirection.Text = SelectedControls(0).GradientDirection
End Sub
```

The subroutine txtGradientDirection_Change() takes place every time the user changes the direction by typing something in the txtGradientDirection text box. By setting the *Changed* variable to True, the code enables the Apply button (which is disabled as long as the GradientDirection property doesn't change value). Visual Basic uses the Changed property to determine when the Apply button must be enabled.

The PropertyPages_ApplyChanges event is triggered every time the Apply button is clicked. From within this event, you must update the control's property. Because the Property Page is a separate Form and can't know the name of the selected control (there could be multiple instances of the same control on the Form), the code uses the SelectedControls(0) object to access the selected control and set its properties.

Finally, the PropertyPage_SelectionChanged() event occurs whenever the user selects another page. This is a good place to insert initialization code. The PropertyPage_SelectionChanged() subroutine's code assigns the current setting of the GradientDirection property to the TextBox control, in which the user is supposed to enter the property's value.

Obviously, we must replace the TextBox control with a ComboBox control, which will display the valid settings for the GradientDirection property and let the user select one of them, just as we did for the Properties window. Follow these steps:

1. To open the Direction Property Page, double-click on its name in the Project window.

2. Select the TextBox control and delete it.

3. Select the ComboBox tool in the Toolbox and draw a ComboBox control on the Form. Adjust the size of the control, and specify a nice font and size for both the ComboBox control and the Label control. You must also change the control's name to something more meaningful than Combo1. I use the name cmbGradientDirection name in the application.

4. Now you are ready to adjust the code. Double-click on the page and enter the following code:

```
Option Explicit

Private Sub cmbGradient_click()
    Changed = True
End Sub

Private Sub PropertyPage_ApplyChanges()
    SelectedControls(0).GradientDirection =
    ➥Val(cmbGradient.Text)
End Sub

Private Sub PropertyPage_SelectionChanged()
    cmbGradient.Clear
    cmbGradient.AddItem "0 - Horizontal"
    cmbGradient.AddItem "1 - Vertical"
    cmbGradient.ListIndex =
    ➥SelectedControls(0).GradientDirection
End Sub
```

Basically, you supply the initial value to the ComboBox control from within the PropertyPage_SelectionChanged() subroutine, and you change the statement of the PropertyPage_ApplyChanges() subroutine so that it assigns the selected value to the property's name. Notice that you take the value of the item selected in the ComboBox (Val(cmbGradientDirection.Text)), which is 0 or 1, because this happens to be the first digit in the property name.

The GradientDirection property is numeric. It's type is Enumerated, which is in essence a numeric data type. You can also perform other types of data validation from within this subroutine, depending on the type of input you expect from the user and the contents of other controls or other property settings.

The adjusted Direction Property Page is shown in Figure 14.18. It looks better than before, but it's quite empty.

FIGURE 14.18

The Direction Property Page after the TextBox control is replaced with a ComboBox

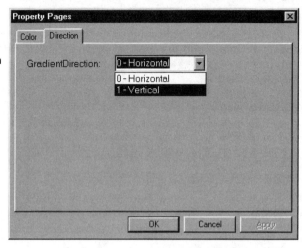

There is not much you can do about it, though, short of squeezing the controls for specifying more properties on the same page (as long as they are related, of course). You could have also created a custom color page, but the one generated by the Wizard is quite nice. As you can see, Property Pages aren't new; they are regular VB Forms, on which you can place all kinds of controls and do all kinds of neat tricks, as long as you observe a few rules inserted in the code by the Wizard:

1. Set the Changed property to True each time a property changes value and you want the Apply button enabled.

2. Update the control's property by using the expression SelectedControls(0) .propertyName, in which the *propertyName* variable is an actual property name.

3. Initialize the properties each time the user switches to a new Property Page from within the PropertyPage_SelectionChanged event.

If you look up the Properties window for the UserControl object, you will see that its PropertyPages property is set to 2 to indicate that two Property Pages were added. Click on the ellipsis button to display the Connect Property Pages dialog box shown in Figure 14.19.

Building a custom ActiveX control isn't a big deal after all. The ActiveX User Interface Wizard takes care of many details for you. It sets up a skeleton for the

FIGURE 14.19

Visual Basic's standard Property Pages are displayed in this dialog box along with the custom page we designed for the Gradient control.

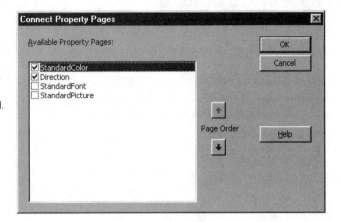

control's code, and you supply the code that actually does something (presumably something that other controls can't do). The code you supply is the type of code you would write for any VB application. There are, however, a few differences between developing Desktop applications and developing controls. The more you familiarize yourself with these differences, the better equipped you will be to develop ActiveX controls. The following section focuses on these differences.

Building a Generic Control

In the first section of this chapter, you learned how to build ActiveX controls with the ActiveX User Interface Wizard. Even though the Wizard took care of many details for you and constructed a functional control, you had to know a few things about a control's modes of operation in order to attach the desired type of functionality. The Wizard creates the skeleton of the control, but you have to flesh it out.

There are a few important topics I didn't cover earlier, and we will look at them in this section, including how to initialize and terminate controls and how to use unique properties, methods, and events. To simplify the discussion, we are not going to build another control. Instead, we'll use a generic control. This time we will not use the Wizard but will implement all the properties and methods manually so that you'll get some experience in editing controls.

Creating a Generic Control

Let's start by creating a generic control. Follow these steps:

1. Choose File ➢ New Project to open the New Project window.

2. Click on the ActiveX Control icon. Visual Basic creates a new project that contains a UserControl, named UserControl1. This is the control's Form on which the visible interface will be built.

3. Choose File ➢ Add Project to add a Standard EXE project. Visual Basic creates a new project with a single Form, named Form1. You'll use Form1 to test the control. (Form1 is frequently called the "test Form," and the project it belongs to is called the "test project.") What you have on your screen now is a generic control.

4. This is a good point at which to rename and save your project's files. For this generic project, use the default names.

5. Close the control's design window to enable the control's icon in the Toolbox.

6. Place an instance of the new control on the Form. The newly created Form doesn't have a background color or a border that will distinguish it from the Form it lies on.

7. With the control selected, open the Properties window.

By default, a UserControl object has the following properties:

DragIcon	DragMode
Height	HelpContextID
Index	Left
TabIndex	TabStop
Tag	ToolTipText
Top	Visible
WhatIsThisHelpID	Width

These properties are actually provided by the container. The Left property is determined by the container and has meaning only in the context of a container. Likewise, the TabIndex and TabStop properties aren't managed by the control itself, because the control doesn't know what other controls exist on the Form. Only the Form does, and therefore the Form must maintain these properties for its controls.

Test a few of these properties. Assign the value "My generic control" to the ToolTipText property. Run the application, and then rest the pointer for a second over the control. The string you entered is displayed in a ToolTip box. In a similar manner, you can test the Tag property by assigning a string to it, or you can test the Index property by creating multiple instances of the same control on the Form with the same name and a different Index value. There's not a single line of code you should add to the control to implement these properties.

Adding a Property

Let's add a property to our generic control. We'll call it Title, and we'll store internally its value to the m_Title private property. Select UserControl1 in the Project window, and in the Code window, insert the following declaration:

```
Private m_Title As String
```

and then the procedures:

```
Public Property Get Title() As String
    Title = m_Title
End Property

Public Property Let Title(ByVal vNewValue As String)
    m_Title = vNewValue
End Property
```

Close the UserControl design window and the Code window, switch to the test Form, select the new control, and look up its new property in the Properties window. The mere presence of the Let and Get procedures is all that Visual Basic needs to add a property to the control. Enter a new value in the Title property's box (for example, "Control Title"). As expected, the title won't appear on the control.

We must also write a few lines of code to display the title. Switch back to the UserControl window, double-click on it to open the Code window, and in the Paint event, enter the following:

```
Private Sub UserControl_Paint()
    UserControl.CurrentX = 0
```

```
        UserControl.CurrentY = 0
        UserControl.Print m_Title
End Sub
```

> **TIP**
> The first two statements aren't really needed to print something at the control's upper left corner, but you must set them accordingly if you want to print something elsewhere on the control.

Switch back to the test Form. If you have followed any of the previous suggestions and experimented with the custom control on the Form, delete all controls on the test Form.

Add an instance of the custom control (it will be automatically named User-Control11 unless you have changed the name of the UserControl object), and then assign a value to the Title property. Set the title to "My Generic Control," for instance. The title won't appear the moment you enter it because the Paint event isn't triggered when a property changes values. You must resize the control to force a Paint event and display the title. If you don't like the font, change the UserControl's Font property (our control doesn't have a Font property yet).

Every time a new property is set, the Property Let procedure is invoked. You must, therefore, call the Paint method from within the Property Let procedure so that the title is printed as soon as its entered. Switch back to the UserControl, and add the following line to the Property Let Title procedure:

```
UserControl_Paint
```

Your VB window should like the one shown in Figure 14.20. Now assign a value to the Title property and watch the string appear on the control.

Now, press F5 to run the application. The title won't appear on the control. It was there at design time, but it disappeared at run time. You probably want to stop the application and look up the value of the Title property to make sure it still contains its value. But you're in for a surprise. The Title property's value is a blank string. It wasn't your fault, so don't repeat the process. Any properties set at design time lose their value at run time. It's a strange behavior, but this is how controls work.

Your experience with Visual Basic tells you that any properties set at design time keep their values at run time. To make this happen, you must first save the property values to the Property Bag. What's not so easy to guess is when an action must take place. Let's explore the control's life cycle.

FIGURE 14.20

The VB window during
the first steps of the
design of the generic
control

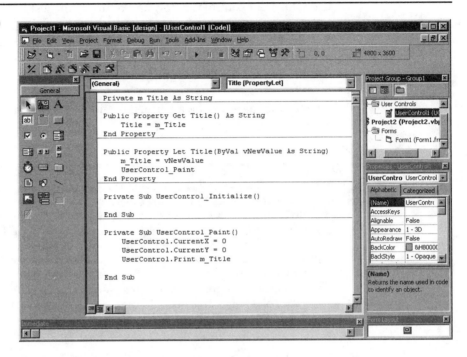

The Life of a Control

Let's experiment a little with the control's key events. Follow these steps:

1. Switch to the UserControl window and double-click on it to open the Code window.

2. Locate the Initialize, InitProperties, and Terminate events in the drop-down list on the right. In each, enter the Debug.Print statement, followed by the event's name, as shown here:

```
Private Sub UserControl_Initialize()
     Debug.Print "initializing control"
End Sub

Private Sub UserControl_InitProperties()
     Debug.Print "initializing properties"
End Sub

Private Sub UserControl_Terminate()
     Debug.Print "terminating control"
End Sub
```

3. Close the UserControl window and return to the test Form. Place an instance of the new control on the Form, and watch the Immediate Execution window. The following messages are displayed:

```
initializing control
initializing properties
```

When you place a control on a Form, it is initialized, and then its properties are initialized.

NOTE   The Print statements executed when you switched from the UserControl to the test Form. Even though you are not running the application, the code is running! To understand this behavior, you must put on your ActiveX designer's hat. When you place a regular ActiveX control, such as a TextBox control, on a Form, some code is executed. This is what you just witnessed. ActiveX controls are always in run mode, regardless of whether the Form they belong to is running. How else would the control's appearance change every time you set a different font or a background color?

4. Now set the Title property and run the test application. Two new messages appear in the Immediate Execution window (clear the current contents of the Immediate Execution window first):

```
terminating control
initializing control
```

The control that was on the Form at design time was terminated, and a new one was initialized. All its properties were initialized to their default values, and the default value for the Title property was a blank string. That's why it disappeared.

If you stop the application now, the following message appears once again in the Debug window:

```
initializing control
```

This time, the run-time instance of the control is terminated, and another design-time instance of the control is initialized. Each time you switch from design-time mode to run-time mode, the instance(s) of the control is(are) terminated, and a new one is created.

During this transition, the properties must be saved somehow. To do so, follow these steps:

1. Switch back to the UserControl Code window and enter a Print statement in the ReadProperties and WriteProperties events.

2. Switch back to the test project, set the Title property, run the application again, and you will see the following sequence of events:

```
writing properties
terminating control
initializing control
reading properties
```

Visual Basic saves the values of the properties in the Properties window and terminates the design-time instance of the control. It then initializes the run-time instance of the control and reads the same properties. This is the life cycle of an ActiveX control.

> **NOTE** But if Visual Basic knows which values to save, why can't it remember them until the new instance of the control is created? Why does Visual Basic save the property values and then read them again? It seems so simple, but notice the Terminate event between the writing and reading of the property values. In between these two instances, the control ceases to exist! Even if this behavior doesn't make sense right now, this is how controls behave.

Let's summarize the events that mark the life of a control. To execute some code at each of these events, place it in the corresponding event handler.

Key Events in a Control's Lifetime

When you place an instance of a control on the Form, the following events take place:

- **Initialize**   Initializes the design-time instance of the control

- **InitProperties**   Assigns initial values to the properties

When you switch from design time to run time, the following events take place:

- **WriteProperties**   Saves the properties listed in the Properties window

- **Terminate**   Terminates the design-time instance of the control

- **Initialize**   Initializes a new, run-time instance of the control

- **ReadProperties**   Reads the saved properties

When you switch from run time to design time, the following events take place:

- **Initialize**   Initializes the design-time instance of the control

- **ReadProperties**   Reads the values from the Properties window and assigns them to the corresponding properties

TIP When you switch from run-time to design-time mode, no WriteProperties event takes place. As expected, Visual Basic doesn't save the properties that changed at run time and resets the ActiveX control to the properties set in the Properties window at design time. In other words, changes made to the control's properties at design time are valid at run time too. The opposite isn't true; changes made at run time are reset when you switch back to design mode.

To maintain the values of the properties when the control switches from design to run time, you must add a few lines of code in the ReadProperties and Write-Properties events. We have looked at how property values are written to and read from the Property Bag object, so here's the code for the Title property:

```
Private Sub UserControl_WriteProperties(PropBag As PropertyBag)
    Debug.Print "writing properties"
    PropBag.WriteProperty "Title", m_Title, "Control Title"
End Sub

Private Sub UserControl_ReadProperties(PropBag As PropertyBag)
    Debug.Print "reading properties"
    Title = PropBag.ReadProperty("Title", "Control Title")
End Sub
```

Initializing the Control and Its Properties

You can use two events to maintain the control—Initialize and InitProperties. The InitProperties event is the place to assign initial values to the various properties.

The ActiveX User Interface Wizard does it so well for us. The Initialize event can be used to enter initialization code that doesn't involve properties. If you attempt to set a property value or do something on the control (for instance, printing the Title on the control with the statement UserControl.Print "Control"), you'll get the following error message:

```
Object Required
```

The UserControl object is being initialized. It doesn't exist yet. That's why the following statement:

```
UserControl.Print "Control"
```

works when executed from within other events, but not from within the Initialize event.

So, what can I do from within this event? Very little. You can assign initial values to the private variables of the control, but you can't access the control's properties, not even the Ambient object.

The event of interest is the InitProperties event, which takes place after the control is created. This behavior may strike you as strange: The Initialize event takes place every time you switch between design and run-time mode, but the Init-Properties event doesn't follow.

TIP

The InitProperties event takes place the first time a control is created and placed on a container. After that, the role of the InitProperties event in the control's life cycle is taken over by the ReadProperties event. If you changed the values of certain properties on the control, it wouldn't make much sense for Visual Basic to reset them to their initial values. Instead, it reads them from the Property Bag, when the ReadProperties event is triggered.

In the InitProperties event, you can insert initialization code that controls the appearance of a "newborn" control. For instance, you can determine what happens if the user places the control on a Form by double-clicking on its icon instead of actually drawing the control on the Form. Visual Basic places an instance of the control on the Form, and it will have a certain size (which is the same for all controls). If your control contains a long default title, a shape, or any element you want to be entirely visible, you can adjust the initial size of the control with a couple of statements such as the following:

```
UserControl.Width = 2400
UserControl.Height = 1200
```

When your control is placed on a Form with a double-click of its icon, its initial size is 2400 by 1200 twips.

The Extender and Ambient objects are also available from within the InitProperties control, because the control has been sited. You can display a title on the control in the same font as the container's font, as follows:

```
Set Font = Ambient.Font
UserControl.Print "FabControl"
```

These two lines display the string "FabControl" in the control's upper left corner, in the font of the container. In addition, your control's font will also be initially set to the Form's font.

> **NOTE**
>
> The title "FabControl" appears on the new instance of the control only if its AutoRedraw property is set to True. The control is created behind the scenes and is actually displayed after all the initialization code has been executed. If the control's AutoRedraw property is False, the string will be printed on the control initially, but when the control is displayed, the string is not part of the persistent bitmap (discussed in Chapter 6, *Drawing and Painting with Visual Basic*) and will be refreshed.

A Control's Key Properties

As you have learned, the UserControl object is basically a Form on which you can place other controls, draw shapes, display text, and detect events. It even has properties such as AutoRedraw and ScaleMode, which make it suitable for drawing at run time. But it's not called Form; it's called UserControl. In addition, it has a few properties that are unique to ActiveX controls, and we are going to look at them in this section.

CanGetFocus Set this property to True if the control can receive the focus, either with the mouse or with the Tab key. A user control can get the focus if the

UserControl object gets the focus or if one of its constituent controls can get the focus. If the control can get the focus, the EnterFocus and ExitFocus events are triggered every time the focus is moved in or out of the control.

Set the CanGetFocus property of the generic control to True and then enter the following lines in the control's EnterFocus and ExitFocus events:

```
Private Sub UserControl_EnterFocus()
UserControl.BackColor = vbRed
End Sub

Private Sub UserControl_ExitFocus()
UserControl.BackColor = vbGreen
End Sub
```

Then switch to the test Form, and place two instances of the new control on it (or one instance of the control and a couple of regular controls). Run the application, and move the focus from one control to the other. The generic control that has the focus is filled with red, and the other control is filled with green.

Custom controls with a visible user interface should be able to receive and handle the focus. If the control contains multiple constituent controls, you should also decide which one takes the focus. By default, the constituent control that was placed first on the user control takes the focus. To set the focus to another constituent control, use the SetFocus method and follow these steps:

1. Go back to the generic control, and place two command buttons on the UserControl. Don't change their names.

2. Add the following lines to move the focus to the Command2 button in the EnterFocus event:

   ```
   Private Sub UserControl_EnterFocus()
       UserControl.BackColor = vbRed
       Command2.SetFocus
   End Sub
   ```

3. Switch to the test Form, delete all controls on the Form, and place an instance of the new control (large enough to display both buttons) and another command button on the Form.

4. Run the project, and check out how the focus is moved from one control to the other. Notice that when the user control takes the focus, it passes it to the Command2 button. You can't move the focus to the Command1 button with the Tab key. The user control is a single entity, and it gets the focus once.

ControlContainer   If this property is set to True, the user control can become a container for other controls. Normally, the controls placed on a container are grouped with the container, and they all move together. When you reposition the container control on the Form, all the controls contained in it are moved along.

By default, a user control is not a container. In other words, it is possible to draw a command button that lies half on the user control and half outside. To change this behavior, set the ControlContainer property to True.

Alignable   If the Alignable property is set to True, the user control has an Align property at design time. The Align property determines whether and how the control is aligned on the Form. The Align property's settings are shown in Table 14.1.

TABLE 14.1   The Values of the Align Property.

VALUE	DESCRIPTION
vbAlignNone	The control is aligned manually (the default).
VbAlignTop	The control is always aligned with the top of the Form.
VbAlignLeft	The control is always aligned with the left edge of the Form.
VbAlignRight	The control is always aligned with the right edge of the Form.
VbAlignBottom	The control is always aligned with the bottom of the Form.

The Align property is not available at design time if the user control's Alignable property is False. Set the Alignable property to True for tool-barlike controls, which must always be aligned with the edges of the container, even when the container is resized.

InvisibleAtRuntime   Some controls, the Timer being the most typical example, are invisible at run time. If your user control does not have a user interface and need not appear on the Form, set its InvisibleAtRuntime property to True.

ToolboxBitmap   Use this property to display a BMP file in the Toolbox in place of the ActiveX Control generic icon. The ToolboxBitmap property's value is a BMP file's path name, but the bitmap is stored in the control and distributed with it.

AccessKeys   You use the AccessKeys property to specify which keys will act as hot keys for the control. If you want the user to move the focus instantly to your control by pressing a hot-key combination (Alt+Key), assign the key value to the AccessKeys property. Follow these steps:

1. Assign the value "A" to the user control's AccessKeys property (without the quotes).

2. Switch to the test Form and run it. Notice that you can switch the focus to the user control by pressing Alt+A.

3. Now stop the application, return to the user control, and open the AccessKeyPress event. This event is invoked every time the access key is pressed. Enter the following lines to print the key's ASCII value:

```
Private Sub UserControl_AccessKeyPress(KeyAscii As Integer)
Debug.Print "Access key pressed " & KeyAscii
End Sub
```

To move the focus to a specific constituent control or to perform some action when the focus is moved to the user control, enter the appropriate code in the AccessKeyPress event. Let's add access keys to the two command buttons of the last example. Follow these steps:

1. Switch to the UserControl, and add two command buttons, Command1 and Command2, as shown in Figure 14.21. (If you have followed the steps of the examples in the section "CanGetFocus," the two command buttons are already on the Form.)

2. Switch to the test Form, and place an instance of the new control, another button, or another VB control on the Form.

3. Run the test project and move the focus back and forth. Notice the following:

   - When you move the focus to the custom control with the mouse, the first command button takes the focus.

   - When you move the focus to the custom control with the Tab key, the ASCII value of the shortcut key is printed in the Immediate Execution window.

FIGURE 14.21

When the focus is moved to a custom control, it is actually moved to one of the constituent controls.

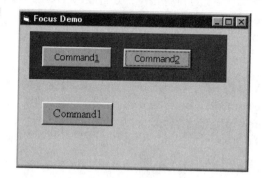

4. Now switch back to the UserControl, and assign shortcut keys to the two command buttons. Change their caption properties to Command&1 and Command&2 so that the keys 1 and 2 will become their access keys.

5. Run the test project, and experiment with moving the focus among the various controls on the Form.

You can use a hot-key combination to access not only the user control, but also the individual constituent components on it. To activate a specific constituent control every time the focus is moved to a custom control, insert the SetFocus method in the UserControl_AccessKeyPress() subroutine. If the custom control contains a text box as a constituent control, you can set the focus to this control each time the user control receives the focus with the following subroutine:

```
Private Sub UserControl_AccessKeyPress(KeyAscii As Integer)
Text1.SetFocus
End Sub
```

VB5 at Work: The Alarm ActiveX Control

The last example in this chapter demonstrates an ActiveX control that contains all three types of members—properties, events, and methods. It's a simple alarm that can be set to go off at a certain time, and when it times out, it triggers a

TimeOut event. Moreover, while the timer is ticking, the control updates a display, showing the time elapsed since the timer started (the property CountDown must be False) or the time left before the alarm goes off (the property CountDown must be True). Figure 14.22 shows the test Form for the Alarm control.

FIGURE 14.22

This is the test Form for the Alarm control.

The Properties

The alarm control will have two custom properties:

- AlarmTime
- CountDown

AlarmTime is the time when the alarm goes off, expressed in AM/PM format. *CountDown* is a True/False property that determines how the timer displays time. If CountDown is True, the alarm displays the time remaining. If you set the alarm to go off at 8:00 PM and you start the timer at 7:46 PM, the control displays 0:14.00, then 0:13.59, and so on until the alarm goes off 14 minutes later. If CountDown is False, the control starts counting at 00:00.00 and counts until the AlarmTime is reached.

The Methods

The Alarm control has two methods for starting and stopping the alarm:

- **StartTimer** starts the alarm.
- **StopTimer** stops the alarm.

The Events

The Alarm control has a TimeOut event which notifies the application that the alarm has gone off (which happens when the time is AlarmTime). The application can use this event to trigger another action or simply to notify the user.

Designing the Alarm Control

Your first step is to design the control's interface. Unlike the Timer control of Visual Basic, the Alarm control has a visible interface. It uses two constituent controls:

- **Timer** updates its display every second.
- **Label** displays the time.

Designing the User Interface

To design the control's interface, follow these steps:

1. Place a Label control on the UserControl Form and set its Font property to a font and size that looks nice for our purposes.

2. Align the Label with the upper left corner of the control and resize the control so that it just fits the label. (Make a note of the values of the control's Width and Height properties. You'll need them later when you write the code to prevent this control from being resized.)

3. Place a Timer control on the UserControl object. It doesn't make any difference where the Timer control is placed; it will be invisible at run time. You can place the timer outside the visible area of the user control or even on top of the label.

4. To complete the design of the control and prevent it from being resized, add the following code to the control's Resize event:

```
Private Sub UserControl_Resize()
    UserControl.Size 1800, 500
End Sub
```

The Size method forces the control to remain at a fixed size. You must change the values 1800 (width) and 500 (height) to the size of the control, according to the size of the Label control.

Now you can test the behavior of your new control. Place it on a Form and try to resize it. Even though you can drag the handles of the control, you won't be able to resize it.

Implementing the Control's Properties, Methods, and Event

Now we are ready to implement the control's properties, its methods, and its event. Let's start with the properties. You have seen how to add properties to a control with the ActiveX Control Interface Wizard and how to do it manually. Now let's look at one more tool. We will do something similar with the Wizard, but this time one property or method at a time.

Let's start with the variables declarations:

```
Private startTime As Date
Private Running As Boolean
Private m_CountDown As Boolean
Private m_AlarmTime As Date
```

As you have guessed, *m_CountDown* and *m_AlarmTime* are the two private variables that will hold the values of the CountDown and AlarmTime properties. The *Running* variable is True while the alarm is running and is declared outside any procedure so that all procedures can access its value. The *startTime* variable is set to the time the alarm starts counting and is used when the control is not counting down (you'll see how it's used shortly).

Follow these steps:

1. Switch to the UserControl window, and double-click on its Form to open the Code window.

2. Choose Tools ➤ Add Procedure to open the Add Procedure dialog box shown in Figure 14.23.

3. Add the name of the CountDown property, and check the Property radio button, as shown in Figure 14.23. The following lines are inserted in the code window:

```
Public Property Get CountDown() As Variant
End Property

Public Property Let CountDown(ByVal vNewValue As Variant)
End Property
```

FIGURE 14.23

The Add Procedure
dialog box

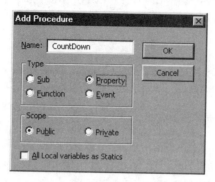

4. Change the property's type to match its declaration, and then supply the
   code for the two Property procedures:

```
Public Property Get CountDown() As Boolean
    CountDown = m_CountDown
End Property

Public Property Let CountDown(ByVal vNewValue As Boolean)
    m_CountDown = vNewValue
End Property
```

> **NOTE**
>
> The code should be quite trivial by now. All Property procedures map the
> property name to a private variable, and they have the same structure.
> You must not forget to change their types from Variant to whatever type
> best describes the variables.

5. Do the same for the *AlarmTime* variable. The procedures for this property
   are as follows:

```
Public Property Get AlarmTime() As Date
    AlarmTime = m_AlarmTime
End Property

Public Property Let AlarmTime(ByVal vNewValue As Date)
    If IsDate(vNewValue) Then m_AlarmTime = vNewValue
End Property
```

This Property procedure validates the property value to make sure you enter a valid time. If you specify a date, the program assumes that the time is 00:00:00 (midnight).

6. Add the two methods. Choose Tools ➤ Add Procedure.

7. Enter the name of the method, StartTimer, but this time check the Sub radio button (see Figure 14.23, earlier in this chapter). The following lines are inserted in the code:

```
Public Sub StartTimer()
End Sub
```

8. Insert this subroutine code, which starts the alarm:

```
Public Sub StartTimer()
    If Not Running Then
        Timer1.Enabled = True
        Running = True
        startTime = Time
        Label1.Caption = "00:00.00"
    End If
End Sub
```

This subroutine doesn't do anything if the alarm is already running. If it isn't, it enables the Timer control and sets the variable *startTimer* to the current time and the display to "00:00:00". The *Running* variable is also set to True to prevent this subroutine from being executed again while the alarm is running.

9. Choose Tools ➤ Add Procedure again to create another public subroutine, the StopTimer subroutine. The code for this subroutine should be the following:

```
Public Sub StopTimer()
    If Running Then
        Timer1.Enabled = False
        Running = False
    End If
End Sub
```

As with the StartTimer method, the alarm stops only if it's running. If that's the case, it disables the Timer control and sets the *Running* variable to False.

10. Last, add the control's event. Chose Tools ➤ Add Procedure to open the Add Procedure dialog box.

11. Specify the name TimeOut, and check the Event radio button. This time, a single line is added to the code, right after the declarations:

```
Event TimeOut()
```

How do you cause this event to take place? With the RaiseEvent statement from any place in your code. Whenever the alarm goes off, you can raise the TimeOut event with the following statement:

```
RaiseEvent TimeOut
```

The TimeOut event is raised from within the Timer's code, which is the core of the control.

You just completed the skeleton of the Alarm control, the kind of thing we did earlier with the ActiveX Control Interface Wizard. But knowing how it can be done manually will help you add a property or two to an existing control, without having to go through all the steps of the ActiveX Control Interface Wizard.

> **TIP**
>
> If you run the ActiveX Control Interface Wizard to update an existing control, you will find that the Wizard comments out some of your code. Always check your code after processing it with the Wizard.

Updating the Display

Now we can write the code that updates the display and raises the TimeOut event. The code we develop in this section has nothing to do with ActiveX control development. It's the type of code you write to implement an alarm as a stand-alone application.

> **TIP**
>
> If you're not quite accustomed to the ActiveX development environment yet, you can develop a regular application that does the job (that is, counts down time, displays elapsed or remaining time on a Label control, and detects when the alarm timed out). Then copy the essential procedures and paste them in the ActiveX project window.

You must supply the code for the Timer control's Timer event, which takes place every second. From within this event, you must update the display and test whether the alarm should go off.

Code 14.7: The Timer Event

```
Private Sub Timer1_Timer()
    If m_CountDown Then
        If Time - m_AlarmTime > 0 Then
            Label1.Caption = "00:00:00"
            RaiseEvent TimeOut
            Timer1.Enabled = False
        Else
            Label1.Caption = Format$(Hour(m_AlarmTime - Time) & ":"
            ➡& Minute(m_AlarmTime - Time) & ":" & Second(m_Alarm-
            ➡Time - Time), "hh:mm:ss")
        End If
    Else
        If Time - m_AlarmTime > 0 Then
            Label1.Caption = "00:00:00"
            RaiseEvent TimeOut
            Timer1.Enabled = False
        Else
            Label1.Caption = Format$(Hour(Time - startTime) & ":" &
            ➡Minute(Time - startTime) & ":" & Second(Time -
            ➡startTime), "hh:mm:ss")
        End If
    End If
End Sub
```

The behavior of the program depends on whether the control is set to count down. When counting down, it displays the time remaining; when counting up, it displays the time elapsed since the timer started (the *startTime* variable set by the StartTimer method) and stops when the AlarmTime is reached.

See how simple it is to generate your own events? Simply call the RaiseEvent method from within your code, and Visual Basic sees that the event is reported to the host application. Any condition in your application can trigger an event at any time. In addition, you must insert the definition of the event, along with the variable definitions at the beginning of the code:

```
Event TimeOut()
```

Testing the Alarm ActiveX Control

The test Form included in the Alarm project demonstrates how to use the Alarm control in your applications. The Form, shown in Figure 14.22, earlier in this chapter, contains two command buttons:

- Start Timer

- Alarm Time

(While the control is counting, the first button's caption becomes Stop Timer, which is what's shown in Figure 14.22.)

The Start Timer button starts the alarm by calling the StartTimer method. When you click on this button, its caption changes to Stop Timer, and when you click on it again, it stops the timer by calling the StopTimer method. Its caption is also reset to StartTimer

The Show Time button retrieves the AlarmTime property's value and displays it in a message box.

Code 14.8: The Start Time and Alarm Time Buttons

```
Private Sub StartButton_Click()

    If StartButton.Caption = "Start Timer" Then
        AlarmCtl1.StartTimer
        StartButton.Caption = "Stop Timer"
    Else
        StartButton.Caption = "Start Timer"
        AlarmCtl1.StopTimer
    End If

End Sub

Private Sub AlarmButton_Click()
    If AlarmCtl1.CountDown Then
        MsgBox "The alarm is ticking..."
    Else
        MsgBox "The alarm will go off at " & AlarmCtl1.AlarmTime
    End If
End Sub
```

Open the test project and set the AlarmTime property a minute or so ahead of your system's time (the current time displayed in the lower right corner of the task bar), and set the CountDown property to True. The Alarm control starts counting downward the difference between the current time and the alarm time. When this difference reaches zero, it informs you that time's up in a message box.

Set the AlarmTime property again to a value ahead of the current time, set the CountDown property to True, and run the application. This time the control counts seconds until time comes for the alarm to go off. If you click on the Alarm Time button, you will see when the alarm is scheduled to go off. When counting down, you know at any moment how much time is left for the alarm to run. The Show Alarm Time button displays the following message:

```
"The alarm is ticking…"
```

NOTE   The Alarm control won't work properly if the AlarmTime is not within the same half-day interval as the current time. If the current time is 9 PM and you set the alarm for 2 AM, the control reports that the alarm has already gone off. The code that would take into consideration changes in date as well is more complicated, and it wouldn't offer any insight into how ActiveX controls work. It's plain VB code that could appear in a standalone application. With some extra programming, you can design an Alarm control that works for any AlarmTime, including a date. If you are not accustomed to the ActiveX control development methodology yet, you can write a standard VB application and then copy the code into the ActiveX control's code.

This example concludes our discussion of ActiveX control design. To summarize, ActiveX controls combine design elements from both standard VB applications and ActiveX component design. Their properties, methods, and events are handled just their counterparts in ActiveX components.

- Properties are private variables, which can be read or set through Property procedures.

- Methods are public subroutines.

- Events can be raised from anywhere in an ActiveX control with the RaiseEvent method.

The control's visible interface is drawn on a UserControl object, which is quite similar to a Form. It supports nearly all of a Form's properties and methods, including the Drawing methods. There are no means for loading and unloading UserControls as there are for Forms, but you can make a control visible or invisible at run time from within your code.

The code of the control resides in key events of the control, such as the Paint and Resize events, and is no different from the code you would use to develop a standalone application with similar functionality.

The integration of an ActiveX control in the development environment is the responsibility of Visual Basic. The properties you attach to the control are automatically displayed in the Properties window, and the syntax of its methods is displayed as you type code (they are incorporated into the QuickInfo feature of the Visual Basic IDE). In short, the development of an ActiveX control is strikingly similar to the development of a standard VB application. The result is a new animal that can live in various environments, including Web pages, as you'll see in the last part of this book.

PART IV

From the Desktop to the Web

Visual Basic and the Web

- Hypertext Markup Language

- ActiveX Control Pad

- Internet Explorer ActiveX controls

- Custom ActiveX controls

- ActiveX documents

15

If there is one technology that caught up literally overnight and has affected more users than any other, it is the Web. The World Wide Web is the set of all Web sites and the documents they can provide to clients. The computers that host Web sites are called *servers*; their service is to provide the documents that clients request. *Clients* are the seemingly endless number of personal computers connected to the Internet. To exploit the Web, all you need is a browser, such as Internet Explorer 3, that can request documents and render them on the client computer.

I assume that most of you are familiar with the Web. This chapter is a compendium of information about how to apply some of the knowledge you acquired in previous chapters to the Web. To use a term that has become quite popular lately, *leverage* your knowledge of Visual Basic by applying it to the Web. To do so, you need a basic understanding of HTML (Hypertext Markup Language), the language used to build Web documents, and the structure of a Web document.

The first section of this chapter briefly discusses HTML tags and shows you how to use HTML to build simple hyperlinked documents. We will look at how to activate Web pages by scripting them with VBScript and adding ActiveX controls to them. In short, you will learn how to turn a static Web page into a highly interactive application. We will also build Web pages that use the custom ActiveX controls we developed in the last chapter.

The second half of this chapter introduces you to a powerful technique for publishing your Visual Basic applications on the Web. To use this technique, you don't even need to know anything about HTML. However, an understanding of the basic concepts of the Web and how browsers work and interact with servers is essential in developing Visual Basic applications for the Web. Without further delay, let's start with a quick introduction to HTML. If you are already familiar with the language, you can safely skip the first part of this chapter.

The Web Also Means Intranets

The information in this chapter isn't addressed only to those of you who are going to publish documents on the Internet. You will also find it useful in building *intranet* applications.

The Web caught on so rapidly because it's really simple to use. One has to wonder why this hypertext model hasn't caught on with personal computers too. The answer is, of course, that computers are much more general tools, but for many people, using a computer means using the Web.

If Web technology simplified a chaotic structure such as the Internet, why not also use it on local networks? Indeed, many local area networks are designed as miniature Internets. An intranet, or corporate Internet, is a local area network that uses Internet technology. On an intranet, you can exploit the Web model to simplify operations, without the security issues you face on the Internet or the limitations imposed by connecting computers with modems.

An HTML Primer

HTML is the language you must use to prepare documents for online publication. HTML documents are also called *Web documents*, and each HTML document is known as a *Web page*. A page is what you see in your browser at any time. Each *Web site*, whether on the Internet or on an intranet, is composed of multiple pages, and you can switch among them by following *hyperlinks* (you'll see more on hyperlinks shortly). The collection of HTML pages out there makes up the *World Wide Web*.

A Web page is basically a text file that contains the text to be displayed and references to elements such as images, sounds, and, of course, hyperlinks to other documents. You can create HTML pages with a text editor such as Notepad or with a WYSIWYG application such as Microsoft FrontPage. In either case, the result is a plain text file that computers can easily exchange. The *browser* displays this text file on the client computer.

Each page is stored on a computer, which acts as a *server*: It provides the page to any computer that requests it. Each server computer has an address that is something like the following:

```
http://www.mycomputer.com
```

The first portion, http, is the protocol used in accessing the server, and www .mycomputer.com is the name of the server on the Internet. All computers on the Internet have a unique numeric address, such as 193.22.103.18. This numeric address is known as the IP (Internet Protocol) address, which is more difficult for us humans to remember than names. Mnemonic names are looked up in tables and translated into IP addresses, which computers use to communicate with one another.

To post an HTML document on a computer so that viewers can access and display it with their browsers, the computer that hosts the document must run a special application called the Web server. The *Web server* acknowledges requests made by other computers, the client computers, and supplies the requested document. The browser, which is the application running on the client computer, gets the document and displays it on the screen.

URLs and Hyperlinks

The key element in a Web page is a *hyperlink*, a special instruction embedded in the text that causes the browser to load another page. To connect to another computer and request a document, the hyperlink must contain the name of the computer that hosts the document and the name of the document. Each computer on the Internet has a unique name, and each document on a computer has a unique name. Thus, each document on the World Wide Web has a unique address, which is called a *URL* (Uniform Resource Locator). The URL for a Web document is something like the following:

```
http://www.someserver.com/docName.htm
```

In this case, `http` is the protocol, which is followed by the name of the server computer, and finally the document's name. Here, `docName.htm` is an HTML file, but it could be an image file, a sound file, a ZIP file, or even (as you will learn in this chapter) the name of a Visual Basic application that can be downloaded and executed on the client computer. (It's not exactly a VB application. It's a so-called ActiveX document, but it's darn close to a VB application, and every application you have developed so far can be converted to an ActiveX document and posted on the Internet.)

TIP You will notice that some URLs end in `htm` and some end in `html`. They are identical, with the exception that the operating system on which the pages with the extension `htm` were developed doesn't support long file names or the author chose to follow the DOS file-naming conventions. The sample pages you'll find on the CD have the extension `htm`, which is a limitation imposed by the CD production process and has nothing to do with the system on which they were developed.

Every piece of information on the World Wide Web has a unique address and can be accessed via its URL. What the browser does depends on the nature of the item. If it's a Web page or an image, the browser displays it. If it's a sound file, the browser plays it back. Some browsers (such as Internet Explorer 3) can process many types of documents. Others can't. When a browser runs into a document it can't handle, it asks whether the user wants to download and save the file on disk or open it with an application that the user specifies.

HTML Tags

No matter what you are going to do on the Web, some basic understanding of HTML is required. HTML is a simple language and certainly easy to learn and use for a VB programmer. The small part of HTML presented here is all you need to build functional, even fancy Web pages. You need to be able to build basic HTML documents in which you can insert ActiveX controls and activate them. If you didn't understand this last statement, keep reading. The topic of this chapter is how to activate your Web pages with ActiveX technology.

HTML commands are called *tags,* and they always appear in pairs of angle brackets. The <HTML> tag denotes the beginning of an HTML document. HTML tags also have a scope, which is marked with the same tag, prefixed with a forward slash. The </HTML> tag denotes the end of the document. In the text, I will frequently refer to them as "tag" and "matching tag."

> **NOTE**
>
> You can enter a tag as <HTML>, <Html>, or <html>. Capitalization doesn't matter; all produce the same effect. Good programming practice, however, is to use one form consistently so that your code is easy to read and understand. HTML tags are capitalized in this chapter to make them stand out in the listings.

The <B> and </B> tags are another example of matching tags. The <B> tag turns on the bold attribute of the text, and the </B> tag turns it off. Everything that appears between these two tags is displayed in bold.

The basic structure of an HTML document is as follows:

```
<HTML>
    <HEAD>
        <TITLE>
            Document title
```

```
        </TITLE>
    </HEAD>
    <BODY>
        The document's body: text, images, sounds, and HTML commands
    </BODY>
</HTML>
```

If you enter these lines in a text file, save it as Test.htm, and then double-click on its icon, Internet Explorer starts and displays the file as shown in Figure 15.1.

FIGURE 15.1

The minimum HTML
document

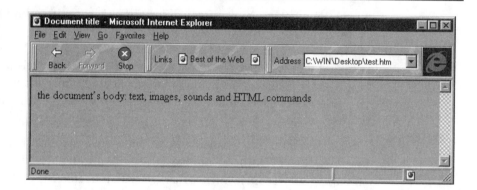

Table 15.1 lists and describes the basic HTML tags. (For Internet Explorer, all these tags are optional, but it's a good idea to write clean, easy-to-understand HTML code that will work with as many browsers as possible.)

TABLE 15.1 The Basic HTML Tags

TAG	DESCRIPTION
HTML	Delimits the entire HTML document. For most browsers, this tag is optional.
HEAD	Contains the initial document information, such as its title, administration tags, and scripts.
TITLE	The page's title. It doesn't appear anywhere in the browser's window, but it's displayed in the browser's title bar.
BODY	Delimits the document's body, which is the largest part of the document. All the text you want to display, formatted with the appropriate HTML tags, appears between the <BODY> and the matching </BODY> tags.

How to Test HTML Tags

Although there are WYSIWYG tools for creating HTML documents, a simple editor such as Notepad is all you need to experiment with the few tags discussed in this chapter. Create a simple text file with the basic HTML document structure listed above. Save the file as Test.htm (use any name, but the extension must be htm). When you save this file for the first time, be sure to select All Files in the Save As Type field of the Save As dialog box. If you don't change the default extension, the TXT extension is appended, and you'll end up with a file named test.htm.txt.

After saving the document, switch to Internet Explorer, and open the document by choosing File ➢ Open. From this point on, you can move back and forth between the text editor and the browser. You can edit the HTML file, save it, switch to the Internet Explorer window, and press F5 to load the updated version of the file, as shown below:

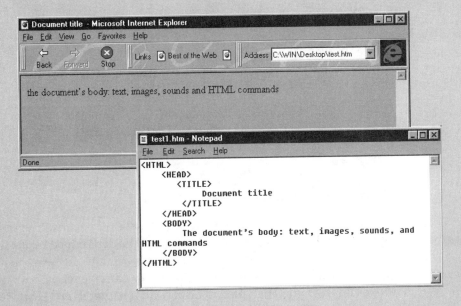

The following are the really necessary tags for creating no-frills HTML documents, grouped by category.

Headers

Headers separate sections of a document. Like documents prepared with a word processor, HTML documents can have headers, which are inserted with the <H*n*> tag. There are six levels of headers, starting with <H1> (the largest) and ending with <H6> (the smallest). To place a level 1 header at the top of the document use the tag <H1>:

```
<H1>Welcome to Our Fabulous Site</H1>
```

A related tag is the <HR> tag, which displays a horizontal rule and is frequently used to separate sections of a document. The document in Figure 15.2, which demonstrates the HTML tags discussed so far, was produced with the following HTML file:

```
<HTML>
    <HEAD>
        <TITLE>
            Document title
        </TITLE>
    </HEAD>
    <BODY>
        <H1>Sample HTML Document</H1>
        <HR>
        <H3>The document's body may contain:</H4>
        <H4>Text, images, sounds and HTML commands</H4>
    </BODY>
</HTML>
```

Paragraph Formatting

HTML won't break lines into paragraphs whenever you insert a carriage return in the text file. The formatting of the paragraphs is determined by the font on the client computer and the size of the browser's window. To force a new paragraph, you must explicitly tell the browser to insert a carriage return with the <P> tag. For example, if you attempted to display this chapter as an HTML document, everything up to the previous line, where the <P> tag appears, is formatted as a single paragraph (see Figure 15.3).

FIGURE 15.2

FIGURE 15.2

A simple HTML document with headers and a rule

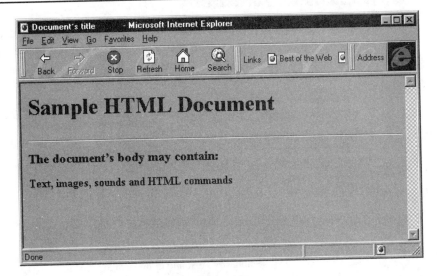

FIGURE 15.3

The first paragraph of this section displayed as an HTML document

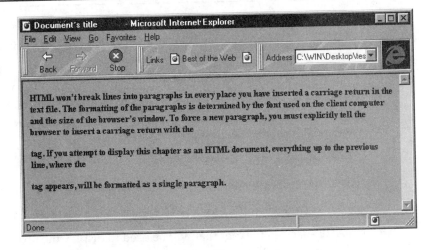

The <P> tag also causes the browser to insert additional vertical space. To format paragraphs without the additional vertical space, use the <BR> tag.

Character Formatting

HTML provides a number of tags for formatting words and characters. Table 15.2 shows the basic character-formatting tags, and following the table is a description of the FONT tag and its arguments.

TABLE 15.2 The Basic HTML Character-Formatting Tags

TAG	WHAT IT DOES
<B>	Turns on the bold attribute.
<I>	Turns on the italic attribute.
<TT>	Turns on the typewriter attribute and is used frequently to display computer code.
<EM>	Emphasizes text and is identical to the I tag.
<CODE>	Displays text in a monospaced font and is used for computer listings.

<FONT> Specifies the name, size, and color of the font to be used. The <FONT> tag takes one or more of the following arguments:

SIZE specifies the size of the text in a relative manner. The value of the SIZE argument is not expressed in points, pixels, or any other absolute unit. Instead, it's a number between 1 (the smallest) and 7 (the largest). The following tag displays the text in the smallest possible size:

```
<FONT SIZE=1>tiny type</FONT>
```

The following tag displays text in the largest possible size:

```
<FONT SIZE=7>HUGE TYPE</FONT>
```

FACE specifies the font that will be used to display the text. If the specified font does not exist on the client computer, the browser substitutes a similar font. The following tag displays the text between FONT and its matching tag in the Comic Sans MS typeface:

```
<FONT FACE = "Comic Sans MS"> Some text </FONT>
```

You can also specify multiple typefaces. The browser uses the one specified first. If it's not available, it tries the next one, and so on, as shown in the following:

```
<FONT FACE = "Comic Sans MS, Arial"> Some text </FONT>
```

If the Comic Sans MS typeface is missing on the client computer, the browser displays the text in Arial (which should not be missing on any Windows machine).

TIP

If you plan to develop Web pages, visit the Microsoft Web site (http://www.microsoft.com/typography) and download a number of new fonts designed by Microsoft specifically for use on the Web.

COLOR specifies the color of the text. You specify colors as hexadecimal numbers (#FF00FF) or by name. Internet Explorer recognizes the following color names:

Black	White
Green	Maroon
Olive	Navy
Purple	Gray
Red	Yellow
Blue	Teal
Lime	Aqua
Fuchsia	Silver

The following displays the text in red:

```
<FONT COLOR=Red>This is red text</FONT>
<FONT COLOR=#FF0000> This is red text</FONT>
```

You can also combine multiple arguments in a single <FONT> tag, as follows:

```
<FONT FACE="Arial, Sans" SIZE=5 COLOR=Red>
```

Hyperlinks

The tag that makes HTML documents come alive is the <A> tag, which inserts hyperlinks in a document. A hyperlink is text that appears in a different color from the rest of the text; when the mouse pointer is over a hyperlink, the pointer turns into a finger (some browsers may display a different pointer, but it will be clear that the text under the pointer is a hyperlink). When you click the mouse button over a hyperlink, the browser requests and displays another document, which could be on the same or another server.

The <A> tag specifies one or more words that will be highlighted as hyperlinks. In addition, you must specify the URL of the hyperlink's destination. For example, the URL of the Sybex home page is:

```
http://www.sybex.com
```

The URL to jump to is indicated with the HREF keyword within the <A> tag. To display the string "Visit the SYBEX home page" and to use the word *SYBEX* as the hyperlink, you must enter the following in your document:

```
Visit the <A HREF="http://www.sybex.com">SYBEX</A> home page
```

This inserts a hyperlink in the document, and each time the user clicks on the SYBEX hyperlink, the browser displays the main page at the specified URL. Notice that you don't specify a document name in the hyperlink. The server supplies the default page, which is known as the *home page*. The home page is usually the entry to a specific site and contains hyperlinks to other pages making up the site.

Hyperlinks need not specify a document on another computer. Most hyperlinks on a typical page jump to other documents that reside on the same server. These hyperlinks usually contain a relative reference to another document on the same server. For example, to specify a hyperlink to the document Images.htm that resides in the same folder as the current page, use the following tag:

```
Click <A HREF=".\Images.htm">here</A> to view the images.
```

If the Images.htm file resides in the folder Bitmaps under the current folder, you use the following statement:

```
Click <A HREF="..\Bitmaps\Images.htm">here</A> to view the images.
```

Frames

The pages you've seen thus far occupy the entire browser window. You can, however, display multiple documents on a page by using frames. You usually create frames with the <FRAMESET> tag. This approach requires some overhead, so I'll describe how to create floating frames using the IFRAME tag. You can place a floating frame, such as an image anywhere on the page, and a page can have multiple floating frames. The user can't resize floating frames, but they are quite adequate for the purposes of this chapter and are easier to implement than frames created with the <FRAMESET> tag.

To insert a floating frame on a page, use the following tag:

```
<IFRAME SRC=url WIDTH=xxx HEIGHT=yyy>
```

The *url* variable is the URL of the document to be displayed on the frame, and *xxx* and *yyy* are the frame's dimensions. To place a floating frame in the middle of a document and display the Sybex home page on it, enter the following lines in an HTML file and then open the file with Internet Explorer:

```
<CENTER>
<H1>Floating Frame Example</H1><BR>
<IFRAME SRC="http://www.sybex.com" WIDTH=500 HEIGHT=300>
</CENTER>
```

The output of this document is shown in Figure 15.4. (The CENTER tag centers on the page everything between the <CENTER> and matching </CENTER> tags.)

FIGURE 15.4

A floating frame displaying the Sybex home page

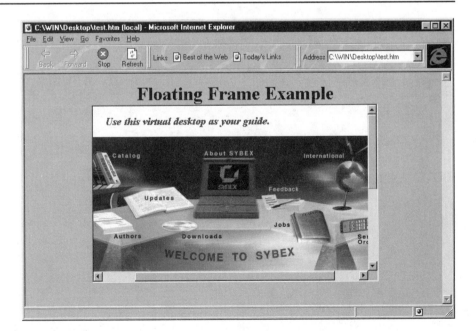

Scripting an HTML Page

The HTML tags of the last section are sufficient for displaying documents that contain images, sounds, and other multimedia elements and for arranging elements on the page in (almost) any way you like, but the documents you can create with these HTML tags are static. There is little that HTML can do to make a page dynamic. A dynamic page changes with time by updating its contents. HTML has been extended with tags that support dynamic content, but HTML started as a document description language.

Scripting allows you to take control of the contents of a page and manipulate them with your program. The first two scripting languages were JavaScript and VBScript. JavaScript is based on SUN's Java, and VBScript is based on Microsoft's Visual Basic. As you can guess, we are going to explore VBScript in this book.

> **TIP**
>
> Shortly before this book was completed, Microsoft announced VBScript 2.0. You can download it freely from `http://www.microsoft.com/vbscript`. The examples in this chapter were tested with this version of VBScript and should work.

A script is a short program that manipulates the elements of a page and is inserted in an HTML document with the <SCRIPT> and </SCRIPT> tags. Typically, you place the SCRIPT portion of a document in the HEAD section. Here's a simple script that sets the page's background color and displays a welcome message:

```
<HTML>
<HEAD>
<TITLE>VBScript Demo</TITLE>
<SCRIPT Language = VBS>
Document.fgColor="hFF0000"
Document.bgColor="h00FFFF"
MsgBox "Welcome to the VBScript Demo Page"
</SCRIPT>
</HEAD>
<BODY>
<H1>VBScript Demo</H1>
</BODY>
</HTML>
```

The *Document* entry is an object that represents the document displayed in the browser's window, and you can access the various properties of the document through the Document object. The properties fgColor and bgColor set (or read) the values of the document's foreground and background colors. The MsgBox() function isn't new to you. There are many similarities between Visual Basic and VBScript, and we need not look at the features of VBScript in detail.

A scripting language such as VBScript made it possible for Web authors to develop dynamic content for their Web pages. But that isn't all. In less than a year after the introduction of VBScript, Microsoft decided to "activate" Web pages; hence, the term *ActiveX*. Since you have the means to program a Web page, why not add programmable objects on it at will? The programmable objects are nothing less than ActiveX controls. If there were a way to place ActiveX controls on a page, you could access their methods and properties from within VBScript and thereby create an active page. An active page is similar to a small application that runs within Internet Explorer.

The next step was to develop ActiveX controls that could be used on Web pages. And Microsoft released a number of those. Now, with Visual Basic 5, you can create your own ActiveX controls for use on Web pages. Later in this chapter, we will test the controls we developed in previous chapters. We will also build one more ActiveX control and test it on a Web page. Finally, we'll look at how you can use some of the ActiveX controls designed for Web pages both in Visual Basic applications and on Web pages.

Inserting an ActiveX Control on a Web Page

The <OBJECT> tag delimits an ActiveX control placed on a Web page. To place an ActiveX control on a Web page, though, you must know its Class ID. This is the number used to register the ActiveX control in the Registry, and it's long number and impossible to remember. Here's the <OBJECT> tag for inserting a command button on a Web page:

```
<OBJECT ID="CommandButton1" WIDTH=96 HEIGHT=32
  CLASSID="CLSID:D7053240-CE69-11CD-A777-00DD01143C57">
    <PARAM NAME="Size" VALUE="2540;846">
    <PARAM NAME="FontCharSet" VALUE="0">
    <PARAM NAME="FontPitchAndFamily" VALUE="2">
    <PARAM NAME="ParagraphAlign" VALUE="3">
    <PARAM NAME="FontWeight" VALUE="0">
</OBJECT>
```

This <OBJECT> tag inserts a command button control at the current location in the HTML document. The control's name is CommandButton1, and you use this name to access the various properties of the control from within the script. For example, you can set the control's caption with the following statement:

```
CommandButton1.Caption = "Click Me!"
```

To program the control to react to the Click event, you must supply the CommandButton1_Click() subroutine, as usual.

The definition of the control is cumbersome. There should be a simpler way to place ActiveX controls on a Web page, an environment similar to the Visual Basic IDE. This environment exists, already, and is similar to the Visual Basic design window. It's called the ActiveX Control Pad, and you can download it from Microsoft's Web site:

```
http://www.microsoft.com/workshop/author/cpad
```

In the next section, we'll look at the ActiveX Control Pad and how to use it to create Layouts and active pages.

The ActiveX Control Pad

After you download and install the ActiveX Control Pad, you can use it to create active Web pages. The ActiveX Control Pad, shown in Figure 15.5, has the following four components:

- A *Text Editor* for editing HTML documents. It's a simple editor that doesn't provide any editing functions for HTML documents.

- An *Object Editor* for visually editing the ActiveX controls you place on the Web page. The Object Editor has a Visual Object Editor, which you can use to change the size of an object, and a Properties window in which you can set the properties of the object.

- An *HTML Layout Editor*, with which you can create HTML Layouts. HTML Layouts are similar to Visual Basic forms and are designed with visual tools similar to the design tools of Visual Basic.

- A *Script Wizard* that automates the creation and editing of scripts.

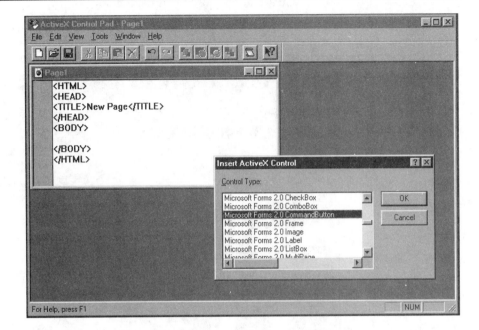

FIGURE 15.5

The ActiveX Control Pad application

The Text Editor

When you start the ActiveX Control Pad, you see the Text Editor with the skeleton of an HTML document already in it, as shown in Figure 15.5 in the previous section. Here you can enter HTML commands and create an HTML page.

The ActiveX Control Pad also inserts Object definitions for you. To place a command button on the HTML document, follow these steps:

1. Choose Edit ➤ Insert ActiveX Control to open the Insert ActiveX Control window, shown in Figure 15.5.

2. Select Microsoft Forms 2.0 CommandButton and click on OK to open the Edit ActiveX Control window and the Properties window, as shown in Figure 15.6.

3. Use the Properties window to set the control's properties. As you do so, the image of the command button in the Edit ActiveX Control window is updated.

4. When you are done, close the Edit ActiveX Control window; the command button's definition appears in the HTML document.

FIGURE 15.6

Editing an ActiveX control with the Control Pad

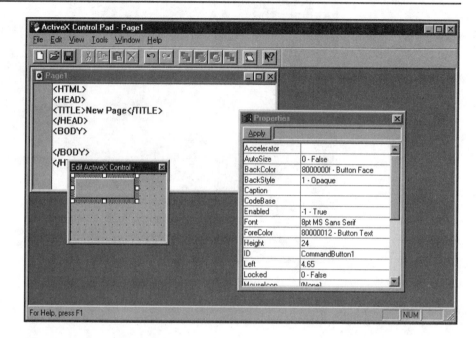

The HTML Layout Editor

Using the HTML Layout Editor, let's create an HTML Layout and see how it can be used from within a Web page. We will build the Dates page (see Figure 15.7), which is in the Example1 folder on the CD.

To build the Dates page, follow these steps:

1. Close the Text Editor window (you don't have to save its contents), and then choose File ➤ Open ➤ New HTML Layout to open the Layout window and the Toolbox window.

The Layout window is the equivalent of a VB Form. Use the tools in the Toolbox to place controls on the Layout and arrange them on it. The Layout will appear on a Web page just as you designed it.

2. To place a command button on the Layout, select its icon in the Toolbox and then draw the button on the Layout. The button will be named Command-Button1.

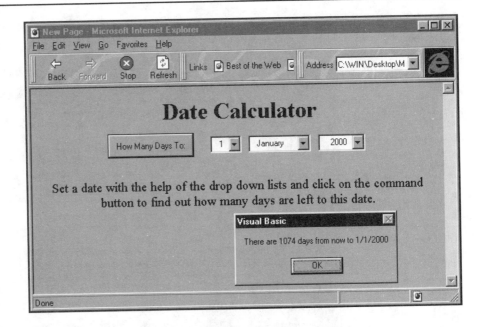

FIGURE 15.7

The Dates Web page demonstrates Web page scripting with VBScript.

3. Right-click on the control and select Properties to display the Properties window. Figure 15.8 shows all three windows.

Now change the dimensions of the control, its caption, and its font.

4. Place three ComboBox controls on the Form, as shown in Figure 15.7, earlier in this chapter. These three controls will hold the numbers 1 through 31 (day numbers), the month names, and the years 1997 through 2003, so size them accordingly.

5. Because the ComboBox control by default doesn't display its first item, set the Text property of the three ComboBox controls to 1, January, and 2000.

6. To arrange the controls on the Layout, use the commands on the Format menu, which is identical to the Format menu of Visual Basic.

You have completed the design of the Layout, which wasn't any more complicated than designing a Form with Visual Basic. You may have noticed that the command button control doesn't have all the properties of a regular Visual Basic command button. This is a new control, developed for the ActiveX Control Pad. Most of the properties of the regular command button are present, however.

FIGURE 15.8

The Toolbox,
Properties, and Layout
windows of the ActiveX
Control Pad

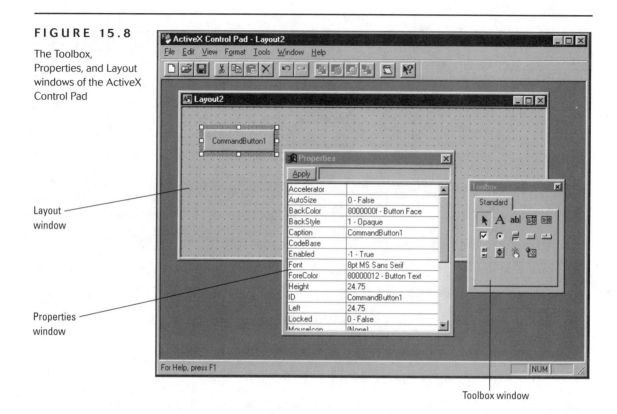

Layout
window

Properties
window

Toolbox window

The Script Wizard

To add the necessary script, right-click somewhere on the Layout, and from the shortcut menu, select Script Wizard to open the Script Wizard window, as shown in Figure 15.9.

The Scripting Wizard has three panes:

- The *Event pane*, in which you select the Control and the event that will be programmed to react to user actions

- The *Action pane*, which contains all the actions that the selected Control can perform or all the properties that can be set

- The *Code pane*, in which the script is displayed

FIGURE 15.9

The Script Wizard
window for the
Dates page

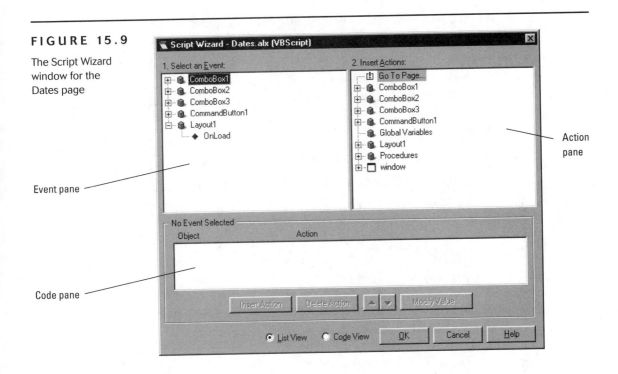

The two Option buttons at the bottom of the window, List View and Code View, determine in which of the two available modes you want to work. List View is the simple mode. In List View mode, you specify the actions to be carried out by the script with point-and-click operations. First, you select a control, and then you select the action to be performed on or by the control. Because this way of developing scripts isn't flexible, we'll focus on the Code View mode. In the Code View mode, you enter the code yourself, as you did with Visual Basic.

NOTE Nonprogrammers may prefer List View mode, but most programmers will find it too simplistic.

In the Event pane, you see the names of the three ComboBox controls, the name of the command button, and the name of the Layout. If you expand these trees, you will see the events that each control can recognize. The Layout control recognizes a single event, onLoad, which takes place when the Layout is loaded.

We are now going to write a script that activates the Dates page. We'll turn this page into a small utility that lets the user specify a date with the help of the ComboBox controls and then find out the number of days between this date and the current date by clicking on the command button. To script the Dates page, follow these steps:

1. Click on the Layout's onLoad event to select it.

2. If the Code View button isn't checked, click on it.

3. In the Code pane, enter the following initialization code:

```
for i=1 to 31
    ComboBox1.AddItem i
next
for i=1997 to 2002
    ComboBox3.AddItem i
next
ComboBox2.Additem "January"
ComboBox2.Additem "February"
ComboBox2.Additem "March"
ComboBox2.Additem "April"
ComboBox2.Additem "May"
ComboBox2.Additem "June"
ComboBox2.Additem "July"
ComboBox2.Additem "August"
ComboBox2.Additem "September"
ComboBox2.Additem "October"
ComboBox2.Additem "November"
ComboBox2.Additem "December"
```

These lines will execute when the Layout is loaded and before it's displayed. They will populate the three ComboBox controls.

4. Expand the CommandButton1 tree and select the Click event. The definition of this event's handler appears at the top of the Code pane.

5. Enter the following lines of VBScript code in the Code pane:

```
ToDate = DateSerial(ComboBox3.Text,
➥ComboBox2.ListIndex+1, ComboBox1.text)
msgbox "There are " & ToDate - Date & " days from now
➥to " & ToDate
```

This is code that you could use in a Visual Basic application. VBScript differs from Visual Basic only in that it doesn't support as many functions and statements.

6. Click on OK, and save the Layout in a new folder. Later, we will save the HTML document that will host the Layout in the same folder.

To display HTML Layouts in Internet Explorer, you must first place them on an HTML document. Let's create an HTML document to host the Layout. Follow these steps:

1. Close all windows in the ActiveX Control Pad, and choose File ➤ New HTML to display the skeleton of an HTML document in the Text Editor's window.

2. Choose Edit ➤ Insert HTML Layout.

3. In the Open dialog box, select the Dates.alx file. The Script Wizard inserts the following object definition in the document's body:

```
<OBJECT CLASSID="CLSID:812AE312-8B8E-11CF-93C8-00AA00C08FDF"
ID="Dates_alx" STYLE="LEFT:0;TOP:0">
<PARAM NAME="ALXPATH" REF VALUE="file:C:\WIN\Desktop\Mastering
VB5\chapter15\Example1\Dates.alx">
➥</OBJECT>
```

Notice that the full path name of the ALX file is inserted. It's always a good idea to make this a relative reference by removing the path name. If you do so, when you move the folder with the project to another location (or to a CD), the references will still work.

4. Now place the title of the page above the layout and the instructions below it, as shown in Figure 15.7, earlier in this chapter.

Code 15.1: The Complete HTML Code of the Dates.htm Document

```
<HTML>
<HEAD>
<TITLE>New Page</TITLE>
</HEAD>
<BODY>
<CENTER>
<H1>Date Calculator</H1>
<BR>

<OBJECT CLASSID="CLSID:812AE312-8B8E-11CF-93C8-00AA00C08FDF"
ID="Dates_alx" STYLE="LEFT:0;TOP:0">
```

```
<PARAM NAME="ALXPATH" REF VALUE="file:Dates.alx">
 </OBJECT>
<FONT SIZE=4>
Set a date with the help of the drop down lists and click on the
 command button to find out how many days are left to this date.
</FONT>
</CENTER>
</BODY>
</HTML>
```

5. Save the HTML file as Dates.htm in the same folder as the Dates Layout file.

Now you are ready to test the project. Start Internet Explorer, open the Dates .htm file, and check out your first Layout. It works just like a Visual Basic application, only it runs from within Internet Explorer. What you have in front of you is an active page—a page that interacts with the user in a way far more complicated than an HTML page with hyperlinks. And what makes it possible are the ActiveX controls and the script.

> **NOTE**
> In a way, VBScript is a language for developing applications that will run in Internet Explorer. For the first time, you can program Web pages that behave like applications. Best of all, VBScript is no different from Visual Basic. It supports a subset of Visual Basic's functions, it manipulates the properties of the various controls, and it's based on the same programming model—event-driven programming.

Internet Explorer ActiveX Controls

In this section, we will look at a few ActiveX controls that Microsoft designed specifically for HTML Layouts. We will even use one of them in a Visual Basic application to see how you can exploit the new controls to build Desktop applications.

The Marquee Control

The Marquee scrolls an HTML document. It can display the document in the same way that a browser displays a document, including the document's images, animation, and sounds. The only browser function that the Marquee control can't perform is to activate hyperlinks. Once the document is downloaded and displayed in the Marquee control, the control can scroll the document contents in all directions, even diagonally. Our Visual Basic application uses the Marquee control to scroll two HTML pages (the Sybex and Microsoft home pages). The user can alternate between them by right-clicking on the Marquee control.

Figure 15.10 shows the Marquee application as it scrolls the Sybex home page. You can click on the Pause button to temporarily stop the scrolling and click on it again to resume the scrolling. Open the Marquee application (you will find it in this chapter's folder on the CD) and run it to see how it works. Be sure you are connected to the Internet before opening the application.

FIGURE 15.10

The AXMarquee application uses the ActiveX Marquee control to scroll any HTML document, local or remote.

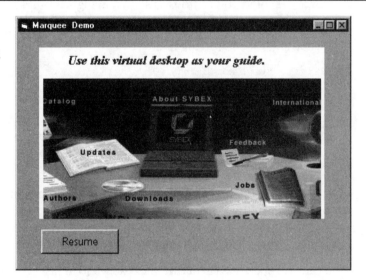

The control's properties and methods are described next, but for the purposes of this example, all you need to know are the following:

- The ScrollDelay property, which specifies how frequently the control's contents will be scrolled

- The ScrollPixelsX and ScrollPixelsY properties, which specify by how much the contents of the Marquee will be scrolled at a time

- The Pause and Resume methods, which obviously pause and resume the scrolling

The document displayed in a Marquee control is moved by ScrollPixelsX and ScrollPixelsY pixels in the two directions every ScrollDelay milliseconds. The Zoom property specifies the zooming factor.

To design the application, follow these steps:

1. Create a new project.

2. To add the Marquee control to the Toolbox, right-click on the Toolbox.

3. In the Components window, select Marquee Control Library, and click on OK.

4. In the Toolbox, select the new tool icon with the mouse and draw a large Marquee on the Form.

5. Place the command buttons as shown in Figure 15.10.

6. Double-click on the Form to open the Code window, and in the Forms' Load event, enter the following lines:

```
Private Sub Form_Load()
    Marquee1.PageFlippingOn = 1
    Marquee1.ScrollPixelsX = 0
    Marquee1.ScrollPixelsY = -5
    Marquee1.insertURL 0, "http://www.microsoft.com"
    Marquee1.insertURL 1, "http://www.sybex.com"
End Sub
```

This Marquee displays two URLs—the Sybex and Microsoft home pages—and alternates between them. Each URL is inserted in a list, with the insertURL method. The first argument of the insertURL method is the order of the URL in the list, after which the new URL is inserted.

You can also specify local HTML files, which load faster. To specify a local file, replace the protocol name with the keyword file, as follows:

```
Marquee1.insertURL 0, "file://c:/windows/desktop/HTMLDoc1.htm"
Marquee1.insertURL 1, "file://c:/windows/desktop/HTMLDoc2.htm"
```

The PageFlippingOn property is set to 1 to allow the user to select to alternate between the two URLs with a click of the right mouse button. Finally, the Scroll-PixelsX and ScrollPixelsY properties are set so that the Marquee scrolls upward.

7. Next, enter the following lines in the Pause command button's Click event:

```
Private Sub PauseButton_Click()
If PauseButton.Caption = "Pause" Then
```

```
        Marquee1.Pause
        PauseButton.Caption = "Resume"
    Else
        Marquee1.Resume
        PauseButton.Caption = "Pause"
    End If

    End Sub
```

This button calls the Pause and Resume methods to pause and resume the scrolling of the document.

The Properties of the Marquee Control

The following paragraphs explain the properties of the Marquee control. Some don't work as expected. All the variations I was able to discover by experimenting with this control are mentioned here.

ScrollStyleX, ScrollStyleY   These properties set the horizontal and vertical scroll style, and their valid values are the strings "Bounce" and "Circular" (default). The Bounce value doesn't work with Internet Explorer or with Visual Basic 5.

ScrollDelay   This property sets the time between each movement of the marquee window's contents in milliseconds. The default value is 100.

LoopsX, LoopsY   If ScrollStyleX is Circular, these properties set the number of times the image scrolls horizontally or vertically. If ScrollStyleX is Bounce, these properties set the number of times the image bounces. The default value is -1, which means the scrolling or bounce never stops.

ScrollPixelsX, ScrollPixelsY   These properties set the number of pixels by which the window's contents move horizontally or vertically every ScrollDelay milliseconds.

szURL   This property specifies the URL of the document to appear in the control. This property doesn't show in the Properties window and can only be set through your code. In the AXMarquee example, I used the insertURL method to insert multiple URLs in a queue, but if you want to display a single HTML document, specify its URL with this property. Visual Basic doesn't recognize the szURL property, but the ActiveX Control Pad does.

DrawImmediately　This property determines whether the document displays progressively. To display the document progressively, set this property to 1, which is the default. This is not a Boolean value; you can't use the True/False values.

Whitespace　This property sets the space between multiple documents and/or tiled images. The default value is zero.

PageFlippingOn　This property determines whether the marquee flips between multiple URLs (instead of scrolling the same document continuously). To switch to another URL, the user right-clicks on the control. You must place the multiple URLs in a list using the insertURL method.

Zoom　This property sets a zooming factor for the current document; the default value is 100 (100%).

WidthOfPage　This property sets the width, in pixels, used to format the text of the URL. The default value is 640.

The Methods of the Marquee Control

The Marquee control's methods let you handle the URLs of the documents displayed on the control. Basically, you can add and remove URLs of documents to be scrolled. You can also stop and resume the scrolling.

Pause　This method stops the scrolling of the marquee.

Resume　This method restarts the scrolling of the paused marquee.

The following methods manipulate the list of URLs that is displayed on the control. To switch to the next URL, the user right-clicks on the control.

insertURL(URLtoInsertAfter, url)　This method inserts a new URL after the existing URL at the position URLtoInsertAfter, which must be a numeric value.

deleteURL(URLtoDelete)　This method deletes the URL at the location URLtoDelete, which must be a numeric value.

queryURL(URLtoGet, strURL) This method gets the URL at location URLtoGet and returns it in strURL argument. The strURL argument must be declared as string.

queryURLCount(urlCount) This method returns the number of URLs in the list in the urlCount argument.

The Events of the Marquee Control

The events of the Marquee control let you handle the succession of multiple URLs by letting your code know when a URL has reached the end of the window, when it's about to bounce, and so on.

OnStartOfImage This event is triggered just before the URL to be scrolled appears in the Marquee window.

OnEndOfImage(HorizontalOrVertical) This event is triggered when the document has been completely scrolled. For example, you can use it to change the contents of another control after the image has stopped moving. The last argument indicates which scrolling came to an end (it's "H" for horizontal and "V" for vertical).

OnBounce(sideBounced) This event is triggered only in Bounce mode, and the image being scrolled bounces off a side. The sideBounced argument returns the side it bounces off ("L" for left, "R" for right, "T" for top, and "B" for bottom).

OnScroll(HorizontalOrVertical) This event is triggered each time the control is about to scroll the URL. The HorizontalOrVertical argument indicates whether the horizontal or vertical scrolling is about to begin again ("H" for horizontal, "V" for vertical).

The HotSpot ActiveX Control

The mouse events supported by the regular ActiveX controls don't include an event that detects when the mouse is moved over a specific area of the document. You can use the MouseMove event to monitor when the pointer is over a specific control, but this means a few lines of code will be executed with each displacement of the mouse, not just when the pointer enters or leaves an area. If you want to find out whether the pointer is over a specific area of an image, the code to be executed from within the MouseMove event becomes complicated.

Some Windows applications seem to react when the mouse enters or leaves a specific area on a page. When the mouse is over a caption or an image, some action takes place—something similar to image maps in the context of the Web. The ActiveX controls we've explored thus far don't generate any events when the mouse enters or leaves their area.

A special ActiveX control, the HotSpot control, monitors the movement of the mouse. The HotSpot control recognizes the MouseEnter and MouseExit events, which occur when the mouse enters and leaves the control. By placing a few lines of VBScript code in these events, you can create dynamic pages whose contents change as the user moves the mouse around. The HotSpot control is installed along with Internet Explorer 3. To use this control in your Visual Basic projects, you must add the component Microsoft ActiveX Layout 1.0 to the project's file. To do so, follow these steps:

1. Choose Project ➢ Components to open the Components dialog box.

2. Check the Microsoft ActiveX Layout 1.0 box.

The HotSpot control is invisible, and you place it over the control(s) whose MouseEnter and MouseExit events you want to monitor. Because the other controls don't recognize these events, you can place a totally invisible HotSpot control on top of them and use the HotSpot control's MouseEnter and MouseExit events to trigger actions when the user moves the pointer over other controls.

Figure 15.11 demonstrates how the HotSpot is used on a Web page. To build this page, I borrowed the image that appears on the Sybex home page and placed HotSpot controls over certain areas of the image (the notebook, the globe, the cellular phone, and the stack of books). Every time the pointer is placed over one of these areas, a different message appears in the Label control at the bottom of the page. When the pointer is on any other part of the image, the string SYBEX is displayed.

The HotSpot page contains an HTML Layout and some text underneath. The Layout contains an Image control, which fills the layout, and a Label control with red background on which the messages are displayed. Four HotSpot controls are on top of the corresponding areas of the image. In Figure 15.11, you can see the handles of the HotSpot control that is over the notebook computer.

FIGURE 15.11

The HotSpot Web page
at design time

The page's script is in the MouseEnter and MouseExit events of the four HotSpot controls.

Code 15.2: The Mouse Events Code for the HotSpot Control

```
Sub BookSpot_MouseEnter()
    Label1.Caption = "Check Out Our Books"
End Sub
Sub BookSpot_MouseExit()
    Label1.Caption = "S Y B E X"
End Sub
```

TIP   The HotSpot application is on the CD, and you can examine the structure of the HTML Layout and the script that drives it.

Using Custom ActiveX Controls on Web Pages

You can use ActiveX Controls for both Desktop and Web applications. This statement is rather brave, though, because the Desktop and the Web have different requirements and it's not always easy to develop controls for both environments. The basic difference in the requirements for the Desktop and the Web is in how the two types of applications are used. Desktop applications can safely assume that all the resources are on the local machine where they are executing. Web applications, on the other hand, are executed on a remote computer, and any additional resources, such as images, sounds, and so on, must be downloaded as needed. Fortunately, most controls you design for the Desktop will also work on Web pages, but don't expect any control you design to work equally well in both environments.

Sometimes, a control will work in one development tool, and not in another. For instance, if you create a plain HTML page and place the Alarm control on it, you can open the page from within Internet Explorer, and it will work fine. If you attempt to use the ActiveX Control Pad to design the page, the control won't work! Obviously, the problem is on the side of the Control Pad. Microsoft will certainly release the tools for uniform development, for both Desktop and Web applications. The striking similarities between the Visual Basic IDE and the ActiveX Control Pad are signs of this approach. But we are still in the early stages of this new technology, and it doesn't quite work as expected.

In the next few sections we are going to see how the custom ActiveX controls we built in the previous chapters can be used on Web pages. Our first attempt will be to place the Alarm control on a Web page. We'll then look at the Gradient control (we'll see why it doesn't work), and we'll build another custom control that reads dates and numbers, based on two of the applications we developed in Chapter 8, *Using Multimedia Elements to Enhance Applications*.

The Alarm Page

Why bother to place an alarm on a Web page? Figure 15.12 shows one reason. This page contains a timer that lets the viewer read a page for 60 seconds. The user can always leave the page by entering another URL in the browser's Address box or by clicking on the Back button. If the user keeps this page open for 60 seconds, however, the script takes him or her to another page automatically.

 An alarm is handy in several situations. For example, you can use an alarm to update a page with literally "live" data, to keep track of time in a game, and so on.

FIGURE 15.12

The Alarm custom control on a Web page

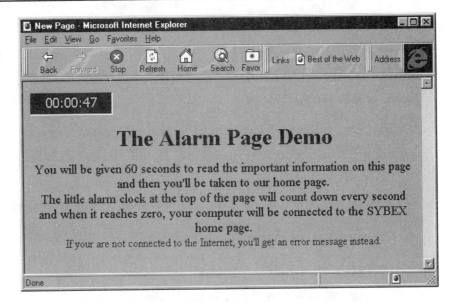

If you are familiar with ActiveX controls for Web development, you know that there is a Timer control you can use on a Web page, but it's not as simple as the Alarm control. For one thing, when you use a Timer control, you must count time from within your program. You must specify the alarm's time-out period in milliseconds, and your script must process timer events many times before it actually decides to do something. Like Visual Basic's Timer control, the ActiveX Timer control has no visible components, and if you want your viewers to know what's happening, you must provide visual feedback from within your script.

To create the page shown in Figure 15.12, follow these steps:

1. Start the ActiveX Control Pad and create a new HTML document.

2. Choose Edit ➢ Insert ActiveX Control to place the Alarm control on the page.

3. In the Insert ActiveX Control dialog box (shown in Figure 15.13), select ALARM.AlarmCtl and click on OK.

FIGURE 15.13

The Insert ActiveX
Control dialog box

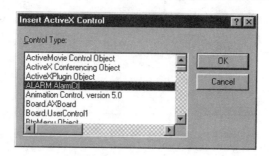

The following definition is inserted in the current document:

```
<OBJECT ID="AlarmCtl1" WIDTH=120 HEIGHT=33
    CLASSID="CLSID:D77B6349-7375-11D0-BB11-444553540000">
        <PARAM NAME="_ExtentX" VALUE="3175">
        <PARAM NAME="_ExtentY" VALUE="873">
        <PARAM NAME="CountDown" VALUE="-1">
    </OBJECT>
```

This definition contains the default values of the control's properties. The Alarm-
Time property doesn't appear in this definition, so you must enter it manually.
You need not specify a value for this property, because you don't know when this
page will be requested and downloaded to a host computer. You must set the
AlarmTime through the page's script each time the page is downloaded.

4. Now type the text you want to appear below the control, along with the
    appropriate HTML formatting commands. Insert the following lines after
    the </OBJECT> tag and before the </BODY> tag:

```
<CENTER>
<H1>The Alarm Page Demo</H1>
<FONT SIZE=4>
You will be given 60 seconds to read the important
    information on this page and then you'll be taken
    to our home page.
<BR>
The little alarm clock at the top of the page will
    count down every second and when it reaches zero,
    your computer will be  connected to the SYBEX home
    page.
<FONT SIZE = 3>
```

```
<BR>
If your are not connected to the Internet, you'll get
    an error message instead.
```

This is the HTML code that produced the page shown in Figure 15.12, earlier in this section. The HTML tags are simple, and even if you are not familiar with HTML, you can understand the code.

Next, we are going to add a script to the page. The script should start the timer as soon as the page is downloaded, and when the alarm times out, it must take the viewer to another page (the Sybex home page, to be exact).

5. Right-click on the page, and from the shortcut menu, choose Script Wizard to open the window shown in Figure 15.14. (The various trees will be collapsed, and the Code pane will initially be empty.)

FIGURE 15.14

The Script Wizard window for the Alarm.htm page

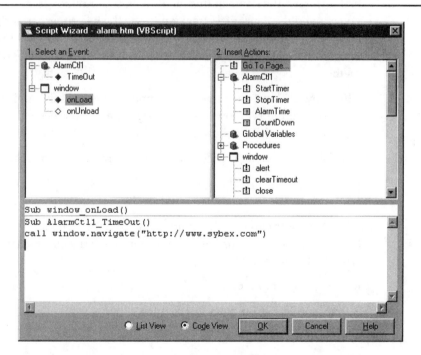

6. Expand the AlarmCtl1 tree to see the events you can program for this control. There is only one event, the TimeOut event (which Script Wizard extracted from the control's OCX file).

7. Now, expand the Window tree in the left pane to see the window's events. The onLoad event takes place when the page is downloaded, and this is where you must start the timer.

8. Click on the onLoad event. The Code pane will be prepared to display the code.

9. Click on the Code View button, and in the Code pane, type the following:

```
Alarmctl1.AlarmTime=time + #00:01.00#
Call AlarmCtl1.StartTimer()
```

The first line sets the control's AlarmTime property to time (which is the time when the page was opened) plus 1 minute. Notice the pound signs around the time specification.

The second line activates the alarm by calling the StartTimer method. If you had forgotten the name of this method, you could look it up in the right pane. If you expand the AlarmCtl1 tree, you'll see the its properties and methods (as shown in Figure 15.14). You can actually make Script Wizard insert the second line in the Code pane for you by double-clicking on the name of the StartTimer method.

10. Now click on the name of the TimeOut event of the AlarmCtl1 control, expand the Window tree in the right pane, and locate the Navigate method (marked with a yellow exclamation point icon).

11. Double-click on the icon, and Script Wizard inserts the following line in the code pane:

```
call window.navigate(url)
```

The *url* argument is a placeholder, and you must replace it with the URL of the location you want the browser to jump to when the alarm times out. Replace *url* with the following:

```
http://www.sybex.com
```

The second line should read as follows:

```
call window.navigate("http://www.sybex.com")
```

12. Click on OK to close the Script Wizard and return to the HTML page. Then save the document. You will find this document in the Alarm folder on the CD.

Code 15.3: The Alarm.htm Page

```
<HTML>
<HEAD>
    <SCRIPT LANGUAGE="VBScript">
<!--
Sub window_onLoad()
AlarmCtl1.AlarmTime = Time + #00:01.00#
call AlarmCtl1.StartTimer()
end sub

Sub AlarmCtl1_TimeOut()
call window.navigate("http://www.sybex.com")
end sub
-->
    </SCRIPT>
<TITLE>New Page</TITLE>
</HEAD>
<BODY>
    <SCRIPT LANGUAGE="VBScript">
<!--
Sub AlarmCtl1_TimeOut()
call window.navigate("http://www.sybex.com")
end sub
-->
    </SCRIPT>
    <OBJECT ID="AlarmCtl1" WIDTH=120 HEIGHT=33
      CLASSID="CLSID:D77B6349-7375-11D0-BB11-444553540000">
        <PARAM NAME="_ExtentX" VALUE="3175">
        <PARAM NAME="_ExtentY" VALUE="873">
        <PARAM NAME="CountDown" VALUE="-1">
    </OBJECT>
<CENTER>
<H1>The Alarm Page Demo</H1>
<FONT SIZE=4>
You will be given 60 seconds to read the important information
on this page and then you'll be taken to our home page.
<BR>
The little alarm clock at the top of the page will count down
 every second and when it reaches zero, your computer will be
 connected to the SYBEX home page.
<FONT SIZE = 3>
<BR>
```

```
If your are not connected to the Internet, you'll get an error
message instead.
</BODY>
</HTML>
```

To see this control in action, follow these steps:

1. Start Internet Explorer.

2. Choose File ➤ Open, and in the dialog box, locate and open the file Alarm.htm.

3. Wait for 60 seconds, and the script loads the Sybex home page.

The Alarm control works nicely in Internet Explorer, and we didn't have to adjust it in any way. It behaves just as it did from within Visual Basic. It even exposed its properties, methods, and events so that the Script Wizard could display them for you in its Events and Actions panes.

The Gradient Control

The Gradient control can't be used as easily on a Web page as it can on the Desktop. Although it's just as easy to insert a Gradient control in an HTML document with the approach described in the last section, you won't be able to place any other controls or text on top of it. And this what the Gradient control is good for: being a backdrop for titles and other design elements. HTML doesn't provide any tags for overlaying its own elements, let alone ActiveX controls.

To overlay a Label control on the gradient, you must use the ActiveX Control Pad to create an HTML Layout. If you place a gradient on an HTML Layout and then attempt to place other controls on top of it (a transparent label is the ideal control), you will see that the Gradient control can't be used as a container. Any controls you place on the Gradient control are covered by it. It is also possible to drag controls placed on the Gradient control outside the control's area, which means that within the environment of the ActiveX Control Pad the Gradient control doesn't act as a container, even though its ControlContainer property is set to True.

Other than that, the Gradient control behaves as expected. You can set its color-related properties from within the Color dialog box (as shown in Figure 15.15), change the direction of the gradient, and so on. You can still use the control as a design element on a page, even change its color from within your application, but you can't place other elements on top of it.

FIGURE 15.15

Designing with the Gradient control from within the ActiveX Control Pad

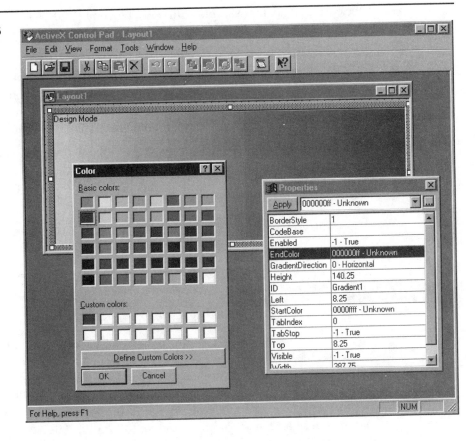

There is, however, something simple you can do about the Gradient control. How about adding a Caption or a Title property and displaying it on the control? The font, size, and style of the text are determined by a Font property, and you can even provide a property for the alignment of the text on the control. The code you will develop must use the Print method, similar to the segment of the existing control that displays the string "Design Mode" on the control. Use the CurrentX and CurrentY properties of the UserControl object to specify the location of the control on the Form.

The Talking Page

The next example is based on the applications we developed in Chapter 8, *Using Multimedia Elements to Enhance Applications*. The ReadDate application reads out the current date, for example, Thursday, November 20, 1997. The ReadNum application reads out numbers; if you pass it the number 345, for example, the program reads out "three hundred forty-five."

In this section, we are going to create a new ActiveX control that combines the functions of the two applications, and then we will use the control to build two demo pages: one that reads out the current date as soon as the page is loaded, and another that reads out numbers entered in a TextBox control.

Let's start by building a new ActiveX control, the ReadCtl control, that can read out dates and numbers. Even if you haven't read Chapter 8, you can easily construct this control by copying all the functions from the ReadDate and ReadNum applications. Follow these steps:

1. Start a new ActiveX Control project, and add a module to it.

NOTE Because this control won't have a visible user interface, all the work will be done by a few functions that we place in a module.

So that the control appears as an icon on the Form at design time, place a small icon on the UserControl object. If you open the ReadCtl project on the CD, you will see that the UserControl object contains the icon of a smiling face. It's size is set to fit exactly around the icon. Figure 15.16 shows the UserControl object on a Form at design time. At run time, the control is invisible.

FIGURE 15.16

The ReadCtl project's test Form with an instance of the ReadCtl control on it

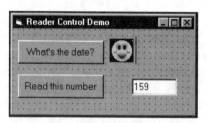

2. Assign a small bitmap to the UserControl's Picture property, and set its InvisibleAtRuntime property to True.

3. Copy the declarations from the Module of the ReadDate or ReadNum application (you will find them in the corresponding folders in the Chapter8 folder) into the project's module:

```
Declare Function mciSendStringA Lib "WinMM" _
        (ByVal mciCommand As String, ByVal returnStr
  As String, _
        ByVal returnLength As Integer, ByVal callBack
  As Integer) As Long

Declare Function mciGetErrorStringA Lib "WinMM" _
        (ByVal error As Long, ByVal buffer
  As String, _
        ByVal length As Integer) As Integer
```

4. Now, copy the functions of both projects and paste them in the project's module. The functions ReadDate() and ReadNumber() must be declared as Public, because they are the control's methods. The functions ReadSingle(), ReadTenths(), and ReadNum() are declared as Private, because they are used internally by the control, and they need not be exposed to other applications.

Test the operation of the new control with the help of the test Form and then create the Reader.ocx control. We can now use it to build the Web page shown in Figure 15.17.

FIGURE 15.17

The Talking Page uses the Reader ActiveX control to read out the current date when it's first loaded.

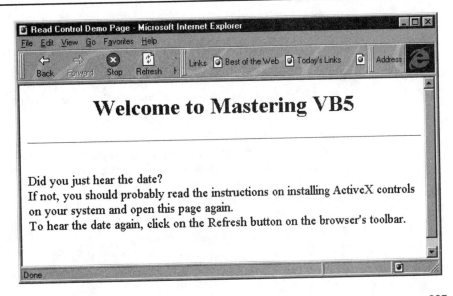

The Talking Page was designed with the ActiveX Control Pad. The ReadCtl control was placed on the page with the Insert ActiveX Control command, and the text and the background were inserted in the Text Editor's window with HTML tags.

Code 15.4: The Talking Page

```
<HTML>
<HEAD>
    <SCRIPT LANGUAGE="VBScript">
<!--
Sub window_onLoad()
call DateCtl1.SayDate()
end sub
-->
    </SCRIPT>
<TITLE>Read Control Demo Page</TITLE>
</HEAD>
<body background="texture.gif" bgcolor="#FFFFFF">
<CENTER>
<H1>Welcome to Mastering VB5</H1>
</CENTER>
<HR>
<BR>
<BR>
<FONT SIZE=4>
Did you just hear the date?
<BR>
If not, you should probably read the instructions on installing
  ActiveX controls on your system and open this page again.
<BR>
To hear the date again, click on the Refresh button on the
  browser's toolbar.
<BODY>
    <OBJECT ID="DateCtl1" WIDTH=41 HEIGHT=39
    CLASSID="CLSID:D77B6437-7375-11D0-BB11-444553540000">
        <PARAM NAME="_ExtentX" VALUE="1085">
        <PARAM NAME="_ExtentY" VALUE="1032">
    </OBJECT>
</BODY>
</HTML>
```

ActiveX Documents

So far in this chapter you have learned how to activate Web pages with ActiveX controls and VBScript. There is one more exciting way to activate your Web documents, namely to use Visual Basic applications as Web documents. One of the cool features of Visual Basic 5 is called ActiveX documents. An ActiveX document is nothing but a Visual Basic application packaged so that it can be displayed on a Web page. In essence, an ActiveX document is an application that runs in Internet Explorer's environment. ActiveX documents can be used in other containers too, such as the Microsoft Office Binder. Here, however, we will explore ActiveX documents in the environment of Internet Explorer, because this is how I believe most users will expose ActiveX documents.

If you start Internet Explorer and open a DOC document (choose File ➤ Open), you will see something similar to Figure 15.18. Word has taken over Internet Explorer's interface and added its own commands to the menu bar; its toolbar is merged with Internet Explorer's toolbar. The result is a new environment for viewing and editing Word documents.

FIGURE 15.18

Editing Word's DOC files from within Internet Explorer

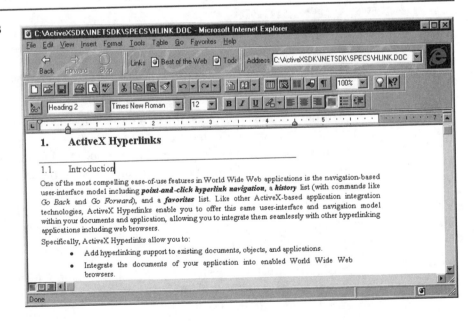

The Word application is an automation server that allows ActiveX containers, such as Internet Explorer, to view and edit DOC documents. The ActiveX container knows nothing about DOC files and can't open them, save them, or manipulate them in any way. It simply contacts the application, which then takes over.

NOTE   The quintessence of ActiveX technology is that it allows developers to write applications that can be activated from within different containers.

Although the DOC file is simply a document, ActiveX documents created with Visual Basic are applications. The "document" is no longer a static document; it's an application with a user interface. The distinction between "documents" and "applications" is blurred. You can think of this as a situation in which the document becomes totally active: It contains both data and code and can be placed on any ActiveX container. Let's look at a few examples.

Converting a VB Application to an ActiveX Document

In this section, we are going to convert the Spiral application, developed in Chapter 6, *Drawing and Painting with Visual Basic*, to an ActiveX document. The Spiral application consists of a Form (Form1) and a module (SpiralMod). Figure 15.19 shows the Spiral ActiveX document opened from within Internet Explorer.

To turn the Spiral application into an ActiveX document, open it with Visual Basic. Select the contents of the module, copy them, and paste them at the top of the Form's code. The two global variables *PenColor* and *BreakNow* need not be global any longer (besides, you can't declare global variables in a Form), so replace the Global keyword with the Dim keyword. (The reason for moving the contents of the module to the Form will be discussed shortly.) Now, follow these steps:

1. Save the project and its components to a new folder.

2. Choose Add-Ins ➤ ActiveX Document Migration Wizard to open the first window of the Wizard which is a welcome screen. Click on Next to see the next window of the Wizard.

FIGURE 15.19

The Spiral application, running in Internet Explorer's window as an ActiveX document

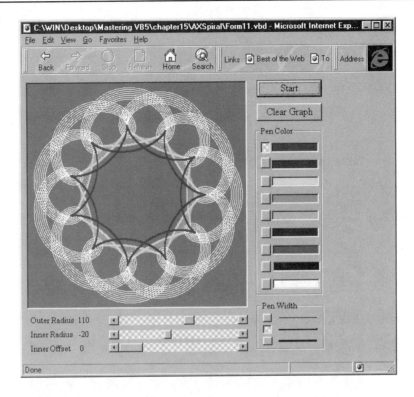

Selecting Forms

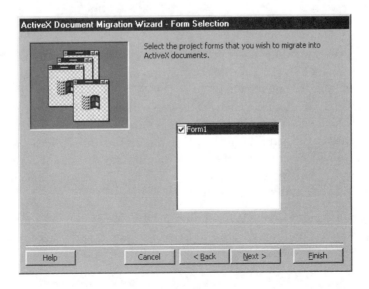

This window displays a list of the Forms in the project. Select the ones you want to convert to ActiveX documents by checking the box in front of their names. In general, you can load multiple Forms in a single project, not necessarily belonging to the same Visual Basic project. Once a Form is converted to a UserDocument object (which is like the UserControl object of an ActiveX control), it's no longer related to the other members of the project. As you will see, a UserDocument object can't directly access the contents of another UserDocument, even if they belong to the same project.

Specifying Options

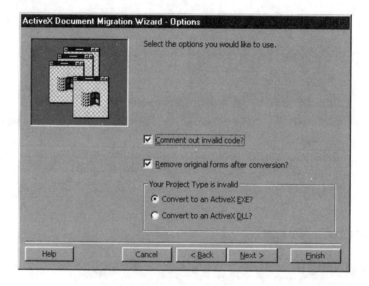

In the second window of the Wizard, you specify various options. Normally, you should ask that invalid code be commented out and that the original Forms be removed after the conversion process. You can keep the original files in the project if you want, but there is a chance that they will interfere with the ActiveX documents. Use the two radio buttons at the bottom of the window to specify whether the Wizard creates an EXE file or a DLL file for the project. This executable file is contacted by the browser and actually displays the document in the browser's window. Any interaction with the user is also be handled by this file. The browser is only the container that hosts the application.

The last window of the Wizard prompts you to click on the Finish button. The Wizard then converts the Forms to UserDocuments, and you can either edit them or open them in Internet Explorer.

Testing the New ActiveX Document

To test the newly created ActiveX document, follow these steps:

1. Choose File ➤ Make Spirals.exe. Visual Basic generates an EXE file that will act as a server. The ActiveX container contacts this EXE file to handle the ActiveX document. In addition, Visual Basic generates the Spirals.vbd file (Visual Basic Document), which is the one you must open from within Internet Explorer.

2. Run the project in Visual Basic by pressing F5.

3. Start Internet Explorer, choose File ➤ Open, and locate the Spirals.vbd file in the folder where you saved the revised project. Open it to see the Spiral application in Internet Explorer's environment.

4. Click on the Start button to draw a new spiral. Visual Basic generates the following error message:

```
"Object Required"
```

Obviously, there is a problem in our application, but nothing really serious. The application is already tested and works as a standalone executable, so the problem is most likely in the translation process. Visual Basic will take you back to the project Code window and highlight the line in which the error occured.

Indeed, the problem is the reference to the Form1 object. There is no such object in our project, so we must either remove the references to the Form1 object or replace them with UserDocument, which is the name of the user object. The prefix Form1 was required when the RouletteDraw() subroutine resided in the module, and we had to use it to access the PictureBox control on the Form.

Turning a Visual Basic application into an ActiveX document is really trivial. The ActiveX Document Migration Wizard takes care of most details. You may have to step in and make a few changes, but in order to do so, you must be aware of the basic differences between Visual Basic applications and ActiveX documents. The example demonstrates the simple conversion process. A typical application differs from the Spiral application in two ways:

- It probably has a menu. Merging the application's menu with Internet Explorer's menu requires a few extra steps.

- It probably has more than one Form. The main Form of the application is the document to be displayed in the browser's window. It's not displayed as a separate window. If a second Form is loaded with the Load or Show method, how will it be displayed? It must replace the existing Form in the browser. Forms and ActiveX documents are not quite the same; that's why ActiveX documents don't have a Show or Hide method.

In developing ActiveX documents, you must take these differences into consideration. Let's convert an application with a menu to an ActiveX document. This time, we will use the QDraw application.

ActiveX Documents with Menus

Open the QDraw application (you will find it in the Chapter 6 folder on the CD), and save the project and its components into a new folder. The ActiveX Document version of the QDraw application is in the QDraw folder under Chapter 15 on the CD.

To prepare the application's menu so that it can be merged with Internet Explorer's menu, follow these steps:

1. Open the Menu Editor window and change the Negotiate Position setting for all top-level commands of the application's menu to 3 - Right, as shown in Figure 15.20.

FIGURE 15.20

To merge the menus of an ActiveX document with the menus of Internet Explorer, you must set the Negotiate Position property to a value other than 0.

The Negotiate Position setting determines how the menus will be merged with the menus of the container application. An application's menu can appear to the left or to the right of the container's menu, but it's common practice to leave the container's menu to the left and append the application menu to the right.

2. Set the Negotiate Position property for the File, Edit, Shape, Width, DrawStyle, and Colors menus to 3, and then close the Menu Editor window.

Now you are ready to convert the application with the ActiveX Document Migration Wizard, as explained earlier. In the process, the Wizard generates a few comments regarding some commands that can't be used with ActiveX documents. As mentioned, ActiveX documents don't recognize the Show and Hide methods. Our application contains a single Form and doesn't ever call these two methods.

The Wizard will complain about the Width and Height properties in the UserDocument's Resize event. It actually inserts comments in the code, indicating the invalid use of certain properties. Here's the Resize subroutine after being processed by the Wizard:

```
Private Sub UserDocument_Resize()

'[AXDW] The following statement is invalid in a User
➥Document:'Width'
    Picture1.Width = UserDocument.Width
'[AXDW] The following statement is invalid in a User
➥Document:'Height'
    Picture1.Height = UserDocument.Height

End Sub
```

Any comments inserted by the Wizard are preceded by the string [AXDW], which is followed by a remark. The Wizard said that the Width and Height properties aren't used properly. The UserDocument's dimensions at run time are determined by the container, and you can't set them as you would with a regular Form. These two properties have values, however, and they can be read. It's not valid to set their value, but you can read their values That's why the Wizard didn't comment out the corresponding lines.

If you look for other [AXDW] comments in the code, you will find one in the Exit command:

```
Private Sub FileExit_Click()

'[AXDW] The following line was commented out by the ActiveX
➥Document Migration Wizard.
'     End

End Sub
```

This time the Wizard has commented out the code too. The End statement can't be used from within a container. An application can't shut down the container (although it *can* shut down Windows). The ActiveX document remains visible in the browser's window until the user decides to open another ActiveX document or move to a URL.

Figure 15.21 shows the QDraw application as an ActiveX document, displayed in Internet Explorer's window. The corresponding files, along with the QDraw .vbd file, which you must open from within the browser in order to load the application, can be found in the QDraw folder on the CD.

FIGURE 15.21

The QDraw application as an ActiveX document

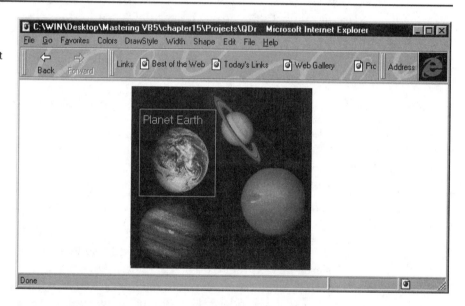

Handling Multiple ActiveX Documents

Now we'll focus on the second major difference between ActiveX documents and Visual Basic applications: How do you convert applications with multiple Forms to ActiveX documents? As mentioned, Forms are displayed directly in the browser's window and not as standalone Forms on the desktop.

ActiveX documents handle multiple Forms in a way similar to the way Internet Explorer handles hyperlinks: by jumping from one to the other. So, in ActiveX terminology, we don't talk about loading or showing other ActiveX documents. We *navigate* from one Form to another.

To navigate among multiple ActiveX documents, you use the Hyperlink object, which is a property of the UserDocument object. The Hyperlink object provides the NavigateTo method, which accepts as argument the URL of the destination document. It can be a valid URL, such as `http://www.microsoft.com`, or it can be the path name to a VBD file. To jump to Microsoft's home page from within an ActiveX document, call the following method:

```
UserDocument.HyperLink.NavigateTo "www.microsoft.com"
```

Likewise, to display another ActiveX document, call the same method as follows:

```
UserDocument.HyperLink.NavigateTo
➥"c:\win\desktop\ActiveX\mydoc.vbd"
```

To return to the document from which the currently displayed document was invoked, use the GoBack method of the HyperLink object:

```
UserDocument.Hyperlink.GoBack
```

You can use the GoBack and GoForward methods to navigate through the history list, similar to the way you use the Back and Forward buttons on the browser's toolbar.

Let's build an ActiveX document that has multiple Forms to demonstrate how the Hyperlink object is used. Our ActiveX document is called UserDocs (you will find it on the CD) and consists of two UserDocument objects: USerDoc1 and UserDoc2. Figure 15.22 shows the first ActiveX document opened with Internet Explorer. This document has a Title property that the user can set in the corresponding TextBox. Clicking on the Show Second Document button displays the second document, which is shown in Figure 15.23.

Start a new ActiveX document (EXE). Visual Basic creates a folder called User Documents in the Project Explorer window and places a UserDocument object in it. The UserDocument object is the Form on which you will draw the ActiveX document's user interface. It is equivalent to the UserControl object of an ActiveX control. Now follow these steps:

1. Choose Project ➢ Add User Document to add a second UserDocument object to the project.

2. Rename the two UserDocument objects to UserDoc1 and UserDoc2.

3. Save the UserDocument objects and the project in a new folder as UserDoc1 and UserDoc2.

FIGURE 15.22

The first
UserDocument object
of the UserDocs
ActiveX document

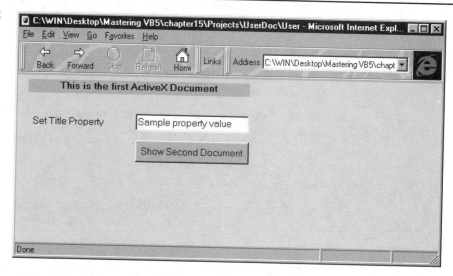

FIGURE 15.23

The second
UserDocument object
of the UserDocs
ActiveX document

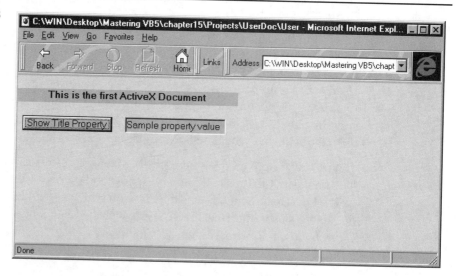

4. Now, double-click on the UserDoc1 object to open it in design mode and place the controls shown in Figure 15.22 on it. There are two Label, one TextBox, and one Command Button controls.

5. Double-click on the command button to see its Click event's subroutine and enter the following line:

```
UserDocument.Hyperlink.NavigateTo
➥"c:\DevStudio\VB\AXDoc\UserDoc2.vbd"
```

This statement opens (or navigates to, if you prefer) the second UserDocument object.

6. Double-click on the second UserDocument object to open it in design mode, and draw the controls you see in Figure 15.23. Place a Label, a TextBox, and a Command Button control on it.

7. In the command button's Click event, enter the following code:

```
Label1.Caption = UserDoc1.TextBox1.Text
```

(It won't work! It's meant to demonstrate the debugging process.)

If UserDoc1 were a Form name, this statement would be valid. It would assign the contents of the TextBox control on the first user document to the Caption property of the Label control.

You are now ready to test your new ActiveX document. As you will see, running and testing ActiveX documents is no different from testing Visual Basic projects. Even though the documents are displayed in Internet Explorer's window, Visual Basic's IDE is active in the background, and you can switch back and forth, change the code in the Visual Basic IDE, and continue execution in Internet Explorer. It may sound complicated, but when you see it in practice, you'll realize that it's quite simple.

Press F5 to run the project. Nothing appears on the screen. You must start Internet Explorer and open the VBD file that Visual Basic generated for the project.

Visual Basic generates one VBD file for each user document in the project. The VBD files have the same name as the UserDocument objects and are stored in the same folder as the project. If you haven't saved the project before running it, the VBD files are placed in Visual Basic's folder.

Now, follow these steps:

1. Start Internet Explorer, and open the UserDoc1.vbd file. You will see the window shown in Figure 15.22, earlier in this section.

2. Click on the Show Second Document button to display the second user document in a new window of Internet Explorer. Unfortunately, the NavigateTo method doesn't let you specify whether the new ActiveX document is displayed in the same or a new window.

Debugging ActiveX Documents

If you click on the Show Title Property button, you will get the following error message:

`"Variable not defined"`

In addition, in the Visual Basic Code window the UserDoc1 string is selected in the button Click event code, as shown in Figure 15.24. The application was interrupted, as usual, and you were switched back to the code window. This would also happen if this were a regular Visual Basic application. The difference with ActiveX documents is that the application is running in Internet Explorer and to edit the code you must switch to the Visual Basic IDE.

FIGURE 15.24

When an error occurs in an ActiveX document, Visual Basic switches you back to the Visual Basic IDE and highlights the offending command.

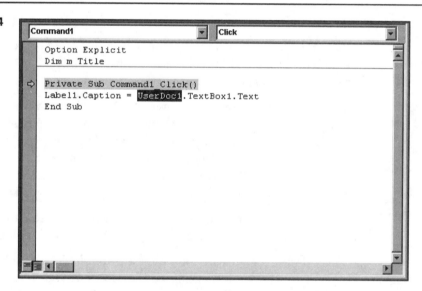

What's wrong with the following expression:

`UserDoc1.TextBox1.Text`

We are trying to read the value of a property of a control on another UserDocument object. Since UserDocument objects are equivalent to Forms, this statement should work, right? But it doesn't, and to understand why, you must know that ActiveX documents are more akin to ActiveX controls than to Visual Basic applications.

What we are trying to do here is rather like trying to read the property of a constituent control on an ActiveX control from outside the control. If you have read the previous chapter, you know that there is no way to read the contents of the Label on the Alarm control with an expression such as the following:

```
AlarmCtl.Label1.Caption
```

The constituent controls on a UserControl object are used internally by the control's code. Outside applications can only access the properties exposed by the UserControl object.

The same thing happens with ActiveX documents. ActiveX documents can have properties and methods, just like ActiveX controls. And this is how ActiveX documents exchange information: by means of their properties. But if ActiveX documents are more like applications, rather than ActiveX controls, why do they behave like controls? Because like controls, ActiveX documents can be hosted on various containers. They should exit on their own and independently of other UserDocuments that exist in the same project.

To access the information on one UserDocument from within another, you must create properties for the various UserDocuments. You can then create a reference to a UserDocument and access its properties.

Stop the application in Visual Basic by choosing Run ➤ End. You will see a message box with the following warning:

```
Other applications are currently accessing an object in your
program. Ending the program now could cause errors in those
programs. End program at this time?
```

The other applications are obviously the instances of Internet Explorer. Click on the Yes button to stop the application and return to the Visual Basic IDE. The two instances of Internet Explorer are orphaned, and their contents are cleared. Switch to them and shut them down, because you must do so later anyway. When you run the modified UserDocs application again, you want Internet Explorer to load the VBD files from the disk instead of from the cache.

Let's implement a property in the UserDoc1 UserDocument through which the other UserDocument can access the value of the TextBox1 control. Follow these steps:

1. Open the Code window for the UserDoc1 object and choose Tools ➤ Add Procedure. Name this property Title. Visual Basic inserts the definitions of the Property Let and Property Get procedures and the declaration of the *m_Title* private variable.

2. Change the type of the property from Variant to String and enter the following code in the procedures:

```
Public Property Get Title() As String
    Title = m_Title
End Property

Public Property Let Title(ByVal vNewValue As String)
    m_Title = vNewValue
End Property
```

3. Next, open the ReadProperties and WriteProperties subroutines for the UserDocument object and insert the following code:

```
Private Sub UserDocument_ReadProperties
(PropBag As PropertyBag)
    m_Title = PropBag.ReadProperty("Title", "")
End Sub

Private Sub UserDocument_WriteProperties
(PropBag As PropertyBag)
    PropBag.WriteProperty "Title", m_Title, ""
End Sub
```

4. The UserDoc1 object has a property named Title. To assign the value of the TextBox control to this property when the user changes the text in the text box, insert the following lines in the control's Change event:

```
Private Sub Text1_Change()
    Set UDoc = Me
    UDoc.Title = Text1.Text
End Sub
```

5. The *Udoc* variable is public and must be declared in a module. Add a new module to the project and enter the following declaration in it:

```
Public UDoc As UserDoc1
```

The UserDoc1 object has a property named Title, and you can now read or set its value from other UserDocument objects. To display the value of the Title property from within the UserDoc2, insert the following line in the command button's Click event:

```
Private Sub Command1_Click()
    Label1.Caption = UDoc.Title

End Sub
```

To access an object on another User Document, you use a public variable. If you have multiple User Documents and you want them to exchange information, you must declare public variables in a separate module, which acts as links between them. Or, you can simply set public variables in the module, but this approach isn't as elegant as the one presented here.

CHAPTER

SIXTEEN

16

The Scripting Model

- The Window object

- The Document object

- The History object

- The Navigator object

- The Location object

- The Links object

In the previous chapter, you learned how to activate your Web pages with VBScript and ActiveX controls. VBScript, however, can do more than manipulate controls: It can manipulate the browser's window in which the document is displayed. Internet Explorer is the environment of VBScript (just as Windows is the environment for Visual Basic applications), and in this chapter we will look at how you can control this environment and interact with it from within your scripts.

The Scripting Model is a hierarchy of objects through which you can access the properties of HTML documents displayed on the browser and the properties of the browser itself. The Scripting Model is not a Visual Basic component, and you can't access it from within your Visual Basic applications. But Visual Basic does provide a control that can render HTML documents, the WebBrowser control (we are going to explore it in the next chapter). The WebBrowser control can host HTML documents, including scripts.

The various flavors of Microsoft's Visual Basic languages are merging, and soon you'll be able to exploit VBScript and active documents from within Visual Basic's environment or ActiveX Documents. In the meantime, you can use the objects of the Scripting Model to activate your Web pages even further, as you will see in the examples of this chapter.

The Objects of the Scripting Model

The Internet Explorer Scripting Model is a hierarchy of objects, with an organization similar to that of the Database Access objects, which were covered in Chapter 11, *Database Programming with Visual Basic*. If you read Chapter 11, you have already seen a hierarchical organization of objects, starting with the Database object at the top. In the Scripting Model, each object has properties, which are themselves objects. As such, they have their own properties (some of them being objects), methods, and events.

The top-level object in the Scripting Model is the Window object. The document is rendered within this object. Some basic properties of the Window object are its name and the location of the document displayed (its URL). Before we look at these and other properties, though, let's look at the objects of the Scripting Model at large and see what they can do for your Web pages.

The most important property of the Window object is another object, the Document object. The Document object represents the HTML document displayed in the window, which in turn has its own properties, such as background color, title, and so on. A window can also contain frames, which in turn can contain documents. To access the document in a frame, you first access the appropriate frame object and then the document object of the specific frame.

NOTE The objects of the Scripting Model and their properties and methods are not case-sensitive. In this chapter, however, I will use initial cap and lowercase for the objects and their members to make these names stand out from the text.

The Properties of the Scripting Objects

The Window is the top-level object and is the container for all other objects. The Window object represents the browser's window, in which HTML documents are displayed. Its properties include the name of the Window and the message displayed in its status bar. To access the name property of the Window object, use a statement such as the following:

```
win1 = Window.name
```

You can use the variable *win1* from within your code to address the window. For example, you can request that another document be displayed in the *win1* window.

To display a welcome message in the browser's status bar, use a statement such as the following:

```
Window.status = "Welcome to our Fabulous Site"
```

You can also include VBScript functions in the definition of the status string, such as the date and time functions:

```
Window.status = "Welcome to our Fabulous Site" & "It is " & date
➥& " and the time is " & time
```

The most important property of the window object is another object, the Document object. Through the Document object, you can access the properties and methods of the document displayed in the browser's window. Two common properties of the Document object are its background color (property bgColor) and its foreground color (fgColor). To change the document's background color to white, for example, you use the following statement:

```
Window.Document.bgColor = white
```

Just as some of the Window object's properties are objects, the Document object has properties that are themselves objects. One of these objects is the Location object, with which you access the properties of the location of the document. The URL of the document in the browser's window is given by the href property of the Location object. You can find out the current document's URL or set this property to the URL of another document. The href property is a property of the Location object, and you access it with the following expression:

```
Location.href
```

The Location object is a property of the Document object, and it must be accessed as follows:

```
Document.Locatiom.href
```

The Document object is a property of the Window object, so the complete expression for accessing the document's URL is the following:

```
Window.Document.Location.href
```

This expression is long, but it's easy to understand. The first-level object is the Window object. The following objects are more specific, and you can step down this hierarchy to reach the desired property. The organization of the scripting objects in a hierarchy simplifies the syntax of its methods and properties.

A window can also contain frames. Frames are accessed though the Frames object, which is an array of objects. The first frame is Frames(0), the second one Frames(1), and so on. To access the document in a specific frame, you start with the Window object and specify the frame whose document you want to access. For example, if you want to access the second frame, you specify the following:

```
Window.Frames(1)
```

Each frame displays a different document and therefore has its own Document property. To access the properties of the document on the second frame, use the following expression:

```
Window.Frames(1).Document
```

What would the background color of this document be? Simply tack on the bgColor property name at the end of the previous expression, and you have it:

```
Window.Frames(1).Document.bgColor
```

As you can see, the same object can be attached to multiple objects. The window has its own Document object, and the document has a Location property. But, if the window contains frames, each frame in the window has its own Location property. You may find this behavior confusing at first, but you'll soon get the hang of it.

The Methods of the Scripting Objects

The scripting objects also have methods. The Document object, for example, provides the Write method, which lets your script place text directly on the Web page. In other words, with the write method you can create Web pages on the fly.

The write method displays a string on the current page. The following statement:

```
Document.Write date()
```

displays the current date on the page. If you use HTML instead, you must hard-code the date and consequently update the document daily. The VBScript date() function returns the current date, but VBScript doesn't provide any methods for actually displaying the date on the page. To display something on a page from within its script, you use the objects of the Scripting Model.

Let's look at an example. Here's a simple HTML document:

```
<HTML>
<BODY BGCOLOR="#H00FF00">
<H1>Welcome to our Active Pages</H1>
</BODY>
</HTML>
```

This document displays a page with a green background and a level 1 heading. You can create the same page with the following VBScript code:

```
<HTML>
<SCRIPT LANGUAGE="VBScript">
Document.bgColor = "#H00FF00"
Document.Write "<H1>Welcome to our Active Pages</H1>"
</SCRIPT>
</HTML>
```

What's the benefit of using the Write method to generate the page? Flexibility. This page is actually generated on the client computer. If you want to display the date and the time this page was opened, you can add the following line of VBScript code:

```
Document.Write "This page was opened on " & date() & ", at " & time()
```

The Write method provides even more flexibility. You can write complicated VBScript code to produce elaborate pages on the fly. For example, you can prompt the user for his or her name and personalize a Web page as follows:

```
UserName = InputBox("Please enter your name")
Document.Write "<H1>Welcome to our Active Pages, " & UserName & "</H1>"
```

The actual heading will be different on each client computer, depending on the user's response to the prompt. Figure 16.1 shows a typical page that this produces.

FIGURE 16.1

Use the Document object's Write method to create HTML documents on the fly.

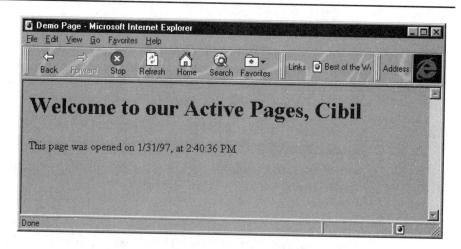

Here is the HTML file that produced the page shown in Figure 16.1:

```
<HTML>
<HEAD>
<TITLE>Demo Page</TITLE>
<SCRIPT LANGUAGE="VBSCRIPT">
UserName = InputBox("Please enter your name")
```

```
Document.Write "<H1>Welcome to our Active Pages, " &
    UserName & "</H1>"
Document.Write "<BR>"
Document.Write "This page was opened on " & date() & ",
    at " & time()
</SCRIPT>
</HEAD>
<BODY>

</BODY>
</HTML>
</BODY>
</HTML>
```

Notice that this document doesn't contain any HTML tags in its BODY section. The entire document was generated from within the page's script section with VBScript commands.

In the following sections, we are going to explore the objects of the Scripting Model, their properties, and their methods, which let you control Internet Explorer's environment from within your code. We'll start with the Window object and one of its most important properties, the Document object. As you will see, the Document object gives you tremendous flexibility over the appearance and function of your Web pages, and we will use it in many of the examples in this section.

The ActiveX Control Pad and the Scripting Model

The objects of the Scripting object we look at in this chapter are not entirely new to you. You may have noticed that the Window object in the Actions window of the ActiveX Control Pad had numerous properties, some of which are shown in Figure 16.2.

The Navigate method, for example, displays another document in the browser's window. If you double-click on this property's name, the following line is inserted in the Code window:

```
call window.navigate(url)
```

The *url* argument is the URL of the new page to be displayed. Set the *url* argument to a document's URL, and when this line is executed, the specified page is displayed. The prompt method is similar to the InputBox function and prompts the user for input. It has the following syntax:

```
call window.prompt(msg, initialTxt)
```

FIGURE 16.2

The expanded view
of the Window object
in ActiveX Control
Pad's Actions window

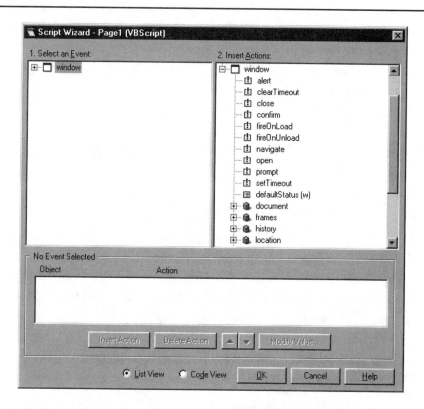

Double-click on its name to insert this definition in the Code window, and then replace the *msg* argument with the prompt and *initialTxt* with the default response. The prompt method can be called as follows:

```
uName = window.prompt("Please enter your name", "Unknown User")
```

You may also notice that, besides properties and methods, the Window object has a number of subordinate objects such as the Document and Frames objects. These objects are properties, and they have their own properties and methods. The Frames object, for instance, represents the frames on the current document.

You need not learn the names and syntax of all the properties and methods in this chapter. Use the ActiveX Control Pad's Actions pane to locate them. Not only that, but various objects in this pane are structured in a way that reflects their organization in the Scripting Model.

> **WARNING**   If you plan to use the objects of the Scripting Model for more than occasional Web page scripting, obtain a copy of the complete documentation that comes with the Internet SDK. You can download the SDK from `http://www.microsoft.com/activex`. The current version of the ActiveX Control Pad is not quite up to date. Some of the Scripting Model's objects are not displayed in the Actions window, but are supported by VBScript.

The Window Object

As mentioned, the Window object is at the top of the Scripting object hierarchy. All other objects in the Scripting Model are properties of the Window object. Here are the most important properties and methods of the Window object.

The Properties of the Window Object

The Window object supports a number of properties that let you manipulate the document displayed in it. The Name property, for example, is the name of the window (a string). The Frames property, though, is another object with its own properties that let you access and manipulate the contents of the frames in the window.

Name   This property returns the name of the window and is read-only. The window's name is specified when a window is created and can't be changed. To create a named window, you use the TARGET attribute with the A HTML tag. The following HTML statement:

```
This is a <A HREF="http://www.sybex.com" TARGET="SYBEX">link</A>
  to SYBEX's home page on the WWW"
```

displays a hyperlink, which, when activated, displays the SYBEX home page in a new Internet Explorer window, named SYBEX.

If a window with the name SYBEX exists already, the document is displayed in it. If such a window doesn't exist, a new window is opened, and the document is displayed in it. You can later refer to this window by its name. For example, you can specify the status string to be displayed in the status bar of this window with the following statement:

```
Sybex.status "Welcome to SYBEX"
```

Another way to create named windows is to use the open method of the Window object, which is discussed later in this chapter.

Opener   This property returns the Window object that opened the current window. The Opener property does not return a window name; it returns another Window object, through which you can access the properties of the window from which the current window was opened. To find the name of the opener window, use the Opener object's Name property as in the following line:

```
MsgBox "My parent window is " & opener.name
```

Top   This property returns a Window object that represents the topmost window. As with the Opener property, the Top property returns a Window object, which you can use to access the properties of the topmost window.

Location   This property is another object in the scripting hierarchy and provides a number of properties through which you can manipulate the URL of the current document. The following statement:

```
MsgBox Window.Location.href
```

displays the URL of the current window in a message box. To jump to another URL, use a statement such as this one:

```
Window.Location.href="www.microsoft.com"
```

> **NOTE**   This is not a hyperlink. It's a VBScript command that causes the browser to jump to the home page of the Microsoft site. You can use the Location object in your code to jump to any URL. For example, you can prompt the user for a favorite URL or select one from a list of URLs.

defaultStatus   This property sets the default text in the status bar. This string is displayed when the browser isn't using the status bar to display some other message.

Status   This property returns or sets the text displayed in the status bar. The following statement:

```
window.status = "Welcome, stranger!"
```

displays a welcome message in the browser's status bar.

Frames   This property is another object that represents the frames in the current window. Individual frames can be accessed either by name or by their order. The first frame on the page is Window.frames(0). If the frame has a name (which was specified in the FRAME tag), the same frame can be accessed as Window.frames("SYBEX").

To find out the background color of the first frame in the current document, use the following command:

```
Window.Frames(0).focument.bgColor
```

The Methods of the Window Object

The Window object supports a few methods that let you interact with the user (similar to the InputBox() and MsgBox() functions), as well as the Navigate method, which causes it to jump to another URL and display a new document.

Alert   This method displays an alert message box that is similar to the message box but has only an OK button.

Confirm   This method displays a message box that has two buttons, OK and Cancel. The confirm method returns True if the OK button is clicked and False if the Cancel button is clicked.

Here's one way to request user input and then use it in your script:

```
scrtPage=window.confirm("Do you want to view our secret page?")
if scrtPage = True Then Window.Location.href="./secretPage.htm"
```

Prompt   This method prompts the user for data and is similar to the InputBox() function. The Prompt method accepts two arguments, the prompt and an optional default response. When the OK button is clicked, the Prompt method the string that the user entered in the dialog box. The following line prompts the user to enter his or her name and provides a generic response for users who don't want to use their real name:

```
UserName=Window.prompt("Please enter your name?", "Unknown user")
```

The user's response is stored in the *UserName* variable and can be used later in the script, as I did in the Page2.htm document you saw earlier in this chapter.

Open   This method opens a window and displays a document in it. The Open method has the following syntax:

```
window.open url, target, "toolbar=bool, location=bool,
   directories=bool, status=bool, menubar=bool, scrollbars=bool,
   resizeable=bool", width, height, top, left
```

The simplest form of the open method is as follows:

```
window.open url, target
```

The *url* variable is the URL of the document to be displayed in the new window, and *target* is the name of the window in which the document will be displayed.

If the window specified with this name exists, this window's contents are replaced with the new document. If not, a new window with this name is opened, and the document is displayed in it. This argument is identical to the TARGET attribute of the HREF tag.

The remaining arguments (shown in Table 16.1) are set to Boolean values (Yes/No or 1/0) and control the appearance of the window. These arguments are literal strings.

T A B L E   1 6 . 1   Arguments of the open Method

ARGUMENT	WHAT IT DOES
Toolbar	Displays/hides the browser's toolbar
Location	Displays/hides the Address box on the browser's toolbar
Directories	Displays/hides the directory list
Menu	Displays/hides the menu bar
Status	Displays/hides the status bar
Scrollbars	Displays/hides the browser's scroll bars

The last four arguments are specified in pixels, and they need not be enclosed in quotes. The arguments *width* and *height* determine the window's dimensions, and the arguments *top* and *left* determine the window's position on the screen, measured from the screen's top left corner.

The return value is a Window object, which can be used later to close the window. The following statement:

```
window.open "http://www.microsoft.com", "MSwindow", "toolbar=no,
menubar=no, resizeable=no",600,400
```

opens the window MSWindow (or creates a new one by that name if it doesn't exist) and displays the home page of the Microsoft Web site in it. The MSWindow window has no toolbar or menu. Furthermore, it is 600 pixels wide and 400 pixels tall, and it can't be resized.

The Open method has a behavior similar to that of hyperlinks inserted with the A tag, except that it gives you more control over the appearance of the new window. The real benefit of using the Open method, though, is that you can specify the target at run time. You must furnish the destination of the A tag at design time, and it can't be changed when the document is viewed. With the Open method, you can navigate to any URL, even a user-supplied one.

Close   This method closes the current window.

Navigate   This method causes the browser to display a new document in the current window. It has the following syntax:

```
Window.navigate url
```

The *url* argument must be set to the URL of the new document and can be a page on the World Wide Web or a local file. The following statement:

```
window.navigate "file:c:\MyPages\VBTricks.htm" [tech changes]
```

opens a local file in the client computer's MyPages folder.

When you jump to another page, the current page is replaced in the browser's window by the new one. The only way to return to the page with the script is by clicking on the Back button.

The Navigate method applies to the Frame object too. If your document has a frame, you can display any other page on the WWW in this frame and still keep the page with the script active. Let's see how this is done.

VB5 at Work: The Open Page

The page shown in Figure 16.3 is called Open, and you will find it in this chapter's folder on the CD. You use the three buttons on the Open page to navigate to the home pages of Sybex, Microsoft, and Netscape.

FIGURE 16.3

The Open page lets you navigate to various URLs and view them in different windows.

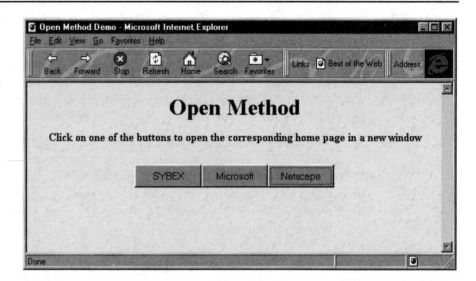

Each URL is displayed in a separate window, with different characteristics. As you can see in Figure 16.4, one of the windows has a menu bar, and the other doesn't. You can specify all the characteristics of each new Internet Explorer window you open under program control by setting the appropriate arguments of the Open method.

I created the Open page with the ActiveX Control Pad and placed the three buttons on the page by choosing Edit ➤ Insert ActiveX Control.

Code 16.1: The SYBEX, Microsoft, and Netscape Buttons

```
<SCRIPT LANGUAGE="VBScript">
<!-
Sub CommandButton1_Click()
    Window.open "http://www.sybex.com", "Win1", "toolbar=0,
    location=0, directories=0, status=0, menubar=0",400,200
end sub
```

FIGURE 16.4

The three smaller windows have different attributes, but they were all opened by the buttons on the Open page.

```
->
    </SCRIPT>
    <OBJECT ID="CommandButton1" WIDTH=96 HEIGHT=32
     CLASSID="CLSID:D7053240-CE69-11CD-A777-00DD01143C57">
        <PARAM NAME="Caption" VALUE="SYBEX">
        <PARAM NAME="Size" VALUE="2540;846">
        <PARAM NAME="FontHeight" VALUE="200">
        <PARAM NAME="FontCharSet" VALUE="0">
        <PARAM NAME="FontPitchAndFamily" VALUE="2">
        <PARAM NAME="ParagraphAlign" VALUE="3">
        <PARAM NAME="FontWeight" VALUE="0">
    </OBJECT>
    <SCRIPT LANGUAGE="VBScript">
<!-
Sub CommandButton2_Click()
    Window.open "http://www.microsoft.com", "Win2", "toolbar=0,
    location=0, directories=1, status=0, menubar=1",300,200
end sub
```

```
->
    </SCRIPT>
    <OBJECT ID="CommandButton2" WIDTH=96 HEIGHT=32
     CLASSID="CLSID:D7053240-CE69-11CD-A777-00DD01143C57">
        <PARAM NAME="Caption" VALUE="Microsoft">
        <PARAM NAME="Size" VALUE="2540;846">
        <PARAM NAME="FontHeight" VALUE="200">
        <PARAM NAME="FontCharSet" VALUE="0">
        <PARAM NAME="FontPitchAndFamily" VALUE="2">
        <PARAM NAME="ParagraphAlign" VALUE="3">
        <PARAM NAME="FontWeight" VALUE="0">
    </OBJECT>
    <SCRIPT LANGUAGE="VBScript">
<!-
Sub CommandButton3_Click()
    Window.open "http://www.netscape.com", "Win3", "toolbar=0,
    location=0, directories=0, status=0, menubar=0",300,200
end sub
->
    </SCRIPT>
    <OBJECT ID="CommandButton3" WIDTH=96 HEIGHT=32
     CLASSID="CLSID:D7053240-CE69-11CD-A777-00DD01143C57">
        <PARAM NAME="Caption" VALUE="NetScape">
        <PARAM NAME="Size" VALUE="2540;846">
        <PARAM NAME="FontHeight" VALUE="200">
        <PARAM NAME="FontCharSet" VALUE="0">
        <PARAM NAME="FontPitchAndFamily" VALUE="2">
        <PARAM NAME="ParagraphAlign" VALUE="3">
        <PARAM NAME="FontWeight" VALUE="0">
    </OBJECT>
```

The three windows on which the corresponding home pages are displayed are called Win1, Win2, and Win3. If one of the windows is already open, clicking on its button doesn't create a new instance of it. Unfortunately, this action doesn't bring the corresponding window on top. If one of the windows is hidden by another one, you must bring it to the front by pressing Alt+Tab or by clicking on its icon in the Desktop's taskbar.

The Document Object

From a programming point of view, the Document object is probably the most important object in the scripting hierarchy. The Document object represents the HTML document displayed in the browser's window or in one of its frames. Through the Document object's properties and methods, you can manipulate the appearance and even the contents of the document. You can use the bgColor property, for example, to read or set the document's background color, and you can use the title property to read the document's title. You use its Write method to specify the document's contents from within the script and, in effect, create documents on the fly. The following section explains the properties of the Document object and provides short examples that demonstrate the syntax of the properties.

The Properties of the Document Object

The Document object provides a few simple properties, which let you set the document's background color, the color of the links, and so on. It also provides a few of the most advanced properties, such as the Cookie property, which lets your script store information on the client computer and read it the next time the document with the script is loaded.

linkColor, aLinkColor, vLinkColor   These properties return or set the color of the links in the document. The linkColor property is the default color of the hyperlinks in the document, aLinkColor is the color of the active hyperlink, and vLinkColor is the color of the hyperlinks already visited. These properties accept color values that can be expressed as hexadecimal numbers or as color names:

```
Window.Document.vLinkColor = #00FFFF
Window.Document.linkColor = blue
```

bgColor, fgColor   These properties return or set the document's background color and foreground color. The foreground color is the color used for rendering text if the HTML code doesn't overwrite this setting. Likewise, the background property can be overwritten by the document if it uses a background image. These properties accept color values.

Title   This property returns the current document's title. This is a read-only property and can't be used to change the document's title at run time.

Cookie   As you know, scripts written in VBScript are executed on the client computer. VBScript, therefore, had to be a safe language. There is no way for VBScript to access the file system of the client computer and tamper with it. That's why VBScript lacks the file I/O commands of Visual Basic. A language that can't store information locally is rather limited. Scripts can't even open or save a few bytes of data on a local file, and for many applications, this is a serious limitation.

The solution to this problem is to use cookies. Cookie is a property of the Document object and is a string that can be stored on the client computer. Cookies are quite safe, though, because they are text files written and read to and from the disk by the browser, and they live in a specific folder. They are not executable files (they present no threat to the rest of the file system), and they can be accessed only by the browser. Cookies can't be considered a substitute for file I/O, but they can save a piece of information on the client computer so that the next time the script is executed, it will find the information there.

The information stored on the client computer by means of cookies is limited. You can't store large files with text or numbers. But you can store customization information such as the user's name and preferences so that the next time the user requests the same page, the script can find the values it stored on the client computer the last time and customize itself for the user.

> **NOTE**   The most common use for cookies is for storing customization data.

Another practical reason for using cookies is to share information among pages. The shopping basket is a typical example. As you know, a script is limited to a single page. If the page with the script loads another page, the script ceases to exist. The script (if any) on the newly loaded page takes over. Some sites let viewers select items to purchase on various pages, and they keep track of the items in the user's shopping basket. If each page is a separate entity and the pages can't share information, how is this done?

The answer is the Cookie property of the Document object. When a page wants to pass some information to other pages, it can leave a cookie on the client computer. The page that needs the information can read it. To the viewer, it appears that the various pages are communicating as if they were Forms of an application, to use a Visual Basic analogy.

VB5 at Work: The Cookie Page

To store a string on the client computer's system and access it from another page or to access it the next time the page is opened, use the Cookie property, as outlined in the Cookie page. The Cookie page, shown in Figure 16.5, is a revision of the Page1 page. This time we prompt the user for his or her name, and then we store it in the Document object's Cookie property. The next time you open this page, the user's name appears automatically.

FIGURE 16.5

Use the Document object's Cookie property to customize your pages.

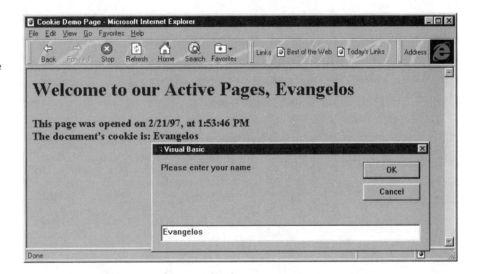

To test the Cookie page, you must have a Web server installed. Opening the Cookie page with Internet Explorer won't do the trick. Cookies are saved on the client computer by the browser and only if they are furnished by a server. You can use any Web server, including the FrontPage Web server or the Personal Web Server.

TIP

The Personal Web Server is part of FrontPage, but it is also separately available as a PowerToy from Microsoft's Web site (http://www .microsoft.com/sitebuilder).

I used the FrontPage Web server to test this example (which works just like the Personal Web Server). Here are the steps to follow to experiment with the cookie property:

1. Copy the Cookie.htm file from the CD to the Cookie folder under the Web server's root folder.

2. Rename it to Index.htm.

3. Start the FrontPage Web server or any other server you have installed on your system (if it's not already running).

4. Start Internet Explorer and connect to the following URL:

    `http://127.0.0.1/Cookie`

    The numerals 127.0.0.1 constitute the IP address of the local server, and Cookie is the name of the folder to which the site has been copied (this site contains a single page).

5. When prompted, enter your name. The script displays it on the page and saves it in the Document object's Cookie property.

6. Connect to another URL by entering it in the browser's Address box.

7. Click on Back to return to the Cookie page. This time you won't be prompted for your name. It's already stored in the Cookie property.

Now, let's look at script of the Cookie.htm page.

Code 16.2: The Cookie.htm Document

```
<HTML>
<HEAD>
<TITLE>Cookie Demo Page</TITLE>
<SCRIPT LANGUAGE="VBSCRIPT">
If Document.Cookie = "" Then
    UserName = InputBox("Please enter your name")
    document.cookie=UserName
Else
    UserName = Document.Cookie
End If
Document.write "<H1>Welcome to our Active Pages, " &
    UserName & "</H1>"
Document.write "<BR>"
Document.write "This page was opened on " & date() & ",
    at " & time()
```

```
Document.write "<BR>"
Document.write "The document's cookie is: " & Document.cookie
</SCRIPT>
</HEAD>
<BODY>

</BODY>
</HTML>
```

The If structure of the script examines the value of the Cookie property. If this property has no value, it prompts the user to enter a name. It then stores the name entered by the user in the Cookie property.

The second time you connect to this page, the Cookie property has a value, and the Else clause executes, which assigns the cookie's value to the *UserName* variable. The rest of the code is the same as that for the Page1 page, with the exception of the last Write method, which displays the current value of the cookie on the page.

Using cookies in this way is slightly unorthodox. Cookies are usually stored as pairs of names and values, separated with a semicolon. A more reasonable cookie value is the following:

```
"UserName = Cibil; Age = 24; Browser=IE3.02"
```

As you can see, you can store many variable values in the cookie, but there are no methods for retrieving the value of a single variable. You must read the entire cookie and then use the string manipulation functions (the InStr(), Mid(), and other string manipulation functions) to isolate each pair and extract the name of the variable and its value.

Cookies Expire

Cookies have an expiration date. If you don't specify an expiration date (I didn't use an expiration date in the Cookie example), the cookie expires after the current session. To create a new session, shut down the Web server and start it again. Shutting down and restarting Internet Explorer won't start a new session.

To specify an expiration date, append a string like this one to the cookie:

```
expires = Thu, 01 Jan 1998 12:00:00 GMT
```

This string must be appended to the cookie as follows:

```
Document.cookie = UserName & " expires = Thu, 01 Jan 1998
12:00:00 GMT"
```

Cookies with expiration dates are actually stored on disk as text files, and you can view them with a text editor. Each Web site's cookies are stored in the Cookies folder under the Windows folder.

Anchor   Anchor is a property of the Document object, and like some other properties, it is also an object. The Length property of the Anchor object returns the number of anchors in the document. The individual anchors are stored in the anchors array, whose elements can be accessed with an index. The name of the first anchor in the document is anchors(0) (its value is the NAME attribute of the A tag that inserted the anchor in the document), anchors(1) is the second anchor, and so on. The following statements display the number of anchors in the current document in a message box:

```
TotalAnchors = Document.Anchors.Length
MsgBox "The document contains "& TotalAnchors & "anchors"
```

You can also scan all the anchors in a document with a loop such as the following:

```
For i=0 to TotalAnchors-1
    ThisAnchor=Document.Anchors(i)
    {do something with this anchor}
Next
```

Scanning the anchors of the current document from within the same document's script section isn't practical. But you can open another document in a frame and access the anchors of the frame with the Frame(1).Document.Anchors array. For another example, see the DocumentLinks example, later in this chapter.

Link   This property is similar to the Anchor property, but instead of representing the anchors, it represents the hyperlinks in the current document. Like the anchors array, the links array is a property of the Document object, which is the only object that can contain links. The basic property of the Link object is the Length property, which returns the number of links in the document.

Each link is a member of the links array. The first link is links(0), the second one is links(1), and so on. Because the hyperlinks in a document are destinations, the link object's properties are identical to the properties of the Location object, but they are read-only.

To obtain the number of links in the document displayed in the browser's window, use the following statement:

```
Window.Document.Links.Length
```

To scan the hyperlinks in the document and examine their destinations, use a loop such as the following:

```
For i=0 to Window.Document.Links.Length-1
     {process the hyperlink}
Next
```

At each iteration of the loop, the current hyperlink is given by the following expression:

```
Window.Dcument.Links(i).href.
```

lastModified This property returns the date the current document was last modified. You can use the lastModified property of the Document object to display the date and time it was last modified, without having to hardcode this information in the document itself.

Referrer This property returns the URL of the referring document.

The Methods of the Document Object

The Document object supports a few methods as well, which let you manipulate its contents. The Document object's methods manipulate the contents of the current document.

Open This method opens the document for output. The current document is cleared, and new strings can be placed on the document with the Write and WriteLn methods.

NOTE The Open method of the Document object opens the current document for output and has nothing to do with the Open method of the Window object, which opens a new instance of Internet Explorer and displays a document in it.

Write string This method writes the *string* variable to the document. The argument is inserted in the current document at the current position, but it doesn't appear until the document is closed with the close method.

WriteLn string This method writes the *string* variable into the current document with a newline character appended to the end. The newline character is ignored by the browser anyway, so the WriteLn string method is practically the same as the Write string method.

Close This method closes the document and causes all the information written to it with the Write and WriteLn methods to be displayed, as if it were placed in an HTML document that is loaded in the browser's window.

Clear This method clears the contents of the document.

Using the Methods

In effect, these methods allow the programmer (or Web author) to create an HTML document from within the script, as the Page1.htm example of the next section demonstrates. The Document object's methods are usually called in the following order:

```
Document.open
Document.write string
. . .
Document.write string
Document.close
```

The *string* variable, or literal, could be anything that normally appears in an HTML document (text, HTML tags, hyperlinks, and so on). Because the Write method's argument can contain HTML tags, you have the flexibility to create Web pages on the fly. The following statements display a level 1 header, centered on the page:

```
Document.write "<CENTER>"
Document.write "<H1>Welcome to our Active Pages</H1>"
Document.write "</CENTER>"
```

If you take the arguments of the Write methods and strip the quotes, you'll get the HTML document that would produce the same page.

The most common use of these methods is to create documents on the fly. If you couple the Write method with the Cookie property of the Document object, you can create customized pages, based on the users' preferences, right on the client computer. The Write method is extremely flexible, and we are going to look at a couple of examples.

VB5 at Work: The Page1 Example

Let's look at another use for the Scripting Model's objects. The Page1.htm document, shown in Figure 16.6, contains a floating frame and three command buttons. The first command button displays the URL of the document currently displayed in the floating frame. The second button displays a user-specified URL in the frame by calling the Window object's Navigate method. The last button also displays the user-specified URL in the frame, only this one uses the Href property of the Location object.

The floating frame was inserted with the following statement:

```
<IFRAME SRC="http://www.sybex.com" WIDTH=500 HEIGHT=300">
```

When the page is first loaded, it displays the SYBEX home page in the floating frame. To display another page, click on one of the command buttons.

I created the Page1.htm document with the ActiveX Control Pad, and I entered the document's body section manually. Here it is:

```
<H1>Welcome to the VBScript page</H1>
<IFRAME SRC="http://www.sybex.com" WIDTH=500 HEIGHT=300">
</IFRAME>
```

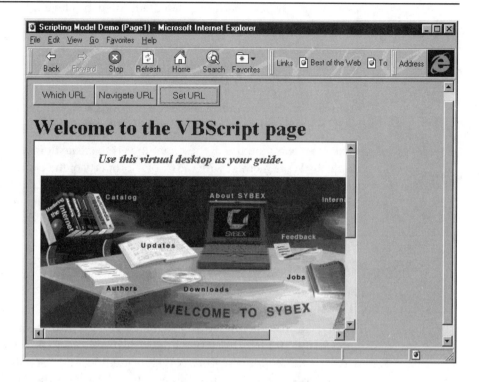

To place the command buttons on the page, choose Edit ➢ Insert ActiveX. As each button is created, resize it and set its Caption property according to Figure 16.2, earlier in this chapter. Then insert the following line in the first button's Click event handler:

```
Sub CommandButton1_Click()
    MsgBox Window.Frames(0).Location.href
End Sub
```

The second button's code sets the frame's destination to a user-specified URL and is as follows:

```
Sub CommandButton2_Click()
    newURL=InputBox("Please enter the URL you want to view")
    Call Window.Frames(0).Navigate(newURL)
End Sub
```

The third button does the same, only this time by setting the Href property, which is equivalent to the Navigate method:

```
Sub CommandButton3_Click()
    newURL=InputBox("Please enter the URL you want to view")
    Window.Frames(0).Location.href=newURL
End Sub
```

VB5 at Work: A Calendar Generator

The page shown in Figure 16.7 was created with a script. The calendar is generated by VBScript code on the client's side and displays the days of the current month. By specifying a different date you can create any month's calendar.

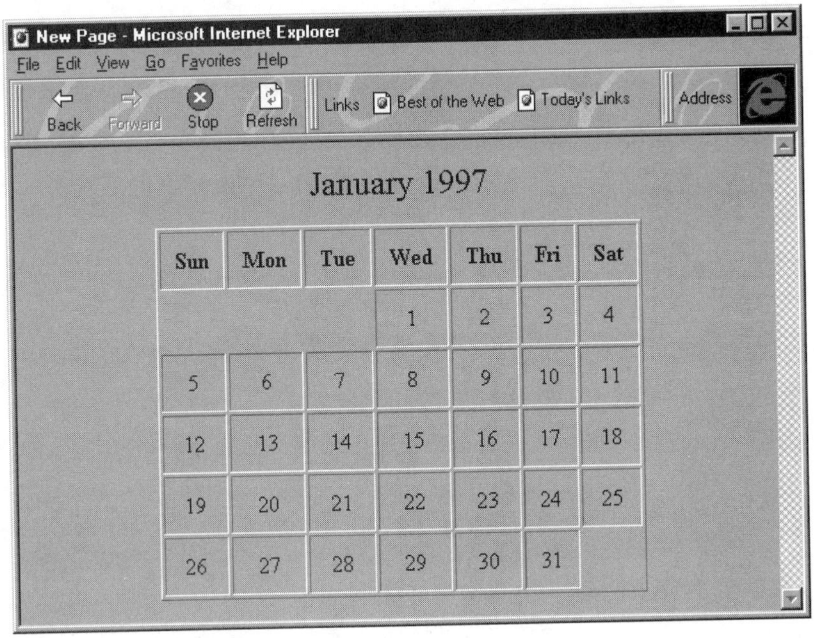

FIGURE 16.7

This calendar was generated with VBScript code.

The actual calendar doesn't react to mouse clicks, but you can easily turn the dates into hyperlinks that point to documents with information specific to each date.

To understand the code of this application, you need a basic knowledge of building tables with HTML tags. If you are familiar with these tags, you'll find the Calendar page's script straightforward.

Code 16.3: The Script for the Calendar Page

```
<SCRIPT LANGUAGE="VBSCRIPT">
Dim imonth, thisdate, nextday, cday
imonth=month(date)
     document.write "<CENTER>"
     document.write "<FONT FACE='Verdana' SIZE=5>"
     document.write format(date, "mmmm") & " " & Year(date)
     document.write "<P>"
     document.write "<TABLE CELLPADDING=10 BORDER><TR>"
     document.write _
"<TD><B>Sun<TD><B>Mon<TD><B>Tue<TD><B>Wed<TD><B>Thu
<TD><B>Fri<TD><B>Sat"
     document.write "<TR>"
     thisdate=DateSerial(year(date), month(date), 1)
     nextday=1
     For cday=1 to 7
         If WeekDay(thisdate)>cday Then
             document.write "<TD></TD>"
         else
             document.write "<TD ALIGN=CENTER><FONT SIZE=3>"
             & nextday & "</TD>"
             nextday=nextday+1
             thisdate=DateSerial(year(date), imonth, nextday)
         End If
     Next
     document.write "<TR>"
     weekDays=1
     while month(thisdate)=imonth
         document.write "<TD ALIGN=CENTER><FONT SIZE=3>" &
         nextday & "</TD>"
         nextday=nextday+1
         weekDays=weekDays+1
         If weekDays>7 then
             WeekDays=1
             document.write "<TR>"
         End If
         thisdate=DateSerial(year(date), imonth, nextday)
```

```
wend
document.write "</TABLE>"
document.write "</CENTER>"

</SCRIPT>
```

WARNING This script will work with version 2.0 of VBScript only. If you don't have the latest version of VBScript, download it from Microsoft's Web site, at http://www.microsoft.com/vbscript.

First, the script displays the week's days as headers:

```
document.write _
"<TD><B>Sun<TD><B>Mon<TD><B>Tue<TD><B>Wed<TD><B>Thu<TD><B>Fri
<TD><B>Sat"
```

Next, the program displays the days of the first week with a For ... Next loop. The first week of the month is frequently incomplete, and the first few cells in the table are likely to be blank. This loop goes through the seven days in the week until it hits the first day in the month.

After the first day in the month is found, the program creates cells in which it places the value of the variable *nextday*, which is increased with every iteration (it goes from 1 to 31). The following string produces a cell with a number:

```
"<TD ALIGN=CENTER><FONT SIZE=3>" & nextday & "</TD>"
```

This is HTML code, and any references to variables are replaced with the actual value of the *nextday* variable. For example, if the value of the *nextday* variable is 24, the following line is actually written to the document:

```
<TD ALIGN=CENTER><FONT SIZE=3>24</TD>
```

After the first week of the calendar is displayed, the program continues with the following weeks. These weeks are complete, except for the last one, of course.

A While ... Wend loop handles the remaining days of the month. With each iteration, the *nextday* variable is increased by one day, and the loop continues to the end of the month.

You can easily turn each day of the month into a hyperlink that points to a file on the server. If you maintain a separate document on the server for each day of the month, you can modify the application so that each day is a hyperlink to this date's file. Instead of writing the number of the day to the output, you can insert the appropriate A tags to turn the day number into a hyperlink. For example, if the current value of the *nextday* variable is 24, the following VBScript line:

```
"<A HREF=" & imonth & "-" & nextday & ".htm>" & nextday & "</A>"
```

writes this string, which is indeed a hyperlink, to the document:

```
<A HREF=1-24.htm>24</A>
```

The names of the files specified in the hyperlinks must also exist on the server or in the same folder as the document that opened them.

The History Object

The History object provides methods for navigating through the browser's history. In other words, it lets you access the functionality of the browser's navigation buttons from within your code.

The Methods of the History Object

The History object of the Scripting Model maintains the list of sites already visited, and you can access them through the History object's methods, which are described next. The History object doesn't have its own properties or events.

Back *n* This method moves back in the history list by *n* steps, as if the user has clicked on the browser's Back button *n* times. To move to the most recently visited URL, use the following statement:

```
call Window.History.back(0)
```

Or simply use this statement:

```
call Window.History.back
```

Forward *n* This method moves forward in the history list by *n* steps, as if the user has clicked on the browser's Forward button *n* times.

Go *n*   This method moves to the *nth* item in the history list. The following statement takes you to the first URL in the list:

```
Window.History.go 1
```

Figure 16.8 shows a revision of the Page1 example, with two additional buttons, Go Back and Go Forward. I placed these two buttons on the page by choosing Edit ➢ Insert ActiveX Control on the ActiveX Control Pad. The following code is behind the Click event of the two buttons:

```
call Window.History.Back(0)
call Window.History.Forward(0)
```

FIGURE 16.8

The revised Page1 document with two navigation buttons

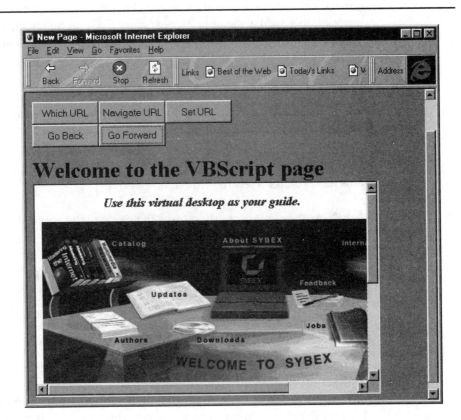

The Navigator Object

The Navigator object returns information about the browser. One of the major problems you will face as a Web author is that the two major browsers (Netscape Navigator and Microsoft Internet Explorer) are not totally compatible. Each supports a few unique features that the other doesn't.The truth is, both Netscape and Microsoft try to catch up with each other instead of attempting to establish new standards.

Developing pages that will work on both browsers is not a trivial task, especially for those who design active pages. Even if you can't design a page that can be rendered on both browsers, you can at least have two sets of pages, one for each browser, and display the appropriate pages. Even for this crude technique to work, you must figure out from within a script which browser is opening the page.

The Properties of the Navigator Object

The properties of the Navigator object are read-only, and they return information about the browser on which the document is viewed.

AppCodeName   This property returns the code name of the application. Internet Explorer 3 returns "Mozilla."

AppName   This property returns the name of the application. Internet Explorer 3 returns "Microsoft Internet Explorer."

AppVersion   This method returns the version of the application. Internet Explorer 3 returns "2.0 (compatible; MSIE 3.0A; Windows 95)."

UserAgent   This method returns the user agent of the application. Internet Explorer 3 returns "2.0 (compatible; MSIE 3.0A; Windows 95)."

Suppose you have prepared an HTML page that can be viewed with any browser (in other words, a generic page), and you have prepared a more advanced version of the same page that includes features supported only by Internet Explorer 3. You can easily detect which browser is running at the client's side, and you can display the advanced page if the browser happens to be Internet Explorer 3 and display the generic HTML page for all other browsers.

VB5 at Work: The Generic.htm Page

The Generic.htm page, shown in Figure 16.9, demonstrates how to display one page for Internet Explorer and another page when the document is opened with another browser.

FIGURE 16.9

The Generic page detects the browser and, if it's not Internet Explorer, displays a generic page.

The script examines the value of the property Window.Navigator.appname, and if it's "Microsoft Internet Explorer," it loads an active page. If not, it displays a generic page.

Code 16.4: The Generic Page

```
<HTML>
<HEAD>
<SCRIPT LANGUAGE=VBS>
If Window.Navigator.appname="Microsoft Internet Explorer" Then
     Window.Navigate("./Page1.htm")
End If
</SCRIPT>
<CENTER>
<H1>This site is optimized for Internet Explorer 3.0</H1>
<P>
```

```
Click <A HREF="http://www.microsoft.com/ie">here</A>
   to download the browser.
<IMG BORDER="0" SRC="./ie_animated.gif" WIDTH="88" HEIGHT="31"
VSPACE="7" ALT="Microsoft Internet Explorer" ></A><BR>
</CENTER>
</HTML>
```

If the browser can handle VBScript , it executes the script and displays the page specified with the Navigate method. Notice that the generic page's contents are listed after the script. This is really important. If you place the contents of the generic page in an Else clause or if you attempt to load the generic page with the window's Navigate method, nothing happens because, chances are, the browser does not understand VBScript. The entire script is, in effect, ignored.

The generic page used in this example is too generic indeed. It doesn't display any content; it simply prompts the viewer to download Internet Explorer and provides a link to the download site. The active page, which is displayed if the page is opened with Internet Explorer, is one of the active pages presented earlier in this chapter (Page1.htm).

The Location Object

The Location object applies to the Window and Frames objects and provides information about the window's (or frame's) current URL. You've already seen examples of the Location object, but we haven't looked at all its properties yet. Here are all the properties of the Location object.

The Properties of the Location Object

The location object's properties return information about the URL of the current document. By setting this object's properties, you can navigate to another document.

href   This property returns or sets the compete URL for the location to be loaded into the browser's window. Use this property to connect to another location through your VBScript code. To display the current document's URL, use a statement such as the following:

```
MsgBox "You are currently viewing " & document.location.href
```

You can also display another document in the window or frame with the following statement:

```
document.location.href="http://www.microsoft.com"
```

As you may recall from the discussion of URLs in the previous chapter, URLs have several parts. The properties shown in Table 16.2 return (or set) these parts.

TABLE 16.2   The Properties That Return or Set URL Parts

PROPERTY	WHAT IT DOES
protocol	Returns or sets the protocol of the URL (usually `http`).
host	Returns or sets the host and port of the URL. The host and port are separated with a colon, as in host:port. The port is optional and rarely used.
hostname	Reads or sets the host of a URL, which can be either a name or an IP address.
port	Returns or sets the port of the URL (you rarely have to specify the port number in a WWW URL).
pathname	Returns or sets the pathname of the URL. Use this property when you want to display a document other than the Web's root document.

The Links Object

Another invisible object is the Link object, which represents a link in an HTML document and exposes properties through which you can find out the destination of the link. The number of hyperlinks in the current document is given by the property Links.Length, and each hyperlink in the document is given by the links array. The URL of the first hyperlink is Links(0), links(1) is the URL of the second hyperlink, and so on up to links(Links.Length-1).

The links array returns a Link object, which in turn provides information about a hyperlink's attributes. The Link object has the properties shown in Table 16.3.

TABLE 16.3   The Properties of the Link Object

PROPERTY	WHAT IT DOES
href	Returns or sets the compete URL for the location to be loaded into the frame.
protocol	Returns or sets the protocol of the URL (usually `http`).
host	Returns or sets the host and port of the URL.
hostname	Reads or sets the host of a URL, which can be either a name or an IP address.
port	Returns or sets the port of the URL.
pathname	Returns or sets the pathname of the URL.
search	Returns or sets the search portion of the URL, if it exists.
hash	Returns or sets the hash portion of the URL.
target	The last property of the Frames object is the target that may have been specified in the `<A>` frame. The target of the link is the window or frame in which the destination object will be displayed.

CHAPTER
SEVENTEEN

17

The Web-Browsing Controls

- The Web Browser control

- The InternetExplorer object

So far, you have seen how to apply Visual Basic to the Web. You learned how to activate Web pages with VBScript, how to use ActiveX controls, and how to use your own custom controls on Web pages. But you still can't use the technology developed for the Web in your Visual Basic applications. Web technology is nothing less than the hypertext model. Being able to interact with an application by clicking on hyperlinks would be a welcome addition to a VB programmer's arsenal of user-interface design tools.

You can use two objects to add Web techniques and hyperlinked documents from within your Visual Basic applications:

- The WebBrowser control

- The InternetExplorer object

The WebBrowser is an ActiveX control you can use to add Internet browsing capabilities to applications and to display Web documents on Visual Basic Forms. Internet Explorer is an OLE Automation object that you can use to control Microsoft Internet Explorer from within an application.

The WebBrowser Control

Simply put, the WebBrowser control is Internet Explorer's window. Any HTML document that can be displayed in Internet Explorer can also be displayed in the WebBrowser control. In other words, the WebBrowser control adds browsing capabilities to your Visual Basic applications. It allows the user to browse sites on the World Wide Web, local files, or ActiveX documents, such as Word or Excel documents. Because the WebBrowser control can function as a container for ActiveX controls, it can handle HTML files that include Layouts (ALX files, discussed in Chapter 15, *Visual Basic and the Web*).

Because the WebBrowser is an ActiveX control, you can place it on any Visual Basic Form. Before you can use it, however, you must add it to the Toolbox. Follow these steps:

1. Right-click on the Toolbox, and from the shortcut menu, select Components to open the Components dialog box, as shown in Figure 17.1.

2. Select Microsoft Internet Controls, and then click on OK. A new icon is added to the Toolbox.

FIGURE 17.1

The Components
dialog box

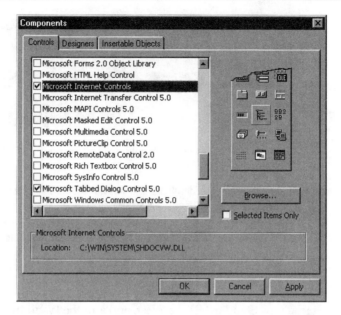

When you place a WebBrowser control on a Form, it's a borderless rectangle that you can size in any way you like. Because the control can't be resized by the user at run time, in your applications you should try to adjust its size according to the size of its container, which is a Visual Basic Form. When the Form is resized by the user, the WebBrowser control should be resized also so that it covers most of the Form.

To display a Web page in the WebBrowser control, use the Navigate method. You can also move through the list of URLs that have been displayed already with the GoBack and GoForward methods. The WebBrowser control automatically maintains the list of visited URLs. We'll look at the control's properties, methods, and events later. Let's start by developing a simple application that demonstrates the basic features of the control.

VB5 at Work: The WebBrwsr Application

The application is called WebBrwsr, and you will find it on the book's CD. Figure 17.2 shows the WebBrwsr application displaying the Microsoft Web site. The user can select a URL from the ComboBox control or select a local HTML file by clicking on the Open HTML File button.

FIGURE 17.2

The WebBrwsr applica-
tion shows how to add
Web-browsing capabili-
ties to a Visual Basic
application.

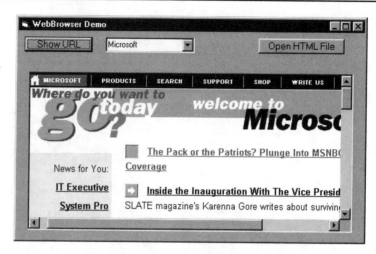

To build the application, follow these steps:

1. Start a new Standard EXE project, and add the WebBrowser control to the Toolbox, as shown earlier in this chapter.

2. Widen the Form and then place an instance of the WebBrowser control on it. Make the control large enough to cover most of the Form's area.

3. Now, place on the Form the other controls you see in Figure 17.2. In addition to the visible controls (two command buttons and a combo box), there is a Common Dialog control, which will be used to display the Open dialog box and in which the user can select local HTML files to display on the WebBrowser control. Also add the Common Dialog control to the Toolbox .

4. Enter the following lines to initialize the ComboBox control when the Form is loaded:

```
Private Sub Form_Load()
Combo1.AddItem "Microsoft"
Combo1.AddItem "SYBEX"
Combo1.AddItem "AltaVista"
Combo1.ListIndex = 0
End Sub
```

You can add your favorite URLs here, as long as the name displayed in the box is the name of a commercial Web server. When the user selects the ServerName in the ComboBox, the program generates the following URL:

```
www.ServerName.com
```

5. The Show URL button creates a complete URL from the computer's name and uses it with the Navigate method to display the specified URL on the WebBrowser control.

Code 17.1: The Show URL Button

```
Private Sub Command1_Click()
WebBrowser1.Navigate "http://www." & Combo1.Text & ".com"
End Sub
```

The Open HTML File button is quite similar, but instead of displaying a remote URL, it prompts the user to select a local HTML file and then renders it on the WebBrowser control.

Code 17.2: The Open HTML File Button

```
Private Sub Command2_Click()
CommonDialog1.CancelError = True
On Error GoTo CancelOpen
CommonDialog1.Filter = "HTML Files|*.HTM|Text Files|*.TXT|All
 Files|*.*"
CommonDialog1.ShowOpen
If CommonDialog1.filename <> "" Then
    WebBrowser1.Navigate CommonDialog1.filename
End If
Exit Sub

CancelOpen:
    Exit Sub
End Sub
```

Run the application and check it out. Try to load the Web pages developed in the previous chapter (they are on the CD). Figure 17.3 shows the HotSpot page, which contains an HTML Layout.

WARNING   If you open a Word document, you will see it as it appears in Word, but you won't see Word's menu and toolbar—which makes it nearly impossible to edit from within the WebBrowser control.

FIGURE 17.3

The WebBrowser control displaying the HotSpot Web page

The InternetExplorer Object

The InternetExplorer object allows you to start an instance of Internet Explorer from within your application and manipulate it through OLE Automation. The InternetExplorer object supports the same properties and methods as the WebBrowser control, plus a few more. We will look at the object's properties and methods shortly, but first let's build an application that controls Internet Explorer. It's called IExplore, and you will find it on the CD.

VB5 at Work: The IExplore Application

To reference Internet Explorer from within your project, you must first add a reference to the InternetExplorer object. Follow these steps:

1.   Start a new project and select Standard EXE as the project type.

2. Choose Project ➤ References to open the References dialog box, as shown in Figure 17.4.

FIGURE 17.4

The References
dialog box

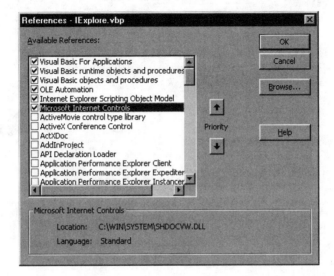

3. Check the Microsoft Internet Controls checkbox.

This time, you won't see a new icon in the Toolbox. But if you open the Object Browser window, you will see that the InternetExplorer class has been added to the project. In the Members window, you will see the properties and methods exposed by the InternetExplorer class, as shown in Figure 17.5, and through these members you can OLE automate the Internet Explorer application.

Let's build an application that will control one or more instances of Internet Explorer. The application is shown in Figure 17.6. The user can select a destination in the ComboBox control in the Visual Basic window and click on the Show URL button to start an instance of Internet Explorer, on which the selected URL is displayed.

FIGURE 17.5

The InternetExplorer
class and its members

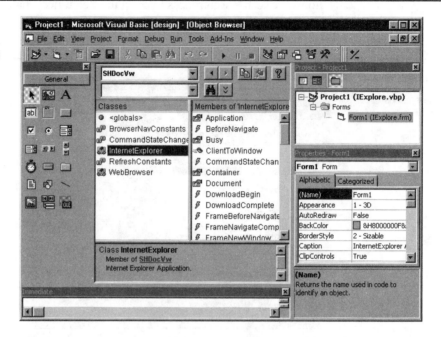

FIGURE 17.6

Use the IExplore applica-
tion to OLE automate
Internet Explorer.

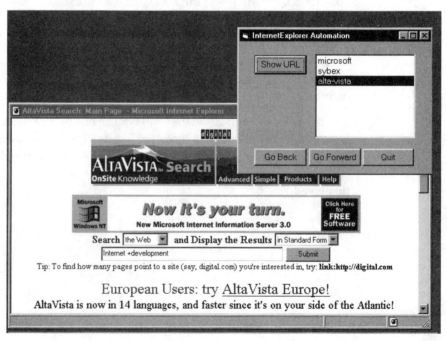

To continue building the application, follow these steps:

4. Design a Form like the one shown in Figure 17.6.

5. Declare a Form-wide object variable, though which you'll be accessing the members of the InternetExplorer class:

```
Dim IE As New InternetExplorer
```

6. Now, add the following initialization code in the Form's Load event:

```
Private Sub Form_Load()
    List1.AddItem "microsoft"
    List1.AddItem "sybex"
    List1.AddItem "altavista"
End Sub
```

The most interesting part of this application is the code behind the Show URL command button, which loads an instance of Internet Explorer and opens the selected URL in its window.

Code 17.3: The Show URL Button

```
Private Sub Command1_Click()
    IE.ToolBar = False
    IE.MenuBar = False
    IE.Visible = True
    IE.Navigate "http://www." & List1.Text & ".com"
End Sub
```

The properties ToolBar and MenuBar determine whether the toolbar and menu bar of Internet Explorer will be visible. Notice that the Internet Explorer window shown in Figure 17.6, earlier in this chapter, has neither.

The Navigate method opens the specified document and displays it in the browser's window. (I'll discuss the properties and the methods of the InternetExplorer object and the WebBrowser control in the next section.)

The Back and Forward buttons are implemented with two methods of the InternetExplorer object, GoBack and GoForward.

Code 17.4: The GoBack and GoForward Methods

```
Private Sub BackBttn_Click()
On Error GoTo NoBack
```

```
        IE.GoBack
        Exit Sub

NoBack:
    MsgBox "There are no URL in the History List"
End Sub

Private Sub ForwardBttn_Click()
On Error GoTo NoForward
    IE.GoForward
    Exit Sub

NoForward:
    MsgBox "There are no URLs in the History List"
End Sub
```

NOTE   We use error-trapping code to prevent run-time errors that will be generated if the user attempts to move in front of or past the history list.

The Properties of the WebBrowser Control and the Internet Explorer Object

In this section and the next two sections, we will look at the most common properties, methods, and events of the WebBrowser control and the Internet Explorer object. Most apply to both. The most common properties of the WebBrowser control and InternetExplorer object are described next.

TIP   The InternetExplorer object has a few additional members, which I won't discuss here. For complete documentation, visit the following site: http://www.microsoft.com/intdev/sdk/docs/scriptom.

Application   This property returns the automation object supported by the application that contains the WebBrowser control.

Busy   This property returns a True/False value specifying whether the control is navigating to a new URL or is downloading a Web page. If the control's Busy property is True for an unusually long time, call the Stop method to cancel the navigation (sever the connection to the server) or the download of a document.

Container   This property returns an object that evaluates to the container of the WebBrowser control, if any. To find out the name of the container, use a statement such as the following:

```
WebBrowser1.Container.Name
```

(The *name* entry is the name of the Form that contains the control.)

Document   This property returns the automation object of the active document, if any. This is not the Document object of the Scripting Model, which was covered in the last chapter. To access the document displayed on the control, you use the following expression:

```
WebBrowser1.Document.Script.Document
```

This expression accesses the active document through the script property of the automation object.

Height, Width   These two properties return the dimensions, in pixels, of the control that contains the WebBrowser control.

Top, Left   These two properties return the location, in pixels, of the control's upper left corner on the Desktop.

LocationName   This property returns the title of the Web page displayed on the WebBrowser control.

LocationURL   This control returns the URL of the page displayed on the WebBrowser control. The LocationName and LocationURL properties retrieve information about the location of the displayed document. If the location is an HTML page on the World Wide Web, LocationName retrieves the page's title, and LocationURL retrieves the URL of that page. If the document displayed is a local file, both LocationName and LocationURL retrieve the full path of the file (or its UNC, if it's located on a network).

Type   This property returns a string that determines the type of the contained document object. The type for HTML documents is "Windows HTML Viewer".

The Methods of the WebBrowser Control and the InternetExplorer Object

The methods of the WebBrowser control and the InternetExplorer object let you navigate to new URLs or to URLs already visited. They are similar to the methods of the Navigate object of the Scripting Model, discussed in the previous chapter.

GoBack, GoForward   These two methods navigate backward or forward one item in the history list, which is maintained automatically by the WebBrowser control or the InternetExplorer object. Attempting to move after the most recent URL or before the first URL in the list generates a run-time error. To prevent this, you must include some error-trapping code, similar to the one you saw in the IExplore application, earlier in this chapter.

GoHome, GoSearch   The GoHome method navigates to the current home page; the GoSearch method navigates to the search page, as specified in the Internet Explorer Options dialog box.

Navigate   This method navigates to the URL or opens an HTML file, as specified in the method's first argument. This method has the following syntax:

```
Navigate URL [Flags,] [TargetFrameName,] [PostData,] [Headers]
```

All the arguments except the first are optional. The *URL* argument is the URL of the resource to be displayed on the control. The *Flags* argument is a constant or a value that specifies whether to add the resource to the history list, whether to read from or write to the cache, and whether to display the resource in a new window. It can be a combination of the values shown in Table 17.1.

TABLE 17.1 The Values of the *Flags* Argument

CONSTANT	VALUE	DESCRIPTION
navOpenInNewWindow	1	Opens the resource or file in a new window.
NavNoHistory	2	Does not add the resource or filename to the history list.
NavNoReadFromCache	4	Does not read from the disk cache for this navigation.
NavNoWriteToCache	8	Does not write the results of this navigation to the disk cache.

The *TargetFrameName* argument is the name of a frame in which the document will be displayed. The *PostData* argument is a string to be sent to the server during the HTTP POST transaction. The POST transaction is used to send data gathered on an HTML Form. If this parameter does not specify any post data, the Navigate method issues an HTTP GET transaction. This parameter is ignored if *URL* is not an HTTP URL (one whose protocol is http).

The *Headers* argument is a value that specifies additional HTTP headers to be sent to the server. These headers are added to the default Internet Explorer headers, and they can specify such things as the action required of the server, the type of data being passed to the server, or a status code. This parameter is ignored if *URL* is not an HTTP URL.

Refresh   This method reloads the page currently displayed on the WebBrowser control.

Refresh2   This method is similar to the Refresh one, but it lets you specify the refresh level. It has the following syntax:

```
WebBrowser1.Refresh2 level
```

The *level* argument can have one of the values shown in Table 17.2.

TABLE 17.2   The Values of the *level* Argument

CONSTANT	VALUE	DESCRIPTION
REFRESH_NORMAL	0	Performs a quick refresh that does not include sending the HTTP "pragma:nocache" header to the server.
REFRESH_IFEXPIRED	1	Performs a quick refresh if the page has expired.
REFRESH_COMPLETELY	3	Performs a full refresh that includes sending a "pragma:nocache" header to the server.

In addition, you can prevent the control from using the cache by specifying the navNoReadFromCache and navNoWriteToCache flags when calling the Navigate method.

Stop   This method cancels any pending navigation or download operation and stops playback of multimedia elements such as background sounds and animations.

The Events of the WebBrowser Control and the InternetExplorer Object

The events of the WebBrowser control and the InternetExplorer object are triggered each time the user moves to another URL with the navigation buttons of Internet Explorer or the WebBrowser control's navigation methods. They also monitor the progress of each download and let your application know when the download of a page is finished.

BeforeNavigate   This event occurs when the WebBrowser control is about to navigate to a different URL. It can be caused by external automation (by calling its Navigate method) or by internal automation from within a script or when the user clicks on a hyperlink in the current document. Your application has an opportunity to cancel the navigation by setting the method's Cancel argument to True.

TIP
The BeforeNavigate event isn't issued unless the hyperlink is valid. In other words, the control first contacts the Web server and then navigates to the specified document.

The BeforeNavigate method has the following syntax:

```
Sub WebBrowser1_BeforeNavigate(ByVal url As String, ByVal Flags
    As Long, ByVal TargetFrameName As String, PostData As Variant,
    ByVal Headers As String, Cancel As Boolean)
```

The *url* argument is the destination URL (specified by the Navigate method or in the hyperlink that was clicked), and *Flags* is a reserved argument. The *TargetFrameName* argument is the name of the frame in which to display the specified document, or it is NULL if the document is to appear on the control, outside any frames. The *PostData* and *Header* arguments are the same as for the Navigate method.

The application can set the *Cancel* argument (notice that it's passed by reference) to cancel the navigation process. If you set this argument to True, the navigation won't even start. To stop a navigation in process, use the Stop method.

NavigateComplete   This event occurs after the control has successfully navigated to the new location. Some of the document's resources may still be downloading (a large image, for instance, may take quite a while), but at least part of the document has been received from the server, and progressive rendering has started already. To interrupt this process, you must call the Stop method.

The NavigateComplete event has the following syntax:

```
Sub WebBrowser1_NavigateComplete(ByVal url As String)
```

The *url* variable is the URL of the document being downloaded.

DownloadBegin   This event occurs when a navigation operation is beginning. It's triggered shortly after the BeforeNavigate event (unless the navigation was canceled), and it signals your application to display a busy message or change the pointer's shape. The DownloadBegin event has the following syntax:

```
Sub WebBrowser1_DownloadBegin ()
```

DownloadComplete   The event DownloadComplete occurs when a navigation operation is finished, halted, or failed. Unlike NavigateComplete, which may not be triggered if the navigation doesn't complete successfully, this event is always triggered after a navigation starts. Any busy indication by your application must end from within this event. The DownloadComplete event has the following syntax:

```
Sub WebBrowser1_DownloadComplete ( )
```

ProgressChange   The WebBrowser control tracks the progress of a download operation and periodically issues the ProgressChange event to inform your application of the progress. The ProgressChange event has the following syntax:

```
Sub WebBrowser1_ProgressChange(ByVal Progress As Long, ByVal
    ProgressMax As Long)
```

Both arguments are long integers. The *Progress* argument is the amount of data downloaded so far, and *ProgressMax* is the total amount of data to be downloaded.

> **TIP**
>
> The percentage of data downloaded is Progress/ProgressMax, but you must always check the value of ProgressMax, because it can be zero (when the control doesn't know the total amount of data to be downloaded). Moreover, the ProgressChange event is triggered for each of the document's resources, and there is no way to know in advance the total size of the components to be downloaded. As you have noticed, Internet Explorer displays the progress of each component's download, and not the progress of the entire document.

StatusTextChange   This event occurs when the message in the status bar of Internet Explorer is about to change. The WebBrowser control doesn't have a status bar, but you can use this information from within your application to update a Caption property. The StatusTextChange event has the following syntax:

```
Sub WebBrowser1_StatusTextChange(ByVal Text As String)
```

The *Text* argument is the string that appears in Internet Explorer's status bar.

TitleChange   This event occurs when the title of the current document changes. The title of an HTML document can change; while the document is being downloaded, the URL of the document is also its title. After the real title (if one was specified with the TITLE tag) is parsed, the TitleChange event is triggered, and you can use it to update the Caption property on your Visual Basic Form. The TitleChange event has the following syntax:

```
Sub WebBrowser1_TitleChange(ByVal Text As String)
```

The *Text* argument is the string that appears in Internet Explorer's caption bar.

NewWindow   Although most hyperlinks result in updating the same window in which the document with the hyperlink is displayed, some hyperlinks specify that a new window be opened to display the destination document. When a new window is about to be created for displaying a new document, the NewWindow event is triggered.

This event can be also be triggered if the user holds down the Shift key and clicks the mouse while the cursor is over a hyperlink or if the user chooses New Window ➤ Open in the hyperlink's shortcut menu. The NewWindow event gives your application the opportunity to halt the creation of the new window. When this event is used with Internet Explorer, the new window is another instance of Internet Explorer.

When the NewWindow event is used with the WebBrowser control, however, your application must either create a new WebBrowser control and display the document there or request that the new document be displayed in the same window. If your application creates a new WebBrowser control, it must pass all the parameters from the NewWindow event directly to the Navigate method on the newly created WebBrowser control. If you decide to display the new document on the same control, you must again pass the parameters from this event to the Navigate method in the existing window.

The NewWindow event has the following syntax:

```
Sub WebBrowser_NewWindow (ByVal url As String, ByVal Flags As
    Long, ByVal TargetFrameName As String, PostData As Variant,
    ByVal Headers As String, Processed As Boolean)
```

The arguments of the NewWindow event are identical to the arguments of the Navigate method, except for the last argument which is a True/False value indicating whether your application will create the new window (set it to True).

FrameBeforeNavigate, FrameNavigateComplete, FrameNewWindow
These three events are identical to the BeforeNavigate, NavigateComplete, and NewWindow events, except that they are triggered from within frames.

Using the WebBrowser Control

You can use the WebBrowser control to build customized Web browsers, because it supports all the browsing functionality of Internet Explorer. You can implement the Back and Forward buttons of Internet Explorer with the GoBack and GoForward methods, capture the jumps to hyperlinks, control which sites the WebBrowser control can visit, and so on.

Of course, the WebBrowser doesn't have all the features of Internet Explorer. The most important limitation is that it can't access the displayed document, and you can't save the current HTML document from within your code. Reading the source code of a Web page is going to become more and more difficult. In the past, Web pages were constructed with plain HTML, and viewers could open and examine them. Active pages now contain HTML Layouts, which you can't read as easily, and ActiveX documents can't be read. They are essentially executable files.

> **NOTE**
>
> If you publish content for the Web, you should be able to keep its source documents to yourself. To viewHTML source files, choose View ➤ Source.

In the last two sections of this chapter, we are going to look at two applications that demonstrate how to use the WebBrowser control from within Visual Basic. The first application is a custom Web browser. The second application demonstrates how to exploit the hypertext model of an HTML document from within Visual Basic applications and how to add hyperlink features to a user interface.

VB5 at Work: A Customized Web Browser

Figure 17.7 shows an interesting approach to customized browsers. The Form shown in this figure contains a TabStrip control, with several pages, each displaying a different URL. The URLs can be local files or pages on remote servers. You can use local help files for an application (step-by-step instructions), or you can connect your application's users to a Web server that has up-to-the-minute information.

FIGURE 17.7

FIGURE 17.7

SuperBrowser is a customized Web browser you can insert in any Visual Basic application.

To create the SuperBrowser application, follow these steps:

1. Start a new Standard EXE project, and add a TabStrip control to the Form. Make the Form larger than its default size, and stretch the TabStrip control to fill as much of the Form as possible. You may want to leave some space for a few command buttons, such as Back and Forward (which aren't implemented in this example).

2. If the Toolbox doesn't contain the WebBrowser icon, add it using the Components dialog box (select Internet Controls from the list of available components). You may have to add the TabStrip control to the Toolbox, using the Components dialog box.

3. In the Toolbox, select the WebBrowser control, and place an instance of the control on each of the TabStrip's tabs. The WebBrowser control should cover nearly all of the tab's area. The three WebBrowser controls are members of the control array WebBrowser1, and their Index values are 0, 1, and 2.

4. Double-click on the Form to open the Code window.

5. In the Form's Load event, enter the following lines, which cause the three WebBrowser controls to navigate to a separate Web site:

```
Private Sub Form_Load()

    WebBrowser1(0).Navigate "http://home.microsoft.com"
    WebBrowser1(1).Navigate "http://www.sybex.com"
    WebBrowser1(2).Navigate "http://www.altavista.com"

End Sub
```

As soon as the Form is loaded, the corresponding WebBrowser controls download the three pages and display them progressively. You can select the page to view by switching to the appropriate tab of the TabStrip control. All three pages continue downloading, as if you had opened three instances of Internet Explorer, each displaying a different document.

You can start the application and watch the three pages being downloaded. The application works fine, but it consumes a number of resources. This is the price of the convenience of having all three pages present at once, as opposed to loading multiple pages on the same control.

Let's add a few lines of code to display the URL of each page on the corresponding tab. Switch back to the Code window, and enter the following line in the WebBrowser control's BeforeNavigate event:

```
Private Sub WebBrowser1_BeforeNavigate(Index As Integer, ByVal
    URL As String, ByVal Flags As Long, ByVal TargetFrameName As
    String, PostData As Variant, ByVal Headers As String, Cancel
    As Boolean)
    SSTab1.TabCaption(Index) = URL
End Sub
```

This line displays the URL of the page that started downloading to the corresponding tab's caption area.

Once the page is downloaded, the WebBrowser control knows its title. At this point, you replace the URL with the actual title. Enter the code to do so in the NavigateComplete event:

```
Private Sub WebBrowser1_NavigateComplete(Index As Integer, ByVal
    URL As String)
    SSTab1.TabCaption(Index) = WebBrowser1(Index).LocationName
End Sub
```

Now run the application and watch how the captions on the TabStrip control reflect the contents of each page.

TIP   You can also add Back and Forward buttons. To do so, use the GoBack and GoForward methods, and also use an On Error statement in case there are no pages in the history list.

Monitoring the Download Progress

This application provides a good opportunity to experiment with the download events. Switch back to the Code window, and enter the following code in the DownloadBegin and DownloadComplete events:

```
Private Sub WebBrowser1_DownloadBegin(Index As Integer)
Debug.Print "Started Download for tab #" & Index
End Sub

Private Sub WebBrowser1_DownloadComplete(Index As Integer)
Debug.Print "Completed download for tab #" & Index
End Sub
```

If you run the application now, you will see the following messages in the Immediate execution window:

```
Started Download for tab #0
Started Download for tab #1
Started Download for tab #2
Completed download for tab #1
Completed download for tab #2
Started Download for tab #1
Started Download for tab #2
Completed download for tab #1
Completed download for tab #0
Started Download for tab #0
Completed download for tab #0
Completed download for tab #2
```

The WebBrowser control starts and completes several downloads for each page. These messages correspond to the downloads of the various elements of each page. If you want to display the progress as well, you must program the ProgressChange event.

To do so, place a Label control on the first tab of the TabStrip control, and enter the following lines in the WebBrowser control's ProgressChange event:

```
Private Sub WebBrowser1_ProgressChange(Index As Integer, ByVal
    Progress As Long, ByVal ProgressMax As Long)
If Index = 0 Then
    If Progress >= 0 Then
        Label1.Caption = "Download Progress " & Progress & "/" &
ProgressMax
    Else
        Label1.Caption = "Page downloaded"
    End If
End If
End Sub
```

> **TIP**
>
> If you have a fast connection to the server on which the documents reside, the messages are displayed for only an instant.

The program monitors the download progress of the first tab only. To monitor the other two pages, you must create an array of three Label controls and place one on each page. Then, instead of updating the Caption property of the Label1 control, update the Label1(Index) control. The Else clause of this If structure displays the following message after the entire page is downloaded:

```
"Page Downloaded"
```

When this happens, the Progress argument is -1, and there's no need for the string "100/100" to remain on the screen.

Adding Other Features to Your Custom Browser

Another interesting feature you can add to your custom browser is to monitor the URLs. For example, you can keep a list of URLs visited frequently by the user. When the user selects one of them, you ask whether the user wants to open the pages from the cache or download them again.

Or you can prevent the user from following links outside a given Web. This isn't as outrageous as it may sound in an intranet environment. In this case, you might want to limit certain users to the company's Web and not let them take the trip of the thousand clicks during business hours.

Using Hyperlinks in Visual Basic Applications

What makes Web pages tick is the hypertext model they use to connect to other pages, anywhere on the World Wide Web. Although you can access the functionality of Web technology from within your Visual Basic applications with objects such as the WebBrowser and InternetExplorer, you still can't exploit this technology by making it an integral part of your Visual Basic application. Things will change soon, and the Web technology will merge with the various technologies you use on your Desktop today.

The WebBrowser controls make it possible to exploit the hyperlink model in your applications, and we'll present an example that uses hyperlinks as part of the user interface of a Visual Basic application.

VB5 at Work: The DemoPage Application

The DemoPage application is shown in Figure 17.8, and you will find it on this book's CD. The DemoPage application consists of two Forms:

- VBForm

- WEBForm

The main Form is VBForm and is used for drawing simple shapes with Visual Basic methods. The WebForm displays an HTML document that contains instructions on the Visual Basic drawing methods. The HTML document contains the instructions and a few hyperlinks. When either hyperlink is activated, it doesn't display another document. Instead, it draws a shape on the first Visual Basic Form.

FIGURE 17.8

The two Forms of the
DemoPage application

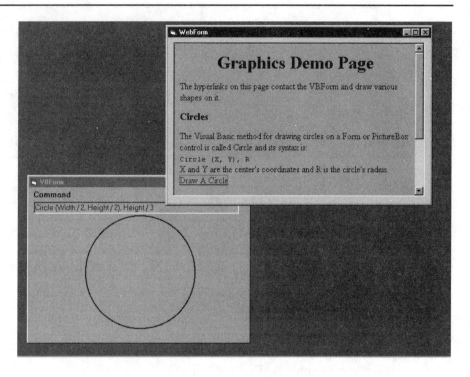

Design the two Forms as shown in Figure 17.8. The main Form contains a
Label control at the top, on which a command is displayed. The second Form
(WebForm) contains a WebBrowser control, on which the Demo.htm page
is displayed.

When the first Form is loaded, it loads the second Form and displays the
HTML document on the WebBrowser control. All the code in the VBForm Form is
located in the Load event.

Code 17.5: The Load Event

```
Private Sub Form_Load()
Dim target

    target = App.Path & "\Demo.htm"
    WEBForm.WebBrowser1.Navigate target
    WEBForm.Show

End Sub
```

To avoid an absolute reference, we use a variable to store the HTML document's name. The name of the HTML document is Demo.htm, and it is stored in the same folder as the project. The complete Demo.htm page is shown in Figure 17.9.

FIGURE 17.9

The entire Demo.htm as displayed by Internet Explorer

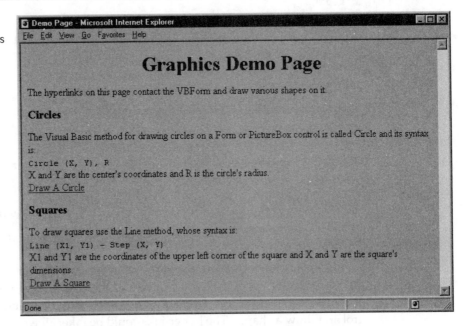

Code 17.6: The DemoPage Application

```
<HTML>
<TITLE>Demo Page</TITLE>

<BODY>
<CENTER>
<H1>Graphics Demo Page</H1>
</CENTER>

The hyperlinks on this page contact the VBForm and draw various
   shapes on it.
<P>
<H3>Circles</H3>
```

```
The Visual Basic method for drawing circles on a Form or
   PictureBox control is called Circle and its syntax is:
<BR>
<CODE>Circle (X, Y), R</CODE>
<BR>
X and Y are the center's coordinates and R is the circle's
   radius.
<BR>
<A HREF="http://127.0.0.1./demo.htm#circle">Draw A Circle</A>
<BR>
<BR>
<H3>Squares</H3>
To draw squares use the Line method, whose syntax is:
<BR>
<CODE>Line (X1, Y1) - Step (X, Y)</CODE>
<BR>
X1 and Y1 are the coordinates of the upper left corner of the
   square and X and Y are the square's dimensions.
<BR>
<A HREF="http://127.0.0.1./demo.htm#box">Draw A Square</A>
</BODY>
</HTML>
```

As you may have guessed, the application exploits the BeforeNavigate event to find out which hyperlink was activated and then cancel the jump to this hyperlink and do something on the first Form (display the command in the Label control and draw a shape). The hyperlinks could be fake; all we need is to know which one was clicked. However, the BeforeNavigate event isn't triggered unless the destination of the hyperlink is a valid URL.

As you can see, the destinations of the hyperlinks include some information about the kind of shape to be drawn on the first Form. The definitions of the two hyperlinks are as follows:

```
<A HREF="http://127.0.0.1./demo.htm#circle">Draw A Circle</A>
<A HREF="http://127.0.0.1./demo.htm#box">Draw A Square</A>
```

The HTML document doesn't contain any anchors named "circle" and "box," and you don't really need them. The WebBrowser control generates an error message, but all you really need is the name of the anchor. The IP address of the local machine is 127.0.0.1 (it's always a valid server name). Let's see how the code of the BeforeNavigate event causes some action to take place on the other Form.

Code 17.7: The BeforeNavigate Event

```
Private Sub WebBrowser1_BeforeNavigate(ByVal URL As String,
ByVal Flags As Long, ByVal TargetFrameName As String,
PostData As Variant, ByVal Headers As String, Cancel As Boolean)

Dim Position, Shape

On Error Resume Next

    If Right$(URL, 8) <> "Demo.htm" Then Cancel = True
    Position = InStr(URL, "#")
    Shape = Mid$(URL, Position + 1)
    If Shape = "circle" Then
        VBForm.Cls
        VBForm.Circle (VBForm.Width/2, VBForm.Height/2),
 VBForm.Height/3
        VBForm.Label1.Caption = "Circle (Width/2, Height/2),
        Height/3"
    End If
    If Shape = "box" Then
        VBForm.Cls
        VBForm.Line (VBForm.Width/4, VBForm.Height/4)-
Step(VBForm.Width/2, VBForm.Height/2), , B
        VBForm.Label1.Caption = "Line (Width/4, Height/4)-
Step(Width/4, Height/4), , B"
    End If

End Sub
```

The first statement is an error-trapping statement; it tells Visual Basic to ignore errors and continue with the next statement. We know that an error will occur because the destinations of the two hyperlinks are invalid. We then cancel the navigation by setting the Cancel argument to True. The If statement makes sure that other (possibly valid) hyperlinks aren't canceled. The program then examines the last part of the hyperlink's destination URL (everything to the right of the pound sign). If this string is "circle", the program draws a circle on the VBForm Form and displays the command used to draw the circle in the Label control. If the string is "box", it draws a square on the Form and displays the corresponding command on the Label.

You can easily modify this application to accommodate more actions, place detailed instructions in the HTML document, and even create demos for your applications. The approach is rather "clumsy," but hyperlinks are not yet part of the Visual Basic interface model. The application does, however, demonstrate how to incorporate the functionality of hyperlinks in your Visual Basic applications.

Built-in Functions

This appendix describes all Visual Basic built-in functions, grouped by category. Table A.1 lists the individual functions by type. In the following sections, you will find detailed descriptions of each function and some simple examples.

TABLE A.1   Functions by Type

TYPE	FUNCTION
Input/Output	InputBox()
	MsgBox()
File I/O	FileAttr()
	GetAttr()
	FileDateTime()
	FileLen()
	FreeFile()
Variable Type	Array()
	LBound()
	Ubound()
	IsArray()
	IsDate()
	IsEmpty()
	IsNull()
	IsNumeric()
	IsObject()
	TypeName()
	VarType()
Variable Type Conversion	CBool()
	CByte()
	CCur()
	CDate()
	CDec()
	CDbl()
	CInt()
	CLng()
	CSng()
	CStr()
	Cvar
String-Handling	Asc()
	Chr()
	LCase()
	InStr()
	InStrB()

TABLE A.1   Functions by Type (continued)

TYPE	FUNCTION
String-Handling	StrComp() Left() Right() Mid() Len() LTrim() Space() String() StrConv() Format$() Ucase() InStr() Str()
Math	Abs() Atn() Cos() Exp() Int() Fix() Log() Oct() Hex() Rnd() Sgn() Sin() Sqr() Tan() Val()
Date andTime	Timer() Date() Time() Now() Day() Weekday() Month() Year() Hour() Minute() Second() DateSerial() DateValue() TimeSerial() TimeValue()

TABLE A.1   Functions by Type (continued)

TYPE	FUNCTION
Date andTime	DateAdd() DateDiff() DatePart()
Financial	IPmt() PPmt() Pmt() FV() PV() NPV() NPer() Rate() IRR() MIRR() DDB() SYD() SLN()
Color	QBColor() RGB()
Miscellaneous	IIF() Switch()

Input/Output Functions

Visual Basic provides two basic functions for displaying (or requesting) informa-tion to the user: MsgBox() and InputBox(). Windows applications should commu-nicate with the user via nicely designed Forms, but the MsgBox() and InputBox() functions are still around and quite useful.

InputBox(prompt[, title][, default][, xpos][, ypos][, helpfile, context])   The InputBox() function displays a dialog box with a prompt and a TextBox control and waits for the user to enter some text and click on the OK or Cancel button. The arguments of the InputBox() function are shown in Table A.2.

TABLE A.2   The Arguments of the InputBox() Function

ARGUMENT	WHAT IT IS	DESCRIPTION
prompt	The prompt that appears in the dialog box	If necessary, the prompt is broken into multiple lines automatically. To control line breaks from within your code, use a carriage return character or a linefeed character (vbCrLf).
title	The title of the dialog box	If you omit this argument, the application's name is displayed as the title.
default	The default input (if any)	If you anticipate the user's response, use this argument to display it when the dialog box is first opened.
xpos, ypos	The coordinates of the upper left corner of the dialog box	Expressed in twips.
helpfile	The name of the Help file	Provides context-sensitive help for the dialog box.
context	The number within the Help file	Assigned to the specific topic.

The simplest format of the InputBox() function is as follows:

```
SSN = InputBox("Please enter your Social Security number")
```

The string that the user enters in the dialog box is assigned to the variable *SSN*. The return value is always a string, even if the user enters numeric information. When prompting for input with the InputBox() function, always check the value returned by the function. At the very least, check for a blank string. Use the IsNumeric() function if you expect the user to enter a number, use the IsDate() function if you expect the user to enter a date, and so on.

```
BDay = InputBox("Please enter your birth date")
If IsDate(Bday) Then
   MsgBox "Preparing your Horoscope"
Else
   MsgBox "Please try again with a valid birth date"
End If
```

MsgBox(prompt[, buttons][, title] [, helpfile, context]) The MsgBox function displays a dialog box with a message and waits for the user to close it by clicking on a button. The message is the first argument (*prompt*). The simplest form of the MsgBox() function is as follows:

```
MsgBox "Your computer is running out of memory!"
```

This function displays a message in a dialog box that has an OK button. The MsgBox() function can display other buttons and/or an icon in the dialog box and return a numeric value, depending on which button was clicked. Table A.3 summarizes the values for the buttons argument.

TABLE A.3 The Values for the Buttons Argument

CONSTANT	VALUE	DESCRIPTION
Button Values		
vbOKOnly	0	Displays OK button only.
VbOKCancel	1	Displays OK and Cancel buttons.
VbAbortRetryIgnore	2	Displays Abort, Retry, and Ignore buttons.
VbYesNoCancel	3	Displays Yes, No, and Cancel buttons.
VbYesNo	4	Displays Yes and No buttons.
VbRetryCancel	5	Displays Retry and Cancel buttons.
Icon Values		
VbCritical	16	Displays Critical Message icon.
VbQuestion	32	Displays Warning Query icon.
VbExclamation	48	Displays Warning Message icon.
VbInformation	64	Displays Information Message icon.

TABLE A.3   The Values for the Buttons Argument (continued)

CONSTANT	VALUE	DESCRIPTION
Default Button		
VbDefaultButton1	0	First button is default.
VbDefaultButton2	256	Second button is default.
VbDefaultButton3	512	Third button is default.
VbDefaultButton4	768	Fourth button is default.
Modality		
VbApplicationModal	0	Application modal; the user must respond to the message box before switching to any of the Forms of the current application.
VbSystemModal	4096	System modal; all applications are suspended until the user responds to the message box.

Button values determine which buttons appear in the dialog box. Notice that you can't choose to display individual buttons; you can only choose groups of buttons.

Icon values determine optional icons you can display in the dialog box. These are the common icons used throughout the Windows user interface to notify the user about an unusual or exceptional event.

Default Button values determine which button is the default; pressing Enter activates this button.

The values 0 and 4096 determine whether the message box is modal.

To combine these settings into a single value, simply add their values.

Finally, the MsgBox() function returns an integer, which indicates the button pressed, according to Table A.4.

TABLE A.4   The Values of the Buttons

CONSTANT	VALUE	DESCRIPTION
vbOK	1	OK
vbCancel	2	Cancel
vbAbort	3	Abort
vbRetry	4	Retry
vbIgnore	5	Ignore
vbYes	6	Yes
vbNo	7	No

To display a dialog box with the OK and Cancel buttons and the Warning Message icon, add the values 1 and 48 as follows:

```
cont = MsgBox("This operation may take several minutes", 48+1);
```

Your application continues with the operation if the value of *cont* is 1 (OK button).

To display a dialog box with the Yes and No buttons and the Critical Message icon, add the values 4 and 16 as follows:

```
cont = MsgBox("Incomplete data. Would you like to retry?", 4 + 16);
If cont = 6 Then      // user clicked Yes
    {prompt again}
Else               // user clicked No
    {exit procedure}
Endif
```

The *title* argument is the title displayed in the message box's title bar. See the description of the InputBox() function for an explanation of the *helpfile* and *context* arguments.

File I/O Functions

The following Visual Basic functions manipulate files (create a new file, open an existing file, read and write to a file, examine a file's properties, and so on).

FileAttr(filenumber, returntype)   The FileAttr() function returns a long integer representing the file mode for files opened using the Open statement. The *filenumber* variable is the number of the file, and *returntype* must be 1. The value returned is one of those in Table A.5.

TABLE A.5   The Values Returned by the FileAttr() Function

VALUE	MODE
1	Input
2	Output
4	Random
8	Append
32	Binary

GetAttr(filename)   This function returns an integer representing the attributes of a file, a directory, or a folder, according to Table A.6.

TABLE A.6   The Values Returned by the GetAttr() Function

CONSTANT	VALUE	DESCRIPTION
vbNormal	0	Normal
vbReadOnly	1	Read-only
vbHidden	2	Hidden
vbSystem	4	System
vbDirectory	16	Directory or folder
vbArchive	32	File has changed since last backup

To determine which attributes are set, use the AND operator to perform a bitwise comparison of the value returned by the GetAttr() function and the value of one or more attributes. If the result is not zero, that attribute is set for the named file. For example, to find out if a file is read-only, use a statement such as the following:

```
Result GetAttr(FName) And vbReadOnly
```

If the *FName* file has its read-only attribute set, Result will be non-zero.

FileDateTime(filename)   This function returns the date and time when a file was created or last modified. The following statement:

```
Print FileDateTime("myDocument.txt")
```

returns a date/time value such as "21/1/97 14:13:02 PM".

FileLen(filename)   The FileLen() function returns a long integer value indicating the file's length. The file whose length you want to find out is passed as an argument to the function. The following statement:

```
MsgBox FileLen(".\docs\myDocument.txt")
```

displays the length of the specified file in a message box.

FreeFile()   Each file opened with Visual Basic must have a unique handle (a number) that is assigned to the file the moment it's opened and is used to refer to the file in future operations. The handle is freed (that is, it becomes available to be used with another file) after its file is closed.

FreeFile() returns an integer representing the next file number available for use by the Open statement. Hard-coding a file number is not considered solid programming practice, so you usually call the FreeFile() function to find out the next available file number and then open the file using the value returned by the FreeFile() function as follows:

```
fileNum = FreeFile
Open "myDocument.txt" For Output As #fileNum
```

The actual value of the file number is unimportant as long you use the variable *fileNum* to refer to the file myDocument.txt.

Variable Type Functions

The following functions determine the type of variables. Some of them let you determine a variable's exact type from within your code, and a series of functions determines the general type of a variable (such as numeric variables, date variables, and so on). In addition, there are three functions that let you populate array elements and quickly check array bounds.

VarType(variable)   The VarType() function returns a value indicating the subtype of a variable, according to Table A.7.

TABLE A.7   The Values Returned by the VarType() Function

CONSTANT	VALUE	DESCRIPTION
vbEmpty	0	Empty (uninitialized)
vbNull	1	Null (no valid data)
vbInteger	2	Integer
vbLong	3	Long integer
vbSingle	4	Single-precision floating-point number
vbDouble	5	Double-precision floating-point number
vbCurrency	6	Currency value
vbDate	7	Date value
vbString	8	String
vbObject	9	Object
vbError	10	Error value
vbBoolean	11	Boolean value
vbVariant	12	Variant (used only with arrays of variants)
vbDataObject	13	A data access object
vbDecimal	14	Decimal value
vbByte	17	Byte value
vbArray	8192	Array

The VarType() function doesn't return the type of an array's elements directly. Instead, the value of the elements' type is added to 8192. If you pass an array of strings to the VarType() function, the return value is 8200 (which is 8192 + 8).

Array(argumentList) This function returns a Variant containing an array whose elements are assigned values from the *argumentList*. The *argumentList* variable is a comma-delimited list of values that are assigned to consecutive elements of the array. Omitting *argumentList* creates an array with no elements. To use it, you must redimension it with the ReDim command. The following statements create an array with the names of the days of the week:

```
Dim WeekDays
WeekDays = Array("Monday", "Tuesday", "Wednesday", "Thursday"
➡"Friday", Saturday", "Sunday")
FirstDay = WeekDays(0)              ' Monday
SecondDay = WeekDays(1)             ' Tuesday
```

The lower bound of an array created using the Array function is always 0. Notice also that the Array function *does not dimension the array*. It only assigns values to its elements.

LBound(arrayname[, dimension]) This function returns the smallest subscript for the indicated dimension of an array. The *arrayName* variable is the name of the array, and *dimension* is an integer indicating the dimension whose lower bound will be returned. If *dimension* is omitted, the first dimension is assumed. The LBound() function is used with the UBound() function, which returns the largest subscript of a dimension of a given array, to determine the size of the array.

UBound(arrayname[, dimension]) This function returns the largest subscript for the indicated dimension of an array. The *arrayName* variable is the name of the array, and *dimension* is an integer indicating the dimension whose upper bound will be returned. If *dimension* is omitted, the first dimension is assumed.

To scan all the elements of a one-dimensional array, use both the LBound() and the UBound() functions. The following statements convert the elements of the string array Strings() to uppercase:

```
Lower = LBound(Strings)
Upper = UBound(Srtings)
```

```
For i = Lower to Upper
    Strings(i) = Ucase(Strings(i))
Next
```

IsArray(variable)   This function returns True if its argument is an array. If the variable *Names* has been defined as:

```
Dim Strings(100)
```

the function:

```
IsArray(Strings)
```

returns True.

IsDate(expression)   This function returns True if *expression* is a valid date. Use the IsDate() function to validate user data. Dates can be specified in various formats, and validating them without the help of the IsDate() function would be a task on its own.

```
Bdate = InputBox("Please enter your birth date")
If IsDate(BDate) Then
        MsgBox "Date accepted"
End If
```

IsEmpty(variable)   This function returns True if the *variable* is empty. An empty variable hasn't been initialized or explicitly set to Empty. After the execution of the following statements:

```
numVar = 0
stringVar = ""
```

the variables *numVar* and *stringVar* are not empty because they have been initialized. If a variable has been declared with a Dim statement but not initialized or otherwise used by your program, it's empty. If a variable must be initialized before it is used, you can find out its status with the IsEmpty() function.

IsNull(expression)   This function returns True if *expression* is Null. A Null value is a nonvalid value and is different from an Empty value. Regular variables can't be Null unless you assign the Null value to them. Object variables can be Null.

IsNumeric(expression)   This function returns True if *expression* is a valid number. Use this function to check the validity of strings containing numeric data as follows:

```
age = InputBox("Please enter your age")
If Not IsNumeric(age) Then
    MsgBox("Please try again, this time with a valid number")
End If
```

IsObject(expression)   This function returns a Boolean (True/False) value indicating whether *expression* represents an object variable. To find out the type of object, use the TypeName() or VarType() functions, which are described next.

TypeName(variable_name)   This function returns a string that identifies the variable's type. It's similar to the VarType() function, but instead of returning an integer, it returns the name of the variable's type. The variable whose type you're examining with the TypeName function may have been declared implicitly or explicitly. Suppose you declare the following variables

```
Dim name As String
Dim a
```

The following statements produce the results shown (you can issue the statements and watch the values they return in the Debug window):

```
Print TypeName(name)
      String
Print TypeName(a)
      Empty
a = "I'm a string"
Print TypeName(a)
      String
a = #5/11/97#
Print TypeName(a)
      Date
Print TypeName(b)
      Empty
```

Notice that the variable *b*, which wasn't declared, is Empty, but not Null.

Variable Type Conversion Functions

These functions convert their numeric argument to the corresponding type. With the introduction of the Variant data type, these functions are of little use. You can use them to document your code and show that the result of an operation should be of the particular type, but keep in mind that all operands in an arithmetic operation are first converted to double-precision numbers for the greatest possible accuracy. Table A.9 lists the Variable Type Conversion functions and describes what they do.

TABLE A.9   The Variable Type Conversion Functions

FUNCTION	WHAT IT DOES
CBool(expression)	Converts its argument to Boolean (True/False) type; evaluates to True if expression evaluates to any nonzero value.
CByte(expression)	Converts its argument to Byte type.
CCur(expression)	Converts its argument to Currency type.
CDate(expression)	Converts its argument to Date type.
CDec(expression)	Converts its argument to Decimal type.
CDbl(expression)	Converts its argument to Double type.
CInt(expression)	Converts its argument to Integer type.
CLng(expression)	Converts its argument to Long type.
CSng(expression)	Converts its argument to Single type.
CStr(expression)	Converts its argument to String type.
CVar(expression)	Converts its argument to Variant type. Numeric expressions are converted to doubles, and alphanumeric expressions are converted to strings.

String-Handling Functions

A typical application spends much of its execution time manipulating strings (validity tests, parsing), and Visual Basic provides numerous functions for that purpose.

Asc(character), AscB(string), AscW(string)   The Asc() function returns the character code corresponding to the character argument, and it works on all systems, regardless of whether they support Unicode characters.

The AscB() function is similar, except that instead of returning the character code for the first character, it returns the first byte.

The AscW() function returns the Unicode character code except on platforms that do not support Unicode, in which case, the behavior is identical to that of the Asc() function.

If you call the Asc() function with a string instead of a character, the character code of the string's first character is returned.

Chr(number), ChrB(number), ChrW(number)   The Chr() function is the inverse of the Asc() function and returns the character associated with the specified character code. Use this function to print characters that don't appear on the keyboard (such as line feeds or special symbols).

The ChrB() function is used with byte data contained in a string. Instead of returning a character, which may be one or two bytes, ChrB() always returns a single byte.

The ChrW() function returns a string containing the Unicode character except on platforms that don't support Unicode, in which case, the behavior is identical to that of the Chr() function.

LCase(string), UCase(string)   The LCase() function accepts a string as an argument and converts it to lowercase; the Ucase() function accepts a string as an argument and converts it to uppercase. After the following statements are executed:

```
Title = "Mastering Visual Basic"
LTitle = LCase(Title)
UTitle = UCase(Title)
```

the variable *LTitle* contains the string "mastering visual basic", and the variable *UTitle* contains the string "MASTERING VISUAL BASIC".

A useful function is one that converts a string to "lower caps." In other words, a function that converts all the characters in the string to lowercase and then converts the first character of each word to uppercase. Now that you've seen all the string manipulation functions, you can write a LowerCaps() function as follows:

```
Function LowerCaps(str As String) As String

position = InStr(str, " ")       ' Locate first space
While position                   ' while there are spaces in the string
    newWord = Left$(str, position)' extract word
```

```
                        ' and convert its first character to upper case
        newStr = newStr & UCase$(Left$(newWord, 1)) & Mid$ (newWord, 2)
        str = Right$(str, Len(str) - position)     ' remove word from
        ➡string
        position = InStr(str, " ")
Wend
newWord = str      ' convert the last word in the string
newStr = newStr & UCase$(Left$(newWord, 1)) & Mid$(newWord, 2)
LowerCaps = newStr      ' return string in Lower Caps

End Function
```

The LowerCaps() function uses the Instr() function to locate successive instances of the space character in the string. It then isolates the words between spaces, changes their first character to uppercase and the rest of the word to lowercase, and appends them to the NewStr string. When the function exits, its value is the original string formatted in lower caps. If you call the LowerCaps() function with the following argument:

```
CompanyName = "ABC industrial, inc."
UCString = LowerCaps(CompanyName)
```

the *UCString* variable's value will be:

```
"ABC Industrial, Inc."
```

InStr([startPos,[string1, string2[, compare]) See the entries Left, Right,and Mid.

InStrB([startPos,] string1, string2[, compare]) The InStr() function returns the position of *string2* within *string1*. The first argument, which is optional, determines where in *string1* the search begins. If the *startPos* argument is omitted, the search begins at the first character of *string1*. If you execute the following statements:

```
str1 = "The quick brown fox jumped over the lazy dog"
str2 = "the"
Pos = Instr(str1, str2)
```

the variable *Pos* will have the value 33. If you search for the string "he" by setting:

```
str2 = "he"
```

the *Pos* variable's value will be 2. If the search begins at the third character in the string, the first instance of the string "he" after the third character will be located:

```
Pos = Instr(3, str1, str2)
```

This time the *Pos* will be 34.

The search is by default case-sensitive. To locate "the", "The", or "THE" in the string, specify the last optional argument whose value is 0 (default) for a case-sensitive search and 1 for a case-insensitive search.

The following statement locates the first occurrence of "the" in the string, regardless of case:

```
str1 = "The quick brown fox jumped over the lazy dog"
str2 = "the"
Pos = Instr(1, str1, str2, 1)
```

The value of *Pos* will be 1. If you set the last argument to 0, the *Pos* variable becomes 33. Notice that if you want to use the last optional argument of the InStr() function, you must also specify the first argument.

The InStrB() function is used with byte data contained in a string. Instead of returning the character position of the first occurrence of one string within another, InStrB() returns the byte position.

StrComp(string1, string2 [, compare])   This function compares two strings and returns a value indicating the result according to Table A.10.

TABLE A.10   The Values That the StrComp() Function Returns

VALUE	DESCRIPTION
-1	*string1* is less than *string2*
0	*string2* is equal to *string2*
1	*string1* is greater than *string2*
Null	*string1* and/or *string2* is Null

The last argument of the StrComp() function determines whether the comparison will be case-sensitive. If compare is 0 (or omitted), the comparison is case-sensitive. If it's 1, the comparison is case-insensitive.

The following function:

```
StrComp("Sybex", "SYBEX")
```

returns 1 ("Sybex" is greater than "SYBEX", because the lowercase y character is after the uppercase Y in the ASCII sequence). The following function:

```
StrComp("Sybex", "SYBEX", 1)
```

returns 0.

Left(string, number), LeftB(string, number)   The Left() function returns a number of characters from the beginning of a string. It accepts two arguments: the string and the number of characters to extract. If the string *date1* starts with the month name, the following Left() function can extract the month's abbreviation from the string, as follows:

```
date1 = "December 25, 1995"
MonthName = Left(date1, 3)
```

The value of the *MonthName* variable is "Dec".

Use the LeftB() function with byte data contained in a string. Instead of specifying the number of characters, the arguments specify numbers of bytes.

Right(string, number), RightB(string, number)   The Right function is similar to the Left function, except that it returns a number of characters from the end of a string. The following statement:

```
Yr = Right(date1, 4)
```

assigns to the *Yr* variable the current year.

Use the RightB() function with byte data contained in a string. Instead of specifying the number of characters, the arguments specify numbers of bytes.

Mid(string, start, [length]), MidB(string, start[, length])   The Mid() function returns a section of a string of *length* characters, starting at position *start*. The following function:

```
Mid("09 February, 1997", 4, 8)
```

extracts the name of the month from the specified string.

If you omit the *length* argument, the Mid() function returns all the characters from the starting position to the end of the string. If the specified length exceeds the number of characters in the string after the start position, the remaining string from the start location is returned.

Use the MidB() function with byte data contained in a string. Instead of specifying the number of characters, the arguments specify numbers of bytes.

Len(string), LenB(string)   The Len() function returns the length of a string. After the following statements execute:

```
Name = InputBox("Enter your first Name")
NameLen = Len(Name)
```

the variable *NameLen* contains the length of the string entered by the user in the Input Box.

The Len() function is frequently used as a first test for invalid input, as in the following lines:

```
If Len(Name) = 0 Then
   MsgBox "NAME field can't be empty"
Else
   MsgBox "Thank you for registering with us"
EndIf
```

Use the LenB() function with byte data contained in a string. Instead of returning the number of characters in a string, LenB() returns the number of bytes used to represent that string.

LTrim(string), RTrim(string), Trim(string)   These functions trim the spaces in front of, after, and on either side of a string. They are frequently used in validating user input, as in the following.

```
If EMail <> "" Then
      MsgBox "Applications without an e-mail address won't be
      ➥processed"
End If
```

The preceding won't, however, catch a string that only has spaces. To detect empty strings, use the Trim() function instead:

```
If Trim(EMail) = "" Then
      MsgBox "Invalid Entry!"
End If
```

Space(number)   This function returns a string consisting of the specified number of spaces. The *number* argument is the number of spaces you want in the string. This function is useful for formatting output and clearing data in fixed-length strings.

String(number, character)   This function returns a string of *number* characters, all of which are *character*. The following function:

```
String(12, "*")
```

returns the string "************". Use the String() function to create long patterns of special symbols.

 StrConv(string, conversion)   This function returns a string variable converted as specified by the conversion argument, whose values are shown in Table A.11.

TABLE A.11   The Values Returned by the StrConv() Function

CONSTANT	VALUE	DESCRIPTION
vbUpperCase	1	Converts the string to uppercase characters.
vbLowerCase	2	Converts the string to lowercase characters.
vbProperCase	3	Converts the first letter of every word in the string to uppercase.
vbWide*	4*	Converts narrow (single-byte) characters in the string to wide (double-byte) characters.
vbNarrow*	8*	Converts wide (double-byte) characters in the string to narrow (single-byte) characters.
vbKatakana*	16*	Converts Hiragana characters in the string to Katakana characters.
vbHiragana*	32*	Converts Katakana characters in the string to Hiragana characters.
vbUnicode	64	Converts the string to Unicode using the default code page of the system.
vbFromUnicode	128	Converts the string from Unicode to the default code page of the system.

*Applies to Far East locales.

To perform multiple conversions, add the corresponding values. To convert a string to lowercase and to Unicode format, use a statement such as the following:

```
newString = StrConv(txt, vbLowerCase + vbUnicode)
```

Format(expression[, format[, firstdayofweek[, firstweekofyear]]])

This function returns a string containing an expression formatted according to instructions contained in a format expression. The *expression* variable is the number, string, or date to be converted, and *format* is a string that tells Visual Basic how to format the value. The string "hh:mm.ss", for example, displays the expression as a time string. The Format() function is used to prepare numbers, dates, and strings for display. If you attempt to print the following expression:

```
Print atn(1)/4
```

the number 3.14159265358979 is displayed. If this value must appear in a text control, chances are that it will overflow the available space.

You can control the number of decimal digits to be displayed with the following call to the Format() function:

```
Print Format(atn(1)*4, "##.####")
```

This statement prints the result 3.1416. If you are doing financial calculations and the result turns out to be 13,454.332345201, it would be best to print it as $13,454.33, with a statement such as the following:

```
amount = 13454.332345201
Print Format(amount, "$###,###.##")
```

These statements print the value $13,454.33, which is a proper dollar amount.

The *firstdayofweek* argument determines which is the week's first day and can have one of the values in Table A.12.

TABLE A.12   The Values of the *firsdayofweek* Argument

CONSTANT	VALUE	DESCRIPTION
vbUseSystem	0	Use NLS API setting
VbSunday	1	Sunday (default)

TABLE A.12   The Values of the *firsdayofweek* Argument (continued)

CONSTANT	VALUE	DESCRIPTION
vbMonday	2	Monday
vbTuesday	3	Tuesday
vbWednesday	4	Wednesday
vbThursday	5	Thursday
vbFriday	6	Friday
vbSaturday	7	Saturday

Similarly, the *firstweekofyear* determines which is the first week of the year, and it can have one of the values in Table A.13.

TABLE A.13   The Values of the *firstweekofyear* Argument

CONSTANT	VALUE	DESCRIPTION
vbUseSystem	0	Uses NLS API setting
vbFirstJan1	1	Starts with the week of January 1
vbFirstFourDays	2	Starts with the week that has at least four days in the year
vbFirstFullWeek	3	Starts with the first full week of the year

The *firstdayofweek* and *firstweekofyear* arguments are used only in formatting dates.

There are many formatting strings for all three types of variables: numeric, string, and date and time. Table A.14, Table A.15, and Table A.16 show them.

TABLE A.14   User-Defined Time and Date Formatting

CHARACTER	DESCRIPTION
:	Time separator. In some locales, other characters may be used to represent the time separator. The time separator separates hours, minutes, and seconds when time values are formatted.
/	Date separator. In some locales, other characters may be used to represent the date separator. The date separator separates the day, month, and year when date values are formatted.
c	Displays date as ddddd and the time as ttttt.
d	Displays day as a number (1 – 31).
dd	Displays day as a number with a leading zero (01 – 31).
ddd	Displays day as an abbreviation (Sun – Sat).
dddd	Displays day as a full name (Sunday – Saturday).
ddddd	Displays complete date (including day, month, and year), formatted according to the system's short date format setting. The default short date format is m/d/y.
dddddd	Displays complete date, formatted according to the long date setting recognized by the system. The default long date format is mmmm dd, yyyy.
w	Displays day of the week as a number (1 for Sunday through 7 for Saturday).
ww	Displays week of the year as a number (1 – 54).
m	Displays month as a number (1 – 12). If m immediately follows h or hh, the minute rather than the month is displayed.
mm	Displays month as a number with a leading zero (01 – 12). If m immediately follows h or hh, the minute rather than the month is displayed.
mmm	Displays month as an abbreviation (Jan – Dec).
mmmm	Displays month as a full month name (January – December).

TABLE A.14 User-Defined Time and Date Formatting (continued)

CHARACTER	DESCRIPTION
q	Displays quarter of the year as a number (1 − 4).
y	Displays day of the year as a number (1 − 366).
yy	Displays year as a 2-digit number (00 − 99).
yyyy	Displays year as a 4-digit number (100 − 9999).
h	Displays hours as a number (0 − 23).
hh	Displays hours with leading zeros (00 − 23).
n	Displays minutes without leading zeros (0 − 59).
nn	Displays minutes with leading zeros (00 − 59).
s	Displays seconds without leading zeros (0 − 59).
ss	Displays seconds with leading zeros (00 − 59).
ttttt	Displays complete time (including hour, minute, and second), formatted using the time separator defined by the time format of the system. The default time format is h:mm:ss.
AM/PM	Uses the 12-hour format and displays the indication AM/PM.
am/pm	Uses the 12-hour format and displays the indication am/pm.
A/P	Uses the 12-hour format and displays the indication A/P.
a/p	Uses the 12-hour format and displays the indication a/p.
AMPM	Uses the 12-hour format and displays the AM/PM string literal as defined by the system. Use the Regional Settings program in the Control Panel to set this literal for your system.

T A B L E A . 1 5 User-Defined Number Formatting

CHARACTER	WHAT IT IS OR DOES	DESCRIPTION
None		Displays the number with no formatting.
0	Digit placeholder	Displays a digit or a zero. If the expression has a digit in the position where the 0 appears in the format string, display it; otherwise, display a zero in that position. If the number has fewer digits than there are zeros in the format expression, leading or trailing zeros are displayed. If the number has more digits to the right of the decimal separator than there are zeros to the right of the decimal separator in the format expression, round the number to as many decimal places as there are zeros. If the number has more digits to the left of the decimal separator than there are zeros to the left of the decimal separator in the format expression, display the extra digits without modification.
#	Digit placeholder	Displays a digit or nothing. If the expression has a digit in the position where the # appears in the format string, display it; otherwise, display nothing in that position. This symbol works like the 0 digit place-holder, except that leading and trailing zeros aren't displayed if the number has the same or fewer digits than there are # characters on either side of the decimal separator in the format expression.
.	Decimal placeholder	The decimal placeholder determines how many digits are displayed to the left and right of the decimal separator. If the format expression contains only number signs to the left of this symbol, numbers smaller than 1 begin with a decimal separator. To display a leading zero displayed with fractional numbers, use 0 as the first digit placeholder to the left of the decimal separator.
%	Percentage placeholder	The expression is multiplied by 100. The percent character (%) is inserted in the position where it appears in the format string.

TABLE A.15 User-Defined Number Formatting (continued)

CHARACTER	WHAT IT IS OR DOES	DESCRIPTION
,	Thousand separator	Separates thousands from hundreds within a number greater than 1000. Two adjacent thousand separators or a thousand separator immediately to the left of the decimal separator (whether or not a decimal is specified) means "scale the number by dividing it by 1000, rounding as needed." For example, you can use the format string "##0," to represent 100 million as 100. Numbers smaller than 1 million are displayed as 0. Two adjacent thousand separators in any position other than immediately to the left of the decimal separator are treated simply as specifying the use of a thousand separator.
:	Time separator	Separates hours, minutes, and seconds when time values are formatted.
/	Date separator	Separates the day, month, and year when date values are formatted.
E+, e-, e+	Scientific format	If the format expression contains at least one digit placeholder (0 or #) to the right of E-, E+, e-, or e+, the number is displayed in scientific format, and E or e is inserted between the number and its exponent. The number of digit placeholders to the right determines the number of digits in the exponent. Use E- or e- to place a minus sign next to negative exponents. Use E+ or e+ to place a minus sign next to negative exponents and a plus sign next to positive exponents.
+ $ (space)	Display a literal character	To display a character other than one of those listed, precede it with a backslash (\) or enclose it in double quotation marks (" ").
\	Displays the next character in the format string	To display a character that has special meaning as a literal character, precede it with a backslash (\). The backslash itself isn't displayed. Using a backslash is the same as enclosing the next character in double quotation marks. To display a backslash, use two backslashes (\\). Examples of characters that can't be displayed as literal characters are the date-formatting and time-formatting characters (a, c, d, h, m, n, p, q, s, t, w, y, / and :), the numeric-formatting characters (#, 0, %, E, e, comma, and period), and the string-formatting characters (@, &, <, >, and !).

TABLE A.15 User-Defined Number Formatting (continued)

CHARACTER	WHAT IT IS OR DOES	DESCRIPTION
"ABC"	Displays the string inside double quotation marks (" ")	To include a string in format from within code, you must use Chr(34) to enclose the text (34 is the character code for a quotation mark).

TABLE A.16 User-Defined String Formatting

CHARACTER	WHAT IT IS OR DOES	DESCRIPTION
@	Character placeholder	Displays a character or a space. If the string has a character in the position where the at symbol (@) appears in the format string, it is displayed. Otherwise, a space in that position is displayed. Placeholders are filled from right to left unless there is an exclamation point character (!) in the format string.
&	Character placeholder	If the string has a character in the position where the ampersand (&) appears, it is displayed. Otherwise, nothing is displayed. Placeholders are filled from right to left unless there is an exclamation point character (!) in the format string.
<	Force lowercase	All characters are first converted to lowercase.
>	Force uppercase	All characters are first converted to uppercase.
!	Scans placeholders from left to right	The default order is to use placeholders from right to left. Use the exclamation point to invert this order.

Math Functions

The following functions perform math operations. Their arguments are double precision values and so are their results.

Abs(expression)   This function returns the absolute value of its argument. Both Abs(1.01) and Abs(-1.01) return the value 1.01.

Atn(expression)   This function returns the arctangent of an angle expressed in radians. The value returned is in radians. To convert it to degrees, multiply by 180/pi, where pi is 3.14159…. To calculate pi with double precision, use the following statement:

```
Atn(1)*4
```

Cos(expression)   This function returns the cosine of an angle expressed in radians. The value returned is in radians. To convert it to degrees, multiply by 180/pi, where pi is 3.14159…. To calculate pi with double precision, use the following statement:

```
Atn(1)*4
```

Exp(expression)   This function returns the base of the natural logarithms to a power. The *expression* variable is the power, and its value can be a noninteger, positive, or negative value. The Exp() function complements the operation of the Log() function and is also called *antilogarithm*.

Int(expression), Fix(expression)   Both these functions accept a numeric argument and return its integer part. If *expression* is positive, both functions behave the same. If it's negative, the Int() function returns the first negative integer less than or equal to *expression*, and Fix returns the first negative integer greater than or equal to *expression*. For example, Int(-1.1) returns -2, and Fix(-1.1) returns -1.

   The functions Int(1.8) and Fix(1.8) both return 1. If you want to get rid of the decimal part of a number and round it as well, use the following expression:

```
Int(value + 0.5)
```

The *value* argument is the number to be rounded. The following function:

```
Int(100.1 + 0.5)
```

returns 100, and the function:

```
Int(100.8 + 0.5)
```

returns 101. This technique works with negative numbers as well. The following function:

```
Int(-100.1 + 0.5)
```

returns -100, and the function:

```
Int(-100.8 + 0.5)
```

returns -101.

Log(expression)   The Log() function returns the natural logarithm of a number. The *expression* variable must be a positive number. The following expression:

```
Log(Exp(N))
```

returns N, and so will this expression:

```
Exp(Log(N))
```

If you combine the logarithm with the antilogarithm, you end up with the same number.

The natural logarithm is the logarithm to the base e, which is approximately 2.718282. The precise value of e is given by the function Exp(1). To calculate logarithms to other bases, divide the natural logarithm of the number by the natural logarithm of the base. The following statement calculates the logarithm of a number in base 10:

```
Log10 = Log(number) / Log(10)
```

Hex(expression), Oct(expression)   These two functions accept a decimal numeric value as an argument and return the octal and hexadecimal representation of the number in a string. The function Hex(47) returns the value "2F", and the function Oct(47) returns the value "57". To specify a hexadecimal number, prefix it with the symbols &H. The equivalent notation for octal numbers is &O. Given the following definitions:

```
Dvalue = 199: Ovalue = &O77
```

the function Oct(Dvalue) returns the string "307", and the function Hex(Ovalue) returns "3F". To display the decimal value of 3F, use a statement such as the following:

```
MsgBox ("The number 3F in decimal is " & &H3F)
```

The actual value that will be printed is 63.

Rnd([expression])   The Rnd() function returns a pseudo-random number in the range 0 to 1. The optional argument is called *seed* and is used as a starting point in the calculations that generate the random number.

If the seed is negative, the Rnd() function always returns the same number. As strange as this behavior may sound, you may need this feature to create repeatable random numbers to test your code. If the seed is positive (or omitted), the Rnd() function returns the next random number in the sequence. Finally, if the seed is zero, the Rnd() function returns the most recently generated random number.

In most cases, you don't need a random number between 0 and 1, but between two other integer values. A playing card's value is an integer in the range 1 to 13. To simulate the throw of a dice, you need a number in the range 1 to 6. To generate a random number in the range *lower* to *upper*, in which both bounds are integer numbers, use the following statement:

```
randomNumber = Int((upper - lower + 1)*rnd() + lower);
```

The following statement displays a random number in the range 1 to 49.

```
Debug.Print Int(Rnd * 48 + 1)
```

Sgn(expression)   This function returns an integer indicating the sign of its argument: 1 if the argument is greater than zero, 0 if the argument is 0, and –1 if the argument is less than zero.

Sin(expression)   This function returns the sine of an angle, specified in radians. See the Cos() entry.

Sqr(expression)   This function returns the square root of a positive number. If the argument number is negative, the Sqr() function causes a run-time error, because by definition the square root of a negative number is undefined. If your program uses the Sqr() function, you must include some error-trapping code such as the following:

```
If var>=0 Then
    sqVar = Sqr(var)
Else
    MsgBox "The result can't be calculated"
End IF
```

Tan(expression)   This function returns the tangent of an angle, which must be expressed in radians.

Val(string)   This function returns the numeric value of a string made up of digits. The Val() function starts reading the string from the left and stops when it reaches a character that isn't part of a number. If the value of the variable *a* is:

```
a = "18:6.05"
```

the following statement:

```
Debug.Print Val(a)
```

returns 18.

Date and Time Functions

The date and time functions report (or set) the system's date and time. Visual Basic understands many formats for the date. Besides the common formats such as 2/9/1999, it recognizes month names. Dates such as "February 1999" and "May 25, 1997" are valid date expressions. See the Format(string) entry for more on date and time formats.

Timer0   This function returns a single number representing the number of seconds elapsed since midnight. It is frequently used for timing purposes, as long as the desired accuracy is not less than a second. To time an operation that takes a while to complete, use a structure such as the following:

```
T1 = Timer
        {lengthy calculations}
Debug.print Int(Timer - T1)
```

The last statement displays the integer part of the difference, which is the number of seconds elapsed since the calculations started.

Date0   This function returns the current date in month/day/year format, unless you specified the UK date format (day/month/year). The following statement:

```
MsgBox "The system date is " & Date()
```

displays a date such as 9/22/1997 in a message box. To set the system date, use the following statement:

```
date = "01/01/97"
```

Time()   This function returns the system's time in AM/PM format. The following statement:

```
MsgBox "The system time is " & Time()
```

displays a time such as 5:13:05 PM in a message box. To set the system time, use the following statement:

```
Time = "13:00.00"
```

Now()   This function returns both the system date and time, in the same format as they are reported by the Date() and Time() functions. The following statement:

```
Debug.print Now()
```

displays a date/time combination such as 9/13/1997 09:23:10 PM in a message box. There's only one space between the date and the time.

The Now function is equivalent to the following pair of functions:

```
Date() & " " & Time()
```

Day(date)   This function returns the day number of the date specified by the argument. The *date* argument must be a valid date (such as the value of the Date() or the Now() function). If the following function were called on 12/01/95, it would return 1.

```
Day(Date())
```

The Day(Now()) function returns the same result.

Weekday(date, [firstdayofweek])   This function returns an integer in the range 1 to 7, representing the day of the week (1 for Sunday, 2 for Monday, and so on). The first argument, *date*, can be any valid date expression. The second argument, which is optional, specifies the first day of the week. Set it to 1 to start counting from Sunday (the default), or set it to 2 to start counting from Monday. The value 3 corresponds to Tuesday, the value 4 corresponds to Wednesday, and so on.

The following code segment prints the name of the day:

```
DayNames = Array("Sunday", "Monday", "Tuesday", "Wednesday",
➥"Thursday", "Friday", "Saturday")
dayname = "Today it is " & DayNames(Weekday(Now)-1)
Debug.Print dayname
```

Notice that the code subtracts 1 from the weekday to account for the array being zero based.

Month(date)   This function returns an integer in the range 1 to 12, representing the number of the month of the specified date. Month(Date) returns the current month number. The following code segment displays the name of the month:

```
MonthNames = Array("January", "February", "March", "April", "May",
➥"June", "July", "August", "September", "October", "November",
➥"December")
monthName = "The current month is " & MonthNames(Month(Now)-1)
Debug.Print monthName
```

Notice that the code subtracts 1 from the month's value to account for the array being zero based.

A Trick with Format$()

You can avoid setting up an entire array for day and month names as I did here, by being creative with the Format$() function. To print the name of the month monthNum (which should be a value in the range 1 to 12), use this trick:

```
Debug.Print Format$(monthNum & "/01/99", "mmmm")
```

This statement prints the string "April". You can use any day in the month and any year in the previous function. The result depends on the month number.

Year(date)   This function returns an integer representing the year of the date passed to it as argument. The following function:

```
Year(Now())
```

returns the current year.

Hour(time)   This function returns an integer in the range 0 to 24 that represents the hour of the specified time. The following statements:

```
Debug.Print Now
Debug.Print Hour(Now)
```

produce something such as:

```
12/27/96 11:32:43 AM
11
```

Minute(time)   This function returns an integer in the range 0 to 60 that represents the minute of the specified time. The following statements:

```
Debug.Print Now
Debug.Print Minute(Now)
```

produce something such as:

```
12/27/96 11:57:13 AM
57
```

Second(time)   This function returns an integer in the range 0 to 60 that represents the seconds of the specified time. The following statements:

```
Debug.Print Now
Debug.Print Second(Now)
```

produce something such as:

```
12/27/96 11:57:03 AM
3
```

DateSerial(year, month, day)   This function accepts three numeric arguments that correspond to a year, a month, and a day value and returns the corresponding date. The following statement:

```
MsgBox DateSerial(1997, 10, 1)
```

displays the string "10/1/97" in a message box.

Although hardly a useful operation, the DateSerial function can handle arithmetic operations with dates. For example, you can find out the date of the 90th day of the year by calling DateSerial() with the following arguments:

```
DateSerial(1996, 1, 90)
```

(3/30/96, if you are curious).

To find out the date 1000 days from now, call the DateSerial function as follows:

```
DateSerial(Year(Date), Month(Date), Day(Date)+1000)
```

You can also add (or subtract) a number of months to the *month* argument and a number of years to the *year* argument.

DateValue(date)   This function returns a variant of type Date. It is handy if you are doing financial calculations based on the number of days between two dates. The difference in the following statement:

```
MsgBox DateValue("12/25/1996") - DateValue("12/25/1993")
```

is the number of days between the two dates, which happens to be 1096 days. You can verify this result by adding 1096 days to the earlier date:

```
MsgBox DateValue("12/25/1993") + 1096
```

or subtracting 1096 days from the later date:

```
MsgBox DateValue("12/25/1996") - 1096
```

TimeSerial(hours, minutes, seconds)   This function returns a time, as specified by the three arguments. The following function:

```
TimeSerial(4, 10, 55)
```

returns:

```
4:10:55 AM
```

The TimeSerial() function is frequently used to calculate relative times. The following call to TimeSerial() returns the time 2 hours, 15 minutes, and 32 seconds before 4:13:40 PM:

```
TimeSerial(16 - 2, 13 - 15, 40 - 32)
```

which is 2:02:08 PM.

TimeValue(time)   This function returns a variant of type Time. Like the DateValue() function, it can be used in operations that involve time. If the variables *Time1* and *Time2* are defined as follows:

```
Time1 = "04.10.55"
Time2 = "18.50.00"
```

you can find out the hours, minutes, and seconds between the two times with the following statements:

```
Diff = TimeValue(Time2) - TimeValue(Time1)
HourDiff = Hour(Diff)
MinDiff = Minute(Diff)
SecDiff = Second(Diff)
```

In this example, the values are:

```
HourDiff=14
MinDiff=25
SecDiff=05
```

 DateAdd(interval, number, date)   This function returns a date that corresponds to a date plus some interval. The *interval* variable is a time unit (days, hours, weeks, and so on), *number* is the number of intervals to be added to the initial date, and *date* is the initial date. If *number* is positive, the date returned by DateAdd is in the future. If it's negative, the date returned is in the past. The interval argument can take one of the values in Table A.17.

TABLE A.17   The Values for the *interval* Argument

VALUE	DESCRIPTION
yyyy	Year
q	Quarter
m	Month
y	Day of year
d	Day
w	Weekday
ww	Week
h	Hour
n	Minute
s	Second

To find out the date one month after January 31, 1996, use the following statement:

```
Print DateAdd("m", 1, "31-Jan-96")
```

The result is:

```
2/29/96
```

and not an invalid date such as February 31.

DateAdd() also takes into consideration leap years. The following statement:

```
Print DateAdd("m", 1, "31-Jan-96")
```

displays the date 2/29/96 in the Immediate window.

The DateAdd() function is similar to the DateSerial() function, but it takes into consideration the actual duration of a month. For DateSerial(), each month has 30 days. The following statements:

```
day1=#1/31/1996#
Print DateSerial(year(day1), month(day1)+1, day(day1))
```

result in:

```
3/2/96
```

which is a date in March, not February.

DateDiff(interval, date1, date2[, firstdayofweek[, firstweekofyear]])

This function is the counterpart of the DateAdd() function and returns the number of intervals between two dates. The *interval* argument is the interval of time you use to calculate the difference between the two dates (see Table A.17, earlier in this appendix, for valid values). The *date1* and *date2* arguments are dates to be used in the calculation, and *firstdayofweek* and *firstweekofyear* are optional arguments that specify the first day of the week and the first week of the year.

Table A.18 shows the valid values for the *firstdayofweek* argument, and Table A.19 shows the valid values for the *firstweekofyear* argument.

TABLE A.18 The Values for the *firstdayofweek* Argument

CONSTANT	VALUE	DESCRIPTION
vbUseSystem	0	Use the NLS API setting
vbSunday	1	Sunday (default)
vbMonday	2	Monday
vbTuesday	3	Tuesday
vbWednesday	4	Wednesday

TABLE A.18 The Values for the *firstdayofweek* Argument (continued)

CONSTANT	VALUE	DESCRIPTION
vbThursday	5	Thursday
vbFriday	6	Friday
vbSaturday	7	Saturday

TABLE A.19 The Values for the *firstweekofyear* Argument

CONSTANT	VALUE	DESCRIPTION
vbUseSystem	0	Use the NLS API setting.
vbFirstJan1	1	Start with week in which January 1 occurs (default).
vbFirstFourDays	2	Start with the first week that has at least four days in the new year.
vbFirstFullWeek	3	Start with first full week of the year.

You can use the DateDiff() function to find how many days, weeks, and even seconds are between two dates. The following statement displays the number of days and minutes until the turn of the century (or the time elapsed after the turn of century, depending on when you execute it):

```
century=#01/01/2000 00:00.00#
Print DateDiff("n", now(), century)
```

If you place this code in a Timer's Timer event, you can update a text control every second or every minute with the countdown to the end of the century. If you use the DateValue() function, as in the following:

```
Print  minute(DateValue("01/01/2000 00:00.00")  - DateValue(now()))
```

the result is a number in the range 0 to 60. You have to consider the difference of years, months, days, hours, and minutes to calculate the correct value.

DatePart(interval, date[,firstdayofweek[, firstweekofyear]]) This function returns the specified part of a given date. The *interval* argument is the desired format in which the part of the date will be returned (see Table A.17, earlier in this appendix, for its values), and *date* is the part of the date you are seeking. The optional arguments *firstdayofweek* and *firstdayofmonth* are the same as for the DateDiff() function. The following Print statements produce the result shown below them:

```
day1=#03/23/1996 15:03.30#
Print DatePart("yyyy", day1)
    1996
Print DatePart("q", day1)
    1
Print DatePart("m", day1)
    3
Print DatePart("d", day1)
    23
Print DatePart("w", day1)
    7
Print DatePart("ww", day1)
    12
Print DatePart("h", day1)
    15
Print DatePart("n", day1)
    3
Print DatePart("s", day1)
    30
```

Financial Functions

You use the following functions to calculate the parameters of a loan or an investment. Included here are only the functions that return the basic parameters of a loan (such as the monthly payment or the loan's duration). The more advanced financial functions are described in the Visual Basic online documentation.

IPmt(rate, per, nper, pv[, fv[, type]]) This function returns the interest payment for a given period of an annuity based on periodic, fixed payments and a fixed interest rate. The result is a Double value.

The *rate* argument is a Double value specifying the interest rate for the payment period. For example, if the loan's annual percentage rate (APR) is 10 percent, paid in monthly installments, the rate per period is 0.1 / 12, or 0.0083.

The *per* argument is a Double value specifying the current payment period; *per* is a number in the range 1 to *nper*.

The *nper* argument is a Double value specifying the total number of payments. For example, if you make monthly payments on a five-year loan, *nper* is 5 * 12 (or 60).

The *Pv* argument is a Double value specifying the principal, or present value. The loan amount is the present value to the lender of the monthly payments.

The *fv* argument is a Variant specifying the future value, or cash balance, after the final payment. The future value of a loan is $0 because that's its value after the final payment. If you want to accumulate $10,000 in your savings account over 5 years, however, the future value is $10,000. If the *fv* argument is omitted, 0 is assumed.

The *type* argument is a Variant specifying when payments are due. Use 0 if payments are due at the end of the payment period; use 1 if payments are due at the beginning of the period. If the *type* argument is omitted, 0 is assumed.

Suppose you borrow $30,000 at an annual percentage rate of 11.5%, to be paid off in 3 years with payments at the end of each month. Here's how you can calculate the total interest, as well as the monthly interest:

```
PVal = 30000&
FVal = 0&
APR = 0.115 / 12
MPayments = 3 * 12
For Period = 1 To Mpayments
    IPayment = IPmt(APR, Period, MPayments, -PVal, FVal, 1)
    Debug.Print IPayment
    TotInt = TotInt + IPayment
Next Period
Debug.Print "Total interest paid: " & TotInt
```

The interest portion of the first payment is $287.50, and the interest portion of the last payment is less than $10. The total interest is $5,614.

PPmt(rate, per, nper, pv[, fv[, type]])   The PPmt() function is similar to the IPmt() function except that it returns the principal payment for a given period of a loan based on periodic, fixed payments and a fixed interest rate. For a description of the function's arguments, see the IPmt entry.

The code for calculating the principal payment of the previous example is nearly the same as that for calculating the interest:

```
PVal = 30000&
FVal = 0&
APR = 0.115 / 12
MPayments = 3 * 12
For Period = 1 To Mpayments
    PPayment = PPmt(APR, Period, MPayments, -PVal, FVal, 1)
    Debug.Print PPayment
    TotPrincipal = TotPrincipal + PPayment
Next Period
Debug.Print "Total principal paid: " & TotPrincipal
```

In this example, the payments increase with time (that's how the total payment remains fixed). The total amount will be equal to the loan's amount, of course, and the fixed payment is the sum of the interest payment (as returned by the IPmt() function) plus the principal payment (as returned by the PPmt() function).

Pmt(rate, nper, pv[, fv[, type]])   This function is a combination of the IPmt() and PPmt() functions. It returns the payment (including both principal and interest) for a loan based on periodic, fixed payments and a fixed interest rate. For a description of the function's arguments, see the IPmt entry. Notice that the Pmt() function doesn't require the *per* argument because all payments are equal.

The code for calculating the monthly payment is similar to the code examples in the IPmt() and PPmt() entries:

```
PVal = 30000&
FVal = 0&
APR = 0.115 / 12
MPayments = 3 * 12
For Period = 1 To Mpayments
    MPayment = Pmt(APR, Period, MPayments, -PVal, FVal, 1)
    Debug.Print MPayment
    TotAmount = TotAmount + MPayment
Next Period
Debug.Print "Total amount paid: " & TotAmount
```

FV(rate, nper, pmt[, pv[, type]])   This function returns the future value of a loan based on periodic, fixed payments and a fixed interest rate. The arguments of the FV() function are explained in the IPmt() entry, and the *pmt* argument is the payment made in each period.

Suppose you want to calculate the future value of an investment with an interest rate of 6.25%, 48 monthly payments of $180, and a present value of $12,000. Use the FV() function with the following arguments:

```
Payment = 180
APR = 6.25 / 100
TotPmts = 48
PVal = 12000
FVal = FV(APR / 12, TotPmts, -Payment, -PVal, PayType)
MsgBox "After " & TotPmts & " your savings will be worth $"& FVal
```

The actual result is close to $25,000.

NPer(rate, pmt, pv[, fv[, type]])   The Nper() function returns the number of periods for a loan based on periodic, fixed payments and a fixed interest rate. For a description of the function's arguments, see the IPmt entry.

Suppose you borrow $25,000 at 11.5%, and you can afford to pay $450 per month. To figure out what this means to your financial state in the future, you would like to know how many years it will take you to pay off the loan. Here's how you can use the Nper() function to do so:

```
FVal = 0
PVal = 25000
APR = 0.115 / 12
Payment = 450
PayType = 0
TotPmts = NPer(APR, -Payment, PVal, FVal, PayType)
If Int(TotPmts) <> TotPmts Then TotPmts = Int(TotPmts) + 1
Debug.Print "The loan's duration will be: " & TotPmts & " months"
```

The actual duration of this loan is 80 months, which corresponds to nearly 6.5 years. If the payment is increased from $450 to $500, the loan's duration will drop to 69 months, and a monthly payment of $550 will bring the loan's duration down to 60 months.

Rate(nper, pmt, pv[, fv[, type[, guess]]])   You use this function to figure out the interest rate per payment period for a loan. Its arguments are the same as with the previous financial functions, except for the *guess* argument, which is the estimated interested rate. If you omit the *guess* argument, the value 0.1 (10%) is assumed.

Suppose you want to borrow $10,000 and pay it off in 48 months with a monthly payment of $400 or less. Here's how you can use the Rate() function to calculate the interest rate:

```
FVal = 0
PVal = 10000
Payment = 400
Payments = 48
PayType = 0
guess = 0.1
IRate = Rate(Payments, -Payment, PVal, FVal, PayType, guess)
Debug.Print "The desired interest rate is: " & Irate * 12 * 100 &
"%"
```

The interest rate is approximately 9.25%. Table A.20 lists the remaining financial functions.

TABLE A.20   The More Advanced Financial Functions

Function	What It Does
PV	Returns a Double specifying the present value of an investment.
NPV	Returns a Double specifying the net present value of an investment based on a series of periodic cash flows and a discount rate.
IRR	Returns the internal rate of return for an investment.
MIRR	Returns a Double specifying the modified internal rate of return for a series of periodic cash flows.
DDB	Returns a Double specifying the depreciation of an asset for a specific time period using the double-declining balance method or some other method you specify.
SYD	Returns a Double specifying the sum-of-years' digits depreciation of an asset for a specified period.
SLN	Returns a Double specifying the straight-line depreciation of an asset for a single period.

Color Functions

The following two functions specify color values that can be used with Visual Basic's drawing methods or with the properties that set the color of various controls (ForeColor, BackColor). The QBColor() function is the simpler one, which is commonly used with business applications.

QBColor(color)   The QBColor() function returns a Long integer representing the RGB color code corresponding to the specified color number. The *color* argument is a number in the range 0 to 15. Each value returns a different color, as shown in Table A.21.

TABLE A.21   The Values for the *color* Argument

NUMBER	COLOR
0	Black
1	Blue
2	Green
3	Cyan
4	Red
5	Magenta
6	Yellow
7	White
8	Gray
9	Light Blue
10	Light Green
11	Light Cyan
12	Light Red
13	Light Magenta

TABLE A.21 The Values for the *color* Argument (continued)

NUMBER	COLOR
14	Light Yellow
15	Bright White

Use the QBColor() function to specify colors if you want to address the needs of users with the least-capable graphics adapter (one that can't display more than the basic 16 colors). Also use it for business applications that don't require many colors.

RGB(red, green, blue)   This function returns a Long integer representing a color value. The *red, green,* and *blue* arguments are integer values in the range 0 to 255, representing the values of the three basic colors. Table A.22 lists some of the most common colors and their corresponding red, green, and blue components. The colors correspond to the eight corners of the RGB color cube.

TABLE A.22 Common Colors and Their Corresponding RGB Components

COLOR	RED	GREEN	BLUE
Black	0	0	0
Blue	0	0	255
Green	0	255	0
Cyan	0	255	255
Red	255	0	0
Magenta	255	0	255
Yellow	255	255	0
White	255	255	255

For a detailed discussion on how to specify colors with the help of the RGB cube, see the section "Specifying Color" in Chapter 6, *Drawing and Painting with Visual Basic.*

The following statement:

```
Text1.BackColor = RGB(255, 0, 0)
```

assigns a pure red color to the background of the Text1 control.

Miscellaneous Functions

This section describes two functions used in controlling program flow: IIf() (a short version of the If Then Else statement) and Switch() (a short version of the Select Case statement).

IIf(expression, truepart, falsepart)   This function returns one of two parts, depending on the evaluation of *expression*. If the *expression* argument is True, the *truepart* argument is returned. If *expression* is not True, the *falsepart* argument is returned. The IIf() function is equivalent to the following If clause:

```
If expression Then
     result = truepart
Else
     result = falsepart
End If
```

In many situations, this logic significantly reduces the amount of code. The Min() and Max() functions, for instance, can be easily implemented with the IIf() function:

```
Min = IIf(a<b, a, b)
Max = IIf(a>b, a, b)
```

Switch(expression1, value1, expression2, value2,....)   This function evaluates a list of expressions and returns a value associated with the first expression in the list that happens to be True. If none of the expressions is True, the function returns Null. The following statement selects the proper quadrant depending on the signs of the variables X and Y:

```
Quadrant = Switch(X>0 and Y>0, 1, X<0 and Y>0, 2, X<0 and Y<0, 3,
➡X<0 and Y<0, 4)
```

If both X and Y are negative, the *Quadrant* variable is assigned the value 1. If X is negative and Y is positive, *Quadrant* becomes 2, and so on. If either X or Y is zero, none of the expressions is True, and *Quadrant* becomes Null (some greater than signs should become greater than or equal).

INDEX

Note to the Reader: Throughout this index **boldface** page numbers indicate primary discussions of a topic. *Italicized* page numbers indicate illustrations.

SYMBOLS

B

C

D

F

H

O

P

T

V

W

SYBEX BOOKS ON THE WEB!

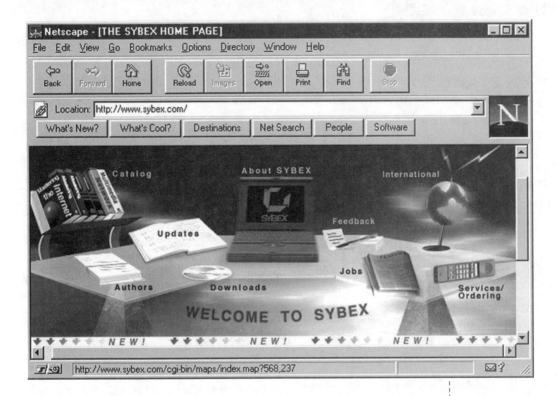

Presenting a truly dynamic environment
that is both fun and informative.

- download useful code
- e-mail your favorite Sybex author
- preview a book you might want to own
- find out about job opportunities at Sybex
- order books
- learn about Sybex
- discover what's new in the computer industry

http://www.sybex.com

SYBEX Inc. • 1151 Marina Village Parkway • Alameda, CA 94501 • 510-523-8233

What's on the CD

Included on this CD in an easy-to-use interface are the following:

- Code for chapter exercises and examples
- New stand-alone VB5 applications built by the author
- Trial versions of third-party ActiveX controls
- Installshield and Demoshield trial software

Custom VB5 Demos by the Author

CDBox   Use this tool to find out how to set up a Font, or a File Open dialog box, without writing a single line of code.

DirMap   Use this application to print the contents of any folder on your hard disk, including its sub-folders, on a RichTextBox control.

FlexGrid   Use this adaptable spreadsheet to create and edit spreadsheets.

FormLoad   The FormLoad demonstrates how to manipulate one Form from within another.

Image   Use this image-processing application as your starting point to build your own custom image-processing techniques.

MDIEdit   The fastest way to get up to speed with Multiple Document Interface (MDI) apps is to use this prebuilt front end.

PaintPic   This simple application demonstrates the various special effects of the PaintPicture methods.

RTFPad   This small application supports the basic features of a word processor; use it as a stand-alone application, incorporate it into your applications, or convert it to an ActiveX document.

Spiral   This application lets you generate and adjust beautiful, mathematically defined curves, controlling their parameters with scrollbar controls.

Wipes   Use the Wipes application as your starting point to set up a slide show on your computer; add any transition effect you can think of.

Third Party Software

ProtoView   WinX Library. The WinX Components Library features a set of 17 ActiveX/OCX files that "snap" into your programming environment.

Crescent Software   FTP Internet Data controls and 16 and 32 bit ActiveX controls.

Dameware   Cal32 ActiveX/OCX control enables you to modify date formats, event notifications, and many "method" functions. The Infotick Information Ticker custom control is a flicker-free timer event with custom controls.

Olympus Software   ImageKnife is a complete solution for acquiring images, processing them in memory, and printing and storing them to either files or databases.

Sheridan   ActiveThreed is a set of seven 32-bit ActiveX controls that make applications look up-to-date and is the easiest way to update existing applications developed using Threed.

Quiksoft   SiteMapper allows webmasters to create an interactive map of their site through which users can navigate. HtmlShow creates a slide show style presentation out of ordinary HTML.

DemoShield   Creating demos to distribute on the Web and on CD-ROMs has never been easier. DemoShield is the easiest way to get your demo done and out doing what it's supposed to: sell your product, train your customers and employees, and create a front end for your CD!

Installshield   Express Professional 1.11 is a 30 day evaluation copy of the full custom installation product for Visual Basic developers.